P9-DFD-637

# Human Migration

PATTERNS AND POLICIES

INDIANA UNIVERSITY PRESS, BLOOMINGTON & LONDON

*Published in association with the American Academy of Arts and Sciences*

# Human Migration

## PATTERNS AND POLICIES

*Edited by*

*William H. McNeill and Ruth S. Adams*

**Library of Congress Cataloging in Publication Data**
Main entry under title:

Human migration.

Papers presented at a conference sponsored by the
Midwest center of the American Academy of Arts and
Sciences and Indiana University; held in New Harmony,
Ind., Apr. 1976.
Includes index.
1. Migration, Internal—Congresses.  2. Emigration
and immigration—Congresses.  I. McNeill, William
Hardy, 1917–     II. Adams, Ruth, 1923–
III. American Academy of Arts and Sciences, Boston.
IV. Indiana. University.
HB1951.H84  1978   301.32  77-23685
ISBN 0-253-32875-6   1 2 3 4 5 82 81 80 79 78

# Contents

# ACKNOWLEDGMENTS

In the context of the Bicentennial of the United States in 1976 it seemed appropriate for the Midwest Council of the American Academy of Arts and Sciences to choose as a special conference topic the role of human migration. Franklin D. Roosevelt's famous greeting to the Daughters of the American Revolution, "Fellow immigrants," underlines the predominantly foreign roots to which we, as a nation, look back. Preliminary discussion among Council members made clear, however, that we could not limit consideration to the American experience. Migration is a worldwide phenomenon—spanning every epoch and encompassing many peoples. Consequently, the Midwest Council, under the chairmanship of Professor William H. McNeill, invited scholars from a number of countries and disciplines to meet to consider the policies, patterns, and implications of migration over time, and across, as well as within, national borders.

The three-day seminar took place in the spring of 1976 at New Harmony, Indiana, site of the early-nineteenth-century utopian communities founded by George Rapp and Robert Owen and now handsomely restored. The choice of that serene setting was fortunate, for it contributed in no small measure to the success of the gathering.

Many individuals and institutions gave invaluable assistance. First and foremost, I should like to thank Indiana University, host for the conference, and in particular Professors Harrison Shull, vice-chancellor for research and graduate development, and George Springer, associate dean, who served on the planning committee. The Lilly Endowment provided the generous grant which made the enterprise a reality. The encouragement of John Voss and Victor Weisskopf, executive officer and president, respectively, of the American Academy of Arts and Sciences, was of inestimable help. Finally, I wish to thank all the participants, as well as Marjorie Veghte of the administrative office of the Department of History, University of Chicago, who gave so freely of her time, and Janet Rabinowitch of Indiana University Press, who skillfully guided and encouraged the authors and editors through the publication process.

Ruth S. Adams

ix

# Introduction

WILLIAM H. McNEILL

The United States is a nation of immigrants. Even the Amerindians among us arrived in the New World only a few thousand years ago, coming from Asia where human life was much older. In fact, the penetration of all the diverse environments of the New World by paleolithic hunters, between about 30,000 and 3000 B.C., followed by a massive change in human occupancy since 1500 when Europeans and Africans first began to come across the ocean in significant numbers, constitute two of the most remarkable demonstrations of the importance of human migration to be found anywhere in the world's history. It is no less true that recent social problems in the United States and in all other countries of the world tie in very closely with the unprecedented scale of recent human migration, sustained, as it is, by massive population growth and by intensified communications nets and cheapened means of transportation.

Nevertheless, in recent decades men of learning have not focused much attention on migration, and different intellectual disciplines have continued to use very different vocabularies and conceptual frames, each according to its own tradition. No one much noticed discrepancies and inadequacies in inherited approaches to the phenomenon. In particular, migration has some-times been conceived of as an exercise of individual decision and choice. Freedom to make such choices may then be elevated to an at least semi-sacred status, and placed among the pantheon of human rights. Lawyers and economists are especially prone to this sort of conceptualization. Anyone

xi

who has in fact moved during his lifetime, pursuing personal goals in accordance with his own best calculation of where private advantage might lie (and who among the readers of this book will not have done so?), is in a weak position to scorn this kind of analysis. Yet sociologists and anthropologists are inclined to take a different tack, looking at social gains and losses that arise from migration. Most of their studies have concentrated on the growing pains that a receiving community experiences when any large number of strangers arrives in its midst. Seldom are the problems of the community whence migrants depart taken seriously, though dying rural communities and ghost towns are familiar enough in American history.

It takes little insight or imagination to recognize that individual rights and self-interest need not coincide with social interests. Whenever a large enough proportion of local population emigrates, the viability of the community of those left behind comes into question. No one intends such a result, least of all the emigrants. Many a European peasant, having come to America in search of a fortune, has comforted himself in times of loneliness with the mental vision of how he would some day return to his native place, able to play the role of rich uncle and bask in the mingled admiration and envy of those he had left behind. If, however, mass departures destroy the village world itself, the migrants may be doubly cheated. Entering an industrial work force at the bottom has few intrinsic charms, yet this is the fate awaiting most peasant emigrants. To submit to such a regimen for years on end in hope of accumulating enough capital to return triumphantly to a village community that no longer survives is to pile illusion upon illusion. Yet this may be exactly what happens when everyone is free to follow his own best guess as to his personal self-interest by migrating wherever and whenever he wishes. Simultaneously, if too massive a hemorrhage of emigration long prevails, those left behind also suffer sharper deprivation—economic, psychological, cultural—than would occur if fewer departed. After all, if only a few left, traditional occupations and ways of life could be more fully sustained, and emigrants' memories of the village past would be less off the mark than when "everyone" goes away. Yet who is to say what an optimal rate of migration might be? And if one sought to define such a concept, from whose point of view would the optimum be defined? Receiving communities obviously have different interests from sending communities, just as employers of labor have different interests from sellers of labor, and these interests differ depending on the direction of migrating movement.

Amidst such perplexities it is perhaps not surprising that scholars as well as the general public find themselves much confused by contradictory values and assumptions. Discrepancies implicit in prevailing attitudes become clear when one asks why it is that within national boundaries the individual right to migrate is accepted as sacred, whereas across national boundaries no such right is recognized to exist. If personal, private decision is and ought to be sovereign within the United States (or any other political jurisdiction), why is it that legal obstacles to movement across political frontiers are acceptable?

As a matter of fact, the effective establishment of political control over international movement was an unexpected and unplanned by-product of World War I. Prior to that time in the United States and western Europe (and therefore in most of the globe which was then still controlled by western European powers), passports and official regulation of migration were re-garded as an improper infringement of personal freedom. The fact that the Russians maintained controls on migration was one of the reproaches that freedom-loving persons regularly made against the Tsar's regime. Consider-ations of military security during World War I persuaded Western govern-ments to imitate the Russians. After the war, official machinery for control of migration was never dismantled. Masses of refugees threatened to put severe strains on industrial society everywhere; and recurrent economic crises made newcomers unwelcome in most lands.

The United States, as is well known, responded to the postwar situation by inaugurating a system of quotas designed to restrict immigration drasti-cally. Eventual liberalization of United States regulations in the 1960s did not alter the principle of official, legal exclusion of some who, in the absence of rules to the contrary, might have come into the country from abroad. Yet since World War II various legal devices that local communities had invented to restrict or prevent immigration of "outsiders" have been declared illegal and strongly reprobated by liberal opinion. Presumably behind such atti-tudes lies the unspoken assumption that all Americans are somehow the same and have identical rights, whereas foreigners are different and do not have the same rights Americans have. Yet human reality scarcely conforms to such a distinction: variability within as well as without the political boundaries of the United States is enormous. The legal barriers to free migration seem more the creation of an administrative and bureaucratic machine than of anything else.

A personal experience in 1966 brought home to me vividly some appar-ent paradoxes of human migration. In that year I visited a number of Greek villages, some of which had become hollow shells because of mass emigration to Germany, where opportunities for work in automobile and other factories had suddenly opened up after 1961, when the erection of the Berlin wall abruptly checked an earlier migration flow from East to West Germany. A few young men ventured away first. Often they were the ne'er-do-wells of the village. When after a year or two such shiftless types returned from Germany driving their own second-hand cars, and backed up this incredible demonstration of wealth with stories of how easy the physical conditions of work were in German factories, all the values and social hierarchy of village life suddenly turned topsy-turvy. What availed a lifetime's work aimed at acquiring enough capital to dower a daughter or purchase a bit of land from an improvident neighbor against the incredible wealth that the young acquired in Germany? What indeed? The only rational response was to follow their example and emigrate, leaving behind only the very young and the very old. Whole villages thus committed suicide in as little as five years time. Yet, with a randomness that is perhaps characteristic of such sudden transformations, other villages close by, situated in almost exactly the same natural environment, sent no one at all to Germany. Some sustained a more modest, local pattern of migration into unskilled occupations in Greek cities; other villages adhered instead to an older, numerically smaller-scale pattern of overseas emigration to Australia, Canada, or the United States. No one encountering the raw wounds that sudden mass emigration sometimes left behind could doubt that in 1966 the full costs of Greek population movement into Germany had not yet been paid, and this despite the fact that the entire migration was conducted under close governmental regulation and in accordance with legal agreements and safeguards devised by German and Greek officials.

By chance, in the same summer of 1966 I also visited some Welsh rural communities situated less than fifty miles from Manchester, the first explosive center of modern industrialism. The contrast was striking indeed, for in the Welsh communities it seemed to me that little had changed since the days of the Tudors. A sharply graded social hierarchy survived, with gentry and simple folk clearly divided yet recognizing each other cordially enough. Moreover, within each class a nicely calculated hierarchy of worth—personal as well as pecuniary—defined each family's place in local society.

Above all, the rural population appeared to be serenely certain of their own superiority to city folk. For generations they had seen the ne'er-do-wells of their society drift off to Manchester and other cities. Most never came back. The few who did were usually failures: their tales of the dirt and distress of urban living reinforced local self esteem. At the top of the social hierarchy, also, a few key individuals spurned careers in town, and proved the superiority of the countryside by preferring the role of country gentleman to anything urban life had to offer. Armored top and bottom by such convincing testimony as to the superiority of their own way of life, therefore, the inhabitants of these Welsh hamlets and villages seemed oblivious to the city lights that so dazzled their Greek counterparts.

Yet mass communications had made their inroad. At least some of the youths of the Welsh countryside were all agog to out-Beatle the Beatles by forming musical groups of their own, more sophisticated, more catchy, more modern than anything that had crawled out of the Liverpool slums to world acclaim. The possibility that the stout self-satisfaction of the rural society of North Wales was nearing a crisis like that which had already descended upon Greek villages could therefore not be ruled out. Like so much else in the contemporary world scene, contrasts and anomalies of the kind that obtruded themselves on my consciousness in 1966 seemed much too sharp to long endure.

Accordingly, ten years later when opportunity offered, it seemed eminently worthwhile to help organize a conference on "Human Migration: Patterns, Implications, and Policies," which took place at New Harmony, Indiana, in April 1976 under the sponsorship of the Midwest Center of the American Academy of Arts and Sciences and Indiana University. In planning the conference, papers were designed to cluster around three foci: (1) a sampling of historical patterns of migration against which to measure more recent manifestations of humanity's penchant for moving about; (2) a survey of migration movements in major segments of the earth since World War II; (3) a weighing of public policies towards migration in the light of the best conceptualization of the process we could bring to bear. In addition, the conference set out to bring together persons of divergent professional background, so that the participants could test each other's approach and see whether discrepancies could stimulate any useful enlargement or correction of received opinions.

As the papers here assembled demonstrate, the encounter of a three-day conference did provoke some of the participants to revise their thinking in significant ways, while others, as one would expect, remained satisfied with the frame of reference from which they had started. Aristide Zolberg's effort to create a theory of state action with respect to migration is by far the most impressive theoretical response to questions raised at the conference; but, in general, the conceptual problems involved in understanding human migration have not here been solved, and far-reaching discrepancies of assumption and outlook remain. Nevertheless, the juxtaposition of historical, legal, economic, anthropological, sociological, geographical, and philosophical vocabularies in what follows underlines the intellectual confusion that needs to be dissipated before any really satisfactory understanding of human migration can develop. In the meanwhile, some interesting and little noted data about what has happened and is happening in many different parts of the world have been gathered together here.

Anyone reading these papers will be impressed by how important migration has been and continues to be in human affairs, in all parts of the world and, so far as one can tell, at all times in the past. Charles Tilly's paper on Europe and James Lee's paper on China will surely dispel the common notion that even if hunters were migratory, traditional agriculturalists were not. The conventional portrait of virtuous if slow-witted peasants, rooted to the soil, living and dying in the village of their birth, tilling land their fore-bears had cultivated before them, generation after generation across untold centuries, seems, indeed, to be romantic fiction, invented by urbanized mi-grants who, looking back upon their own rural childhoods, rashly assumed that no one had ever left home before they did so themselves.

A second widespread misconception will be dispelled, or at least chal-lenged, by McGee's paper on Southeast Asia. From what he has to say, it seems entirely implausible to believe that the pattern of rural exodus and mass urbanization that prevailed in much of western Europe and the United States during the past two hundred years will be recapitulated in Asia. The Asian peasantry is too massive, the urban absorptive capacity is too limited for that to happen; moreover "empty" overseas spaces which played a part, even if only a minor one, in cushioning Europeans' encounter with the modern population explosion, are not very obvious in the world today. Any Asian emigration sufficient to relieve population pressures in any significant degree would overwhelm receiving lands, e.g., Australia, in a way sure to arouse strenuous political opposition.

Patterns of accommodation to the changes modernity has brought will therefore be different. There exists no single, standard pattern of moderniza-tion to which all peoples must conform, and this despite a habit of mind that remains widespread in English-speaking lands and that expects all peoples to follow along a path already trodden by Britain and the United States. But just as Greek villagers in 1966 reacted to opportunities of urban industrial employment in a way fundamentally different from the way Welsh rural folk had reacted to similar opportunities dating back to the eighteenth century, so, too, peoples with different cultural traditions and different contemporary patterns of life can be expected to react to all the novelties that modernity brings into their lives in ways divergent from the way that English-speakers reacted to innovations of times past, even when the innovations in question appear to be similar.

A third general point emerges from several of the papers that follow: to wit, that modern efforts by states to control and direct migration have led to the appearance in many different countries of a subpolitical class compris-ing recent immigrants. In some cases, as in the United States, such immi-grants are illegal, and for that reason do not have ordinary access to political rights. In other cases, the immigrants are fully legal, but their status remains subpolitical because both the country of origin and the country of destination prefer to arrange things that way. This is the case, for instance, in Germany and Switzerland, as H. J. Hoffmann-Nowotny's paper makes clear. It is no less the case in Argentina, and in several parts of Africa, as Carl Solberg's and Philip Curtin's essays explain. A contrasting political differentiation occurs in the Soviet Union, where Russian emigrants enjoy specially privileged positions in regions of that country where other nationalities prevail. Alexandre Bennigsen and Enders Wimbush explore some of the strains that result from this old-fashioned "imperial" pattern.

Comparison of recent political assumptions with the practice of traditional polyethnic imperial societies suggests that the tendency towards the development of a subpolitical class composed of recent immigrants is more in line with past precedents than we are prone to suppose. Socially uniform states, comprising in principle if never quite in practice only persons of the same nationality and culture, are exceptional in civilized history. Single nationality states are, indeed, characteristically barbarian. Civilization normally generated polyethnic societies, often divided hierarchically between a ruling and various occupationally differentiated subordinate nationalities. What seems to be happening in diverse parts of the earth since World War II may therefore turn out to be a belated and still very limited retreat from the barbarian principle of ethnic uniformity up and down the social scale.

Finally, Zolberg's and Janet Abu-Lughod's papers make explicit what others touch on only tangentially: the fact that although most writing about migration in English assumes that free choices made by individuals or families govern human movements, the fact is that much human migration does not conform to this pattern in the least. Instead, political violence and threat of violence have often compelled whole populations to flee. Sometimes in the deeper past, entire peoples discovered that their military power was such that they could afford to invade neighboring lands and travel at will, seeking plunder and a suitably attractive place in which to settle down.

Mass movements of this kind, directly connected with the exercise of force or the threat of force, have played a critically important role in times past. The European penetration of the Americas could not have occurred without military (as well as epidemiological) superiority over the previous inhabitants. Indeed, the territorial base of almost all existing nationalities of the world can usually be traced back to some ancient mass migratory movement of a similar kind, carried through at sword's point. Such movements have by no means ceased in our time, even though the character of warfare has altered profoundly from the age of the European *Völkerwanderung*. Millions of political refugees had to be settled in new homes after World Wars I and II. Indeed every angry confrontation of hostile masses that leads to organized violence can be counted on to generate a new flood of refugees in a world as densely inhabited as ours has become. No theory of migration that omits this side of human movement can be adequate to the facts, any more than a theory that views human action as solely the result of individual decision can do justice to the side effects massive migratory movements generate, quite apart from and often in contradiction of anybody's conscious intention.

To have challenged commonly held opinions on four such basic points as these makes this collection of essays intellectually worthwhile, even though the numerous discrepancies as between one paper and the next underline the many unsolved problems of conceptualization that remain. No single conference nor any collection of essays from different hands can be expected to resolve such obscurities. But by making some of the difficulties clearer than before and by assembling information across a broad range of space and time so that a reader can survey the phenomena of migration from a wider perspective than has commonly been attempted previously, this volume may nevertheless play an appropriate part in provoking others to think more clearly about and to understand more thoroughly what assuredly continues to be, as it has been in the past, one of the most significant manifestations of the human condition.

# Human Migration

PATTERNS AND POLICIES

*Part One*

---

# Patterns of Migration:
# Times Past

# [1]

## Human Migration: A Historical Overview

WILLIAM H. McNEILL

Defending hearth and home against strangers, on the one hand, and roving to far places in search of food and excitement, on the other, have always been opposing poles of human experience. They tend to manifest themselves most strongly at different stages of the life cycle: roving being an affair of youth, home-keeping of adulthood as well as of infancy and old age. The roving pattern of behavior has obvious biological advantages: apart from expanding the range of genetic mingling and variation, rovers occasionally discovered new foods and in rare instances even opened up new ecological niches for human occupancy. Their restless movements continually probed for new possibilities and tested old barriers, usually finding nothing of importance to other human beings, but every so often opening the way for critically important technological, geographical, and/or social breakthroughs.

Roving behavior, therefore, had an important role in human (and prehuman) evolution. Humankind could not have become the earth-girdling, dominant species we are without roving and without the migrations that followed successful discovery of new possibilities made manifest by such roving. Human occupation of the Americas and of previously islanded lands of Oceania is only the most recent—and geographically most extensive—example of processes that are as old as humankind.

The earliest phases of prehuman and human evolution are too little known for us to speculate usefully about the importance of roving and migration in those remote ages. But once skilled human hunters had mastered the

3

art of killing big game and had discovered how to maintain a subtropical micro-environment next to their hairless bodies by wearing clothes, a truly remarkable globe-girdling migratory expansion began. Human hunting bands moved across the Bering Straits and all the way south to Tierra del Fuego within a few thousand years, and simultaneously filled up all the other corners of the globe where suitably large-bodied game animals could be found.

About 8000 B.C. this vast migration began to reach inelastic limits. This led many different human communities to intensify their search for food, diversifying diet so that humans again became omnivorous. Intensified food searches soon provoked the invention of agriculture in several different parts of the earth where suitably nourishing plants could be artificially propagated. Early agriculturalists were not necessarily sessile: in the Middle East, for example, where wheat and barley were the principal initial crops, slash-and-burn cultivation required farming communities to remove to new ground every few years; and since suitable new ground could only be found beneath the canopy of a deciduous forest, this meant periodic migration across distances that may sometimes have been considerable. Other styles of early cultivation—in particular the millet cultivation of the Chinese loess soils—do not seem to have required removal to new ground; perhaps for that reason, the Middle Eastern pattern of grain cultivation came to occupy a much larger region of the Old World—from the Atlantic face of Europe and north Africa to northwest India—than was true of other, more sessile early styles of agriculture.

Movement by boat also became significant for human society before cities and civilization appeared. The horizon for this kind of movement in the Mediterranean seems to have been about 4000 B.C.; I am not aware of what the best estimates for the beginning of navigation in the southern seas and oceans may be, but coastal movement (and occasional long-range migration by sea) affected human occupancy of the shores of the Indian Ocean long before civilized societies established themselves in those parts.

There are systematic and persistent differences between movement by ship and movement overland; and the cultural reactions to contacts initiated by sea are systematically different from reactions to land contacts. This is not the place to try to define such differences in any detail. Suffice it to say that ships, being capable of carrying men and goods in relatively large quantities for long distances at relatively little cost, may initiate intense but intermittent encounters across cultural frontiers. Contacts overland are likely to be more continuous, and the samples of an alien style of life that can be carried on a man's back or on the back of pack animals are more rigorously selected than are the contents of a ship. The result is a longer lasting, more dilute encounter across cultural boundaries. Consequently, contact overland characteristically produces different reactions from overseas contacts between alien societies.

In this connection it is interesting to note that the earliest civilization known to archaeologists seems to have arisen as a result of sea-borne migration of the people we know as Sumerians into Mesopotamia from somewhere south, presumably along the shores of the Persian Gulf. The newcomers established themselves as rulers of whoever may have lived in the marshy estuaries of the Tigris-Euphrates before they got there, and soon began to develop new skills and techniques for exploiting the agricultural as well as the fishing and fowling possibilities of that exceptional environment. The result was the emergence of cities and civilization by about 3000 B.C.

Other parts of the globe became seats of early civilizations not very long afterwards. The valleys of the Nile, the Indus, and the Yellow River were the most important sites of such early civilizations in Eurasia. Different patterns seem to have prevailed in the Americas and in Africa, partly because crops and climates differed, but also—and perhaps chiefly—because epidemiological conditions created by the emergence of civilizations were different in Africa and in the Americas from those prevailing in the temperate zones of Eurasia. In what follows, I will endeavor to sketch a pattern of migration that I believe to have been characteristic of traditional Eurasian civilizations: Middle Eastern, Indian, Chinese, and European alike. I will *not* try to say anything about the Amerindian civilizations nor about the various high cultures that developed in Africa where the Eurasian migration patterns did not, I think, prevail; and if other patterns did, I do not know enough even to guess what they may have been.

My thesis is that from Sumerian times until the latter decades of the nineteenth century—almost throughout civilized history in other words— four currents of migration can be distinguished and were, indeed, necessary for the maintenance of Eurasian civilized society. These four currents of migration divide into movements affecting the unskilled—primarily peasants or ex-peasants—and movements of elites.

First, consider mass migration patterns. My hypothesis rests on the idea that differential patterns of mortality were created by the conditions of city life. This in turn permanently drew migrants from their places of birth—into cities, on the one hand, and off towards the frontiers of settlement, on the other. How epidemiology could create and sustain such a double pattern of die-off and compensatory migration requires a little explanation.[1] When comparatively large numbers of human beings began to live in cities, many different infections became more common because proximity multiplied opportunities for parasitic organisms to pass from one human host to another. Not only this: when human numbers attained a critical threshold (sometimes in the hundreds of thousands), entirely new forms of infection that passed directly from human to human with no intermediate host or dormant form of the infectious organism became viable. These infections constitute the array of familiar childhood diseases of the recent past: smallpox, measles, mumps, and the like. Such diseases could survive only within civilized societies, since only there were human numbers and frequency of contact sufficient to allow the infectious organism to find an unceasing succession of new hosts.

This class of infections provokes antibody formation in infected humans so that one exposure to the disease will create immunity for many years, usually for a lifetime. In a disease-experienced population, therefore, only children are suitable hosts for these infections. But among inexperienced populations this is not the case. In such societies adults are just as vulnerable as children to infection and death. Thus the impact of these civilized diseases upon disease-experienced populations is entirely different from their impact upon virgin populations: a fact of enormous import for human history.

A result of the intensification of infection that urban conditions of life induced was that until the latter part of the nineteenth century cities were population sumps. Eighteenth-century London, for instance, required an in-migration of an average of 6,000 persons per annum simply to maintain itself—a sum of 600,000 for the entire century, which was more than the entire population of the city in 1700.[2] No comparably reliable figures exist for earlier ages; but I believe this necessity for recruiting urban population from the countryside—what we can perhaps call the Dick Whittington syndrome —is about as old as cities themselves.

The reasons for saying this are twofold. Early (ca. 2000 B.C.) Mesopotamian texts such as the Epic of Gilgamesh refer casually to lethal epidemic infection as an evidence of divine power. This shows that conspicuous and demographically significant epidemic infections had become routine aspects of urbanism by 2000 B.C., i.e., within the first millennium of city living. Secondly, the language of administration and record-keeping in the cities of southern Mesopotamia shifted during the third millennium from Sumerian to Akkadian. I believe that this shift registered the result of in-migration to the (initially) Sumerian-speaking cities from the Akkadian-speaking countryside—a pattern of migration that at some point must have assumed such velocity as to make it unnecessary for the in-migrants to learn the language of the established managers of the city. A modern parallel from European history is the way in which Prague and Budapest ceased to be German-speaking cities when the pace of in-migration from the Czech- and Magyar-speaking countryside assumed an increased velocity in the course of the nineteenth century, partly in response to industrial expansion, and partly as an aftermath of cholera (and other epidemic) die-off of German-speaking urban dwellers. It seems possible, therefore, that the linguistic shift in ancient Mesopotamia (which had no apparent political or military base) attests the existence in remote antiquity of the same rural to urban migration current that played such a prominent role in eighteenth-century London and nineteenth-century Prague and Budapest.[3]

Armies constituted another significant population sump for civilized societies. They assumed demographically significant roles about a thousand years after cities first came into existence. It is, indeed, useful to think of armies as mobile cities, exercising power over the countryside from a movable focus in much the same way that cities were accustomed to exercise power over their rural hinterlands from a fixed location. And like cities, the human density of armies (and of people fleeing before their ravages) induced intensified infections that were far more lethal than weapons. In modern times, when figures become more or less accurate, soldiers' deaths from disease far outranked deaths in action until after the Boer War, 1901–3.

Rural emigrants had, accordingly, two alternative paths of migration available to them: either moving into the city to make their fortunes as chance and aptitude and places opened by die-off of older urban populations might permit, or serving in an army—voluntarily or by conscription—and pursuing a career under arms, where life expectancy was even shorter than in town and the pattern whereby fresh recruits moved into slots vacated by veterans' deaths was a good deal more obvious and immediate—speedier and more massive in other words—than was commonly the case in cities.

A second traditional current of mass migration from the peasant countryside ran in an opposite direction: towards the frontier of settlement. This may perhaps be termed the Daniel Boone syndrome. Lands towards the periphery of civilized styles of living were ordinarily made available for settlement by intensified die-off of partially isolated populations resulting from contacts with disease-experienced city folk. This phenomenon was massively apparent in the Americas, where contacts with white men regularly decimated Indian populations. Similar processes prevailed in the deeper past, at the fringes of other civilized communities, from the time that the characteristic diseases of civilization established themselves in cities, and thereby conferred upon disease-experienced civilized communities an epidemiological weapon wherewith to mow down isolated, disease-inexperienced communities.

Innumerable instances of how an unfamiliar infection can play havoc in isolated communities are known from recent times. When measles was first introduced into Fiji, for instance, twenty-five percent of the population died of the infection within a few weeks; the English doctor who observed these appalling effects published what became a classical account of this sort of virgin-soil epidemic in 1877.[4] To give a more recent illustration: when the Alcan highway was opened in 1942, a previously isolated Alaskan community experienced nine different, serious infections within the first nine months that trucks began to move through their community. Had the sick not been spirited away to modern hospitals as soon as a new infection appeared among them, it is impossible to believe that this tiny community of some 130 individuals could have survived the catastrophic exposure to diseases of civilization the Alcan highway meant for them.[5]

Obviously, such epidemics opened the way for relatively easy expansion of civilized settlement, if climate and soils and other natural conditions made it possible for familiar ways of exploiting the environment to be applied in the newly emptied landscapes. Indeed civilized expansion of this kind resembles the growth patterns of bread mold on an agar jelly, whereby the mold excretes a substance—penicillin—lethal to rival forms of life. Civilized communities do the same merely by breathing in the presence of disease-inexperienced human adults.

Thus while endemic disease in urban centers maintained a flow of migrants from countryside into town, epidemic disease operating towards the periphery of the civilized region sporadically depopulated frontier zones, which thus became available for pioneer settlement by other migrants from the same rural hinterland. An inward flow of relatively low skilled ex-peasants towards cities (and armies) thus matched an outward flow towards unsettled frontiers on the part of the same population. (See Figure 1.)

This, I think, was the fundamental pattern of human migration in China, India, the Middle East, and Europe; and its operation had much to do with the fact that in these regions a single style of civilized life (or closely related variants upon a single style, like the differences between Latin and Orthodox Christendom in medieval times, or between German and French civilization in the nineteenth century) tended to assert itself and maintain recognizable identity across relatively very large times and spaces. In parts of the earth where these two basic patterns of migration did not assert their homogenizing force, high urban cultures exerted a less long-lived and less territorially extensive effect. Their rise and fall could be and apparently was more rapid and may have affected rural life less intimately than was the case in the temperate zones of the Old World.

Two more migration patterns nevertheless also deserve attention though they affected smaller numbers of persons, being an affair of elites and ruling classes rather than of the masses. As before, one such current moved inward toward the centers of urban life and civilization, and a second moved outward toward (and beyond) civilizational frontiers. I wish to consider the latter pattern first, since I believe it manifested itself before the contrary migration of elites inward toward the center of civilization set in.

From the earliest days of the river-valley civilizations of the Near East it is clear that certain important raw materials had to be brought into the

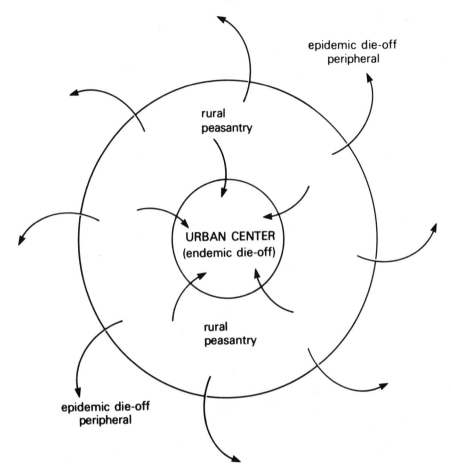

FIGURE 1. Standard mass migration pattern for traditional civilization

emerging cities and court centers from afar. Mesopotamia and Egypt both lacked timber and metals. Mesopotamia also lacked stone. Yet these commodities played a critical role in early civilized technology. Trade expeditions, often undistinguishable from raids, were necessary to assure a supply of these and other valued raw materials.

This economic motive for penetrating distant regions was supplemented from quite early times by missionary impulses, perhaps sustained by the fact that a missionary preaching some doctrine valued for religious reasons might also expect to secure for himself an honored and relatively comfortable status among the barbarian populations who received him and accepted his message. Thus the spread of the so-called megalithic tomb and other structures around the coasts of western Europe as far as the Baltic during the third millennium B.C. seems to have been accomplished by missionaries of a faith that taught life after death and set great store by accurate astronomical observations.

Often, too, trade and conversion went hand-in-hand. Merchants and raiders carried ideas as well as goods; and if those ideas somehow illumined reality as experienced by distant and alien peoples among whom they penetrated, ideational borrowing and adaptation could and did occur in quite the same way that technological traits and skills might also diffuse outward from a civilized center along routes of trade—always within limits set by the receptivity of the distant community to the imports from the civilized center.

Among the skills exported from civilized communities were those of organized violence. As long as human communities did not produce more than was needed to keep alive, raiding and robbery were relatively unrewarding. Moral inhibitions against seizing what one had not himself labored to make available for human consumption must, I think, have been very strong in early agricultural communities; and in the absence of food surpluses, a community that tried to live by robbery and pillage would speedily kill off its victims and thus find itself unable to live any longer by rapine. Only when populations came into existence that habitually produced more than they themselves consumed did a predatory pattern of life become practicable. And it was only when urban elites had come into being and learned how to feed themselves by extracting foodstuffs from agriculturalists that populations which habitually produced more food than they needed for their own use came into existence.

Eventually, however, dwellers-round-about discovered that they could rival city elites in preying upon the rural peasantry, seizing food and other commodities on a hit-and-run basis. With luck, a raiding party could expect to get in ahead of civilized tax and rent collectors or armies living off the countryside. As militarization of the barbarian world proceeded, such raiders became rivals and potential heirs to civilized ruling classes. In Eurasia, the main reservoir of barbarian prowess established itself on the grasslands of the steppe, with a secondary center in the drier zone that shades off into desert south of the steppe. Recorded political history largely turns upon how one wave of barbarian invaders after another coming off the steppe or in from the deserts of the Middle East and Central Asia conquered civilized lands and established themselves as rulers. Successful conquerors, of course, set out as best they could to prevent others from following directly in their rear, overthrowing their power. Diplomatic missions, tribute payments, punitive military expeditions, elaborate border defenseworks to shelter standing armies or, alternatively, local self-defense of civilized landscapes by peasant militias or by professionalized warrior classes living in the countryside: all these and more were tried. And all, sooner or later, failed to check fresh invasion and conquest from the barbarian fringes. This Genghis Khan syndrome therefore matched and opposed the Marco Polo/Dr. Livingstone trade-missionary syndrome, each affecting relatively small elites, and pulling them in opposite directions. (See Figure 2.)

The historical importance of these patterns of elite migration seem very considerable. Efforts at defense and no less persistent efforts at raid and conquest provided a fertile stimulus to administrative and technical innovation, from the time the war chariot burst upon civilized communities with initially irresistible force until the present. In addition, the far-ranging movements of warrior, trading, and missionary elites spread familiarity with a considerable variety of high skills across otherwise unbridgeable distances.

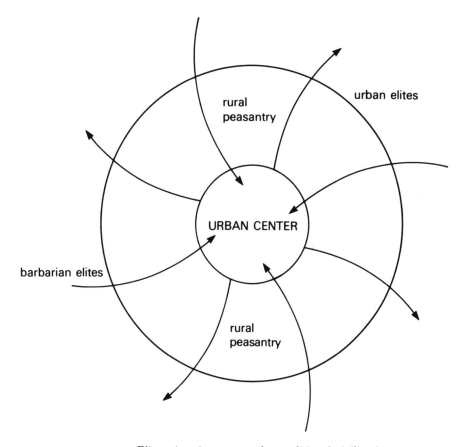

FIGURE 2. Elite migration pattern for traditional civilization

Skills of China could and did seep westward along paths of communication, just as Roman or Middle Eastern and Indian skills and ideas could move in the opposite direction along the same communications paths.

Whenever established institutions and ideas of a particular civilization failed to function satisfactorily, the possibility of taking alien notions and skills seriously arose. Much of the cultural history of civilized societies in the Eurasian world turned upon such sporadic receptivity on the part of one civilization for things imported (and in the process normally also distorted) from an alien, distant civilized center. From this point of view, the massive interaction between western civilization and the various other high cultures of the earth which has been such a conspicuous feature of the last two to three centuries is no more than the most recent (though perhaps the most dramatic and drastic) such process.

Inter-civilizational exchange and stimulus provided a major—perhaps *the* major—stimulus to change within civilized communities ever since the plurality of civilized cultures became knowable to suitably located and strategically situated individuals. The ancient Greeks' encounter with the Orient, so tellingly recorded in Herodotus' pages, and the initial Chinese encounter with the Middle East, more briefly recorded in the pages of the Ssu-ma Ch'ien, the founder of Chinese historiography, have the advantage of being accessible to us through surviving texts. Other similar encounters ran all the way back to the time when predynastic Egyptians met ideas and skills emanating from Sumer and saw that they were good, some time before 3000 B.C. Such stimuli drastically altered patterns of cultural growth and often accelerated developments or turned them into new paths. Or so I argued in *The Rise of the West: A History of the Human Community*,[6] which, with its emphasis upon cultural diffusion, may be read as a paean to the world historical significance of elite migration. (See Figure 3.)

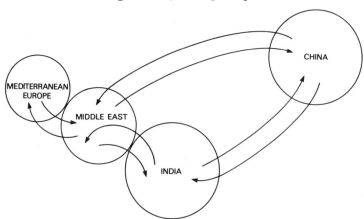

FIGURE 3. Elite migration linkages by ca. 1 A.D.

Two observations about these migration patterns seem worth making. First, mass migration was not always a matter of a more or less free individual or group response to their perceptions of the world and its opportunities. Obviously, the existence of civilization and cities, with the patterns of human migration these communities created, put extraordinary strain upon the rural food-producing peasantry. Their efforts sustained the city folk in a most direct fashion by raising the food the citizens consumed. They also supported cities and rulers by exporting a portion of their offspring after having borne all the costs of raising them from infancy to adolescence. It follows that high rural birth rates, as well as the regular production of a lot more food than the village population of working age itself required, were preconditions for the maintenance of civilized patterns of life.

If one reflects upon the hardships and difficulties such requirements placed upon the peasantry, it is not surprising that population shortages in the countryside could and sometimes did threaten the survival of city life and civilization. In such cases, legal enactment often sought to assure fulfillment of vital functions by assigning individuals to specific jobs and roles in society. A second possibility was to recruit labor by organizing slave raids aimed at bringing additional manpower to bear on tasks for which an adequate supply of local personnel was not available. Slave soldieries and household servants were sometimes more prominent in the past than slave cultivators; but since slaves seldom reproduced themselves, all three kinds of slavery depended on the availability of a supply of enslaveable people somewhere at a distance.

Wherever such pools of enslaveable population were discovered and exploited—whether in Africa or on the Turkish steppes or in Russian villages —they constituted a sort of auxiliary reservoir of manpower for civilized societies, supplementing the peasant manpower resources available closer at hand which had proved insufficient to man all the posts and perform all the functions the civilized ruling classes wanted or needed to have performed.

Secondly, it made a good deal of difference whether the circulatory patterns of migration I have described were entered upon by isolated individuals and small family groups that left their native place and moved to the city, into an army, or to the frontier as a result of individual decision, or whether such channels of migration were instead entered upon by larger social groups—whole tribes or villages—that entered into the circulatory system of civilized society as organized communities, so that they could maintain, e.g., a linguistic identity of their own in novel situations, and perpetuate distinctive cultural characteristics even after they had entered into the very heart and core of civilized society. The Jews who wept by the waters of Babylon in the time of Nebuchadnezzar and the Visigoths and Vandals who sacked Rome in the fifth century A.D. sufficiently illustrate the difference that migration in organized groupings can make to the historic role such migrants may play as against anything possible for isolated individuals and small family groupings.

Finally, I should point out that the fourfold pattern of civilized migration in Eurasia that I have sketched did not exclude other remarkable migratory movements during the historic age. Among peoples but little affected by acquaintance with the skills of civilization, some quite extraordinary migratory dispersals are known to have occurred. The Indonesian migration from Borneo to Madagascar, the Polynesian migration through the islands of the central Pacific, the Eskimo circumpolar migration and the Bantu migration within Africa each allowed human communities to penetrate and exploit in new ways hitherto uninhabited or very thinly inhabited landscapes. As such, they partook of the process described in my first pages—pushing human occupancy ever closer to absolute geographic limits.

From about 1700 the patterns of civilized migration outlined above began to encounter fundamentally new circumstances. It can be argued, indeed, that the world of our own time is only beginning to come to grips with the changed conditions of migration that began to manifest themselves in the eighteenth century, and became massive human realities in the course of the nineteenth.

What were the new circumstances? First and most widely experienced was a change in population dynamics that resulted in an unprecedentedly massive and prolonged population growth, approximating to a rate of about one percent per annum. In many parts of the world, reception of American food crops—maize, potatoes, peanuts, etc.—played a part by expanding available food supplies. Diminution of local violence as a result of the easier monopolization of superior force that the invention and spread of cannon involved may have diminished deaths from human agency. But by all odds the most powerful disturber of older balances was surely the increasingly effective homogenization of civilized infections. This meant that in city after city and in one rural community after another in contact with such cities, epidemic was succeeded by endemic forms of disease. As wider and wider territories were merged into a more nearly homogeneous disease pool by a heightened frequency and range of communications, the conditions that in earlier times had allowed a ring of rural communities close by city disease-centers to produce a population surplus on a regular basis for the replenishment of urban numbers began to apply to larger territories. As all important lethal infections became endemic within the limits set by climate and other natural conditions, the possibility of epidemic die-off of adult populations diminished. Consequently human communities, traditionally adjusted to withstand sporadic epidemic die-offs, found themselves multiplying incontinently. In practice, this meant that the major civilized regions of Eurasia all witnessed the first phases of the modern population explosion during the eighteenth century, though in some lands the effect was quickly dampened by food shortages or political disorder.

Correspondingly, the epidemiological process whereby previously isolated peoples were exposed to death-dealing civilized infections accelerated, since the same intensified pattern of communication that assured homogenization of diseases in civilized lands also increased the risk of exposure to infections for populations without previous experience of the disease in question.

Thus from about 1700 onward, an accelerated rate of epidemiological destruction of primitive communities accompanied an accelerating rate of civilized population growth. At first, Europeans were by far the best situated to take advantage of this new circumstance. They manned the ships that plied the high seas, carrying infections as well as goods and ideas. Since they controlled the ships, it was relatively easy for Europeans to initiate settlements overseas in lands emptied or partially emptied of their previous inhabitants by the action of civilized infections. This process had of course begun in the sixteenth century with the European discovery of America; it expanded to South Africa (first Dutch settlement 1652), Australia (first English settlement 1788), New Zealand (first European settlement 1790s, but organized British colonization only from 1840), and to many lesser islands and shore stations in other remote regions of the earth. Overseas European colonial settlements in turn built up trade and intensified exchange patterns across the oceans, thus accelerating epidemiological destruction of remote populations while forwarding the general process of European expansion—economically, technologically, and demographically all at once. (See Figure 4.)

On top of this already sharply disbalanced world situation, Europeans began to pioneer the discovery and administration of effective public health measures. Two horizons seem especially significant here: the development of vaccination against smallpox at the very end of the eighteenth century, and the introduction of an arterial-venous system of water supply and waste disposal, beginning in the 1850s. Urban water supplies that were guarded against amoebic and bacterial contamination sharply diminished infectious disease transmitted through drinking water. Sanitary sewage disposal inhibited yet other infections propagated by contact with faeces. Soon afterward came the discovery of disease-causing germs, and of ways to check the chain of infection by scientifically tested and often not very expensive forms of prophylaxis. Such revolutionary changes in public health meant that Europeans were abruptly freed from a long series of previously significant diseases—smallpox, dysenteries, diphtheria, plague, and others—while relatively effective means were simultaneously devised to keep more stubborn

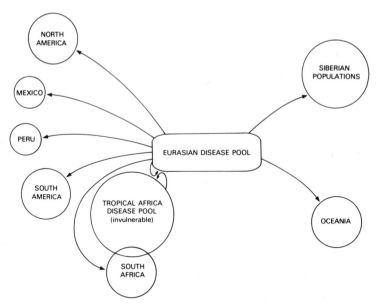

FIGURE 4. Spread of Eurasian disease pool, with resulting die-offs, 1500–1800

infections at least partially in check, tuberculosis and malaria chief among them.

Other parts of the civilized world lagged behind Europe—sometimes only by a few decades and sometimes, when the medical improvement required heavy capital expenditure, as the installation of a flow-through water and sewer system always did, for an indefinite length of time. The swarming of civilized populations in Asia and Africa therefore lagged somewhat behind the European pattern, but not far behind; and when it got fully in train, the larger base from which such population-swarming started meant that its scale and mass eclipsed what European lands had known.

Such a population surge was further complicated by the changed demographic regime in the cities and along the frontiers of civilized lands. As infectious disease circulation became more nearly worldwide and more nearly uniform (within climatic limits), the phenomenon of marginal die-off became trifling. By the beginning of the twentieth century only a few tiny and remote communities remained to be mowed down by an initial exposure to the infectious diseases of civilization; and the regions in which such populations lived—the Arctic north and the Amazon jungle, for instance—are not regions easily available for occupancy by migrating peasants, however crowded they may find themselves in their native land.

Similarly, as urban concentrations of humanity ceased to be lethal through the implementation of elementary public health measures, city folk became capable not merely of reproducing themselves, but of sustaining natural increase. Thereby opportunities for migrants from the countryside to enter urban occupational roles met a new obstacle. Newcomers from rural communities had to compete with a far greater number of persons born and bred in the city, whose skills were often better adapted to city existence than those of uprooted peasants could be. To be sure, cities could and do continue to grow and migrants from crowded countrysides do continue to move into town—or at least to the ring of squatters' shanties that surround many, perhaps most, of the world's cities. Such areas constitute a sort of visual evidence of the increased difficulty rural migrants face in insinuating themselves into the tissues of urban society, thanks to the cessation of an age-old pattern of urban die-off that has resulted from the new practices of public health administration.

Hence the peoples of Asia, Africa, and Latin America face a fundamentally altered circumstance as they move toward the cresting of their population explosions. Absorption of rural migrants has begun to require far more intensive applications of capital investment—educational investment as well as material investment in machines and the like that alone can render their labor usable in urban settings.

The magnitude of the problem boggles the mind, so much so that I find it hard to imagine any peaceable, happy resolution of the current population explosion. For the foreseeable future it seems sure that overcrowded and impoverished lands, in which traditional patterns of migration and modes for utilizing (and consuming) rural surplus populations have been interrupted, will share the earth with far less densely populated lands, in which the standard of living is immensely higher; and the gap between such regions is more likely to widen than to narrow in the immediate future. This in turn means, I think, that pressures for migration into the richer, emptier lands will mount, and only an increasingly ruthless application of force is likely to prevent such movements.

I freely confess that I do not see the path of wisdom in such a situation. Free migration across as well as within state boundaries would speedily result in catastrophic collisions between in-migrants and older populations—collisions which would dwarf the recent problems of American cities where in-migrant blacks have confronted older immigrant classes in what remains an only precariously peaceful fashion.

Closed frontiers do not appeal to me either, for they can only remain closed by resort to brutal police methods, or some kind of Big Brother supervision of every individual person within state boundaries.

Whether any intermediate policy can be formulated whereby some concept of optimal rates of migration from poor to richer lands could be defined so as to permit migration only on such a scale as to minimize damages to all the parties concerned seems to me dubious. And even if such a policy

could be defined in the abstract, application in detail would open the way
to extraordinary acts of arbitrary judgment by those officials entrusted with
its administration. For if hundreds wish to migrate and policy dictates that
only scores shall do so, who decides which applicants should be preferred?

Contemplating the world situation, who can say confidently that intelligent management and deliberate policy will be able to alleviate the problems of migration arising from the extraordinary differences of wealth that
currently exist between different parts of the earth? Instead, I suspect that
age-old controls on humanity are likely to assert their sovereign power, so
that some combination of violence, famine, and disease will again, as so often
in the past, reduce the extremes of contrast that today exist.

In such an anticipation I by no means exclude the possibility of catastrophic collapse within the United States, where our dependence on machine agriculture, with its complex flow-technology, makes us highly
vulnerable to catastrophic loss of an entire year's crop any time the supply
of gasoline, fertilizers, pesticides, or spare parts for tractors and combines
should break down. The time-tried methods of Asian peasants, however
laborious, are far more reliable in the sense that they can survive social
upheaval and disruption of trade nets for indefinite periods of time. In future
years the current patterns of food production in the United States and similar
lands may seem like an extraordinary legerdemain. We have, extraordinarily,
turned the social pyramid on its head, so that a mere five percent of the
population feeds the other ninety-five percent. By comparison, the instabili-
ties of Asian, African, and Latin American societies, painful though they be,
may prove far less precarious, since they have remained closer to long-
standing civilized norms.

Yet I do not despair of the possibility of using intelligence to mitigate an
intractable and probably insoluble problem. To understand better may not
permit control and resolution of all difficulties; it may, nevertheless, allow us
to navigate the current of contemporary world history a bit more skillfully,
dodge some of the rocks, and perhaps soften some of the sharpest hurts that
current conditions inflict and seem likely to inflict in time to come. Intelligence has never done more than that in human affairs; to do less would be
unworthy of our humanity.

NOTES

1. For a fuller discussion see W. H. McNeill, *Plagues and Peoples* (New York,
1976).

2. This calculation is based on the famous London Bills of Mortality. Cf. C. F. Brockington, *World Health,* 2nd ed. (Boston, 1968), p. 99.

3. For instructive details regarding the severity of urban die-offs in early modern times in Europe see R. Mols, *Introduction à la démographie historique des villes d'Europe du XIIIe au XVIIIe siècle,* 3 vols. (Louvain, 1954–56). Until I read this work I had no idea how severe were plagues and other epidemics in European cities of the early modern age. The loss of up to half a city's population in a single season was a routine disaster that called for no more than ordinary ritual prophylaxis and an accelerated in-migration from the countryside for a few years to restore things to normal.

4. William Squire, "On Measles in Fiji," *Transactions of the Epidemiological Society of London,* 4 (1877), pp. 72–74.

5. John F. Marchand, "Tribal Epidemics in the Yukon," *A.M.A. Journal,* 123 (18 December 1943), pp. 1019–20. In fact, only seven persons died: three from measles and four from meningitis.

6. Chicago: University of Chicago Press, 1963.

# [2]

## Migration and Expansion in Chinese History

Migration built China as a geographic and multiethnic entity. Yet this theme has been largely neglected in recent scholarship. Most modern scholars have explained China's growth as a purely political and military expansion of the capital area, dictated from above by the imperial court and carried out from below by its officials and armies. At the same time, scholars have remained generally indifferent to the demographic and geographic settings that conditioned these state policies; they have disregarded the interaction, intersettlement, and interfusion of migrant Han and non-Han peoples that preceded and followed military conquest and that made long-term political integration possible.[1]

Chinese migration was in good part an occupation of empty land, an expansion of the frontiers of Chinese settlement. Indeed, only the settlement of the American West and Tsarist Russia's expansion towards Central Asia and Siberia are comparable in geographic scale to Chinese migration. Present-day China, whose area has shrunk considerably from the maximum attained during the eighteenth century, is still as large as the continent of Europe from the Atlantic to the Urals.

Yet, the mere extent of land settled by Chinese migrants is less striking than the extraordinary historical dimensions of China's population movement. Whereas the American frontier reached its end by the turn of the nineteenth century and Russian eastward expansion began in the late seventeenth century, major private Chinese migrations date from the beginning

20

of China's traceable prehistory and have continued to the present. Chinese government-planned migrations date at least from the early second millennium B.C.[2] Even today Chinese are moving in increasing numbers towards such vast outlying areas as Sinkiang (Chinese Turkestan), Ch'ing-hai (Kokonor), Manchuria, and Tibet.

The role played by migration in the expansion of the sinitic world from its original nucleus in the southeastern portion of the loess highlands, starting in the early fifth millennium B.C., possibly even earlier, is clearly implied in Professor Ping-ti Ho's recent book, *The Cradle of the East.*[3] More systematic historical records pertaining to migration began to become available, however, only in the Chou period (1027–256 B.C.). This paper will, therefore, describe migration processes from about 1000 B.C.

## GOVERNMENT-PLANNED MIGRATION

The continuous role of government initiative, encouragement, organization, and aid constitutes one of the distinctive characteristics of Chinese migration. Throughout Chinese history the state repeatedly used migration as a major tool to further its policies of political and social integration, economic development, popular relief, and control of the rich and powerful. The Duke of Chou, who played a key role in the Chou conquest of Shang, remarked: "When a calamity struck the Yin dynasty [ca. 1600–1027 B.C.] . . . they always transferred population in the interests of the people."[4] The *Rites of Chou,* a compendium of statements on early political institutions and policies probably completed in the second century B.C., reiterates: "When a principality is struck by famine the rule is . . . to order the local population moved and relief supplies distributed."[5] This may have been a rationalization, but it had a factual basis.

Almost all migrations mentioned in early Chinese historical sources were government sponsored and linked to border control. As feudal lords expanded their states during the period of the Western Chou (1027–771 B.C.), they often organized colonists under new fiefs and sent them to settle recently conquered territory. The early kings of Western Chou established more than fifty of these colonies along their borders, including such states, later to become important, as Chin in modern Shansi, Lu and Cheng in modern Honan, and Ch'i in modern Shantung.[6]

By the Warring States period (455–221 B.C.) the government relied on migration not only to garrison and develop newly won border areas but also to facilitate their eventual political and social integration with the rest of China. In keeping with this goal, the state of Ch'in, the eventual unifier of China, systematically settled conquered non-Han Chinese areas before establishing its territorial administrations, known as *chün* and *hsien*.[7] Thus in 221 B.C. Ch'in Shih-huang ordered over five hundred thousand military colonists south to modern Hunan, Kiangsi, Kuangsi, and Kuangtung[8] "to settle on unoccupied land,"[9] and "live among the various Yüeh peoples,"[10] the native inhabitants of that area. Not until 214 B.C. did he establish the southern commanderies of Hsiang, Kuei-lin, and Nan-hai in these colonized territories. Native polities continued to exist in the more sparsely settled or politically resistant areas, and preserved their local autonomy until later dynasties integrated them with the rest of the empire by sending still other settlers into their territories. Emperor Kao-tsu of the Former Han later praised this use of migration for its partial sinicization of the Yüeh people.[11]

Subsequent Chinese dynasties followed these and other early examples. Government migration took many forms besides border settlement—from the forced migration of the rich and powerful to imperially controlled towns, to the voluntary settlement of famine victims or the poor on government-owned lands. Figures 1 and 2 showing instances of large-scale government migration from 225 B.C. to 1650 A.D. suggest the magnitude of this sustained policy of planned migration. The figures, based on government records, are thoroughly reliable, although they are doubtless incomplete: not all instances for which a record has survived are included and there were many more instances for which records did not survive.[12] Gaps in the graph may represent a lack of information rather than an absence of planned migration. Nevertheless the graphs demonstrate that from the second century B.C. to the seventeenth century A.D. the flow of planned migration, with its fixed directional character, was a constant, and occasionally perhaps even a predominant, feature of Chinese population movement.

With the continuous use of migration as a policy tool, the government developed a vast body of techniques for planning and financing population movements and solving settlement problems. The settlement of China's northern borders during the Han dynasties, one of the earliest well-documented government migrations, serves as a good illustration. Between the second century B.C. and the first century A.D. the Han emperors moved over one and a half million migrants north. Ch'ao Ts'o, a well-known statesman of the second century B.C., described the care they took:

> In the past when the government moved people to far-away areas and settled the broad wasteland, they examined the climatic and water conditions [of the proposed site], inspected the local topography, and checked the supply of forest and pasture land. Only then did they organize camps and build cities, draw street and house foundation lines, build roads to the fields, and map the property boundaries. [After that] they first built houses for the migrants: they provided each with a two-room house, a door that shut prop-

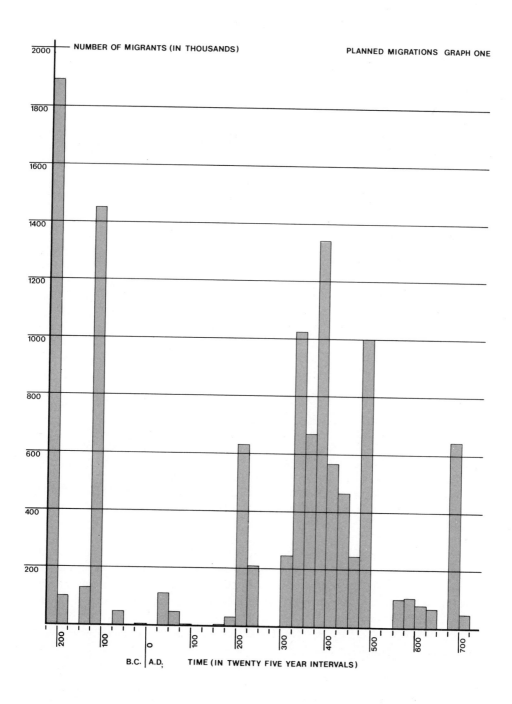

FIGURE 1. Planned migrations in China, 225 B.C.–725 A.D.

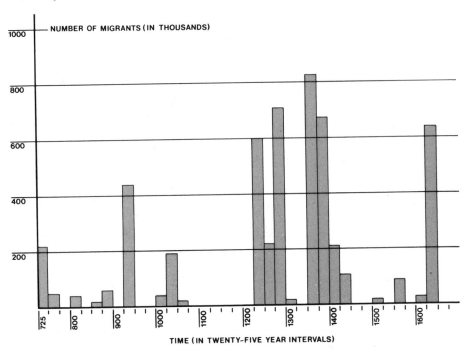

FIGURE 2. Planned migrations in China, 725 A.D.–1650 A.D.

erly, and farm tools. Thus when the migrants arrived, they had a place to live. When the time came to farm, they had land and agricultural tools. Only in this way could the government easily move people from their original homes and encourage them to move to the new cities.... Only in this way would the migrants like their new homes and be willing to settle there permanently.[13]

During these migrations, the Han government provided housing, transportation, food, clothing, and occasionally even travel allowances to the northern colonists.[14] Special taxes met the migration costs. In 120 B.C., for example, Emperor Wu of the Former Han evacuated seven hundred twenty-five thousand people from present-day Honan, Hopei, and Shantung. Of these, one hundred fifty-five thousand went south to Kiangsu and northern Chekiang;[15] the other five hundred eighty thousand were sent to Kansu, Ninghsia, and Inner Mongolia. To finance this massive evacuation the emperor created a new tribute tax, levied on all nobility, called the "white deerskin money" and issued China's first recorded silver currency.[16]

Archeological remains attest to the success of these early planned migrations. Since 1949 Chinese archeologists have uncovered over forty Western

Han cities in Inner Mongolia.[17] Averaging perhaps one thousand families, each represents a former government colony.[18] According to epigraphical evidence almost all of these cities date from the second century B.C. Several appear to have been built for the migrants of 120 B.C. Aerial photographs of Sinkiang in the northwest clearly show the remains of field and boundary lines created by early Han pioneer settlements and agricultural colonies.[19] Excavations in the Tarim Basin have revealed ancient canal systems over one hundred kilometers in length from the first century B.C. Indeed, the Ch'in and Han government cared so much about such settlement projects that many of the earliest irrigation and canal networks in China were constructed to accommodate border migration.[20] So well built were these canals of the Ch'in and Han period that even today some of them continue to irrigate millions of acres of land.[21]

Frequently, the army was the major organizer of government migration. Most government migrants were placed on state-owned farms and agricultural colonies similar to those in Inner Mongolia and Sinkiang; at different times these units were called *t'un-t'ien, kung-t'ien, ying-t'ien, ch'ing-t'ien,* and *ch'i-t'ien.* These state-owned farms, normally attached to the army, supplied provisions to local military units.[22] The farming households served terms as active soldiers and constituted a hereditary occupational group, legally registered as military households (*ping-hu, ying-hu, fu-hu* or *chün-hu*).[23] In peacetime the majority of these soldiers worked with their families as agricultural colonists.

With the exception of the militia, military units were rarely composed of local recruits. Most dynasties preferred to station troops away from their native districts permanently, in units of mixed geographical origin.[24] The handful of recruitment lists remaining from various dynastic periods provide evidence on this point. Han bamboo strips from the second century B.C. recently discovered in northwest China show the presence there of recruits from modern Honan, Shensi, Shantung, Hopei, and as far away as Szechwan to the southwest and Anhui and southern Hunan, two thousand kilometers to the southeast.[25] In turn, T'ang stone inscriptions from the eighth century A.D. reveal that men from northwest China were serving in the capital armies.[26] Two lists from the sixteenth century are particularly illuminating: one of 621 soldier households (*chün-hu*) from Kao-ling county in Shensi, the other of 6,898 soldier households from Hai-ning county in Chekiang.[27] The lists indicate that the recruits from these counties were regularly assigned to as many as five hundred garrison posts stretching from Manchuria to the Yunnan-Burmese border and that very few were stationed in districts neighboring their places of origin. According to this sample, Ming soldiers were permanently stationed with their families in places at least five hundred kilometers from their ancestral homes. As Yang Shih-ch'i, the Grand Secretary and President of the Board of War, remarked in the 1430s: "Natives from [north China] . . . now serve along the borders furthest south, while people from [south China] . . . serve along the extreme northern frontier. . . . Each garrison is thus seven or eight thousand *li* away from its place of registration or commanding unit. . . . The road is long and hard. Many die before they reach their unit."[28]

Often the government enlisted colonists from the more populous areas in the empire. Planned migration simultaneously alleviated population pressure and social unrest and made tremendous contributions to the development and settlement of China's internal frontiers. Three examples are illustrative. In the early third century A.D. four hundred thousand Han Chinese and Yüeh military settlers, conscripted from their homes in the then overpopulated mountain regions of southeast China, were moved one thousand kilometers west to establish more than thirty farm complexes along the middle and lower course of the Yangtze (Figure 3).[29] By the thirteenth century other colonists of similar background had reclaimed thousands of acres of polder land along the coasts of Kiangsu.[30] Within the first three decades of the Ming dynasty (1368–1644) military farmers of various ethnic backgrounds, assembled from all over China, had cleared at least two million *mou* (one *mou* equals approximately one-sixth of an English acre) in Yunnan and Kueichou provinces alone.[31]

Government-planned migration, of course, assumed still other forms which cannot be discussed in detail here: from the mass transferral of captured border peoples from their native lands[32] to the steady flow of convict and conscripted labor toward provincial and national capitals.[33] In all of these migrations the result was the forced homogenization that characterized army migration.

## PRIVATE MIGRATION

Modern scholars generally believe that because of the progressive dissemination of Confucian teachings about filiality, the Chinese were usually reluctant to leave their ancestral homes;[34] nevertheless, there was considerable private migration at all times. The widespread but obsolete view that agrarian life in traditional China was sedentary and static certainly conflicts with the documentary evidence. Ideally, peasants may have preferred to live and die in their native districts, but in reality overpopulation, war, famine, epidemics, natural catastrophes, and government oppression often forced them to seek a living elsewhere. Refugees were a perennial preoccupation of every imperial government, an indication that bad times, though mostly localized or regional, were frequent.[35]

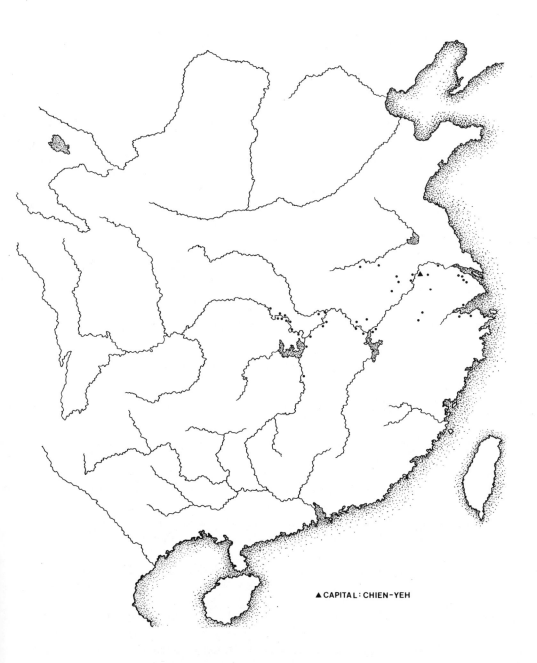

FIGURE 3. Agricultural colonies of the Sun-Wu Kingdom, 221–265 A.D.

CAPITAL: CHIEN-YEH

Even during peaceful times many rural inhabitants of early China moved. Not only was there a large seminomadic population of herdsmen *(mu-min)* and slash-and-burn agriculturalists *(she-min)* in the north and south; but also throughout China, merchants, itinerant craftsmen, vagabonds, and, numerically most important, an ever-increasing number of migrant laborers moved about the countryside. They fed a steady stream of local and circular migration, mainly between villages or market towns, and occasionally into the cities. Recent studies of hired labor during the Han dynasties suggest that as early as the second century B.C. rural society was geographically highly mobile.[36] Farm workers appear commonly to have traveled long distances. Even in underdeveloped parts of the empire such as northern Szechwan seasonal labor migrations extended over several hundred kilometers. Fan Yeh, a noted historian of the fifth century A.D., wrote: "In the Eastern Han [25–220 A.D.] the climate of northern Szechwan was so cold that in the summer not all the ice would melt. Every winter, to avoid the freezing weather, the native Yi peoples all migrated to Shu [approximately three hundred fifty kilometers away] as hired laborers and returned home only in summer."[37] According to Sung gazetteers this seasonal migration from northern Szechwan to Shu continued for at least eight hundred years, through the late tenth century.[38] Clearly, such migrations comprised an enduring part of China's demographic structure.

In tracing these private migrations special care must be paid to the institutional context of tax and corvée registers, a commonly assumed index of population change.[39] No Chinese government, with the possible exception of the present one, ever successfully registered all of China's population. Underregistration was chronic.[40] Moreover, until the twentieth century there existed in north and south China large, politically semiautonomous native polities, known at different times as *tao, shu-kuo, tso-chün, chi-mi-chou,* and *t'u-ch'ü,* that owed little or no tax to the central government and consequently had no obligation to register their population. According to the *Hou-hu chih,* the Board of Revenue manual on population registration compiled in 1513, even the reliable censuses of the early Ming dynasty excused the native officials in Yunnan, Kueichou, and much of Szechwan from registering the local population.[41]

The lack of government-registered population figures for such areas does not reflect their actual demographic condition. Many native polities had a thriving population of both indigenous peoples and Han Chinese who had immigrated because of the greater availability of land and freedom from imperial oppression. Fukien, for example, registered no population in the well-known census of A.D. 2. Archeological studies of Fukien, however, have uncovered evidence of a sizable indigenous population and of Han Chinese immigration during this period.[42] Particularly impressive among the seven

Former Han settlements uncovered so far in Fukien is a hitherto unknown city near modern Ch'ung-an, the perimeter of whose extant city walls measures almost two and a half kilometers.[43]

Changes in tax figures are often an indication of fluctuation in government control rather than an accurate reflection of population growth and migration. Between the second and sixth centuries A.D. the absence of strong centralized government in south China led to a drastic decline in registered population—from twenty million in A.D. 140 to slightly over five million in A.D. 464. This chaotic period was, nevertheless, one of unparalleled southern migration and population growth.[44] My own study of dynastic histories of the second to the fourth century A.D. suggests that at least three million people —approximately one tenth of the registered northern population in the second century A.D.—may have fled south during this period: half a million during the late second century, half a million during the late third century, and two million during the fourth century.[45]

The great migrations of the Age of Disunion are good examples of the sustained widespread population movement that occurred in early China. First, most of this migration was either rural-rural or urban-rural. After the fall of the Western Chin in A.D. 316, as natural catastrophe, local famine, political upheaval, and war became commonplace in the north, the urban population fled in great numbers to the countryside and joined other rural migrants in forts and mountain fortresses called *wu* and *pao* and in far away villages.[46] Second, much of this migration, though we do not know how much, was local, not regional. Even so, clan and village ties did facilitate long-distance migration for many families, poor as well as rich. The histories record numerous examples of local magnates such as Hsü Teng-chih who, in the early fourth century A.D., led his clansmen and over one thousand families of all economic strata from Shantung to southern Kiangsu, a distance of more than five hundred kilometers.[47]

Chain migration sustained much of the population movement during this period. In the second and third centuries A.D., when over two million non-Han tribesmen moved into the central plains from the northern steppe,[48] hundreds of thousands of Chinese fled before their advance. Between A.D. 289 and 312 almost two thirds of the original 59,200 registered households of Ping-chou in modern western Shansi emigrated.[49] Not all the migrants headed south. Although we lack statistics, most migrants probably moved within the north. So while the Shansi refugees fled east to Hopei, many Hopei refugees fled north to Liaotung (Figure 4). The scope of this chain migration was very significant. By the early fourth century two hundred thousand households of Han Chinese had moved to Manchuria,[50] perhaps doubling the population or even more.

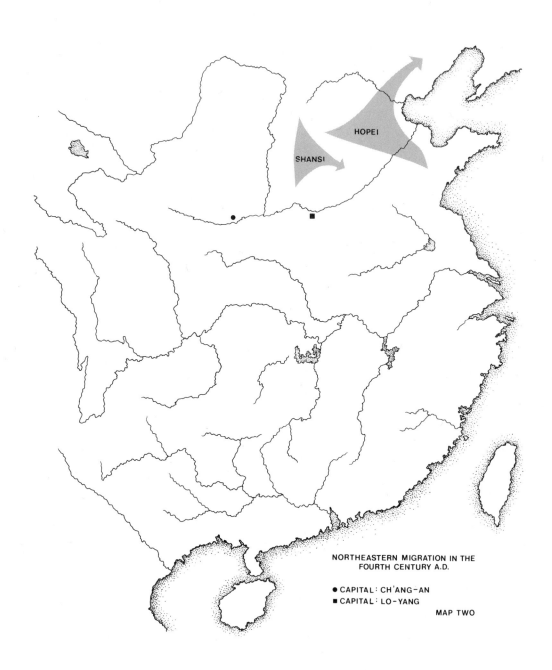

NORTHEASTERN MIGRATION IN THE
FOURTH CENTURY A.D.

● CAPITAL: CH'ANG-AN
■ CAPITAL: LO-YANG

MAP TWO

FIGURE 4. Northeastern migration in the fourth century A.D.

The pattern of population movement was as dynamic in the south as in the north, with migrants traveling in all directions. At the turn of the fourth century several hundred thousand Ti and Han Chinese refugees fled south from southern Shensi to Szechwan and Yunnan. Their arrival forced tens of thousands of northern Szechwan residents to move east to Hunan and Hupei. Similarly large numbers took refuge in the northeastern mountains near modern Ch'ung-ch'ing. As the northern invaders went south they drove the P'u, an indigenous people from southeastern Szechwan, into Yunnan and Kueichou. This led to the eastward and then the northward migration of the Liao, who originally lived in Yunnan and western Kuangsi, and then later provoked the eastern migration of the Lin-chun Man, who formerly inhabited Hunan and southern Hupei. By the middle of the fourth century an estimated one hundred thousand households *(lo)* of the Liao had infiltrated into northern Szechwan.[51] Tens of thousands of Lin-chun Man had settled in western Anhui north of the Yangtze River (Figure 5).[52]

Political and geographic conditions generally favored southbound over northbound migration. In the first place the south was more attractive than the north because of its more readily available agricultural land. Secondly, the strict passport requirements that attended political boundaries in China tended to be less rigidly enforced in the south than in the north. In addition, geographic and climatic changes within the last millennium pushed the Chinese back from such early settled areas as the northern Ulan Boha desert. These factors explain, in part, why the southeast, a mere hinterland as late as the second century A.D., had by the twelfth century become China's demographic, economic, and cultural center.[53]

The migration of the Hakka, literally "guest people," is a spectacular example of this southward migration pattern.[54] We first hear of the Hakka in the fourth century when, because of northern rebellions, they fled south from Shansi and Honan to the Huai River valley and southern Anhui. In the ninth century, when rebellion broke out in that area, the Hakka moved again, first southward past the T'ung-t'ing lake area and then down the Kan River to southern Kiangsi and southwestern Fukien. Later in the thirteenth century increasing northern migration pressure because of the Mongol invasion forced the Hakkas to move into the poor hill country of northeastern Kuangtung. Life in this area was hard, and by the seventeenth and eighteenth centuries many of the Hakka had left for Kuangsi and the rich coastline of Kuangtung, while others migrated as far as the upper Yangtze River area, particularly Szechwan (Figure 6).

The Hakka emigration to Szechwan reflects the many-sided social and economic changes that developed in China from the eleventh century on. Of course, migration alone does not explain the "medieval revolution" which began during this period. Such important changes as the gradual dissolution

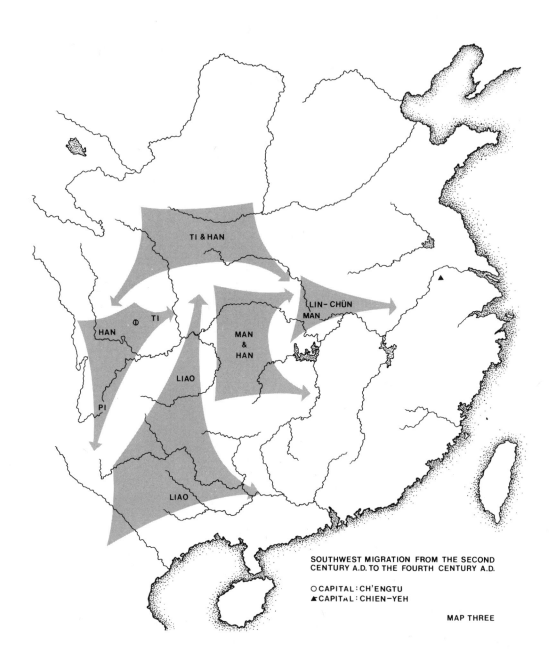

TI & HAN

LIN-CHÜN
MAN

TI

HAN

MAN
&
HAN

LIAO

PI

LIAO

SOUTHWEST MIGRATION FROM THE SECOND
CENTURY A.D. TO THE FOURTH CENTURY A.D.

○ CAPITAL : CH'ENGTU
▲ CAPITaL : CHIEN—YEH

MAP THREE

FIGURE 5. Southwest migration from the second century A.D. to the fourth
century A.D.

32]

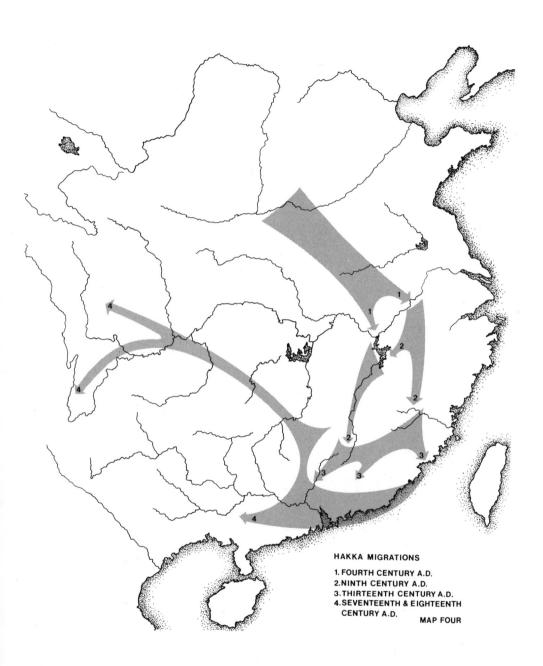

HAKKA MIGRATIONS

1. FOURTH CENTURY A.D.
2. NINTH CENTURY A.D.
3. THIRTEENTH CENTURY A.D.
4. SEVENTEENTH & EIGHTEENTH
   CENTURY A.D.
                    MAP FOUR

FIGURE 6. Hakka migrations

[33

of a manorial economy; the growth of handicraft industries, particularly in textiles; the development of an extensive network of rural markets; the dissemination of new agricultural technology and crops; the consequent rise in the living standard of the common peasant; and the dramatic though by no means steady rise in China's population to approximately one hundred million in A.D. 1200, 150 million in A.D. 1700, 275 million in 1780 and 430 million in 1850—all these and much more, combined to make Chinese society more mobile geographically.

As we have seen, during the Ming and Ch'ing dynasties, good land and the prospect of economic betterment enticed many of the Hakka to move fifteen hundred kilometers from Kuangtung west to Szechwan. Although detailed research on migration in this period has yet to be done, recent studies have suggested that from the eleventh century on the character of migration tended increasingly toward voluntary and occasionally longer population movements. Indeed, the very pace of migration may have quickened.[55] After A.D. 1000 the volume of private migration almost consistently appears to have been greater than government-planned migration.

Most migration was rural. While some restraints on city-bound career migration may have remained through the early Ming, all legal restraints on rural population movements were gradually abolished.[56] Beginning in southeast China in the twelfth century and culminating in an edict affecting the entire empire in the eighteenth century, the imperial court abrogated all laws tying tenants to the land.[57] By the mid-fifteenth century, the Ming government even gave up its attempts to confine the Chinese to hereditary occupational groups and geographical areas.[58] In turn, this abolition of forced permanent settlement encouraged freer, and perhaps more frequent, migration.

New agricultural technology and crops also encouraged the settlement of previously underdeveloped and underpopulated areas in the Chinese countryside. From the Sung onward, new methods of drainage and land reclamation facilitated the cultivation of the large marshland areas in the lower Yangtze River valley. Terraced fields with paddy rice as the main crop (t'i-t'ien), apparently first developed in Fukien,[59] also played an important role in the Sung, Yuan, and Ming settlement of western Fukien, southern Kiangsi, northern Kuang-tung, Szechwan, and Yunnan. Equally significant were the increased use of new strains of early ripening rice and millet and the introduction of such dryland American food plants as the peanut, the sweet potato, and maize in the sixteenth century. These technological developments allowed the Chinese for the first time to farm profitably the dry hill-country of southwest China.[60]

The consequent large scale development of southwest China and particularly the upper Yangtze River valley and its tributaries characterized Chinese migration during the Ming and early Ch'ing. Farmers from all over the empire flocked to the southwest. In 1477 the Ming government registered 438,644 recent immigrants in Hupei province alone.[61] The diverse origins of these immigrants is illustrated by the widespread mixture of voluntary associations based on common geographic origin.[62] In Tang-yang county, Hupei, for instance, immigrants from five other provinces—Hunan, Shansi, Shensi, Kiangsu, and Fukien—established regional associations called *hui-kuan.* The highest density of these organizations was in Szechwan, where practically every county had a few, and some counties had as many as forty or fifty. Although the headquarters of these associations were urban-based for convenience, their membership, reflecting the rural nature of southwestern migration, was drawn predominantly from the countryside. By aiding immigrants, these regional associations, developed to facilitate social integration, also came to promote population change.

Clan ties, like the regional associations, were a further spur to migration, offering clansmen support during their journey and sometimes after their arrival.[63] During the Ming and Ch'ing period, as migrants traveled unusually long distances—often one thousand kilometers or more—clan ties proliferated over wide geographical areas. Through the clan association the relatively poor achieved a degree of mobility they seem to have lacked in other countries. Thus in China, in contrast, for example, with eighteenth-century France, long-distance migration was not confined to the rich.[64]

## MIGRATION AND THE FORMATION OF THE HAN CHINESE

Migration was most important in shaping the cohesive identity of the Chinese people. However, it is impossible to distinguish the role of migration in this process from that of other forces. Many factors intermingled in transforming China from a world of separate peoples and independent polities in the first millennium B.C. to a politically consolidated, culturally homogeneous nation. But to a degree unequaled elsewhere, massive and recurrent migrations in China facilitated cultural interchange between host and immigrant peoples. Over and over, large-scale migrations acted as catalysts for subsequent acculturation and assimilation.

In 1000 B.C. the land now known as China was inhabited by many diverse peoples. The Han Chinese, the present-day dominant ethnic group in China, did not exist. Their predecessors, the sinitic Hua-hsia, lived mainly within the confines of the loess area of north China, less than one tenth of China's present area. Most of China was inhabited by other peoples known generically as I, Man, Jung, and Ti whose own states and civilizations developed partly independently of the Hua-hsia. Rigid ethnic boundaries reinforced the political divisions of early China. As a lord of the Chiang-jung, a nonsinitic people who lived originally in western Honan, said in B.C. 559: "Our Jung drink, our food, our clothes are all different from those of the Hua. We do not exchange offerings with them. Our languages are mutually incomprehensible."[65]

With the beginnings of wide-scale migration after B.C. 1027 the ethnic map changed radically. Migrations affected all of China. We have mentioned the frontier settlement of north China by the Hua-hsia peoples. During this period as well the Yüeh in southern Kiangsu, Chekiang, and Fukien conquered the Li people of Kuangtung and eastern Kuangsi;[66] the Shu extended their Szechwan kingdom into Kueichou, northern Yunnan, and western Kuangsi;[67] and the Ch'iang moved from Kansu into Ch'ing-hai, northern Szechwan, and western Yunnan.[68] Frequent intermarriage accompanied migrations and accelerated further change. According to archeological evidence, from the first millennium B.C. physical differences between such people as the sinitic Hua-hsia and the Tungusic Shan-jung began to disappear.[69] Throughout north China, as states slowly merged to form a politically united China by the third century B.C., the Hua-hsia, Shan-jung, and Chiang-jung peoples, among others, fused to form the Han Chinese.

The establishment of a common cultural base shared by all Chinese peoples during this period reflected their new identity. For example, the present Chinese writing system, a distinctive, historically binding cultural force, gradually spread with the Chou migration at the expense of native scripts. As early as the seventh century B.C., the Hsü-jung, a nonsinitic people who lived in central eastern China, composed bronze inscriptions in Chinese.[70] In some cases Chinese characters appeared first as loan words intermixed with native script. The fourth century B.C. sites of the Kingdom of Pa in northeastern Szechwan provide evidence that Chinese characters were first used for titles such as *wang* (king) or for abstract concepts such as *jen* (virtue) and *kuei* (nobility).[71] Pa writing, a pictographic script similar to modern Mo-sie,[72] continued in use until the second century B.C. when, perhaps partly by government fiat, the Han Chinese writing system totally replaced the native characters.

Large-scale migrations also caused other linguistic changes. Although little is known about the early indigenous languages of China, their variant dialects, or the processes of change, historians and linguists agree that by the late second century A.D. many Chinese, including the Han, the Ti in Kansu to the northwest, the Shu and Pa in Szechwan, and the Ai-lao in Yunnan, spoke a common language.[73] Even when non-Han peoples preserved their native languages, the upper classes often appear to have been fluent in Chinese.[74]

Changes in the Han Chinese dialect caused by migration are better documented. In the first century A.D., for example, Yang Hsiung, the eminent early authority on the Chinese language, divided north China into five dialect areas.[75] By the fourth century, however, as the people of north China migrated and intermixed to an unprecedented degree, they were led to adopt a mutually intelligible dialect. Eventually, major differences among northern dialects disappeared totally. Although provincial accents have remained, the population of the whole of north China has since spoken a common dialect.[76] Much of the homogeneity of modern north China can thus be traced to the Chinese *Völkerwanderung.*

Material remains testify to the gradual development of a relatively homogeneous civilization. Throughout the Eastern Chou (770–256 B.C.) many migrant ethnic groups were distinguished by their characteristic cultural assemblages and burial styles. Archeologists have been able to identify third century B.C. Pa and Ch'iang migrants within Shu political borders in northern Szechwan,[77] as well as Han Chinese migrants in Manchuria and north Korea.[78] By the end of the second century A.D., however, tombs known through epigraphical evidence to be non-Han Chinese can no longer be distinguished by their structure and contents.[79]

Although the flow of Chinese migration began early, the pace of integration was slow. Throughout Chinese history many non-Han Chinese continued in varying degrees to preserve their native customs, languages, and political autonomy. Indeed, over forty million non-Han "minority" peoples still live within China's present political boundaries, grouped in "semiautonomous regions."

Historically, these inner frontier areas initially attracted Chinese migration because land was available along with the prospect of freedom from imperial government oppression. Han Chinese migration thus usually moved ahead of tighter political control. Recent historical studies of such non-Han peoples as the Man who lived in the middle reaches of the Yangtze River valley, the Po-man who lived in northern Yunnan, and the Shan-yüeh who lived in southeast China reveal that many "native" peoples were actually descended from Han Chinese refugees.[80] As Shen Yüeh, a keen observer of the early sixth century A.D., wrote: "With the burden of tax and corvée, the poor people of the Sung [A.D. 420–479] found life intolerable. Many fled to the Man [non-Han Chinese] regions [in Hunan and Hupei], as the Man people do not have to perform corvée and the strong among them do not pay tax. ... The total number of these [non-Han and Han Chinese] households cannot be known."[81] In general these Han Chinese refugees were numerically too weak to displace the native population. Instead they settled in native villages and intermixed and intermarried with the native population. Only rarely did they arrive in such force as to allow separate communities or the establishment of an independent city.

Because of its escapist nature, there is little mention of refugee or village-bound migration in the dynastic histories, the major literary source for
the study of China before the tenth century A.D. As a result, most scholars
have ignored early refugee and village migration and have concentrated
instead on the role of urban migration and settlement in Chinese frontier
history. In the view of one important group of historians,[82] the Chinese did
not develop village settlements until the late second century A.D. Before this
period the ancient Chinese lived entirely in planned walled cities. Thus in
early China migration occurred from city to city, not from village to village.
This pattern was especially true of planned military migration which, these
scholars suggest, was invariably accompanied by the construction of a walled
city. Accordingly, expansion of China's borders meant the spread of urban
culture. Conflict between migrant and native implied urban-rural collision.

Archeological evidence contests this interpretation. Excavations currently underway in the People's Republic of China are uncovering villages
dating from the second century B.C. and earlier.[83] Many are from frontier
areas. Several were inhabited by Han Chinese and natives. Most appear to
antedate urban development. Two newly discovered maps of China's southern frontier drawn in the early second century B.C. are especially important
in this context.[84] They show over fifty rural communes, scattered across
southern Hunan and northern Kuangsi, ranging in size from hamlets of
twelve households to villages of eighty-one households. All of these villages
appear to have developed prior to the establishment of imperial control.
Their place names indicate that several were inhabited by both natives and
Han Chinese.[85] We can therefore conclude that in these areas China expanded through village-bound frontier migration, not urban development.

Planned military migration followed in the wake of village settlement
and modeled itself after the village settlement pattern. Although local military headquarters normally centered in forts and cities, many dynasties such
as the Ch'in, Northern Wei, Yuan, Ming, and Ch'ing also scattered troops in
open hamlets called *shao* or *hsün* by the native population.[86] In these periods there was no geographic barrier between natives and soldiers. Thus, for
instance, in the late fourteenth century, when the Ming government moved
more than seven hundred thousand "soldier" households assembled from all
over China to government-owned land in Yunnan, many military farms
"bordered on native lands."[87] In the eighteenth century, when the Ch'ing
moved an additional one hundred thousand soldier-colonists and their families to Yunnan, it divided them among three thousand five hundred settlements scattered across the province "like the pieces on a *go* board."[88] Hsü
Hsia-k'o, the famous seventeenth-century geographer, observed the consequent assimilation of military immigrants and natives during his travels in
southwest China. In his diary he described "military farms *[wei-t'un]* infil-

trated with Miao natives" and villages where "Han Chinese military settlers lived side by side with Lo-lo [also called Yi]."[89] According to Fang Kuo-yü, the leading modern historian of Yunnan, several present-day Yi (non-Han Chinese) clans possess Ming and Ch'ing military migrant registration papers among their family heirlooms.[90]

By reducing the barriers between immigrant and native, village migration allowed relatively peaceful frontier integration. Early Han Chinese migrants thus found it easy to intermix and intermarry with the native population. Subsequent assimilation, in turn, paved the way for basic steps toward acculturation such as the adoption of the Chinese script.

Migration thus facilitated *from below* the later growth of China into a unified political state. The ancient Chinese were well aware of this historical process. In the fifth century A.D. Fan Yeh wrote: "Although in the reign of Wang Mang [A.D. 9–25] the imperial court established its administrative districts in Chiao-chih [southern Kuangsi and northern Vietnam], nevertheless the native language was very different from Chinese. It required several translators to make oneself understood. The indigenous people behaved like animals. . . . Only later when the government exiled Han Chinese criminals to this area and made them live among the local inhabitants, did the natives gradually learn Chinese and become sinicized."[91]

Throughout Chinese history major migrations played an important role as both an instrument and an index of historical change. This high degree of geographic mobility requires us to reconsider many of our preconceptions about early Chinese society. First, rural migration did not always involve short-distance or evanescent population movement. The planned rural migrations of the third century B.C., the widespread chain migrations of the fourth century A.D., and the sustained southwestern rural pioneer movements of the fifteenth century A.D. were, by any definition, three great periods of migration. Second, throughout these periods most population movement in China was from village to village rather than from village to city. It was this village-bound migration that expanded China's frontiers and settled her borders. Indeed, it is interesting to note that, in general, the "bright lights" phenomenon of urban-bound migration appears to have been a late development in China (perhaps only since the sixteenth century).[92] Chinese migrations then and now have been predominantly rural rather than urban. Even today, in the People's Republic of China, the major population flow is directed "down to the countryside and up into the mountains." Many of these modern rural migrants now live in semiautonomous non-Han inhabited areas of China.

Periods of radical population change occurred repeatedly in China's past and often lasted for centuries. Through the intermingling of peoples the modern Chinese state and people evolved. Though the detailed mechanics of this cultural and political fusion are still not well understood, it is certain that for Chinese history, migrations were of far-reaching and long-lasting significance.

## NOTES

I would like to thank my teachers and fellow students for their generous help in preparing this paper. Many people gave advice and criticism freely, among them: Roger DesForges, Paul Ho, Tim Hornquist who drew the maps and tables, Susan Mann Jones, Philip Kuhn, William H. McNeill, Martin Powers, Stewart Oost, and Shiba Yoshinobu. My main debts of gratitude are to Professor Ping-ti Ho, whose intellectual guidance and personal inspiration were a major influence on my study, and to Professor Michael Dalby, who displayed unusual patience, acumen, and learning in detecting numerous errors of style and fact.

1. Han refers to the present dominant ethnic group in China.

2. Yü Hsing-wu, "Ts'ung chia-ku-wen k'an Shang-tai ti nung-t'ien k'en-chih" [Agricultural Colonies in the Shang Dynasty as seen from the Oracle Bone Records], *K'ao-ku* [Archeology], 1972/4:40–41, 45 (hereafter cited as *KK*).

3. Ping-ti Ho, *The Cradle of the East: An Inquiry into the Indigenous Origins of Techniques and Ideas of Neolithic and Early Historic China, 5000–1000 B.C.*, Hong Kong: The Chinese University of Hong Kong Press, 1975.

4. *Chou-King*, translated by F. S. Couvreur, Ho Kien Fu: Imprimerie de la Mission Catholique, 1920, 2, ch. 7, 2, 4–6.

5. *Chou-li* [Rituals of the Chou Dynasty], Ts'ung-shu chi-ch'eng edition, 9:239.

6. Hsü Chung-shu, "Yin Chou chih-chi shih-chi chih chien-t'ao" [An Examination of the Historical Data from the Transitional Period between Yin and Chou], *Chung-yang yen-chiu yüan li-shih yü-yen yen-chiu so chi-k'an* [Bulletin of the Institute of History and Philology, Academia Sinica], 7/2 (1936):137–164 (hereafter cited as *BIHP*).

7. For a vivid and detailed example of Ch'in planned migration in conjunction with the establishment of a *hsien* see Chang Chu (ca. 347), *Hua-yang kuo-chih* [Records of the Principality of Hua-yang], Shanghai Commercial Press, 1938 edition, 3:29 (hereafter cited as *Hua-yang kuo-chih*), together with Yang Hsiung (53 B.C.–A.D. 18), *Shu-wang pen-chi* [Annals of the Kings of Shu], in Yen K'o-chün (1762–1843), editor, *Ch'uan Han-wen* [The Complete Prose Works of the Han Dynasties], 53:5b, Peking: Chung-hua shu-chü, 1958 edition, 414.

8. Liu An (d. 122 B.C.), *Huai-nan tzu* [The Book of the Prince of Huai-nan], Shanghai Commercial Press, 1931 edition, 175.

9. Pan Ku (32–92), *Ch'ien Han shu* [History of the Former Han Dynasty], Peking: Chung-hua shu-chü, 1962 edition, 64:2783 (hereafter cited as *Ch'ien Han shu*).

10. *Ch'ien Han shu*, 1b:73.

11. *Ch'ien Han shu*, 1b:73.

12. In compiling these tables I consulted the twenty-four dynastic histories, the various *hui-yao* or Collections of Important Documents, and The Veritable Records of the Ming and Ch'ing dynasties. Household figures were computed at four individuals per family, except in a few cases where other estimates seemed more reasonable: e.g., Shih Yün-chün, "Ming-ch'u Yünnan an-ting chü-mien ti ch'u-hsien ho nung-t'ien shui-li shih-yeh ti fa-chan" [The Pacification of Yunnan and the Development of Agricultural Irrigation in the Early Ming dynasty], *Ssu-hsiang chan-hsien* [Ideological Struggle], 1975/6:66, estimates the early Ming military colonists stationed in Yunnan at three members per family. Because of the quantity of government documents available after 1000 A.D., Figure 2 is much less comprehensive than figure 1.

13. *Ch'ien Han shu*, 49:2288.

14. *Ch'ien Han shu*, 6:178; Fan Yeh (398–446), *Hou Han shu* [History of the Latter Han Dynasty], Peking: Chung-hua shu-chü, 1965 edition, 2:99, 109, 3:145 (hereafter cited as *Hou Han shu*).

15. Wang Ming-sheng (1722–1798), *Shih-ch'i shih shang-ch'üeh* [Assessments on the Seventeen Dynastic Histories], Ts'ung-shu chi-ch'eng edition, 9:71.

16. *Ch'ien Han shu*, 6:178.

17. *KK*, 1958/3:14–22, 1959/3:154, 1961/4:212–213, 1961/6:340, 1965/7:347–351, and especially Hou Jen-chih and Yü Wei-ch'ao, "Wu-lan pu-ho sha-mo ti k'ao-ku fa-hsien ho ti-li huan-ching ti pien-ch'ien" [The Archeological Finds in the Ulan Boha Desert and the Changes in the Geographical Environment], *KK*, 1973/2:92–107, and by the same authors with Li Pao-t'ien, "Wu-lan-pu-ho sha-mo pei-pu ti Han-tai k'en-ch'ü [The Cultivated Areas of the Northern Ulan Boha Desert during the Han Dynasties], *Chih-sha-yen-chiu* [Research in Desert Control], 1965:15–34.

18. *Ch'ien Han shu*, 49:2286.

19. Meng Ch'ih, "Ts'ung Hsin-chiang li-shih wen-wu k'an Han-tai tsai hsi-yü ti cheng-chih shih-hsuan ho ching-chi chien shih" [Han Dynasty Political Measures and Economic Construction in the Western Regions as Reflected in the Historical Remains from Sinkiang], *Wen-wu* [Objects of Cultural Interest], 1975/7:29 (hereafter cited as *WW*).

20. See Joseph Needham et al., *Science and Civilization in China*, Cambridge, England, 1971, 4/3:272, 288, 299–306, for a discussion of the irrigation systems at Kuan-hsien in Szechwan, and Ning-hsia and the Ling-chü canal in Kuangsi.

21. Fang Chi, *Wo-kuo ku-tai ti shui-li kung-ch'eng* [Hydraulic Engineering in Ancient China], Shanghai, 1955, 20–23.

22. There exists a large literature on government farms and agricultural colonies. The best work in English is D. C. Twitchett, "Lands under State Cultivation during the T'ang Dynasty," *Journal of Economic and Social History of the Orient*, 2 (1959):162–203. In Chinese: for the Han dynasties, Ch'en Chih, "Lun Liang Han t'un

shu yen-chiu" [Research on Garrison Colonies during the two Han dynasties], *Liang Han ching-chi shih-liao lun-ts'ung* [A Collection of Essays on Economic History during the Two Han Dynasties], Sian, 1958, 1–76; for the Period of Disunion, Wang Chung-lo, *Wei Chin Nan-pei ch'ao Sui ch'u-T'ang shih* [A History of the Wei, Chin, Period of Disunion, Sui, and early Tang Dynasties], Shanghai, 1961, 22–24, 43–44, 89–97, 416–418 (hereafter cited as Wang Chung-lo); for the Yuan, Kuo Ch'ing-ch'ang, "Yuan-tai ti chün-t'un chih-tu" [The Military Farm System of the Yuan Dynasty], *Li-shih chiao-hsüeh* [Teaching History], 1961/11, 12:39–45; for the Ming, Wang Yü-ch'uan, *Ming-tai ti chün-t'un* [Military Colonies during the Ming Dynasty], Peking, 1965 (hereafter cited as Wang Yü-ch'üan).

23. Not all the *chün-hu* were hereditary. The T'ang *fu-ping*, for example, was a draft army. See Ku Chi-kuang, *Fu-ping chih-tu k'ao-shih* [An Examination of the *Fu-ping* System], Shanghai, 1962, 191.

24. See the general discussion of this governmental policy in Chou I-liang, "Wei Chin ping-chih ti yi ko wen-t'i" [One Question on the Military Systems of the Wei and Chin Dynasties], *Wei Chin Nan-pei-ch'ao shih lun chi* [A Collection of Essays on the History of the Wei, Chin and Period of Disunion Dynasties], Peking, 1963, 1–11. To my knowledge the Chin *chung-chün*, the T'ang *fu-ping*, and the Ch'ing Green Standard military systems were the only major long-standing national armies that systematically stationed all recruits in their native districts. The Ming *wei-so* system followed this policy only in Fukien. Even in these armies the exigencies of war often required soldiers to be transferred away from their original units. Thus in the fourteenth century the Ming stationed almost thirty thousand native Fukien troops in Yunnan (see *Ming shih lu: yu kuan Yunnan li-shih tzu-liao ch'e-ch'ao* [A Selection of Historical Material Concerning Yunnan in the Ming Veritable Records], Kunming, 1959, 46). For further examples see Lo Erh-kang, *Lü-ying ping-chih* [A Treatise on the Army of the Green Standard], Chungking, 1945, 41, 177–179. I should point out that according to Chao Yen-wei (ca. 1163), *Yün-li man lu*, Shanghai: Ku-tien wen-hsüeh, 1957 edition, 12:177, although the Sung *hsiang-chün* army recruits were never stationed in their native districts, they were also never assigned permanently to any one provincial post.

25. *Chü-yen Han chien chia pien* [Han Bamboo Strips from Chü-yen: Volume one], Peking, 1959: Honan, nos. 439, 881, 938, 1022, 1122, 1675, 1776, 1789, 1941, 1944, 2087, 2108, 2167, 2224, 2257, 2278; Shensi, nos. 266, 519, 539, 1198, 1596; Hopei, nos. 682, 1530, 1752, 1778, 2370, 2415; Shantung, nos. 1588, 2029, 2292; Anhui, nos. 1941, 2116; southern Hunan, no. 933. For recruitment strips from Szechwan see Ch'en Chih, "Kuan-yü Chü-yen Han-chien ti fa-hsien ho yen-chiu yi-wen ti shang-ch'üeh" [An Evaluation of the Essay "The Discovery and Research on the Han Bamboo Strips from Chü-yen], *KK*, 1960/10:38.

26. Hsia Nai, "Wu-wei T'ang-tai T'u-yu-hun mu-jung shih mu chih" [Funeral Stelae Newly Discovered from the T'ang Cemetery of the Tu-yü hun Tribe at Wu-wei Kansu], *K'ao-ku hsüeh lun-wen chi* [A Collection of Essays on Archaeology], Peking, 1961, 95–116.

27. Lu Nan (1479–1542), *Kao-ling hsien-chih* [Local Gazetteer of Kao-ling County], 1541 edition, 2:12b–24; Chang Chih, *Hai-ning hsien-chih* [Local Gazetteer of Hai-ning County], 2:16b–23, Peking NLB Rare Book Collection, microfilm 848.

28. *Huang Ming ching-shih wen-p'ien* [A Collection of State Papers from the Ming Dynasty], Hong Kong reprint, 15:109.

29. My calculations based on Ch'en Shou (233–297), *San-kuo chih* [Records of the Three Kingdoms], Peking: Chung-hua shu-chü, 1959 edition, 47:1118, 1119, 1140, 1146; 51:1214; 53:1253; 54:1264, 1266, 1271, 1276, 1277; 55:1293, 1298, 1299, 1301, 1303; 60:1385.

30. *Sung hui-yao chi-pen* [A Collection of Important Documents on the Sung], Taipei, 1964 edition.

31. Wang Yü-ch'üan, 31, 35.

32. See for example, Ise Sentaro, "T'ang-ch'ao tui sai wai hsi-nei hsi-min tsu chih chi-pen t'ai-tu" [The Basic Attitude of the T'ang Government to the Immigration of Border Peoples], translated by Ch'iu Kung-sheng, *Ta-lu tsa-chih* [The Continental Magazine], 36/11 (1968):29–33.

33. See Chung-kuo k'ao-ku so Lo-yang kung-tso tui, "Tung Han Lo-yang ch'eng nan chiao ti hsing-t'u mu" [The Eastern Han Graveyard of Convicts in the Southern Suburbs of Loyang], *KK*, 1972/4:2–19. The 522 convict laborers buried in this site came from 39 of the 103 commanderies in the Eastern Han Empire, including some from Shan-yang county in northeastern Chekiang almost one thousand kilometers away!

34. A typical example is Lü Ssu-mien, *Sui T'ang Wu-tai shih* [A History of the Sui, T'ang and Five Dynasty Period], Peking, 1959, 769–776.

35. As in the case of the government-owned farms there exists a vast literature on refugee migration and vagrancy. Note especially: for the Han and Period of Disunion, Wang Chung-lo, 5–8, 11–34, 142–155; for the T'ang and Sung, Nakagawa Manabu, "Tō Sō no kyakko ni kansuru shokenkyu" [Research on the "Guest Households" of the Tang and Sung Dynasties], *Tōyō gakuhō*, 46/2 (1963):97–110; for the Ming, Wei Ch'ing-yuan, *Ming-tai huang-ts'e chih-tu* [The Yellow Register System of the Ming Dynasty], Peking, 1961, 194–232 (hereafter cited as Wei Ch'ing-yuan).

36. Chien Po-ts'an, "Liang Han shih-ch'i ti ku-yung lao-tung" [Hired Labor in the Two Han Dynasties], *Pei-ching ta-hsüeh hsüeh-pao: jen-wen k'o-hsüeh* [Peking University Review], 1959/1:51–56; Lao Kan, "Han-tai ku-yung lao-tung chih-tu" [The Hired Labor System in the Two Han Dynasties], *BIHP*, 23 (1951):77–87.

37. *Hou Han shu*, 86:2858; *Hua-yang kuo-chih*, 3:40 records an almost identical description of seasonal migration from northern Szechwan in the fourth century A.D.

38. Yueh Shih (930–1007), *T'ai-p'ing huan-yü chi* [Gazetteer of the World during the T'ai-p'ing Period 976–983], Taipei, Wen-hai reprint, 78:3b, 599.

39. The early classic works of Aoyama Sadao, "Zui Tō Sō san-dai ni okeru kosu no chi-ikiteki kosatsu" [A Geographical Study of the Household Figures in the Sui, Tang and Sung Dynasties], *Rekishi gaku* [Historical Studies], 6/4 (1936):59–94, and Hans Bielenstein, "The Census of China during the Period 2–742 A.D.," *Bulletin of the Museum of Far Eastern Antiquities*, Stockholm, 19 (1947):125–163, among others, rely heavily on tax registers.

40. Chao Kuan (ca. 1513), *Hou-hu chih*, 1611 edition, 10:29b–30, Peking NLB Rare Book Collection, microfilm 1146 (hereafter cited as *Hou-hu chih*), in a typical memorial dated 1442 records underregistration in parts of Kiangsi, Hukuang, Kuangtung, Kuangsi, Szechwan, Kueichou, and Honan.

41. *Hou-hu chih*, 4:3, 7; also see *Ta Ming hui-tien* [Collected Statutes of the Ming], Taipei, 1964 reprint, 20:10.

42. Ch'en Chih, "Fu-chien Ch'ung-an ch'eng ts'un Han ch'eng yi-chih shih-tai ti t'ui-tse" [An Investigation on the Dates of the Han City Remains at Ch'ung-an Fukien), *KK*, 1961/4:219–221.

43. Fu-chien sheng wen-wu kuan-li wei-yuan-hui, "Fu-chien Ch'ung-an ch'eng ts'un Han ch'eng yi-chih" [The Remains of a Han City at Ch'ung-an Fukien), *KK*, 1960/10:1–9, 52.

44. Wang Chung-lo, 111–134, 142–155.

45. For the late second century note especially: *San-kuo chih*, 21:610; 47:1118–1119, 1121; 52:1219. For the late third century: Fang Hsüan-ling (578–648), et al., *Chin-shu* [The History of the Chin Dynasties], Peking: Chung-hua shu-chü, 1974 edition, 120:3023 (hereafter cited as *Chin shu*) and Ssu-ma Kuang (1019–1086), *Tz'u-chih t'ung-chien* [Comprehensive Mirror for Aid in Government], 86:2621–2622, 2718.

46. Miyagawa Hisashi, *Rikuchōshi kenkyu* [Research on the History of the Six Dynasties], Tokyo, 1956, 437–472.

47. *Chin shu*, 91:1356.

48. Ma Ch'ang-shou, *Pei-ti yü Hsiung-nu* [The Northern Ti and the Hsiung-nu], Shanghai, 1962, 81–93 (hereafter cited as Ma Ch'ang-shou, *Pei-ti yü Hsiung-nu*).

49. Wang Chung-lo, 143, 151 n. 2.

50. Ma Ch'ang-shou, *Wu-huan yü Hsien-pei* [The Wu-huan and the Hsien-pei], Shanghai, 1962, 36–38 (hereafter cited as Ma Ch'ang-shou, *Wu-huan yü Hsien-pei*).

51. Miao Yüeh, "Pa Shu wen-hua ch'u-lun shang-ch'üeh" [An Assessment of "Preliminary Discussions on Pa and Shu Culture"], *Tu-shih ts'un-kao* [Draft Notes in Reading History], Peking, 1963, 108–113.

52. Chang Kuan-ying, "Liang Chin Nan-pei ch'ao shih ch'i min-tsu ta pien-tung chung ti Lin-chün Man" [The Lin-chün Man during the Great Ethnic Changes of the Wei Chin and Period of Disunion], *Li-shih yen-chiu*, 1957/2:67–85 (hereafter cited as Chang Kuan-ying).

53. On southward migration in early times see Hsiao Fan, *Ch'un-ch'iu chih Liang Han shih-ch'i Chung-kuo hsiang nan-fang ti fa-chan* [China's Southward Expansion from 770 B.C. to 220 A.D.], Taipei, 1973; Chang Chia-chü, *Sung-tai she-hui chung hsin nan-ch'ien shih* [The History of the Southward Movement of Sung Society], Canton, 1944, and by the same author, *Liang Sung ching-chi chung-hsin ti nan-yi* [The Southward Movement of the Economic Heartland of the Sung Dynasties], Wuhan, 1957.

54. The following discussion of the Hakka is based exclusively on Lo Hsiang-lin, *K'o-chia yüan-liu k'ao* [An Analysis of the Development of the Hakka People], Taipei, 1973.

55. Miyazaki Ichisada, "Sō-dai igo no tochi shoyū keitai" [The Demesne in China from the Sung Period and Later], *Tōyōshi kenkyū*, 12/2 (1952):1–34; and by the same author, translated by Tu Cheng-sheng, "Ts'ung pu-ch'ü tao tien-k'o" [From Dependent to Tenant], *Shih-huo* 3/9 (1973):427–443, 3/10 (1974):473–492 (hereafter cited as Miyazaki Ichisada, "Ts'ung pu-ch'ü tao tien-k'o").

56. This is suggested by Lai Chia-tu, *Ming-tai Yün-yang nung-min ch'i-yi* [The Peasant Rebellion in Yun-yang (Hupei) during the Ming Dynasty], Wuhan, 1956, 13

(hereafter cited as Lai Chia-tu). Lai stresses the government obstacles to commercial urban-bound migration.

57. Miyazaki Ichisada, "Ts'ung pu-ch'ü tao tien-k'o," 479–486.

58. Wei Ch'ing-yüan, 215.

59. Ho Ping-ti, *Huang-t'u yü Chung-kuo nung-yeh ti ch'i-yüan* [The Loess Soil and the Rise of Chinese Agriculture], Hong Kong: The Chinese University of Hong Kong Press, 1969, 100–101.

60. Ping-ti Ho, *Studies on the Population of China: 1368–1953,* Cambridge, Mass., 1959, 147.

61. *Ming Shih-lu,* Taipei reprint, 1962–66, 2925; Lai Chia-tu, 9–24, 52–65, has a general discussion on immigration to Hupei during Ming times.

62. The following discussion of *hui-kuan* is based on Ho Ping-ti, *Chung-kuo hui-kuan shih-lun* [A Historical Survey of *Landsmannschaften* in China], Taipei, 1966.

63. Fu I-ling, *Ming Ch'ing shih-tai shang-jen chi shang-yeh tzu-pen* [Merchants and Commercial Capital during the Ming and Ch'ing Dynasties], Peking, 1965, 75–77; Fujii Hiroshi, "Hsin-an shō nin no kenkyū" [Research on the Merchants of Hsin-an], *Tōyō gakuhō,* 36/3 (1953):77. A translation of the latter article into Chinese by Fu I-ling and Huang Huan-tsung is available in *An-hui shih-hsüeh t'ung-hsün* [The Historical Bulletin of the University of Anhui], 2, 9 (1959):11–41, 10 (1959):55–71.

64. Jean-Pierre Poussou, "Le Mouvement migratoire en France," *Annales de Démographie Historique,* 1970, 43.

65. My translation is based on Legge, tr., *The Ch'un Ts'ew with the Tso Chuen,* 460.

66. Tan Ch'i-hsiang, "Ao-tung ch'u-min k'ao" [An Analysis of the Early People of Canton], *Yü-kung,* 7/1, 2, 3 (1937):45.

67. Li Tao-yüan (d. 527), *Shui-ching chu* [Commentaries on the Water Classic], Shanghai Commercial Press, 1929 edition, 37:62–63; *Hua-yang kuo-chih,* 3:28.

68. Yu Chung, "Tui Ch'in yi-ch'ien hsi-nan ko tsu li-shih yüan-liu ti k'uei-t'an" [An Investigation into the Historical Origins of the Ethnic Groups in Southwest China before the Ch'in Dynasty], *Jen-wen k'o-hsüeh* [Humanistic Sciences], 1957/4:70–71.

69. Chung-kuo k'o-hsüeh yuan k'ao-ku yen-chiu so t'i-chih jen-lei hsüeh tsu [Physical Anthropology section, Institute of Archeology, Academia Sinica], "Ch'ih-feng Ning-ch'eng Hsia-chia tien shang-ts'eng wen-hua jen-ku yen-chiu" [Studies on the Human Skeletal Remains of the Upper Hsia-chia-tien Culture Unearthed at Ning-ch'eng and Ch'ih-feng], *K'ao-ku hsüeh-pao* [*Archeological Review*], 1975/2:157–169 (hereafter cited as *KKHP*).

70. Kuo Mo-jo, *Liang Chou chin-wen tz'u ta-hsi t'u-lu k'ao shih* [A General Illustrated Catalogue of the Bronze Inscriptions of the Two Chou Dynasties], Peking, 1958 edition, 184; and Feng Yün-p'eng (ca. 1821), *Chin shih-so* [An Examination of Inscriptions on Bronze and Stone], Shanghai Commercial Press, 1929 edition, 1: 95–96.

71. There is a large literature on the Pa tombs. See, for example, Ssu-ch'uan sheng po-wu-kuan, *Ssu-ch'uan ch'uan-kuan tsang fa-chüeh pao-kao* [The Excavation Report of the Boat Grave Sites in Szechwan], Peking, 1960, 59–62 (hereafter cited as

*Ssu-ch'uan ch'uan-kuan fa-chüeh pao-kao*); and T'ung En-cheng and Kung T'ing-wan, "Ts'ung Ssu-ch'uan liang chien t'ung k'o shang ti ming-wen k'an Ch'in mie Pa Shu hou t'ung-i wen-tzu ti chin-pu ts'u-shih" [The Unification of the Chinese Written Language after the Ch'in Conquest of Pa and Shu as Seen in the Inscriptions on Two Bronze Halberds from Szechwan], *WW*, 1976/7:82–85.

72. Hsü Chung-shu, "Pa Shu wen-hua ch'u-lun" [A Preliminary Discussion on Pa and Shu Culture], *Ssu-ch'uan ta-hsüeh hsüeh pao* [The University of Szechwan Review], 1959/2:40–44.

73. Lo Ch'ang-p'ei and Chou Tsu-mo, *Han Wei Chin Nan-pei ch'ao yün pu yen-chiu* [Research on Phonetic Change in the Han, Wei, Chin and Period of Disunion], Peking, 1958, 70 (hereafter cited as Lo Ch'ang-p'ei and Chou Tsu-mo); Meng Wen-t'ung, "Pa Shu shih wen-t'i" [Questions on the History of Pa and Shu], *Ssu-ch'uan ta-hsüeh hsüeh pao*, 1959/5:40.

74. Chang Kuan-ying, 79–80; Ma Ch'ang-shou, *Wu-huan yü Hsien-pei*, 55–59, and by the same author, *Pei-ti yü Hsiung-nu*, 46–50.

75. Lo Ch'ang-p'ei and Chou Tsu-mo, 71.

76. Pang-hsin Ting, *Chinese Phonology of the Wei Chin Period*, Taipei, 1975, 262.

77. *Ssu-ch'uan ch'uan kuan tsang fa-chüeh pao-kao*, 86; Feng Han-chi et al., "Min-chiang shang-yu ti shih kuan-tsang" [The Stone Cist Burials on the Upper-course of the Min River], *KKHP*, 1973/2:41–60.

78. Tung Chu-ch'en, "K'ao-ku hsüeh-shang Han-tai chi Han tai chih ch'ien ti tung-pei chiang-yü" [The Han and Pre-Han Northeastern Border Regions in the Light of Archeology] *KKHP*, 1956/1:29–43.

79. Yun-nan sheng wen-wu kung-tso tui, "Yun-nan Chao-t'ung kuei-chia yüan chih Tung Han mu fa-chüeh" [The Excavation of an Eastern Han Period Tomb at Chao-t'ung kuei-chia yuan in Yunnan], *KK*, 1962/8:399.

80. On the Po-Man see *Yun-nan Po-tsu ti ch'i-yuan ho hsing ch'eng lun-wen-chi* [A Collection of Essays on the Origins and Formation of the Po People of Yunnan], K'un-ming, 1957; on the Shan-yüeh see Ch'en K'o-wei, "Tung-yüeh shan-yüeh ti lai-yuan ho fa-chan" [The Origin and Expansion of the Eastern Yüeh and the Mountain Yüeh], *Li-shih lun-ts'ung* [Historical Review], 1 (1964):161–176.

81. Shen Yüeh (441–513), *Sung shu* [History of the Liu Sung Dynasty], Peking: Chung-hua shu-chü, 1974 edition, 91:1356.

82. This major school of historians is well represented by Miyazaki Ichisada's "Chūgoku ni okeru son-sei no nari-tachi" [On the Appearance of Villages in China: An Aspect of the Ruin of the Ancient Empire], *Tōyōshi kenkyū*, 18/4 (1960):50–72. For a general bibliography on urban studies see Shiba Yoshinobu, "Chūgoku toshi o meguru kenkyu gaiyō" [An Outline of the Research on Chinese Urban Studies], *Hosei shi kenkyu* [Legal History Review], 23 (1973):185–206.

83. See p. 40 n. 17, and p. 43 n. 42.

84. The two most important articles on these maps (with detailed reproductions) are T'an Ch'i-hsiang, "Erh-ch'ien yi-pai to nien ti yi-fu ti-t'u" [A Two-Thousand-One-Hundred-Year-Old Map], *WW*, 1975/2:43–48, and Tan Li-po, "Ma-wang-tui Han-mu ch'u-t'u ti shou-pei t'u t'an-t'ao" [An Examination of the Defense Map Excavated at Ma-wang-tui], *WW*, 1976/1:22–27.

85. Note for example Shen-chün li village on the map reproduced in *WW*, 1975 /2, between pages 46 and 47. In private correspondence T'an Ch'i-hsiang, a senior scholar in the People's Republic of China and one of the first historians to study these maps, expressed agreement that this village probably contained both Han and non-Han Chinese inhabitants.

86. On the Ch'in military settlement pattern see p. 38 n. 9 and 10. On the Northern Wei settlement pattern see T'ang Chang-ju, "Shih-lun Wei-mo pei-chen chen-min pao-tung ti hsing-chih" [A Preliminary Discussion on the Character of the Riots by the Northern Garrison Soldiers in the late Wei Dynasty], *Li-shih yen-chiu*, 1964/1:97–114.

87. Li Yuan-yang (1497–1580), *Yun-nan t'ung-chih* [A Local Gazetteer of Yunnan], 1574 edition, 7:1.

88. Li Ch'eng (1778–1844), *Yun-nan t'ung-chih* [A Local Gazetteer of Yunnan], 1835 edition, 43:1.

89. Hsü Hsia-k'o (1585–1641), edited by Ting Wen-chiang, *Ting chiao pen Hsü Hsia-k'o yu-chi* [The Travel Diaries of Hsü Hsia-k'o edited by Ting Wen-chiang], Taipei: Ting-wen, 1974 reprint, 8:385; 10:446.

90. Fang Kuo-yü and Miao Luan-ho, "Ch'ing tai Yun-nan ko-tsu lao-tung jen-min tui shan-ch'ü ti k'ai-fa" [The Settlement of Mountain Areas in the Ch'ing Dynasty by the Multi-ethnic Working-class People of Yunnan], *Ssu-hsiang chan-hsien*, 1976/1:74.

91. *Hou Han shu*, 86:2836.

92. See Hsü Ta-ling, "Shih-liu shih-chi shih-ch'i shih-chi ch'u-ch'i Chung-kuo feng-chien she-hui nei-pu tzu-pen chu-yi ti meng ya" [The Buds of Capitalism within the Chinese Feudal System of the Sixteenth and Early Seventeenth Centuries], *Chung-kuo tzu-pen chu-yi meng-ya wen-t'i t'ao lun-chi* [A Collection of Papers on the Question of the Buds of Capitalism in China], Peking, 1957, 897–946.

# [3]

## Migration in Modern European History

### WHAT IS MIGRATION?

Some apparently crisp concepts owe their crispness to bureaucracy. After many centuries in which workers had now and then walked off the job to put pressure on the boss, only in the nineteenth century did firms, unions, and governments coerce each other into precise definitions of the strike. Thenceforth the strike became routinized, and strike statistics based on standard definitions proliferated. Slowdowns, wildcats, demonstrations, tardiness, absenteeism, unauthorized holidays, sabotage, mass resignation came to seem distinct alternatives to the strike. Most of the organized parties came to consider these other forms of action less desirable than the strike because they were riskier and less routine. Yet in the eighteenth century the boundaries among these ways of behaving had been unclear indeed. Bureaucracies, by defining the strike as a distinctive form of action, helped create the modern strike.

Other commonly employed and frequently statisticized concepts owe the same debt to bureaucracy: unemployment, employment, production, consumption, perhaps marriage and illegitimacy as well. Twenty-five years ago Oskar Morgenstern pointed out that fluttering definitions introduce significant errors into economic statistics. But Morgenstern thought the main problems were theoretical:

There is often lack of definition or classification of the phenomenon to be measured or recorded, and in addition, there is the difficulty of applying correctly even a faultless system of classification. The theoretical characteristics of, say, an industry or simply of a "price" are less well established than those of a wave length. Almost everything turns around the question of classification. This is a well known difficulty and much effort has been directed towards the establishment of uniform classifications, of employment categories and commodities in foreign trade. But there are large fields where very little has been done and where deep theoretical problems await solution before classification can be significantly improved (Morgenstern, 1963, p. 35).

Morgenstern shows appropriate indignation when faced with evidence that organizations actually fabricate or manipulate definitions for their own purposes:

Perhaps equally important is the often arbitrary, willful, and frequently politically determined procedure employed by customs officials. In spite of a perfectly definite classification scheme, commodities are sometimes put into a similar category carrying higher duties in order to impede their import (or, as the case may be, into one that will make the import cheaper). This plays havoc, of course, with statistical accuracy (Morgenstern, 1963, pp. 37–38).

Here is a less testy, but more cynical, interpretation: bureaucracies first produce definitions to serve their own purpose. Economists come along later to rationalize the definitions.

The concept of migration faces the same difficulties. From the continuous locomotion of human beings, to pick out some moves as more definitive than others reflects the concern of bureaucrats to attach people to domiciles where they can be registered, enumerated, taxed, drafted and watched. A vagrant—a person without a domicile—gives trouble not only to the police but also to definitions of migration. Are gypsies migrants? The crisp definitions and statistics essential to an answer emerged with the consolidation of national states and state bureaucracies.

With rare exceptions, both practical definitions and available evidence concerning migration state the answers to some combination of these three questions:

1. Who lives here *now*?
2. Where did they live *then*?
3. Who else lived *here* then?

A single enumeration of the population can produce answers to the first two questions. The third question requires enumerations at more than one point in time. But all three can be answered within a single administrative unit. Only rarely do we find an answer to a fourth obvious question in the series: Where do they live *now*? That requires two difficult operations: looking in several places, and tracing people forward in time. Counts of migration therefore consist mainly of comparisons, one place at a time, (a) between the answers to questions 1 and 2; (b) among the answers to questions 1, 2, and 3.

All the elements—who, where, when—are problematic. All are quite vulnerable to the administrative vagaries that vexed Oskar Morgenstern. "Who" may refer to heads of households, workers, citizens, legal residents, or everyone on hand. "Where" may mean in some particular dwelling, in some particular parish, or in some much larger administrative unit. "When" is the most elusive of all. For the innocent theorist, to live somewhere sometime implies a durable attachment to the place. For the actual collector of the information, however, physical presence on census day, or mere registry as an inhabitant, whether the person is physically present or not, is commonly all that matters. As a consequence, both our conceptions of migration and our evidence concerning it emphasize changes of legal domicile and crossings of administrative boundaries.

In order to make sense of the long-run changes in European migration patterns, we must therefore add social content to our measures and classifications. Whatever else migration is about, it is about moves that are relatively long and relatively definitive. Figure 1 presents a simple classification scheme based on length and definitiveness. It classifies moves of individuals, households, or other social units. Its first dimension is distance: we have the choice of simple geographic distance, time, expense, cultural distance, or some combination of them. Below some minimum distance, no move (however definitive) constitutes migration. Although any such minimum is arbitrary, we are unlikely ever to consider a move from one house to the house next door to qualify as migration.

The second dimension is the extent of the social unit's break with the area of origin. At the one extreme lie moves that entail no breaking of social ties; at the other, the complete rupture of ties at the move's place of origin. Below some minimum amount of rupture, no move (however distant) constitutes migration. Such a minimum requirement corresponds readily to our intuitive reluctance to consider a long round-the-world voyage as migration; to our intuitions, the maintenance of a household "back home" says that too few ties have been broken.

Given the two dimensions, most moves—a walk around the block, a vacation trip to London, the daily trip to the factory and back—involve too little distance and/or too little break with the place of origin to count as migration at all. The diagram labels those moves "mobility." It includes them to emphasize that the line between mobility and migration is arbitrary. The point may be obvious, but it is important. For example, historians working with village population registers frequently encounter individuals who kept the same legal domicile for years while working in distant cities; before calculating migration rates and describing the characteristics of the village's "resident" population, historians must decide on which side of the curved line to put those vagrant individuals.

## LOCAL, CIRCULAR, CHAIN, AND CAREER MIGRATION

The most interesting distinctions appear within the shaded migration area. They depend on the social organization of the move in question. Local migration shifts an individual or a household within a geographically contiguous market—a labor market, a land market, or perhaps a marriage market. In local migration the distance moved is small by definition; the extent of break with the place of origin is also likely to be small. On the whole, the

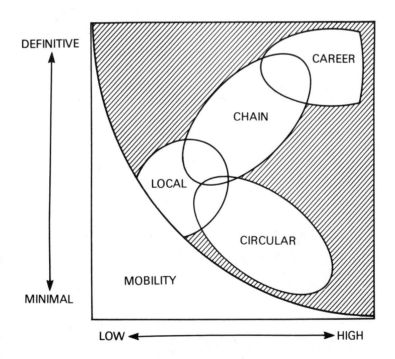

FIGURE 1. Four standard migration patterns

migrant is already quite familiar with the destination before making the move; he or she therefore has relatively little learning of a new environment to do after the move.

Take Uppsala-Nås, an agricultural parish near Uppsala, Sweden, for an example. There, the continuous population registers make it possible to pinpoint different types of moves from 1881 to 1885. There were many moves. Calculated as rates per year per hundred persons who could have moved, the figures (Eriksson and Rogers, 1973, p. 67) are:

| | |
|---|---|
| moves into or out of the parish | 35.2 |
| moves within the parish | 40.6 |
| movers into or out of the parish | 25.1 |
| movers within the parish | 26.9 |

In 1882, an ordinary year, in a parish whose population remained a little under 500, 76 in-migrants arrived, 93 people left the parish, and 27 more moved within the parish. If the parish boundary is the line between "local mobility" and "migration," migrants were equal to about a third of the total population. In 1883, the figure went up to about two-fifths. Yet the occupational structure remained fairly constant, no devastating social change occurred, and the great bulk of the migrants moved to or from other parishes in the immediate vicinity. Although many migrants tried their hands in Uppsala or Stockholm at one time or another, Eriksson and Rogers suggest that the structure of local agriculture accounted for most of the movement:

> Large estates required hired labor, and a landless proletariat quickly developed, which in turn contributed to a higher rate of movement. Landless and almost entirely restricted to agricultural occupations, these groups had little chance for social advancement until the breakthrough of industry, bringing changes in society and new opportunities (Eriksson and Rogers, 1973, p. 79).

The local migration rates for this one well-studied Swedish parish were probably above average for Europe as a whole. Yet where hired labor and a landless proletariat prevailed, local migration rates on the same order seem to have been common.

"Circular" migration takes a social unit to a destination through a set of arrangements which returns it to the origin after a well-defined interval. Seasonal work on harvests, pastoral transhumance, the sending of young people into domestic service before they married, and the circuits of Alpine villagers who served long years in the lowlands as schoolteachers, soldiers, or craftsmen before their long-planned return to the mountains with the accumulated capital all represent variants of circular migration. Today many Turks, Algerians, West Indians, Spaniards, and Portuguese are traveling in similar circles.

In Limousin in the nineteenth century, for example, there were a number of cantons in which a quarter, two-fifths, or even three-fifths of the adult males reported their occupations as "mason" (Corbin, 1975, p. 197). That was possible only because each spring thousands of men who worked on Limousin farms during the winter months walked off to earn money in construction elsewhere, and each fall most of them returned with the bulk of their earnings hidden in their knapsacks. Taking all trades together, at mid-century some 50,000 Limousins joined each year's circular migration. In Paris, "mason" and "Limousin" were nearly synonymous.

Because of their migratory regularity, the Limousins bore the nickname Swallows. Although the road from Limoges to Paris was close to 200 miles, before the railroad offered a cheap alternative hundreds of village bands tramped most of it together each year. The famous mason-become-politico Martin Nadaud took his first trip in 1830, when he was fourteen. He, his father, and other masons from their village walked the roughly 150 miles of back roads and woods to Orleans in four days before boarding their hired coaches for the last leg to Paris. Once in Paris, the Limousin masons gathered for the construction season in cheap, dingy rooming houses run by their countrymen. During the great Parisian workers' insurrection of June 1848, 575 masons were among the roughly 11,600 people arrested and charged. Of those 575 masons, 246 were from northern Limousin. The great bulk of them lived in central-city lodging houses, especially in the narrow streets behind the Hotel de Ville.* The Limousin masons were at once countrymen, migrants, and active participants in Parisian life.

"Chain" migration is our third type. Chain migration moves sets of related individuals or households from one place to another via a set of social arrangements in which people at the destination provide aid, information, and encouragement to new migrants. Such arrangements tend to produce a considerable proportion of experimental moves and a large backflow to the place of origin. At the destination, they also tend to produce durable clusters of people linked by common origin. At the extreme, the migrants form urban villages. In Medieval and Renaissance Europe, cities often permitted or even required these clusters of people to organize as "nations" sharing well-defined privileges and bearing collective responsibility for the policing and welfare of their members. In those cities, migrants of one nationality or another frequently established a quasi-monopoly of some particular trade. In

*Computed from dossiers in Archives Nationales (Paris), F7 2586 and in Archives Historiques de l' Armée (Vincennes), series A.

sixteenth-century Rome, for example, the most successful courtesans were Spanish. So well known was this fact that in 1592 other members of "the Spanish nation," no doubt wishing their reputation to rest on other accomplishments, formally petitioned Pope Clement VIII to banish Spanish courtesans from Rome (Delumeau, 1957, I, p. 201). To this day, the old university of Uppsala is organized in Nations representing the major provinces of Sweden. But most chain migrants have formed and reformed their communities without the benefit of such formal recognition of their common origin.

When the chain works well as a transmission belt, it continues to stretch from origin to destination until no members are left at the origin. In the 1950s and 1960s, for example, chain migration was emptying Tierra de Campos, a Castillian agricultural region of some 120,000 people in 178 small settlements. In one sample of out-migrants interrogated by Victor Perez Díaz, 60 percent of the migrants already knew someone at the destination before they left home. Once departed, the migrants sent back letters and remittances at an impressive rate: a reported average of 40 letters and 8,000 pesetas per year (Perez Díaz, 1971, pp. 148–53). In general, the more distant and costly the migration, the more people rely on others at the destination to ease the way. The extreme—for the case of Tierra de Campos and for the migration of poor Europeans in general—is overseas migration, where the great majority of moves belong to well-defined chains.

"Career" migration, finally, has persons or households making more or less definitive moves in response to opportunities to change position within or among large structures: organized trades, firms, governments, mercantile networks, armies, and the like. If there is a circuit, it is based not on the social bonds at the migrant's place of origin, but on the logic of the large structure itself. If people within the migrant mass help and encourage each other, they are generally colleagues, not neighbors or kinsmen. The migrations of scientists, technicians, military officers, priests, and bureaucrats commonly fall into this type rather than into local, circular or chain migration.

Sixteenth-century migrants to Canterbury and other towns of Kent, according to Peter Clark, consisted mainly of two groups: poor people from the countryside who moved relatively long distances to take up unskilled urban work, and more comfortable people from other towns and the nearby countryside who entered crafts and other fairly skilled urban employment. Both of these groups probably consisted chiefly of chain migrants. But with the economic expansion of the sixteenth century, another category was becoming more important: itinerant professionals, craftsmen, and other specialists. As Clark puts it:

> If the itinerant craftsman or specialist had also been a medieval figure the
> expansion of this kind of professional migration in the sixteenth century in
> response to the needs of an increasingly sophisticated social and economic

order had a new, radical importance—both in numbers and impact. The growth of internal trade entailed a major increase in the numbers of pedlars, chapmen and other itinerant retailers with their own trade routes across countries (Clark, 1972, 146).

In the same general category were clergymen seeking new posts. None of those people were undergoing the sorts of station-to-station transfers that became the common experience of employees in big twentieth-century organizations. Yet as compared with the other migrants to Kentish towns, they were clearly migrating in response to career opportunities.

The types overlap. Sometimes they change from one to another. For example, most systems of circular migration leave a residue of migrants at the destination. The stayers include both successful people who make a good thing of mediating between their mobile countrymen and the local population, and failures who die before accumulating the capital to go back home. A circular system with a rising residue eventually becomes a chain. In migration from the high Alps, for example, the peddler-migrants who made good tended to establish shops in lowland towns, and to provide the contacts for subsequent migrants from the uplands (Merlin, 1971, p. 34).

In another overlap, local migration systems sometimes provide the basis for long-distance chain migration. One of the most spectacular examples is the local system of labor migration around seventeenth-century Tourouvre-au-Perche: it extended into the long chain which, through transatlantic migration, North American propagation, and subsequent migration within Canada, gave ancestors to much of Quebec's contemporary population. Some 300 migrants from the small region of Tourouvre-au-Perche left for Canada in the seventeenth century, especially toward 1650. Labor recruiters encouraged the move to Quebec, and drew a disproportionate number of men in their twenties. Despite the unbalanced sex ratio, the migrants married and bore children in exceptional numbers. Some migrated as families, some sent later for families already begun in France, some returned to marry in the region of Tourouvre, and almost all the rest married in Canada soon after arrival (Charbonneau, 1970).

Despite the overlap, the systems have some characteristic differences. On the whole, circular migration is very sex-selective: practically all-male or all-female, depending on the occupation at the destination. Chain migration's sex-selectivity tends to change over time. One typical arrangement is for single males to make up the vanguard, with single females and then whole families joining them later. Local and career migration, in contrast, are not generally very selective by sex; either whole households migrate or the stream comprises both men and women.

The geographic pattern also varies from one type to another. Chain migration tends to link a particular origin with no more than a handful of possible destinations. But those destinations are often at a considerable distance. Circular migration may do the same thing, but it is somewhat more likely to disperse the available workers among a number of opportunities. Local migration involves many destinations within a circumscribed range. Career migration, finally, tends to spread people far and wide. The geographic differences suggest the following grouping of the migration patterns:

|  | Supply of Relevant Skills | |
|---|---|---|
|  | General | Special |
| Cost of Information About Opportunities  High | chain | circular |
| Low | local | career |

Chain and circular migration are ways of combatting high costs of information about opportunities for employment, proprietorship, and other desired ends. Circular and career migration respond to situations in which the skills the migrants exercise are not generally available—because they are hard to learn, because the migrants have monopolized them, or because other people are unwilling to work at them. Thus as the cost of information about job opportunities declines, chain and circular migration give way to local and career migration. But to the extent that all job skills are unevenly distributed, circular and career migration tend to supplant chain and local migration.

The rough classification of migration into local, circular, chain, and career does not exhaust the significant distinctions one might make. For example, it catches quite imperfectly the important difference between individual and collective migration; although on the whole chain and circular migration involve single individuals less frequently than do local and career migration, there are individual and collective versions of all four types. The classification does not embody the distinction between forced and voluntary migration; it therefore deals awkwardly with the expulsion of the Huguenots from France and the flight of Jews from eastern European pogroms. Since it concentrates on particular moves, it does not easily separate two rather different relationships between a major city and its hinterland: the rare pattern in which migrants come directly to the city from the distant countryside, and the common pattern in which country people move to nearby small towns, small town people move to large towns, and so on step by step to the metropolis. The classification into local, circular, chain, and career migrations separates some significantly different social arrangements from each other, but it does not make all the distinctions one might wish to employ.

The sorts of administratively produced evidence we have concerning European migration do not permit us to distinguish easily among local, circular, chain, and career migration. To do so, one needs life histories, detailed accounts of intentions and social relations at the time of moves, or both.

Records of official changes of domicile yield the former with great difficulty, and the latter not at all. On the basis of the scattered evidence available, nevertheless, it seems safe to say that in the age of industrialization the general character of European migration shifted from the lower left to the upper right of our diagram: away from local and short-distance circular migration, toward longer-distance, more definitive chain and career migration. It also seems safe to say that the *pace* of migration changed much less than its *character*. The history of Europe shows us not so much periods of immobility and mobility as decisive shifts among types of mobility.

## THE GREAT FLOWS

William McNeill has portrayed the repeated sweeps of conquering bands across the continent. He has also recounted the less dramatic, but no less momentous, flows of agricultural settlers into the continent's emptier spaces. Before the last millennium, large-scale movements of armed men and tribute-takers set the rhythm of European political history. Armed men and tribute-takers have thrived into our own time, but on the whole they have fixed themselves in space, reduced the scale and duration of their movements, and worked harder and harder at controlling the flows of people and goods into and out of their own fixed territories. Within Europe, long-distance flows of agricultural settlers continued, although their relative volume seems to have declined irregularly with the approach of our own time.

The last massive migration of agricultural workers within Europe was the Medieval flow of German-speakers into the East and South of the continent. That flow continued past 1500. But by then its volume had greatly diminished. By that time German-speaking migrants consisted mainly of one variety or another of conqueror: officials, managers, merchants, and landlords. The seventeenth- and eighteenth-century expansion of the Prussian state formally incorporated a number of eastern German enclaves and took in a good deal of predominantly Slavic population. It did not, however, produce movements of population comparable to those of three or four centuries earlier. Despite Frederick the Great's strenuous efforts at settlement, for example, Silesia remained predominantly Polish-speaking. Further south, the Austrians also sought to settle German speakers to their east by such straightforward devices as dispossessing the Czech landlords of Moravia. Although such planned migrations were of the greatest political importance, the numbers involved were relatively small. Indeed, they bucked the long-range trend, which was for Slavic-speakers, given weight by their generally higher levels of natural increase, to push westward into areas earlier occupied by Finns, Swedes, and Germans. On either side of the linguistic frontier, massive long-distance rural-to-rural migration became less prevalent after 1500.

Long-distance moves of workers into nonagricultural employment are a different matter. They accelerated some two hundred years ago, and have remained important since then. The migration of Poles into the mining areas of western Germany and eastern France and the rush of Irishmen to Liverpool and London illustrate the importance of long-distance migration within industrial Europe. Contrary to first impressions, few of these long-distance migrants moved directly from farm to factory. For the most part, the farmers who moved to cities found low-level employment in services and commerce. The apparent exceptions were commonly small-town artisans or rural industrial workers rather than peasants or farm laborers. Indeed, over the last two centuries the most important single category of urban employment for rural-to-urban migrants within Europe has most likely been domestic service. Only an undue concentration on males and on manufacturing has obscured that fact.

During the period of swift natural increase from the mid-eighteenth century to the end of the nineteenth, Europe also sent millions of its residents to the agricultural and industrial areas of the Americas and of Oceania. The great flows of the nineteenth and twentieth centuries followed smaller but still important migratory movements which accompanied European colonial expansion during the three previous centuries. In this great overseas migration, millions of rural Europeans *did* migrate to farms. French migrants peopled rural Quebec as well as Quebec City and Montreal. Portuguese emigrants became Brazilian farmers as well as residents of São Paulo and Rio de Janeiro. Later, more than two million Germans and Scandinavians sailed to America. There, many of them settled on frontier farms.

Altogether, Europe's net migration from 1800 to World War I was on the order of fifty million persons. Given the frequent returns of chain migrants, a much larger number must have made the trip at one time or another. Since a return rate of 30 percent is plausible, the true number could easily be 65 million sometime emigrants. Over half of all European emigrants in that period went to the United States.

The British Isles—especially Ireland—were the champion exporters of humankind, and the chief purveyors to America. About three-quarters of nineteenth-century emigrants from Britain went to North America. As a result, at least a third of all American immigrants in that century were native speakers of English. Nevertheless, Germany, Greece, Italy, and the Scandinavian countries all became major sources of overseas migrants at some time during the nineteenth century.

One of the best-documented cases is Denmark. With a total population in the range of two million, Denmark sent over 300,000 migrants overseas between 1840 and 1914 (Hvidt, 1975, p. 9). Over 90 percent went to North America. Within that small country, rates of emigration differed dramatically from one district to another. On the whole, they were much higher in the southeast than elsewhere. More generally, urban areas sent migrants at a significantly higher pace than rural areas did. Yet where urban growth and industrialization were vigorous, relatively little emigration occurred.

The ideal origin for Danish emigrants seems to have been the stagnant town in which underemployed long-term migrants from nearby rural areas were accumulating. Landless laborers and servants were especially good prospects for emigration. Kristian Hvidt quotes a letter describing the situation on the high-migration island of Bornholm:

> The Bornholm farmers pay their small-holding laborers much too poorly in relation to the prices of necessities. But the huge number of immigrating Swedes rules out a rise in wages. An ordinary laborer who is not a craftsman has often only the choice between America or the poorhouse (Hvidt, 1975, p. 129).

Chain migration was the predominant pattern among the 300,000 Danes who left Denmark. Toward the end of the nineteenth century, around a quarter of all Danish migrants to the United States came on steamship tickets prepaid by migrants already in America. (The comparable figures for Norway and Sweden run from 40 to 50 percent.) "Letters, money, and prepaid tickets came in a constant stream, the volume of which would quite likely surprise most people," writes Hvidt,

> since the emigrants were generally believed to have formed the poorest part of the population and to have been characterized by intellectual narrowness and insufficient education. Improved economic conditions in the United States combined with the emotional longings inherent in emigration furthered both letter writing and sending tickets home. These personal contacts with the Old Country may well be sufficient explanation of why mass emigration accelerated whenever economic conditions permitted (Hvidt, 1975, p. 194).

Indeed, it was partly *because* they were poor and uneducated that the Danish emigrants relied on their compatriots for aid, encouragement, and information in the long migration to America.

In the period after World War I, with declining European rates of natural increase and rising American resistance to immigration, the pace of European emigration diminished. Nevertheless, Canada, Argentina, Brazil, Australia, and New Zealand continued to receive large numbers of European migrants. In that period, as Table 1 shows, the British Isles

Table 1

Percentage of All European Overseas Emigrants Leaving from
Selected Countries, 1846–1963

| Countries | Period | | | |
|---|---|---|---|---|
| | 1846–90 | 1891–1920 | 1921–39 | 1946–63 |
| British Isles | 47.9 | 17.7 | 29.0 | 27.7 |
| Germany | 20.2 | 3.4 | 9.8 | 15.7 |
| Sweden, Denmark, Norway | 6.9 | 3.8 | 3.8 | 2.1 |
| France, Switzerland, Nether-lands | 4.2 | 1.5 | 2.5 | 14.9 |
| Italy | 8.2 | 27.0 | 18.6 | 19.0 |
| Austria, Hungary, Czecho-slovakia | 3.7 | 15.9 | 4.1 | ? |
| Russia, Poland, Lithuania, Estonia, Finland | 2.1 | 13.0 | 12.0 | ? |
| Spain, Portugal | 6.9 | 15.3 | 15.0 | 12.1 |
| Total emigrants from Europe per year (× 1,000) | 376 | 910 | 366 | 585 |

The figures describe gross migration, not net loss through migration. Boundaries as of the 1960s apply to all periods.

Source: Calculated from Kosinski 1970: 57.

regained the predominance they had lost to Italy during the period 1891 to 1920. Poorer areas of the British Isles, such as the declining Welsh mining region, sent their surplus labor overseas in the company of a smaller number of highly educated people from all over Britain. Since the table deals only with the total number of overseas emigrants, it conceals an important countercurrent: while the poor areas of northwestern Europe continued to send migrants overseas, the more prosperous areas began to bring in migrants from elsewhere in Europe.

Since World War II, northwestern Europe has become an even more active importer of migrants. Yugoslavia, Spain, Portugal, Italy, Ireland, and Turkey became major suppliers to the highly industrialized regions of Europe. This last shift has its ironies: we see the nations which peopled the rest of the western world with their poor now drawing their unskilled labor from poor immigrants, and fretting about the disruption such migrations may cause. Switzerland, which long disposed of its surplus men as mercenaries in European armies, now has a sixth of its population foreign-born. Great Britain, which flooded America with English-speaking families, now debates the desirability of its 5 percent born elsewhere. According to Stephen Castles and Godula Kosack, France, West Germany, Switzerland, and Great Britain, among others, have come to rely almost entirely on foreigners to do their dirty work. Yet they have proved quite hostile to granting the newcomers a permanent stake in their host countries. Xenophobia is nothing new. But the backing it has received from West European states in recent years is unusual.

## THE IMPACTS OF WAR AND POLITICS

The most dramatic twentieth-century change in European migration patterns was not the northwest's shift from export to import of migrants. It was the expanding role of political pressures and political controls. Politics impinged on migration in three distinct ways: through war, through deliberate relocation of ethnic minorities, and through stringent national controls over immigration and emigration.

During the twentieth century, in more senses than one, war became the prime mover. Earlier, such continental conflicts as the Thirty Years' War and the Napoleonic Wars had produced hordes of refugees. They also produced some long-term displacement of population away from the war zones. But World Wars I and II produced incomparably greater migratory currents in Europe. According to Eugene Kulischer's compilation (Kulischer, 1948, pp. 248–49), the largest flows within Europe and the adjacent sections of Asia from 1918 to 1939 were:

1.2 million Greeks to Greece from Turkey (1922–1923)
1.15 million Russians to Europe outside the Soviet Union (1918–1922)
1.1 million repatriated from Russia to Poland (1918–1925)
900 thousand Poles from former Russian and Austrian Poland to former German Poland (1918–1921)
700 thousand Germans from Western Poland, Danzig and Memel to Germany (1918–1925)

Only then do we arrive at migratory streams in which the war and the peace settlement did not play a large, direct part: the estimated 650 thousand Italians who went from Italy to France over the 21 years from 1919 to 1939, and the estimated 450 thousand Poles who made the move to France over the same period. (These are net figures; according to Polish statistics, for example, 622 thousand Poles went to France from 1919 through 1939, but 200 thousand returned to Poland, for a net of 422 thousand migrants: Kosínski, 1970, pp. 79–80.)

These numbers are large. They are, however, modest compared to the figures for World War II and its aftermath. To take again the leaders in Kulischer's compilation (Kulischer, 1948, pp. 302–4):

6 million Reich Germans from New Poland to Germany (1944–1947)

5 million Jews from Germany to extermination camps in Poland and elsewhere (1940–1944)

4 million Reich Germans from the Soviet Zone to the U.S. and British Zones (1945–1946)

3 million Poles from Old Poland to New Poland (1945–1947)

2.7 million ethnic Germans from Czechoslovakia to Germany and Austria (1945–1946)

1.8 million Czechs and Slovaks from Inner Czechoslovakia to the former Sudetenland (1946–1947)

1 million ethnic Germans from Old Poland to Germany (1944–1945)

The list goes on. However approximate these figures are, and however much double-counting they include, they portray World War II and—especially—the postwar settlement as one of the greatest demographic whirlwinds ever to sweep the earth.

Some of these migrants fled from war zones. Many more of them moved at the behest of governments. On the whole, the refugees contributed to the diversity of population at their destinations. When states deliberately relocated people, however, they tended to homogenize the language and culture of the people within any particular set of national boundaries. The net effect of the migrations surrounding the two world wars was therefore to homogenize nation-states and probably to increase their capacity for nationalism.

Heightened nationalism and the recurrent labor shortages of the richer European countries have combined to produce a contradictory situation. On the one hand, such countries as Switzerland, West Germany, and France have become sorely dependent on poorer countries for supplies of unskilled labor. On the other hand, those same countries and their neighbors have greatly increased their controls over immigration and emigration. There is, to be sure, a sharp difference between eastern and western Europe in those regards. On the whole, the richer western European countries have encouraged circular migration of low-wage workers from elsewhere but have made it difficult for them to become long-time residents and, especially, to acquire citizenship. The Soviet Union and other Communist states have simply made all forms of entry and exit difficult.

The last five centuries of European long-distance migration show us three major factors at work: (1) a changing geographic distribution of opportunities for employment; (2) alterations of regional differentials in natural increase; (3) actions and policies of national states—notably making war, controlling migration and deliberately recruiting, expelling, or relocating specific ethnic and religious groups. The first two factors have shaped migration throughout the five hundred years. To explain why and how they worked is to trace out the expansion of capitalism, the proletarianization of the European population as a whole, the march of urbanization and industrialization. The third factor—actions and policies of national states—gained importance as the five centuries wore on. By the twentieth century, wars and their settlements rivaled the interplay of employment and natural increase as incentives to long-distance migration.

## THE LOCAL FLOWS

No one has given us a comprehensive statistical atlas of long-distance migration within, from, and to the European continent. That would be a useful enterprise. But at least the existence and broad directions of the long-distance flows are well known. In the present state of our knowledge, local migration provides more puzzles.

Recent work on the historical demography of Europe has experienced a nice dialectic. The fastidious methods for reconstructing precensus demographic characteristics developed by such scholars as Louis Henry and E. A. Wrigley sometimes assume, and always apply more easily to, relatively immobile populations. Yet one of the most impressive and consistent findings of the historical demographers has been the high level of local mobility among preindustrial European people. In studies of eighteenth-century agricultural villages, it is not unusual to find over a tenth of the population making a significant change of residence each year. If the sheer frequency of moves (rather than the distance moved) is the criterion, it is not at all clear that industrialization produced a major increase in the European population's mobility.

The findings coming in jar our preconceptions concerning the settled peasant world that industrialization is supposed to have broken up. Still, the idea of a settled peasant world is not so much wrong as incomplete. Let us consider "peasants" to be members of households whose major activity is farming, households which produce a major share of the goods and services they consume, which exercise substantial control over the land they farm, and which supply the major part of their labor requirements from their own energies. If that is what we mean by peasants, a majority of the European population was probably peasant until late in the eighteenth century. The true peasant population was, so far as we know, relatively immobile.

But the extrapolation of peasant immobility to the European population as a whole errs in several ways. A substantial minority of the population was *not* peasant. From the later eighteenth century, the nonpeasants were probably a majority. Among the nonpeasants were significant groups of traders and artisans for whom movement was a way of life. Less obvious among them was a large, growing mass of landless laborers. (To take one of the extreme cases, Gregory King estimated for the England of 1688 that only 350 thousand of the 1.2 million families in agriculture lived from their own land: Pollard and Crossley, 1968, p. 154.)

The landless and land-poor moved frequently, sometimes seasonally, in response to the demand for wage-labor. As Paul Slack points out, the seventeenth-century English local authorities regularly whipped the "vagrants" who were multiplying in the countryside and sent them back to their parishes of origin. But those "vagrants" were only a minority of the many landless laborers then on the roads. They were the ones who had failed to find work. As enclosures and population growth swelled the numbers of people who had no place on the land in their home villages, many migrated in search of employment elsewhere. Local authorities treated them ambivalently: welcoming their labor if the parish needed it and could control it, but striving to make sure the wanderers gained no claims on parish welfare funds. Hence the whip.

Contrary to ideas linking high mobility to industrialization, however, the spread of rural industry seems to have helped the landless to settle down. It meant they could piece together starvation wages from industrial and agricultural work in their own villages. In his rich study of the Zurich uplands during early industrialization, Rudolf Braun shows us exactly this fixing of the proletarian population in place via cottage industry. Whereas the surplus hands of previous generations had walked off to military careers, domestic service, or another kind of unskilled work elsewhere, the villagers of the eighteenth century began to stay on the land, spinning and weaving. Take, for example, the Leicestershire village of Shepshed, where cottage industry grew considerably during the eighteenth century:

> In pre-industrial Shepshed just 46% of the families entering the observation had been married in the parish whereas during protoindustrialization the proportion of parochial marriage rose so that after 1810 76.9% of all families had been married in the village church (Levine, 1977, p. 40).

As opportunities for industrial employment expanded in Shepshed, more people lived out their lives in the parish, and saw their children do the same.

Some true peasant households were also quite mobile. It is doubtful that the majority of European peasant households owned the bulk of the land they farmed before some time in the nineteenth century. Most were tenants of one type or another. Tenancy meant turnover. Annual, quinquennial, or even nine-year leases brought the significant possibility of a move when the lease expired. The scattered studies in historical demography that have been able to make the essential distinctions with respect to control of land have found tenants migrating to and from villages in significant numbers. During the nineteenth- and twentieth-century "rural exodus," landless laborers were generally the first to leave the countryside, tenants next, and owners quite slow to depart.

## DEMOGRAPHIC STIMULI TO MIGRATION

In addition to the effects of tenancy and employment, old-regime demographic conditions provided their own spurs to migration. The best-known of those demographic conditions was the enormous death rate in cities. The rates were high enough that before the nineteenth century large cities could maintain their populations only through substantial in-migration, and could grow only through massive recruitment of outsiders. For example, in the little North Sea port of Husum from 1765 to 1804 the crude birth rate was about 26.6 and the crude death rate about 28.9, for a natural *decrease* of about 2.3 persons per thousand per year. That was true despite an age structure favorable to low mortality. In the forty years after 1804, by contrast, the crude birth rate rose a trifle to 27.1, while the crude death rate declined to 24.8. That produced a natural *increase* of about 2.3 per thousand (computed from Momsen, 1969, pp. 58, 66). In actual numbers, the breakdown of Husum's growth in the two periods ran like this:

| Period | Population Change | Births–Deaths | Net Migration |
|---|---|---|---|
| 1769–1802 | +165 | −345 | +510 |
| 1803–1844 | +249 | +358 | −110 |

Thus in the early nineteenth century natural increase more than supplied Husum's need for new hands and a surplus migrated elsewhere. But in the eighteenth century the city had to bring in migrants simply to maintain its population.

Husum and other small cities generally drew the bulk of their migrants from their immediate hinterlands. In most cases, a small city's radius of intensive attraction was no more than ten or fifteen miles (see Patten, 1973). Before the rising natural increase of the eighteenth and nineteenth centuries, the supply of migrants behaved a good deal like the supply of food: cities consumed more than they produced; they drew the hard-won surplus from many surrounding communities, and thus affected those communities deeply; they drew more specialized supplies from greater distances via other cities; when they grew fast, that growth generated a demand which reverberated through more and more of the hinterland.

Large cities drew on correspondingly larger areas of supply. In times of relatively rapid urban growth, such as significant parts of the sixteenth and eighteenth centuries, major cities drew their increments from vast hinterlands. London grew from about 400 thousand in 1650 to about 650 thousand a century later. That growth had a large impact on the food production of southern England. It also altered English migration systems, despite the fact that they were already centered in London. E. A. Wrigley speculates that in the high-growth century from 1650 to 1750 a sixth of the entire adult population of England spent some part of their lives in London (Wrigley, 1967, p. 49). The high-mortality metropolis stuffed itself with an entire country's demographic surplus.

Urban natural decrease was not the only important demographic condition. In a time of high, fluctuating fertility and high, unstable mortality, households that had relatively inelastic labor requirements often found their supply and demand badly matched. Artisans with an expensive stock in trade and peasants with fixed allotments of land, for instance, tended to develop a well-defined household division of labor by age, sex, and marital status. They could absorb an extra hand or do without one of the standard household members only at great strain. Either the death of a mother or the survival of an extra child jostled a delicate equilibrium. In the short run, such households used migration to adjust the supply to the demand. Extra children migrated, temporarily or definitively, into domestic service, armies, peddling. The household made up shortages by bringing in servants and/or kinsmen from elsewhere. A very high proportion of all individual migration before the twentieth century consisted of these transfers of labor among households.

In quantitative terms, however, marriage and the termination of marriage were probably the most significant demographic spurs to migration. Throughout the centuries, almost every European marriage has required at least one spouse to make a definitive change of residence. With some lags and exceptions due to co-residence with parents, the great majority have led to the formation of a new household in a new location. As nuptiality rose in the nineteenth century, the frequency of marriage-linked migration rose as well. The termination of marriages through divorce or death played a smaller part, but not a negligible one, in causing migration. To know whether its importance increased or decreased, we need not only to grasp the trends in the divorce rates, but also to balance off the migration-inducing effects of remarriages against the changing likelihood that a bereaved spouse will remain in the household she or he already occupies. We do not now have the necessary evidence. My speculation is that the termination of marriages became a less important occasion for migration in Europe after the eighteenth century.

## QUALIFICATIONS AND CONCLUSIONS

Over the five centuries or so we have been reviewing, most migrants have moved short distances. Most moves have responded to demographic imbalances and changing employment opportunities. Both conditions remained true during the nineteenth century with its massive overseas migration and during the twentieth century with its major displacements by war. Furthermore, local systems of migration often provided the bases of subsequent longer-range migration. That happened in circular migration systems which included cities; if opportunity rose in the city and declined in the countryside, the system started depositing a permanent residue of migrants in the city. It also happened in some essentially rural systems of labor migration to which an overseas destination became available: mobile agricultural workers in Denmark or Portugal found themselves working, in the company of their compatriots, in New York or Toronto. The long-run trend of European migration ran from local and circular migration to chain and career migration. The average distances moved and the definitiveness of breaks with the place of origin both increased. But the continuities between the older and newer forms of migration were impressive.

I have stressed the high mobility of European populations before the nineteenth century because it requires us to rethink the relationship between industrialization and mobility. If I have given the impression that nothing changed in the nineteenth and twentieth centuries, however, that is wrong. The average distances of migration rose dramatically with large-scale industrialization. The unprecedented concentration of opportunities for employment in large cities oriented migration to those cities as never before. The growing power of national states impinged on twentieth-century migration through war and through deliberate controls over entries and exits. Those are novelties of the modern world.

The high mobility of the preindustrial world also requires some qualification. In general, the distances involved in rural migration or in migration to small cities were small. The bulk of the migrants to any locality typically came from within five or ten miles. Only larger cities regularly escaped from that rule. If we were to set a local labor market as the limit within which a move counts as "mobility" instead of "migration," we would eliminate many of the extremely high rates of migration now coming in from demographic studies of preindustrial European populations. The generalization would then read: before large-scale industrialization, rural labor markets were typically larger than a single village; they were often very active, especially where tenancy and/or wage labor prevailed; people moved frequently within those labor markets in response to demographic imbalances and shifting opportunities for livelihood.

We might speculate, in fact, that despite all the reverence for the village, the parish, or the commune which European historians have developed, the fundamental local unit was larger than any of them. The area served by a single market has turned out to be the basic building block of traditional China (Skinner, 1964, 1965). It defined the familiar world, the world of labor exchange, marriage, social mobility, local solidarity. Perhaps local market areas played a similar role in traditional Europe. The village, parish, or commune then may have acquired importance only when national states required mutually exclusive administrative units which they could hold collectively responsible for taxation, conscription, road labor, the provision of food and the maintenance of public order.

To the degree that we expand the definition of local mobility and become more stringent in our definition of migration, the era of large-scale industrialization and massive expansion of national states separates from the previous era. Long-distance, definitive migration did increase with industrialization and statemaking. Gross and net flows of migrants from rural to urban areas came to dominate the migration map as never before. As urban mortality declined, large rural-urban flows increasingly meant rapid urban growth. As rural natural increase declined, large rural-urban flows increasingly meant a depletion of the rural population. As national states grew, wars, peace settlements, and national policies acted more and more powerfully as spurs and checks to migration. In the same era, local mobility did not increase significantly; in rural areas and small towns, it probably declined.

The study of migration, then, gets us into the homely adjustments ordinary Europeans made among their own life plans and the labor requirements of the various organizations which had claims on them, or on which they had claims. Organizational structure, life plans, demography: changes in any of these three large elements eventually affect the character of the other two. Every major change in European organizational structure, life plans, and demography has produced a durable transformation of European migration patterns. As time has gone on, national states have increasingly shaped and reshaped those patterns—by deliberately controlling the possibilities of migration, by intentionally relocating ethnic minorities, and by destructively making war. The history of European migration is the history of European social life.

## NOTE

I am grateful to Martha Guest for assistance in my search of the literature and to Louise Tilly for comments on earlier drafts. An early draft of this paper circulated as a Discussion Paper of the Center for Western European Studies, University of Michigan, under the title "Preliminary Notes on European Migration." The Horace Rackham School of Graduate Studies, University of Michigan, gave financial support to the research in European historical demography which underlies some parts of this paper. The National Science Foundation supported other parts of the work.

## REFERENCES

Anderson, Grace. 1974. *Networks of Contact: The Portuguese and Toronto.* Waterloo, Ontario: Wilfred Laurier University Press.

Aymard, Maurice. 1974. "La Sicile, Terre d'Immigration," in M. Aymard et al., *Les migrations dans les pays méditerranéens au XVIIIe et au debut du XIXème.* Nice: Centre de la Méditerranée Moderne et Contemporaine.

Banks, J. A. 1968. "Population Change and the Victorian City." *Victorian Studies,* 11, pp. 277–289.

Beijer, G. 1963. *Rural Migrants in Urban Setting: An Analysis of the Literature on the Problem Consequent on the Internal Migration from Rural to Urban Places in European Countries (1945–1961).* The Hague: Nijhoff.

Blaschke, Karlheinz. 1967. *Bevölkerungsgeschichte von Sachsen bis zur industriellen Revolution.* Weimar: Böhlhaus.

Brandes, Stanley H. 1975. *Migration, Kinship, and Community: Tradition and Transition in a Spanish Village.* New York: Academic Press.

Braun, Rudolf. 1960. *Industrialisierung und Volksleben: Die Veränderung der Lebensformen in einem landlichen Industriegebiet vor 1800 (Züricher Oberland).* Zürich: Rentsch.

———. 1970. *Sozio-kulturelle Probleme der Eingliederung italienischer Arbeitskräfte in der Schweiz.* Zurich: Rentsch.

Buckatzsch, C. J. 1949–1950. "Places of Origin of a Group of Immigrants into Sheffield, 1624–1799." *Economic History Review,* second series, 2, pp. 303–6.

———. 1951. "The Constancy of Local Populations and Migration in England before 1800." *Population Studies,* pp. 62–69.

Butcher, A. F. 1974. "The Origins of Romney Freemen, 1433–1523." *Economic History Review,* second series, 27, pp. 16–27.

Castles, Stephen, and Kosack, Godula. 1973. *Immigrant Workers and Class Structure in Western Europe.* London: Oxford University Press.

Chambers, J. D. 1965. "Three Essays on the Population and Economy of the Midlands." In D. V. Glass and D. E. C. Eversley (eds.), *Population in History: Essays in Historical Demography.* Chicago: Aldine.

Charbonneau, Hubert. 1970. *Tourouvre-au-Perche aux XVIIe et XVIIIe siècles.* Paris: Presses Universitaires de France. Institut National d'Etudes Démographiques, Travaux et Documents, Cahier 55.

Chevalier, Louis. 1950. *La formation de la population parisienne au XIXe siècle.* Paris: Presses Universitaires de France.

Clark, Peter. 1972. "The Migrant in Kentish Towns 1580–1640." In Peter Clark and

Paul Slack (eds.), *Crisis and Order in English Towns, 1500–1700.* London: Routledge & Kegan Paul.

Corbin, Alain. 1975. *Archaisme et modernité en Limousin au XIXe siècle.* Paris: Marcel Rivière. 2 vols.

Cornwall, Julian. 1967. "Evidence of Population Mobility in the Seventeenth Century." *Bulletin of the Institute of Historical Research,* 40, pp. 143–152.

Delumeau, Jean. 1957. *Vie économique et socialè de Rome dans la seconde moitié du XVIe siècle.* Paris: Boccard. 2 vols.

Eriksson, Ingrid, and Rogers, John. 1973. "Mobility in an Agrarian Community. Practical and Methodological Considerations." In Kurt Ågren et al., *Aristocrats, Farmers, Proletarians: Essays in Swedish Demographic History.* Uppsala: Scandinavian University Books. Studia Historica Upsaliensa, 47.

Friedl, Ernestine. 1976. "Kinship, Class and Selective Migration." In J. G. Peristiany (ed.), *Mediterranean Family Structures.* Cambridge: Cambridge University Press.

Goreux, L. M. 1956. "Les migrations agricoles en France depuis un siècle et leur relation avec certains facteurs économiques." *Etudes et Conjoncture,* 11, pp. 327–376.

Hammer, Carl. 1976. "The Mobility of Skilled Labour in Late Medieval England. Some Oxford Evidence." *Vierteljahrschrift für Sozial- und Wirtschaftsgeschichte,* 63, pp. 194–210.

Hannan, Damian. 1970. *Rural Exodus.* London: Geoffrey Chapman.

Henry, Louis. 1967. *Manuel de démographie historique.* Geneva & Paris: Droz.

———. 1972. *Démographie, analyse et modèles.* Paris: Larousse.

Hesse, Sharlene. 1975. "Migrants as Actors: A Case Study of Life-Cycle and Geographical Mobility in Sweden." Doctoral dissertation, Department of Sociology, University of Michigan.

Hollingsworth, T. H. 1971. "Historical Studies of Migration." *Annales de Démographie Historique 1970,* pp. 87–96.

Hvidt, Kristian. 1975. *Flight to America: The Social Background of 300,000 Danish Emigrants.* New York: Academic Press.

Iatsounski, V. K. 1971. "Le rôle des migrations et de l'accroissement naturel dans la colonisation des nouvelles régions de la Russie." *Annales de Démographie Historique 1970,* pp. 302–8.

Kasdan, Leonard. 1965. "Family Structure, Migration and the Entrepreneur," *Comparative Studies in Society and History,* 7, pp. 345–57.

Kollmann, Wolfgang. 1959. "Industrialisierung, Binnenwanderung, und 'Soziale Frage,'" *Vierteljahrschrift für Sozial- und Wirtschaftsgeschichte,* 46, pp. 45–70.

Kosínski, Leszek A. 1970. *The Population of Europe: A Geographic Perspective.* London: Longman.

Kulischer, Eugene M. 1948. *Europe on the Move: War and Population Changes, 1917–47.* New York: Columbia University Press.

Laslett, Peter. 1968. "Le brassage de la population en France et en Angleterre aux XVIIe et XVIIIe siècles." *Annales de Démographie Historique 1968,* pp. 99–109.

Levi, Giovanni. 1971. "Migrazioni e popolazione nella Francia del XVII e XVIII secolo." *Rivista Storica Italiana,* 83, pp. 95–123.

———. 1974. "Sviluppo urbano e flussi migratori nel Piemonte nel 1600." In M.

Aymard et al., *Les migrations dans les pays méditerranéens au XVIIIeme et au début du XIXème.* Nice: Centre de la Méditerránee Moderne et Contemporaine.

Levine, David. 1977. *Family Formation in an Age of Nascent Capitalism.* New York: Academic Press.

Liang, Hsi-Huey. 1970. "Lower-Class Immigrants in Wilhelmine Berlin," *Central European History.* 3, pp. 94–111.

Lopreato, Joseph. 1962. "Economic Development and Cultural Change: The Role of Emigration." *Human Organization,* 21, pp. 182–86.

MacDonald, John S., and MacDonald, Leatrice D. 1964. "Chain Migration, Ethnic Neighborhood Formation, and Social Networks." *Milbank Memorial Fund Quarterly,* 42, pp. 82–97.

McNeill, William H. 1963. *The Rise of the West: A History of the Human Community.* Chicago: University of Chicago Press.

Merlin, Pierre, et al. 1971. *L'exode rural, suivi de deux études sur les migrations.* Paris: Presses Universitaires de France. Institut National d'Etudes Démographiques, Travaux et Documents, Cahier 59.

Momsen, Ingwer Ernst. 1969. *Die Bevölkerung der Stadt Husum von 1769 bis 1860.* Kiel: Selbstverlag des Geographischen Instituts der Universität Keil.

Morgenstern, Oskar. 1963. *On the Accuracy of Economic Observations.* Princeton: Princeton University Press. 2d ed.

Morrill, Richard L. 1965. *Migration and the Spread and Growth of Urban Settlement.* Lund: Gleerup. Lund Studies in Geography, Series B, no. 26.

Norberg, Anders, and Åkerman, Sune. 1973. "Migration and the Building of Families: Studies on the Rise of the Lumber Industry in Sweden." In Kurt Ågren et al., *Aristocrats, Farmers, Proletarians: Essays in Swedish Demographic History.* Uppsala: Scandinavian University Books. Studia Historica Upsaliensia, 47.

Öhngren, Bo. 1974. *Folk i rörelse. Samhallsutveckling, flyttningsmönster och folkrörelser i Eskilstuna 1870–1900.* Uppsala: Almqvist and Wiksell. Studia Historica Upsaliensia, 55.

Pasigli, Stefano. 1969. *Emigrazione e compartamento politico.* Bologna: Il Mulino.

Patten, John. 1973. *Rural-Urban Migration in Pre-Industrial England.* Oxford: School of Geography. Research Papers No. 6.

———. 1976. "Patterns of Migration and Movement of Labour to 3 Pre-Industrial East Anglian Towns." *Journal of Historical Geography,* 2, pp. 111–19.

Perez Díaz, Victor. 1971. *Emigración y cambio social: Procesos migratorios y vida rural en Castilla.* Barcelona: Ariel. 2d ed.

Perrenoud, Alfred. 1971. "Les migrations en Suisse sous l'Ancien Régime: Quelques problèmes." *Annales de Démographie Historique 1970,* pp. 251–59.

Pitié, Jean. 1971. *Exode rural et migrations intérieures en France: L'exemple de la Vienne et du Poitou-Charentes.* Poitiers: Norois.

Pollard, Sidney, and Crossley, David W. 1968. *The Wealth of Britain.* London: Batsford.

Pourcher, Guy. 1964. *Le peuplement de Paris.* Paris: Presses Universitaires de France. Institut National d'Etudes Démographiques, Travaux et Documents, Cahier 43.

Poussou, Jean-Pierre. 1971. "Les mouvements migratoires en France et à partir de la

France de la fin du XVe siècle au début du XIXe siècle: Approches pour une synthèse." *Annales de Démographie Historique 1970*, pp. 111–78.

————. 1974. "Introduction à l'étude des mouvements migratoires en Espagne, Italie et France méditerranéenne au XVIIIe siècle." In M. Aymard et al., *Les migrations dans les pays méditerranéens au XVIIIème et au début du XIXème*. Nice: Centre de la Méditerranée Moderne et Comtemporaine.

Pred, Allen. 1961. *The External Relations of Cities During 'Industrial Revolution.'* Chicago: Department of Geography, University of Chicago.

Redford, Arthur. 1964. *Labor Migration in England, 1800–1850*. W. H. Chaloner (ed.). Manchester: Manchester University Press. 2d ed.

Reinhard, Marcel R.; Armengaud, André; and Dupâquier, Jacques. 1968. *Histoire générale de la population mondiale*. Paris: Montchrestien.

Roof, Michael K. and Leedy, Frederick A. 1959. "Population Redistribution in the Soviet Union, 1939–1956." *Geographical Review*, 49, pp. 208–21.

Russell, J. C. 1959. "Medieval Midland and Northern Migration to London, 1100–1365." *Speculum*, 34, 641–45.

Sabean, David. 1971. "Household Formation and Geographic Mobility: A Family Register Study in a Wurttemberg Village 1760–1900." *Annales de Démographie Historique 1970*, pp. 275–94.

Saville, John. 1957. *Rural Depopulation in England and Wales, 1851–1951*. London: Routledge and Kegan Paul.

Schofield, R. S. 1971. "Age-Specific Mobility in an Eighteenth-Century Rural English Parish." *Annales de Démographie Historique 1970*, pp. 261–74.

Schon, Lennart. 1972. "Västernorrland in the Middle of the Nineteenth Century: A Study in the Transition from Small-Scale to Capitalistic Production." *Economy and History*, 15, pp. 83–111.

Shaw, R. Paul. 1975. *Migration Theory and Fact: A Review and Bibliography of Current Literature*. Philadelphia: Regional Science Research Institute. Bibliography Series, No. 5.

Skinner, G. William. 1964–1965. "Marketing and Social Structure in Rural China," Parts I, II, III. *Journal of Asian Studies*, 24, pp. 3–43, 195–228, 363–99.

Slack, Paul A. 1974. "Vagrants and Vagrancy in England, 1598–1664." *Economic History Review*, 2d series, 27, pp. 360–79.

Smith, C. T. 1968. *An Historical Geography of Western Europe before 1800*. London: Longmans.

Tauriaienen, Juhani, and Koivula, Samuli. 1973. *The Conditions in and Problems of Rural Depopulation Areas*. Helsinki: Department for Social Research, Ministry of Social Affairs and Health. Official Statistics of Finland, Series 32, no. 33.

Willcox, Walter F. 1929–1931. Ed., *International Migrations*. New York: National Bureau of Economic Research. 2 vols. Publications of the National Bureau of Economic Research, nos. 14 & 18.

Wrigley, E. A. 1966. Ed., *An Introduction to English Historical Demography*. London: Weidenfeld & Nicholson.

————. 1967. "A Simple Model of London's Importance in Changing English Society and Economy, 1650–1750." *Past and Present*, 37, pp. 44–70.

————. 1969. *Population and History*. New York: McGraw-Hill.

*Part Two*

---

# Patterns of Migration:
# Europe and the Americas

# [4]

## The Image of "Elsewhere" in the American Tradition of Migration

PETER A. MORRISON AND JUDITH P. WHEELER

"In the United States, there is more room where nobody is than where anybody is. That is what makes America what it is." Gertrude Stein's pronouncement is whimsical, but it strongly parallels the famous thesis of Frederick Jackson Turner concerning America's western frontier. Turner suggested that the frontier was the key force shaping American intellectual style, national character, and political institutions. When he first proposed it, the idea stimulated a flurry of scholarly studies, but eventually it wilted under historians' critical scrutiny. Instead of a central driving force, they concluded, the frontier was "a hazy and shifting concept riddled with internal contradictions"—actually a cluster of causes united in a single term.[1]

Whatever the limitations of his thesis in explaining the national character, Turner surely enriched the national mythology: the captivating image of the frontier as a place, but also as a process, was magnified into a legend with continuing intuitive appeal.[2] Students of the American experience continue to interpret it because they sense in it some kernel of wisdom.

Fifteen years ago, demographer Everett Lee reexamined the frontier theory and suggested that Turner actually had in mind a special case of a more general theory of migration.[3] Most of the effects that Turner attributed to the frontier, Lee said, can equally be attributed to migration, even the development of that "coarseness and strength combined with acuteness and inquisitiveness; that practical, inventive turn of mind, quick to find expedients; ... that restless, nervous energy; that dominant individualism."[4] In

75

Lee's view, these traits were made manifest through and nurtured by the migratory experience as well as by Turner's prairie. Moreover, migration has persisted where the frontier did not.

Lee's perspective has been sharpened over the last fifteen years by new findings from research by geographers, quantitative urban historians, sociologists, demographers, and others. The extraordinary volume of migration and its consequences for people and places can be discerned more clearly now —in particular its role in redistributing population in response to economic growth patterns. But how are we to explain all this coming and going, so vast in comparison with the net redistribution accomplished and so much greater than what the rate of national economic growth would seem to require? The evidence for any answer to this question is too slim to warrant more than suggestive speculation. And the course we follow in this paper is deliberately speculative; we generalize Turner's concern with American national character and apply it to contemporary patterns of migration behavior.

Extending Lee's perspective, we might ask whether Turner's thesis is attractive not so much for what it tells us about the frontier of the Old West, but because it introduces the frontier concept—or perhaps fantasy—as a compelling force in American development. One might suppose, for example, that the highly selective process of migration, in sorting both people and places according to an array of recognizable characteristics, perpetuates those characteristics in the American consciousness. One of the most deeply ingrained of these characteristics seems to be the sense that one can always "pick up and go"—not necessarily where nobody is, just "elsewhere." It may be, then, that the true safety valve for Turner's discontented Eastern masses was not the free lands of the West, but a kind of frontier of the mind—the image of an "elsewhere" with its idealized possibilities—created and sustained by a tradition of unhindered migration. Migrants, who seem to live life as a perpetual odyssey, may be carriers of some fundamental impulse that inspirits the whole society and continues to define the American experience as one of freedom and opportunity through migration, whether one migrates or not. Every American has at least that choice.

## THE VOLUME OF MIGRATION

Until quite recently, the full extent and consequences of the population's comings and goings were severely understated. Statistics were inadequate to register the magnitude of actual movement; only its residue was recorded in the measure known as net migration. There are, of course, no "net migrants," but, rather, people who are arriving at places or leaving them.

The importance of the distinction between net and gross movement has been highlighted in a number of recent historical studies focusing on individual American cities, mostly during the nineteenth century.[5] These studies have been virtually unanimous in demonstrating a high degree of impermanence in the population during that period owing to migration. The net change in a city's population typically concealed a massive volume of gross migration. Over the course of a decade or so, the total number of *different* people residing in these cities was perhaps five or ten times the population recorded at any time. The static view of cities as growing somewhat like brick piles has been replaced by a dynamic view: cities are more like sieves, snagging occasional new settlers out of the rush of people passing through.

Demographic analyses of contemporary migratory experience accord well with this historical evidence and afford a more detailed view of the population's astonishing impermanence. The barely six percent of the citizenry that each year moves across a county line—and thus qualifies for migrant status in the Census Bureau's definition—actually produces almost enough people on the move to depopulate, within five years, all 223 current U.S. metropolitan areas with under one million residents. How this gross movement can produce so little net change is well illustrated by Albuquerque, New Mexico, during the 1960s. Metropolitan Albuquerque's 1970 population of about a third of a million included a gain of just twenty-two "net migrants" since 1960. That net figure revealed nothing of what had been going on in Albuquerque: in a typical year throughout the decade, some 44,000 people—more than one-sixth of the population—moved to the metropolitan area, replacing 44,000 who left for somewhere else. More generally, contemporary U.S. metropolitan areas annually gain from five to twenty in-migrants per hundred residents and lose a roughly similar number of out-migrants (refer to Table 1).[6]

## THE INDIVIDUAL AND SPATIAL SELECTIVITY OF MIGRATION

Recent research has also examined: (1) the distinctive characteristics of migrants, through which it is possible to discern some of the principles which govern individual selectivity, and (2) the social structures which, by establishing relationships between the migrant and the receiving community before he moves, delimit the spatial pattern of movement.

The decision to migrate is triggered in certain kinds of people by economic and social influences, mainly those associated with life-cycle stage, occupation, employment status, educational attainment, and past mobility experience.

*Life-cycle patterns in migration.* Migration is often induced by transitions from one stage of the life cycle to another. Migration rates vary sharply

Table 1

Average Annual In-Migration and Out-Migration Rates,
Selected Large Metropolitan Areas[a]

| Metropolitan Area[b] | Rate Per Hundred | | Metropolitan Area[b] | Rate Per Hundred | |
|---|---|---|---|---|---|
| | In-Migration | Out-Migration | | In-Migration | Out-Migration |
| Akron | 6.9 | 7.4 | Miami | 14.1 | 15.0 |
| Albany | 7.0 | 6.2 | Milwaukee | 5.3 | 5.6 |
| Albuquerque | 14.4 | 14.8 | Minneapolis | 7.0 | 6.8 |
| Allentown | 5.7 | 6.1 | Mobile | 11.2 | 11.9 |
| Atlanta | 11.4 | 11.4 | Nashville | 9.0 | 9.4 |
| Bakersfield | 15.1 | 15.1 | Newark | 9.0 | 9.8 |
| Baltimore | 5.3 | 5.9 | New Haven | 7.4 | 8.3 |
| Birmingham | 8.6 | 10.4 | New Orleans | 10.4 | 10.3 |
| Boston | 5.8 | 6.3 | New York | 5.6 | 5.8 |
| Bridgeport | 8.0 | 8.0 | Norfolk | 11.1 | 11.8 |
| Buffalo | 4.8 | 5.9 | Oklahoma City | 13.0 | 13.0 |
| Canton | 5.9 | 5.7 | Omaha | 10.0 | 9.8 |
| Charleston (W. Va.) | 9.1 | 10.1 | Orlando | 19.1 | 17.5 |
| Charlotte | 12.8 | 13.7 | Paterson | 11.2 | 11.6 |
| Chattanooga | 7.8 | 8.9 | Peoria | 7.5 | 7.0 |
| Chicago | 5.6 | 5.9 | Philadelphia | 5.8 | 6.4 |
| Cincinnati | 6.2 | 7.0 | Phoenix | 15.2 | 13.4 |
| Cleveland | 6.9 | 7.1 | Pittsburgh | 5.5 | 5.7 |
| Columbia (S.C.) | 10.5 | 11.1 | Portland (Ore.) | 9.6 | 9.4 |
| Columbus | 9.0 | 9.2 | Providence | 5.6 | 6.5 |
| Dallas | 13.0 | 12.5 | Reading | 6.2 | 6.4 |
| Davenport | 8.2 | 7.2 | Richmond | 9.4 | 9.5 |
| Dayton | 7.0 | 6.9 | Rochester (N.Y.) | 6.1 | 5.5 |
| Denver | 12.4 | 11.1 | Sacramento | 16.0 | 12.3 |
| Des Moines | 9.8 | 11.2 | St. Louis | 6.4 | 6.4 |
| Detroit | 4.7 | 5.5 | Salt Lake City | 9.9 | 9.8 |
| Duluth-Superior | 6.9 | 8.1 | San Antonio | 9.8 | 10.6 |
| Erie | 5.1 | 6.2 | San Bernardino | 17.4 | 16.6 |
| Flint | 5.1 | 5.1 | San Diego | 11.5 | 12.7 |
| Ft. Lauderdale | 20.1 | 19.7 | San Francisco | 12.3 | 12.1 |
| Fresno | 14.2 | 14.7 | San Jose | 19.6 | 17.6 |
| Gary-Hammond | 6.6 | 7.6 | Seattle | 8.8 | 9.2 |
| Grand Rapids | 6.7 | 6.9 | Shreveport | 14.4 | 13.9 |
| Harrisburg | 9.0 | 8.7 | Spokane | 9.8 | 11.2 |
| Hartford | 7.6 | 7.3 | Springfield (Mass.) | 6.9 | 7.4 |
| Honolulu | 6.9 | 6.3 | Syracuse | 7.4 | 8.2 |
| Houston | 12.8 | 12.5 | Tacoma | 10.9 | 10.9 |
| Huntington | 8.3 | 9.7 | Tampa | 13.3 | 13.3 |
| Indianapolis | 7.8 | 8.2 | Toledo | 6.5 | 7.0 |
| Jacksonville | 16.1 | 15.3 | Trenton | 9.3 | 8.4 |
| Jersey City | 11.6 | 12.9 | Tucson | 14.6 | 13.1 |
| Johnstown | 5.7 | 6.8 | Tulsa | 12.6 | 11.7 |
| Kansas City | 9.2 | 9.3 | Utica | 6.9 | 7.5 |
| Knoxville | 9.4 | 7.9 | Washington | 10.9 | 9.7 |
| Lancaster | 6.1 | 6.2 | Wichita | 9.7 | 11.0 |
| Lansing | 7.4 | 8.1 | Wilkes-Barre | 8.3 | 8.2 |
| Los Angeles | 9.7 | 8.3 | Wilmington (Del.) | 11.0 | 10.3 |
| Louisville | 7.1 | 7.4 | Worcester | 6.6 | 7.0 |
| Memphis | 9.5 | 9.9 | Youngstown | 5.8 | 7.8 |

[a] Average is the mean of annual rates per hundred resident wage and salary workers of a metropolitan area for each year between 1959 and 1965. Migrants entering or leaving military service are excluded.

[b] Most of the metropolitan areas listed are defined according to the Office of Management and Budget's definition as of 1970. For technical reasons, some areas are defined slightly differently.

Source: Social Security Continuous Work History Sample, covering approximately 9 in 10 wage and salary workers in a typical metropolitan area. For further technical detail, refer to Peter A. Morrison and Daniel A. Relles, *Recent Research Insights into Local Migration Flows*, The Rand Corporation, P-5379, February 1975.

78]

and with nearly universal regularity according to age groups, with young adults predominating. U.S. rates are highest for people in their early twenties, reflecting the changes, adjustments, and initial commitments that accompany early adulthood. Large numbers of these people are completing their formal schooling, entering the labor market for the first time, serving in the armed forces, and marrying and forming families. These activities predispose people to move frequently until they are well into their thirties.

Changes in marital status accentuate the effect of age. Migration is closely linked in time to marriage and family formation, and the first few years after marriage are a period of frequent movement. The dissolution of marriage through separation or divorce is also frequently accompanied by movement.

*Occupation and employment status.* Whereas unskilled jobs are usually filled by local residents, highly skilled or specialized jobs tend to be filled through regionwide or even nationwide competition and recruitment. Occupational differentials in migration reflect the scope of this competition and recruitment. White-collar workers migrate more frequently than manual and service workers. Within the white-collar category, professional workers (especially those who are salaried rather than self-employed) tend to be the most migratory. Professionals' migration stems from the more nearly nationwide labor markets in which such people find jobs; it also reflects the variety of relatively short-term residences that accompany higher education and internship or other apprenticelike arrangements. The least migratory occupational groups tend to be service workers and farmers and farm managers. Retirement from the labor force may also stimulate migration over considerable distances.

*Educational attainment.* Education is also related to the propensity to move. People with at least some college education, for example, are considerably more migratory overall than those with only an elementary education, and nearly four times as likely to migrate across a state line. In general, each successively higher increment of education between these extremes is associated with a higher rate of migration.

*Past migration experience.* Migration is frequently a repetitive episode, and observed mobility rates tend to reflect repeated and frequent moves by the same people rather than single moves by others. Consequently, people with a history of past moves show a disposition to move again—possibly because some of the characteristics that make people likely to move are persistent characteristics, because successful moves may lead to attempts to achieve further success by moving again, or because not all moves are made with the expectation of a permanent stay at the destination.

These motives and predisposing factors associated with migration for the most part display obvious opportunities being exploited or purposes being fulfilled, but they fail to explain the reasons why: (1) of those who have similar characteristics and purposes, only some choose to migrate, and (2) those who have migrated once are highly likely to migrate again fairly soon. If migration served solely as a readjustment to life's contingencies, almost everyone might be expected to migrate at some point in his or her life, but not everyone does. And, paradoxically, movers do not necessarily become stayers once they have fulfilled their stated or ostensible purpose for moving. On the contrary, research shows that a large part of the moving is done by a small part of the population who move repeatedly and frequently. What it seems to come down to is that migration may be purely self-selective, chosen perhaps by "pioneer individuals"—persons with a wider vision of the possibilities offered by unknown areas and a perspective toward the future wholly different from that of their nonmigrating counterparts.

The paradoxical quality of migrants' behavior is further underlined by the circumstances under which they are found to leave and the way they select the places to which they go. It has long been recognized that the typical migrant is not entirely objective and rational in choosing a destination, and that the migrant's information system is highly selective. Survey data suggest that migrants generally are seeking economic opportunity, but that they consider only a very narrow range of possible locales. They give little or no thought to the many alternative destinations where their purposes might be served; instead, they migrate to places where family and friends have settled—so-called "chain migration."[7] It is as though *where* the individual will go is a long-standing assumption. The decision to move automatically activates the mental map; the only question is *when.*[8]

As a result of this spatial selectivity, migration flows exhibit relatively permanent geographic patterns—patterns that amount to a cumulative record of the population movements by which regions were settled and cities were formed. For example, migrants continue to flow between California and the rural Ozark-Ouachita region of Arkansas, Missouri, and Oklahoma, reflecting kinship ties sustained since the Dust Bowl migration of the 1930s. (Interestingly, the direction of this movement has reversed in recent years, suggesting how past movements of population may shape contemporary ones.)[9] Over time, the geographic patterns of migration flow shift in response to economic and technological change: migrants in today's urban economy for the most part circulate among cities, in contrast to the nineteenth-century migrants who headed for open land and those bends in the road that were to become today's cities. But it will still be true that, because of the sociological links between origins and destinations, certain places receive a vastly disproportionate share of the migrants departing from certain other places. These migration paths are broadened and deepened by each new migrant, whose arrival at a destination establishes yet another reference point for the population remaining at origin.

Given such spatial selectivity, economically thriving migratory focal points—Phoenix, Fort Collins, Tucson, and their like—would balloon out of control except for migrants' peculiar proclivity for moving on. What the evidence shows is that migrants on the whole flock toward economic growth areas, but they also *leave* such areas even more readily than they leave those with ailing economies.[10] Successive waves of migration appear to move *through* a select few boom areas, so that although the net population change of those areas is well above average, it is still modest in comparison with the magnitude of the flow-through.

This fact can be demonstrated with further reference to the Social Security Continuous Work History Sample on migration for contemporary metropolitan areas. The eight representative areas shown in Table 2 range from rapidly growing Ft. Lauderdale and San Jose to slowly growing Buffalo and Milwaukee. The data have been tabulated so as to distinguish two segments within the out-migrant stream from each area. One segment comprises persons who had resided elsewhere two years before (i.e., were recent in-migrants to this area). This "revolving" element, exemplifying repetitive migration in its most immediate form, is composed of people who seem chronically disposed to migrate. The remaining segment is more heterogeneous: some of those departing are natives, while others are repeat migrants who have remained in the area for more than a year.

Table 2

Rate and Composition of Out-Migration by Migrants' Residential History, for Eight Representative Metropolitan Areas

| Metropolitan Area | Persons Residing Elsewhere Two Years Before | | Persons Residing in Same Area Two Years Before | | Both Segments | |
|---|---|---|---|---|---|---|
| | Annual Out-Migration Rate | Percent of All Out-Migrants | Annual Out-Migration Rate | Percent of All Out-Migrants | Annual Out-Migration Rate | Percent of All Out-Migrants |
| Fort Lauderdale | 41.1 | 45 | 12.1 | 55 | 18.0 | 100 |
| San Jose | 34.7 | 40 | 12.5 | 60 | 16.8 | 100 |
| Bakersfield | 43.8 | 43 | 9.1 | 57 | 14.7 | 100 |
| Kansas City | 33.6 | 35 | 5.9 | 65 | 8.6 | 100 |
| Indianapolis | 32.1 | 32 | 5.4 | 68 | 7.5 | 100 |
| Louisville | 33.6 | 34 | 4.5 | 66 | 6.5 | 100 |
| Buffalo | 31.8 | 27 | 4.2 | 73 | 5.5 | 100 |
| Milwaukee | 25.0 | 25 | 4.0 | 75 | 5.1 | 100 |

Note: Rates and percentages are arithmetic means of values for each year 1959 through 1965.

Source: Social Security Continuous Work History Sample.

This distinction affords only a crude separation of repetitive and non-repetitive migrants, but it is an important one. The data in Table 2[11] show that persons who resided elsewhere two years before are much more prone to subsequent migration than are the longer-term residents. Upwards of 25.0 percent (Milwaukee) to 43.8 percent (Bakersfield) of the former group out-migrate, compared with only 4.0 percent (Milwaukee) to 12.5 percent (San Jose) of the latter group. The propensity of recent in-migrants to move repeatedly is evident.

Can we attribute this paradoxical "moving on" to the existence of a kind of migratory inheritance whereby (for some people) the promise of a new frontier competes with any particular well-being here and now? The phenomenon of repeat migration tempts the thought that, to the pioneering personality, almost any place will do so long as it is *another* place. Novelty, in short, may be as alluring as economic opportunity.

The sense of promise and opportunity attached to "moving on" has been seen as an especially American trait handed down since the first European settlers landed.[12] It is striking that migration should continue in such magnitude long after the stimulation afforded by an open frontier and waves of immigration from abroad ended. We have postulated that the allure of an "elsewhere" with its idealized possibilities may be what, in the last analysis, distinguishes the migrant from the nonmigrant and accounts at least partially for the phenomenon of repetitive migration. We further suggest that this mental conception is a peculiarly *American* legacy—an outgrowth of the historical readiness to migrate which reinforces that tradition today. For any individual, of whatever station in life, that legacy has the power to construct a frontier of the mind—an abiding vision of some other *place* where the past can be discounted and the future shaped at will. The promise embodied in that legacy induces movement for a certain few, and their movement keeps the promise alive for all.

The American culture, more than others, is a repository of the mental conceptions tied to other places on which internal migration feeds. The superintendent of the 1850 census attributed Americans' restlessness to "the peculiar condition of their country" and took comfort in his prediction that they would eventually settle down:

> When men of scanty means cannot by a mere change of location acquire a homestead, the inhabitants of each State will become comparatively stationary; and our countrymen will exhibit that attachment to the homes of their childhood, the want of which is sometimes cited as an unfavorable trait in our national character.

History did not bear out Superintendent Kennedy's prediction. We suggest here that a major cause has been the persistence of images rooted in the

American past. Admittedly, it is a difficult thesis to prove; we must join with Turner, who, in speaking of his own thesis, observed that its strength or weakness ultimately "lies in interpretation, correlation, in the elucidation of large tendencies to bring out new points of view."

## NOTES

This paper draws on research supported in part by a grant from the National Institute of Child Health and Human Development. The authors thank Rand Corporation colleagues Will Harriss and Joanne Hasslinger for comments on an earlier draft of this paper. The views expressed here are the authors' own, and are not necessarily shared by Rand or its research sponsors.

1. George W. Pierson, "The Frontier and Frontiersman of Turner's Essay," *Pennsylvania Magazine of History and Biography*, 64 (October 1940), p. 478; idem, "The Frontier and American Institutions: A Criticism of the Turner Theory," *The Turner Thesis*, ed. George R. Taylor (Boston, 1956), p. 63.

2. William Coleman, "Science and Symbol in the Turner Frontier Hypothesis," *American Historical Review*, 62 (October 1966), pp. 22–49.

3. Everett S. Lee, "The Turner Thesis Reexamined," *American Quarterly*, Spring, 1961, pp. 77–83.

4. Turner, as quoted in ibid., pp. 77–78.

5. Among these studies are: Gunther Barth, *Instant Cities: Urbanization and the Rise of San Francisco and Denver* (New York: Oxford University Press, 1975); Howard P. Chudacoff, *Mobile Americans: Residential and Social Mobility in Omaha, 1880–1920* (New York: Oxford University Press, 1972); Howard M. Gitelman, *Workingmen of Waltham: Mobility in American Urban Industrial Development, 1850–1890* (Baltimore: Johns Hopkins University Press, 1974); Richard J. Hopkins, "Status, Mobility, and the Dimensions of Change in a Southern City: Atlanta, 1870–1910," in Kenneth T. Jackson and Stanley K. Schultz (eds.), *Cities in American History* (New York: Alfred A. Knopf, 1972), pp. 216–231; Stephan Thernstrom, *The Other Bostonians: Poverty and Progress in the American Metropolis, 1880–1970* (Cambridge: Harvard University Press, 1973), p. 27. Useful comparative reviews of recent studies are given in S. L. Engerman, "Up or Out: Social and Geographic Mobility in the United States," *Journal of Interdisciplinary History*, 3 (1975), pp. 469–489; and James P. Allen, "Geographic Mobility Trends in the United States," mimeo., 1975.

6. Data shown in Table 1 are average annual rates of in- and out-migration by the civilian labor force for each of ninety-eight metropolitan areas between 1959 and 1965. Data are based on the Social Security Continuous Work History Sample, which

refers to a subset of the entire population—employed workers covered by Social Security. To our knowledge they are the only annual rates of gross migration available for individual metropolitan areas.

Migration rates for the working-age population are taken here as a surrogate for rates for the entire population. Much of the civilian migration not directly reflected in these rates is derivative migration, i.e., moves attributable to the spouse and children of a worker covered by Social Security. For a fuller discussion of these data, see Peter A. Morrison and Daniel A. Relles, *Recent Research Insights into Local Migration Flows*, The Rand Corporation, P-5379, February 1975.

7. A major national survey of migrants conducted in the early 1960s disclosed that: (1) two-thirds of all migrants considered no other destinations than the places to which they actually moved, and (2) job information was most frequently obtained from friends and relatives (49 percent). John B. Lansing and Eva Mueller, *The Geographic Mobility of Labor* (Ann Arbor: Survey Research Center, Institute for Social Research, 1967).

8. For example, see the descriptions contained in James S. Brown, et al., "Kentucky Mountain Migration and the Stem-family: An American Variation on a Theme by Le Play," *Rural Sociology*, March 1963, pp. 48–69; Harry K. Schwarzweller, et al., *Mountain Families in Transition* (University Park, Pa.: Pennsylvania State University Press, 1971); Harvey M. Choldin, "Kinship Networks in the Migration Process," *International Migration Review*, 7, no. 2 (Summer 1973), pp. 163–175.

9. According to census data, the Ozark-Ouachita region now withdraws many more migrants *from* California than it sends there: between 1965 and 1970, two persons migrated from California to this region for every one who followed the traditional path leading west. During that period, over one-third of the region's net migratory gain originated in California alone.

10. Research findings, although not fully in agreement, indicate that migrants flock to locales where the economy is growing and labor is in demand (the economically "correct" destinations). However, they do not depart so readily from places where labor is in oversupply (the economically "correct" origins).

Much of the net in-migration that feeds the growth in U.S. metropolitan areas is confined to a few rapidly growing centers containing a comparatively small part of the nation's population. For example, consider the twenty-three metropolitan areas to which net in-migration, 1960–1970, added twenty or more new residents per hundred population in 1960. They contained only 11 percent of the entire metropolitan population in 1965, yet they drew 71 percent of the cumulative net migration that fed metropolitan growth during the decade. Further details are given in Peter A. Morrison, "Population Movements and the Shape of Urban Growth: Implications for Public Policy," in John Friedmann and William Alonso (eds.), *Regional Policy: Readings in Theory and Applications* (Cambridge: MIT Press, 1975), pp. 221–243.

11. Only a few representative metropolitan areas are shown here, but the patterns are typical of all the areas in Table 1.

12. We acknowledge a debt to George W. Pierson, whose suggestive discussion of psychological aspects of migration in *The Moving Americans* (New York: Alfred A. Knopf, 1973) is extended here.

# [5]

## European Migration after World War II

HANS-JOACHIM HOFFMANN-NOWOTNY

I.

Migrations have characterized human groups and societies since mankind's earliest history. Historically, migrations have come in waves—times of large migrations have followed, irregularly, upon epochs of relative calm. Today, even a superficial analysis shows that throughout the world large legal international migrations have almost disappeared. To be sure, an explanation of this disappearance must take into account the present economic recession. But in the case of Europe—as we will show— migrations decreased before the recession set in. In short, international migrations drastically declined not because their determinants disappeared but because immigration countries closed their borders as a result of internal problems.

Although completely accurate statistical information is very difficult to obtain, it may be affirmed that European migrations after World War II were one of the largest movements of the kind in history. Today, about 12 million aliens are living in the Western European immigration countries; and if one could count those who have returned to their home countries after some time, or those who work on a seasonal basis, one could add several million more. These numbers do not take into account migrations which may have been direct or indirect consequences of wars: the numbers of refugees transcends the aforementioned figure.

The problem of obtaining accurate statistics is not new in migration research. Even when such statistics are available—which is not the case in many countries—accurate comparisons are difficult, owing to the different categorization of migrants. Unfortunately, too, it has been impossible to obtain data on European migration streams; thus, we have had to rely on data giving only the number of aliens in the immigration countries. Nevertheless, these data have proved sufficient for the present analysis.

What is new, on the other hand, are the problems of terminology one encounters in describing these migrations. Speaking about migrations in Europe after World War II in terms of "emigrant" or "immigrant," "country of emigration" or "country of immigration," "emigration policy" or "immigration policy," has become difficult. It is the very paradox of European migrations today that millions of people who are living in foreign countries are not designated as "immigrants"; nor do these countries see themselves as immigration countries. And vice versa, very few of the countries that send millions of their citizens to work abroad consider themselves "emigration countries" in the narrow sense. Instead of the term "immigrant," words such as "foreign worker," "guest worker," "foreign employee," or "migrant worker" are used.

Since neither emigration nor immigration countries admit that they are such, there are no well-defined or codified immigration or emigration policies. Consequently, a situation that has lasted for thirty years remains "provisory." In the present paper I will attempt to show that many of the problems related to European migration in the period after World War II are a consequence of this paradox. After a statistical description of the development and present state of European migrations, I will show that the existence of policies that do not conform to realities, along with the rules and laws that these policies engender, reinforce this anomic situation. Finally, even though emigration and immigration countries do not designate themselves in this way and do not call immigrants or emigrants by those names, we will nonetheless use the terms here, for simplicity's sake, as well as for intellectual honesty and the social science perspective underlying the following analysis.

II.

The countries designated "immigration countries" in this paper are the Federal Republic of Germany, Switzerland, Belgium, Sweden, Norway, the Netherlands, France, Austria, and Denmark. Great Britain has been marginal to intra-European migrations, and the same is true for the Eastern European countries, if they can be called immigration countries at all. While it is well known that Poland has sent workers to the German Democratic

Republic, there is no reliable information about duration of stay or size of this work force; an analysis is therefore impossible. However, there can be no doubt that if the borders within Eastern Europe—let alone the ones between Eastern and Western Europe—could be freely crossed, strong migratory movements would set in.

The European countries designated "emigration countries" are Italy, Finland, Spain, Portugal, Yugoslavia, and Greece, although Morocco, Tunisia, Algeria, and Turkey also play an important part in European migration. It should be pointed out that Yugoslavia is the only Eastern European country that not only permits but encourages free emigration.

In order to interpret the migration data presented in the tables, a few theoretical considerations are necessary. Macro-sociologists emphasize that modern migrations usually follow developmental gaps between societal contexts.[1] This applies to internal as well as to international migrations. Thus, those modern migrations to be discussed here seem to be a result of developmental differences existing in the system formed by international society. But on the behavioral (micro) level, they are also—and this is sometimes overlooked—a result of the fact that, because value integration is an important characteristic of the system, these differences have deeply affected the awareness and behavior of individuals in the countries in question. By value integration, we mean that modern acquisitive values (like "development," or "standard of living") have become an integrative part of most cultures in our day, and that practically all cultures have become homogeneous as far as these values are concerned. This does not, of course, imply that fulfillment of the aspirations based on these values has also become homogeneous.

From a sociological point of view, the "integration of values" means an enlargement of the structure relevant to social actors and their orientations. Value integration is accelerated by politico-economic integration—for instance, the removal of barriers preventing the exchange of ideas and people, as is the case within the European Community. At the same time, however, the problems of underprivileged groups and regions become problems of the larger societal system, which has to deal with the claims of the underprivileged for a share in the goods that represent the values of the system.

To change its situation, an underprivileged group theoretically has two possibilities: collective action and individual mobility. In the first case, an attempt is made to improve the individual's situation by improving the whole group's situation—for instance, by developing one's region or nation. In the second case, an attempt is made to improve one's own personal situation—for instance, by emigration from a less developed to a more developed country.

The high level of emigration from the less developed parts of Europe, and from Turkey and North Africa, to the highly developed European countries suggests that millions of people are no longer willing to wait for the success of collective efforts in their home countries and that they prefer to migrate. These mass migrations create ethnic, racial, and class problems as soon as the people involved penetrate ethnically different and more highly developed groups. On the other hand, because of their developmental lead and the capital accumulation made possible by it, the highly developed countries are able to use developmental gaps for recruiting workers who are considered a kind of industrial reserve army by the political authorities as well as by the entrepreneurs and broad segments of the native work forces.

III.

A first look at the migration data shows that migrations do follow developmental gaps, although this is not demonstrated here in detail by means of development indicators. Moreover, the data show that developmental gaps do not lead to an equal distribution of emigrants among immigration countries. Rather, there are specific migration flows between certain emigration and immigration countries, and these flows vary considerably in duration and size. In the postwar years, for instance, Italy, the classic emigration country, accounted for the largest share of migrants in the most important immigration countries (Germany, France, Belgium, and Switzerland). While this is still true for Switzerland and Belgium, Italian immigrants in other countries have lost their leading position, even if their absolute numbers have continued to increase. In Germany, Yugoslav immigrants made up the largest share for a while, but they have now been replaced by the Turks. In France, not only the relative share but also the absolute number of Italians have decreased; today Algerians make up the largest share, followed by Portuguese. In Belgium, too, the relative share of Italian immigrants has decreased, but they are still the largest group, as in Switzerland. Although Belgium and the Netherlands are neighbors and together with Italy belong to the European Community (EC), the Netherlands, surprisingly enough, has never had a strong Italian immigration. The large number of Germans and Belgians who went there during the early years of immigration after World War II shows that during this phase the Netherlands recruited its immigrants from neighboring countries. In Switzerland, Italians have formed the largest group of immigrants since World War II, and although their share has slightly decreased since 1960, they still represent more than half of the foreign residents today. Recently, the Spanish share of immigrants in Switzerland has increased. Sweden is the country that deviates from this roughly uniform picture: here, it is Finland that provides by far the largest part of the migrants, doubtless because of geographical proximity. Obviously the geographical factor is important for all the migration flows discussed above.

Disregarding the nationality of the migrants and considering instead the total size of migrations in absolute and relative terms, the following picture emerges: excepting the smallest European immigration countries, Liechtenstein and Luxembourg,[2] it may be affirmed that the Swiss share of foreigners, about 17 percent of the total resident population, is the largest in Europe. The absolute number of immigrants there, which was over 200,000 in 1950, tripled by 1960; between 1960 and 1974 the number doubled again. A distant second behind Switzerland is Belgium, whose relative share of foreigners is 8 percent, equal in absolute numbers to 775,000. France is third with 7.7 percent, equal to roughly 4 million persons. As to the growth of the number of foreigners in France, it must be noted that this number was already quite high (1.8 million) just after the war; the number decreased slightly by 1960, but increased again from then on. Between 1960 and 1970 the number of foreigners in France doubled, and from 1970 to 1974 there was a further increase of roughly 650,000 persons.

In the German Federal Republic the proportion of foreigners today is roughly 7 percent, equal to about 4 million. Between 1951 and 1961 the number of immigrants was almost stagnant, but it increased by 600 percent between 1961 and 1974. This does not mean, however, that until 1961 Germany had no need for immigrants. Rather, at that time Germany (or the three zones occupied by the Western powers) took in about 10 million people expelled from the former German East, and later on took in about 3.5 million refugees from the German Democratic Republic. After the construction of the Berlin Wall in 1961 the large flow of refugees suddenly stopped, and the expanding German economy was forced to recruit foreign immigrants. If people expelled from the East and refugees are also counted as immigrants (which is not officially the case), it may be said that the Federal Republic of Germany has received the largest number of immigrants since the war, both absolutely and relatively.

With a foreign population of roughly 5 percent, or 401,000 persons, Sweden, too, has had considerable immigration. In the other Western European immigration countries—the Netherlands, Austria, Denmark, and Norway—the foreign share today is below 2.5 percent.

If Spain and Italy are looked at as immigration instead of emigration countries, the thesis that migrants mainly follow developmental gaps seems to apply there too. Both countries have received immigrants from still less developed countries. Besides Portuguese immigrants in Spain, both countries have a considerable number of immigrants from North Africa. These latter, however, are statistically nonexistent since they enter the country illegally. The same situation occurs in Greece.

A more differentiated consideration of European migrations, on the one hand, and the hypothesis concerning the connection between developmental gaps and migration, on the other, suggest a qualitative difference in

## Table 1

### Total and Foreign Population of
### European Immigration Countries Since World War II

| Year | Total Population | Number of Aliens | Aliens as Percentage of Total Population |
|------|------------------|------------------|-------------------------------------------|
| *Switzerland* | | | |
| 1941 | 4,265,703 | 223,554 | 5.24 |
| 1950 | 4,714,992 | 285,446 | 6.05 |
| 1960 | 5,429,061 | 569,935 | 10.50 |
| 1965 | 5,945,500 | 810,243 | 13.47 |
| 1968 | 6,147,000 | 933,142 | 15.21 |
| 1970 | 6,269,783 | 982,887 | 15.68 |
| 1974 | 6,442,800 | 1,064,526 | 16.52 |
| *Belgium* | | | |
| 1947 | 8,388,526 | 367,619 | 4.38 |
| 1954 | 8,840,704 | 379,528 | 4.29 |
| 1961 | 9,189,741 | 453,486 | 4.93 |
| 1965 | 9,499,234 | 636,749 | 6.70 |
| 1970 | 9,650,944 | 696,282 | 7.21 |
| 1973 | 9,756,590 | 775,185 | 7.94 |
| *France* | | | |
| 1946 | 40,125,000 | 1,743,619 | 4.35 |
| 1954 | 43,228,000 | 1,766,100 | 4.09 |
| 1958 | 45,015,000 | 1,621,075 | 3.60 |
| 1960 | 45,904,000 | 1,633,410 | 3.56 |
| 1965 | 48,954,000 | 2,683,490 | 5.48 |
| 1970 | 51,012,000 | 3,393,457 | 6.65 |
| 1972 | 51,921,000 | 3,775,804 | 7.21 |
| 1974 | 53,614,441 | 4,128,312 | 7.70 |
| *Federal Republic of Germany* | | | |
| 1951 | 50,241,400 | 485,763 | 0.99 |
| 1955 | 52,383,000 | 484,819 | 0.92 |
| 1961 | 56,175,000 | 686,160 | 1.22 |
| 1968 | 60,184,000 | 2,381,100 | 3.96 |
| 1970 | 60,651,000 | 2,976,500 | 4.90 |
| 1972 | 61,672,000 | 3,438,700 | 5.58 |
| 1974 | 62,054,000 | 4,127,400 | 6.65 |
| *Sweden* | | | |
| 1945 | 6,673,749 | 35,111 | 0.53 |
| 1950 | 7,041,829 | 123,720 | 1.76 |
| 1954 | 7,234,664 | 111,111 | 1.54 |
| 1960 | 7,497,967 | 190,621 | 2.54 |

Table 1 (Continued)

| Year | Total Population | Number of Aliens | Aliens as Percentage of Total Population |
|------|------------------|------------------|------------------------------------------|
| *Sweden (continued)* | | | |
| 1968 | 7,931,659 | 320,580 | 4.04 |
| 1970 | 8,081,229 | 411,280 | 5.09 |
| 1974 | 8,176,691 | 401,158 | 4.91 |
| *Austria* | | | |
| 1961 | 7,073,807 | 102,159 | 1.44 |
| 1971 | 7,456,000 | 176,773 | 2.37 |
| *Netherlands* | | | |
| 1947 | 9,715,890 | 113,871 | 1.17 |
| 1956 | 10,957,040 | 106,480 | 0.98 |
| 1960 | 11,556,008 | 107,018 | 0.93 |
| 1964 | 12,212,269 | 134,792 | 1.12 |
| 1968 | 12,798,346 | 181,376 | 1.43 |
| 1973 | 13,491,020 | 282,361 | 2.11 |
| *Norway* | | | |
| 1946 | 3,156,950 | 15,912 | 0.50 |
| 1950 | 3,278,546 | 15,797 | 0.48 |
| 1960 | 3,591,234 | 24,828 | 0.69 |
| *Denmark* | | | |
| 1950 | 4,281,275 | 77,970 | 1.82 |
| 1960 | 4,585,256 | 16,637 | 0.36 |
| 1964 | 4,741,000 | 23,645 | 0.50 |
| 1968 | 4,855,300 | 32,286 | 0.66 |
| 1970 | 4,920,966 | 49,811 | 1.01 |
| 1972 | 5,007,538 | 54,716 | 1.10 |
| 1974 | 5,036,184 | 49,727 | 0.99 |

migrations. Migrations may result in what I shall call *Unterschichtung* or *Ueberschichtung.*

By *Unterschichtung* I mean that immigrants form a new social stratum beneath the existing social structure of the immigration country. This stratum is ethnically different, its members have no political rights, and with regard to stratum characteristics, they do not conform to the general developmental level of the immigration country. This means, first, that the social distances existing in the society increase, and second, that a highly developed society once again has to deal with problems specific to different (i.e., lower)

Table 2

Aliens in Switzerland by Country of Origin (in Numbers and as Percentage of Total)

| Year | Total | Federal Republic of Germany | France | Italy | Austria | Spain | Greece | Yugoslavia | Turkey | Other Countries |
|---|---|---|---|---|---|---|---|---|---|---|
| 1941 | 223,554 | 78,274[a] | 24,397 | 96,018 | — | — | — | — | — | 24,866 |
|  | 100 | 35.00 | 10.90 | 43.00 |  |  |  |  |  | 11.12 |
| 1950 | 285,446 | 55,437 | 27,470 | 140,280 | 22,153 | — | — | — | — | 40,106 |
|  | 100 | 19.40 | 9.60 | 49.10 | 7.80 |  |  |  |  | 14.05 |
| 1960 | 584,739 | 93,406 | 31,328 | 346,223 | 37,762 | — | — | — | — | 76,020 |
|  | 100 | 16.00 | 5.40 | 59.20 | 6.50 |  |  |  |  | 13.00 |
| 1964 | 793,351 | 113,776 | 39,417 | 437,212 | 40,865 | — | — | — | — | 162,081 |
|  | 100 | 14.34 | 4.97 | 55.11 | 5.15 |  |  |  |  | 20.42 |
| 1968 | 933,142 | 114,658 | 47,233 | 522,638 | 41,911 | 87,724 | 7,997 | 7,216 | 7,777 | 87,106 |
|  | 100 | 12.30 | 5.10 | 56.00 | 4.50 | 9.40 | 0.90 | 0.90 | 0.80 | 9.30 |
| 1970 | 982,887 | 115,564 | 51,396 | 526,579 | 43,143 | 102,341 | 9,029 | 22,972 | 12,137 | 99,726 |
|  | 100 | 11.80 | 5.20 | 53.60 | 4.40 | 10.40 | 0.90 | 2.30 | 1.20 | 10.20 |
| 1972 | 1,032,285 | 114,896 | 53,137 | 544,903 | 43,298 | 114,106 | 9,870 | 28,072 | 18,966 | 105,037 |
|  | 100 | 11.13 | 5.14 | 52.78 | 4.19 | 11.05 | 0.95 | 2.71 | 1.83 | 10.17 |
| 1974 | 1,064,526 | 110,507 | 53,000 | 554,925 | 42,597 | 112,555 | 10,810 | 34,669 | 27,000 | 145,463 |
|  | 100 | 10.38 | 4.90 | 52.10 | 4.00 | 10.50 | 1.00 | 3.20 | 2.50 | 13.66 |

[a] Including Austria

Source: *Statistisches Jahrbuch der Schweiz*, Bern.

levels of development—problems that it believed were resolved long before. For instance, many of the immigrants may have had little or no formal education, while the host country utilizes mostly written communication.

While *Unterschichtung* is the consequence of migrations from less developed countries to more highly developed countries—i.e., migrations that run counter to the gradient of development—*Ueberschichtung* is the result of migrations from more highly developed countries into less developed countries. This type of migration can be purely sectoral—for instance, from highly developed into less developed sectors of countries at the same developmental level. The concept of *Ueberschichtung* refers to the fact that leading positions in certain sectors or countries are occupied by immigrants. Quite a considerable part of the migrations among the highly developed European immigration countries can be considered as *Ueberschichtung*. In this connection it should be pointed out that developmental differences among the different emigration countries give rise to a reproduction of the stratification of international society in the immigration country. This refers not only to *Unterschichtung* of the native society by immigrants but also to the stratification of immigrants according to their national origin and the developmental level of their home countries. But I shall not discuss this phenomenon here. Since the socio-structural and the socio-psychological problems of *Unterschichtung* are much more serious than the problems of *Ueberschichtung,* we will deal mainly with the former. But first we will have a brief look at immigration and emigration policies, since these policies have decisive consequences for migrations and embody the paradox mentioned at the beginning.


IV.


While the immigration patterns of the classic immigration countries are, or were, subject to certain population policies—immigrants serve or served to rapidly increase the size of an originally small population and to make use of empty space and other resources—these conditions are absent in the new European immigration countries. These countries are characterized by high population density, and their primary resource is accumulated capital not yet productively used. Conforming to the two goals mentioned above, the immigration policies of the classic immigration countries (even if highly selective as in the case of the United States) are oriented toward viewing the immigrant as a permanent member and citizen-to-be of the immigration country's society, while the immigration policies of the European immigration countries are directed toward preventing permanent residence as well as naturalization. For this reason it is impossible to speak of an immigration policy in these countries. It is more adequate—and the term is also used officially—to designate the rules concerning immigrants as an "alien policy."

It would lead us too far afield to discuss in detail the "alien policies" of all European immigration countries, so we will discuss only those of Switzerland and the Federal Republic of Germany. The liberal residence policy followed by Switzerland and other European countries in the second half of the nineteenth century, originally established to facilitate emigration, later encouraged a strong increase in the number of foreigners in Switzerland after large-scale emigration had come to a stop. In 1914 the percentage of foreigners in the total Swiss population was 15.4. This situation then, as now, caused a widespread uneasiness for which, just as today, the term *Ueberfremdung* (over-foreignization) was used. But unlike today, this uneasiness did not give rise to demands for immigration quotas or for reducing the number of foreigners. Rather, it was thought that foreigners should be integrated through naturalization. A change in this attitude occurred only after World War I, when the liberal residence treaties were canceled and the minimum period of residence required for becoming a citizen was prolonged from two

Table 3

Aliens in Federal Republic of Germany by Country of Origin
(in Numbers and as Percentage of Total)

| Year | Total | Greece | Spain | Italy | Yugoslavia | Turkey | Portugal | Belgium |
|------|-------|--------|-------|-------|------------|--------|----------|---------|
| 1952 | 466,200 | 3,398 | 1,673 | 24,470 | 21,175 | 1,309 | 102 | 6,297 |
|      | 100 | 0.72 | 0.35 | 5.24 | 4.54 | 0.28 | 0.02 | 1.35 |
| 1954 | 484,819 | 3,796 | 2,071 | 25,802 | 20,997 | 1,683 | 160 | 6,357 |
|      | 100 | 0.78 | 0.43 | 5.32 | 4.33 | 0.35 | 0.03 | 1.31 |
| 1961 | 686,160 | 42,090 | 44,183 | 196,672 | 16,404 | 6,679 | — | 6,501 |
|      | 100 | 6.13 | 6.44 | 28.66 | 2.39 | 0.97 |  | 0.95 |
| 1968 | 2,381,100 | 271,300 | 206,900 | 514,600 | 331,600 | 322,400 | 37,500 | 12,000 |
|      | 100 | 11.39 | 8.69 | 21.61 | 13.92 | 13.54 | 1.57 | 0.50 |
| 1970 | 2,976,500 | 342,900 | 245,200 | 553,600 | 514,600 | 469,200 | 54,500 | 12,900 |
|      | 100 | 11.52 | 8.23 | 18.59 | 17.28 | 15.76 | 1.83 | 0.43 |
| 1971 | 3,430,700 | 394,900 | 270,400 | 589,800 | 594,300 | 652,800 | 75,200 | 13,800 |
|      | 100 | 11.48 | 7.86 | 17.15 | 17.28 | 18.98 | 2.18 | 0.40 |
| 1974 | 4,127,400 | 406,400 | 272,700 | 629,600 | 707,800 | 1,027,800 | 121,500 | — |
|      | 100 | 9.85 | 6.60 | 15.25 | 17.15 | 24.90 | 2.94 |  |

Source: *Statistisches Jahrbuch für die Bundesrepublik Deutschland*, Statistisches Amt Wiesbaden.

to six years. (In 1952, when immigration resumed after World War II, this waiting period was increased to twelve years.) Between 1931 and 1934 a new law concerning aliens came into force, which provided that no foreigner had a legal claim to a residence permit. Before conceding residence permits, Swiss authorities were to take into account the cultural and economic interests of the country, especially the condition of the job market. Moreover, the authorities had the right to prevent an immigrant from bringing his family into the country or to permit his family to come only after he had been there for several years.

After World War II, there were hardly any barriers to immigration as such. Based on the laws just mentioned, which in part were made even stricter through executive orders, the "alien policy" in Switzerland was directed simultaneously toward maximizing immigration and minimizing the foreigner's chances of integration. Immigrants were explicitly designated as "boom cushions," and the official though not very successful policy was to generate as high a rotation of immigrants as possible.

As Table 4 shows, the rotation which was fairly high in the first twenty years of postwar immigration decreased constantly after 1969. However, in looking at these data, one must take into account that today about two-thirds of the foreign population have stayed in Switzerland for more than ten years. This suggests that only a small segment of the foreign population rotates,

Table 3 (Continued)

| Bulgaria | Denmark | France | United Kingdom | Netherlands | Austria | Poland | Switzerland | Other |
|---|---|---|---|---|---|---|---|---|
| 1,819 | 4,280 | 11,713 | 6,136 | 77,200 | 54,576 | 78,330 | 13,704 | 160,010 |
| 0.39 | 0.91 | 2.51 | 1.31 | 16.55 | 11.70 | 16.80 | 2.94 | 34.32 |
| 1,877 | 4,179 | 14,949 | 7,401 | 79,028 | 66,686 | 81,292 | 17,124 | 151,410 |
| 0.39 | 0.86 | 3.08 | 1.53 | 16.30 | 13.75 | 16.76 | 3.58 | 31.23 |
| — | 3,667 | 20,066 | 9,058 | 65,423 | | | 15,950 | 259,460 |
| | 0.53 | 2.92 | 1.32 | 9.53 | — | — | 2.32 | 37.81 |
| — | 7,600 | 42,100 | 29,500 | 99,100 | 121,000 | | 25,300 | 360,200 |
| | 0.32 | 1.77 | 1.24 | 4.16 | 5.08 | — | 1.06 | 15.13 |
| — | 8,100 | 47,100 | 34,300 | 103,900 | 143,100 | | 26,700 | 420,400 |
| | 0.27 | 1.58 | 1.15 | 3.49 | 4.81 | — | 0.90 | 14.12 |
| — | 9,000 | 53,800 | 39,500 | 108,700 | 163,300 | | 27,800 | 445,400 |
| | 0.26 | 1.56 | 1.15 | 3.16 | 4.75 | — | 0.81 | 12.95 |
| — | — | — | — | 109,900 | 177,000 | | | 674,700 |
| | | | | 2.66 | 4.29 | — | — | 16.35 |

Table 4

Number of Aliens in Switzerland, Arrivals and Departures

| Year | Foreigners with Permits | Arrivals (including children of alien parents) | Departures (including deaths) | Net Gain or Loss | Departures as Percentage of Total |
|------|------|------|------|------|------|
| 1968 | 933,000 | | | | |
| 1969 | 972,000 | 170,000 | 131,000 | + 39,000 | 13.5 |
| 1970 | 983,000 | 133,000 | 122,000 | + 11,000 | 12.4 |
| 1971 | 999,000 | 114,000 | 98,000 | + 16,000 | 9.8 |
| 1972 | 1,032,000 | 119,000 | 86,000 | + 33,000 | 8.3 |
| 1973 | 1,053,000 | 117,000 | 96,000 | + 21,000 | 9.1 |
| 1974 | 1,065,000 | 95,000 | 83,000 | + 12,000 | 7.8 |
| 1975[a] | 1,033,920 | 49,566 | 80,646 | − 31,080 | 7.8 |

[a] End of August.

Source: *Statistisches Jahrbuch der Schweiz*, Bern.

while most of the foreigners who come to Switzerland are really permanent immigrants.

After 1960, when the foreigners' share of the population exceeded 10 percent, voices began to be heard demanding a limit to immigration, and the authorities tried to take this pressure from below into account in various ways. In 1963 the Swiss government launched a so-called stabilization policy whose aim was to prevent a further increase in the foreign population. Since industrial enterprises did not cooperate, the proportion of foreigners kept increasing; in 1970 it reached 16 percent. This attempt at stabilization was accompanied by strict measures concerning the mobility of immigrants. In 1968 foreigners were barred from changing their employers, their occupations, or the canton where they lived for five years. Beginning in 1968, several popular initiatives were launched which demanded that the proportion of foreigners be limited by a constitutional article, and the government was forced to take stricter measures for limiting immigration. After 1970 immigration was stopped except for small quotas, and the government promised not only to limit but also to reduce the proportion of foreigners. At the same time, the five-year restriction mentioned above was gradually reduced to one year for employment changes and to two years for changing one's occupation or canton. In this respect, conditions for foreigners have improved. In summary, the Swiss "alien policy" in recent years has been characterized by a transition from unhampered immigration to a very restrictive line and differential integration. Although discrimination has gradually been reduced on the employment and social levels, only a few foreigners have the chance to become integrated politically.

In Germany, as in Switzerland, immigration is tolerated as a necessary evil, with the emphasis on "evil."[3] The employment of foreign workers in Germany is not new. At the beginning of industrialization in the second half of the nineteenth century, Germany employed several hundred thousand foreigners. Although the number of foreigners is much higher today, Germany has not developed an immigration policy; as in Switzerland, there is only an "alien policy." According to the present law, foreigners desiring to live in Germany need a residence permit. Immigrants from countries not belonging to the EC have no legal claim to enter the country or to receive a residence permit. Nor can such a legal claim be based on bilateral residence treaties signed with non-EC members, even though such treaties usually state that entry and residence of the signatories' citizens should be facilitated. The legal situation is different only for immigrants from EC member countries, who are allowed to enter EC countries without having to apply for a work permit. If an immigrant from an EC country receives a work contract, he has a legal claim to a residence permit valid for at least five years.

A brief look at German naturalization laws shows that the employment of foreigners is not considered a prelude to permanent immigration. According to these laws, a foreigner can be naturalized provided he has no criminal record and is able to maintain his family. The minimum residence period is ten years, after which the foreigner still has no legal claim to be naturalized. As Fritz Franz has written: "Naturalization is considered an act of grace, and since grace comes from God but rarely from the state, it is not practiced vis-à-vis foreign workers unless they are married to a German."[4]

In Germany as in Switzerland, there are many barriers to the foreigner's mobility. A work permit may state that for a period of up to five years special permission must be given before one can change one's job. If an immigrant tries to change his job without such permission, he risks the loss of his work permit and expulsion from the country. Apart from this, the foreigner, at least in theory, has the same social and employment rights as the citizen. In actuality, however, foreigners are discriminated against in many ways. It is hardly an exaggeration to say that foreigners are subject to police authority rather than to the law, since laws concerning foreigners leave the authorities considerable latitude.[5] This discretionary power, which is hardly ever used in favor of foreigners, is responsible for the fact that foreigners rarely carry their complaints to the authorities. Both in Germany and in Switzerland foreigners who lose their jobs must queue up behind unemployed citizens when seeking another job (this does not apply to foreigners from EC countries). Foreigners are employed only if the employer can prove that no citizen is available for the job in question. Also, foreigners can be forced to accept new jobs which pay less than their former jobs or even less than unemployment insurance; if a foreigner rejects such offers twice, unemployment pay may be withheld.[6]

That the Federal Republic is not an immigration country has been made clear by the German government on various occasions. The policy of the federal government explicitly aims at the rotation of foreigners and the postponement of integration. The government expects that after a while immigrants will return to their home countries and will be replaced, if the labor market permits it, by new immigrants. This expectation is visible in the treatment of foreign children. After attending preparatory classes, foreign children go to school with German children but in addition they must attend lessons given by a teacher of their own nationality in their native language for five hours a week. The embassy of the home country usually offers another five hours of training in the mother tongue. This procedure is quite consistent if the return of the immigrants to their home countries is assumed. However, the double task assigned to schools—integrating the children into German society and culture while maintaining a link to their native society and culture—yields unsatisfactory results in both fields. The foreign children's study load is so large that they are neither integrated into the society of the immigration country nor properly prepared for reintegration into their home country.[7]

In October 1973, Germany, like Switzerland a few years earlier, practically put a stop to immigration. The other EC countries followed suit, and from this point of view the EC may also be considered a closed employment market. In Germany as in Switzerland, the immigrant is seen as a production factor hired for a certain time. Even if official statements do not clearly say so, the countries of the Mediterranean periphery are perceived as sources of an industrial reserve army which is available to highly developed Western Europe in times of need. Just as in Switzerland, the employment of immigrants in Germany must be considered a permanent phenomenon, in spite of the present recession, so the question arises whether the "alien policy" should not at last take this reality into account in order to avoid the wild growth of problems created in large part by the existing policy itself. In what follows we will take a brief look at some of these problems.[8]

V.

The immigrants' situation is made difficult in many ways. Cultural, structural, and psychological problems exert pressures which are all the harder to bear if the immigrant does not know how long he may be allowed to stay in a given place and lives in fear of losing his residence permit. In addition, immigrants have no political rights and thus cannot articulate their political interests in an aggregate form. Under these conditions there is little hope that their situation will change by acquiring citizenship in the immigration country. In addition, political parties lack incentive to do anything for the immigrants since there is no indication that such action will win votes for the future.

Apart from these institutional realities, the collective expression of interests by the immigrants is also hampered by the fact that a large proportion belong to the lowest strata. A study carried out by the *Deutsche Bundesanstalt für Arbeit* (German Federal Labor Office) showed that 95 percent of all Italians living in Germany, 97 percent of the Greeks, 96 percent of the Spaniards, 98 percent of the Portuguese, and 95 percent of the Yugoslavs are workers. Only 20 percent of the men and 3 percent of the women could be described as skilled workers.[9] As to the educational level, 6 percent of the men and 9 percent of the women were totally illiterate, and 54 percent of the men and 51 percent of the women had a maximum of six years' schooling.[10] According to my own research, about half of those who attended school for six years worked at a regular job during that time. The same finding applies to the other European immigration countries.

Integration and assimilation of the immigrants in Western Europe are thus made difficult by at least two groups of factors, even in cases where permanent immigration results in spite of official policy. The barriers to integration and assimilation are consequences, on the one hand, of the "alien policy," and on the other, of the immigrants' own past. A third barrier indirectly affecting the immigrants results from structural factors affecting the native population. As a consequence of *Unterschichtung*—the fact that immigrants settle at the very bottom of the social structure—the mobility opportunities of the native population have considerably improved, and this is in addition to improved mobility chances brought about by the considerable growth of the tertiary (service) sector of the economy, which means a corresponding increase in white collar jobs. Table 5, based on a study done in the city of Zürich, shows the extent of upward mobility among the native population.

The concept of mobility opportunities refers to the fact that upward social mobility is differential. Sociologically speaking, this creates problems for two categories of citizens. First, there are those unable to take advantage of mobility opportunities. This category consists mainly of unskilled and/or older people who perceive themselves as being on the same social level as the immigrants and interpret this as a relative loss of status, i.e., downward social mobility. This situation is a direct consequence of the projection of international stratification onto the consciousness of the individual who, seeing himself on the same level as the immigrants, experiences a sense of neglect and deprivation. For him, only an internal stratification identical to

Table 5

Intra-Generational Occupational Mobility Among
Swiss Men, 18–65

| Occupation | Percentage | | %d |
| | Past | Present | |
| --- | --- | --- | --- |
| Worker | 58.7 | 23.1 | − 35.6 |
| White collar | 38.1 | 64.5 | + 26.4 |
| Independent | 2.7 | 11.0 | +  8.3 |
| Other | 0.5 | 1.4 | |
| Total (N = 473) | 100.0 | 100.0 | |

Source: Hans-Joachim Hoffmann-Nowotny, *Soziologie des Fremdarbeiterproblems: Eine theoretische und empirische Analyse am Beispiel der Schweiz* (Stuttgart, 1973), p. 70.

the international stratification is acceptable. Tendentially, the greater the developmental distance between the immigrants' country of origin and the immigration country, the greater is the feeling of loss of status on the part of the citizen who has to live on the same social level as the immigrants. This explains why social tensions between citizens and immigrants exist not only when both groups compete for scarce jobs but also during economic booms.

Second, there are also problems for citizens who, as a consequence of *Unterschichtung*, have moved upward very rapidly but unevenly: those whose income status greatly exceeds their educational and qualificational status. Such individuals not only live under continuous pressure but also run the permanent risk of downward social mobility.

I have shown elsewhere that both these categories of citizens see society as anomic.[11] Individuals of the first category perceive themselves as excluded from certain goals (upward social mobility), since they do not have the means (qualifications) to reach them. Individuals of the second category have reached these goals (income, occupational position) but experience a disequilibrium between the achieved status and the means (qualifications) to equilibrate their status configuration. In both cases the consequence is anomia: sociologically, a state characterized by the divergence of goals and means. This form of anomia is added to that endemic to modern industrial societies in general. On the individual level, anomia takes the form of uncertainty, disorientation, fear, and frustration, which may result in a diffuse kind of aggression. As a number of studies have shown, individual anomia is linked to, among other things, social prejudice and discrimination against minorities —in this case, the foreign workers.

Both categories of citizens resist the integration of immigrants, although to a different extent; both would like to see them become as marginal to society as possible. While the first category demands that immigrants be expelled (this was the attitude expressed in the Swiss constitutional initiatives mentioned above), the second category displays a "neofeudal" syndrome. While individuals exhibiting this syndrome are ready to accept the presence of immigrants, they refuse to grant them integration or full-fledged status in the immigration country; on the basis of ascribed criteria (ethnic membership), they wish to prevent the immigrants from participating in the values of their society. This suggests the introduction of a traditional feudal element into a modern society where, at least according to the predominant ideology, the degree of participation in social values depends on the achieved criteria of performance. The attempt to replace achievable by ascribed criteria of status distribution is paralleled on the political level by strong nationalist or even chauvinist currents. It is these currents, much more than the economic recession, that have caused the European governments in question to call a halt to immigration.

It should be pointed out that while the European immigration countries treat immigration as a temporary phenomenon, a considerable number of the foreign immigrants take this view as well. A study I have made recently in Zürich reveals that at the time of their entry into Switzerland, 41 percent of the immigrants intended to go back to their home countries within about five years. But two-thirds of these have now lived in Switzerland for ten years or more, and still 29 percent of the interviewees state that they intend to return home within the next five years. The intention to return accompanied by the failure to do so have been described by Rudolf Braun as *Heimkehrillusion* (illusion of returning).[12] To be sure, the proximity of immigration and emigration countries would seem to facilitate temporary emigration; it also allows the immigrant continually to postpone the decision about whether emigration is to be temporary or permanent. But there is also evidence that the "return illusion" functions as a defensive mechanism, permitting the immigrant to reduce anxiety about the duration of his stay by telling himself that he does not really care about staying for good. Of course, this mechanism, which may be interpreted as an adaptation to an anomic situation, does not affect the actual uncertainty of the foreigner's situation.

Another anomic adaptive strategy is a tendency on the part of immigrants to reduce their aspirations in order to bridge the gap between their claim to membership status, integration, and social mobility, on the one hand, and the reality of their marginal situation on the other. Their own repressed aspirations are then somehow transformed into totally unrealistic aspirations for their children. A third strategy is the tendency to emphasize consumption as a kind of compensation. Finally, many immigrants gradually develop attitudes complementary to the neofeudal attitudes of the natives: if the latter set themselves apart by looking down on the immigrants, the former set themselves apart by looking up at the natives. Thus, many immigrants, by recognizing the ascribed criterion of nationality as a basis for the distribution of occupations, are willing to accept the principle that natives *a priori* get higher positions than they do.

## VI.

It is obvious that recession and unemployment are important issues in contemporary discussions of migration in Europe. Accordingly, it is argued that the Western European immigration countries are not really immigration countries and that immigration is exclusively connected with the needs of the labor market. Those who take this view seem to forget that immigration was halted at a time when the market could absorb more immigrants and when there were as yet no signs of a recession. It is understandable that unemployment, a phenomenon practically unknown in Europe since the war, is today the predominant political problem and that it also dominates the immigration question. But it is unfortunate that the discussion of related problems, which was gradually beginning at the time that immigration was stopped, has also come to a halt. These related issues include the basic structural problems created by rapid immigration and their consequences for a future "alien" or immigration policy. This is all the more unfortunate since it has already become clear that in spite of unemployment and recession the number of foreigners willing to return is much smaller than was anticipated by many politicians who took no notice of the structural factors.

From a structural point of view it is not surprising that the Federal Republic of Germany, for instance, still employs two million foreigners in spite of the fact that there are one million unemployed Germans. What we had said earlier about *Unterschichtung* and the differential upward mobility of citizens reveals that a large number of unemployed citizens would experience strong downward mobility if labor authorities tried to force them to accept the inferior positions occupied by immigrants. Such a measure would be only partly successful anyway, even if unemployment were to run totally out of control, politically and financially. Since this will hardly be the case, a realistic "alien policy" should confront the fact that there may be no large reduction in the number of immigrants. To be sure, the predictions by Luisa Danieli,[13] based on data of the United Nations Economic Commission for Europe (ECE), sound rather improbable. In 1971 Danieli predicted that the Western European immigration countries would need between 4.7 and 12.8 million workers before 1980, while Southern Europe, the North African emigration countries, and Turkey would have an excess of between 7.6 and 10.5 million workers, which Western Europe would be able to absorb. The estimate of excess is probably correct, but not so the estimate of need, and even less so the idea that this excess could be absorbed. It seems much more probable that in the near future, just as at present, European migrations will be limited; in any case there will be no new widening of borders by the immigration countries. Evidence for this prediction is provided by the socio-structural factors mentioned above as well as by the continuing recession and unemployment.

In addition, the immigration countries' own potential labor forces will increase until about 1985–1990. Youth unemployment, already widespread, suggests that it will not be easy to find jobs for the young natives who reach the labor market each year. Only around 1990 will the steady decline of the native birthrate since 1965 be reflected in a corresponding reduction of the economically active population. Estimates based on the present decline of the birthrate show that the population of some Western European countries will be considerably smaller by the year 2000. Long-range analyses, which apparently have not yet been taken into consideration by political leaders, thus ask whether the population decrease could be compensated for by new immigration.[14] For instance, estimates for Germany show that without counting migration gains or losses today's population of 61 million will be reduced to 57 or 58 million in the year 2000. However, these predictions, based on fertility rates for 1972 and 1975, respectively, are probably too high, since fertility rates have since declined.

If there were a long-range population decrease in other Western European immigration countries, which at the moment seems possible, new arguments would probably be introduced into the discussion of "alien" or immigration policy: positions based on the needs of the labor market might yield to population considerations. In that case there might be interesting parallels to the classic immigration countries. If an immigration policy aimed at recruiting not only workers but also potential new citizens were instituted, Western European governments would have to consider the criteria by which immigrants would be selected. Since the population deficit to be expected toward the end of the century probably cannot be filled by immigrants from the EC countries alone, the extent to which immigrants from Southern Europe, North Africa, and Turkey should be admitted must also be discussed. This is, of course, a potentially explosive question, both internally and externally. Since the less-developed countries will continue to have an excess of births, and since they will hardly be able to bridge the development gap between themselves and the immigration countries in this interval, the number of potential emigrants will exceed the labor needs of the Western European countries; thus the difficult problem of selecting immigrants by nationality and occupational qualifications will arise.

In conclusion it seems reasonable to ask, both on humanitarian grounds and from a social and political point of view, that the "alien policy" of immigration countries such as Switzerland and Germany be replaced by an immigration policy. By "immigration policy" I mean a clearly defined set of laws that specify which categories of people are to be accepted as permanent immigrants and under what conditions. Such rules may differ with regard to their degree of restrictiveness. But even restrictive rules at least assure those who are accepted that they may stay permanently and that they are considered potential citizens.

## NOTES

1. See the migration theories discussed in Hans-Joachim Hoffmann-Nowotny, *Migration: Ein Beitrag zu einer soziologischen Erklärung* (Stuttgart: Ferd. Enke Verlag, 1970).

2. The proportion of foreigners in Luxembourg is 23.6 percent, in Liechtenstein, 37.3 percent.

3. See *Fremde unter uns*, Sekretariat für Migration, Oekumenischer Rat der Kirchen (ed.) (Geneva, 1964).

4. Fritz Franz, "Die Rechtsstellung der ausländischen Arbeitnehmer in der Bundesrepublik Deutschland," in *Gastarbeiter, Analysen und Berichte*, Ernst Klee (ed.) (Frankfurt: Suhrkamp Verlag, 1972), p. 42.

5. E.g., Franz, pp. 38ff.

6. See Jürgen Kühl, "Die Bedeutung der ausländischen Arbeitnehmer für die Bundesrepublik Deutschland," in H. and H. Reimann (eds.), *Gastarbeiter* (München: Wilh. Goldmann Verlag, 1976), p. 24.

7. See Franz Domhof, "Vorschulische und schulische Situation ausländischer Kinder in der Bundesrepublik Deutschland," in Deutsche UNESCO-Kommission (ed.), *Arbeitnehmer im Ausland* (Pullach bei München, 1974), p. 25.

8. For the following section see Hans-Joachim Hoffmann-Nowotny, *Soziologie des Fremdarbeiterproblems: Eine theoretische und empirische Analyse am Beispiel der Schweiz* (Stuttgart: Ferd. Enke Verlag, 1973).

9. See Stefan Harant, "Schulprobleme von Gastarbeitern," in H. and H. Reimann (eds.), p. 167.

10. E.g., Harant, p. 153.

11. E.g., Hoffmann-Nowotny (1973), pp. 67–138.

12. See Rudolf Braun. *Sozio-kulturelle Probleme der Eingliederung italienischer Arbeitskräfte in der Schweiz* (Zürich: Erlenbach, 1970).

13. See Luisa Danieli, *Labour Scarcities and Labour Redundancies in Europe by 1980: An Experimental Study* (Florence, 1971).

14. See Franz-Xaver Kaufmann (ed.), *Bevölkerungsbewegung zwischen Quantität und Qualität, Beiträge zum Problem einer Bevölkerungspolitik in industriellen Gesellschaften* (Stuttgart: Ferd. Enke Verlag, 1975); also H.-J. Hoffmann-Nowotny, *Sozialstrukturelle Konsequenzen der Kompensation eines Geburtenrückgangs durch Einwanderung*, in F. X. Kaufmann, pp. 72–81.

# [6]

## Migration in Caribbean Societies: Socioeconomic and Symbolic Resource

ORLANDO PATTERSON

Almost all societies have been shaped, at least to some extent, by migration. Only a small minority, however, have had histories in which, due solely to migration, drastic periodic changes have taken place in the demographic structure of their populations. And in only very few cases has migration become a basic means of individual and societal survival. Caribbean societies belong to this last category of unusual populations.

It is the thesis of this paper that in Caribbean societies, especially the Afro-Caribbean islands, the process of migration has long been institutionalized. In several of them it is the overriding institution: without external migration they would cease to exist. In all of them, except postrevolutionary Cuba, migration has become a primary socioeconomic resource, a social good, access to which determines and is seen to determine the economic and social fate of individuals and groups. Indeed, throughout Caribbean history the control of access to the resource of migration, and the struggle against such control, have been focal points of conflict between the main classes.

Like all enduring, primary processes, the institution of migration is self-sustaining. It is both cause and effect in these societies, historically and structurally. Furthermore, as I hope to show, migration is the referent for the most dominant symbols in these societies. The major themes of West Indian culture reflect, and in turn shape, the attitude toward and experience of migration. In art, folklore, literature, and religion, the migration symbol finds expression as a dominant theme.

106

Finally, the basic modes of human interaction reflect the binary opposition inherent in the migratory symbol; they are indeed an acting out of this opposition. In social life also, there are elaborate rituals of migration, some directly related to the migration process, others expressing the dominant theme in ways not immediately obvious.

Clearly, we are dealing with an extraordinary situation, which goes beyond demography and the computerized oversimplifications of socioeconomic surveys. My approach, therefore, will be, first, to present a review of the migratory experience of Caribbean societies and, second, to attempt an interpretation of this experience with a view to showing the critical role of migration not only in the economic life of these societies but in their social systems and symbolic elaborations as well.

## THE MIGRATORY EXPERIENCE: A SURVEY

All Caribbean societies share the property of being small. Apart from the seven "bigger" states—Cuba, Puerto Rico, the Dominican Republic, Haiti, Jamaica, Trinidad–Tobago, and Guyana—the numerous little island states and colonies average less than 250 square miles. Jamaica, which is considered "big," has only 4,207 square miles, a good part of which is uncultivable. This elementary geographical fact brings into question the viability of these societies.

After asking this question, one is then led to wonder why it is that all of these islands have such high population densities: Barbados, with over 1,300 persons per square mile, has one of the highest densities in the world. The answer is to be found in another geographical fact—their common tropical location—and in the history of European imperial expansion. The suitability of the soil for the production of sugar and other highly desired crops such as coffee, and later tobacco, created conditions which were ripe for exploitation during the second half of the seventeenth century. By the first decade of the eighteenth century all except the Latin areas were converted from the seventeenth-century pattern of white colonial settlement to plantation colonies. Based on slave labor, the latter produced the "brown gold," or sugar, the profits from which played such a crucial role in the accumulation of the commercial capital that, later, partly fed the industrial revolution of northwestern Europe.[1] It is hard to imagine today the incredible wealth generated by these tiny islands in the eighteenth century, and the enormous role they played in the political and economic life of the major European imperial states, as well as in the development of prerevolutionary America.[2]

These observations lead us to note another common feature of Caribbean societies: the absolutely critical role of migration throughout their histories. At this point, however, it is necessary to distinguish between the Latin Caribbean and what may be called the Afro-Caribbean societies: the former include Cuba, Puerto Rico, and the Dominican Republic; the latter include the remainder of the West Indian states as well as Guyana.

Two factors stand out in the history of Spain's activities in the area. First, Spain discovered the Caribbean and colonized all the major islands of the Greater Antilles; second, Spain neglected the area, once it was discovered that there were no precious ores to be found there. By the mid-sixteenth century the islands were of only military value to Spain: they served as shipping depots and as military bases to protect the Spanish sea lanes between the mainland and Spain. The result was the emergence of atrophied colonies of poor white settlers. Until about the last third of the eighteenth century the Spanish Caribbean populations either were stagnant or were areas of out-migration to the more prosperous mainland colonies. While conditions were to change radically, especially in Cuba, by the turn of the nineteenth century, the first three hundred years of Spanish rule in the area set the tone of the creole societies that were to emerge into the modern period of Caribbean history.[3]

Cuba was the first to change. After refusing for over a century to follow the other West European states in the profitable business of growing sugar, Spain, in the last quarter of the eighteenth century, decided to follow their lead; this was about the time that the other European colonies were beginning to go through a period of economic decline. To some extent Spain was taking advantage of this decline. She was also exploiting the vast virgin lands of Cuba for the first time. Between 1780 and 1880 the economy of Cuba underwent a drastic change, as it shifted from a white colony of settlement to a slave plantation society.[4]

This change was accompanied by a radical transformation in the demographic structure of Cuba, brought about almost entirely by external migration. From a population that was predominantly white and free, it became one that was predominantly nonwhite and unfree. Thus in 1774, 56 percent of the population was white, 20 percent was free colored, and 23 percent were black slaves. By 1841 only 42 percent of the population was white, 15 percent was free colored, and 43 percent were slaves. At the same time there was an absolute growth in the population of all segments, the total population moving from 171,620 in 1774 to 1,007,624 in 1841.[5] This growth was due completely to immigration, since the blacks almost all came from Africa, in spite of the British opposition to the slave trade. Cuban developments in the late eighteenth and nineteenth centuries were simply a replay of developments that had begun a hundred years earlier in the northwestern European colonies (those of the British, French, Dutch, and Danes), and it is to these that we must now turn.

The collapse of the northwestern European settlement colonies and the emergence of the monocrop slave economy were accompanied by two population movements. One involved an out-migration of white settlers who had tried and failed to develop settlements along the lines of colonial New England. Most of them re-migrated to the American colonies; a few went back home. Those that remained were supplemented by a new type of white migrant who came, not to settle, but to make his fortune. Together they formed the bulk of the white middle class who became the overseers and bookkeepers on the plantations. A small minority, invariably by cheating their employers, succeeded in becoming plantation owners. Throughout the eighteenth century the white population remained a small and declining proportion of the total population. In a few of the islands there was even an absolute decline during the early decades of the eighteenth century. The white share of the total population rarely exceeded 15 percent and in the largest of the colonies dipped well below 10 percent.[6]

There was another small but significant migration pattern among the whites. Beginning about the first quarter of the eighteenth century, the elite segment of the white populations—those who owned slaves and plantations, as well as the wealthy attorneys and merchants—began to migrate back home to the metropolitan center. By the second half of the eighteenth century the majority of Caribbean property (outside the Latin areas) was owned by absentee landlords resident in Europe. By the beginning of the nineteenth century less than 20 percent of the slaveholder class, at the most conservative estimate, was resident in the islands.[7]

Absenteeism, as I and others have argued elsewhere, had a devastating impact on the economies and the societies of the Caribbean slave systems, accounting for the chronic inefficiency that was the ultimate cause of their collapse, and for the brutality and cultural degradation of all parties that had the misfortune to reside in them—the slaves most obviously, but also the whites, who abandoned all canons of decency and civility, both secular and sacred, in their pursuit of the "brown gold."

After the abolition of slavery in the 1830s (the French slave colony of St. Domingue—Haiti—had won its freedom at the end of the eighteenth century in the only known successful slave revolt in recorded history), the non-Latin plantation systems went through the first of a series of collapses that have marked the economic history of the Caribbean. When Britain opted for free trade in 1846 the collapse was complete in the older islands, especially Jamaica and Barbados.[8] The newer, ceded islands gained from France, with their less heavily exploited soil, suffered much less in this economic decline.[9]

The post-abolition period ushered in both a new social order and new patterns of migration throughout the region. In the larger Afro-Caribbean British colonies, the available backlands and abandoned plantations were

bought up by ex-slaves and became the material base for the development
of peasant economies. This type of development was particularly marked in
Jamaica and Guyana, although a similar trend took hold in several of the
smaller islands, especially those, such as Nevis and Dominica, which had
never been highly successful as plantation colonies. In Barbados, St. Kitts,
and Trinidad there was relatively less available land, due either to geography
or to the greater efficiency of cane-growing. Even so, a smaller but equally
viable peasantry did emerge.[10]

On the whole, Philip Curtin's model of developments in Jamaica is valid,
though in varying degrees, for most of the Afro-Caribbean areas.[11] Where
Curtin speaks of "two Jamaicas," one may speak of two subcultures evolving
in the Afro-Caribbean belt: the subculture of the peasants based on small-
scale hill farming and that of the white elite, committed to a reconstructed
wage-based plantation. The peasant sector developed a syncretic subculture
composed of reinterpreted Africanisms and of West Indian creolized European culture. The Europeans developed a creolized version of their parent
cultures that differed in style, if not in substance, from the European model.
Between the two groups stood a third caste of mixed-race coloreds who were
culturally Euro–West Indian and highly committed to the economic and
political interests of the white elite.[12]

In the light of these developments, we can now look at population
movements during the nineteenth and first half of the twentieth centuries.
Let us begin with external migration. The reluctance of the ex-slaves to work
on the plantations, now indelibly stamped with the taint of slavery, led to the
first wave of internal migration in the region: the movement of the black
population from the coastal, level, cane-growing regions to the mountainous
or inland areas. This migration created a labor crisis for the planters who
were trying to revive the plantation system. It is important to note that the
whites viewed the internal migration of the blacks as a vicious political and
symbolic action. They retaliated in the traditional manner, by turning to
external sources of labor.[13]

At first, European laborers were sought. This led to a small influx of
Portuguese in Guyana and of Germans in Jamaica. Both groups of migrants
turned out to be failures as plantation laborers. The Portuguese in Guyana,
however, quickly seized opportunities for small-scale trading presented by
the post-emancipation economy, built up this base, and have continued to
maintain their grip on Guyanese commerce to this day.[14] The Germans failed
not only as plantation laborers but also as tropical peasant farmers; they
eventually withdrew into small poverty-stricken enclaves, where they intermarried to a genetically dangerous degree. Recent evidence suggests that
they have begun to show signs of physical degeneracy and extinction.

The planters next brought over several thousand Chinese coolies, some from China, others from Central America. This indentured immigration, which began in earnest in the 1850s, was a complete failure and the Chinese population rapidly died out. A second wave of Chinese coolies was imported during the 1860s and last quarter of the nineteenth century. Once again, the Chinese proved unsuccessful as plantation workers. However, this second wave of Chinese immigrants, who went to Guyana, Trinidad, and Jamaica, survived, especially in Jamaica, through the simple expedient of taking black peasant concubines. The Afro-Chinese offspring were then shipped off to mainland China and Hong Kong in one of the most bizarre migrations in human history. In China, the half-black children were enculturated to Chinese ways and language by kinsmen of the West Indian immigrants, and in early manhood (only males were sent) they returned to the Caribbean with Chinese wives. As I have argued elsewhere,[15] the Chinese West Indians substituted cultural for racial purity as a means of ethnic survival. However, once the population became demographically viable, it promptly shifted back toward racial purity through endogamous marriage and the immigration of Chinese women. The Chinese were able to accomplish this because, like the Portuguese in Guyana, they quickly seized the opportunities for small-scale trading offered by the Jamaican economy. Like the Portuguese, they have continued to monopolize this sector of the economy, branching out into the wholesale and supermarket business in recent years.

The Chinese in Guyana did not find the same opportunities as those in Jamaica since the Portuguese migrants had monopolized the retail trade by the time they arrived. They therefore opted for acculturation into the Afro-Creole culture of the emerging black middle class. They have not maintained any ethnic solidarity and are fast disappearing as a distinct group in Guyana.

More important demographically was the immigration of Indian coolies into Guyana, Trinidad, and Jamaica.[16] Unlike the Chinese, the Indians proved successful as plantation workers. Today Indians constitute over 50 percent of the Guyanese population and over 40 percent of the Trinidad population, and they are still overwhelmingly rural. In Jamaica the immigration was only moderately successful: Indians presently constitute less than 5 percent of the total Jamaican population.[17]

Black inhabitants perceived these immigrations as an economic retaliation by the whites, and vented their hostility on the immigrants.[18] In 1865, land shortage and drought in Jamaica led to a peasant revolt, which was brutally put down.[19] Violence directed at oriental immigrants by blacks in Trinidad and Guyana was also severely dealt with. This led to a massive wave of black emigration in the late nineteenth century.[20] Many black West Indians migrated to Panama, where they constituted the bulk of the labor force that dug the Panama Canal. A substantial number stayed in Panama after the Canal was completed and others spread out over Central America. This was the period of the United Fruit Company's rapid expansion in both Central America and the Latin Caribbean islands, and the West Indians took advantage of the increased demand for agricultural labor in these societies. Thus a black West Indian diaspora emerged throughout the Latin Caribbean. Some black West Indians settled in Central America, especially in Costa Rica, where they joined the migrants who had gone there after digging the Canal. Others went to the island states. Enclaves of West Indians still exist in all of these Latin American societies. Worsening economic conditions in the early 1920s led to a new wave of external migration, directed at the United States. Over 100,000 West Indians settled there, the Jamaicans mainly in New York, the Barbadians in Boston. The Jamaicans very soon made their presence felt in New York, where Marcus Garvey, who had re-migrated from Panama, led the first mass movement of urban black Americans. The movement was crushed by U.S. authorities, and Garvey, the eternal exile, died several years later in Britain.[21]

Emigration, which had declined during the Depression and World War II, began to pick up again during the late 1940s; it intensified during the early 1950s and attained mass proportions between 1955 and 1962. This movement was directed mainly at Britain, where substantial West Indian populations now live. David Lowenthal summed up this migration as follows:

> Owing to the net outflow of 200,000 during the 1950's and 1960's, one Jamaican in ten now lives abroad. But emigrant proportions are higher in the eastern Caribbean. The years 1959–61 saw almost 6,000 people depart from St. Kitts-Nevis, 10 percent of the inhabitants; Montserrat lost 5 to 10 percent of its people *each year* over the same period. On small islands where migration is endemic, still larger proportions may be away. One Carriacouan in four is normally off the island, and Anguilla, with only 600 residents, keeps close ties with nearly 8,000 Anguillians living elsewhere.[22]

It should be noted that accompanying this movement out of the Afro-Caribbean region was a very active movement from the poorer and smaller islands of the Eastern Caribbean to more prosperous islands such as Trinidad and Curaçao. According to Lowenthal 50,000 Barbadians and other emigrants from the Eastern Caribbean went to Curaçao to take advantage of the employment offered by the oil refineries there; today the population of Curaçao is still 15 percent foreign born.[23] Barbadian emigration to other islands is particularly striking in this respect. George Roberts has found that one-eighth of all emigration into the region was contributed by Barbados.[24] Counteracting these outflows have been periodic waves of inflows, as emigrants return to their native islands. Thus in spite of continuing heavy outmigration, between 1921 and 1955 the total population of Barbados actually

Table 1

Migration to the United Kingdom from Jamaica

|      | Emigrants | | | | Migrants Returning from U. K. | | | |
|------|-------|--------|---------|----------|-------|-------|---------|----------|
|      | Total | Males | Females | Children | Total | Males | Females | Children |
| 1953 | 2,210 | 1,284 | 875 | 51 | 133 | 73 | 60 | — |
| 1954 | 8,149 | 5,178 | 2,861 | 110 | 182 | 108 | 74 | — |
| 1955 | 17,257 | 10,911 | 6,145 | 201 | 99 | 65 | 34 | — |
| 1956 | 17,302 | 9,144 | 7,577 | 581 | 757 | n.a. | n.a. | n.a. |
| 1957 | 13,087 | 6,257 | 6,097 | 733 | 1,376 | 700 | 439 | 237 |
| 1958 | 9,992 | 4,425 | 4,509 | 1,058 | 1,992 | 935 | 614 | 443 |
| 1959 | 12,796 | 6,410 | 4,955 | 1,431 | 2,318 | 833 | 816 | 619 |
| 1960 | 32,060 | 18,372 | 11,258 | 2,430 | 1,791 | 751 | 611 | 429 |
| 1961 | 39,203 | 19,181 | 16,276 | 3,746 | 1,558 | 705 | 493 | 360 |
| 1962 | 22,779 | 8,434 | 10,207 | 4,138 | 2,868 | 1,196 | 959 | 713 |

Source: G. Tidrick, "Some Aspects of Jamaican Migration to the United Kingdom, 1953–1962," *Social and Economic Studies*, 15, no. 1 (1966), p. 26.

increased each year, partly as a result of returning migrants. External migration on this massive scale naturally influences total population growth both directly and indirectly through its effect on fertility rates. Thus during the massive out-migration of Barbadians during the period 1904 to 1921 to build the Panama Canal, there was a sharp decline in the birthrate. Between net outflow and natural decline, the total Barbadian population declined at an average annual rate of o.6 percent during this period. However, between 1921 and 1953 the population once again began to grow, the rate increasing from 0.2 to 1.9 due partly to in-migration and partly to natural increase.

We must now move to internal migration patterns. As one would expect, peoples so willing to migrate out of their societies are equally prone to move within them. The data on internal migration bear this out. Indeed one might say that in many instances internal migration is a kind of test-run for external migration. The rate of internal movement in Jamaica and Trinidad is phenomenal, considering the preindustrial nature of their economies. In Jamaica, if we take the proportion of the population with duration of residence under one year as an index of internal mobility, it will be found that the percentage for 1943 is 12.9; for 1953, 36.8; and for 1960, 37.2.[25] The same increasing rates of internal migration are found in Trinidad, where according to Joy Simpson,

> in the earlier census period (1936–1946) approximately 58,500 persons moved from their place of birth to other areas within the region, between 1946 and 1960 a total of approximately 146,000 persons changed from their place of birth.[26]

A substantial proportion of internal migration involves movement from one rural area to another—in particular, movement between the peasant and plantation belts. In discussing internal migration, two patterns of seasonal migration should be given special attention. One is the annual migration induced by the seasonality of labor demand in the plantation belt. This factor largely accounts for the high levels of social disorganization in these areas, as reflected, for example, in the large number of female-headed households without the extended kin support traditional in peasant areas.[27] Of more recent origin is the pattern of seasonal migration created by the tourist industry. Indeed, no sooner had the sugar industry begun to wane in the larger islands than the tourist industry took its place in reimposing an equally dislocating pattern of annual internal movement.

A third pattern of seasonal movement involves external migration. For several decades the fruit-producing areas of the United States have entered into contracts with various West Indian governments to supply farm laborers for the harvest. Each year, for example, some 10,000 peasants migrate from Jamaica to the United States, where they reside for about four months, after which they are returned to their rural communities. Naturally, this experience makes such peasants more prone to migrate permanently, so that this seasonal external pattern of movement bears directly on longer-term internal—especially rural-urban—movements and external movements.

To return to purely internal movements, Table 2 summarizes the most recent census data on internal migration in five West Indian societies. The number of moves between major divisions can be taken as a crude index of internal migration. These major divisions are, with the exception of Guyana, "divisions recognized as administrative units, and as such carry official designations as for instance the parishes of Jamaica and Barbados."[28] While this approach has enormous advantages for the study of internal migration over time within each of the societies, it presents almost insuperable problems for comparative work in view of the varying sizes of the major divisions and of the countries concerned. Guyana merely complicates the issue since its huge size obliged the West Indian Census Bureau to artificially divide the natural administrative units used in the other islands. At the same time, it should be noted that these major divisions are not only administrative units but are perceived by the inhabitants as meaningful social units. As such, one may argue that there has been a kind of institutional weighing of the divisions. That is to say, while the distance between two parishes may be much smaller in Barbados than in Jamaica, the perceived distance between them may be much the same. To the extent that one finds it possible to accept such an anthropological weighing of the major boundaries, one may regard the data as being in some way intuitively comparable.

Two observations immediately impress us on examining Table 2. First, in every society the majority of the population has made at least two major moves; in two of them—Trinidad and Guyana—the great majority has made three moves. Second, in all but one of these societies (Guyana, the data on which are questionable), women move more than men. The difference is greatest in Jamaica and in British Honduras. The greater propensity of women to move is a pattern peculiar to the New World, and it has been reported in some Latin American societies. But the degree of this female propensity to move seems to be much greater in the Caribbean than in any other region.

Let us examine more closely the experience of migration in the Caribbean by looking briefly at the most important kind of internal migration, namely, rural-urban movements. All the larger Caribbean societies are experiencing rapid urbanization. Table 3 summarizes data on nine of these societies, grouped by per capita income, from the World Bank and from my own sources. It will be seen that all but two of them were over 35 percent urban in 1968, and that two, Trinidad and Cuba, were more than 50 percent urban. There is a close correlation between per capita income and degree of urbanization, but the relationship is actually quite complex and no facile generalizations should be drawn.

Even more striking is the urbanization rate in the larger societies. Table 4 summarizes the data on four Caribbean societies. In all of them, the average annual growth rate of the urban population is much greater than that of the total population between 1960 and 1970; in Jamaica it is twice that of total population growth and in Trinidad more than double. Given the fact that, unlike Asian and many South American societies, the urban sectors are already quite large, it will be seen that within the next two decades or so, the great majority of the inhabitants of these Caribbean societies will be living in urban areas.

A closer look at Trinidad and Jamaica will be useful. Joy Simpson has found that urbanization in Trinidad is now largely the result of internal migration rather than of immigration from other islands, which apparently used to be the case.[29] A striking feature of Trinidad's urbanization, repeated in Jamaica, is the phenomenon of urban sprawl in the central or primate city. Thus, while the three main towns contributed 23 percent of the total population in 1946, by 1960 they made up only 17 percent. However, when the suburban spread of these towns is taken into account, the rate rises to 36 percent, with the suburban spread accounting for 18 percent. The situation is even more acute in Port of Spain; there, the suburban sprawl has converged with the spread of neighboring towns to produce a long string of connected urban settlements, twelve miles in length, along the major highway of the country—the so-called Eastern Main Road Strip. This vast metropolitan strip now accounts for 41 percent of the total Trinidadian population.

## Table 2

### Internal Migration: Number of Major Moves of Migrants by Society

| No. of Major Moves | Jamaica | | | Trinidad and Tobago | | | Guyana | | | Barbados | | | British Honduras | | |
|---|---|---|---|---|---|---|---|---|---|---|---|---|---|---|---|
| | Male | Female | Total | Male | Female | Total | Male | Female | Total | Male | Female | Total | Male | Female | Total |
| 1 | 233 | 274 | 507 | 0 | 0 | 0 | 0 | 0 | 0 | 1 | 0 | 1 | 0 | 0 | 0 |
| 2 | 16,499 | 24,019 | 40,518 | 6 | 9 | 15 | 5,044 | 2,924 | 7,968 | 907 | 1,054 | 1,961 | 2 | 2 | 4 |
| 3 | 1,334 | 2,012 | 3,346 | 4,306 | 5,775 | 10,081 | 1,020 | 689 | 1,709 | 108 | 137 | 245 | 2,519 | 3,438 | 5,957 |
| 4 | 178 | 171 | 349 | 665 | 914 | 1,579 | 88 | 71 | 159 | 7 | 5 | 12 | 257 | 299 | 556 |
| 5 | 48 | 37 | 85 | 119 | 115 | 234 | 30 | 25 | 55 | 1 | 3 | 4 | 41 | 54 | 95 |
| 6 | 17 | 6 | 23 | 31 | 39 | 70 | 15 | 9 | 24 | 0 | 0 | 0 | 13 | 15 | 28 |
| 7 | 9 | 5 | 14 | 7 | 9 | 16 | 5 | 4 | 9 | 0 | 0 | 0 | 6 | 3 | 9 |
| 8 | 4 | 5 | 9 | 4 | 4 | 8 | 1 | 0 | 1 | 0 | 0 | 0 | 4 | 2 | 6 |
| 9 or more | 16 | 17 | 33 | 1 | 5 | 6 | 4 | 9 | 13 | 0 | 0 | 0 | 0 | 0 | 0 |
| Total Population | 860,024 | 906,521 | 1,766,545 | 429,316 | 439,698 | 869,014 | 340,360 | 346,564 | 685,924 | 104,452 | 117,461 | 221,913 | 54,458 | 55,313 | 109,771 |

Source: *1970 Population Census of the Commonwealth Caribbean*, Vol. 5 (Kingston, 1975).

Table 3

Percentage Population Urban by Gross National Product
Per Capita, 1968

| Under $100 | $200–500 | $500–1,000 | Over $1,000 |
|---|---|---|---|
| Haiti 18% | Dominican Republic 37% Surinam 38% Barbados 45% Cuba 58% | Jamaica 40% | Puerto Rico 48% Trinidad and Tobago 53% |

Source: World Bank, *Urbanization*, Sector Working Paper, 1972, p. 81; Orlando Patterson, *The Condition of the Low Income Population in the Kingston Metropolitan Area*, Government Report, Kingston, Jamaica, 1972.

Much the same situation exists in Jamaica with respect to Kingston and the Kingston metropolitan area. Table 5 summarizes the relevant data. According to these projections, the majority of Jamaicans will be urbanites by 1980. The metropolitan area will continue to grow in absolute terms, but it will account for less and less of the total urban population. This is due to the growth of smaller urban areas around the country and in particular of the other major cities—May Pen, Mandeville, and Montego Bay.

To return to the Latin areas, it will be recalled that the Cuban population changed dramatically at the turn of the nineteenth century. After the war of independence with Spain and with the growth of American influence, especially in the economic sphere, during the latter part of the nineteenth century, the pattern of massive in-migration was intensified.[30] There were two reasons for this development. The first was a purely economic demand for cheap labor on the modernized and expanded *centrales* of the multinationals, which had taken over Cuban cane cultivation after independence. The second was fear by whites that they would be swamped by the growing number of blacks, since blacks and mulattos now outnumbered whites. From the mid-nineteenth century a special effort was therefore made to encourage Asian and white immigrants. The experiment with Asians failed, but white immigrants came in substantial numbers, especially from Spain, during the latter half of the nineteenth and the first decade of the twentieth century.

Until 1932, Cuba received more immigrants than all other Latin American countries in the hemisphere, except Argentina and Brazil. Between 1907 and 1919 half a million immigrants arrived, of whom 60 percent were Spanish, 10 percent Jamaican, 6 percent from the United States, 6 percent from Haiti, and 2 percent from Puerto Rico. Between 1919 and 1931 another 600,000 arrived, mainly to work on the sugar plantations. Then came the Depression and the beginning of the decline of the Cuban economy, as sugar production

Table 4

Urbanization and Population Growth in Four Caribbean Societies, 1960–1970

| Country | Total Population, 1960 | Annual Growth Rate | Urban Population, 1960 | Annual Growth Rate | Percentage Urban 1960 | Percentage Urban 1970 | Principal City | Population of City, 1960 | Growth Rate | Principal City Population as Percentage of Total Urban |
|---|---|---|---|---|---|---|---|---|---|---|
| Dominican Republic | 4,324,000 | 3.6 | 1,601,000 | 5.7 | 31 | 37 | San Jose | 435,000 | 5.4 | 68 |
| Guyana | 737,000 | 2.8 | 221,000 | 3.2 | 29 | 30 | Georgetown | 200,000 | 3.1 | 41 |
| Jamaica | 2,020,000 | 2.2 | 727,000 | 4.3 | 29 | 36 | Kingston | 560,000 | 5.0 | 77 |
| Trinidad and Tobago | 1,106,000 | 2.9 | 589,000 | 6.0 | 40 | 53 | Port of Spain | — | — | — |

Source: World Bank, *Urbanization*, Sector Working Paper, 1972, pp. 76–79.

Table 5

Proportion of Population: Rural, Urban, and
Kingston Metropolitan Area, 1943–1980

| Year | Jamaica Population | Percentage of Total | Rural Population | Percentage of Total | Urban Population | Percentage of Total | Kingston Metropolitan Area Population | Percentage of Total | Percentage of Urban Population |
|---|---|---|---|---|---|---|---|---|---|
| 1943 | 1,237,100 | 100.0 | 960,200 | 77.6 | 276,900 | 22.4 | 201,900 | 16.3 | 72.1 |
| 1960 | 1,609,800 | 100.0 | 1,069,311 | 65.3 | 558,200 | 34.7 | 419,400 | 26.1 | 69.7 |
| 1970 | 1,848,500 | 100.0 | 1,071,369 | 57.9 | 777,131 | 42.1 | 475,548 | 26.2 | 63.3 |
| 1980 | 2,115,440 | 100.0 | 1,064,939 | 50.2 | 1,050,501 | 49.8 | 597,734 | 28.2 | 56.9 |

Source: Orlando Patterson, *The Condition of the Low Income Population in the Kingston Metropolitan Area*, Government Report, Kingston, Jamaica, 1972.

once again underwent a periodic collapse. Between 1931 and 1943 only 20,000 came, and there was an out-migration of most, though not all, of the West Indian blacks to their native islands. After this, racist migration laws, along the lines laid down in several South American countries, were passed, putting a permanent stop to immigration from other parts of the Caribbean. The Cuban economy stagnated until the socialist revolution, and there was little population movement during this period. It might be wondered why, apart from the black West Indians, more people did not leave Cuba during this anterevolutionary period. To a great extent this can be explained by factors mentioned earlier, especially that the Latin areas were originally colonies of settlement. The migrant population, apart from the black West Indians, easily settled down and soon developed sufficient commitment to their new home to stay there, even during the hard times that began in the 1930s. Cuba, in short, had a viable culture that could absorb and assimilate its immigrants and win their loyalties. In this respect, the view of the British economist Dudley Sears that "the surplus labor force lacked both legal possibilities and sufficient education to emigrate on a large scale"[31] is wide of the mark. The black West Indians had even less education than the Cubans, and for racial reasons, they faced greater legal barriers; yet they migrated during this period at a much greater rate than the Cubans. Clearly then, the stability of the Cuban population must be explained in cultural rather than in purely economic or legal terms.

During the period just discussed with respect to Cuba, the Dominican Republic, in spite of similar political changes and similar American influence, remained essentially as it had been for most of its history: a depressed semi-insular zone of feudal stagnation, its population a backward tropical hybrid exhibiting extreme color prejudice and a skin-toned pecking order rigidly perpetuated by its small Hispanic elite.[32] Between 1897 and 1928 the population declined by 43 percent, mainly as a result of emigration. From time to time, the government issued optimistic calls for immigrants. The black West Indians, always willing to try another country at least once, were the only people to respond, but even most of those who went did not stay for long.

Puerto Rico followed the Cuban pattern of development. Arturo Morales-Carrión, in his fine study, *Puerto Rico and the Non-Hispanic Caribbean*, has observed:

> Spanish neglect in developing Puerto Rico into a tropical colony of exploitation, as the French and English had done in their Caribbean islands, contributed to the evolution of a society with less racial tensions and a more homogeneous population than in the neighboring establishments. The levelling force of poverty had given rise to a rustic equality (impossible) in the sugar colonies of the capitalistic empires. This legacy persisted as an influential factor in the new period when urban development and economic productivity began to bridge the gap between the walled city and the rural interior.[33]

With the royal *cédula* of 1815—the so-called *cédula de gracias*—Spain, encouraged by developments in Cuba, changed its policy of exclusivism with regard to Puerto Rico, opening the island not only to foreign trade but also to immigrants. A modest number came, mainly whites, although the 83 loyalists who arrived from Louisiana in 1815 brought quite a few slaves with them. On the whole, Puerto Rico was spared the sociological agony of overnight transformation into a slave-based migration economy. As the Puerto Rican historian Manuel Maldonado-Denis points out, Puerto Rico was able to develop, especially during the nineteenth century, a highly integrated culture with a viable economy.[34]

All this was to change with the coming of the Americans, after Puerto Rico was ceded to the new imperial power in the aftermath of the war with Spain. The American multinationals, aided by the American colonial government, set about systematically dismantling the institutional bases of traditional Puerto Rican life. On the one hand, the stable traditional economy was destroyed by the depression of the price of coffee and the concentration of landownership in the hands of a few absentee American landlords. On the other hand, the colonial government, through its educational policy, subverted the traditional culture to the point where teachers, some of them barely able to speak English, were forced to teach it as the first language in Puerto Rican schools.[35]

A few facts will illustrate the economic transformation that occurred. In 1898 Puerto Ricans owned 93 percent of their land, with the majority of holdings in the hands of middle-sized and small farmers. Forty percent of cultivable land went into coffee, 32 percent into locally consumed commodities, and only 15 percent into sugar. By 1930, 44 percent of all cultivable land was in sugar production, and 60 percent of this area was held by four absentee American owners. Maldonado-Denis's summary of developments during this period bears a striking resemblance to what took place in earlier centuries in other parts of the Caribbean:

> The move toward the concentration of property in the hands of a few absentee corporations went hand in hand with the creation of a cash-crop, monoculture plantation type economy. The demise of the coffee plantations ... that came on the heels of the American occupation led to the unfolding of a process in which the campensinos of the coffee subculture were forced to such jobs on the great sugar plantations and centrales. This led to the creation of a rural proletariat whose life chances were geared to the major factories, and by the conclusion of the first three decades of American rule, Puerto Rico had become—within the international division of labor—an economy basically dependent upon the price of sugar in the world market.[36]

Even so, the integrity of traditional ante-American Puerto Rican culture was such that in spite of this dramatic change in its economic base and the systematic assault on its language and values, there was only a marginal movement of its population to other lands. There was some movement within the Caribbean from Puerto Rico to the American Virgin Islands after 1927, and Puerto Ricans today constitute a significant segment of the skilled workers and small-scale commercial sector of this other American colony. Emigration to the United States between 1899 and 1946, however, was well below what might have been expected, given the fact that Puerto Ricans had been made citizens of the United States. Four thousand Puerto Ricans went to Hawaii in 1900, but many of these later re-migrated to California. In the half century or so after 1900 Puerto Ricans went to the mainland at an annual average rate of only about 2,000 persons.

Table 6

Migratory Flow from and to Puerto Rico (years ending in March)

|  | Annual Averages | | | | | | |
|---|---|---|---|---|---|---|---|
|  | 1951–55 | 1956–60 | 1961–63 | 1964 | 1965 | 1966 | 1967 |
| Emigration | 60,000 | 55,400 | 38,000 | 43,000 | 66,000 | 79,600 | 76,700 |
| Immigration | 10,000 | 15,400 | 29,000 | 51,000 | 50,000 | 49,600 | 42,700 |
|  | −50,000 | −40,000 | − 9,000 | + 8,000 | −16,000 | −30,000 | −34,000 |

Source: H. C. Borton, Jr., "The Employment Situation in Puerto Rico and Migratory Movements Between Puerto Rico and the United States," cited in J. P. Fitzpatrick, *Puerto Rican Americans: The Meaning of Migration to the Mainland* (Englewood Cliffs, N.J.: Prentice-Hall, 1971), p. 13.

How then can we explain the massive out-migration from Puerto Rico that began in the early 1950s? While only approximately 106,000 persons migrated to the United States in the half-century up to 1946, over a million streamed to the mainland between 1946 and 1972. Between 1955 and 1970 approximately a third of the entire Puerto Rican population migrated to the United States, where more than 70 percent of them settled in New York City. Over 1.5 million Puerto Ricans now live in the United States.

One important factor triggering this mass migration was the collapse of the sugar industry during the depression years. Because the Puerto Rican economy was now tied to that of the mainland, a depression there was magnified into an economic disaster for the island. The impact was delayed, however, since people were simply too poor and communications between the island and the mainland still too expensive to permit any mass migration. Besides, mass migrations usually begin with a slowly sloping curve, as the first group of migrants settle in and form the nucleus for future groups.

By the time the emigration curve had reached the take-off point, another development intervened to further stimulate the mass exodus: the program of planned industrialization known as "Operation Bootstrap."[37] Within a decade, Puerto Rico changed from a predominantly rural to a primarily urban society. Urbanization, of course, partly paved the way for the second migration to the mainland, although most of the emigrants were to come from the rural areas. More important, rapid Americanization brought images of a far more affluent society. The modernization process, accompanied by careless educational planning, led to the usual rapid escalation of expectations, which could not be met by the opportunities created by industrialization. Population growth, brought about mainly by decreasing mortality rates, aggravated the situation. But the major cause of the migration was the increasing rate of unemployment generated by both modernization and industrialization. As in other parts of Latin America and the Caribbean, industrialization in Puerto Rico has been far more efficient in dislocating traditional sources of employment than in creating new jobs. Fifteen years after Operation Bootstrap began, the unemployment rate was higher than it had been in the early 1940s.[38] A further factor reinforcing the mass exodus of Puerto Ricans was the encouragement of emigration by the planners of Operation Bootstrap, who saw it as a "safety valve." Moreover, the dislocation of the rural labor force became an incentive for the multinationals who were invited to invest in the country.

There are now, as Kal Wagenheim has observed, "two Puerto Ricos": one in the island, the other on the mainland.[39] Both are beset with problems. The immigrants have become an alienated, slum-dwelling, welfare-dependent population, desperately trying to come to terms with life in the big city by every means possible, from organized protests and academic ethnic studies to politically conscious street gangs. The Puerto Ricans in the United States are a homeless people, rejected by the mainland society, yet tragically cut off from their island home. As Maldonado-Denis has pointed out, "When in search for roots they return to Puerto Rico, they find that they are not at home on our island; they are frequently rejected in Puerto Rico, not because they are not American enough, but because they are not Puerto Rican enough."[40] Drugs, petty crime, and violence, usually directed inwards, often seem the only answers.

Neo-colonial modernization and Americanization have, together, created a tendency toward structural convergence in the experiences of Puerto Rico and the larger Afro-Caribbean societies. In Puerto Rico, the more integrated cultural base, however fragmented by recent developments, and the relative recency of the dependency on migration account for the absence of any deep-seated symbolic elaboration of the migratory experience; there has been only a partial institutionalization of this experience. In the Dominican Republic and Cuba, stagnation and revolution, respectively, have made migration an insignificant social pattern. The interpretation in the next section therefore will be concerned mainly with the Afro-Caribbean societies, where migration has become fully institutionalized. Before proceeding with our analysis let us glance briefly at postwar developments in the Afro-Caribbean societies.

The postwar years brought about major changes in these societies. Politically, there was the independence movement. Economically, we find the same pattern of modernization as in Puerto Rico. Indeed Operation Bootstrap was used as a model by planners in the larger Afro-Caribbean islands with the same disastrous consequences: dislocation of the rural population, urban sprawl, massive internal and external migration, and a growing rate of unemployment. Internal migration has, ironically, recreated the two-tiered polarization of the slave period. Racial, ethnic, and other vertical cleavages are fast giving way to the emergence of a two-class society consisting of an affluent, newly emerged elite and a large, unsettled, increasingly angry urban lumpen proletariat. Once again, too, these societies are totally dependent on external economies. Slight ripples in the North American metropolis become major economic disasters in the islands. One bad tourist season could wipe out the entire economies of the Bahamas, the Bermudas, and the Virgin Islands. In 1976, a fall in tourist arrivals and the world price of bauxite created havoc in Jamaica. A fall in the price of sugar means more mass misery in St. Kitts and St. Vincent. If the British eat fewer bananas, the rural proletariat of St. Lucia suffers. Several of these economies have already passed the point of recovery and simply cannot survive in the modern age. Montserrat, St. Vincent, possibly Grenada and Dominica are all bankrupt. Haiti has learned to live with ruin. Some of these little states are so poor that the income they generate cannot even pay the administration that collects it. They are, literally, welfare states of Britain.

Migration is seemingly the only solution. But migration is itself becoming a scarce resource. Doors are closing everywhere. Post-industrial society does not need a Marxian reserve army. The two remaining outlets are Canada and the United States, but Canada is now cutting back on its immigrant intake, and both countries, by the selective nature of their immigration policies, offer an outlet for the middle classes mainly. The middle classes have been quick to see the significance of this and now use the migration resource, which they monopolize, as a weapon in their struggle against all policies aimed at equalization of wealth. This is most clearly evident in Jamaica, where the entire middle class is in a state of mass panic as a result of the progressive policies of the Manley government, policies aimed at averting disaster and class warfare. There, the middle classes have retaliated, through their conservative party, the Jamaica Labor Party, by systematically attempting to undermine the economy and discredit the government. Thus the 1976 riots in Kingston were not the result of radicals mobilizing the restless masses toward Castro-type revolution, as the U.S. press claimed, but were deliberate instigations by political thugs from the conservative, elitist pro-American party.

Middle-class panic has led to middle-class flight as well as to a withdrawal of the capital of the multinationals, both of which have simply reinforced the economic crisis. A recent study of the Chinese community in Jamaica concludes that over 40 percent of the Jamaican Chinese community have taken out papers preparatory to migration. Hard on their heels are the light-skinned and brown middle classes, terrified of the urban masses and the egalitarian policies of the Manley government.

## THE MIGRATORY EXPERIENCE: AN INTERPRETATION

The demographer E. Gordon Ericksen, in his study, *The West Indies Population Problem*, has argued that "whatever structure is involved in demographic phenomena is vitally influenced by human assessments."[41] That is, "so-called external forces become forces only insofar as they are made socially significant. This bare statement merely sketches the fundamental fact that *demographic phenomena in the Islands are intrinsically unstable and inherently disposed toward rearrangement.*"[42]

If one agrees that economic forces have been ultimately responsible for the Caribbean propensity toward migration, then what have been the effects of this sustained history of migration on the cultures and societies of the Caribbean? How has the high propensity to migrate been translated into meaningful human terms? To pose the problem more formally, first, has the tradition of migration affected individuals, their perceptions of each other, and their interactions in groups? Second, how has the migratory tradition affected the systems that emerged from such individual and group interactions? Third, how do these two sets of effects relate to each other?

In an effort to suggest some answers to these large and difficult questions within the confines of a brief essay, I propose to argue that the propensity to migrate has become fully institutionalized in Afro-Caribbean societies. In becoming institutionalized, migration ceases to be simply one of several social processes, to be treated as just another option available to individuals in their struggle to survive. In all Afro–West Indian societies, migration has always been the *main* option for all but the least ambitious, and in a good number of them—the smaller states of the Eastern Caribbean, where over 60 percent of the total male labor force are migrants—it is the *only* option.[43] Migration is thus a major institution: as such, it dominates and defines the social structure, it is a matter of central preoccupation for individuals, and it constitutes a dominant theme in the cultural and symbolic structures of the societies under consideration.

We must pause to say something about the nature of symbolization, since we will be drawing heavily on this area of anthropological theory in what follows. A symbol, Raymond Firth argues, is a special kind of sign, the latter being anything—thought, object, behavior—that stands for or represents something else. A symbol exists "where a sign has a complex series of associations, often of emotional kind, and difficult . . . to describe in terms other than partial representation. The aspect of personal or social construction in meaning may be marked, so no sensory likeness of symbol to object may be apparent to an observer, and imputation of relationship may seem arbitrary."[44]

Firth goes on to point out that symbols are often used as "instruments of control and power." As symbols are powerful modes of expression and communication, those who control them control the means of influencing others. This brings us to what Victor Turner calls the "dominant symbols" of a society. Such "pivotal" or emphatic symbols are often complex and relate to the central preoccupations of a culture. They are "centers of organization in cultural systems" and "constitute sematic systems in their own right." A symbol has a single, central *signan* (the sign or vehicle of expression) but may have several *signatia* (that which is signified).[45] A dominant symbol will be made up of a cluster of related signantia, each signifying some signatum or dimension of meaning of the dominant symbol.

Another important feature of symbols is their tendency toward binary opposition, this being particularly true of dominant symbols. I shall take this to mean the convergence of opposite signata or meanings in a single signan.

In this way, existing and potential conflicts, whether on the cultural or the psychological level, are expressed and resolved by means of symbolic association.

Most important is Firth's distinction between what he calls public and private symbols. The former refer to "the symbolism of a collectivity—of myth, of ritual, of social structure."[46] The latter refer to the personal symbols of individuals as revealed in dreams, artistic creations, and the like. Both kinds of symbols are capable of influencing each other, although public symbols have tended to do most of the influencing and "have been regarded as having power to regulate individual behavior, to express personal sentiments, and to dictate forms in which private symbols present themselves."[47] This is so precisely because public symbols, especially dominant ones, express and communicate as well as encapsulate or "condense" the most urgent experiences collectively shared by a people, and are often distillations of what is most critical about their heritage.

The work of the psychologist Abram Kardiner[48] suggests that between public and private symbols there exists a third category of symbols whose role is to link the other two. I shall refer to them as the symbolic modalities or connectors of a society. Through them, we can recognize the ways in which the sociocultural system connects with the personality systems of individuals. Such symbolic modalities are unique and vital in that they are clusters of signantia which represent both personality signata, especially modal personality signata, and sociocultural signata. On the one hand, such signantia recur in the private symbolism of members of the community, referring to personal crises experienced individually by all. On the other hand, they happen to be, purely by coincidence, the very signantia that best represent the dominant themes of the culture. The coincidence is a happy one, but there is nothing extraordinary about it. Given the vast number of symbols in every society, there is always a high statistical likelihood that some symbols will emerge with this dual signifying and, as such, connecting quality. Their dual symbolic quality, however, makes such modalities powerful intermediaries, linking, by association, the most structurally significant meanings of a culture with the deepest psychic wishes of its individual members. In traditional, pre-industrial cultures, folklore—songs, tales, and games as opposed to myth and ritual—constitutes the major repository for such symbolic connectors.

I propose to consider migration as such a symbolic connector in Caribbean societies. As we have seen, migration has always been, and continues to be, a powerful social resource. Like any other social good, individuals and groups have struggled over the right to it and the enjoyment of it. In West Indian societies, both slave and slaveholder populations were maintained and increased by means of migration.[49] Migration was the means whereby the slaveholder classes developed and maintained their socially destructive and economically productive economies. As a resource, migration was largely closed to the slaves. Indeed, a slave may be defined as a person incapable of exploiting the resource of migration. But while the migration resource was denied to the slaves, they did not always accept this deprivation. To an unusual degree, West Indian slaves seized this resource by rebelling and migrating to the hills, where in several of the islands they formed maroon communities.[50] The relationship between revolt and retreat by migration is significant: the two impulses were to become powerfully linked in a kind of binary psychic opposition in the minds of West Indians.

Migration, initially a resource and a weapon in the conflict between the two main classes, was thus institutionalized; internalized by the masses as a special binary mode of interaction, it became a weapon and a resource in the relations between individuals. We know too little about the personal interactions of the slaves to do more than speculate on the basis of indirect evidence. From the available evidence, we know that relationships between the slaves were extremely "fickle," to use a contemporary description, and that they constantly shifted between aggression and withdrawal. The response to crises in personal relations seems to have been restricted to the polarities of rebellion and retreat. When conflicts arose, individuals either quarreled violently or withdrew and sulked. The terms of abuse used by the slaves were loaded with images of migration, suggesting strongly the individuation of the archetypal migratory master-slave relationship. Thus the two most common terms of abuse in Jamaica were "salt water negro" and "Guinea bird." In both cases the emphasis is not so much on Africa (hence the simplistic explanation that such terms merely reflect a superiority complex about Africa should be rejected) as on movement and flight: thus, "salt water," with its reference to the migration across the middle passage, and "bird," with its immediate suggestion of flight. Evasiveness, dissimulation, lying, and withdrawal (images of migration), combined with aggression and cunning (images of rebellion), were the two sets of character traits most frequently commented on by those who wrote about the slaves.[51]

The migration experience involved the master class as much as the slaves. Absenteeism, as we mentioned earler, was chronic among the slaveholders and was both a cause and effect of the disintegration of cultural patterns in the islands, and of the brutality of the system. Those whites who remained were obsessed with one goal: to make their fortunes and return home. Their sense of exile was acute, and in their haste to repatriate, they drove the slaves beyond the limits of endurance.

The migration-induced Hobbesian nightmares, which West Indian societies became, could obviously be held together only by force. And so they were. But no group of human beings in any sustained pattern of interaction, however close to the Hobbesian state of nature, can exist without generating, if not a culture, then at least some symbolic patterns to give some minimum human support, if not comfort, to their condition. There is an instinctive drive to create, however minimally, symbolic patterns to give meaning and to guide action. Indeed the very absence of a rich, complex traditional culture places a premium on symbolic behavior. Cultures take great spans of time to emerge; in the creation of symbols, every person is an artist. In creating symbols, human beings are overwhelmingly influenced by what is central to their experience. And what was most central in the experience of West Indians during the seventeenth and eighteenth centuries? Obviously, migration. For the slaves, in particular, there was the terrible trauma of the migrations from their villages to the coast, then the even greater trauma of the middle passage. But the situation was not much different for the whites: the passage to the islands from Europe was no joy ride. More important, there was the constant sense of exile, the yearning to succeed and to migrate back home. Whether out of fear or out of hope, all individuals who lived in these societies were obsessed with the experiences of migration and exile. It is logical then that symbolic creations should have focused on this central experience, come to terms with it psychologically, acted it out in ritual social behavior, and sublimated it in symbolic thought.

In the slaves' festivals and in the rituals associated with death and religion, we find the signatum of migration occupying a central place. Thus travelers to Jamaica observed that the most popular event at the Christmas and Easter festivals of the slaves was the John Canoe: a figure who wore on his head a large image of a boat. Monk Lewis, an early nineteenth-century gothic novelist, described the John Canoe personage as "a merry Andrew dressed in a striped doublet and bearing on his head a kind of pasteboard houseboat filled with puppets representing some sailors, others soldiers, others again shown at work on the plantation."[52] A more obvious symbol of migration is simply unimaginable.

One of the earliest accounts of the island, by Charles Leslie, contains a detailed description of the death rituals of the slaves.[53] Leslie tells us that the slaves believed that, on death, the spirit returned to Africa. At the funeral ceremony, the dead slave was bade farewell and wished a happy journey back home. The living also asked the dead to take greetings back to Africa. To assist the dead on the return migration, food and other items useful on the long journey were placed in the grave. This tradition continued throughout the period of slavery.

It is not unreasonable to assume that the collective memory of the migratory traumas of the slave period would have been encapsulated and distilled during the process of institutionalization that followed the emancipation, and that such encapsulation and distillation of memory would have been achieved in the manner typical of all human cultures, namely by means of dominant condensation symbols.

Evidence for such development is found in the repository of symbolic modalities of the Afro-Caribbean peoples: their folktales, songs, proverbs, games, and, where possible, recorded dreams and communal attitudes toward dreams.[54] It should be noted that almost all these folk traditions originated during the period of slavery and that their contents were borrowed from both African and European sources. In some cases, indeed, it is possible to keep track of certain of the major symbolic patterns and to observe how their signata either changed or were reinforced during the process of institutionalization. Let us begin by examining the process of symbolic institutionalization in the rituals of death, spirit beliefs, and festive behavior. I shall concentrate on the largest of the Afro-Caribbean societies, Jamaica, not only because of space limitations, but also because it is the society for which the richest data are available.

The Jamaican folk still believe in the existence of spirits, or "duppies." This is true of most traditional societies, and it is certainly so of the West African societies from which the slaves came. What is significant, however, is the category of spirits selected for emphasis by the Jamaican migrants and their descendants. Elsewhere, I have traced the origin of the word *duppy* back to a word used by the Osudoku people of the Shai plain of Ghana.[55] The Osudoku have two categories of spirits. As Field has informed us, there is the "black" kind, which are worshipped as deities with their own cults, and which perform positive integral functions in the culture of these people. There are also the "red" spirits: these "dwarfs, believed malicious, are propitiated annually with food and other rites outside the town, a barrier being across the path to prevent entering";[56] they are evil, migrating spirits whose annual migration back to the village must be prevented. It is striking that the Osudoku name for these spirits is *adope*, and it is remarkable that it is precisely this category of migratory spirits that survived in the island, and that became the general name for all spirits in Afro-Jamaican creole language, namely *duppy*. There are no good or "black" spirits in Jamaica, no spirits that perform integrative cultural functions. *All* spirits are evil wanderers, and *all* ritual behavior is concerned with the sole purpose of keeping them away. In this regard, it is significant that the belief in the haunted house, which is of European origin, plays only a minor role in West Indian spirit beliefs.

The migratory theme inherent in West Indian spirit beliefs is strikingly illustrated by the two places that ghosts are most likely to be encountered: the silk cotton tree and the mouth of a river. The migratory symbolism becomes immediately obvious when it is pointed out that the silk cotton tree is the main tree used by the folk for making canoes. The symbolism of a river's mouth as a migratory signan is evident. Finally, the three animals in which spirits most commonly invest themselves are all powerful migration symbols: the "rolling (wandering) calf," the "three-legged horse," and the "doctor," or hummingbird.

One final point is worth noting with respect to West Indian spirit beliefs. The dead are feared, it seems to me, not so much for what they may do to the living as for what life may do to the dead. In this respect, it is important to note that West Indians do not fear death, as such. Indeed, death is cele-brated. For death is the final escape from the most tragic consequence of life: eternal exile, the migratory agony of the eternal return. So powerful is the exilic hold on life, however, that the dead themselves must be prevented from re-succumbing to it. The dead must be helped to free themselves by remaining dead. Thus, on the one hand, they are celebrated for their good fortune, while on the other hand, they must be "tied down," to use the Jamaican expression, just in case they get any crazy ideas.

In the Afro-Caribbean revivalist cults of the folk, images of flight are dominant. When possessed, nearly all West Indian cultists flap their arms like the wings of birds.[57] Informants who reported on their first "conversion" experience to Martha Beckwith in the 1920s all depicted the experience as similar to flight. Thus, an informant who was converted in the late nine-teenth century said that he was "taken away in the spirit to Brown's Town. I didn't walk 'pon the earth; I flew in the air to Brown's Town, I and the Master in the spirit."[58]

The most popular Sankey and Moody hymn (hymns are the main source of songs in the revivalist rituals, although adapted to Afro-Jamaican rhythms) is "Wish I had the wings of a dove." So popular is the song that Jamaicans have secularized it, and it is now standard in the repertory of the urban lower-class reggae singers.

The earliest millenarian West Indian cult, the Bedwardites, created a sensation in Jamaica at the turn of the century. Members of the cult con-verged with their leader, Shepherd Bedward, on a small village in the out-skirts of Kingston now known as the August Town. There they awaited the day when they would all fly to heaven. One woman was actually tied to a tree and told to practice the art of flying. Bedward was eventually consigned to a mental asylum.[59]

Consistent with the dominance of the migratory signatum is the fact that flight is a dominant signan among the Jamaican folk. Flight, in its turn, is signified among the folk mainly by the bird, although there are other sig-nantia. We know from the psychoanalytic literature that flight, and its main signifier, the bird, are among the most powerful symbols of sexuality.[60] Flight, and its signifier, bird, thus become one of the major symbolic connec-tors of Afro–West Indian culture, expressing the deepest anxieties, which were modal in the collectivity, and the major signatum of its culture.[61] Illustrative of this symbol is the following tale (one of a category of "moral tales") recorded in the 1940s by the late British social psychologist Madeline Kerr, while she worked among the Jamaican folk:

### "What Happened to the Little Boy Who Would Shoot Birds"

There was once a little boy who would shoot birds on Sunday, although his grandmother kept telling him not to do it. After a time the grandmother died. The next Sunday the little boy went out and saw a bird on a tree. He got out his sling and shot it. The stone hit the bird on the head and it fell. As it fell it sang:

"Pick me up, pick me up, Lemon Boy."
He picked it up as he was told. The bird then said:
"Pluck me, pluck me, Lemon Boy."
The boy plucked the bird. The bird then said:
"Gut me, gut me, Lemon Boy."
The boy did this. The bird said:
"Roast me, roast me, Lemon Boy."
The boy put the bird on the pot and roasted it. The bird said:
"Eat me, eat me, Lemon Boy."
The boy then ate the bird. The bird said:
"Make up your bed, make up your bed, Lemon Boy."
The boy did this and lay down. The bird said:
"Go to sleep, go to sleep, Lemon Boy."

The boy went to sleep. The bird then bored a hole out of his belly and flew away. The boy lay dead.[62]

It should be noted that the informant, an elderly woman, told Kerr that the bird was the grandmother. As Beckwith had learned in her field researches a quarter of a century earlier, Jamaicans "are quite aware of the import of this symbolism."[63] This tale is an excellent example of the symbolic modality discussed above. It is an expression of private anxieties, fears, and wishes that are commonly experienced. Partly because of the high illegitimacy rate (over 80 percent, though a substantial proportion of unions are permanent though consensual), and because fathers frequently abandon their children, many mothers fall back on their kin, especially their own mothers, for support in childrearing. Caribbean anthropologists have established that the high illegitimacy rate does not imply, at least among the folk (the argument no longer holds for the urban lower classes, as my own researches show), that most unions are unstable; not only are the majority of unions consensually stable, they eventually become legalized, though long after children are born.[64] Still, the "outside child" presents a problem for the mother when she finally settles down in a stable union. An examination of the distribution of children within households always reveals that a substantial proportion of all children are being cared for by their maternal grandmothers, since the stepfather invariably rejects such children.

While outwardly the relations between grandmother and her ward might appear harmonious, ethnographers have noted that there is tremendous tension in this relationship. Grandmothers usually resent the burden placed on them by their daughters but feel obliged to repress their resentment. The child, furthermore, is a constant reminder to the grandmother of the sexual "wickedness" and disgrace of her daughter, or, as the Jamaican folk put it, of the daughter's "fall." The tension and animosity toward the daughter is invariably displaced to the child. Jamaican grandmothers are notoriously brutal in their childrearing methods.

There is yet another source of anxiety and repression: while brutal in their day-to-day relationships with their wards, grandmothers in Jamaica exhibit the same patterned familiarity between members of the opposite sex of alternate generations that anthropologists have reported all over the world.[65] This familiarity borders on, but rarely results in, overt sexuality. Thus at dances in rural Jamaica, grandmothers will pull their young wards onto the dance floor and proceed to dance with them in a lewd manner, to the amusement of the younger adults. There are obviously strongly repressed incestual urges in the relationship. Another source of anxiety is the grandmother's feeling that, as mother surrogate, she should have a legal as well as a physical right to the child. Yet this is not the case. After the grandmother has cared for the child for years, he may be taken back abruptly by the mother.

With this social background in mind, let us return to the tale. Clearly, the bird is a symbol of mother, both the real mother and the surrogate. The real mother has flown from her nest. That the boy is allowed to kill birds on all days except Sunday represents hostility toward the mother on the part of the grandmother. The mother, however, is not to be killed on Sunday, the day of repression. The grandmother dies, and the next Sunday, as she knew he would, the boy kills her. What follows is obviously a seduction scene (the term "lemon boy" means "sweet man" or "sweetheart"). The grandmother's wishes are fulfilled symbolically. In one fell swoop she becomes mother and seducer. But she also gets her revenge on her daughter by killing the boy in the very act of seducing him, and she averts guilt by placing the blame for the incest and his death on the boy's disobedience. Furthermore, not only does she punish the mother by killing the boy, but she also fulfills her wish to own the boy, since he now joins her in the spirit world. Thus securing him, she achieves her greatest wish, which is to "fly away," enjoying eternal sex with the boy.

This short tale sums up volumes of anthropological literature on one of the major personal problems of the West Indian folk and condenses exquisitely a central preoccupation of the Jamaican peasant's modal personality. Let us now see how the tale relates to the dominant migratory symbol of the culture. Not only is the bird a universal symbol of sexuality, it is also the most powerful signan for the signatum of migration. On the cultural level, the grandmother ceases to be a signatum and becomes a signan, or signifier, since the old always symbolize the traditions of a people, as living embodiments of the past. On this level of interpretation, the boy symbolizes the anthropological present. The tale now becomes a complex symbolic modality connecting two sets of binary oppositions. There is, most obviously, the convergence of flight and aggression as basic interdependent modes of interaction, each serving as a trigger for the other. Secondly, the tale symbolizes the cultural tension between the emphasis on migration and its opposite, the idealized quest for home. In the killing of the bird, the cultural emphasis on migration is temporarily destroyed—but only temporarily, for in so doing, the structural basis of the culture is destroyed. You cannot kill the bird that lays the golden egg, the tale seems to say, even if the egg is nine parts lead and grief. Migration brings disaster, but it is the only path to survival. So the bird rises phoenix-like from the belly of the dead present, to fly again. Migration will prevail. The bird must win in the end.

A final message is revealed in a second statement of the binary opposition of migration and home, which is signified in the single, triumphant final flight of the bird. For while the bird is a symbol of migration, it is also a symbol of home. We associate birds with flight, but we also associate them with nests. So the ultimate meaning of the tale seems to be this: home is a place to which the West Indian returns after every season, but it is equally a place to be left at the start of every season; home is an eternal return which you build from the belly of the homeless present, the present that must constantly destroy and eat its past.

One final area of the folk culture to be examined is the trickster-hero cycle of tales. The trickster is the *only* folk hero among the Afro-Caribbean folk. Among many West Indian societies, the trickster takes the form of the spider, *Anancy*, a word derived from the Akan, *Ananse*,[66] where the spider-hero cycle is also found. The first thing that strikes us in examining the cultural history of the Afro-Caribbean societies is that the trickster-hero cycle was the only one selected. Given the rich and varied cycles of tales in West Africa, among which the trickster-hero cycle is merely one,[67] what has been discarded in the migration becomes as important as what has been retained. Clearly, a trickster-hero has many adaptive functions for a slave population.[68]

The trickster-hero is found among black communities all over the New World. But there are differences in the symbolism of the trickster, depending on the specific culture of a particular area. In this regard, a comparison of the symbolism among the nonmigratory U.S. slaves and postbellum Southern blacks with the symbolism of migratory West Indian blacks is extremely instructive. In the United States the rabbit is the trickster hero, whereas in the West Indies it is primarily the spider. The symbolic implications of this difference are quite profound. The rabbit is a sedentary, homely creature who lives in a cozy warren: the perfect symbol of home, residence, and demographic stability. The spider is a migrant. It can live anywhere, in trees or houses or caves or nowhere in particular, for the spider carries its home, its only real home, buried in its belly.

Second, the rabbit, faced with a crisis, withdraws to its warren. The cunning of Br'er Rabbit is the cunning of evasion. It is devoid of violence. There is no convergence of opposite qualities in the symbol. The spider, on the other hand, is not just cunning, it is venomous. It bites. It kills. It is predatory. It lives by its wits and its venom. It sucks the blood of its victims. But if the crisis set off by its aggression becomes more than it can manage, the spider can also resort to flight. Of all animals, the spider is the only creature which, without any aerodynamic qualities, is capable of flying. Appropriately, it flies by means of the very same material it uses to build its temporary homes. Home is a means of departure and escape, not a warren in which to be cornered.

I strongly suspect that the Br'er Rabbit trickster, far from being a dominant symbol among black Americans, was simply a minor theme, expressive only of the sedentary nature of Southern rural black life. It would seem, too, that the cycle was reserved mainly for communication with whites, something Uncle Remus told Miss Ann. It was what the whites wanted to hear and they heard it. Other tales were for other times.[69] In the Caribbean, the trickster-hero, in the form of the spider-man, was definitely part of the dominant symbology of the folk culture. It became so because it represented with tremendous potency the central structural emphasis of the culture: the sustained experience of migration.

Turning now to the modern period, we shall see that migration has been intensified as the dominant symbol of Afro-Caribbean societies. The culture of these societies is far more complex and sophisticated than the rustic, post-emancipation folk culture we have just discussed. New signantia or signifiers have developed to express the heightened significance of migration. As a symbol, it dominates all aspects of life, from the most sophisticated novels and poems, to the new urban cults and reggae music of the masses.

The first thing to note about the contemporary West Indian literary scene is that, with several exceptions, almost all the novelists and poets are in exile or have written their best works while in exile.[70] Whether or not they are in exile, however, the migration symbol dominates their writings, and is expressed in the themes of exile, alienation, homelessness, and endless search.[71] All of George Lamming's novels, not just *The Emigrants*, are concerned with this theme. Indeed, one of Lamming's most recent novels, *Natives of My Person*, is a complex symbolic exploration of the theme of migration.[72] Samuel Selvon, the gentle Trinidadian satirist, deals directly with the theme of migration, both internal and external, especially in such works as *The Lonely Londoners*,[73] and *An Island is a World*.[74] Andrew Salkey, a Jamaican, explores the same theme in his *Escape to An Autumn Pavement*;[75] Neville Dawes, before going (for good he claimed) in search of his roots in Africa, wrote *The Last Enchantment*,[76] which explored the ambivalence of the West Indian intellectual to his society. V. S. Naipaul, a Trinidadian, generally considered not only the best West Indian novelist but among the four or five best novelists writing in the English language, is the novelist of alienation par excellence. In spite of his contempt for his native island—a trait shared by most writers in exile—Naipaul cannot tear himself away from the exilic theme. Naipaul's finest novel, *A House for Mr. Biswas*,[77] is a dark predestinarian tragedy about an Indian Trinidadian, struggling with his closed, clammy ethnic world, its broken rituals and its vicious little spites, in his search for a house, a search which in the end is just not worth it. Biswas's death, announced at the very beginning of the novel, hangs, as it is meant to do, over his search like the bird in "The Rime of the Ancient Mariner." Life is a meaningless, preordained round of pointless search, painful forebodings, and endlessly unrealized wishes.[78] In his somewhat over-praised nonfiction work, *The Loss of El Dorado*,[79] Naipaul takes on the subject of migration and search directly, using history as materials for his symbolism. El Dorado is, of course, the perfect symbol of vain and foolhardy searching. A mirage, however, is something to migrate toward, even if its consequences are disastrous. To lose the mirage is to be left only with its disasters. This, as far as Naipaul is concerned, is the present state of Trinidadian society: a cultural disaster zone. Writing, toward the end of the work, about his native city, Port of Spain, he says: "Today I am a stranger in the city myself . . . when I was at school there . . . it felt like a place at the rim of the world . . . Port of Spain was a place where things had happened and nothing showed. Only people remained."[80]

The exilic theme is even more pronounced in poetry. Negritude is essentially a French West Indian movement.[81] The negritude of Senghor disappeared when he left his fellow West Indians who returned to Guadeloupe and Martinique. There, as Sartre pointed out, they found themselves in what was supposed to be their native islands, exiles twice over from Western culture and from the African culture they yearned for. West Indians, however, are not Africans, as all of them discover when they make the journey "home." To insist on finding the lost "âme noir" there is to guarantee an endless voyage, which perhaps is what the poets subconsciously desire.[82]

In the English-speaking West Indies, the Barbadian poet Edward Brath-waite has most thoroughly explored the migration signatia. In his epic trilogy,[83] Brathwaite follows the "explorations of the worm" through all its wanderings over the entire range of the West Indian diaspora. After taking stock in the first volume, *Rights of Passage*, a deliberate and revealing play on the term "rites of passage," Brathwaite goes on an imaginary migration of the soul across the ocean and backwards in time in a search for roots in Africa. Having accomplished this in the second volume, *Masks*, Brathwaite returns to the Caribbean in *Islands*, and lovingly sets about rebuilding, poetically, the creole civilization which he insists exists in the islands.[84]

The classic West Indian novelist and poet, however, is the Jamaican Claude McKay. McKay combines the aggressiveness and the withdrawal inherent in the psychological dimension of the migration symbol to a greater extent than any other West Indian writer.[85] McKay was a triple exile. He felt himself an exile in Harlem, in spite of his involvement with the "Harlem Renaissance," and he wrote many novels and poems partly romanticizing Jamaica, partly mourning that "I shall return, I shall return again," which he never did. McKay knew that he was an exile in his own island, which is why he left and did not return. He also felt that he was an exile from Africa. To some extent, McKay played off his exilic experiences against each other, to attain a tenuous belief in the possibility of home. Thus, in America, he idealized Jamaica. That was home. In Jamaica, he idealized Africa. That, really, was home. Eventually, McKay came to realize that Africa was not home, that he was born "out of time," and that "the great western world holds me in fee."

When we move from the high culture of the intellectual elite to the culture of the modern urban proletariat, we find that in Kingston a most remarkable religion has been created out of the migratory chaos of shanty-town life. This is the cult of Ras Tafari.[86] Originally, the cult was millenarian and worshipped Haile Selassie, the late Emperor of Ethiopia, as "the true and living God"; its members prepared themselves for the return migration to Ethiopia. The emperor, they claimed, would come for them in his ship. When the millennium failed to materialize, the cultists spread out over Kingston and other parts of Jamaica. The creed was reinterpreted, becoming theologi-cally more sophisticated. The violently antiwhite doctrines of the Ras Tafari-ans were either dropped or considerably toned down, although black pride continued to be emphasized; above all, the Ras Tafarians began to reinter-pret their condition in class, rather than in racial, terms. For them, Africa stands as a symbol of spiritual salvation, and there is a theological split be-tween those who deny and those who accept the divinity of Selassie: to return to Africa is to find oneself; to know Selassie is to discover "peace and love." It helps, of course, if the "holy weed," *ganja* (marijuana) is used. In the meantime, the withdrawal emphasis of the early cult has been replaced by a primitive, aggressive Marxian ideology. The political system is rejected, but the society is redeemable. Only through a revolution will "Babylon" fall and will the real Jews (the Ras Tafarians) find and make their new Jerusalem in Jamaica.

The significance of the Ras Tafarians goes far beyond their numbers. Their ideology, a mixture of refined back-to-Africa nationalism and Old Testament exilic writings, can no longer be called bizarre. The cult has given a whole system of symbols and direct meanings to the urban masses who, even if not members, think in Rasta terms. They have also greatly influenced the thriving working-class reggae music. The most articulate and politically conscious songs are invariably of Rasta origins, and they all stress the migratory themes of exile, alienation, and oppression. Increasingly, however, they also stress the coming apocalypse, the "burning fire," during which those who are now "on the right" will be no longer "in the right."

Finally, it should be noted that migration is given symbolic expression not only in cultural artifacts but in ritualized social relations. Stuart B. Philpott[87] in his fine study of Montserratian migration found:

> The significance of migration and the migrant are given ceremonial expression. Aside from the rites de passage at birth, marriage and death, *the only major ceremonial occasions are those connected with migration*. [Emphasis added.]

The Montserratian's departure is not viewed as a break with his society but "as a stage in his social maturity," and "references to a man's migration—even when referring to middle aged married men—are often couched in terms which imply the attainment of adulthood: 'He went out to make himself a man,' or 'I was only half a man before I went out.' " Significantly, the ceremonial feasts connected with the migration rites "represent offerings to the *jumbies* or spirits of dead family members and friends,"[88] in order to placate them and to solicit their assistance in the migration. Similar ceremonies have been observed in Jamaica, especially among rural migrants.

## CONCLUSION

In this essay I have tried to demonstrate the dominant role of migration in the origin, development, and present life of Caribbean societies. I have argued that in the Afro-Caribbean areas the propensity to migrate has become fully institutionalized and, both directly and indirectly, influences the socioeconomic base as well as the dominant public and private symbols of these cultures. I have treated migration mainly as an independent variable in this analysis, but the propensity to migrate is, in turn, the consequence of other, especially economic, factors,

The consequences of the institutionalization of migration have been to a large extent deleterious. In economic terms, it has reinforced the external orientation and chronic dependence of these societies on foreign economies, and it has stifled the emergence of alternative strategies of development. Culturally, it has sustained the uprooted quality of life that was produced by the mass migration during the period of slavery, and it has led to the emergence of a modal personality syndrome devoid of trust and seemingly incapable of compromise.

Such a modal personality syndrome provides poor support for political structures. When one adds to this the lack of commitment on the part of the elite, and its willingness to use migration as a weapon against any progressive policy aimed at correcting the conditions that make migration both possible and necessary, the problems of government become formidable. The proximity of a world power that is sociologically insensitive to underlying realities and politically inept in the local forces it supports transforms the formidable into the impossible.

As a dominant symbol, migration has perhaps retarded the development of other, healthier symbolic systems in these societies. The cluster of themes that express the migration signatum may well have had too pervasive an impact on the minds of the most creative members of West Indian societies, repressing the symbolization of other important themes.

And yet, the influence of migration has not been all bad. It is no accident that the ancient Greeks were inveterate migrants and that, like the modern West Indians, they were quick to use migration as the first response to crisis. Many social scientists and historians have drawn parallels between the Mediterranean and the Caribbean: their small scale, their insularity, the role of the sea for both, as a barrier and as an aid to communication, and their ability to survive and create from minimal resources.

For West Indians are an exceptionally creative people. In spite of the chaos and discontinuity of their histories, these societies appear remarkable in world-historical terms. In less than a century and a half West Indians have risen from the ruins of slavery and from a catastrophic history of mass migration and detribalization. Their literary productions are, as a body, comparable in quality to those of Canada, Australia, and New Zealand with their incomparably greater populations and resources. In under two decades the West Indian urban proletariat, amid the chaos of shanty-towns, has created and refined a radical proletarian religion and produced a popular musical form—the reggae—which has made Kingston the second capital of popular music in the Western Hemisphere, outside the United States.

Actually, it is *because of* these chronic discontinuities in their traditions that the West Indians have made such striking creations. It is discontinuity that forces the uprooted to create. West Indians have in abundance the "mental mobility" that Barnes[89] and others speak of in accounting for great cultural advances. In institutionalizing migration, West Indians have eschewed continuity and have placed all their cultural cards on flight and on their wits. There has been no accumulation, no steady process of cultural accretion. Like a child playing with creative blocks, each new cultural model, however original, involves the destruction of the one built earlier. Each generation must start from scratch, create anew. Only the propensity to destroy, retreat, and create again continues.

Now there are, as population biologists have shown us, evolutionary advantages for a species in not being too perfectly adapted to its environment, especially when that environment is subject to violent periodic changes. In human terms, there are marked advantages for a people who are not too closely tied to their past and whose culture is not too perfectly adapted to its environment. As an Englishman, Francis Bacon, wrote at the dawn of the British drive toward cultural ascendancy over Europe and the rest of the world, "A veneration of custom is as turbulent a thing as an innovation, and they that reverence too much old-times are but a scorn to the new."[90]

Still, the principle of creative nonadaptation, if I may so call it, can be taken too far. Sooner or later, the evolutionary advantage must be seized and translated into relatively stable structures. Otherwise the advantage ceases and becomes instead the means of self-destruction. The model of the spider living by a combination of aggressive cunning and creative flight is ultimately a dangerous one for human beings.

The legends and myths of ancient Greece and Rome suggest two solutions to the crisis of migration: those of Daedalus and of Odysseus. The tragedy of Afro–West Indian society was to have chosen Daedalus over Odysseus. For the West Indians, banished to this miserable archipelago, creative flight seemed, too easily, the only path to freedom. But flying is a risky business, never meant for people, and "the homeless mind," like the bird with waxed-on feathers, will, in its endless search for heaven, still forget the sun. Now that Icarus is seen to be truly dead, it is no use following Daedalus, cursing the "art that had so spited him," as for example, did Claude McKay when he lamented:

> Something in me is lost, forever lost,
> Some vital thing has gone out of my heart,
> And I must walk the way of life a ghost
> Among the sons of earth, a thing apart.

More recently, Derek Walcott, writing in the West Indies, echoed the same sentiment:

> Something inside is laid wide like a wound,
> some open passage that has cleft the brain,
> some deep, amnesiac blow. We left
> somewhere a life we never found,
>
> customs and gods that are not born again,
> some crib, some grill of light
> clanged shut on us in bondage, and withheld
> us from that world below us and beyond
> and in its swaddling cerements we're still bound

Maybe so. But at least one Caribbean society, Cuba, has followed the lead of Odysseus. There is no reason to believe that others, still, cannot.

## NOTES

1. Richard Sheridan, "The Development of the Plantations to 1750," *Chapters in Caribbean History* (Barbados: Caribbean Universities Press, 1970).

2. See Frank W. Pitman, *The Development of the British West Indies, 1700–1763* (New Haven, 1917), and Richard Pares, *Yankees and Creoles* (London, 1956).

3. See Sidney Mintz, "Caribbean Society," in the *Encyclopedia of the Social Sciences,* 2 (New York, 1968), pp. 306–19.

4. Ramiro Guerra y Sanchez, *Sugar and Society in the Caribbean* (New Haven, 1964), chap. 6.

5. Franklin W. Knight, *Slave Society in Cuba During the Nineteenth Century* (Madison: University of Wisconsin Press, 1970). For a different view, see J. E. Eblen, "On the Natural Increase of Slave Populations: The Example of the Cuban Black Population," in S. L. Engerman and E. D. Genovese (eds.), *Race and Slavery in the Western Hemisphere* (Princeton: Princeton University Press, 1975), pp. 211–47.

6. Sheridan, chap. 1.

7. Douglas Hall, "Absentee Proprietorship in the British West Indies to about 1850," *Jamaica Historical Review,* 4 (1964), pp. 15–35; L. R. Ragatz, *Absentee Landlordism in the British Caribbean, 1750–1833* (privately published, 1931).

8. For Jamaica, see Douglas Hall, *Free Jamaica, 1838–1865: An Economic History* (New Haven: Yale University Press, 1959).

9. For Trinidad, see Donald Wood, *Trinidad in Transition: The Years after Slavery* (New York, 1968).

10. On the formation of these peasantries see Rawle Farley, "The Rise of the Village Settlement in British Guiana," *Caribbean Quarterly,* 3, no. 2 (1953); Rawle Farley, "The Rise of the Peasantry in British Guiana," *Social and Economic Studies,*

2, no. 4 (1954); Sidney Mintz, "Historical Sociology of the Jamaican Church-Founded Free Village System," *West-Indische Gids,* 38 (1958); Hugh Paget, "The Free Village System in Jamaica," *Caribbean Quarterly,* 1, no. 4 (1951).

11. Philip D. Curtin, *Two Jamaicas* (Cambridge: Harvard University Press, 1955).

12. See Sheila J. Duncker, "The Free Coloureds and their Fight for Civil Rights in Jamaica, 1800–1830" (M.A. thesis, University of London, 1961); Mavis Campbell, *Edward Jordan and the Free Coloureds of Jamaica* (Ph.D. diss., University of London, 1970).

13. See Raymond T. Smith, "Some Social Characteristics of Indian Immigrants to British Guiana," *Population Studies,* 13 (1959); Judith Ann Weller, *The East Indian Indenture in Trinidad,* Caribbean Monograph Series, no. 4 (Rio Piedras: ICS, 1968); Orlando Patterson, "Context and Choice in Ethnic Allegiance," in N. Glazer and D. P. Moynihan, *Ethnicity: Theory and Experience* (Cambridge: Harvard University Press, 1975), pp. 305–49.

14. K. O. Lawrence, "The Establishment of the Portuguese Community in British Guiana," *Jamaica Historical Review,* 5, no. 2 (November 1965), pp. 50–74; David Lowenthal, *West Indian Societies* (Oxford: Oxford University Press, 1972), pp. 198–202.

15. See Patterson, "Context and Choice in Ethnic Allegiance"; Lowenthal, *West Indian Societies,* pp. 202–8.

16. Weller, *The East Indian Indenture in Trinidad;* Morton Klass, *East Indians in Trinidad,* (New York, 1961); Allen S. Ehrlich, "History, Ecology, and Demography in the British Caribbean: An Analysis of East Indian Ethnicity," *South Western Journal of Anthropology,* 27, no. 2 (1971), pp. 166–80.

17. Patterson, "Context and Choice in Ethnic Allegiance."

18. Lowenthal, chap. 4.

19. On the Morant Bay peasant revolt, see Ansell Hart, *The Life of George William Gordon* (Kingston: Institute of Jamaica, n.d.); Bernard Simmel, *Jamaican Blood and Victorian Conscience,* (Boston, 1963).

20. George W. Roberts, *The Population of Jamaica* (Cambridge: Cambridge University Press, 1957), especially pp. 133–41.

21. E. David Cronon, *Marcus Garvey* (Madison: University of Wisconsin Press, 1972).

22. Lowenthal, p. 217. For more detailed and technical discussions of this movement, see: R. B. Davison, *West Indian Migrants* (London: Institute of Race Relations, 1962); Ceri Peach, *West Indian Migration to Britain* (Oxford: Oxford University Press, 1968); G. W. Roberts and D. O. Mills, *Study of External Migration Affecting Jamaica: 1953–1955,* Suppl. to *Social and Economic Studies,* 7, no. 3; Gene Tidrik, "Some Aspects of Jamaican Emigration to the United Kingdom: 1953–1962," *Social and Economic Studies,* 15, no. 1 (1966), pp. 22–39; W. F. Maunder, "The New Jamaican Emigration," *Social and Economic Studies,* 41, no. 1 (1955), pp. 38–63.

23. Lowenthal, p. 217.

24. G. W. Roberts, "Emigration from the Island of Barbados," *Social and Economic Studies,* 4 (1955), pp. 242–88; Howard Johnson, "Barbadian Immigrants to Trinidad," *Caribbean Studies,* 13, no. 3 (1973), pp. 5–30; for a detailed treatment of

inter-island migration in the Commonwealth Caribbean, see E. P. Reubens, *Migration and Development in the West Indies,* Studies in Federal Economics, no. 3 (Jamaica: Institute of Social and Economic Research, [1962?]).

25. Kalman Tekse, *Internal Migration in Jamaica* (Jamaica: Department of Statistics, 1967), pp. 8–13; see also Nassau A. Adams, "Internal Migration in Jamaica: An Economic Analysis," *Social and Economic Studies,* 18, no. 2 (1969), pp. 137–51.

26. Joy M. Simpson, *Internal Migration in Trinidad and Tobago* (Kingston: University of the West Indies, 1973).

27. See Edith Clarke, *My Mother Who Fathered Me* (London: George Allen & Unwin, 1966); G. E. Cumper, "Labour Demand and Supply in the Jamaican Sugar Industry, 1830–1950," *Social and Economic Studies,* 2, no. 4 (1954).

28. Introduction, *1970 Population Census of the Commonwealth Caribbean,* 5 (Kingston, 1975).

29. Simpson, *Internal Migration in Trinidad and Tobago.*

30. See Alfonso Gonzalez, "The Population of Cuba," *Caribbean Studies,* 11, no. 2 (1971), pp. 74–84.

31. See the paper by Dudley Sears in R. F. Smith (ed.), *Background to Revolution* (New York, 1966), p. 212.

32. Harry Hoetink "The Dominican Republic in the Nineteenth Century: Some Notes on Stratification, Immigration and Race," in Magnus Morner (ed.), *Race and Class in Latin America* (New York: Columbia University Press, 1971), pp. 96–121.

33. Arturo Morales-Carrión, *Puerto Rico and the Non-Hispanic Caribbean* (Rio Piedras, Puerto Rico, 1952), p. 143.

34. Manuel Maldonado-Denis, *Puerto Rico: An Historic Social Interpretation,* translated by Elena Vialo (New York: Random House, 1972). See also A. G. Quintero Riverla, "Background to Emergence of Capitalism: Puerto Rico," *Caribbean Studies,* 13, no. 3 (1973), pp. 31–63.

35. On the Americanization of Puerto Rico, see Gordon K. Lewis, *Puerto Rico: Freedom and Power in the Caribbean* (New York: Monthly Review, 1968), chaps. 3, 11.

36. Maldonado-Denis, p. 306.

37. Lewis, chaps. 6, 7. For a favorable neo-classical view of the effect of migration on Puerto Rican development see Stanley Friedlander, *Labor Migration and Economic Growth: A Case Study of Puerto Rico* (Cambridge: MIT Press, 1965).

38. See Edwardo Seda-Bonilla, "Dependence as an Obstacle to Development: Puerto Rico," in N. Girvan and O. Jefferson (eds.), *Readings in the Political Economy of the Caribbean* (Kingston: New World Group, 1971), pp. 103–8.

39. Kal Wagenheim, *The Puerto Ricans: A Documentary History* (New York: Praeger, 1973). For a suggestive discussion of the varying responses of Puerto Ricans to different host societies, see Sidney Mintz, "Puerto Rican Emigration: A Threefold Comparison," *Social and Economic Studies,* 4, no. 4 (1955), pp. 311–25. And for a more recent study see Joseph P. Fitzpatrick, *Puerto Rican Americans: The Meaning of Migration to the Mainland* (Englewood Cliffs, N.J.: Prentice-Hall, 1971).

40. Maldonado-Denis, p. 320.

41. E. Gordon Ericksen, *The West Indies Population Problem* (University of

Kansas, 1962), pp. 43–44. See also R. W. Palmer, "A Decade of West Indian Migration to the United States, 1962–1972: An Economic Analysis," *Social and Economic Studies*, 23, no. 4 (1974), pp. 571–86.

42. Ericksen, p. 18.

43. See Stuart B. Philpott, "Remittance Obligations, Social Networks and Choice among Monserratian Migrants in Britain," *Man*, N.S., 3 (1968), pp. 465–676.

44. Raymond Firth, *Symbols: Public and Private* (Ithaca: Cornell University Press, 1973), p. 75.

45. Victor Turner, "Symbolic Studies," *Annual Review of Anthropology*, 4 (1975), pp. 145–61.

46. Firth, p. 207.

47. Ibid., pp. 76–91.

48. A. Kardiner, "The Concept of Basic Personality Structure as an Operational Tool in the Social Sciences," in R. Lindon (ed.), *The Science of Man in the World Crisis* (New York, 1945).

49. Philip D. Curtin, *The Atlantic Slave Trade: A Census* (Madison: University of Wisconsin Press, 1969). R. W. Fogel and Stanley Engerman, *Time on the Cross*, 2 vols. (Boston: Little, Brown, 1974), 1, chap. 1.

50. See Richard Price (ed.), *Maroon Societies* (New York: Doubleday, 1973).

51. See the discussion of slave personality in Orlando Patterson, *The Sociology of Slavery* (Rutherford, N.J.: Fairleigh Dickenson University Press, 1970), chap. 5, section 5.

52. Matthew Lewis, *Journal of a West Indian Proprietor* (London, 1823), p. 51.

53. Charles Leslie, *A New History of Jamaica* (London, 1740), pp. 307–10.

54. Fortunately, there are several excellent monographs on this period, starting with the last quarter of the nineteenth century. Toward the end of this period (the early 1940s) we have the work of professional anthropologists and social psychologists. See the following: Martha W. Beckwith, *Black Roadways* (Chapel Hill: University of North Carolina Press, 1929); Martha Beckwith, *Jamaica Anonsi Stories*, Memoirs of the American Folklore Society, 21 (New York, 1928); Martha Beckwith, *Christmas Mummings in Jamaica* (Poughkeepsie, N.Y.: Folklore Foundation, Vassar College, 1923); Walter Jekyll, *Jamaica Song and Story* (London, 1907); Madeline Kerr, *Personality and Conflict in Jamaica* (London, 1963); Daniel J. Crowley, *I Could Talk Old-Story Good: Creativity in Bahamian Folklore* (Berkeley: University of California Press, 1966).

55. Patterson, *The Sociology of Slavery*, chap. 7.

56. M. J. Field, *Search For Security: An Ethno-Psychiatric Study of Rural Ghana* (London, 1960), p. 44.

57. See George E. Simpson, "Jamaican Revivalist Cults," *Social and Economic Studies*, 5, no. 4 (1956); see also his "Baptismal, Mourning and Building Ceremonies of the Shouters in Trinidad," *Journal of American Folklore*, 79 (1966).

58. Beckwith, *Black Roadways*, p. 166.

59. Beckwith, *Black Roadways*, pp. 170–71.

60. Sigmund Freud, "Leonardo Da Vinci and A Memory of His Childhood," in J. Strachey and A. Freud (eds.), *The Standard Edition of the Complete Psychological Works*, vol. 11 (London, 1957), pp. 125–27.

61. Firth, *Symbols,* pp. 237–40.

62. Madeline Kerr, *Personality and Conflict in Jamaica*, p. 152.

63. Martha Beckwith, *Jamaica Proverbs* (Poughkeepsie, N.Y.: Vassar College, 1925), p. 6.

64. Clarke, *My Mother Who Fathered Me;* see also W. Davenport, "The Family System in Jamaica," *Social and Economic Studies,* 10, no. 4 (1961), pp. 420–54.

65. A. R. Radcliffe-Brown, "On Joking Relationships," in *Structure and Function in Primitive Society* (London, 1952), especially pp. 96–97. See also Raymond Firth, *We, the Tikopia* (Oxford: Oxford University Press, 1930).

66. See Robert S. Rattray, *Akan-Ashanti Folktales* (Oxford: Oxford University Press, 1930).

67. See the introduction to Paul Radin and James J. Sweeney, *African Folktales and Sculpture* (New York, 1952). See also M. J. Herskovits, *Dahomean Narrative* (Evanston: Northwestern University Press, 1958).

68. Folktales also change faster than other traditional areas of culture over the years acquiring new meanings as they adapt to new settings. On the means by which dominant symbols "shed and gain signata through time," see Victor Turner, "Symbolic Studies."

69. See Norman E. Whitten, Jr., and John F. Szwed (eds.), *Afro-American Anthropology* (New York: Free Press, 1970), Introduction. On the effect of migration on West Indian racial consciousness, see C. R. Sutton and S. R. Makiesky, "Migration and West Indian Racial Consciousness," in H. I. Safa and B. DuToit (eds.), *Migration and Development* (The Hague, 1975).

70. For two valuable introductions to West Indian literature, see K. Ramchand, *The West Indian Novel and its Background* (London, 1970); G. R. Coulthard, *Race and Colour in Caribbean Literature* (Oxford: Oxford University Press, 1962).

71. See the introduction to Louis James (ed.), *The Islands in Between: Essays on West Indian Literature* (Oxford: Oxford University Press, 1968).

72. George Lanning, *Natives of my Person* (New York, 1972).

73. Samuel Selvon, *The Lonely Londoners* (London, 1956).

74. Samuel Selvon, *An Island is a World* (London, 1965).

75. Andrew Salkey, *Escape to an Autumn Pavement* (London, 1960).

76. Neville Dawes, *The Last Enchantment* (London, 1960).

77. V. S. Naipaul, *A House for Mr. Biswas* (London, 1969).

78. See the critical study of this work by F. G. Rohlehr, "Predestination, Frustration and Symbolic Darkness, in Naipaul's *A House for Mr. Biswas,*" *Caribbean Quarterly,* 10, no. 1 (1964), pp. 3–11.

79. V. S. Naipaul, *The Loss of El Dorado* (New York, 1970).

80. Ibid., pp. 318–19.

81. See Jean-Paul Sartre, *Black Orpheus* (Paris, n.d.); Orlando Patterson, "Twilight of a Dark Myth," *The Times Literary Supplement,* 316, September 16, 1965.

82. This is particularly true of the Haitian poet Leon Laleau. For a critical appraisal, see Naomi M. Garret, *The Renaissance of Haitian Poetry* (Paris, 1963).

83. For an interesting study of the theme of ancestral loss and rediscovery in Brathwaite's work see Samuel Omo Asein, "A Study of Some Ancestral Elements in

Brathwaite's Trilogy," *African Studies Association of the West Indies,* Bulletin no. 4 (December 1971), pp. 9–38.

84. Edward Brathwaite, *Rights of Passage* (Oxford: Oxford University Press, 1967); *Masks* (Oxford: Oxford University Press, 1968); *Islands* (Oxford: Oxford University Press, 1969). On Brathwaite's theory of creolization see his *Creole Society in Jamaica* (Oxford: Clarendon Press, 1971), pp. 296–305.

85. For a critical discussion of McKay, see Ramchand, pp. 239–73.

86. There is an impressive body of literature on this cult. See G. E. Simpson, "Political Cultism in West Kingston, Jamaica," *Social and Economic Studies,* 3, no. 4 (1955); G. E. Simpson, "The Rastafarian Movement in Jamaica," *Social and Economic Studies* (1956); M. G. Smith, Roy Lugier, and Rex Nettleford, "The Ras Tafari Movement in Kingston, Jamaica," *Social and Economic Studies* (1956); Leonard E. Barrett, *The Rastafarians* (Puerto Rico: Institute of Caribbean Studies, 1968); Orlando Patterson, "Ras Tafari: Cult of Outcasts," *New Society,* no. 111 (November 1964).

87. Philpott, p. 467.

88. Ibid.

89. Howard Becker and Elmer Barnes, *Social Thought From Lore to Science* (New York, 1961), vol. 1, ch. II.

90. Cited in J. H. M. Salmon (ed.), *François Hotman's Francogallia* (Cambridge: Cambridge University Press, 1972), p. xxiv.

# [7]

## Mass Migrations in Argentina, 1870–1970

CARL SOLBERG

For nearly a century, Argentina was one of the principal countries of immigration in the modern world. By the outbreak of World War I, no other major country, not even the United States, contained as high a proportion of foreign-born residents as did South America's second largest republic. The impact of the millions of European immigrants was profound and transformed numerous aspects of Argentine life. Nonetheless, immigration did not fundamentally alter the country's economic structure. A peculiar aspect of Argentine immigration, and one that distinguished Argentina from most other important immigrant countries, is that large-scale immigration took place in an economy that remained structurally dependent for markets and capital on a decaying European power—Great Britain. When the negative implications of this dependency—that is, social and economic stagnation—became apparent after 1955, European immigration into Argentina all but ceased. Still, massive internal migrations, both within Argentina and from the neighboring countries, have continued to change Argentine demographic patterns radically. During the past decade, as the clouds of economic despair and political chaos have settled ominously over Argentina, the country also has begun to lose a significant proportion of its skilled and professional labor force. The negative implications of this "brain drain" underscore the severity of the Argentine crisis. Whatever may be Argentina's future, the country's experience with human migration during the past century presents an important case study of relationships between population movements and basic economic structures, and analysis of Argentine immigration and emigration may provide lessons for other dependent countries experiencing major population transfers.

## THE IMMIGRATION BOOM, 1 8 7 0 – 1 9 3 0

Argentina's immigration boom, which lasted with few interruptions from 1870 to 1930, was directly related to the country's emergence as an economic appendage of Great Britain. Convulsed by civil wars since independence from Spain in 1816, Argentina was a sparsely populated economic backwater as late as 1870. But consolidation of political power in the hands of an export-oriented landed elite, along with the rapid growth of the English market for food products and of technological innovations ranging from barbed wire to refrigerated ships, led to Argentina's thorough integration into Great Britain's economic sphere. Between 1880 and 1913, foreign investment, two-thirds of it British, flowed into the pampas and reached a total of about 3.2 billion gold pesos by the outbreak of World War I. Foreign investors built a modern railway network and financed extensive modernization of ports and utilities in the burgeoning "commercial-bureaucratic cities," particularly Buenos Aires; they also structured the new Argentine economy around production of agricultural products for the export market.[1]

The alliance of British investors and the Argentine landed elite achieved remarkable short-term success. By the eve of World War I, Argentina had become one of the world's principal agricultural countries. It led as an exporter of corn and linseed, placed third or fourth among world wheat exporters, and was by far the largest source of beef for the British market. While exports rose from 47 million gold pesos in 1872 to 519 million in 1913, hectares under cultivation increased from half a million to 24.1 million.[2] The Argentine economy appeared to be a true success story, a Cinderella of the liberal international economic system. The fact that the country had little industry other than the processing of rural products for export did not alarm the liberals and positivists who dominated Argentine economic thinking prior to the First World War.

The export economy presented a golden opportunity to the Argentine landed elite, which enjoyed a near monopoly of landownership in the rich pampa provinces. As late as 1928, 1,041 estates occupied one-third of the vast province of Buenos Aires and included much of its best grazing and farm land.[3] In the atmosphere of skyrocketing land values that accompanied the boom, the landed elite, securely in control of the national government until 1916, made no effort to relinquish its hold over the country's best soil; with few exceptions, it leased its holdings to sharecroppers and tenant farmers. To satisfy the growing demand for rural labor, the elites turned to European immigration. A substantial displaced native-born population, descendants of mestizo gaucho horsemen, already inhabited the pampas, but it was an unskilled population, and the elites disdained it as semibarbarian and racially inferior.[4] In 1876 the landowners translated into legislation their desire to populate the pampas with what they hoped would be hard-working, thrifty, and orderly European farmers. In that year the national government en-

Table 1

Argentine Immigration, 1870–1964[a] (Five-year Totals)

| Period | Net Immigration[b] |
|--------|--------------------|
| 1870–74 | 81,059 |
| 1875–79 | 35,868 |
| 1880–84 | 124,818 |
| 1885–89 | 505,943 |
| 1890–94 | 156,950 |
| 1895–99 | 297,327 |
| 1900–04 | 246,190 |
| 1905–09 | 786,323 |
| 1910–14 | 794,776 |
| 1915–19 | −78,681 |
| 1920–24 | 493,564 |
| 1925–29 | 457,787 |
| 1930–34 | 80,057 |
| 1935–39 | 99,370 |
| 1940–44 | 20,357 |
| 1945–49 | 329,095 |
| 1950–54 | 418,492 |
| 1955–59 | 250,419 |
| 1960–64 | 218,300 |
| 1965–69 | 141,186 |
| Total | 5,537,881 |

[a]These are the official statistics of the Argentine government's Dirección National de Migraciones, as reported in the sources below. Immigration statistics used in the present essay rely on government sources unless otherwise noted. Clandestine immigration, which government statistics do not include, always has been large in Argentina.
[b]Net immigration refers to the excess of in-migrant arrivals over departures.

Sources: Argentine Republic, Consejo Federal de Inversiones, *Aspectos jurídicos, económicos y sociales de la colonización con inmigrantes* (Buenos Aires, 1963), pp. 205–6, 209, 214; "Immigration into Argentina from Neighboring Countries," *Migration Facts and Figures*, no. 74 (May–June 1970), p. 2; Ofelia I. Stahringer de Caramuti, *La política migratoria argentina* (Buenos Aires: Ediciones Depalma, 1975), p. 99.

acted an Immigration Law which opened Argentina to the virtually unrestricted entrance of Europeans. Social Darwinist ideologies, then in vogue
among the republic's intellectuals, justified this policy of recruiting labor
from Europe rather than undertaking the more arduous (and expensive) task
of settling the native born in agricultural colonies.

Although most Argentine leaders of the period believed that northern
Europeans would make the most desirable immigrants, the vast bulk of the
four million Europeans who settled in Argentina between 1870 and 1930
were Latins. About 40 percent were Italians and 35 percent Spanish. Smaller
currents of immigration poured into Argentina from other European countries. A significant influx of Poles arrived in the 1920s; Germans, Frenchmen,
and displaced Russian Jews also came in significant numbers.[5] But it was the
Spanish and the Italians who spurred the dramatic growth in the Argentine
population, which doubled between each of the first four national censuses

Table 2

Foreign-Born Population Resident in Argentina,
Census Years 1914–1960, by Country of Origin

| Origin | 1914 | | 1947 | | 1960 | |
|---|---|---|---|---|---|---|
| | Number | Percent | Number | Percent | Number | Percent |
| Italy | 929,863 | 39.4 | 786,207 | 32.3 | 878,298 | 33.7 |
| Spain | 829,701 | 35.2 | 749,392 | 30.8 | 715,685 | 27.5 |
| Poland[a] | — | — | 111,024 | 4.6 | 107,915 | 4.1 |
| Russia | 93,634 | 4.1 | 89,983 | 3.7 | 51,197 | 2.0 |
| France | 79,491 | 3.4 | 33,465 | 1.4 | 21,183 | 0.8 |
| Syria[b] | 64,369 | 2.7 | 32,789 | 1.3 | 23,344 | 0.9 |
| United Kingdom | 27,692 | 1.2 | 11,425 | 0.5 | 6,628 | 0.2 |
| Germany | 26,995 | 1.1 | 51,618 | 2.1 | 48,157 | 1.8 |
| Japan[c] | — | — | 5,244 | 0.2 | 7,606 | 0.3 |
| Bolivia | 17,993 | 0.8 | 47,774 | 2.0 | 89,155 | 3.4 |
| Brazil | 36,442 | 1.5 | 47,039 | 1.9 | 48,737 | 1.9 |
| Chile | 34,217 | 1.4 | 51,563 | 2.1 | 118,165 | 4.5 |
| Paraguay | 28,049 | 1.2 | 93,248 | 3.8 | 155,169 | 6.0 |
| Uruguay | 86,428 | 3.7 | 73,640 | 3.0 | 55,934 | 2.1 |
| Others | 102,178 | 4.3 | 251,516 | 10.3 | 277,174 | 10.6 |
| Totals | 2,357,052 | 100.0 | 2,435,927 | 100.0 | 2,604,447 | 99.8 |

[a] In 1914 statistics Poland is included in Russia.
[b] In 1914 census Syria is listed under "Ottoman Empire."
[c] In 1914 Japan is included in "Others."

Sources: Argentine Republic, *Tercer censo nacional, levantado el 1° de junio de 1914*, 10 vols.
(Buenos Aires, 1916–17), I, pp. 205–6; N. Eriksson, "Immigration Policy-II," *The Review of the
River Plate*, 145 (May 31, 1969), p. 783.

(see Table 3). Between 1850 and 1930 no other major country experienced such rapid population growth. Similarly, Argentina led the world in the rate of foreigners as a percentage of total population.[6]

The elites had encouraged this flood of migrants with the expectation that most of them would enter agriculture, but by 1914 only about 30 percent of the Europeans in Argentina lived in rural areas.[7] The extremely bleak working and living conditions on the pampas discouraged rural immigration. With the exception of several early colonization schemes in Santa Fe, Entre Ríos, and Córdoba provinces, few European immigrants to the pampas were able to acquire their own land, and about 70 percent of immigrant farmers worked as renters or sharecroppers.[8] The landed elite treated the immigrants as factors of production and required them to farm on short-term, often highly exploitative contracts. Technically backward and lacking modern storage or marketing systems, Argentine agriculture relegated the immigrant farmers to a marginal and insecure status. Dependent on uncertain world prices and fickle weather conditions, Argentine agriculture became a speculative business, a "game of chance," as one observer noted.[9] A few immigrant tenants succeeded and purchased their own land, but the bulk faced a dreary life of isolation, hardship, and constant economic insecurity.[10] Another feature of rural Argentine immigration was the seasonal arrival of about 30,000 Spanish and Italian harvest workers during the pre-World War I period. These *golondrinas* (swallows) contributed greatly to the spectacular rural production increases recorded in the century's opening years.[11]

Table 3

Growth of the Argentine Population, 1869–1970

| Census Year | Total Population | Annual Rate of Growth (Percent) | Percent of Foreign-Born Population |
|---|---|---|---|
| 1869 | 1,736,923 | — | 12.1 |
| 1895 | 3,954,911 | 3.0 | 25.5 |
| 1914 | 7,885,237 | 3.5 | 29.9 |
| 1947 | 15,893,827 | 2.0 | 15.8 |
| 1960 | 20,010,539 | 1.7 | 12.8 |
| 1970 | 23,364,431 | 1.5 | 9.3 |

Sources: Juan C. Elizaga, "La evolución de la población de la Argentina en los últimos cien años," *Desarrollo Economico*, 12 (January–March 1973), p. 796; Nicolás Sánchez-Albornoz, *The Population of Latin America: A History*, trans. W. A. R. Robertson (Berkeley, Los Angeles, and London: University of California Press, 1974), p. 164; Argentine Republic, Instituto Nacional de Estadística y Censos, *Censo nacional de poblacion, familias y viviendas—1970: Resultados preliminares* (Buenos Aires, 1971), pp. 16, 34.

While the landed elite profited fabulously from this rural productive system, the bulk of Argentine immigrants, unable to establish themselves on the land, gathered in the rapidly growing cities, particularly the capital. Its economy mobilized by the export trade, Buenos Aires became Latin America's most flourishing commercial emporium. The seat of the national government as well as the principal port, Buenos Aires attained a population of over 1.5 million by 1914 and furnished great opportunity for ambitious immigrants, particularly for those with education, skills, or capital. Immigration gave Buenos Aires the flavor of a European city during this period. On the eve of World War I, about 50 percent of the city's population was foreign born, as were almost 80 percent of its male inhabitants over 20.[12] Immigrant entrepreneurs, who owned over 80 percent of the capital's commercial establishments and over 60 percent of the artisan shops and light industries, soon composed the majority of the urban middle class outside the government bureaucracy.[13] First and second generation immigrants, moreover, entered the universities, achieved professional positions, and began to penetrate traditional institutions, including the church and the military.

The bulk of the urban working class of Buenos Aires, as well as of other large coastal cities such as Rosario and La Plata, was also largely recruited from immigrants. Railway workers, draymen, longshoremen, packing-house laborers, and other workers who transported and handled the rich produce of Argentine farm and pasture were primarily Spaniards and Italians. Their living conditions were not much brighter than those of their brethren on the pampas. Although wages were better than in southern Europe, Argentine prices were extremely high (a loaf of bread cost more in Buenos Aires in 1910 than in London, Paris, or New York City), and housing was abominable.[14] Crowded five or six to a room in the squalid *conventillos* (tenements) that housed the capital city's working class, Spanish and Italian immigrants formed vigorous anarchist and syndicalist labor movements. Massive general strikes that occurred during the century's first two decades deeply alarmed the ruling elites about the potential social consequences of immigration. After 1900, upper-class writers and politicians responded to the growth of the labor movement with nativist and anti-Semitic ideologies.[15]

But while the traditional international economic system functioned, the elites remained convinced that immigration was an essential ingredient of the country's prosperity and allowed it to continue virtually unrestricted. Immigrant labor "agitators" were dealt with by special expulsion legislation passed in 1902 and strengthened in 1910. The elites also continued to ignore the situation of the "other half" of the Argentine population, the native-born poor who were largely of mestizo stock and who inhabited the interior provinces or lived on the margins of social and economic life in the pampa region. Neglected by the educational system and consequently often functionally or totally illiterate, the native-born rural poor also suffered from debilitating diseases and from the stigma of a high illegitimacy rate, which reached 203 per thousand live births in Santa Fe province and 390 per thousand in Entre Ríos as late as 1937.[16] Vocational training or practical mass-level education programs were not available; in 1935 there were only 6,032 students in Argentine technical and vocational schools. By means of comparison, Canada, whose population was one million less than that of Argentina, enrolled 86,000 students in its vocational schools in 1925.[17] Their upward mobility blocked by the government's neglect of education, the native-born poor remained a marginal class, composed largely of transient workers and harvest laborers, whether in the sugar plantations of the north-west or the wheat fields of the pampas. Their exploitation, particularly in the sugar industry, was extreme, but governments did nothing to improve their status.

## THE GREAT DEPRESSION AND INTERNAL MIGRATION

The Great Depression shook Argentina to its foundations. In 1930, a right-wing military clique overthrew the liberal political system that had been established in 1912. The most conservative sectors of the elite allied themselves with the military and employed fraudulent elections to remain in power until 1943. The eclipse of Argentine political democracy reflected the country's severe economic crisis. Between 1928 and 1930, the value of exports fell more than 40 percent, and it continued to decline until 1933. The country's entire economy had developed a structure geared to the production of exports, and suddenly the market had shrunk drastically. Cut off from traditional sources of foreign exchange, Argentina began a process of import substitution to supply a vast array of consumer products previously purchased abroad. By 1943, manufacturing and construction provided, for the first time in the country's history, a larger share of the Gross Domestic Product (GDP) than agriculture and livestock combined. Employment in manufacturing grew rapidly, from 890,000 in 1925–29 to 1,310,000 in 1940–44. Industrial wages, however, remained very low and labor unions were weak.[18]

During the Depression, Argentine governments ended the traditional policy of admitting all able-bodied European immigrants. In 1932, the government imposed sharp immigration restrictions that required prospective newcomers to secure employment in Argentina before their arrival. Unemployment, which reached 334,000 in 1932, was partially responsible for these restrictions, but elite anti-Semitism also shaped the rigid immigration policy of the 1930s. When the large Argentine Jewish community urged admission of refugees fleeing fascist repression in Europe, the regime in Buenos Aires instead decreed more restrictive entrance procedures requiring prospective immigrants to win approval from a special Immigration Review Commission in Buenos Aires.[19] Under these severe restrictions, the government permitted the entrance of only about 9,000 European Jewish refugees between 1933 and 1941, although thousands more were able to enter Argentina clandestinely from neighboring countries.[20]

During the 1930s, internal migration assumed a much more important role than foreign immigration as a source of labor for the new light industries that surrounded Buenos Aires and the other coastal cities. Between 1936 and 1943, a net total of about 72,000 migrants from the rest of the country settled in the Greater Buenos Aires region annually, and the total rose to a net annual migration of 117,000 between 1943 and 1947.[21] By 1947, about 37 percent of the population of the capital's metropolitan area was composed of migrants, of whom about half came from outside the province of Buenos Aires.[22] Although rural poverty, the bleak employment outlook in agriculture, and the attraction of the industrializing cities stimulated migration from all parts of Argentina, the majority came from the pampa provinces. Many were women for whom urban employment in the service sector, particularly as domestics, offered hope of escape from the poverty and boredom of the pampa towns.[23] This internal migration, which not only continued but accelerated through the 1950s and 1960s, created demographic changes of enormous importance for Argentina. Increasingly, the country's population became concentrated in the Greater Buenos Aires region, while the population of the rest of the country, with the exception of Mendoza in the far west, Patagonia in the far south, and Misiones in the far north, consistently declined as a percentage of the national total.

Although the native-born Argentine poor accounted for much of the internal migration, rural immigrants also streamed to the cities in the 1930s and 1940s. The experience of the Jewish agricultural colonies in western Buenos Aires province and in Entre Ríos provides examples. Founded in the 1890s by philanthropist Baron Maurice Hirsch to settle Russian Jews who had been victims of Czarist pogroms, the Argentine Jewish agricultural colonies reached their peak population by the late 1920s. Subsequently, rural poverty, the general unprofitability of agriculture, and the desire for education and opportunity stimulated a major out-migration from the colonies to the cities, particularly among younger people. The propensity to migrate from the colonies was particularly high among women.[24]

## THE PERÓN ERA

Because Juan Perón rose to power at a time when internal migration was reshaping Argentina's demographic structure, several analysts, particularly sociologist Gino Germani, have surmised that Perón based his electoral victory in 1946 on the support of newly arrived marginal urban groups. This interpretation of the rise of Peronism, which assumes that most of the migrants were mestizos from the interior and that they were easily swayed by charismatic leaders, is open to serious question. For one thing, as noted above, the bulk of the internal migrants came from the pampa provinces and included many immigrants or their descendants. Moreover, analysis of the 1946 vote suggests that Perón's victory was based primarily not on urban marginal groups but on the working classes throughout the nation. Since 1930, the Argentine masses, whether of immigrant background or of native stock, had suffered exclusion from meaningful political participation and had not shared the fruits of the new industrialization. The principles of social justice and economic nationalism proclaimed by Perón attracted widespread support from all sectors of the working classes and from portions of the middle class as well. Although mestizo internal migrants voted for Perón, they were only one segment of the broadly based national coalition on which he rose to power.[25]

Despite Perón's ambitious plans to industrialize Argentina, nationalize foreign investments, and reduce the country's economic dependency, Argentina's economic structure had not changed significantly by 1955. Spurred by the government's redistribution of income to the workers and by its industrial promotion policies, manufacturing production rose, although not at as rapid a rate as during the 1936–46 period.[26] Argentina still relied on exports as the motor force of its economic growth, but the decline of markets able to pay in convertible currency was becoming a major threat to the country's export economy.[27] The British market remained crucial. During the boom years 1945–48, when exports jumped from 700 to 1,500 million dollars, Argentina prospered and the annual growth rate of GDP was about 10 percent. But after 1949, the terms of trade moved against Argentina, acute foreign-exchange shortages appeared, and per capita income declined. Meanwhile, Argentine agriculture remained on the whole technologically backward.[28]

Within this context of short-lived economic boom followed by stagnation, Argentina's most recent experiment with large-scale European immigration took place. In the decade 1938–48, manufacturing employment had grown about 6 percent annually, the highest rate among the thirty most industrialized countries in the world,[29] and during the postwar boom years the country faced a severe labor shortage. Entrepreneurial groups, particularly the Unión Industrial Argentina (UIA), the principal national association of industrialists, urged the government to reopen Argentina's gates to massive European immigration. In a lengthy analysis of population policy, the UIA complained that Argentine population growth was sluggish and that the restrictive policies followed since the 1930s violated "the letter and the spirit" of the 1853 Constitution, which charged Argentine governments to encourage immigration.[30] Determined to foster industrial growth, the Perón government responded quickly to these pleas from the business sector.

Perón's first Five-Year Plan, published in 1946, announced the government's intention to stimulate immigration of craftsmen, technicians, and farmers. To promote a resurgence of foreign settlement in Argentina's rural areas, the government proclaimed its intention to grant land on generous terms to immigrant farmers. During the next two years, Perón began to implement these plans selectively. A series of decrees streamlined admission procedures, authorized the entrance of foreigners with relatives in Argentina, and set up agencies in Italy to recruit immigrants and to pay their ocean fare.[31] Moreover, the Perón government cooperated closely with the International Refugee Organization (IRO) and adopted what Jacques Vernant praised as the most liberal refugee entrance procedures in Latin America.[32] Although the government also permitted several hundred technicians and military officers from Nazi Germany to enter Argentina during 1946 and 1947, this migration was of marginal significance in comparison with the large-scale entrance of other European refugees between 1947 and 1951.[33]

The first refugees transported to Argentina by the IRO began to arrive in 1946. During the next five years, the organization sponsored 32,712 refugee immigrants, primarily Yugoslavs, Poles, and Hungarians, among whom were thousands of Jews. The government of the United Kingdom sponsored an additional migration of 17,500 Poles, including many ex-officers and soldiers of the Polish army in exile. When Perón tightened his refugee policy in 1948, requiring refugees to prove that they had first-degree blood relatives in Argentina, refugee immigrants began to enter Argentina clandestinely, primarily from neighboring countries. As many as 30,000 had taken this route by 1951.[34]

Refugees formed only a small portion of the massive European immigration to Argentina during the postwar boom. Between 1946 and 1955, Argentina ranked fourth, behind the United States, Canada, and Australia, as a destination for European immigrants. Most of the approximately 806,000 Europeans who arrived and remained during this period came from the traditional sources of Argentine immigration. Net Italian immigration reached about 365,000 (about 45 percent of the total), while net Spanish immigration amounted to 184,000 (about 23 percent of the total).[35] Another traditional pattern that reappeared during this period of Argentine immigration was the high proportion of males (56 percent) among the newcomers.[36]

Perón also followed the historic lines of Argentine immigration policy when he failed to implement the promises, made in the Five-Year Plan, of government-sponsored land grants and colonization projects for immigrant settlement. Perón sponsored no major land reforms, and the land-tenure pattern of the pampa provinces changed little during his administration. The

1947 census revealed that tenants and sharecroppers still produced 70 percent of Argentina's corn and 65 percent of its cereal and worked 53 percent of the total surface of the nation's rural properties. The 1.2 percent of Argentina's landowners with properties 5,000 hectares or larger still controlled 41.4 percent of Argentina's total rural land, and of course this included the country's best agricultural land.[37] In view of the stagnant rural land-tenure system as well as the urban labor shortage, it is not surprising that as many as two-thirds of the postwar immigrants settled in the Greater Buenos Aires region.[38]

## EASE OF ASSIMILATION

Like earlier generations of Argentine immigrants, the post-World War II arrivals assimilated to Argentine culture with remarkable ease. Because of their Latin background, Catholic religion, and the similarity of their languages to Argentine Spanish, the bulk of the immigrants found it much easier to become acculturated than did immigrants to the United States. Perhaps the one most important avenue of assimilation in Argentina was the high proportion of single male immigrants who married Argentine women. Although isolated ethnic communities, usually composed of northern Europeans, have survived in Argentina, the general trend, particularly among urban working-class Spaniards and Italians, has been toward intermarriage and thorough identification with the new national society.[39] Sociologist Juan Marsal's recently published autobiography of a Spanish immigrant, "J. S.," illustrates the ease with which Argentina assimilated its Latin immigrants. Arriving in 1927, J. S. found that the common people, both Argentine and foreigners, were friendly; the women were warm; and the Catholic church was always close at hand.[40] Studies of Japanese and Jewish immigrants suggest that Argentina has been able to acculturate and assimilate non-Latin immigrants as well. Among the Japanese, for example, mixed marriages and adoption of the Catholic religion have been widespread. Argentina, not the United States, may well be the true modern immigrant "melting pot."[41]

During the Perón administration assimilation was extended to the highest levels, as sons of European immigrants occupied many leading positions in government and the professions. Prior to Perón, particularly during the period of conservative dominance between 1930 and 1943, the political elite had come primarily from the traditional upper class. But after 1946, cabinet ministers were recruited largely from the sons of Spanish and Italian immigrant professionals, businessmen, and farmers. For the first time in Argentine history, a high presidential adviser was Jewish. Moreover, sons of immigrants occupied 42 percent of the seats in the 1946 Chamber of Deputies. Among

the political parties, the proportion of second-generation immigrant deputies was highest among Perón's own party, although the opposition Radical
Party also counted many "new Argentines" in its ranks. The influx of second-
generation Europeans into the political elite continued after Perón's fall. In
the Frondizi government of 1961, for example, half the top officials were sons
of foreigners.[42]

Similar evidence of rapid immigrant assimilation and upward mobility
appeared in two other key institutions of Argentine society—the army and
the Catholic church. Sociologist José Luis de Imaz reported that in 1963, 77
percent of Argentine bishops were sons of immigrants, primarily Italians. In
the army, 44 percent of the active-duty generals between 1946 and 1951 were
sons of Italian, Spanish, German, or other immigrants. "It is very unlikely,"
Imaz concluded, "that percentages such as these have occurred anywhere
else in the world at the highest military levels."[43]

Although assimilation has proceeded rapidly, the rate of naturalization
remains low and the rate of return to Europe always has been very high. This
seeming paradox has characterized Argentine immigration throughout its
history. The 1914 census revealed that 2.2 percent of the foreign-born population had become citizens; by 1946 this proportion had risen only to 7 percent.
In Argentina, naturalization took place far more slowly than in other immigrant countries such as the United States and Canada, primarily because,
under the terms of the 1853 Argentine Constitution, foreigners enjoyed full
civil rights as well as exemption from military service.[44] Consequently, many
immigrants perceived naturalization as disadvantageous. Moreover, the political elite did not actively encourage naturalization of the foreign-born
population, nor did the major political parties attempt to build immigrant-
based political machines. Procedures for obtaining citizenship were time-
consuming and bureaucratic.[45]

The low rate of naturalization was also related to the highly transitory
nature of much of Argentina's immigration. Between 1870 and 1924, according to Juan Marsal's research, 43 percent of European immigrant arrivals left
the country. During 1947–60, the proportion of returning Europeans rose to
56.7 percent of arrivals.[46] These statistics suggest that a vast number of
European migrants to Argentina intended to "Hacer la América" (make it
in America) but not to stay there. Typically, Italian and Spanish migrants
planned to work a few months or years in the Argentine and then return to
Europe with substantial savings. Once in Argentina, they found themselves
subject to the violent and pronounced fluctuations of Argentina's dependent
economy. Consequently, when depression or economic stagnation hit the
country, the rate of return rose sharply. Available research strongly suggests
that economics, not problems connected with assimilation, was the main
determinant of re-emigration.[47]

## IMMIGRATION FROM THE NEIGHBORING COUNTRIES

While much of Argentina's immigration during the Perón regime followed traditional patterns, one highly significant new trend emerged—immigration on a large scale from neighboring countries, particularly Paraguay and Bolivia. Throughout its history, Argentina had attracted South American migrants, but they had composed only 8.7 percent of the total foreign-born population in 1914. During the 1930s and 1940s, however, Paraguayans and Bolivians began to stream into Argentina, and by 1947 the census revealed that South American migrants composed 12.8 percent of the foreign-born population. This migration intensified during the Perón government, and the proportion of migrants from neighboring countries rose steadily. Much of this immigration came illegally, but the Perón government, like other Argentine administrations, tolerated it as a source of cheap labor. The 1960 census counted 521,000 Argentine residents born in the neighboring countries, or 17.9 percent of the foreign-born population, but these figures are obviously low. Taking account of the large number of illegal immigrants from the neighboring countries, a more accurate estimate for 1960 would be around 900,000.[48]

In many respects this population movement was part of the general rural-urban internal migration that swept southern South America after 1930. The extreme social and economic underdevelopment of both Bolivia and Paraguay, along with their archaic agricultural sectors and their high rates of population growth, combined to push young people toward the industrializing Argentine urban regions. In Paraguay in 1965, for example, only about 60 percent of the rural work force actually was employed, 70 percent of the farms occupied less than 10 hectares, and only 32 percent of the farmers held definitive titles.[49]

Immigration from the neighboring countries has tended to follow the "step process" characteristic of internal migrations. Prior to 1947, most of the Paraguayan migrants settled in the northeastern Argentine provinces adjacent to their homeland, while the Bolivians remained in the northwestern provinces of Salta, Jujuy, and Tucumán, the center of the Argentine sugar industry. Contracted by the sugar companies as harvest labor, often through illegal means and on the most exploitative terms, tens of thousands of Bolivians trekked to Argentina yearly. Because of the duplicity of the labor contractors who organized this migration, many workers fell into virtual debt peonage, a "kind of slavery," as the Bolivian writer Edgar Avila Echazú described it. While the Argentine population of the northwest gradually migrated towards Buenos Aires, the Bolivian migrants tended to remain. This trend worked to the advantage of the sugar industry, which often evaded the Perón government's labor and social legislation when dealing

with this largely clandestine immigration. By the early 1950s both Paraguayans and Bolivians, having experienced the exploitative working conditions in
the northern provinces, began to join the general march of the Argentine
population towards the coastal cities.[50] Chileans composed the third important current of South American immigration during the postwar period.
Primarily, they migrated across the low southern Andean passes to work in
the oil fields and sheep ranches of the Patagonian provinces. Like the Bolivians in the sugar provinces, the Chileans have been the lowest paid and worst
treated workers in Patagonia.[51]

Political events in the neighboring countries strongly influenced the
migrant flow to Argentina. A civil war in Paraguay in 1947, the most serious
and prolonged conflict of modern Paraguayan history, pitted against each
other the country's two major traditional political parties, the Liberals and
the Colorados, both based strongly among the peasantry. Following their
victory, the Colorados, who have remained in power since, began to purge
and in some cases to liquidate the opposition, which fled *en masse* to Argentina. In 1947, at least 150,000 Paraguayans crossed the border, often clandestinely in canoes or launches. The rise to power of the Colorado dictator
Alfredo Stroessner in 1954 produced a new wave of political refugees, and
by 1958 an estimated 500,000 Paraguayans were living in Argentina. The
population of Paraguay at that time was about 1.5 million.[52] In Bolivia, on the
other hand, migration to Argentina dropped temporarily after the 1952 social
revolution and the subsequent land reform, which held out hope for better
conditions in their own country to the Bolivian masses.[53]

## THE POST–PERÓN ERA

Since the fall of Perón in 1955, Argentina has remained a divided and
confused country politically, and with the exception of a few short periods
of prosperity, a stagnant country economically. Although manufacturing output (primarily of consumer goods) rose at a steady rate, Argentine heavy
industry grew slowly, and production of traditional exportables was only 3
percent higher in 1960–64 than in 1935–39. Trapped by falling terms of trade
between agrarian and industrial goods internationally, Argentina also lost
many of its historic markets, including much of the British market, as a result
of protectionism practiced by the European Common Market. Moreover, the
rural productive structure remained archaic. Within this economic context,
Argentina has faced continual crises in its balance of payments as well as
rampant inflation for the last twenty years. While generals and conservative
politicians fought for power, the huge Peronist movement, virtually out-
lawed between 1955 and 1973, remained remarkably loyal to its exiled leader.

The regressive income distribution policies imposed by a succession of governments between 1955 and 1970 only solidified working-class support for Peronism. While wage income had accounted for 42 percent of Gross Domestic Product in 1950–55, by 1959–61 it had fallen to 36 percent. Not until the mid-1960s did average family incomes exceed the postwar peak year 1949.[54]

This bleak political and economic situation did not present a very attractive picture to prospective overseas immigrants, particularly in the context of Europe's postwar revival. Net immigration from outside South America declined from 84,000 during 1955–59 to 17,000 between 1960 and 1964. (See Table 4.) The dearth of overseas migrants has continued into the 1970s. In modern Argentine history, the only comparable period of such low immigration occurred during the two World Wars.[55]

One of the few groups from outside South America to migrate to Argentina in recent years consists of Japanese and Ryukyuans. A trickle of Japanese had entered Argentina since 1886 to work primarily in truck farming, floriculture, and the dry-cleaning business, but when Japan regained sovereign status in 1952, its government adopted an energetic emigration policy to South America. Anxious to promote closer economic links with Japan and to encourage Japanese investment, the Frondizi government signed an immigration agreement with Tokyo in 1961. The Japan Overseas Emigrant Promotion Company, a government agency, purchased land in semitropical Misiones province and began colonizing these holdings with immigrant

Table 4

Origins of Argentine Immigration, 1945–1964[a]
(Five-year totals in thousands of persons)

| Origin | 1945–49 | 1950–54 | 1955–59 | 1960–64 |
|---|---|---|---|---|
| Italians and Spaniards | 256.3 | 276.1 | 73.9 | 3.9 |
| Neighboring Countries | | | | |
| Paraguayans | 16.1 | 41.1 | 104.2 | 87.1 |
| Bolivians | 1.0 | 6.6 | 31.9 | 62.6 |
| Chileans | 8.3 | 23.5 | 9.6 | 39.0 |
| Brazilians | 4.7 | 9.5 | 1.4 | 6.7 |
| Uruguayans | −33.8 | 9.0 | 19.3 | 6.0 |
| (Sub-totals) | −3.6 | 89.5 | 166.4 | 201.4 |
| Other Countries | 76.3 | 52.8 | 10.1 | 13.0 |
| Totals | 329.0 | 418.4 | 250.4 | 218.3 |

[a]Clandestine immigration is not included.

Source: "Immigration into Argentina from Neighboring Countries," *Migration Facts and Figures*, no. 74 (May–June 1970), p. 2.

farmers. About 1,000 Japanese immigrants arrived annually during the 1960s, and the Misiones settlements prospered.[56]

Although no longer a favored destination of European migrants, Argentina continues to attract immigrants from the neighboring countries in increasing numbers. After a careful study in 1969, the International Catholic Migration Commission estimated that 1,580,000 South American immigrants resided in Argentina, or about 6.5 percent of the total population (Table 5). As in previous decades at least 60 percent came illegally, and the government continued to tolerate them.[57] On three occasions in the mid-1960s the government granted amnesty to illegal immigrants who regularized their status. Although over 200,000 took advantage of this offer, probably at least half a million clandestine South American immigrants did not. In 1967 the government prohibited the employment of illegal residents, but the decree was enforced sporadically, and the influx continued. Private economic interests tacitly supported the illegal immigration, whose members did not unionize, were not covered by labor legislation, and worked for low wages. The prominent Buenos Aires newspaper *La Nación* openly applauded South American migration as a means to revive Argentina's low rate of population growth (1.5 percent).[58]

Paraguayans continued to predominate among the South American immigrants. By 1969 at least 600,000 lived in Argentina. During the 1960s, Paraguay experienced a population explosion. The growth rate averaged 3.6 percent throughout the decade, and population rose by 556,000 to a total of 2.4 million between the 1962 and 1970 censuses. At the same time, the country's primitive rural sector remained unchanged, and labor productivity

Table 5

Immigrant Population from Neighboring Countries
Residing in Argentina, 1969[a]

| Origin | Population |
|--------|-----------|
| Paraguayans | 600,000 |
| Bolivians | 450,000 |
| Chileans | 350,000 |
| Uruguayans | 100,000 |
| Brazilians | 80,000 |
| Total | 1,580,000 |

[a]These statistics are the estimates of a joint mission sent to Argentina in 1969 by the International Catholic Migration Commission and Caritas Internationalis.

Source: "Immigration into Argentina from Neighboring Countries," *Migration Facts and Figures*; no. 74 (May–June 1970), p. 1.

in agriculture declined. In these circumstances, mass illegal emigration to Argentina became virtually institutionalized in Paraguayan life. The new wave of Paraguayan immigrants no longer remained in the frontier provinces of Argentina but migrated directly to the Buenos Aires region. The mammoth *villas miserias* (shanty towns) around the capital city now house at least 250,000 Paraguayans.[59]

The second largest South American immigrant group is the Bolivians, whose total reached 450,000 by 1969. After the late 1950s, it became clear that the Bolivian land reform had left at least one-third of the peasantry no better off than before. Isolated on marginal and unproductive lands and excluded from technical assistance or credit, the poorer segments of the Bolivian peasantry again turned to emigration. An estimated 250,000 to 300,000 Bolivians from the southern provinces of Potosí, Chuquisaca, and Tarija emigrated to Argentina between 1954 and 1963. About 50 percent remained in Argentina, and about 90 percent of these were there illegally. To reduce the proportion of seasonal migrants staying on in Argentina, the Bolivian and Argentine governments signed a Migrant Labor Convention in 1964, but the Argentine sugar industry continued to connive with labor contractors and corrupt government officials to import Bolivian labor illegally. Like the Paraguayans, Bolivians are gathering increasingly in the Buenos Aires region.[60]

The economic crisis that afflicted the River Plate basin for the past twenty years hit Argentina's small neighbor Uruguay with devastating severity. Once regarded, somewhat mistakenly, as the Denmark or Switzerland of South America because of its high urban living standards, democratic political system, and comprehensive social welfare plans, Uruguay suffered economic collapse and the death of democracy. Highly dependent on exports of wool for its foreign exchange, the Uruguayan economy was unable to recover from the depression which hit the world wool trade after the Korean War. Exports fell, imports remained high, and inflation ravaged the country. Between 1957 and 1967, working-class real wages in Montevideo fell 25 percent. Unable to control the Tupamaro urban guerrillas, the government gradually resorted to states of siege, until a right-wing military clique seized power in 1973 and began systematically to terrorize its opposition. These tragic events unleashed a major emigration, particularly among Uruguay's large and sophisticated urban middle class. Emigration reached 1,000 monthly by 1968, and although many emigrants sought to go to the United States or Canada, the majority got no farther than Argentina. By 1969, 100,000 Uruguayans resided in the country across the River Plate, and the total has grown steadily. This has been a bitter and tragic migration. Many of those who crossed to Argentina had emigrated to Uruguay from Spain or Italy earlier in the century. They had established businesses, homes, and families, and then had lost these gains during the twenty-year depression that converted Montevideo from a thriving capital to a bleak grey skeleton.[61]

Joining the Uruguayan emigrés in Argentina are an estimated 150,000 Chileans who fled their homeland following the military coup that overthrew President Salvador Allende's government in September 1973. The Chileans migrated for a variety of compelling reasons. The military junta's vicious repression forced thousands of politically active citizens to flee for their lives, while the regime's austere economic policies compelled many others to emigrate to earn their livelihood. Icami, the Catholic migration organization, estimates that 30 percent of Chile's professionals have left or are leaving.[62]

## THE BRAIN DRAIN

While migrants poured into Argentina from the depressed surrounding republics, the Argentine middle class began to flee the country. The United States Immigration and Naturalization Service reported 31,743 immigrants from Argentina during the 1965–74 decade (Table 6). Many others migrated to Canada, Brazil, Venezuela, and Europe. Professionals, technicians, and skilled workers were particularly numerous among this emigration. Between 1950 and 1964, 13,804 Argentines from these categories emigrated legally to the United States alone, but this number, according to Dr. Bernardo Houssay, Argentina's leading scientist and winner of a 1947 Nobel Prize, "defi-

Table 6

Legal Argentine Emigration to the
United States, 1965–1974

| Year | Arrivals |
|------|----------|
| 1965 | 6,124 |
| 1966 | 4,414 |
| 1967 | 2,477 |
| 1968 | 3,425 |
| 1969 | 3,938 |
| 1970 | 3,443 |
| 1971 | 1,992 |
| 1972 | 1,819 |
| 1973 | 2,034 |
| 1974 | 2,077 |
| Total | 31,743 |

Source: United States, Department of Justice, Immigration and Naturalization Service, *1974 Annual Report* (Washington, 1974), p. 59.

nitely is far less than the actual total." Houssay estimates that emigration of high-level personnel to all countries totaled 34 to 39 thousand during 1950–64.[63] All observers agree that Argentina has lost thousands of its most talented engineers, scientists, university professors, and technical workers.

The causes of this brain drain are rooted primarily in the structural weaknesses of the Argentine economy. Emigrating engineers, scientists, and physicians often identify low salaries, high inflation, and poor research facilities as factors that influenced them to leave.[64] Argentine universities produce more graduates than there are available positions, causing what sociologist Jorge Graciarena calls the "pauperization of the new professionals." But these problems are only symptoms of a deeper malaise. Exaggerated external dependency, both in trade and in capital investment, not only has subjected the economy to slow growth and violent cyclical fluctuations but also has permitted multinational corporations to absorb much of the Argentine industrial sector. Argentine analysts of the brain drain strongly emphasize this last factor. The development strategy of several Argentine governments between 1958 and 1970 attempted to revive the economy with large-scale foreign investments, particularly in the petroleum and manufacturing sectors. At least $640 million in new investment, 70 percent of it from the United States, entered the country during this period. As part of this process, the multinationals took control of Argentine industry. As David Rock points out, in 1956, of the hundred companies in Argentina with the highest value turnover, 75 were Argentine; by 1970, this number had fallen to 39. Only 20 of the 50 largest companies were nationally owned.[65]

The multinationals carry out little basic research in Argentina, importing their own technology instead. This situation allows few positions for researchers. In 1968 only two Argentine physicists were employed by the industrial sector. While in industrially advanced countries, the industrial sector typically employs about 75 percent of the engineers, in Argentina industry employed about 7,000 engineers in 1964, or about half the country's practicing engineers. The lack of industrial positions for scientists and engineers in Argentina leaves them practically no place to work other than the poorly funded and unstable universities. Government research institutes employ a lucky few.[66]

Political and ideological persecution also has played a role in stimulating the emigration of high-level professionals and skilled workers. Major changes of regime immediately reverberated in the universities. At least 1,250 university professors were fired or resigned when Perón first came to power, an event which began the modern Argentine brain drain. When Perón fell, another round of firings took place, and 800 were dismissed.[67] The largest academic purge took place on July 29, 1966. The new right-wing military regime of General Juan Carlos Onganía stripped the universities of their autonomy, ordered an invasion of them by the police during which forty-nine persons (including a visiting MIT professor) were injured, and demanded the resignations of 1,378 faculty members. Anyone suspected of hostility to the ultra-Catholic and pro-U.S. Onganía lost his or her job. The government closed the entire sociology department at the University of Buenos Aires and thus ended promising research in progress on the economic and social roots of Argentine underdevelopment. The purge also carried strong anti-Semitic overtones. Again, hundreds of professors and researchers, including some of Argentina's best minds, went into exile in Europe, the United States, Chile, and Venezuela.[68]

Some U.S. academicians have attempted to discount the negative economic impact of the brain drain on the development of countries like Argentina, and a few economists even have argued that emigration of high-level personnel was in the best interests of the underdeveloped countries, but Argentine analysts have dismissed these theories as sophistry.[69] Overwhelmingly, Argentine scientific leaders and economists have condemned the emigration of high-level manpower as a serious setback to the country's struggle to promote industrial development and to reduce economic dependency. Houssay and others viewed the emigration as a loss of human capital for whose education and training the country had sacrificed heavily. "To lose this capital is suicidal for the country's future," lamented Dr. Juan J. Giambiagi, professor of theoretical physics at the University of Buenos Aires. Houssay blamed United States policy for what he considered the catastrophic effects of the brain drain. After suggesting that the United States train its own professionals rather than import them, Houssay argued that the United States "is despoiling us of our most precious raw material." He calculated that Argentina had exported over $400 million in human capital to the United States between 1950 and 1964.[70]

Besides organizing a program to repatriate emigré scientists, an effort which met with indifferent success, neither the Argentine intellectual elite nor the government has done much to stop the outward flow of skilled manpower.[71] Although this emigration declined after 1970 when the U.S. economy began to experience surpluses of skilled manpower, the brain drain continues and will probably increase again when rapid economic growth returns to North America. Barring the unlikely advent of a totalitarian regime in Argentina, emigration of professionals and technicians will be a permanent fixture on the Argentine scene as long as the labor market in the United States and Europe is open and as long as the Argentine economy stagnates.

Historically, massive overseas immigration accompanied periods of export boom in Argentina. But in today's hungry world, Argentina's export trade is depressed and European immigration is nil. The social inequities that accompanied Argentine economic history led to the political mobilization of the huge Peronist working-class movement whose demands for economic and social justice have brought the country to the verge of civil war. Until Argentina resolves its political crisis, the economy will stagnate, overseas immigrants will stay away, high-level manpower will emigrate, and urban shantytowns will be filled with an unskilled, illiterate population fleeing from the rural desperation of southern South America.

NOTES

1. The value of the gold peso until 1933 was US $.9648. For the concept of the "commercial-bureaucratic city," see James R. Scobie, "Buenos Aires as a Commercial-Bureaucratic City, 1880–1910: Characteristics of a City's Orientation," *The American Historical Review,* 77 (October 1972), pp. 1035–73.

2. Ernesto Tornquist & Cía. Ltda., *El desarrollo económico de la República Argentina en los últimos cincuenta años* (Buenos Aires: Ernesto Tornquist & Cía., 1920), pp. 20, 134; Vernon L. Phelps, *The International Economic Position of Argentina* (Philadelphia: University of Pennsylvania Press, 1938), p. 141; Laurel Duvall, "The Production and Handling of Grain in Argentina," in *Yearbook of the Department of Agriculture* (Washington: United States Department of Agriculture, 1915), pp. 284–85.

3. Jacinto Oddone, *La burguesía terrateniente argentina,* 3rd ed. (Buenos Aires: Ediciones Populares Argentinas, 1956), pp. 182–85.

4. Carl Solberg, "Farm Workers and the Myth of Export-Led Development in Argentina," *The Americas,* 31 (October, 1974), p. 20.

5. José Panettieri, *Inmigración en la Argentina* (Buenos Aires: Ediciones Macchi, 1970), p. 38.

6. Juan C. Elizaga, "La evolución de la población de la Argentina en los últimos cien años," *Desarrollo Económico,* 12 (January–March 1973), p. 799; Nicolás Sánchez-Albornoz, *The Population of Latin America: A History,* trans. W. A. R. Robertson (Berkeley, Los Angeles and London: University of California Press, 1974), p. 164; Oscar Cornblit, "Inmigrantes y empresarios en la política argentina," in Torcuato S. Di Tella and Tulio Halperín Donghi (eds.), *Los fragmentos del poder: De la oligarquía a la poliarquía argentina* (Buenos Aires: Editorial Jorge Alvarez, S.A., 1969), pp. 394–95.

7. Cornblit, "Inmigrantes y empresarios," p. 399.

8. Carl Solberg, "Rural Unrest and Agrarian Policy in Argentina, 1912–1930," *Journal of Inter-American Studies and World Affairs,* 13 (January 1971), p. 20.

9. Juan Bialet Massé, *Informe sobre el estado de las clases obreras en el interior de la República,* 3 vols. (Buenos Aires: Imprenta y Casa Editora de Adolfo Grau, 1904), I, p. 120.

10. James R. Scobie, *Revolution on the Pampas: A Social History of Argentine Wheat, 1860–1910* (Austin and London: University of Texas Press, 1964), pp. 55–70; Solberg, "Rural Unrest," pp. 18–23.

11. Mark Jefferson, *Peopling the Argentine Pampa* (New York: American Geographical Society, 1926), p. 183.

12. Gino Germani, "La movilidad social en la Argentina," in Seymour Martin Lipset and Reinhard Bendix (eds.), *Movilidad social en la sociedad industrial* (Buenos Aires: Editorial Universitaria de Buenos Aires, 1963), p. 80.

13. Carl Solberg, *Immigration and Nationalism: Argentina and Chile, 1890–1914* (Austin and London: University of Texas Press, 1970), pp. 51, 53, 60.

14. James R. Scobie, *Buenos Aires: Plaza to Suburb, 1870–1910* (New York: Oxford University Press, 1974), pp. 141–42.

15. Solberg, *Immigration and Nationalism*, pp. 93–116.

16. Carl C. Taylor, *Rural Life in Argentina* (Baton Rouge: Louisiana State University Press, 1948), p. 334; Ramón J. Cárcano, *800.000 analfabetos. Aldeas escolares* (Buenos Aires: Roldán-Editor, 1933), pp. 9–13.

17. Daniel Weinberg, *La enseñanza técnica industrial en la Argentina, 1936–1965* (Buenos Aires: Instituto Torcuato di Tella, Centro de Investigaciones Económicas, 1967), p. 9. For the comparison with Canada, see Alejandro E. Bunge, *The Cost of Living in the Argentine Republic: Wages and Output* (Buenos Aires, n.p., 1928), p. 23.

18. Carlos F. Díaz Alejandro, *Essays on the Economic History of the Argentine Republic* (New Haven and London: Yale University Press, 1970), p. 406; Walter Little, "The Popular Origins of Peronism," in David Rock (ed.), *Argentina in the Twentieth Century* (Pittsburgh: University of Pittsburgh Press, 1975), p. 167; Guido Di Tella and Manuel Zymelman, *Las etapas del desarrollo económico argentino* (Buenos Aires: Editorial Universitaria de Buenos Aires, 1967), p. 81.

19. "A Matter for Close Attention and Complete Familiarity with the Facts: Argentina's Present Immigration Regulations," *The Review of the River Plate*, 86 (March 3, 1939), p. 45. For background on immigration legislation and decrees of the 1930s, see Fernando Arturo Bidabehere, *El problema inmigratorio* (Buenos Aires: Talleres Gráficos Porter Hnos., 1940), pp. 40–45. This influential work, which won a University of Buenos Aires prize, utilized heavy doses of anti-Semitic ideology to justify restriction of refugee admission. See pp. 94–98.

20. Ira Rosenswaike, "The Jewish Population of Argentina: Census and Estimate, 1887–1947," *Jewish Social Studies*, 22 (October 1960), p. 205; Jacques Vernant, *The Refugee in the Post-War World* (London: George Allen & Unwin, 1953), p. 602.

21. Gino Germani, *Estructura social de la Argentina: Análisis estadístico* (Buenos Aires: Editorial Raigal, 1955), p. 75.

22. Zulma L. Recchini de Lattes and Alfredo E. Lattes, *Migraciones en la Argentina* (Buenos Aires: Instituto Torcuato di Tella, Centro de Investigaciones Sociales, 1969), p. 48; Germani, *Estructura social*, p. 77.

23. Little, "The Popular Origins," pp. 164–65; Gino Germani, "El surgimiento del peronismo: El rol de los obreros y de los migrantes internos," *Desarrollo Económico*, 14 (January–March 1975), pp. 457–61.

24. Morton D. Winsberg, *Colonia Baron Hirsch: A Jewish Agricultural Colony in Argentina* (Gainesville: University of Florida Press, 1963), pp. 11–12, 52–53; Morton D. Winsberg, "Jewish Agricultural Colonization in Entre Ríos, Argentina," *The American Journal of Economics and Sociology,* 27 (October 1968), pp. 426–27; 28 (April 1969), pp. 180–81.

25. For Germani's arguments, see "El surgimiento del peronismo," pp. 435–88. For other analysis of the class basis of Peronism, see Little, "The Popular Origins," pp. 162–78; Tulio Halperín Donghi, "Algunas observaciones sobre Germani, el surgimiento del peronismo y los migrantes internos," *Desarrollo Económico,* 14 (January–March 1975), pp. 765–81; and Peter H. Smith, "The Social Base of Peronism," *Hispanic American Historical Review,* 52 (February 1972), pp. 55–73.

26. Díaz Alejandro, *Essays,* p. 446.

27. Jorge Fodor, "Perón's Policies for Agricultural Exports, 1946–1948: Dogmatism or Commonsense?" in Rock (ed.), *Argentina in the Twentieth Century,* pp. 142–51.

28. David Rock, "The Survival and Restoration of Peronism," in Rock (ed.), *Argentina in the Twentieth Century,* pp. 186–90.

29. Díaz Alejandro, *Essays,* pp. 238–39.

30. "El estancamiento de la población impone cambiar la política inmigratoria restrictiva seguida en el país durante los últimos años," *Revista de la Unión Industrial Argentina,* 59 (March 1946), p. 12. For a similar view see Eduardo Crespo, "Argentina's Vital Problem: The Need to Encourage Suitable Immigration," *The Review of the River Plate,* 99 (September 7, 1945), pp. 14–18.

31. For the Five-Year Plan's immigration provisions, see "The Five-Year Plan: Immigration and Colonization. Proposed Basis of Legislation," *The Review of the River Plate,* 101 (November 8, 1946), pp. 21–22. The Perón government's immigration decrees are discussed in Argentine Republic, Consejo Federal de Inversiones, *Aspectos jurídicos, económicos y sociales de la colonización con inmigrantes* (Buenos Aires: Consejo Federal de Inversiones, 1963), pp. 21, 39.

32. Vernant, *The Refugee,* pp. 602, 605.

33. Juan José Sebreli, *La cuestión judía en la Argentina* (Buenos Aires: Editorial Tiempo Contemporáneo, 1969), pp. 20–21.

34. Vernant, *The Refugee,* pp. 595–98, 603–5.

35. Statistics in Argentine Republic, *Aspectos,* pp. 214, 220, 228.

36. N. Eriksson, "The Economics of Population, Part III," *The Review of the River Plate,* 143 (March 30, 1968), p. 476.

37. Argentine Republic, *Aspectos,* pp. 154–55.

38. N. Eriksson, "Immigration Policy—I," *The Review of the River Plate,* 145 (May 22, 1969), p. 721; Vernant, *The Refugee,* p. 605.

39. Juan F. Marsal, "El caso J.S. y la inmigración en Argentina," in Juan F. Marsal (ed.), *Hacer la América: Autobiografía de un inmigrante español en la Argentina* (Buenos Aires: Editorial del Instituto, 1969), pp. 30–31; Francis Korn, "Algunos aspectos de la asimilación de inmigrantes en Buenos Aires," *América Latina,* 8 (April–June 1965), pp. 78–83; Panettieri, *Inmigración,* p. 40.

40. Marsal (ed.), *Hacer la América,* p. 254 and passim.

41. Winsberg, *Colonia Baron Hirsch,* pp. 58–59; James Lawrence Tigner, "The Ryukyuans in Argentina," *Hispanic American Historical Review,* 47 (May 1967), pp. 209–11. Also see Marsal, "El caso J.S.," pp. 30–31.

42. Dario Cantón, *El parlamento argentino en épocas de cambio: 1890, 1916 y 1946* (Buenos Aires: Editorial del Instituto Torcuato di Tella, 1966), pp. 43–46, 66; José Luis de Imaz, *Los que mandan (Those Who Rule),* trans. C. A. Astiz (Albany: State University of New York Press, 1969), pp. 15–19; Sebreli, *La cuestión judía,* pp. 238–39.

43. Imaz, *Los que mandan,* pp. 59, 60, 182. The quoted passage is on p. 60.

44. Solberg, *Immigration and Nationalism,* p. 42; Germani, "El surgimiento del peronismo," p. 447; Cornblit, "Inmigrantes y empresarios," pp. 417–19.

45. Cantón, *El parlamento,* pp. 113–15; Solberg, *Immigration and Nationalism,* pp. 124–25; Marsal, "El caso J.S.," p. 36.

46. Juan F. Marsal, "Retorno de inmigrantes españoles de la Argentina," in Marsal (ed.), *Hacer la América,* pp. 378, 381.

47. Marsal, "Retorno de inmigrantes," pp. 384–405. The author bases his conclusions on extensive survey research among Spaniards returning to the homeland from Argentina between 1946 and 1960.

48. N. Eriksson, "Immigration Policy—II," *The Review of the River Plate,* 145 (May 31, 1969), p. 783; Andrés Flores Colombino, *La fuga de intelectuales: Emigración paraguaya* (Montevideo: n.p., 1972), p. 45.

49. Domingo F. Rivarola, "Aspectos de la migración paraguaya," *Aportes,* no. 3 (January 1967), pp. 38–45; Mario Margulis, "Sociología de las migraciones," *Aportes,* no. 3 (January 1967), p. 19.

50. For a penetrating study of Bolivian migration, see Edgar Avila Echazú, "Las migraciones de braceros bolivianos a la Argentina," *Mundo Nuevo,* no. 30 (1968), pp. 21–30. The quoted passage appears on p. 22. For the early stages of Paraguayan migration, see Flores Colombino, *La fuga,* pp. 65–75.

51. Lelio Mármora, *Migración al sur (argentinos y chilenos en Comodoro Rivadavia)* (Buenos Aires: Ediciones Libera, 1968), pp. 85–103.

52. Flores Colombino, *La fuga,* pp. 45, 75–76; Rivarola, "Aspectos," p. 57.

53. Avila Echazú, "Las migraciones," p. 46.

54. Rock, "The Survival," pp. 194–96; Díaz Alejandro, *Essays,* pp. 443, 519.

55. "Immigration into Argentina from Neighboring Countries," *Migration Facts and Figures,* no. 74 (May–June 1970), p. 2.

56. Tigner, "The Ryukyuans," p. 223; Argentine Republic, *Aspectos,* pp. 242–47; Robert C. Eidt, *Pioneer Settlement in Northeast Argentina* (Madison, Milwaukee, and London: University of Wisconsin Press, 1971), pp. 172–81.

57. "Immigration into Argentina from Neighboring Countries," pp. 1–2.

58. The *La Nación* article of January 23, 1968, is quoted in Flores Colombino, *La fuga,* p. 80. Also see Eriksson, "Immigration Policy—I," p. 720.

59. Rivarola, "Aspectos," pp. 38–45, 58, 63; "Immigration into Argentina from Neighboring Countries," pp. 1–4; Nassim Yampay, "Expatriación y salud mental," *Revista Paraguaya de Sociología,* 2 (September–December 1965), pp. 41–42.

60. Avila Ecuazú, "Las migraciones," pp. 22–27; "Immigration into Argentina from Neighboring Countries," pp. 1, 3.

61. "Uruguayan Emigration Rises Fourfold in Growing Inflation," *The New York Times,* May 14, 1968, p. 2.

62. "Chile: The Unhappy Middle," *Latin America Political Report,* 11 (June 17, 1977), p. 180.

63. Enrique Otieza, "La emigración de ingenieros de la Argentina: Un caso de 'brain drain' latinoamericano," in Di Tella and Halperín Donghi (eds.), *Los fragmentos,* p. 506; Bernardo A. Houssay, *La emigración de científicos, profesionales y técnicos de la Argentina* (Buenos Aires: n.p., 1966), p. 7; Morris A. Horowitz, *La emigración de profesionales y técnicos argentinos* (Buenos Aires: Editorial del Instituto, 1962), p. 3; Bernardo Canal-Feijoó, "Los éxodos selectos," *Revista de la Universidad de Buenos Aires,* 5th epoch, 8 (April–June 1963), pp. 300–301.

64. In 1962, salaries for beginning engineers in Argentina averaged US $3,910 per year. In the United States, the comparable average salary was $9,100. Enrique Otieza, *La ingeniería y el desarrollo económico en la Argentina,* 2nd ed. (Buenos Aires: Instituto Torcuato di Tella, Centro de Investigaciones Económicas, 1965), p. 53. Also see Enrique Otieza, "Emigración de profesionales, técnicos y obreros calificados argentinos a los Estados Unidos," *Desarrollo Económico,* 10 (January–March 1971), pp. 449–50; "Exodo de técnicos y científicos," *Revista de la Universidad de Buenos Aires,* 5th epoch, 8 (April–June 1963), pp. 310–14.

65. Rock, "The Survival," p. 198. For Graciarena's quote, see "Exodo de técnicos y científicos," p. 318.

66. Nilda Sito y Luis Stuhlman, *La emigración de científicos de la Argentina* (San Carlos de Bariloche: Fundación Bariloche, Departamento de Sociología, 1968), pp. 14, 30; Otieza, "Emigración de profesionales," pp. 447–48; "Exodo de técnicos," pp. 316–17; Fidel Alsina, *¿Qué hacer por la física en la Argentina?* (San Carlos de Bariloche: Fundación Bariloche, 1968), pp. 17–23.

67. Houssay, *La emigración,* pp. 2–3; Marta Slemenson (ed.), *Emigración de científicos argentinos: Organización de un éxodo a América Latina. Historia y consecuencias de una crisis política-universitaria* (Buenos Aires: Instituto Torcuato di Tella, 1970), pp. 23, 105.

68. Sito and Stuhlman, *La emigración,* p. 7; Slemenson (ed.), *Emigración,* pp. 1–18.

69. Robert G. Myers, *Education and Emigration: Study Abroad and the Migration of Human Resources* (New York: David McKay, 1972), pp. 156–61, 321; Hla Myint, "The Underdeveloped Countries: A Less Alarmist View," in Walter Adams (ed.), *The Brain Drain* (New York: Macmillan, 1968), pp. 236–38; Harry G. Johnson, "An 'Internationalist' Model," in Adams (ed.), *The Brain Drain,* pp. 69–89.

70. Houssay, *La emigración,* p. 11; Enrique Otieza, "A Differential Push-Pull Approach," in Adams (ed.), *The Brain Drain,* p. 134; Sito and Stuhlman, *La emigración,* pp. 3–23. The Giambiagi quote is in "Exodo de técnicos," p. 311.

71. For the repatriation program, see Houssay, *La emigración,* p. 14; and Charles V. Kidd, "Migration of Highly Trained Professionals from Latin America to the United States," in The Committee on the International Migration of Talent, *The International Migration of High-Level Manpower: Its Impact on the Development Process* (New York: Praeger Publishers, 1970), p. 474.

*Part Three*

---

# Patterns of Migration:
# Asia and Africa

# [8]

## Migration and Political Control: Soviet Europeans in Soviet Central Asia

ALEXANDRE A. BENNIGSEN AND
S. ENDERS WIMBUSH

Prominent among the characteristics of population distribution in the Soviet Union is the presence of large numbers of Russians, Ukrainians, and other "European" Soviet citizens in areas other than their official ethnic territories. In 1970 more than 25 million Slavs were living outside the borders of their respective republics: 20 million Russians (or 16.5 percent of their total number), 5.5 million Ukrainians (13.4 percent of the total), and 1.5 million Belorussians (19.5 percent of the total). These populations have migrated over the course of many years to their current locations, the peak periods of movement coming in the years immediately following the Stolypin reforms of 1908 and during the Khrushchev campaign in the late 1950s to settle the virgin lands of Soviet Central Asia and Kazakhstan.

If we ignore the rural-urban migration and the migration within national units—for instance, the migration of Great Russians from central Russia to another area of the RSFSR, or the migration of Ukrainians from the eastern russianized Ukraine to the western "uniate" areas which were annexed in 1945—and if we discount the regular political deportation of individuals and of entire ethnic groups during World War II, we can say that since 1945 some 10 to 12 million Soviet citizens have changed their place of residence; that is, they have moved from one national area to another.[1]

The focus of this study is the large migration of Soviet citizens from the "European" parts of the Soviet state (primarily Great Russians and Ukrainians, but including members of smaller ethnic groups such as Moldavians,

Latvians, Estonians, and Lithuanians) to the four Central Asian republics (Uzbekistan, Kirghizia, Tadzhikistan, and Turkmenia) and Kazakhstan. We are concerned mostly with the political and ethnic aspects of this migration. It is well to remind the reader that the Soviet Union is not an ethnically homogeneous Great Russian nation but a large and diverse multi-ethnic empire consisting of some 140 ethnic groups speaking and writing more than one hundred literary languages. The Great Russians *(Velikorosy)* are the largest—and dominant—ethnic group in the Soviet state: about 53 percent of the total population in 1970 and now probably slightly less than half. Thus, to use the designation "Russia" to refer to its conglomerate of inhabitants is inaccurate and, if said to non-Russians, is often highly insulting.

Serious ethnic problems exist in the Soviet Union: in fact, the "national problem" may well be the greatest single obstacle to Soviet state-builders. In general, the most violent ethnic reactions arise from the confluence of Great Russians and non-Slavic minorities. This tension is especially acute in Soviet Central Asia. The problem of "European" migration into these republics is definitely a destabilizing factor and consequently should be viewed as an important element of this larger problem.

Historically, people migrate for many reasons. Among the most often cited are: to search for better employment and employment opportunities, to secure better educational opportunities for their children, to find a more congenial climate, to escape some kind of repression or persecution, or simply because of wanderlust. Surely all of these reasons figure in the migration of European Soviet citizens to the Central Asian Muslim borderlands. Yet this migration is distinguished by its strong support and organization from above. Unlike most migrations, it is not spontaneous, inasmuch as it is largely the product of a conscientious and consistent plan of the Great Russian leadership to establish coethnics in positions of authority and control in non-Russian areas as a way of ensuring Russian political dominance.

The Great Russians have a compelling reason for holding a tight political leash in Central Asia and Kazakhstan: these republics share a major section of the world's longest land frontier with the foremost enemy of the Soviet state—the People's Republic of China. In fact, propaganda aimed at securing the loyalty or neutrality of the ethnic groups of this border area is intensive and sustained from both sides of the frontier. Despite a substantial degree of economic integration into the Soviet system, the loyalty of the inhabitants of these areas—as both sides recognize—cannot be taken for granted.[2]

In addition to their concern with this area in matters of defense, Soviet planners have often looked covetously upon the lands of Central Asia, and particularly the extensive, albeit barren, Kazakhstan steppe, as a potential solution to the state's severe agricultural shortages. Khrushchev's ill-fated virgin lands campaign of the late 1950s is the most emphatic attempt to unite theory and practice along these lines. But regardless of the success or failure of this or like undertakings, there is a substantial body of evidence, as well as a strong feeling among Central Asians themselves, that resources for development and the actual fruits of their labors are allocated disproportionately in favor of the western Soviet Union, especially the major Russian population centers.[3] The "European" migrants (as we shall henceforth refer to those who migrate from the western Soviet Union) often are compared to their predecessors of the Russian Empire; that is, they appear as representatives of a colonial power whose aim is the exploitation of less powerful peoples for the benefit of the mother country. Soviet leaders and orthodox academics, of course, hotly reject the idea that they are merely disguising historical Russian colonialism in a new ideological cloak.[4]

The most recent censal projections (1975) based upon the 1970 All-Union census estimate the total population of the five Central Asian republics at 37 million;[5] in 1970 approximately 11 million inhabitants were Soviet Europeans. The big jump in the European community occurred after 1945; in fact, by 1970 it had grown by some 7 million persons—more than half of this number coming directly from new immigration. Between 1959 and 1970 (censal years), the European community increased by about 2.7 million, of whom at least 1.5 million were immigrants (see Table 1). It should be noted, however, that from 1959 to 1970 the total proportion of natives to Europeans in each of the five republics increased for the first time in recorded censal findings (see Table 2). One reason for this change is certainly the high birth rate among Central Asians; but it may also indicate that the flow of immi-

Table 1

European Population in Central Asia: Natural Increase and
Immigration, 1959–1970 (in thousands)

| Central Asian Republics | European Population | | Increase | | Natural Increase (Average 13 Percent) | New Immigrants |
|---|---|---|---|---|---|---|
| | 1959 | 1970 | Number | Percent | | |
| Uzbekistan | 1,586 | 1,835 | 249 | 15.60 | 206 | 43 |
| Kazakhstan | 5,573 | 7,593 | 2,020 | 36.24 | 725 | 1,295 |
| Kirghizia | 801 | 1,066 | 265 | 33.08 | 104 | 161 |
| Tadzhikistan | 334 | 429 | 95 | 28.44 | 43 | 52 |
| Turkmenistan | 304 | 371 | 67 | 22.03 | 40 | 27 |
| Total | 8,598 | 11,294 | 2,696 | 31.35 | 1,118 | 1,578 |

Sources: Data for all tables are taken from the following sources: *Itogi vsesoyuznoi perepisi naseleniia 1959* (Moscow: Gosstatizdat, 1962); *Itogi vsesoyuznoi perepisi naseleniia 1970* (Moscow: Statistika, 1972).

grants has peaked. Unfortunately, Soviet statisticians are reluctant to provide exact data by nationality concerning the numbers of migrants. We must await the next census for a more general synopsis of this trend, possibly in 1981. If the change is too dramatic, of course, it is possible that Soviet authorities may choose to obfuscate the evidence.

In the three southern oasis republics (Uzbekistan, Tadzhikistan, and Turkmenia) agricultural land is scarce, and hence immigration is essentially a city phenomenon (see Tables 3 and 4). The capital cities have about equal percentages of Russians and natives. European rural communities in the oasis republics often are remnants of old immigrations, such as religious dissidents (Old Believers and members of various sects) who fled to Turkestan in the nineteenth century to escape persecution, or political deportees of the late 1930s.

Table 2

Russian and Native Population in Central Asia, 1959–1970

| | Russians | | | Local Nationalities | | |
|---|---|---|---|---|---|---|
| | Percent of Total Population | | Percent Decrease | Percent of Total Population | | Percent Increase |
| Republics | 1959 | 1970 | 1959–1970 | 1959 | 1970 | 1959–1970 |
| Uzbekistan | 13.5 | 12.5 | 1.0 | 62.1 | 65.5 | 3.4 |
| Kazakhstan | 42.7 | 42.4 | 0.3 | 30.0 | 32.6 | 2.6 |
| Kirghizia | 30.2 | 29.2 | 1.0 | 40.5 | 43.8 | 3.3 |
| Tazhikistan | 13.3 | 11.9 | 1.4 | 53.1 | 56.2 | 3.1 |
| Turkmenistan | 17.3 | 14.5 | 2.8 | 60.9 | 65.6 | 4.7 |
| Azerbaidzhan | 13.6 | 10.0 | 3.6 | 67.5 | 73.8 | 6.3 |

Table 3

Russian Urban and Rural Population in Central Asia, 1970

| | | Urban | | Rural | |
|---|---|---|---|---|---|
| Republics | Number (in thousands) | Number (in thousands) | Percent | Number (in thousands) | Percent |
| Kazakhstan | 5,522 | 3,818 | 69 | 1,704 | 31 |
| Kirghizia | 856 | 564 | 66 | 292 | 34 |
| *Oasis Republics* | | | | | |
| Uzbekistan | 1,473 | 1,312 | 89 | 161 | 11 |
| Tadzhikistan | 334 | 323 | 94 | 21 | 6 |
| Turkmenistan | 313 | 299 | 96 | 14 | 4 |
| Total | 8,498 | 6,316 | | 2,192 | |

Table 4

Ukrainian Urban and Rural Population in Central Asia, 1970

| | | Urban | | Rural | |
|---|---|---|---|---|---|
| Republics | Number (in thousands) | Number (in thousands) | Percent | Number (in thousands) | Percent |
| Kazakhstan | 933 | 501 | 54 | 432 | 46 |
| Kirghizia | 120 | 61 | 51 | 59 | 49 |
| *Oasis Republics* | | | | | |
| Uzbekistan | 112 | 97 | 87 | 15 | 13 |
| Tadzhikistan | 31 | 29 | 94 | 2 | 6 |
| Turkmenistan | 35 | 29 | 83 | 6 | 13 |
| Total | 1,231 | 717 | 58 | 514 | 42 |

In the two northern republics (Kazakhstan and Kirghizia), on the other hand, agricultural land is more abundant; and in fact European Soviets have tended to settle both in these areas and in the cities. The European settlement pattern in Kazakhstan (Table 5) is particularly interesting, as it reflects Moscow's unease about the ethnic situation along the Chinese border. In border regions (the Eastern, Northern, and Central territories) Europeans are in the clear majority; in the nonborder territories natives are more numerous.

The European immigrants belong to many ethnic groups, but the most important are Great Russians, Ukrainians, Belorussians, Estonians, Latvians, Lithuanians, Moldavians, Poles, Germans, and Jews. Great Russians constitute the bulk of both urban and rural immigrants, with Russian urban settlers outnumbering rural settlers by about 3 to 1 (Table 3). This is approximately the same ratio as in the RSFSR. Great Russians, in fact, constitute 45 percent of the total urban population of Central Asia and Kazakhstan, followed by Ukrainians (5.1 percent), Volga Germans (3 percent), and Jews (0.9 percent). In Kazakhstan the proportion of Russians among the urban immigration is even greater—77 percent, or 60 percent of the total urban population.

In general, urban immigrants are middle-level administrative and technical cadres, skilled industrial workers, specialists, and bureaucrats. A large proportion are Communist Party members. On the whole they are well paid and housed (the latter an especially welcome incentive in the chronically housing-short cities of Central Asia). Depending upon the nature of their work, their status in the Party, and their relations with their superiors, European immigrants often receive other special privileges. Some immigrants come to Central Asia on their own, seeking better employment. Most—and particularly those at the upper levels of their profession—are chosen for their

Table 5

European Population of Kazakhstan by Region, 1970

| Region (*oblast'*) | Total Population | European Population | Percentage of Europeans | | |
|---|---|---|---|---|---|
| | | | Total | Urban | Rural |
| *European Majority* | | | | | |
| Eastern territories | | | | | |
| Taldy Kurgan | 610,046 | 311,310 | 51.0 | 75.6 | 35.4 |
| East Kazakhstan | 845,251 | 630,263 | 74.5 | 89.3 | 54.6 |
| Semipalatinsk | 713,827 | 364,163 | 51.0 | 68.1 | 37.4 |
| Northern territories | | | | | |
| Pavlodar | 697,947 | 492,110 | 70.5 | 82.1 | 75.3 |
| North Kazakhstan | 555,830 | 443,778 | 79.8 | 87.1 | 75.3 |
| Kustanay | 889,621 | 717,101 | 80.6 | 89.9 | 74.0 |
| Central territories | | | | | |
| Karaganda | 1,552,056 | 1,160,538 | 74.7 | 81.4 | 45.6 |
| Tselinograd | 754,955 | 574,699 | 76.1 | 80.2 | 71.5 |
| Kokčetav | 589,204 | 432,927 | 73.4 | 80.7 | 70.3 |
| Turgay | 221,441 | 134,817 | 60.9 | 73.8 | 56.3 |
| *Native Majority* | | | | | |
| Western territories | | | | | |
| Ural'sk | 513,077 | 241,521 | 47.0 | 82.3 | 31.4 |
| Aktubiusk | 550,582 | 261,051 | 47.4 | 66.5 | 31.8 |
| Gur'ev | 499,577 | 160,302 | 32.0 | 44.8 | 7.2 |
| Southern territories | | | | | |
| Alma Ata | 712,148 | 328,833 | 46.2 | 78.9 | 38.7 |
| Djambul | 794,320 | 373,758 | 47.0 | 69.6 | 31.9 |
| Kyzyl Orda | 491,780 | 123,992 | 25.2 | 41.0 | 5.6 |
| Chimkent | 1,287,431 | 386,014 | 29.9 | 53.2 | 15.2 |
| Alma Ata City | 729,633 | 581,739 | 79.7 | — | — |

political loyalty and their ability to implement directives from the center. One of the most important tasks of the Europeans is to arrest expressions of native nationalism and dissent at the source. In this respect, their ultimate responsibility is not unlike that of their Russian predecessors during the revolt of the nomad tribes of 1916 and the Civil War and its aftermath (1918–1928).

While the urban immigrants are largely from the privileged strata of Soviet society, rural immigrants often come from groups that have been displaced and/or dispossessed by the regime. In many cases they remain potential adversaries. Of a total rural population of slightly less than 19 mil-

Table 6

Urban and Rural European Population of
Kazakhstan, 1970

| Nationalities | Total Population | Percentage Urban | Percentage Rural |
|---|---|---|---|
| Jews | 27,689 | 95 | 5 |
| Tatars | 858,077 | 71 | 29 |
| Russians | 5,521,917 | 69 | 31 |
| Lithuanians | 14,194 | 64 | 36 |
| Moldavians | 26,025 | 55 | 45 |
| Ukrainians | 933,461 | 54 | 46 |
| Belorussians | 198,275 | 48 | 52 |
| Germans | 858,077 | 40 | 60 |

lion in 1970, European immigrants accounted for 3.5 million. Of these, Russians numbered 2,190,000; Ukrainians 515,000; Volga Germans nearly 600,000; and there were smaller groups of Moldavians, Belorussians, and Poles. These peoples were not necessarily peasants prior to their arrival in Central Asia; they became such only after their banishment or deportation to remote rural areas, where their survival was regarded by the Soviet regime as unimportant, and their successes, if any, were achieved as an unexpected bonus in the fight against "the idiocy of rural life." Rural immigrants in this category include the Volga Germans, who were deported en masse in 1941; Ukrainian Uniates from western Galicia, many of whom fought against the Red Army in Bandera's partisan detachments after 1945; Moldavians from former Rumanian Bessarabia; Belorussian Uniates; Catholic Poles from western Belorussia; and various Russian political and religious dissidents. Among the Russian rural immigrants the proportion of Baptists and members of other Protestant sects and of Orthodox believers is unusually high. In their new settlements the immigrants are "re-educated": that is, they are indoctrinated with the benefits of Soviet citizenship. Undoubtedly, this process is aided by the Chinese specter just across the border and by the hostility of the former Muslim nomads upon whose land they have been settled. These permanent rural settlers are augmented by temporary immigrants, usually young and from the cities, who must serve in some state-specified capacity for periods of up to three years.

Persuading people to immigrate to Central Asia (when they have a choice) is a difficult and delicate task. Some, as mentioned earlier, undertake this move for personal reasons. For most, however, the matter of choice is more ambiguous. As Martin Marty has written, "the line between voluntary and involuntary migration is normally vague and thin in historical experience." This assessment would seem to be particularly true in the Soviet experience, where personal choice is often intertwined with what the state considers to be the duty of its citizens. Without going into the complexities of the mechanism, we can point to some of the methods employed by Soviet planners to help "get them out there."

*Propaganda.* In recent years, and particularly under Khrushchev, many of the resources of the Soviet propaganda machine have been devoted to convincing those possessing particular skills that both their future and the state's would best be served if they were to migrate to Central Asia. Films, documentaries, novels, plays, thousands of articles in newspapers and various periodicals, public speeches, and other means of public and private *agitatsiia* have been used to assist this mobilization. Such propaganda attempts to create an atmosphere of "pioneer spirit," unlimited adventure, and heroic effort on behalf of a sacred cause. Often stressed is the idea that participation in large-scale collective projects goes "back to Lenin": that is, such participation embodies the spirit of self-sacrifice common to the Old Bolsheviks who undertook Herculean tasks out of true dedication to the principles of Marxism-Leninism. The periods of the Civil War, the first Five-Year plans, the construction of the White Sea Canal and the Dneprostroi Dam, and (currently) the building of BAM—the Baikal-Amur Railroad—are cited as great moments of collective sacrifice.

Some of the arguments are crude, others sophisticated. In the abstract they praise socialism, especially the Soviet variety. Maoist deviationists are condemned and vilified. On a less subtle plane, often in literature, defense of the Russian motherland is championed against the potential onslaught of the yellow hordes—the Chinese and, by implication, their "nonwhite" Asian brothers, the Central Asian Muslims. It is significant that a current Soviet campaign extols the history, valor, and readiness of the *pogranichnye voiska* —the Soviet Border Forces who patrol the Soviet-Chinese border—as if to reassure the immigrants that their security is a high official priority.

Ultimately the advertising for any commercial venture is only as good as the product it represents. It is doubtful whether immigration actually provides its adherents with the color and drama portrayed on the posters. When asked about the romance and adventure depicted on the BAM posters, for example, most young Russians, many of whom have friends or relatives who were persuaded by the propaganda early on, speak only of the waist-deep mud and the enormous man-eating mosquitoes of central Siberia. There is little Jack London adventure and lots of back-breaking work. So it is with these inducements to venture into Central Asia. Few are enticed by the glamor, which they know to be marginal. As is true of so many other propaganda drives in the Soviet Union, the propagandists of Central Asian migration soon find that they are speaking only to each other.

*Material incentives.* Prospective immigrants, particularly specialists, technicians, scientists, and others with needed skills, most of whom will settle in Central Asian cities, are lured with various secular incentives: higher salaries, rapid advancement, a freer hand in individual research, good housing, tax exemptions, access to unobtainable foreign products and scarce Soviet ones, educational advantages for their children, and other attractive bonuses. Many immigrants accept these conditions for a specified period of employment, at the end of which their contract is renegotiable.

*Compulsory measures.* Deportation of political and religious dissidents, criminals, and entire ethnic groups has already been noted. Other less punitive, but equally effective methods are used. Junior members of the Communist Party bureaucracy often are required to begin their careers in undesirable posts in Central Asia. The same is true for many academics. These posts, far from the more attractive European centers (Moscow, Leningrad, and Kiev), are training grounds for cadres who eventually hope to return to the western Soviet Union. In Central Asia their ability to endure hardships, their subservience to superiors, and their political loyalty are tested and evaluated. To be allowed to return to Moscow after an extended stay in the East is considered by most to be the ultimate reward for faithful service. Some, of course, decide to stay; but, as we shall see, this usually means that they have achieved an effective isolation from the native environment.

Perhaps the most comprehensive compulsory measure is the requirement that all graduates of institutes of higher education in the major cities of the western Soviet Union (there are some regional variations, although this obligation is supposed to be universal) serve for three years in a place of the state's choosing before seeking employment in an area of their own preference, usually a major western Soviet city. Many graduates are dispatched to Central Asia. A substantial portion of these sneak back to European Russia before their time is up. It is not unusual to encounter them living in Moscow from friend to friend (because they cannot obtain a residence permit) long before their obligation expires. They leave for many reasons, among them the climate, the nature of the work, homesickness, and better living conditions in the capital. One of the most common reasons is the inability and/or unwillingness of Europeans to accept local standards of behavior and cultural norms. Because they are very junior in their places of employment they do not receive the same material benefits as their superiors, hence they cannot achieve the same measure of isolation from the native environment. In short they are unable to live like Russians, a condition which for most of them is almost as unthinkable as learning the native language.

## MIGRATION AND SOVIET NATIONALITIES POLICY

Internal migration, according to one expert, "is an instrument of cultural diffusion and social integration. The person who migrates from one community to another unites in himself two cultures."[6] Eventually he assimilates to the culture of his new environment.

This concept of internal migration does little to explain the migration of European Soviets to Central Asia. First, instead of cultural diffusion there has developed a polarity of cultures: Russian on one side and native on the other. Second, social integration has been extremely limited. Europeans and natives live in separate communities even within the same cities. There is little social mixing and considerable antagonism. Each group retains its own social values and eschews those of the other. Third, European immigrants to Central Asia, with rare exceptions, do not assimilate to the native culture. Soviet policy dictates precisely the opposite: that the European (read "Russian") cultural presence in these areas is a good thing because it promotes russianization of the borderlands. Thus the paradox of this internal migration: the native is supposed to assimilate to the immigrant.

Theory and practice diverge widely in Soviet nationalities policy. According to the former, each of the officially recognized nations *(natsiia)* and smaller, incompletely consolidated ethnic communities *(narodnost')* is entitled to fulfill freely its national development, as long as that development stresses the positive aspects of national consciousness and avoids the pitfalls of chauvinistic ethnic nationalism. What constitutes positive national consciousness, and when the threshold between consciousness and nationalism is breached, have always been distinctions left to the Russians, in Moscow.

For many years the professed ethnic strategy of Soviet state-builders has been embodied in the terms *sblizhenie* and *sliianie*. *Sblizhenie* means the "coming together" of different ethnic groups; *sliianie* means their final "merging"—including biological assimilation—into one homogeneous mass, the "Soviet People." In recent years the latter term has been dropped as the failure of Russian-Asian biological assimilation has become apparent. Its place has been taken by the idea of "internationalism." Internationalism, a term once reserved for describing the *weltanshauung* of proletarians of all nations, now is employed as an adjunct to Soviet nationalities policy. In short, its message is the opposite of *sliianie:* Soviet nations will not merge but will remain distinct; and each ethnic group will continue to celebrate what is unique in its culture while honoring that which is unique in the culture of its neighbor. The feeling of unity between Soviet nationalities that is created by this mutual respect and the commitment to move forward as one People under the banner of Lenin and guided by the Communist Party of the Soviet Union is called "Soviet Patriotism." Not surprisingly, "internationalism" implies an inordinate respect for Russian culture, the culture of the *starshii brat* —the elder brother—of all Soviet peoples.

Each migrant is viewed as a representative of this civilizing mission, the spreading of Russian culture, although many non-Russian migrants from the European Soviet Union may not have been russianized themselves before immigration. Once having immigrated to Central Asia, however, they have a choice of assimilating to Russian culture—the culture of the greatest number of immigrants—or to the native culture. Linguistic data (never conclusive but at least a general indicator of assimilation patterns) indicate that the immigrants are rapidly becoming russianized. Linguistic assimilation to native culture, on the other hand, is almost nonexistent. Thus, an important aspect of the migration of Europeans to Central Asia is the gradual russianization of the new immigrants and, consequently, the development of an extended Russian cultural presence in this area.

To support and encourage this process Soviet authorities have created an extensive network of Russian schools, publishing houses, and cultural institutions in the east. In Kazakhstan, for example, there are both Russian and Kazakh schools, local newspapers are printed in Russian and Kazakh, and both languages are used in administrative institutions and in institutions of higher education. (Russian alone is used in Party institutions, the army, and in security organs.) This pattern is repeated in each of the eastern republics. So it is that Russian immigrants to these areas, as well as non-Russian European immigrants who assimilate to Russian culture, reap the benefits of a comprehensive extraterritorial cultural autonomy, much along the lines envisaged by Otto Bauer in the early twentieth century. Russians, in fact, are the only ethnic group in the Soviet Union to enjoy this arrangement. It is both a reminder of their political dominance and a strong intimation of what the future could hold.

We must be a bit more cautious when considering the possible assimilation of Central Asian natives to the Russian culture of the European immigrants. Language data are deceiving because most of the Turkic inhabitants of this region have employed several languages interchangeably for centuries. The Uzbeks are a case in point. Many Uzbeks speak both Uzbek (a Turkic language) and Tadzhik (an Iranian language); and, in some areas of Uzbekistan, they are likely to utilize the two languages in different situations. Russian is viewed as a tool to be employed when necessary; few Uzbeks would agree that the use of another language in any way diluted their special ethnic consciousness. This is true for the majority of the Turkic- and Persian-speaking natives of Central Asia. For these people, tribal and religious affiliations, for example, are considerably more important than language in determining ethnic self-identity.

Yet another interesting trend concerns Muslim immigrants to Central Asia. In spite of the close kinship between the various Turkic languages and their common cultural background with Central Asian natives, these immigrants tend to adopt Russian, and not the local tongue whenever they claim a first language other than their native language. This can be explained, perhaps, by their inclination to settle in Central Asian cities where Russian is used by a large part of the population. Some of the Tatars may indeed be Christians, hence their attachment to Russian culture. In any event, the total number of Muslim immigrants who adopt another first language remains relatively small.

Another measure of assimilation, mixed marriages, is probably more revealing, but once again we must be cautious about extrapolating. Political attitudes often are not reflected in statistical data. Moreover, Soviet data on mixed marriages are incomplete, perhaps intentionally (the 1970 Soviet census is the first to present data of any kind on mixed marriages). For example, figures published in the 1970 census gave only the total number of mixed marriages in various republics without regard for the specific ethnic nature of these unions. Thus, the statistics on mixed marriages in Uzbekistan did not indicate whether these were marriages between Uzbeks and Russians, Russians and Ukrainians, Tadzhiks and Uzbeks, etc. From firsthand knowledge of the area, however, we can state that the incidence of marriage between Europeans and natives is very low. When such marriages occur, they are almost always between a European woman and a native man and almost never between a European man and a native woman. The 1970 figures, therefore, with few exceptions, probably represented marriages between Russians and Ukrainians, Uzbeks and Tadzhiks, etc.: that is, between marriage partners speaking the same or similar languages and of the same general cultural background, race, and religious affiliation. A Soviet study of homogeneous marriage by nationality (1969) bears out this generalization: it shows that the highest percentages of marital homogeneity in the Soviet Union are found among the Kirghiz, Kazakhs, Turkmens, Azerbaidzhanis, and Uzbeks—all Turkic Muslims.[7]

## SOURCES OF FUTURE TENSION

One typical characteristic of internal migration is movement from areas of low opportunity and high population to areas of greater opportunity and low population. Here again European migration to Central Asia differs from the norm in several respects. First, Central Asia is a labor-surplus area, and while the European center has provided much-needed skilled labor to important cities like Tashkent, it can be argued that this has been at the expense of developing a sufficient reserve of native specialists.[8] In some areas, notably in Uzbekistan, the native elite has begun to assert itself, asking for a larger share of key professional and technical positions. The rivalry for these positions—and for the political power invested in them—is certain to increase as the native societies mature economically and grow numerically.

Second, the population of Central Asia, already large, is increasing rapidly, thus creating the specter of heightened conflict over scarce employment resources. Compared to the Russian fertility rate of 863 (about the same as the French), and to the Ukrainian rate of about 700 (among the lowest in the world), the fertility rate of Soviet Central Asians, among the highest in the world, ranges from approximately 1,800 to 2,200 (the world's record is held by the Soviet North Caucasian Chechens, also Muslims—about 2,300). The reasons for this rapid increase are complex, but they include strict traditional sexual customs, a high proportion of rural dwellers, the persistence of patriarchal family traditions, and, at least among some segments of the population, a conscious desire to expand the national population and displace the Russians. In relative terms, for the intercensal period 1959–1970 the Russian population increased by about 13 percent and the Ukrainians about 10 percent. Central Asian Muslims, on the other hand, registered the following increases: Tadzhiks, 52.9 percent; Uzbeks, 52.8 percent; Turkmens, 52.3 percent; Kirghiz, 50 percent; and Kazakhs, 46.3 percent. (Smaller groups had even greater increases: Uighurs, 82 percent; Dungans, 76 percent; and even the Karakalpaks, despite heavy assimilation by Uzbeks, 37 percent.) According to Soviet demographers, these exceptionally prolific birth rates will continue until the end of the century. At that time, barring the unforeseen, Central Asian Muslims will number more than 100 million.

It has been suggested by several Western geographers that the impending labor surplus problem in Central Asia will find its natural safety valve in the Soviet north as greater and greater demands for labor are made on other Soviet regions to offset the shortages in Siberia. Central Asian Muslims, this theory goes, will find this an attractive labor market and will migrate north. Without going into an extensive explanation, we are extremely skeptical that there will be significant out-migration of Central Asians. In this case we believe that deep-seated cultural traditions will outweigh "scientific data" based upon Western development models. In any event, this movement is not yet upon us. In 1970, less than 1 percent of the Muslim population of Central Asia—200,000 persons against a total population of more than 20 million—was living outside the Central Asian republics.

In recent years ethnic tensions have risen sharply. The net result has been the intensification of local nationalisms. Lines are clearly drawn: on one side stand the "Russians"—as all nonnative immigrants from the European Soviet Union are referred to—and on the other the natives. An increasingly active native intelligentsia, especially among Uzbeks in Tashkent, has begun to agitate against what is viewed as colonial encroachment. Many Central Asians, probably the majority, feel that their future can be guided best by members of their own intelligentsia, who presumably would attach greater importance to native cultural traditions, social norms, and local desires. Lenin's nationalities program has promised the Central Asian nationalities many things which have not come to pass and which, they are beginning to realize, are unlikely to be achieved in the future. As a result, both Lenin's doctrine and its bearers, the European immigrants, are increasingly suspect in the eyes of those for whom a "nationalities policy" was created.

William McNeill writes of the capital city as a locus for the assimilation of a barbaric elite. In the Soviet Union, Moscow has assumed this function only to a limited degree. Instead, Soviet strategy in Central Asia is aimed at establishing several provincial "capital cities"—Tashkent is the most notable example—where, with the help of a large Russian immigration, native elites can be assimilated—that is, sovietized and russianized. But since assimilation is problematic, so is the efficacy of this strategy. In the final analysis this is native territory, conferring on the local inhabitants a substantial hometown advantage.

Several Soviet ethnographers recently have hinted at what has long been known but impossible to say in the Soviet Union: that intensified contact between ethnic groups may lead not to ethnic harmony and homogenization, but to the opposite—ethnic conflict and a strengthening of a sense of ethnic particularism.[9] This is indeed the case in Central Asia, and awareness of it has prompted propagandists to step up appeals for adherence to the principles of "internationalism" by all Soviet peoples. Few barriers have been lowered; to the contrary, new ones have been raised and old ones reinforced. Significantly, the European presence in Central Asia is acting as a catalyst for a renewed dialogue among Central Asians themselves. It will not be surprising if Central Asians become less inclined to accommodate the demands of their European "elder brothers," and less willing to think of themselves as residents of a "European" outpost in a Muslim world.

## NOTES

1. These and subsequent figures, unless otherwise noted, are taken from the 1970 All-Union Soviet Census.

2. Cf. David Hooson, *The Soviet Union: People and Regions* (Belmont, Calif.: Wadsworth Publishing Company, 1972), pp. 272–94. See also by the same author, "The

Outlook for Regional Development in the Soviet Union," *Slavic Review*, 31, no. 3 (September 1972), pp. 535–54; and the commentaries by Ann Sheehy, ibid., pp. 555–63, and V. Stanly Vardys, ibid., pp. 564–70.

3. See, for example, articles by Leslie Dienes: "Investment Priorities in Soviet Regions," *Annals of the Association of American Geographers*, 62, no. 3 (1972), pp. 437–54; and "Issues in Soviet Energy Policy and Conflicts Over Fuel Costs in Regional Development," *Soviet Studies*, 23, no. 1 (July 1971), pp. 26–58. Also informative are Violet Conolly, *Beyond the Urals* (London, 1967), p. 123; and Gertrude Schroeder, "Regional Differences in Incomes and Levels of Living in the USSR," in J. N. Bandera and Z. L. Melnyk (eds.), *The Soviet Economy in Regional Perspective* (New York: Praeger Publishers, 1973).

4. A typical example is V. A. Shlilyuk, *Mezhrespublikanskaia migratsiia i sblizhenie natsii v SSSR* (L'vov, 1975), pp. 140–46.

5. *The USSR in Figures for 1974* (Moscow: Statistika Publishers, 1975), pp. 10–11.

6. Donald J. Bogue, "Internal Migration," in Philip M. Hauser and Otis Dudley Duncan (eds.), *The Study of Population: An Inventory and Appraisal* (Chicago: University of Chicago Press, 1959), p. 487.

7. L. V. Chuiko, *Braki i razvody* (Moscow, 1975), p. 76.

8. Robert A. Lewis, Richard H. Rowland, and Ralph S. Clem, "Modernization, Population Change and Nationality in Soviet Central Asia and Kazakhstan," *Canadian Slavonic Papers*, 17, nos. 2 and 3 (Summer and Fall 1975), pp. 294–99.

9. Viktor Perevedentsev, for example, has suggested this quite strongly in some of his more recent works on urbanization and ethnic processes.

# [9]

## Postwar Migrations in Sub-Saharan Africa

Historically, migration within sub-Saharan Africa has been mainly from the north to the south. With the dessication of the Sahara between about 3000 and 1000 B.C., people were forced southward into the Sudanic savanna belt. In about the millennium before Christ, these migrants and other savanna peoples moved into the West African forest, while the spread of the Bantu-speaking peoples into the whole southern bulge of the continent also began. By about 1400 A.D., the Bantu-speakers appear to have occupied most of the land they occupy today, and population movements became less clearly unidirectional. The flow of people out of Africa by way of the slave trade became more important—in all three branches: the Atlantic slave trade, the overland trade to Egypt and North Africa, and the Indian Ocean trade to Arabia, the Persian Gulf, and India. Some movements of people within Africa had important cultural consequences. The Maghrib, western Sahara, and Nilotic Sudan all became Arabic speaking through the influence of migrants from Arabia who arrived in the eleventh to the thirteenth centuries. The transhumant drift of the Fulbe across West Africa from the Senegal basin to Lake Chad also had cultural consequences far outweighing the comparatively small numbers involved.

With the European conquests of the 1880s and later, the north-to-south migrations resumed, mainly because the resource endowment of the tropical forest and of South Africa could then be exploited as a reflex of European industrialization. Rubber and palm oil were among the natural forest products in demand early in the colonial period. Food production in the forest zone had been increasing slowly since the sixteenth century with the gradual introduction of maize and manioc from the Americas, while coffee and cocoa and new varieties of cotton began to be produced for export. Along the east-west Gulf of Guinea coast, the forest zone was also the coastal zone, easiest to reach from the ports, the natural place to develop the kind of export-oriented economy Europeans fancied at that time. In southern Africa, mineral deposits, especially those of the Transvaal goldfields, encouraged the only substantial investment Europeans made in Africa during the colonial period. By 1936–38, per capita investment reached £56 sterling in South Africa, £38 in the Rhodesias (Zimbabwe and Zambia), and £13 in the Belgian Congo (Zaïre)—but no more than £10 per capita anywhere else in sub-Saharan Africa.[1] All these mining centers with their subsidiary industrial development attracted people in large numbers, and the weight of movement followed the weight of investment toward the Transvaal.

The patterns of migration created in the early colonial period were to persist into the postwar period, and one of the most persistent was the special kind of labor migration that came into existence in southern Africa. Elsewhere, and especially in the tropical world at large during the early twentieth century, workers were drawn away from agriculture into new towns, mines, and plantations, often on a temporary basis. But the South African pattern was not merely labor migration: it was labor migration that turned into a regular and systematic oscillation between periods of nearly self-subsistent farming and periods of wage work for European enterprises.

The origins of oscillating labor go back to the 1840s when the Afrikaners first occupied the high veld and parts of Natal in the wake of the Zulu *Mfecane.* They found themselves with two partly contradictory goals in regard to the Africans they had conquered. One was to seize legal ownership of the best land, which called for a policy of driving away its African owners. At the same time, they wanted Africans to do the actual agricultural work, but just enough Africans and no more. Before the end of the nineteenth century, these goals were spelled out in legislation as contradictory as the goals themselves. Some of it, such as the vagrancy laws, was designed to give the European farmers command over the labor they wanted. Other legislation limited the number of Africans who were allowed to farm as squatters on "white" land, while special taxation was applied to Africans in the reserves so as to increase the "push" factor driving them to seek work on European-owned farms. The taxes usually took the form of hut or poll taxes and were first applied in Natal in 1849, later spreading in one form or another to virtually all of sub-Saharan Africa. The theory was that regressive taxation would force honest labor from people who were otherwise prone to work only enough for their bare subsistence.[2] The rate of taxation was therefore set quite high, often demanding the value of a month's wages in a single annual payment, or even more. The rate could also be varied to serve more specific goals. In the Transvaal, for example, one of the earliest laws, passed in 1870, provided that Africans in the service of Europeans and resident on their farms paid only £.125 sterling a year, while those in European service but nonresident paid £.25, and those who did not work directly for a European paid £.50.

In the 1890s, after the opening of the Witwatersrand gold mines, labor recruitment became more systematic. Alongside the pull of wages and the push of taxes, the Chamber of Mines set up a central recruiting organization that served the industry and began to reach outside Transvaal and beyond the British South African colonies. By 1910, the annual number of non–South African recruits was already about 100,000 and the proportion of Africans from beyond the borders never dropped below 60 percent thereafter. The Land Act of 1913 and the Urban Areas Act of 1923 spelled out in explicit legislation principles that were already understood: cities, European farms, and mining areas—indeed, nearly 90 percent of the Union of South Africa —were declared to be "white man's country" where Africans might live as temporary sojourners. Their permission to stay was never treated as a right, but was contingent on the Europeans' need for African labor. Otherwise, Africans had to live on the reserves set aside for them, and, even in the towns, they were supposed to live in racially segregated "locations."

Neither the legislation nor the theory behind it implied that labor migration was necessarily oscillating, but it became so, partly because of the form of contract used to recruit mine labor, partly by international agreement with neighbors like Portuguese Mozambique, and in time by the internal dynamics of the system. A recent study by Francis Wilson of the University of Cape Town[3] shows the way in which economics and custom combined to make for alternating pushes and pulls. As population grew, the land in the reserves could no longer support the population, and men had to leave in search of wage labor. But low wages and bad living conditions in towns rarely made it possible for the laborer to take wife or children with him. They stayed on the reserve, working the land, so that, in time, women's agricultural work in the reserves made it possible to pay low wages—in effect subsidizing the mining industry. After a period in the city or mining camp, usually about a year, the contract expired and the worker was drawn back to the reserve. His absence would have been missed, and his work was needed for a time to catch up on all the postponable chores that had come due while he was away. His presence was also essential for the sake of social continuity and to preserve his right to work a part of the land, but the fact remained that the land would not actually support the whole family. Soon the pull of wages would exceed the need for labor at home, and the migrant would set off for another period in the European towns or farms.

Although oscillating labor made it possible to pay extremely low wages, the system as a whole was far from cheap. Short-term migrants were unskilled and often inefficient workers. Mining companies early came to the conclusion that while the wage rate might be low, the cost per unit of work performed by oscillating labor was high. In the early 1920s, Union Minière du Haut Katanga decided to abandon oscillating labor in favor of "stabilized" labor, where workers were encouraged to move to the mining settlement with their wives and to become semipermanent, professional miners. Annual labor turnover dropped from 96 percent in the early 1920s to 7 percent in the early 1930s. Mining companies in the Copper Belt of Northern Rhodesia (now Zambia) changed over to stabilized labor in the early 1930s, with similar success.[4] These experiments were well known in South African mining circles, but the mining firms were conservative. The whole structure of the industry and of supporting South African legislation, pressure of "white" trade unions, and the social goals of the dominant minority have conspired to preserve oscillating labor as the dominant labor system until the present.[5]

As a result, oscillating labor in southern Africa has kept its predominant place in the pattern of sub-Saharan migration. Total interterritorial migration in 1960—that is migrants crossing frontiers—was estimated at more than 25 percent of the total wage-labor force, about 1.25 million people—of whom 560,000 moved in southern Africa, 440,000 in west Africa, 137,000 in east Africa, and 40 to 50,000 in Zaïre. But interterritorial migration represents only a part of the picture in southern Africa. Most mine labor for South Africa came from other territories, but the reserves within South Africa itself supplied the bulk of non-mine labor. In 1951, the Tomlinson Commission estimated that 503,000 African men were absent at any one time from the reserves within the Union of South Africa, working in "white" parts of the country. This represented 40 percent of all males between the ages of 15 and 65. In addition, some 630,000 workers from other territories could be found in South Africa, about two-thirds in the mining industry, one-third in South African agriculture. For South Africa alone, this implies that more than 2 million men spent their lives oscillating between wage work in the Union (later the Republic) and relatively inefficient agriculture in the reserves or in neighboring countries.[6]

Rhodesia, Nyasaland, the former High Commission Territories, and Mozambique were caught up in this oscillating labor pattern. Mozambique, Lesotho, and Botswana exported but did not import labor, just as South Africa imported but did not export. Others both exported and imported. Nyasaland (later Malawi) sent men to Rhodesia, Zambia, and Katanga as well as South Africa, but it also received some agricultural workers from Mozambique—and more than half of all Nyasalanders in wage employment in 1956 were actually working outside the country. Swaziland was also both an importer and exporter of labor, but with a comparatively small net export in most years, at the opposite extreme from Lesotho, whose labor exports were the highest per capita in Africa. In 1960, 131,000 people were temporarily absent in South Africa, out of a total population of 800,000.[7]

In tropical Africa, oscillation was important in the early years of economic development. It was only natural for those who were unaccustomed to wage employment to return to their villages after the initial experience. Some never went back; others developed the habit of occasional employment in the wage sector; while others went to town and settled there permanently. Connections with the home village might continue over several decades, but the tendency over time was for an individual to begin as an occasional labor migrant, making more and more frequent oscillations until he finally settled as a permanent townsman.

During the colonial period, political factors were comparatively unimportant, and Africans could wander back and forth across most colonial frontiers without passports, visas, and other paraphernalia necessary to interterritorial migration in Europe or America. Those who had a usable primary education were somewhat limited to the anglophone, lusophone, or francophone zones, but the less skilled or more skilled moved more easily. Buganda Province of Uganda, for example, drew very heavily on francophone Rwanda, while Ghana drew more workers from francophone Upper Volta than from any other territory. Since independence, however, some of this freedom has been curtailed, though not enough, perhaps, to keep Africa from being exceptional in the degree of freedom of its people to move about.

The greatest exception to this relative freedom is a rash of refugee movements and mass expulsions of aliens since independence. Some of these mass movements were voluntary or nearly so, like the retreat of the *pieds noirs* from Algeria, which brought about the "repatriation" of as many as 900,000 people to France over the decade 1954 to 1964. Other flights from possible persecution, less provoked, also involved tens of thousands of people, such as the flight of the Tutsi from Rwanda between 1962 and 1966, that of the Hutu from Burundi in the late 1960s, or that of southern Sudanese into Uganda during that same period. By 1971, some 100,000 Rwandans and 80,000 Sudanese were living as refugees in Uganda alone.

The line between voluntary flight from persecution and legal expulsion may be narrow, but the expulsion of aliens—normally for reasons of economic rivalry—has been increasingly common. Some instances took place as long ago as 1958, when several thousand Dahomeans (Béninois) were expelled from the Ivory Coast even before formal independence; Nigerians were expelled from Cameroon in 1967. Indians still resident in East African countries have been subject to various and subtle pressures to emigrate since the early 1960s, but in 1971 Idi Amin's expulsion of some 80,000 Indians who carried British, not Ugandan passports brought the expulsion of Indians to the level of a mass movement. Even earlier, between December 1969 and June 1970, Ghana expelled more than 200,000 resident foreigners, many of whom had been living in Ghana for decades. But even this was only about half the number of foreign-born Africans in Ghana, who made up about 10 percent of the 1960 population.[8] Nor were all major changes of this kind on the initiative of the receiving state. Early in 1966, Nigeria announced a withdrawal of Nigerian migrant workers on the island of Fernando Po (Macias Nguema) in Equatorial Guinea, where they made up about 75 percent of the total population. It is worth noting that the expulsion of aliens from Ghana and of Indians from Uganda were seriously damaging to the economy of the expelling states, and that Nigeria's move was designed to put pressure on Equatorial Guinea.

In West Africa, more than anywhere else, the early pattern of oscillation has given way to permanent relocation, but the pattern of relocation is variable within the region. One pattern prevails from Dahomey and Niger westward to Cape Verde, where the main flow has been a southward drift toward the coastal towns, and from the savanna into the tropical forest. Part of this drift has been by seasonal migrants who practice a form of oscillation different from the South African pattern. With a dry season of six months or more in the savanna country, agricultural labor was seasonally underemployed and men could move south to find work, but only for four to seven months in contrast to the typical southern African contract of one year or eighteen months. Seasonal labor migration for the period 1920–1970 has been estimated at an annual average of 240,000 per year in West Africa west of Nigeria. In addition, about 60,000 people a year moved south to stay. Though the annual total is smaller, it should be kept in mind that it is nevertheless about the size of the whole Atlantic slave trade at its peak, and its contribution to a redistributed West African population was really important. Before about 1920, these coastal regions west of Nigeria had about a third of the total population. Today, they have about half. A total of about 3 million migrants over the half-century ending in 1970 made a population contribution to the south of some 4.8 million people or about a fifth of the coastal population. The most important receiving regions were southern Ghana, southern and central Ivory Coast, and the Cape Verde region of Senegal, in that order of importance. The outstanding supply zone was Upper Volta, which sent most in proportion to its total population, followed by other savanna states.[9]

The Nigerian pattern was different, mainly because of the denser populations and because mining and export agriculture were more evenly distributed between savanna and forest. Some of the recent Nigerian censuses have been falsified beyond any value to demographic history, but Akin Mabogunje's analysis of the census of 1952–53 points up the main trends. As a point of departure, Nigeria was comparatively weak as a magnet for interterritorial migration, having a foreign-born African population equal to only about 4.5 percent of the total. Nigeria's internal migrations fall into two different patterns, one dominant before about 1950 and the other dominant afterwards. The patterns are distinguished partly by size: permanent migration among the three Nigerian regions was only about 30,000 a year before the 1950s, rising to 200,000 and more per year from the late 1950s onward. The patterns can also be distinguished as "colonization migration" in the earlier phase and "urbanization migration" in the later one, with the difference in type being mainly a matter of income levels in the sending and receiving regions. Colonization is recognized when people leave a region of comparatively high incomes for another where incomes are lower, skill levels are sometimes lower, but untapped resources or skilled employment make the move attractive. The prime example in Nigeria was the movement of Ibo from the Eastern Region to the North, which may have accounted for as much as 70 percent of interregional migration over the past fifty years. Other colonization migration took place within a single region, such as the movement of people in the North from the central zone around Kano and Katsina into the relatively unpopulated "middle belt" further south—or northeast to Bornu and Adamawa. But movements of this kind have been outweighed in the past two decades by the drift toward the cities in all regions, or toward developing agricultural centers like the cocoa belt in the Western Region.

One final type of large-scale southward migration was the flight from famine involving the whole sahelian zone from the Cape Verde Islands to the Red Sea and the horn of Africa. The sahelian drought of the late 1960s and early 1970s was the only postwar occurrence, but the pattern of periodic droughts followed by the partial depopulation of this zone has been a regular pattern with especially severe occurrences in the 1640s and the 1750s. The latest phase has apparently ended with the generally good harvests of 1975, but not all the people who fled have returned to their old homes and the former nomads have not had an opportunity to rebuild their herds. Nor has the movement been studied yet for its demographic repercussions. It is clear, however, that it affected millions and perhaps tens of millions of people. And it is not necessarily only a temporary move. The refugees from past droughts often found new homes, and their relocation can be traced in important aspects of the cultural geography of the Sudan. There is no reason to suppose that a return to the sahel will be more complete this time.

At the other extreme in size but not significance has been small-scale movement of the highly skilled or highly educated, including Europeans moving both into and out of Africa. The coming of independence brought the gradual replacement of colonial administrators by local people, but not a net flow of Europeans away from Africa, other than the French exodus from Algeria. In many countries of tropical Africa, the number of Europeans increased after independence because of a combination of new business openings and a flood of temporary personnel in a variety of technical assistance programs. Settlers also continued to flow in from Europe—especially to South Africa, Rhodesia, Kenya, and Angola—and some interesting exchanges of European population took place in the sixties, when liberal South Africans sometimes sought posts in the newly independent countries, while pro-colonialist settlers in places like Kenya tended to move to South Africa.

Other migratory streams involved the African educated elite. African universities were staffed almost entirely by expatriates in the immediate postwar decade, but by the early 1970s some parts of Africa were exporting some of their most qualified people. There were more Dahomeans and Togolese with university degrees working in France in recent years than French with university degrees working in Togo and Dahomey. There are more Nigerians employed today in American universities than Americans in Nigerian universities.

One very important but virtually unstudied aspect of migration within Africa in the past century is its epidemiological consequences. It is generally recognized that movement into an unfamiliar disease environment exacts some price in the form of increased morbidity and mortality for the migrants —sometimes for the receiving population as well. It is also recognized that this price is higher in some proportion to the previous degree of isolation of the sending from the receiving population. The disease cost of migration within a single continent or region could therefore be expected to be highest where the populations were comparatively isolated from one another and lowest where the general level of intercommunication was most intense. Since the general level of intercommunication in Africa at the beginning of the twentieth century was markedly lower than it was in most of Asia, Europe, or the Americas, African migration in the early colonial period implied increased mortality among the migrants—with mortality rates sometimes running as high as 100 to 300 per thousand per annum. Without more systematic study of African demographic history in this century, it is hard to know how long this phenomenon persisted, but it probably went on at a low level even after the Second World War. For earlier decades it seems likely, though not yet demonstrated, that African cities had a substantial excess of deaths over births, as did all other growth centers that attracted migratory labor. New diseases or strains of disease may have reached their home villages as well, and some recently published research suggests that the opening up of new trade routes had significant epidemiological consequences.[10]

People's ideas about migration are also a part of migration history, and in Africa these have changed in significant ways between the late 1940s and the early 1970s. In the immediate postwar years, some African voices protested against some aspects of labor migration, but the vocal African leadership had other concerns. For European economic planners, migration was a subhead under the general rubric, "Labor Problems," and the most generalized labor problem was a shortage of people to work for the wages European firms and governments wanted to offer.[11] Some economists had protested the inefficiency of oscillating labor in southern Africa far back into the interwar period, and the protests reappeared in the postwar era with increased strength but limited effectiveness. Other objections had to do with the social costs of having drastically unbalanced sex ratios both at the source and at the destination of the migrants. But it was not until the 1960s that African leadership began to be seriously alarmed by the extremely rapid growth of urban centers, at a time when urban rates of unemployment were often higher than 50 percent.

The search for an explanation and a remedy took several directions. Perhaps the earliest response of neoclassical economics was to point out that the people who flooded into the towns made their own assessments of the costs and the benefits; if they had not thought it worthwhile, they would not have come. And it was argued that, while oscillating migration on the South African model was wasteful, the free movement permitted in most of West Africa was a benefit to the sending and receiving regions alike.[12] By the late 1960s, however, other economists and sociologists began to be concerned with the seeming irrationality of the economic lure of higher urban wages, if the chance of a newcomer actually landing a job was poor indeed. The excitement of urban life, the "bright lights," the chance that "something might turn up" had to be added to the equation—along with the "Vegas principle" that people will gamble, even when they know the house takes its cut, leaving no chance at all of being a net winner after a long period of play. A few governments in tropical Africa, Kenya among them, began to take a serious look at future planning for urban growth with the explicit objective of reducing the flow of migrants to the capital. And the possibility of "influx control" on the South African model crossed the minds of some planners, even though it would have been politically disastrous to identify the precedent.

More recently, some of the younger economists of a vaguely neo-Marxian persuasion have begun another kind of reconsideration, drawing some of their ideas from "dependency theory" developed in the context of Latin America's relations with the more developed world. In 1972, Professor Samir Amin, a Franco-Egyptian who was then Director of the UN-sponsored Institut Africain de Développement et Planification (IDEP), held a conference in Dakar and edited a volume of its proceedings.[13] He and his colleagues argued that the neoclassical economists had made a mistake in concentrating on the cost-benefit assessment of the migrants themselves. Migrants played with cards stacked against them by the previous investment of capital, placed so as to maximize the return to European capitalists as a group, rather than the return from a particular investment. It was claimed that European planners and investors in Africa were consciously or unconsciously following a strategy that would concentrate on the export sector at the expense of the whole economy. The remedy proposed was to change the development strategy to one that would increase employment opportunities where people actually lived, rather than attracting migrants to new growth poles. Not only would this decrease economic dependence on Europe, it would also decrease economic dependence of the poorer parts of Africa on the richer. Some critics in this group argue that the piling up of unemployed migrants in the capital cities and port towns was not even an efficient way of exploiting African labor, but rather that it was one of the "contradictions" in the system. This unfortunate situation resulted when Europeans who had set out to attract people into wage labor with a combination of carrots and sticks discovered, like the apprentice sorcerer, that the stream was easier to start than to stop.

## NOTES

1. Colin W. Newbury, "Historical Aspects of Manpower and Migration in African South of the Sahara," in Peter Duignan and L. H. Gann, *Colonialism in Africa* (1969–75), 4:523–545, p. 536, based on data from S. Herbert Frankel, *Capital Investment in Africa* (London, 1938, p. 170). For recent general studies of African population and migration see John C. Caldwell and Chukuka Okonjo (eds.), *The Population of Tropical Africa* (New York, 1968), and William A. Hance, *Population, Migration, and Urbanization in Africa* (New York, 1970).

2. The classic statement of this case in a policy document is the despatch of the Third Earl Grey to the Governor of Ceylon, later copied into the instructions sent to other colonial governors. See Grey to Torrington, no. 22, 24 October 1848, printed in House of Commons Sessional Papers, 1849, xxxvi (1018), pp. 342–45, reprinted more recently in P. D. Curtin, *Imperialism* (New York, 1971), pp. 165–70. For the early history of taxation and forced migration see F. E. Sanderson, "The Development of Labour Migration from Nyasaland, 1891–1914," *Journal of African History*, 2:259–271.

3. Francis Wilson, *Labour in the South African Gold Mines 1911–1969* (Cambridge, 1972).

4. Simon E. Katzenellenbogen, "The Miner's Frontier, Transport and General Economic Development," in Duignan and Gann, *Colonialism in Africa*, 4:360–426, p. 416.

5. D. Hobart Houghton, *The South African Economy* (Cape Town, 1964), pp. 89–96.

6. Houghton, *South African Economy,* pp. 84–87.

7. Newbury, "Manpower and Migration," p. 530; Chandler Morse, Gordon Hadow, C. G. Hawes, O. T. Jenkins, and J. F. V. Philips, *Basutoland, Bechuanaland Protectorate and Swaziland: Report of an Economic Survey Mission* (London, 1960), pp. 365, 446–47.

8. J. Adomako-Sarfoh, "The Effects of the Expulsion of Migrant Workers on Ghana's Economy, with Particular Reference to the Cocoa Industry," in Samir Amin (ed.), *Modern Migrations in Western Africa,* (London, 1975), pp. 138–52.

9. Samir Amin, *Modern Migrations,* pp. 70–79.

10. Gerald W. Hartwig, "Economic Consequences of Long-Distance Trade in East Africa: The Disease Factor," *The African Studies Review,* 18:63–73 (September 1975); R. Mansell Prothero, *Migrants and Malaria in Africa* (Pittsburgh, 1965).

11. See, for example, Lord Hailey, *An African Survey Revised 1856* (London, 1957), pp. 1357ff.

12. Elliot J. Berg, "The Economics of the Migrant Labor System," in Hilda Kuper (ed.), *Urbanization and Migration in West Africa* (Berkeley, 1965), pp. 160–81.

13. Samir Amin, *Modern Migrations.*

# [10]

## Rural-Urban Mobility in South and Southeast Asia: Different Formulations, Different Answers

T. G. McGEE

And so the diversion of the population from agriculture is expressed in Russia, in the growth of towns . . ., suburbs, factory and commercial and industrial villages and townships, as well as non-agricultural migration. All these processes which have been and are rapidly developing in breadth and depth in the post-Reform period, are necessary components of capitalist development and are profoundly progressive as compared with the old forms of life.
—V. I. Lenin, *The Development of Capitalism in Russia*

## INTRODUCTION

The preceding quotation occurs at the conclusion of some twenty pages of analysis on a similar theme, which if read out of context might appear as a panegyric on the beneficial effects of capitalist development in moving population from agricultural to nonagricultural activities. The purpose of introducing the quotation is not to suggest that Lenin was a defender of capitalism; nor is it to argue that the experience of Russia before 1900 is identical to that of the countries of South and Southeast Asia which are the subject of this paper. Rather, the quotation catches the basic theme of the

199

paper: that an understanding of the reasons for and the features of internal mobility[1] within states of South and Southeast Asia rests upon the delineation of the broad processes of capitalist penetration of the region.

In *The Development of Capitalism in Russia,* Lenin shows how the growth of capitalism led to radical changes in the organization and production of agriculture and industry. The development of a commodity market for agricultural produce broke down the old precapitalist relationships and set up an economic differentiation among the peasantry, which created a basic dislocation force. At the same time, the growth of large-scale industry offered employment opportunities in urban areas and produced goods which began to put rural domestic producers out of operation. This forced another group from the countryside. These developments were associated with a growth in the means of transportation, which greatly facilitated the circulation of commodities as well as population mobility. For example, the length of the Russian railway system increased from 3,819 kilometers in 1865 to 29,063 kilometers by 1890; passengers increased from 10.6 million to 123.6 million in approximately the same period, and there was a considerable growth in the volume of freight on inland waterways. The growth of the nonagricultural population dislocated from the rural areas was clearly shown in the growth of towns. Thus between 1863 and 1897 towns in European Russia with populations of over 50,000 increased by 31. The population of these towns grew from 1.6 million to 6.3 million, at a rate almost double that of the total population. (See Lenin, 1899, pp. 556–668.)

The changes induced by the growth of capitalism which produced this substantial rural-urban mobility in nineteenth-century Russia are now occurring in South and Southeast Asia. This does not mean that the process of capitalist penetration is the same as that experienced in Russia, for in these countries it is *peripheral capitalism* that is at work. In addition, the demographic, economic, and social components of these Asian societies are different from those of nineteenth-century Russia, which caused the penetration of capitalism to vary in its impact. However, an important group of studies in the political economy of the Third World by such writers as Baran (1957), Frank (1967), and Amin (1974a) has begun to delineate the major features of peripheral capitalism, making it possible to graft these ideas onto the earlier formulations of Lenin. In addition, the conceptual framework of the peasant systems suggested by Chayanov (1966) and Franklin (1965; 1967) greatly aid the analysis of internal mobility in South and Southeast Asia.

It would have been impossible to present a comprehensive review of internal mobility in a region as large as South and Southeast Asia. Instead, I have had to be selective—theoretically, geographically, and in the type of mobility that I have chosen to study. Theoretically, I have attempted to formulate an explanatory model that focuses first upon processive change, and only secondarily upon situational change, as the major force inducing mobility. Geographically, I have generally limited my examples to the two largest countries of the region, Indonesia and India, where I have some intuition for the value of data. Finally, I have concentrated upon rural-urban mobility, since I consider this the most important type of mobility in South and Southeast Asia. It is important not only because of the volume of migrants engaged in this form of mobility but also because of its major significance for the future development of these societies.

With these limitations, the present essay is divided into four main parts. In the first section I will discuss the limitations of conventional approaches to the study of internal mobility. In the second section there is a brief discussion of the pattern of urbanization in the region to provide a setting for the introduction of an alternative model for the study of rural-urban mobility. Finally, one example of rural-urban mobility—circulatory migration in West Java—is described in some detail as an illustration of a type of mobility that may become widespread in countries where economic development is slow, population is dense, and employment prospects are limited.

## CONVENTIONAL APPROACHES TO THE STUDY OF MOBILITY

Three main theoretical frameworks have provided the set of assumptions underlying the major studies of rural-urban mobility: (1) the conventional economic approach, (2) the situational approach, and (3) the historical approach.

*The conventional economic approach.*[2] This approach to the study of rural-urban mobility takes the unequal geographic distribution of the "factors" of production (e.g., labor, capital, natural resources, and land) as a given apriori and assumes that this will determine the unequal remuneration of these factors. Thus labor will move from a region where it is abundant and where capital is scarce to a region where labor is scarce and capital is abundant, assuming that natural resources are equally distributed. This approach assumes some form of economically "rational" choice on the part of the migrant involved in the labor transfer. A rather more sophisticated formulation is the basis of the influential work of Todaro (1969; 1971). Todaro's model assumes that the decision of the migrant to relocate is the function of two variables: the gap in income between the city and the countryside, and the possibility of finding employment in the city. A knowledge of these variables enables us to predict likely migratory behavior.

Amin (1974*b*) offers the following critique of Todaro's model. First, the approach is descriptive, not explanatory. The geographic distribution of factors is primarily the result of the development pattern, which in the case of South and Southeast Asia has been characterized by capitalist penetration within the political framework of colonialism. Thus, for example, the marked differences in the income levels of the population of the West-coast states of peninsular Malaysia and the East and Far North are a consequence of the pattern of colonial development. It has not led to major flows of migration from the poorer states to the richer regions, as Todaro's model would predict. Indeed Todaro's model is nothing more than the increasingly criticized push-pull hypothesis of migration dressed-up in economic jargon.[3]

Second, the approach assumes economic rationality on the part of the migrant. The decision to migrate is presumably made with full knowledge of the variables of income and potential employment. Surely this is an inaccurate assumption. Migrants from the countryside in South and Southeast Asia are moving to cities, where the rates of growth are double that of the national population, where unemployment (particularly in specific age groups) is high, and where poverty and squalor are a major part of city life. Yet they continue to move to the cities, dislocated by processes deriving from the pattern of capitalist penetration over time. The introduction of individual land ownership, the development of cash crops for export, the increased monetization of the South and Southeast Asian countryside, technological changes, and the marketing of the cheap industrial products manufactured in the developed countries have all led to new patterns of social and productive relationships in the countryside. This process has made some groups marginal, forcing them to migrate, and has created affluence among others, who have also migrated to the cities in a process of upward mobility. It is among this latter group that economic rationality may be a more important factor. Unfortunately, there is no comprehensive study of this process throughout the region.[4] Certainly it can be argued that rural-urban migrants are reacting to the impact of these broader processes, which are part of the national system, and that their decisions are a consequence of the system.

*The situational approach.* The majority of studies of rural-urban mobility are characterized by the situational approach. Broadly, these studies have two theoretical thrusts. The first rests upon the model of rural-urban differences and focuses upon the problems of migrant adaptation, as migrants move from one milieu to another. The second prong of this research concentrates upon the decisions of the migrants. I will not cite the familiar inadequacies that characterize the model of rural-urban differences developed out of Western experience when it is applied to South and Southeast Asia.[5] Suffice it to say that one of the major criticisms of the rural-urban continuum is that it does not accurately describe the movement of people from rural to urban areas. Such movement brings to the city people whose values, attitudes, and institutions have been developed in the countryside. These personal attributes do not simply disappear in the urban environment, especially when the rural migrant moves within a network of close personal ties and information which aids his assimilation into the urban environment. In other words, the model of urban and rural differences is inaccurate.

The second thrust within this broad situational approach focuses upon the decisions of the migrant involved in movement. In particular, the work of the geographer Wolpert (1965), drawing on the research of other social scientists, is representative of this approach. In his 1965 paper, Wolpert postulated a framework in which potential migrants are perceived as receiving a number of negative and positive impulses from different potential destinations as well as from their present environment. In this situation the individual's decision to move will be formulated in terms of the concept of "place utility," which is defined as "the net composite utility derived from the individual's integration at some position in space." The utility of a new location must be greater than the present location for migration to occur. Wolpert's theories have had some impact on migration studies in South and Southeast Asia. For instance, Mukherji expanded Wolpert's ideas in a study of internal migration in India (Mukherji, 1975; see also Du Toit, 1975).

However, most of the studies of population movement in South and Southeast Asia have been carried out within the framework of ideas developed in the model of the rural-urban continuum. In this category I would also place a majority of the many excellent empirical studies of internal migration in the region that have emerged over the last twenty years, despite their focus upon largely demographic research such as migration differentials and flows.[6]

Of course, the strongest argument in favor of the situational approach is that external determinants such as population density and political and social structures will vary from situation to situation. Thus a particular constellation of these determinants is often an important element inducing migration. For instance, there is ample evidence from my studies of the internal migration of Malays in West Malaysia that the traditional cultural practice of *merantau,* in which men left a matrilineal society for periods of time to travel, was well adapted to the patterns of short-term labor recruitment into government jobs introduced by the British in the nineteenth century; men from Minangkabau areas figured prominently in the migration streams (McGee, 1969). The problem is that there is no way of predicting that two similar situations will not have different rates of out-migration. Only through an understanding of the manner in which processive forces such as education, technological change, and changing forms of production diffuse into each situation can the real causes of mobility be investigated. The problem of giving priority to each situation, and within each situation to the decision-making process of the individual migrant, is that individual motivations are nothing more than rationalizations of behavior within a system. This does not take account of the fact that this behavior is caused by the system of which the individual is part.

*The historical approach.* There have been many historical models of population movement through time, often concentrating upon typologies,[7] but few have attempted to relate population movements through time to the model of the "demographic transition." An ambitious attempt made by Zelinsky (1971) has had considerable impact on geographic studies of migration in the Third World.[8] Zelinsky has developed an evolutionary model of spatial behavior which argues:

> There are definite, patterned regularities in the growth of personal mobility through space-time during recent history, and these regularities comprise an essential component of the modernization process.
>
>                                        [Zelinsky, 1971, pp. 221–22.]

He then goes on to postulate unilinear stages of the mobility transition, which are related to levels of socioeconomic development that are linked to a phase in the demographic transition. Five main stages are delineated. First, there is a preindustrial, traditional phase of low residential mobility and natural increase. Second, there is the early transitional phase, in which a sudden increase in fertility is accompanied by large-scale rural-urban migration and the colonization of domestic and other areas. The late transitional phase is characterized by a decline in the rates of natural increase and of rural-urban and rural-rural migration. Various forms of residential circulation increase, particularly inter- and intraurban movement. The fourth phase, the advanced industrial society, experiences a leveling off of rates of natural increase, and a further decline in rural-urban and rural-rural migration. Finally, the super-advanced society of the future will probably have a substantial decline in residential mobility because communication developments will allow place of work to be brought closer to place of residence. In some cases place of work and of residence will be the same.

Most of the countries in the region under discussion are clearly in the early transitional phase. To quote Zelinsky:

> The onset of modernization (or more precisely the onset of major changes in the reproductive budget in Phase B, along with the general rise in material welfare or expectations and improvements in transport and communications) brings with it a great shaking loose of migrants from the countryside.
>
>                                        [Zelinsky, 1971, p. 236.]

This is the process analyzed by Lenin which was paraphrased in the introduction to this essay.

But the empirical evidence for the mobility patterns being experienced by these societies raises questions as to whether they are experiencing the same mobility transition. First, the theory of the mobility transition assumes that the same processes of modernization are occurring in this region as occurred in Western Europe—in fact, the processes that produced societies in which the majority of people became urban dwellers. While the impact of colonial powers in the Asian region certainly developed a large number of urban settlements, particularly large port cities such as Bombay, Madras, Calcutta, Singapore, and Batavia, the period of colonial rule did not see "a great shaking loose of migrants" from the countryside of the various states. Rather, selective and often recruited labor migration (much of it international) was the main feature of rural-urban and rural-rural migration. Overall patterns of mobility continued at the first phase of the mobility transition. In the period of colonial devolution since the end of World War II, rural-urban migration has considerably accelerated, particularly in the early part of the period, in countries such as India, Pakistan, Burma, Malaya, and Indonesia, where political disturbance in the countryside was often the major dislocating force. Since 1955, with the exception of the former French colonies of Indochina, political disturbance has not played such a significant role in dislocating rural populations, and processes connected with the form of economic development have become more important. (See McGee, 1967 and 1971*b*.) In the heavily populated countries of the region—India, Indonesia, Sri Lanka, and more recently Bangladesh—the level of urbanization has increased only slowly. In other countries, such as Malaysia and the Philippines, the level of urbanization has risen during the period since 1955, although it has led to an increased concentration of urban population in the largest metropolitan area. Thus the mobility transition appears to have some applicability to these latter countries but is of no great value in the heavily populated countries such as India, Indonesia, and Bangladesh.

Zelinsky's model suffers from the assumption that societies will necessarily pass through these various phases and will experience the same set of processes. At least in demographic terms none of these societies in South and Southeast Asia has the possibility of emigration, as did the societies of Western Europe. Secondly, demographic processes are different: natural increase is higher in the cities and this contributes an important part of urban increase. At the same time the ability of the cities to absorb the rural population into viable occupations is inadequate, and the rates of unemployment and underemployment reinforce this observation. Is it possible then that one will see a dual pattern in South and Southeast Asia, in which one group of countries will bog down in the early transitional phase while the other group will move beyond it? The analysis of urbanization in the Asian region that will be presented in the next section lends credence to this view.

This brief review of the major conventional approaches to the study of mobility has presented a broad critique of the theoretical underpinnings of the major approaches to the study of rural-urban mobility. The major critique presented is that the approaches either ignore or misinterpret the broad processive changes at a societal level which can be subsumed within the process of the penetration of capitalism. In the next section an attempt is made to review the facts concerning the urbanization process in the region as a basis for the structural model of rural-urban movement which is presented in the following part.

## PATTERNS OF URBANIZATION IN SOUTH AND SOUTHEAST ASIA

As Table 1 shows, South and Southeast Asia is one of the least urbanized regions in the underdeveloped world. Only Middle and Southern Africa and East Africa have lower levels of urbanization. What is more, the proportion of population in the rural areas of the region has fallen slowly in the last twenty years. Thus if Kingsley Davis's estimates are correct, the percentage of Southeast Asia's population in rural areas has decreased only from 86 percent in 1950 to 80 percent in 1970. The proportion for South Central Asia fell by 2.3 percent in the same period. These figures are, of course, subject

Table 1

Trends in Urban Population in the Underdeveloped World, 1950–1970

| Region | Percentage Urban | | | Change in Percentage Urban | |
|---|---|---|---|---|---|
| | 1950 | 1960 | 1970 | 1950–70 | 1960–70 |
| Northern Africa | 24.6 | 29.6 | 34.6 | 10.0 | 5.0 |
| Western Africa | 10.6 | 14.7 | 19.7 | 9.1 | 5.0 |
| Eastern Africa | 5.5 | 7.5 | 9.9 | 4.4 | 2.4 |
| Middle and Southern Africa | 6.6 | 11.6 | 15.4 | 8.8 | 3.8 |
| Middle America | 39.2 | 46.2 | 53.0 | 13.8 | 6.8 |
| Caribbean | 35.2 | 38.5 | 42.5 | 7.3 | 4.0 |
| Tropical South America | 35.8 | 44.7 | 53.1 | 17.3 | 8.4 |
| East Asia (excl. Japan) | 12.1 | 18.0 | 25.3 | 13.2 | 7.3 |
| *Southeast Asia* | 13.6 | 16.6 | 20.1 | 6.5 | 3.5 |
| Southwest Asia | 24.3 | 29.5 | 35.5 | 11.3 | 6.0 |
| *South Central Asia* | 15.4 | 16.4 | 17.7 | 2.3 | 1.3 |

Source: Kingsley Davis, *World Urbanization 1950-70*. Volume I: *Basic Data for Cities, Countries, and Regions*, Population Monograph Series no. 4 (Berkeley: University of California Press, 1969).

to revision, but the available census data from the 1970–71 round of censuses in the region support this picture. Thus the level of urbanization in India, which makes up a major portion of the population of this region, increased by only 1.9 percent in the period between 1961 and 1971 to reach a level of 19.8 percent. Census figures for Sri Lanka reveal a similar trend, which leads one analyst of these data to conclude that "there has been no perceptible acceleration in the rate of urban growth in the period between 1963 and 1971" (Gunatilleke, 1972, p. 1). In Indonesia, which contains 42 percent of the population of Southeast Asia, urban dwellers increased from 14.9 percent in 1961 to 18.8 percent in 1971. Although I have not been able to extract figures for Bangladesh, I suspect that a smilar trend exists.

Thus in considering the four countries that make up almost 82 percent of the population of the region under discussion, three main points emerge. First, urbanization levels have increased only slowly. Second, the countryside has absorbed a major part of the total population increase; in India, for example, nonurban areas absorbed 78.6 million of the 108.3 million total population increase in the period 1961–71. Third, despite the fact that the population resident in urban areas grew considerably from rural-urban migration, natural increase, and urban reclassification, the actual volume of net rural-urban migration was only a small trickle out of the potential sending population. This is well illustrated in the case of India where between 1951 and 1961 net rural-urban migration amounted to only 6 million of a potential rural sending population of 350 million.

In these heavily populated countries, therefore, the urbanization process—"that great shaking loose of migrants from the countryside," to use Zelinsky's phrase—has hardly begun. This raises many questions concerning the future of urban centers in this region. Even allowing for the hopeful (perhaps excessively hopeful) possibility that birth control programs will reduce rates of population increase, it does appear that the long-term perspective is for increasingly large metropoli.[9] Fairly conservative estimates suggest that Bangkok-Thonburi will reach 13 million by 2000 A.D., that Jakarta could reach 20 million, and that the prospect for Indian cities could approach science fiction—e.g., a Calcutta of 66 million. It may be that as new urban hierarchies develop, the urbanizing population will be funneled into new and medium-sized towns. But present trends do not give much credence to this possibility.

The incipient nature of this rural-urban migration raises questions about the possibility of providing employment for these urban populations. Already, the cities of these countries have high unemployment rates, and large proportions of the population are eking out an existence in the low-income "informal sectors" of the cities' economic structures. Despite the growth of industrialization in such a country as India, there is no indication that Indian

centers can create viable employment opportunities if the rural-urban movement accelerates and releases the very large volume of rural migrants that
would be involved in lifting the urbanization level even to 50 percent.

Faced with this sort of future, planners have reacted in two ways. The
first is an optimistic, pragmatic reaction that seeks to develop strategies
designed to cope with these developments. One example of this approach is
a plan described by Jones which

> would have Java with an area of less than a quarter of France and about a
> third of Japan, sustaining about 7 "million" cities and two massive "urban
> corridors," one from Jakarta through Bogor to Bandung (comparable in
> population to the present Boston-Washington metropolis in the U.S.), and
> the other in the Surabaja-Malang-Kediri triangle. A third agglomeration
> could well develop linking Jogjakarta and Surakarta in Central Java. And it
> is important to recognise that despite such massive urban development, the
> rural population of Java would still be larger than it is at the moment, barring
> catastrophies or highly unlikely trends in fertility.
>
> [Jones, 1972, p. 15.]

This spatial planning strategy offers no critique of an overall developmental strategy which assumes rapid urbanization. It is often associated
(indeed it must be associated) with programs designed to increase agricultural productivity to feed these rapidly growing urban populations. But only
too frequently the effect of these programs is to dislocate rural populations.

The other reaction, represented in a recent article by Kingsley Davis
(1975), can only be described as fatalistic. The following citations will indicate
its general thread.

> If development is the goal, a policy of trying to keep Asia's rapidly expanding
> population in the countryside is misguided. The cities are also overcrowded,
> but for reasons well known in location theory, they are the chief seats of
> growth-sensitive activities."
>
> [Davis, 1975, p. 84.]

> How can giant cities be crowded and have a high level of consumption at
> the same time? . . .
>
> One must therefore face the possibility that in Asia "development" and
> "personal consumption" will part company. . . . Further massive growth in
> urban populations rules out a democratic consumer-sovereign adaptation
> leading instead to a minutely regulated communal dictatorship with lower
> personal consumption and high collective use of whatever resources and
> surpluses are available.
>
> [Davis, 1975, pp. 84–85.]

> Development without prosperity, urbanization without opulence, without
> sophistication, without urbanity—that is apparently the path.
>
> [Davis, 1975, p. 85.]

The first group of planners envisions these countries following along the capitalist path to the consumer-orientated affluence of full urbanized Western capitalist societies. The second body of thought does not consider this possible and foresees an inevitable persistence of poverty, which will force political and social reorganization. It may be argued that the incipient rural-urban migration pattern of the countries already discussed is not so grave a problem in other countries of the region. Singapore, a city-state, is in the fortunate position of being able to close its boundaries to international migration; with a rapid fall in the rate of natural increase in the 1970s, it should not be faced with severe problems of creating employment or managing its urban environment.[10] Malaysia, while still faced with grave problems of creating sufficient urban employment opportunities for its Malay majority, has already exceeded a 50 percent level of urbanization and has embarked on ambitious programs of rural development, designed to siphon off rural population from overpopulated areas (Pryor, 1975*b*). The Philippines and Thailand will still experience considerable rural-urban migration over the next thirty years, but assuming that political conditions improve, there is a possibility that they can manage the urban transformation. Finally, the former French Indochinese territories are now developing within socialist frameworks; at the moment they are all experiencing deurbanization (except for North Vietnam), and we can expect that the major spatial focus will be on the socialist transformation of the countryside in the first few years.[11]

To summarize, it appears that the major problems and potential of rural-urban mobility are likely to occur in the heavily populated countries of Bangladesh, India, Sri Lanka, and Indonesia. Despite the adoption by these countries of differing mixes of foreign aid, state involvement, and priorities in their development plans, their central goal is still to move toward industrialized, urbanized, high mass-consumption societies similar to those of the rich countries.[12] However, the demographic and economic facts appear to be that this can be accomplished only within the structural context of a continuing increase in the agricultural work force, at least in the next fifty years. At the same time there will be some shift in the industrial structure toward industry and services. Thus this developmental strategy involves the creation of massive employment opportunities in both rural and urban areas. Given the fact that in all these countries there already exist what Bose (1971) labels "pools" of underemployed and unemployed populations, this will exacerbate any effort to increase employment opportunities.

Of course, there is nothing new in emphasizing the employment problem in the Third World. From the mid-1960s, a rapid proliferation of papers by individual writers and by such international organizations as the International Labor Office and United Nations' regional organizations (see Morse, 1970; Lewis, 1967; and Grant, 1971) has drawn attention to the fact that an increasing proportion of the labor force of the rapidly growing cities of the

Third World is not being absorbed into what has been labeled "full productive employment" (see Friedmann and Sullivan, 1972, p. 1). In addition to high rates of unemployment among the urban populations, often young and relatively well educated, there is "a reserve army of low-productivity workers in rural and urban areas, among whom the waste of human potential is massive" (Turnham and Jaeger, 1971, p. 10). What is more, this pattern does not appear to vary greatly between the countries of the Third World that have experienced rapid economic growth and those that have had slower rates of development. For instance, in Brazil, despite comparatively high rates of economic growth in the 1960s, unemployment and underemployment have increased during the 1950s and 1960s (see Diégues, 1966). By contrast, in Indonesia, with comparatively low rates of economic growth, unemployment has also increased (see Keddie, 1973).

The statistics presented by a group of studies focusing on this problem in the three continents of the Third World, even if subject to the problems of the applicability of data, all tell the same story—a picture of a rapidly increasing labor force in both rural and urban areas, increasing rates of unemployment, and absorption into low-productivity informal activities in urban areas, which will accelerate in the 1970s and 1980s in most of the Third World countries.[13] Thus, in 1970 the International Labor Office estimated that in the 1970s over 300 million new jobs would be needed in the underdeveloped world, outside agriculture. The reasons for this situation are well known: population explosion, urban growth, and limited employment opportunities generated by capital-intensive industrialization have combined to create the problem. For instance, the Economic Commission for Latin America estimates that while industrial production has increased its share of the Gross Domestic Product from 11 percent in 1925 to 23 percent in 1967, the proportion of the total labor force employed in industry has remained stable at 14 percent. At the same time, employment in agriculture and mining has declined from 60 percent of the labor force in 1925 to 43 percent in 1969. As a consequence, the construction and service sectors have absorbed the redistribution of the labor force, increasing from 26 percent in 1925 to 43 percent in 1969, of which approximately 50 percent are in the categories of "other services" and "unspecified activities," in which many of the urban informal sector participants are located (Frank, 1972, citing publications of the Economic Commission for Latin America). Similar patterns have been observed in Africa and Asia, but they have not yet reached the level of Latin America. As Weeks has perceptively commented, the failure to create employment structures that can successfully absorb labor in high-productivity activity is also a symptom "of a development strategy seeking to reproduce a Western consumer goods economy" (Weeks, 1971, p. 69) in the less-developed countries which rely on Western-derived capital-intensive techniques.

It must be obvious that I am skeptical about urbanization levels increasing to more than 50 percent in the heavily populated countries of Asia in the next fifty years. Assuming that there is no structural transformation and that various mixtures of state capitalism continue, I envisage increasing labor involution in countryside and cities: that is, a continuing absorption of labor into low-productivity, labor-intensive activities, which the International Labor Organization has labeled rather inadequately the "informal sector." There is nothing new in this position, which was first developed in 1968 (see Armstrong and McGee, 1968), but the prospect of continuing rural-urban involution raises important questions of the types and patterns of rural-urban mobility that will prevail over the next few decades. In the next section, I will present a structural model of rural-urban mobility that takes account of the processes delineated in this section.

## A STRUCTURAL MODEL OF RURAL-URBAN MOBILITY

In the introduction I observed that many of the conventional approaches to the study of rural-urban mobility were inadequate because they failed to recognize the important role of processes operating at international and national levels. By far the most important process is the penetration of capitalism into the precapitalist system of production that I illustrated by reference to Lenin's study of Russia. In the context of the peripheral economies of South and Southeast Asia, this process appears to be best conceptualized within the framework of the well-established dualistic model of the economic organization of these underdeveloped countries. Initially this dualistic model, developed by Boeke (1953) and Lewis (1958), distinguished between capitalist towns and subsistence countryside, but the work of Geertz drew attention to the existence of a dual economic structure in urban areas as well. In his work on a Javanese town he pointed out that the town was divided between a *firm-centered* economic sector

> where trade and industry occur through a set of impersonally defined social institutions which organize a variety of specialized occupations with respect to some particular productive or distributive end, and a second sector labelled the *bazaar economy* based on . . . the independent activities of a set of highly competitive traders who relate to one another mainly by means of an incredible volume of *ad hoc* acts of exchange.
>
> [Geertz, 1963a, p. 28.]

This model has been greatly expanded in the work of Santos (1971 and 1975).

From the point of view of rural-urban migration, the most fruitful concepts arise out of the work of Chayanov (1966) and Franklin (1965; 1969), which distinguished between three main systems of production, in which "the fundamental differentiator is the labour commitment of the enterprise" (Franklin, 1965, p. 148). In this framework the peasant economy is characterized by the commitment of the *chef d'enterprise* to the utilization of his family (kin). The capitalist and socialist systems of production are different because "labour becomes a commodity to be hired and dismissed by the enterprise" (Franklin, 1965, p. 148). This is a scheme which, as Franklin points out, is not impinged upon by the agricultural-industrial division, or by the rural-urban division. I have used this conceptual model for much of my research on street vendors in Hong Kong and other Southeast Asian cities. (see McGee, 1973; 1974*a*; 1975*a*; 1976.) The concept has not gone without criticism (see Isaac, 1974, and McGee, 1974*b*), but I would still argue that peasant systems of production exist in the majority of these cities.

If this conceptual framework is accepted, then it is possible to suggest a model for the analysis of rural-urban mobility, as set forth in Figure 1. In the diagram, the relative proportions of the capitalist sector and the peasant sector in the countryside and in the city represent the number of workers in each system. It should be stressed that this is primarily a model of labor mobility, although some other types of mobility, such as retirement to the rural peasant sector from the urban capitalist sector, may be regarded as a

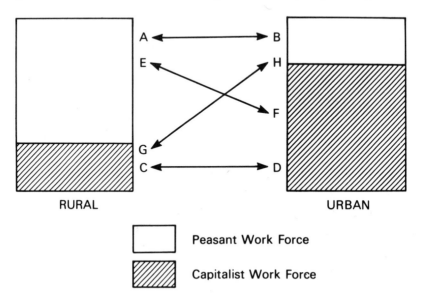

RURAL                                                                                    URBAN

▢  Peasant Work Force

▨  Capitalist Work Force

FIGURE 1. Structural setting of rural-urban/urban-rural mobility

form of social movement. A further feature is that the rural capitalist sector would include plantations, mineral works, and smaller towns between 5,000 and 20,000. Some rural peasant workers such as street vendors would be resident in these towns. In urban areas it is difficult to place some types of occupations in the correct sector; thus daily laborers who earn wages and also work as hawkers, for instance, would be in the capitalist system and the peasant system at the same time. But the majority of the labor force can be clearly placed in one of the four sectors. Government employees are something of a problem but I have assumed that they are part of the capitalist sector.

Figure 1 suggests that there are five main types of rural-urban mobility. The first, A——B movement, is most frequently circulatory or seasonal migration and involves two-way movement between the peasant sectors of countryside and city. In this type of mobility there will also be permanent migration, in both directions. The second type of rural-urban mobility, C——D, involves a shift from the capitalist sector of the countryside to the capitalist sector of urban areas. In my work in Malaysia I found that transfer of government servants was a major component of this type of migration. Third, there is a movement from the rural peasant sector to the urban capitalist sector, E——F. This was the major migratory stream occurring during the urban transformation of the Western countries. In South and Southeast Asia at the moment this form of migration appears to be made up of two main types of migrants: the first type are migrants who have been educated too well for the countryside; the second type are unskilled persons who have been forced off the land. Traditionally, during the colonial period there was a certain amount of circulatory migration in response to recruited labor, and this continues for instance in India. (See Bose, 1971.) There are potential problems of work adjustment in this type of mobility, but in general in this Asian region they do not appear to have been severe. Movement from the urban capitalist sector back to the rural peasant sector, F——E, is largely retirement migration. Finally, movement between the capitalist sector of the countryside and the informal sector of the urban areas, G——H, is not common, except when prices of primary produce fall dramatically. This model, of course, takes no account of mobility within the urban and the rural sectors, but this movement may be quite significant. Thus, my research on the occupational mobility of street vendors in Hong Kong indicates a prior occupational history of factory work in the capitalist sector. There is also ample evidence that peasants in the countryside are recruited to work on plantations, i.e., in the rural capitalist sector.

Figure 1 is, of course, a static model, describing various types of rural-urban mobility. Figure 2 is an attempt to present a dynamic model of possible migratory results that could occur according to the rates of growth of the labor force in the capitalist and peasant sectors during a fifty-year period. The assumptions upon which these projections are based are very simple and can easily be criticized, but they are open to modification. The diagram is constructed on the following assumptions: (1) that the urban and the rural labor force will have equal rates of natural increase during the fifty years; (2) that the labor force will double every twenty-five years.

The diagram presents three possible developmental sequences in a hypothetical country that has 100 million workers in 1975. Structural setting A assumes that the rural and urban capitalist sectors will absorb a large proportion of the labor force increase as the urbanization level increases from 20 to 60 percent. This would mean that 248 million additional workers would be added to the capitalist sector in this fifty-year period, while the peasant rural sector would also grow. But the major migratory stream would be from the rural peasant sector to the urban capitalist sector. This developmental path could be accomplished only with massive industrialization and a very high rate of economic growth.

Structural setting B assumes a much slower increase in the urbanization level, to only 40 percent; consequently the peasant sector in rural and urban areas would be expected to absorb much more of the labor increase. There would still have to be an expansion of jobs in the capitalist sectors, both in the rural and urban areas, of some 128 million. Thus there would be a reduction in the volume of migration from peasant-rural to urban-capitalist, but peasant rural to peasant urban migration would become more important. This developmental path assumes a slower rate of economic growth than structural setting A.

Finally, structural setting C represents a truly involutionary situation, in which neither the level of urbanization nor the proportion of workers in the various sectors changes over the fifty-year period. In this highly unlikely situation, the peasant sector would have to absorb a majority of the labor force. Even so, the capitalist sector would have to provide 72 million jobs in a situation of very limited economic growth.

Of course, this dynamic model of rural-urban mobility takes no account of such factors as a fall in the birthrate or technological developments which would allow greater agricultural productivity. Nor does it take into account the contradictions that emerge with the penetration of capitalism, e.g., that new techniques of agricultural productivity can force people to leave the rural peasant sector, or that the expansion of capital-intensive industrial production provides insufficient capacity to absorb more than a small proportion of the future labor force. Of the three developmental sequences, the migration pattern described in structural setting B most closely approaches the situation of the heavily populated Asian countries described above. Indeed a case study carried out by Dr. Shekhar Mukherji, in which this struc-

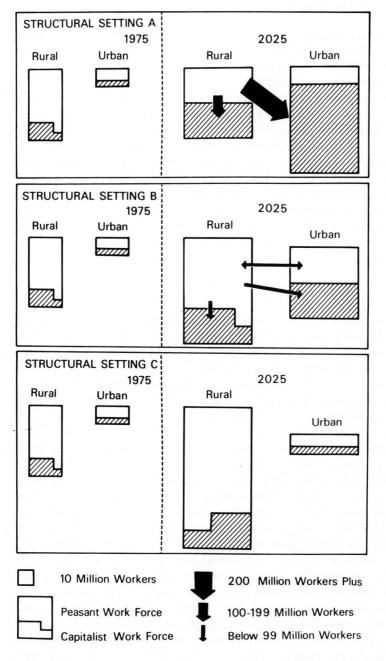

FIGURE 2. Dynamic model of structural setting of rural-urban mobility, 1975 and 2025

tural model was applied to India, and which assumed the continuation of
trends of the past twenty years in urbanization, migration, natural increase,
and redistribution within the various sectors of the labor force, strongly
supported structural setting B.[14]

In this setting, there would have to be continued absorption of the rural
labor force in both capitalist and peasant sectors as well as substantial growth
of the labor force in both sectors of the urban areas. In such a situation
circulatory migration between the peasant sectors of the countryside and the
city would greatly aid the process of absorption, while permanent movement
from countryside to city would also be of help. Because the former type of
movement has been little documented in Asia and because it may become
a crucial mechanism in the process of labor absorption in a situation of slow
economic growth in these labor surplus economies, the next section will be
devoted to a case study of circulatory migration in West Java.

## THE CASE OF WEST JAVA[15]

The island of Java is one of the most densely populated regions in South
and Southeast Asia. In 1971 it contained almost 63 percent of Indonesia's
population in only 7 percent of its area. This gave rise to extremely high
population densities of 477 per square kilometer, compared to the Indonesian average of 51 persons per square kilometer. By comparison, India had
170 persons and Sri Lanka 192 persons per square kilometer in 1970. The
western third of the island of Java, which includes the province of West Java
and the special capital district of Jakarta, contains only 2.5 percent of the land
area and 22 percent of the population of 120 million. It is a classic underdeveloped area, with an annual per capita income of less than U.S. $50, and
with the bulk of the labor force engaged in subsistence agriculture. With
limited access to medical care and post-primary education, it is not surprising
that the annual rate of population growth is 2.1 percent and that life expectancy at birth is only 44. Nevertheless this region is one of the most urbanized
in Indonesia, with 27 percent of its population resident in urban areas in 1971.
The presence of Jakarta, the national capital, with a population of 4.5 million
in 1971, contributes significantly to this urbanization level. If Jakarta is removed from the urban hierarchy, the urbanization level sinks to 12 percent.
There are, however, several other sizeable urban settlements, notably Bandung (1971, 1.2 million); Bogor (1971, 196,000); Cirebon (1971, 179,000); Taksik-
malaya (1971, 136,000), and some other smaller centers below 100,000. In 1971
agriculture and trade dominated the labor force in the rural areas, while
trade and services prevailed in the urban areas. Hugo estimated that between one-half and two-thirds of the labor force were in the "informal sec-

tor," which can be equated with the urban and rural peasant sectors. The structural setting is thus very similar to structural setting B in Figure 2.

Together with Java, West Java has increased its population dramatically since Dutch colonial rule began. In 1815, Java's population was estimated at 4.6 million; by 1930 it had increased to 41.7 million and by 1971 to 76.1 million. Urban increase has accounted for only a small proportion of this population increase; much of the growth has been absorbed in agricultural areas, in a process that Geertz has described as agricultural involution (Geertz, 1963b). West Java's experience was somewhat similar; its population increased from 10.8 million in 1930 to 21.6 million in 1971. In the same period the urban population of the region grew from 1 million to 7.2 million. Much of the increase was due to the growth of Jakarta, which increased from 0.5 million in 1930 to 4.5 million in 1970. This increase did not serve as a safety valve for the West Java rural population, as the proportion of West Javan migrants declined from 73.7 percent to 42.2 percent of all migrants.

Three main types of rural-urban movement have characterized the region: (1) daily commuting from the peri-urban areas of Jakarta and Bandung, involving return to locations outside the cities' boundaries each evening; (2) permanent migration, involving continuing residence within the cities for more than six months; (3) circular migration, involving people who circulate between the villages and the cities without ever taking up permanent residence. It is this last category which has increased in volume and importance over the last five or six years. Hugo has shown how the rapid growth of cheap public transportation involving small buses has been the technological development that enabled circulatory migration to become so important. Also, the strongly seasonal nature of rice growing creates periods of labor slackness when the landless have to seek work elsewhere. Political problems associated with in-migration restrictions and the inadequacy of census data have precluded a reliable estimate of the contribution of circular migration to the total migration streams flowing into and out of Jakarta. But there are strong indications that the majority of circulatory migrants are moving between the rural and urban peasant sectors. One survey in Bandung showed that 66 percent of the West Javan migrants had entered "traditional occupations" compared to 44 percent of the migrants outside West Java.

In an effort to describe in detail the features of this circulatory migration, Hugo surveyed fourteen villages chosen from a wide spectrum of situations. F'e found that in nine of the surveyed villages circular migration was the major strategy adopted by migrants. In two other villages, close to Jakarta a\ud Bandung, commuting dominated; in only three villages, some distance fiom the urban areas, was permanent migration dominant. It must be stressed that these villages are an average of 190 kilometers from Jakarta and 129 kilometers from Bandung. Hugo found that in virtually all these villages, growing population pressure, the limited success of the green revolution, and the replacement of the traditional *ani-ani* harvesting knives by sickles meant that more than 75 percent of the household heads in the villages had been forced to seek employment off the land. Because rural employment opportunities were limited, they turned mostly to work in Jakarta and to a lesser extent in Bandung.

The pattern of circular migration that has developed relies on village groups. Migrants travel in groups to the city; their entry into the city is facilitated by groups from their village already present; jobs are found (or created) for them by fellow villagers; villagers often live together, sleeping ten to a room or alternating the use of sleeping space. This is predominantly single migration, and the majority of these migrants are males. Most enter bazaar-type activities, such as street trading and *becak* driving. Some also engage in illegal activities such as prostitution. Each village tends to specialize in one occupation or one activity, such as bread-making. City authorities have attempted to eliminate these activities, which are regarded as unproductive and unsightly. This naturally leads to rampant bribery. Circulatory migrants maintain very close contact with their families in the villages. The average frequency of return is once every three weeks, but there is a constant flow of remittances and information back to the villages. Hugo calculates that remittances make up half the total income of the circulatory migrants' households.

Obviously the movement of a majority of circulatory migrants between the rural and urban areas facilitates a migration strategy designed to cut overhead costs. Migrants leave their families behind but operate in groups, sharing travel, accommodations, and their means of livelihood such as vending stalls or *becaks*. Given the urbanization patterns of the other heavily populated countries of South and Southeast Asia, it is not unreasonable to predict that this mobility pattern will become widespread.

## CONCLUSION

The urbanization and rural-urban mobility patterns that now prevail throughout much of South and Southeast Asia present policy-makers with a dilemma. The situation is most dramatic in the heavily populated countries of India, Bangladesh, Sri Lanka, and Indonesia. In these countries, if planners push ahead with goals based on assumed development of capitalism, dislocation of population from the countryside will be accentuated. Conversely, if planners try to restrict these processes, they will retard economic growth, and while the involutionary capacity of these societies to absorb both rural and urban labor is considerable, it is not infinite.

In the face of this situation it appears highly likely that the experience of socialist Asian countries, notably China, may offer an alternative. By placing emphasis on the creation of employment in rural and urban areas, Chinese planners have avoided some of the worst contradictions that have hastened rural-urban drift in other countries in Asia. It should be emphasized, however, that the Chinese have not completely checked the growth of urban centers. This process was most marked in the period prior to 1960, but since then the Chinese have adopted a series of measures that have successfully slowed the rate of urbanization. These measures include urban dispersal campaigns, designed to resettle unproductive urbanites in the countryside; the limitation of movement, brought about through systems of registration and ration certificates; organizational innovations, such as the creation of service networks, that reduce urban-rural differentials; and most significantly, the development of a national ideology that emphasizes the rural worker's role in national development.[16] All this, of course, has been accomplished within the structural setting of a socialist society. That such measures can be carried out within a capitalist or even a mixed economic system is very doubtful.

Marx was wrong in his prediction that employment-destroying innovations would exceed employment-creating innovations in nineteenth-century Europe. But it does not follow that he will be proved wrong about the heavily populated countries of South and Southeast Asia, particularly as the demographic situation is now on his side. This conclusion puts Marx and Malthus in the same bed. Strange bedfellows indeed!

NOTES

1. I have used the term *mobility* rather than *migration,* which is the theme of this symposium, because it offers more conceptual breadth, encompassing all types of geographic, social, and economic mobility. Demographers have chosen to define migration more rigorously as a permanent change of residence operationally defined by locational and temporal criteria. (See Zelinsky, 1971; United Nations, 1970.)

2. The summary of this approach follows closely that of Amin (1974*b*), pp. 85ff.

3. For earlier statements on the push-pull hypothesis see Thomas (1938), Hauser (1957), and Bogue (1959).

4. I have attempted to analyse these processes and their impact on migration in McGee (1969) and (1972). See also Arrighi (1973).

5. I have attempted a review of these inadequacies in McGee (1971*a*) and (1975*b*, pp. 35–63). A more recent publication edited by B. M. Du Toit and H. I. Safa

(1975) provides many empirical studies that indicate the inadequacy of the rural-urban continuum approach.

6. To cite a few of the more important: Davis (1951); Zachiariah (1960); Visid Prachuabmoh et al. (1972); Goldstein et al. (1974); Caldwell (1962); Pryor (1972, 1974, 1975a, 1975b); Temple (1974); McNicoll (1968); Hugo (1975); and Yun Kim (1972).

7. See, for instance, Petersen (1958) and more recently Eichenbaum (1975).

8. See, for instance, the heavy reliance on the use of Zelinsky's model in several papers in Kosinski and Prothero, eds. (1975).

9. On the problems of the implementation of birth control programs see the excellent study by Mamdani (1972). Natural increase will therefore be an important component of population growth in urban centers.

10. For a contrary view see Buchanan (1972).

11. For a description of this process see Austerlitz (1976).

12. For critical commentaries of these development plans see Myrdal (1968), Bettleheim (1968), and Mortimer (1973).

13. See, for instance, Oshima (1970–71) for Asia; Hofmeister, 1971, for Africa; also Turnham and Jaeger (1971) for a broad overview.

14. This work will emerge in a much larger study presently being written by Dr. Mukherji.

15. I am grateful to Graeme Hugo for permission to utilize material from his unpublished Ph.D. thesis (Hugo, 1975).

16. A much more detailed discussion of the Chinese experience can be found in the following: Salaff (1967); Buchanan (1970); Chen (1972); Onoye (1970); Salter (1973) and (1974).

# REFERENCES

Amin, Samir. 1974a. *Accumulation on a World Scale: A Critique of the Theory of Underdevelopment.* 2 vols. New York and London.
———. 1974b. "Introduction." In Amin, Samir (ed.), *Modern Migration in West Africa,* pp. 65–124. Oxford.
Armstrong, W. R., and McGee, T. G. 1968. "Revolutionary Change and The Third World City: A Theory of Urban Involution." *Civilisations,* 18, no. 3, pp. 353–78.
Arrighi, Giovanni. 1973. "Labour Supplies in Historical Perspective: A Study of the Proletarianization of the African Peasantry in Rhodesia." In Arrighi, G., and Saul, J. S., *Essays on the Political Economy of Africa,* pp. 180–234. New York and London.
Austerlitz, Max. 1976. "Vietnamizing South Vietnam." *New York Times Magazine,* April 25, pp. 31ff.
Baran, P. A. 1957. *The Political Economy of Growth.* New York and London.
Bettelheim, Charles. 1968. *India Independent.* New York.
Boeke, J. H. 1953. *Economics and Economic Policy of Dual Societies as Exemplified by Indonesia.* Haarlem.

Bogue, Donald J. 1959. "Internal Migration." In Hauser, P. M., and Duncan, O. D. (eds.), *The Study of Population: An Inventory and Appraisal,* pp. 486–509. Chicago.

Bose, Ashish. 1971. "The Urbanization Process in South and Southeast Asia." In Jacobson, Leo, and Prakash, Ved (eds.), *Urbanization and National Development,* pp. 81–109. Beverly Hills.

Buchanan, Iain. 1972. *Singapore in Southeast Asia: An Economic and Political Appraisal.* London.

Buchanan, Keith. 1970. *The Transformation of the Chinese Earth.* London.

Caldwell, J. C. 1962. "The Population of Malaya." Ph.D dissertation, Department of Demography, Australian National University, Canberra.

Chayanov, A. V. 1966. *The Theory of Peasant Economy.* Homewood, Illinois.

Chen, Pi-chao. 1972. "Overurbanization, Rustication of Urban-Educated Youths, and Politics of Rural Transformation." *Comparative Politics,* 4, no. 3, pp. 361–86.

Davis, Kingsley. 1951. *The Population of India and Pakistan.* Princeton.

———. 1969. *World Urbanization 1950–1970.* Volume 1: *Basic Data for Cities, Countries and Regions.* Population Monograph Series no. 4. Berkeley.

———. 1975. "Asia's Cities: Problems and Options." *Population and Development Review,* 1, no. 1, pp. 71–86.

Diégues, Manuel. 1966. "Urban Employment in Brazil." *International Labour Review,* 93, no. 6, pp. 643–57.

Du Toit, Brian M. 1975. "A Decision-Making Model for the Study of Migration." In Du Toit, B. M., and Safa, H. I. (eds.), *Migration and Urbanization Models and Adaptive Strategies,* pp. 49–76. The Hague, Paris.

Eichenbaum, Jacob. 1975. "A Matrix of Human Movement." *International Migration,* 13, no. 1/2, pp. 21–41.

Frank, A. G. 1967. *Capitalism and Underdevelopment in Latin America.* New York.

———. 1972. *Lumpenbourgeoisie: Lumpendevelopment, Dependence, Class and Politics in Latin America.* New York.

Frank, Charles R., Jr. 1971. "The Problem of Urban Unemployment in Africa." In Ridker, Ronald G., and Lubell, Harold, *Employment and Unemployment Problems of the Near East and South Asia,* pp. 738–818. Bombay.

Franklin, S. H. 1965. "Systems of Production: Systems of Appropriation." *Pacific Viewpoint,* 6, no. 2, pp. 145–66.

———. 1969. *The European Peasantry: The Final Phase.* London.

Friedmann, John, and Sullivan, Flora. 1972. "The Absorption of Labour in the Urban Economy: The Case of Developing Countries." School of Architecture and Urban Planning, University of California, Los Angeles.

Geertz, Clifford. 1963a. *Peddlers and Princes: Social Change and Economic Modernization in Two Indonesian Towns.* Chicago.

———. 1963b. *Agricultural Involution: The Processes of Ecological Change in Indonesia.* Berkeley.

Goldstein, Sydney, et al. 1974. "Urban-Rural Migration Differentials in Thailand." Research Report No. 12, Institute of Population Studies, Chulalongkorn University, Bangkok.

Grant, J. 1971. "Marginal Men." *Foreign Affairs,* 50, no. 1, pp. 112–24.

Gunatilleke, Godfrey. 1972. "Rural-Urban Balance and Development: The Experience of Ceylon." Unpublished paper presented to a seminar on "Population Change and Development: The Urban Focus," sponsored by Southeast Asian Development Advisory Group.

Hauser, Philip M., ed. 1957. *Urbanization in Asia and the Far East.* Calcutta.

Hofmeister, Ralph H. 1971. "Growth with Unemployment in Latin America: Some Implications for Asia." In Ridker, Ronald G., and Lubell, Harold (eds.), *Employment and Unemployment Problems of the Near East and South Asia,* pp. 819–48. Bombay.

Hugo, G. J. 1975. "Population Mobility in West Java, Indonesia." Ph.D. dissertation, Department of Demography, Australian National University, Canberra.

Isaac, Barry L. 1974. "Peasants in the Cities: Ingenious Paradox or Conceptual Muddle." *Human Organization,* 33, no. 3, pp. 248–57.

Jones, Gavin W. 1968. "Underutilisation of Manpower and Demographic Trends in Latin America." *International Labour Review,* 98, no. 5, pp. 451–69.

———. 1972. "Implications of Prospective Urbanization for Development Planning in Southeast Asia." *Southeast Asian Development Advisory Group Papers on Problems of Development in Southeast Asia.* New York.

Keddie, James. 1973. "The Mass Unemployment Explosion." *Far Eastern Economic Review,* 82, no. 52, pp. 41–43.

Kosinski, Leszek, and Prothero, Mansell R., eds. 1975. *People on the Move: Studies in Internal Migration.* London.

Lenin, V. I. 1899. *Collected Works.* Volume 3: *The Development of Capitalism in Russia.* Moscow, 1960.

Lewis, W. Arthur. 1958. "Economic Development with Unlimited Supplies of Labour." In Agarwala, A. N., and Singh, S. P. (eds.), *Economics of Underdevelopment.* Bombay.

———. 1967. "Unemployment in Developing Countries." *The World Today,* vol. 23, pp. 13–22.

McGee, T. G. 1967. *The Southeast Asian City.* London.

———. 1969. "Malays in Kuala Lumpur City: A Geographical Study of the Process of Urbanization." Ph.D dissertation, Victoria University of Wellington.

———. 1971a. *The Urbanization Process in the Third World: Explorations in Search of a Theory.* London.

———. 1971b. "Tetes-de-ponts et enclaves: Le problème urbain et le processus d'urbanisation dans l'Asie de Sud-Est depuis 1945." *Revue Tiers Monde,* 12, no. 45, pp. 115–44.

———. 1972. "Rural-Urban Migration in a Plural Society: A Case Study of Malays in West Malaysia." In Dwyer, D. J. (ed.), *The City as a Centre of Change in Asia,* pp. 108–24. Hong Kong.

———. 1973. "Peasants in the Cities: A Paradox, A Paradox, A Most Ingenious Paradox." *Human Organization,* 32, no. 2, pp. 135–42.

———. 1974a. *Hawkers in Hong Kong: A Study of Policy and Planning in the Third World City.* Hong Kong.

————. 1974*b*. "Peasants in the Cities: A Rejoinder." *Human Organization,* 33, no. 3, pp. 258–60.

————. 1975*a. Hawkers in Southeast Asian Cities.* Final Report to the International Development Research Centre, Ottawa.

————. 1975*b*. "Malay Migration to Kuala Lumpur City: Individual Adaptation to the City." In Du Toit, B., and Safa, H. I. (eds.), *Migration and Urbanization Models and Adaptive Strategies,* pp. 143–78. The Hague, Paris.

————. 1976. "Hawkers and Hookers Making Out in the Third World City: Some Southeast Asian Examples." *Manpower and Unemployment Research,* 9, no. 1, pp. 3–21.

McNicoll, G. 1968. "Internal Migration in Indonesia." *Indonesia,* no. 5, pp. 29–92.

Mamdani, Mahmood. 1972. *The Myth of Population Control.* New York.

Morse, David A. 1970. "Unemployment in Developing Countries." *Political Science Quarterly,* 85, no. 1, pp. 1–13.

Mortimer, Rex, ed. 1973. *Showcase State: The Illusion of Indonesia's "Accelerated Modernisation".* Sydney.

Mukherji, Shekhar. 1975. "The Mobility Field Theory of Human Spatial Behaviour: A Spatial-Behavioural Foundation to the Movement Dynamics." Unpublished seminar paper, Department of Human Geography, Australian National University, Canberra.

Myrdal, Gunnar. 1968. *Asian Drama: An Inquiry into the Poverty of Nations.* 3 vols. New York.

Onoye, Etsuzo. 1970. "Regional Distribution of Urban Population in China." *Developing Economies,* 8, pp. 93–127.

Oshima, H. 1970–71. "Labour Force Explosion: The Labour Intensive Sector in Asian Growth." *Economic Development and Cultural Change,* 19, pp. 161–83.

Petersen, W. 1958. "A General Typology of Migration." *American Sociological Review,* 23, pp. 246–266.

Pryor, Robin J. 1972. "Malaysians on the Move: A Study of Internal Migration in West Malaysia." Ph.D dissertation, Department of Geography, University of Malaya.

————. 1974. *Spatial Analysis of Internal Migration, West Malaysia.* Monograph Series no. 5, Geography Department, James Cook University, Townsville, Australia.

————. 1975*a*. "The Migrant to the City in Southeast Asia: Can and Should We Generalize?" Unpublished seminar paper, Department of Demography, Australian National University, Canberra.

————. 1975*b*. "Migration Trends, Population Redistribution Policies and Development Strategies in Malaysia." Paper presented at the Symposium on Alternatives for Development Strategies in Asia and the Pacific, 46th Congress, Australian and New Zealand Association for the Advancement of Science. Canberra.

Salaff, Janet. 1967. "The Urban Communes and Anti-City Experiment in Communist China." *China Quarterly,* no. 29.

Salter, Christopher L. 1973. "Chinese Mechanisms for Diminishing the Rural-Urban Migration Flow." Working paper, Subcommittee on Comparative Urbanization, University of California, Los Angeles.

————. 1974. "Chinese Experiments in Urban Space: The Quest for an Agropolitan China." In *Proceedings of the Second Annual Colloquium,* sponsored by the Subcommittee on Comparative Urbanization, University of California, Los Angeles, pp. 101–25.

Santos, Milton. 1971. *Les Villes du tiers monde*. Paris.

———. 1975. *L'Espace partagé: Les deux circuits de l'economie urbaine des pays sous-développés*. Paris.

Temple, Gordon P. 1974. "Migration to Jakarta: Empirical Search for Theory." Ph.D dissertation, University of Wisconsin.

Thomas, D. S. 1938. *Research Memorandum on Migration Differentials*. New York.

Todaro, M. P. 1969. "A Model of Labour Migration and Urban Unemployment in Less Developed Countries." *American Economic Review*, 59, pp. 138–48.

———. 1971. "Income Expectations, Rural Urban Migration and Employment in Africa." *International Labour Review*, 104, no. 5, pp. 387–414.

Turnham, D., and Jaeger, Ingelies. 1971. *The Employment Problem in Less Developed Countries*. Paris.

United Nations. 1970. *Methods of Measuring Internal Migration*. Population Studies no. 47, New York.

Visid, Prachuabmoh et al. 1972. "The Rural and Urban Populations of Thailand." Research Report no. 8, Institute of Population Studies, Chulalongkorn University, Bangkok.

Weeks, John. 1971. "Does Employment Matter?" *Manpower and Unemployment Research in Africa*, 4, no. 1, pp. 67–70.

Wolpert, J. 1965. "Behavioural Aspects of the Decision to Migrate." *Regional Science Association Papers and Proceedings*, no. 15, pp. 159–69.

Yun Kim. 1972. "Net Internal Migration in the Philippines 1960–1970." Technical Paper no. 2, The Philippines Bureau of the Census and Statistics.

Zachariah, K. C. 1960. *Internal Migration in India: 1941–51*. Bombay.

Zelinsky, Wilbur. 1971. "The Hypothesis of the Mobility Transition." *The Geographical Review*, 61, pp. 219–49.

# [11]

## Recent Migrations in the Arab World

JANET ABU-LUGHOD

From its inception, migration theory has had pretensions toward a "natural science." Migratory movements have been viewed as physical events shaped by environmental forces. Thus, within the positivistic or even ecological-evolutionary paradigms that dominated nineteenth-century thought, it was assumed that human migrations could be predicted by mechanistic models. Gravity metaphors abounded. The work of Ravenstein was but one in a long series of such attempts to "pass" abstract and preferably mathematical "laws" for human migrations. Translated into the behavioral language of our day, this same mechanistic paradigm has generated a new model of "forces," this time couched in the tragically inelegant metaphor of "push and pull."

Historical evidence—from not only the nineteenth century but much farther back as well—could easily have refuted such an approach to migration, had anyone stopped to examine it critically. But it is one of the amazing facts about paradigms that they blind selectively in direct proportion to their power to illuminate. It would have been impossible, for example, to predict from any mechanistic model the tremendous population upheavals that occurred in fourteenth-century Europe, wracked as it was by plagues and economic dislocations of enormous magnitude. Yet out of these culture-shattering peregrinations emerged fundamental and irreversible transformations in Europe's social order. Similarly, the redistributions of population in much of the Third World during the nineteenth century, under the impact

225

of world colonialism, altered the basic parameters within which the future of many countries could evolve, but no one in his right mind would choose to label these events "natural."

It may be that the geographers' models fit best when the parameters remain relatively constant and that their explanatory power decreases in direct proportion to the magnitude of changes in the larger system of political economy. Certainly, this generalization would apply to the contemporary era in the Middle East, since the substantial movements of population in that region during the past few decades could never have been accounted for or predicted, either in nature or degree, by the usual "causes" with which social scientists (but, admittedly, *not* historians) traditionally work. Seldom do we find in the migration models of social scientists the two factors that this paper will stress: (1) military events and forced migrations; and (2) the world power system of economic dependence.

Present migrations in the Arab World are largely accounted for by these two factors so often overlooked in conventional theory. War-induced migrations have chiefly affected the area of the Fertile Crescent and, since 1967 at least, Egypt. This situation has combined with changes in the world economic system to generate population movements into the principalities of the Arabian Gulf, into Saudi Arabia, and into Libya. And an inversion of this latter process has been largely responsible for the movement of population out of the rest of North Africa.[1]

This paper explores some of these events and causes but makes only a tentative and preliminary estimate of the magnitude of their impact.[2] It is, of course, impossible to generalize about the Arab World (much less the entire Middle East), since the zone is vast (from the Atlantic to the Indian Ocean), populous (over 140 million), and fragmented into a score of separate governmental jurisdictions which periodically raise and lower their barriers to migration, depending upon somewhat capricious shifts in economic demand and political-ideological expedience. Rather than group these countries by geographic proximity, our analysis groups them by their "migration circumstances," a classification having only rough correspondence to geographic subregion.

## WAR ZONES

Into this first "migration circumstance" category might be placed those states whose population movements have been significantly influenced by the continuing state of war endemic to the region of Palestine. The influx of Jews into Palestine, partly in response to Hitler's persecutions of the 1930s, led to war and the subsequent dislodging of over 700,000 Palestinian Arabs in 1947–48.[3] This set in motion a chain of migration which continues to generate profound changes in the Middle East.

The major impact was felt first in the portions of Palestine that remained outside Israeli control: eastern Palestine, which subsequently came to be called the "West Bank," and the Gaza Strip. Refugees who crowded into the latter zone were trapped there; those who had sought refuge in eastern Palestine either remained, many of them in camps, or pressed on in search of a more viable existence. Large numbers went to the Jordanian capital of 'Amman which, in consequence, exploded from a modest market town of under 60,000 in 1945 to a metropolis of about 200,000 by the early 1950s, by which time the first wave had been absorbed.[4]

Where individual Palestinians fled was affected by geographic routes and by kinship channels. Those from the northern part of Palestine tended to move to Syria or Lebanon. While large numbers were initially housed in refugee camps, the fortunate few with connections to landed families in these countries made a relatively easy transition into new citizenship and economic roles. Another large minority struggled to gain a foothold in the commercial and professional sectors of the economy and in the cities to which they had migrated. Palestinians settled chiefly on inhospitable land at the urban periphery—several unserviced hills beyond built-up 'Amman (Hacker, 1960), the open sandy zone of Hamra in Beirut (Khalaf, 1973), and the dry lands around Damascus.

Regardless of where the war victims went, their "migration" affected the rural-urban balance in the region. While most Palestinians had followed farming occupations at home, this avenue of economic activity was completely blocked in the situations into which they moved. They thus became, overnight and perforce, an urbanized population. Mobility through nonagricultural activities was the only avenue open—and this avenue was available *only* in urban areas. What has gone unrecognized (and indeed could not have been noted under the old paradigm) is that a good proportion of the "urban growth" of Lebanon and Jordan was unintentional: essentially, the movement of war victims who had no place to go *except* into cities.

The case of 'Amman is totally inexplicable without reference to this state of affairs. The more modest growth of Damascus during the same period is, in part at least, due to the same phenomenon. And the extravagant blossoming of Beirut between 1948 and 1974, not only in demographic but even more so in economic terms, cannot be understood without reference to the war of 1947–1948. Prior to the establishment of Israel, the major port for international trade in the Fertile Crescent had been Haifa, located in northern Palestine. After the war, these activities, along with the expanded commercial, entrepreneurial, and banking activities associated with increased trade (more and more linked to the Gulf and Peninsula oil as time went by), came to be centered in Beirut, then the only major Arab capital whose economy expanded at a rate substantially faster than its population growth. Beirut was to grow from several hundred thousand in the late 1940s to over a million, counting the suburbs, in the quarter of a century following the war. (The brittle quality of its growth has recently been demonstrated by the internecine war that has temporarily if not permanently "killed" the city; hundreds of thousands of Beirutis sought safety in nearby countries, while Syrian and other foreign workers in the capital simply "went home.")

During the 1950s there also occurred shifts in international demand and trade which stimulated developments in Saudi Arabia and the Gulf (at that time, almost exclusively the city-state of Kuwait). The exploitation of oil resources, which had hitherto been on a more modest scale and achieved chiefly through the importation of temporary personnel from Europe and the United States, was dramatically expanded and, at the same time, "indigenized." But the population in these places was not yet adequate in numbers or skills to take up the slack. Palestinians moved into the expanding levels of the technocracy and bureaucracy, becoming the largest minority after the Kuwaitis themselves in the newly rich kingdom of Kuwait, and constituting a small but at the time valued minority in Saudi Arabia.

However, whereas Palestinians had been granted complete citizenship in Jordan after annexation of the West Bank and whereas kinship connections had enabled many more to obtain Lebanese or Syrian passports, neither the Saudis nor the Kuwaitis extended this privilege to the other Arabs (then chiefly from the Fertile Crescent area) who joined their expanding economies as a "stop-gap" labor force. Although ideologically more acceptable and cheaper than Europeans, in the last analysis, the newcomers were expendable once local citizens achieved the education and training required to supplant them.

While I would roughly estimate that the population dislocations in the late 1940s and early 1950s which were directly or secondarily the result of the first Palestine War would probably not exceed one million, on a population base of the combined populations of Palestine, Lebanon, Syria, and Jordan (during that period under 7 million), this accounts for almost 15 percent of the total. More relevant would be the urban base into which most of this dislocation flowed, and in this accounting the relocation had formidable impact—infusing the existing cities with perhaps twice as many urbanites as before.

The June 1967 war was even more significant in generating population migrations than the earlier and geographically more confined conflict had been. Israeli occupation of the entire East bank of the Suez Canal and the heavy bombardment sustained by the major Egyptian settlements strung out along the canal—namely, Port Said which, according to the census of 1966, contained a resident population of 313,000; Ismailiyah, midway along the canal, with a 1966 population of 345,000; and Suez at the southern end, with a 1966 population of 315,000—led to an internal migration of refugees within Egypt. While, proportionate to population, this migration was not nearly so traumatic as the earlier Palestinian displacement, it was greater in terms of the number of persons affected. With the destruction of large sections of these cities in the bombardment, and with the canal, which had provided the economic base for their existence, closed indefinitely to traffic, there was a relocation of perhaps a million persons to other parts of Egypt. While this dislocation is generally ignored in scholarly as well as popular accounts, it was undoubtedly a major factor in pushing Cairo's population substantially over the projected figure of 5–6 million by the early 1970s. This unpredicted (and indeed unpredictable) source of "urban growth" helped to swell Greater Cairo to its current level in excess of nine million.[5] Far from the stereotypical rural-to-urban migration, this was a war-induced migration of urban people to the capital, the only place in the country that could absorb such numbers, albeit with incredible difficulty.

The 1967 war also left the Egyptian economy badly undermined. Loss of the oil fields, which were just beginning to yield, coupled with the loss of at least 95 million Egyptian pounds per year (1966, as compared with only 24 million in 1957) from the canal tolls, contributed to the depressed economic conditions. While there had been some outmigration from Egypt since the early 1950s (relatively unprecedented before that, since Egyptians have been notorious for their reluctance to migrate), after 1967 her export of trained manpower—doctors, teachers, administrators, and the like—increased markedly. To some extent this new migration could be attributed indirectly to the hostilities and the war losses of 1967.

The same war caused further reverberations in Palestine, Jordan, Syria, and, eventually, in Lebanon. The Israeli occupation of the Gaza Strip caused some residents to flee across the Sinai with the retreating Egyptian forces; subsequently there have been systematic expulsions and "facilitated" emigrations of Palestinians from that zone, although accurate estimates of their number cannot be obtained. On the so-called West Bank, which was completely occupied by Israel in 1967, flight was easier and indeed "facilitated" by the occupying forces. It is estimated that at the time of the war 150,000 to 250,000 crossed the Jordan River heading for reception centers in the vicinity of 'Amman. Soon after the war, that city's population rose to half a million, as contrasted with its census population of 323,000 in 1966. The more settled population attempted to remain and to resist the imposition of Israeli rule. However, expulsions, the destruction of homes and whole villages, and the expropriation of lands to accommodate new Jewish settlements have driven out several hundred thousand more. The growing pattern of dependence upon remittances from sons working in the Gulf area and elsewhere intensified as the economy became increasingly dependent on Israel. The residual population of the occupied areas is now disproportionately old and/or female.

On the Syrian front, the Israeli conquest of the Golan Heights resulted in the complete destruction of the Syrian city of Kuneitra (which had a population of some 60,000 before the war) and the "clearing" of agricultural regions that have subsequently become the sites of paramilitary Israeli settlements. About 100,000 Syrians have been displaced from this area, most of them finding refuge in Damascus, along with Palestinians retreating from the West Bank.

As before, those refugees who could sought the economic opportunities most readily available to them in Lebanon, where the economy continued to boom, and in the Gulf areas, where new oil finds began to stimulate a demand for labor in the smaller sheikhdoms south of Kuwait. There they ran into greater competition from the Egyptians, who were also fanning out in search of jobs.

These trends continued through the 1973 war which left the Egyptian and Syrian situations relatively unchanged but began finally to have an effect upon Lebanon. Events there were to culminate in a civil war of long duration and bloody proportion. The 1973 ceasefire was followed not by a quieting of frontiers with Lebanon, a nonbelligerent, but by increased tension. The southern portion of Lebanon was subject to frequent incursions and even the construction of a military highway through Lebanese territory by Israeli troops who thus gained leverage and control over portions they did not yet occupy. Israeli aircraft flew over Beirut at will, well above the range of air defenses.

Endemic tensions among religious factions, political groups, and locally based paramilitary bands were exacerbated by the defenselessness of the country which, like Switzerland, had counted on its noninvolvement for protection. As tensions mounted, Israeli incursions increased, not only in the south, which by that time had lost much of its population, but also more boldly by air bombardments near major cities. Finally, the outbreak of street fighting in the major cities interrupted trade, the economic activity upon which Lebanon's viability was based. Western-based financial, banking, and other business firms withdrew to set up alternate Middle East headquarters in Athens, 'Amman, and even Damascus. And there was a major flight of population to safer areas. While the magnitude of this temporary emigration cannot be estimated accurately nor its long-term effects predicted, this most recent war-induced migration on the order of half a million or more (at least one-sixth of the total population), is unfortunately not without precedent in the Middle East.

One difficulty in dealing with such migrations is that just as their origins are unpredictable, so also are their reversals. For example, with preliminary Sinai agreements and the recovery by Egypt of her Canal Zone, plans are being carried out to reconstruct the major cities of that zone. In March 1976 I observed almost complete population recovery, even before rebuilding had been completed. Certainly, once the situation in Lebanon subsides, most of the population temporarily in other capitals will return, but whether prosperity and the foreign firms will follow is another matter. Should the economy recover, Beirut will again become a magnet for population; should it not, one may expect additional out-migration. Possible destinations would be whichever capital inherits Beirut's commercial role (Cairo, Damascus, and 'Amman are all vying), the Gulf area (although immigration restrictions are now closing down this haven), and Iraq whose recent economic growth has been remarkable and which is encouraging immigration of other Arabs through offers of citizenship and other inducements.

Even this brief survey should indicate how hard it is to apply "theories" of migration to the Middle East, where events have been governed more by local and international politics and war than by internal environmental/economic factors, i.e., the types of variables usually treated as central. Where such events take place in a more visible arena and at a somewhat larger scale (for example, during World War II in Europe), migration theories are of course suspended. It is remarkable that scholars forget to suspend them in studying the Middle East. Because of the permanent state of tension in the area, some of the population movements that are having so marked an effect on the region are not caught by the theories. We cannot afford to suspend the "real laws" indefinitely; we will have to conceptualize new ones to fit the abnormal conditions which are *not* abnormal in the Middle East.

The traditional theories are somewhat more germane for the other two "migration circumstance" categories to be discussed: economic expansions leading to in-migration, tied to the world economic system; and changes of an involutionary character, similarly tied to that system. In the first category are the *nouveau riche* oil producers of the Gulf, the Arabian Peninsula, and Libya—all resource-rich but population-poor—and two additional cases, Iraq and Algeria, both of which have begun to develop diversified economic bases supplemented by oil and which have ample human resources that can now be utilized, given this new stimulus to prosperity. In the second category are the remaining countries of the Maghreb, Morocco and Tunisia (as well as Algeria still to some extent), whose economic development remains involuted and tied in a dependent relationship to the Metropole economy, despite the fact that French political domination ended some time ago. These countries have traditionally served as providers of cheap labor to the European, chiefly French, industrial system and continue to export labor to the continent.

## OIL ZONES

Because of the affinity between deserts and petroleum reserves, the relatively unpopulated arid reaches of the Arabian Peninsula and Arabian Gulf as well as the Saharan interiors of Libya and Algeria have been the locations of the richest oil strikes of recent times. Oil was first drilled in Kuwait in 1936 and in Saudi Arabia in 1939, but production did not really expand in these places until after World War II. Libya's oil strikes came in the late 1950s and significant production not until the 1960s. Algeria's modest production began later. These countries have since been joined by the various small principalities on the Arabian Gulf. By 1974, Arab oil production reached a billion metric tons annually (Johns, 1974:83) and the income to Arab countries from oil in that year approached $54 billion. The future continues to hold promise since, according to the *BP Statistical Review 1973*, the Middle East has almost half of the world's known reserves of oil still under the ground. (See Table 1 for oil production and revenues.)

Virtually all these countries (with the exception of Algeria and Iraq, which will be discussed later) had very small and sparse populations before the advent of oil. The transition from nomadism to industrialism has taken time (albeit less than one might have predicted), and in the interim white collar and technical personnel were in great demand—needed immediately to build an administrative and technical apparatus to serve oil extraction and to administer the financial responsibilities and powers that oil generated.

This gap was filled primarily by Arabs from other regions. For example, the population of Kuwait before the discovery of oil was estimated at about 100,000. By 1973 the population residing in Kuwait exceeded 800,000, only 360,000 of whom were Kuwaiti citizens. The remainder were members of the labor force and their families who came in from outside to fill second-level administrative and technical jobs (chiefly Palestinians, Lebanese, Syrians, Jordanians) or to do the menial labor disdained by Kuwaitis (chiefly Iranians and some Indians and Pakistanis). In Libya, the small population of under a million (1950) in pre-oil days has been expanded by the importation of Arab labor. Most recently, the United Arab Emirates and Qatar have been offering opportunities to skilled manpower as their oil production expands. In the latter countries, Pakistani and other Asian laborers have been used to fill needs at the bottom while Palestinians, Egyptians and, most recently, Lebanese have assisted at the middle levels. These situations seem to be recapitulating the earlier case of Kuwait where skilled Arab "outsiders" have been used until citizens can be trained for the better positions, while non-Arab outsiders have been substituted increasingly at the bottom to fill the least desirable jobs. The results are distressing, since the generous benefits of the welfare state are concentrated on citizens; noncitizens earn less and

Table 1

Arab Oil Production and Revenues in 1963, 1964, and 1973

| Country | Crude Oil Production (million metric tons) | | Oil Revenues (million $ U.S.) | |
|---|---|---|---|---|
| | 1963 | 1973 | 1964 | 1973 |
| Saudi Arabia | 80.5 | 364.7 | 561 | 4,900 |
| Kuwait | 97.2 | 138.4 | 655 | 2,000 |
| Iraq | 56.7 | 97.1 | 353 | 1,300 |
| Abu-Dhabi | 2.6 | 62.6 | 12 | 1,000 |
| Qatar | 9.1 | 27.3 | 66 | 400 |
| Neutral Zone[a] | 16.7 | 26.5 | | |
| Oman | — | 14.7 | | |
| Dubai | — | 11.0 | | |
| Syria | — | 5.5 | | |
| Bahrein | 2.2 | 3.4 | | |
| Libya | 22.4 | 105.1 | 197 | 2,200 |
| Algeria | 23.9 | 51.0 | ? | 1,100 |
| Egypt[b] | 5.7 | 9.5 | | |

[a] Neutral zone shared equally by Saudi Arabia and Kuwait.
[b] Includes output of the Sinai wells occupied by Israel in 1967.

Source: See Richard Johns, "Oil in the Middle East and North Africa," in *The Middle East and North Africa, 1974–75* (London: Europa Publications, Ltd., 1974), pp. 69–93. Data have been compiled from tables on pp. 83–84.

often must pay for services provided without cost to citizens. Nevertheless, in the short run, this expansion of demand for skilled labor and administrators has opened up opportunities that immigrants have seized, yielding another major source of population redistribution.

Thus far, oil extraction has not created the kind of economic multiplier effect that is necessary if the present phenomenal growth in GNP (30 percent per annum in the United Arab Emirates, 25 percent per annum in Libya, 11 percent per annum in Saudi Arabia in 1960–1970, and now of course much higher) is to be used to establish these countries on a course of permanent self-sustained economic development. Oil extraction is notoriously capital intensive, as are some of the industries related to oil-processing. One scientist has estimated that only 100,000 workers in the entire Middle East are directly associated with the oil industry (Zahlan, 1974). The potential for additional labor absorption is certainly there, if these countries were to become engaged in the manufacture of consumer items from petroleum by-products, but this has not yet occurred. Unless more diversified industrialization takes place, one can certainly predict a decline in the amount of migrant-labor the oil countries will demand and possibly a "nativistic" movement which will seek to repatriate "guest workers," once the need for their assistance has finished.

Clearly, the economist's model of the free flow of productive forces and the redistribution of population in relation to demand is not working perfectly in the case of the oil-wealthy states, largely because of political factors. A united federated Arab world where factors of production could move freely to where they are needed would present a much different picture from the present one. Currently, capital is generated in highly concentrated amounts within a few relatively underpopulated countries which cannot absorb it. For political as much as for economic reasons, this capital does not flow into other regions of the Middle East which have large population surpluses but little capital (e.g., Egypt), but rather has been drained off for "recycling" in the developed world, which depends upon oil imports. Instead of capital being brought to labor, labor has gravitated to capital in the form of migrations to the oil-wealthy countries. Since this labor is not viewed as being within the same market as that of the "citizens" of these countries, all sorts of barriers are developing; these will eventually lead either to the substitution of "native" labor or to the formal crystallization of the migrants into a permanent under-caste.

Without pressures from the world economic system, unification of political entities and hence rational combination of productive factors and equalization of resources throughout the Arab world might have been feasible. Given the interest of the Western world in assuring a continued flow of reasonably priced oil and absorbing the capital generated by such purchases through reinvestment in the purchasers' economies, this chance seems to have been temporarily foreclosed.

The case of Iraq diverges quite radically from the preceding scenario, and increasingly it seems that Algeria is changing from her past position as a dependent, labor-exporting country to an autonomous, internally developing country like Iraq. In both cases, oil exploitation, in conjunction with disciplined economic planning and a stance of political independence, is the variable that is making the difference. In both countries, an ample supply of labor, albeit still lacking in some essential skills, is being combined with high levels of capital accumulation from oil export in order to effect major developments in the agricultural and industrial sectors of an expanding economy. Because of these rapid strides, Iraq is now able to absorb domestic increases in the labor force as well as additional workers who are actively sought elsewhere. (An attempt was recently made, for example, to recruit Egyptian farmers to regions of land reclamation near new irrigation projects.) Algeria finally seems to be reversing the trend which for so long kept a large percent of her able-bodied labor force in France rather than at home, and net migration is beginning to swing in the direction of repatriation.[6] Up to now, her case would have fallen in the final "migration circumstance" to which we shall turn, that of the labor exporters.

## ECONOMIC INVOLUTION IN THE DEPENDENT ZONES

In a few remaining portions of the decolonized Arab world, the economic hold of neocolonialism still continues along classic lines. While planning for economic development is ostensibly within the province of national regimes, foreign capital investments are so overwhelming and technological dependence so great that the autonomy required to set new priorities is seriously compromised. This remains the situation in Tunisia and Morocco. In both countries large-scale, capital-intensive, multinational ventures are combined with labor-intensive service developments connected with tourism. Modest-scale, indigenously financed, labor-intensive industries—i.e., those types of growth most likely to contribute to labor absorption and greater economic independence—are relatively neglected. The result has been economic involution, whether in the form of capital importation which converts the labor force to a kind of "putting-out system" for European firms, or in the form of labor exportation, which moves that labor force directly to plants in the metropole. The former has no effect on migration and therefore will be ignored in this discussion. The latter has direct implications for migration and must concern us here.

During a recent trip to Aix-en-Provence, I was startled to note that all voices from below ground level and most manual-labor ground level voices were speaking Arabic. It was at this time that race riots broke out in nearby Marseilles, between French and North African residents. According to the estimates of an Algerian anthropologist (Bennoune, 1975) studying North African workers in Europe, in 1973 there were some 1.1 million Moroccan, Tunisian, and Algerian workers in France where they provided a poorly paid and exploited underclass to industry and services. A French survey of industrial and commercial workers in 1967 indicated that over 85 percent of the North African workers were unskilled or semiskilled. Their situation is not unique. Millions of low-paid laborers have been drawn to the core industrial zone from the periphery—and the periphery today consists of Portugal (almost as many workers outside as inside), Turkey (mostly in Germany), Italy (chiefly in northern Europe), and North Africa, whose expatriates are chiefly in France. Such labor supplies are assured by the involution which North African economies have undergone first under colonialism and now under neocolonialism. It is hard to predict how and when these movements will be reversed. Given the proximity between that portion of the lesser-developed world and the European core, the established channels that make it simpler to travel from North Africa to Europe than to other parts of the Arab world, and the prevailing underemployment and wide wage differentials, labor flows will continue toward Europe unless migration barriers are raised or development proceeds in the home countries at very high rates. The latter is an unlikely prospect, so long as Tunisia remains resource-poor and Morocco remains dependent.

## CONCLUSION

In this paper we have ignored the issue usually discussed when the topic is migration—namely the redistribution of population *within* countries that transforms them from predominantly rural to increasingly urban. Certainly this trend is not absent in the Middle East. Using the definition of 100,000 as the lower limit for "urban," we find that some 30 percent of Egypt's and the rest of the Fertile Crescent's population is now urban, that about one quarter of North Africa's population resides in cities, and that even in Saudi Arabia the rate is some 10 percent. The reasons for this have been thoroughly discussed elsewhere. In this paper we have chosen to explore those aspects of population movement which tend to be overlooked in other discussions, but which cannot be left out if one is to understand the present migrations that are reshaping the Arab world.

We might mention in conclusion one of the overlooked implications of the flow of populations across national boundaries. Despite all the barriers, competitions, and indeed even conflicts that these flows have engendered, they have helped to forge a new unified identity which may be reflected increasingly in the political arena. Just as an internationally caused war began the process of mobility, so unification of political policies seems to be taking place first at the international level. The cultural and economic effects of this intermingling, however, may be of more lasting and far-reaching signifi-cance.

## NOTES

1. I shall ignore in this paper both the emigration of non-Arabs from the Middle East and North Africa which accompanied decolonization and also the relocation of Arabs of the Jewish faith into Israeli-held Palestine. While estimations of the magni-tude of these emigrations lie beyond the purview of this paper, the two cases offer additional evidence for the basic thesis that war and politics constitute underlying

factors in Middle Eastern migrations. During and after the Algerian war of national liberation, perhaps a million French *colons* relocated, chiefly in southern France. After the more peacefully gained independence of Morocco and Tunisia, substantial numbers of French and Spanish colonists left North Africa. To some extent, the decrease in the number of Jews in that region paralleled the exodus of foreigners, as the following figures from Morocco illustrate.

| | | Population of Residents by Nationality and Religion | | | | | |
|---|---|---|---|---|---|---|---|
| | | Moroccan Muslim | | Moroccan Jewish | | Foreign | |
| Year | Total | Number | Percent | Number | Percent | Number | Percent |
| 1935* | 7,040,000 | 6,590,000 | 93.4 | 185,000 | 2.6 | 265,000 | 3.8 |
| 1952* | 9,342,000 | 8,585,000 | 91.9 | 218,000 | 2.3 | 539,000 | 5.8 |
| 1960 | 11,626,232 | 11,067,929 | 95.6 | 162,420 | 1.4 | 395,883 | 3.4 |
| 1971 | 15,410,378 | 15,267,350 | 99.1 | 31,119 | 0.2 | 111,909 | 0.7 |

*We have combined the populations in the French and Spanish Zones to make the data equivalent to that of later years.

Percentages have been rounded and do not add to 100.

The preceding table was assembled from the following sources: *Résultats du Recensement de 1960,* Volume I on nationality, sex and age, (Rabat: 1965), p. 9, Table I–2, giving data for 1935, 1952, and 1960; *Population Légale du Maroc,* according to the general census of population and housing in 1971 (Rabat: December 1971), Table I, p. 4.

2. In this paper I have made no attempt to derive precise demographic estimates but rather have concentrated on more general factors which might guide the collection and processing (as well as interpretation) of such data.

3. This is a precise estimate, based upon careful demographic analysis. Detailed estimates appear in Janet Abu-Lughod, "The Demographic Transformation of Palestine," in *The Transformation of Palestine,* edited by Ibrahim Abu-Lughod (Evanston, Ill.: Northwestern University Press, 1971).

4. Official figures for the post-1950 period appear to be gross underestimates, according to Jane Hacker. See her *Modern Amman: A Social Survey* (University of Durham, Department of Geography, Research Paper no. 3, 1960), especially pp. 60 –65.

5. Estimates provided to the author in March 1976 by Egyptian government officials.

6. The most complete source on the changing magnitudes, patterns and constraining circumstances of Algerian workers in France is Ahsène Zehraoui, *Les travailleurs algériens en France: Étude sociologique de quelques aspects de la vie familiale* (Paris: Maspero, new edition, 1976). From a peak of a million Algerian workers in the 1960s, the total number of Algerians in France has dropped to 800,000, despite the natural increase that has occurred as the result of a shift from the earlier pattern of single male migrants to the present typical pattern of the movement of nuclear families.

## NOTE ON SOURCES

I have intentionally not cluttered this position paper with footnotes nor do I wish to append a lengthy bibliography. Frankly, there are not a great many sources that I trust. Issues of rural-to-urban migration in the Middle East have been critically examined in my article, "Problems and Policy Implications of Middle Eastern Urbanization," in *Studies on Development Problems in Selected Countries of the Middle East,* 1972 (New York: United Nations, 1973), pp. 42–62. I have, therefore, not repeated this argument or the data here.

The following sources are cited in the text:

Bennoune, Mahfoud. "Maghribin Workers in France." MERIP Reports, no. 34 (August 1975), pp. 1–12, 30.

Hacker, Jane M. *Modern Amman: A Social Study.* University of Durham, Department of Geography, Research Paper no. 3, 1960.

Khalaf, Samir, and Per Kongstad. *Hamra of Beirut: A Case of Rapid Urbanization.* Leiden: E. J. Brill, 1973.

Johns, Richard. "Oil in the Middle East and North Africa." In *The Middle East and North Africa 1974–75.* London: Europa Publications, 1974. Pp. 69–93.

Zahlan, A. (ed.). *Arab World: Year 2000.* Beirut: Arab Projects and Development, 1975.

Zehraoui, Ahsène. *Les travailleurs algériens en France: Étude sociologique de quelques aspects de la vie familiale.* Paris: Maspero, new edition, 1976.

*Part Four*

---

# Problems of Theory and Policy

# [12]

## International Migration Policies in a Changing World System

ARISTIDE  R.  ZOLBERG

### INTRODUCTION

The task I have set myself is drawn from the aphorism with which Kingsley Davis concluded a recent overview of human migrations from prehistoric times to the present: "Whether migration is controlled by those who send, by those who go, or by those who receive, it mirrors the world as it is at the time."[1] Among other things, this formulation draws attention to changes over time in the respective contributions to the total migratory flow, of individuals, seeking to maximize benefits by moving, and of societies, seeking to control population movements in accordance with interests of their own. It also suggests that these changes can be understood as consequences of changes of a more general nature occurring in the world as a whole.

A more substantive observation follows from the preceding. Although Davis and other demographers or economists view intrasocietal migrations and movement of people between societies as aspects of the same phenomenon, to which a single body of theory is therefore applicable, in the modern world an increasing differentiation has grown between the two segments of the total migratory flow. On the whole, in a world of states, internal migration is controlled to a considerable extent by "those who go"; as for international migration, the choices of individuals are very much constrained by the preferences of "those who send" and "those who receive."

241

Although specialists on migrations have long acknowledged this reality —as is shown, among other things, by the fact that the present essay is based almost entirely on their work—I believe that they have not dealt with it satisfactorily. The more analytic among them seldom take it into account in the elaboration of theories, most of which are founded on the axiom of individual choice. From that vantage point, the obstacles that states of putative origin and destination erect in the path of many who want to go, as well as the coercive measures that produce departures among many who would prefer to stay, are treated as events that lie beyond the explanatory domain of migration theories, as residual error does in an equation. But since the residual error accounts for more of the variance than does the equation, migration theories of this sort are, at best, useful as counterfactual models, suggesting what might occur under conditions of relatively free movement, and, at worst, trivial or even ideologically misleading. In contrast, the specialists who deal with the residual error component—emigration policies, forced population exchanges, expulsions, immigration policies and their concomitants such as naturalization law—tend to be a-theoretic. Produced mostly by historians or political scientists interested in a segment of social reality within specified time limits and in particular countries, by specialists of international law, and by students of international organization, the literature on these matters constitutes an array of discrete bits.[2]

It is my contention that these bits can be viewed as pieces of a puzzle and that the puzzle, if reconstituted, would transform the residual error of economic and sociological migration theories into an equation of its own. As for the time being only *some* of the pieces are available, the puzzle cannot be reconstructed. The mere demonstration that a puzzle exists can nevertheless be useful because the literature does not suggest that this is the case; if persuasive, the demonstration would lead to a search for missing pieces that would otherwise not be undertaken.

What follows can be viewed as the preliminary statement of a framework suitable for the analysis of past and present migrations. For each of three periods, spanning the emergence of a state system in Europe and its overseas expansion in the sixteenth century to the recent past, I shall attempt, first of all, to account for the emergence of a zone of exchange defined by some major population-receiving states and their principal suppliers. Second, I shall assess the relative contributions of the aggregate calculus of opportunity made by individuals and of the actions of states in shaping the intersocietal migrations under consideration. Third, focusing on the actions of states, I shall identify patterns of policy and seek to account for them in terms of the promotion of certain interests. Defined as a consequence of the activities of domestic groups, these interests are related to the situation of states in an international social system of which they are units, and whose structures and processes states attempt to modify to their advantage.

My somewhat unconventional use of the term "policy" and the concept "international social system" requires some clarification. "Policy" is used here in a very broad sense, which includes permissive indifference or "benign neglect"—the absence of specific legislation—with respect to a social phenomenon, as well as attempts to shape and to control it; policy includes not only formal rules and regulations, but also administrative practices concerning them, as well as related incentives and sanctions. The domain of such policies, or perhaps more appropriately, "postures," is that of intersocietal population movements. It covers, on the "exit" side, not only policies concerning emigration properly speaking (ranging perhaps from the distribution of positive incentives to severely sanctioned total prohibition), but also the expulsion of individuals or groups, and even the use of individuals as commodities in some form of international trade. On the "entry" side, the domain extends from immigration in the narrow sense (ranging once again from positive incentives to effectively enforced prohibitions), including purchase and capture, to policies concerning the treatment of arrivals in the receiving society such as naturalization law. When speaking of postures, I am by no means assuming, however, that at any one time a given state can be characterized as having a consistent policy with respect to all aspects of either exit or entry; inconsistencies or even contradictions may constitute a significant aspect of its overall posture and provide some clues toward an understanding of the interests which shaped it.

The concept of an "international social system" is no mere theoretical construct: the universality of population movements from one society to another demonstrates that societies are always parts of a larger sociobiological whole. As used in this essay, however, the concept refers to a specific historical phenomenon, the rise of a worldwide economic and political order under European hegemony in the sixteenth century and its expansion to encompass most of the globe by the end of the nineteenth. Whereas the existence of such a world system is generally acknowledged and the major features of its history are well known, there does not exist a completely satisfactory theoretical framework for its analysis. For the present purpose I shall posit, without elaborating its theoretical details, a world system that combines aspects of the sociobiological dimension emphasized by demographers, of the "international political system" elaborated by students of international relations, and of the "world capitalist system" recently constructed by Immanuel Wallerstein from the vantage point of political economy.[3] My somewhat eclectic approach resembles that of Geoffrey Barraclough in *An Introduction to Contemporary History.*[4]

The world system, described in some detail for each relevant period, is a stratified system of states, whose position in it is determined by a combination of political (diplomatic, military) and economic relationships that are somewhat autonomous from each other to a degree which varies over time, and whose interests with respect to the system are therefore complex. The system of states operates in a global environment characterized by a particular structure of spatially uneven distribution of population, physical resources, and opportunities. This unevenness produces among other things intersocietal population movements and state actions concerning them. With respect to the latter, the present conceptualization points to two general processes relevant to the analysis of migration policies: (1) The behavior of any given state in the system becomes an element in the interest-calculus of others; (2) Economic and political considerations may produce complementary or contradictory orientations among states with respect to the movement of human beings across their borders. That such movements not only matter greatly to the human beings involved but are of vital import to states as well is shown by the emergence, shortly after the world system under consideration originated, of a system of international law in whose sphere, Hannah Arendt pointed out, "sovereignty is nowhere more absolute than in matters of 'emigration, naturalization, nationality, and expulsion.' "[5]

## STATE-BUILDING AND MERCANTILISM, SIXTEENTH–EIGHTEENTH CENTURIES

The emergence of a new world system under European hegemony in the sixteenth and seventeenth centuries was accompanied by a profound transformation of human migrations in which the policies of major European states played a leading role. "The discovery of the sea," J. H. Parry has written, in the sense of discovery by Europeans of continuous sea-passage from ocean to ocean,

> inaugurated a new age, in which control of the world's trade and to a considerable extent also political control, fell gradually into the hands of a small group of states, mostly in Western Europe, which could build enough reliable ships to operate in all the oceans at once, and move at will from ocean to ocean. They created maritime empires, networks of trade, influence and power, on a scale formerly undreamt of.[6]

The process resulted in the institutionalization of a world capitalist system with a core initially dominated by Britain and the Netherlands, in relation to which outlying regions constituted a semi-periphery and a periphery. Simultaneously, the rulers of European states were struggling to assert their authority over home territories and populations. Europe became an arena for political and military competition among a limited number of sovereigns acknowledging each other's legitimacy, a process expressed in the birth of international law and in the elusive search for a balance of power.

These changes produced a concurrent transformation of population movements. As Kingsley Davis has put it, "In the sixteenth and seventeenth centuries, for the first time, the world began to be one migratory network dominated by a single group of technologically advanced and culturally similar states."[7] That the policies of states, reflecting persistent interests adjusted to the varying geographical and demographic configurations encountered in different regions, were more determinative than the preferences of migrants can be inferred from a brief overview of these movements.

From a quantitative point of view, the most important displacements occurred outside of Europe. As regions hitherto outside the system were incorporated into it as the periphery, states of the core displaced non-European populations from one region to another at their own convenience. Whereas inaccessible and sparsely inhabited territories were generally left in abeyance, tropical and subtropical regions, accessible by sea, were immediately exploited to produce commodities complementing Europe's. The requirement of huge inputs of cheap labor was fulfilled by massive involuntary migrations, among which the best known is the importation of West Africans as slaves into the Americas. Live arrivals grew from an estimated 1,800 a year for the period 1451–1600, to 13,400 for 1601–1700, and 55,000 for 1701–1810, a total of about 7.7 million altogether.[8] Accessible but thickly populated regions were handled more indirectly, often through a system of estate agriculture based on indentured labor which produced large-scale migrations within regions. The establishment of plantations also produced a limited flow of European migrations, mostly voluntary and temporary, to provide supervisory personnel. The most visible legacy of these migrations and of structurally similar ones in the nineteenth and early twentieth centuries are the "plural societies" of the colonial world, identified by J. S. Furnivall as amalgams of racially distinct groups bound together by a hierarchical division of labor.[9] (Many of them were to produce migrations again when the whites who controlled them were forced to relinquish their authority.)

Only the accessible, lightly populated, but temperate regions attracted permanent European migrants. For nearly three centuries, however, the transoceanic European populations remained limited to the coastal zones, where they grew mostly by the high natural increase of a small number of migrants. Davis suggests that so few went not only because "few people were so poor or so persecuted that they wanted to transfer to a wild area to live under subsistence conditions and battle savages" but also because there was little interest in fostering migrations to these territories so long as European populations grew slowly. These factors would account for a relatively steady trickle, i.e., for migration at a very low rate, over a long period. In fact, however, the migrations appear to have been concentrated in specific periods, distinct for different countries, during which they sometimes occurred at a relatively high rate. It has been recently suggested, for example, that "the rate of emigration in England between 1630 and 1700 averaged 7,000 per annum of a population of some seven million, an even higher rate of emigration per head of the population than prevailed in Spain during the sixteenth and seventeenth centuries."[10] The pattern points toward variation among factors governing European migration to the colonies, including the policy outlook mentioned by Davis.

Within Europe, to the endemic mobility of journeymen, mercenaries, and merchants, must be added migrations attributable to the deliberate actions of political authorities, eastward movements to settle colonies within the continent, and displacements resulting from great crises or measures of collective expulsion. Estimates of the numbers involved in the latter vary considerably; but on the whole, "it is certain that those displaced are numbered in several hundreds of thousand during the following crises: the expulsion of Jews and Moriscos in Spain; the emigration of the Protestants of the Spanish Netherlands; the departure of the Huguenots after the Revocation of the Edict of Nantes."[11]

The actions that produced most of these movements can be understood in terms of a very general policy founded on a belief in the absolute value of population to the sovereign except under very special conditions. In the sixteenth century, there was still much talk of overpopulation. But as European states engaged in state-building and colonial expansion under conditions of slow demographic growth, of labor-intensive production, and of equally labor-intensive warfare, population came to be perceived as a scarce resource. This perception was signaled by an awakening of demographic curiosity, "the joint achievement of four different groups: humanists, geographers, politicians, and economists."[12] Among the latter, Jean Bodin concisely summarized the doctrine that was to become an axiom until well into the nineteenth century: *Il n'est force ni richesse que d'hommes.*[13] The basic objectives of states constituted a form of primitive accumulation: keeping the indigenous population within the sovereign's possessions, maximizing its size, while acquiring a surplus from elsewhere in the system or even outside of it at the lowest possible cost. Within this framework, some were more valuable than others. At a time "when the mystery of trades lay in the heads of skilled workers, migration provided the means by which specialized skills could be transferred."[14]

As personal allegiance to lords and bonding, which usually implied very limited geographical mobility, shifted to the obligations of subjects to sovereigns—i.e., of the inhabitants of a larger territory to the ruler who exercised legitimate authority over that territory—the sovereign reinforced controls over the movements of goods and people across the boundaries of the home state and of its possessions. The principles of international law enunciated by Grotius and Pufendorf, on which law concerning exit, entry, and citizenship is founded, were devised in part for this very purpose.[15] It was also for the sovereign to determine who was more useful at home and who in the colonies. Concern for physical control of populations was coupled with concern for moral control as a foundation for allegiance, usually denoted by conformity with the sovereign's religious choice, but extending as well into other spheres.[16] When dissenters arose, the preferred solution was their forcible reconversion. If this failed, however, states might have to tolerate them or incur some loss by destroying or expelling them.

In keeping with a calculus of interests founded on considerations such as these, in the seventeenth and eighteenth centuries many states sought to encourage a higher rate of human reproduction in their home territories, to prevent the departure of especially productive subjects, and to attract productive foreigners.[17] As early as 1623, Spain encouraged foreigners to engage in agricultural and industrial pursuits by exempting them from various taxes, much as is often done now for foreign investors; incentives elsewhere included easy naturalization and dowries for the immigrants' daughters. In 1666, France restricted the number of celibate priests and nuns, granted tax exemptions for early marriages, and even provided a sort of allocation to encourage the raising of families, which was extended to Canadian colonists in 1669. International conflict fostered the imposition of severe restrictions on exit. Also in 1669, France raised sanctions against the emigration of navigators, shipbuilders, sailors and fishermen—many of them Huguenots—and sought to encourage their return if they had emigrated. Beginning in 1720, Britain also restricted the emigration of its seamen, artificers, and skilled workmen.

Although craftsmen often followed the pull of locational opportunities known to them through merchants from their own region or cultural group already active abroad, it is well known that many of them were deviants and dissenters who were expelled or who escaped. With every state seeking to retain its population, "an opportunity for international movement [of Europeans] on a large scale arose only when religious intolerance proved stronger than economic or political considerations."[18] The economic irrationality of intolerance was perceived very early. The Sultan Bajazet is reported to have exclaimed when the Spanish Jews began to arrive, "What! Call ye this Ferdinand 'wise'—he who depopulates his own dominions in order to enrich mine?"[19]

How did it come about that states created the very conditions which produced the departure of valuable populations? John Armstrong has identified the process which ultimately led to the expulsion of the Jews from Spain, and which is relevant to "mobilized diasporas" in general, as follows.[20] When there is a sharp overall rise in social mobilization among the dominant ethnic population, the previously established symbiotic relationship between the dominant ethnic elite and the mobilized diaspora is upset because the "impurity" of the upper stratum threatens to become a ground for drastic turnover in elites. Ferdinand, an erstwhile protector of the Jews, "sanctioned the Inquisition to quiet populist rumors assailing his Jewish ancestry." This process involves "frustrations" and "scapegoating," but not just *any* frustrations and *any* scapegoat, since the social mobilization that alters what Armstrong calls the "terms of exchange" between relevant actors and groups is itself occasioned by the more ambitious activities of states in a changing world system such as the one under consideration.

The cases of Protestants in the Spanish Netherlands and Huguenots in France seem to be attributable more precisely to what would now be termed a concern with internal security. Given the configuration of international conflict in the latter part of the sixteenth century and throughout the seventeenth, French Calvinists and those living under Spanish rule in the southern Low Countries (now Belgium) might be torn between allegiance to their native land and allegiance to the United Provinces, homeland of their revolution. The behavior of Spain and France with respect to Calvinists, irrational from an economic point of view, was much less so from a strategic one.

Countries competed with one another for valuable Protestant refugees. France received many of them, particularly from the Spanish Low Countries, until the mid-seventeenth century; when they were opposed by indigenous guilds in Protestant countries, "the State intervened in their favour, not for humanitarian reasons, but in order to keep them at work."[21] In the long run, this competition contributed to the beginnings of religious toleration. Austria's Patent of Tolerance (1781), which gave Protestants the same rights as Catholic subjects, reflected a desire to develop manufactures by attracting to the realm immigrants with appropriate skills and capital.[22]

Formulation of migration policies toward various overseas colonies involved not only the European states but also the companies they chartered and often the colonies themselves. To piece together the widely scattered information concerning this subject requires a large-scale research task I have not undertaken. Policies appear to have been governed by general demographic estimates, by the economic conjuncture of the home territory, and by strategic considerations. For example, so long as it was believed that the population exceeded home needs and that the surplus produced social and political disturbances, colonial emigration of the populace was generally encouraged; but rotation was preferred for people of quality acting as supervisory personnel in the plantations and as imperial guards.[23] When and where overseas expansion itself produced economic growth at home, however, the surplus turned into a shortage. This occurred in Britain in the second half of the seventeenth century.[24] It was now argued that the emigration of Englishmen to the colonies was warranted only if the colonies could be compelled to confine their trade to the mother country and if their activities provided labor for the homeland, as mercantilists believed was the case in the plantation belt where Englishmen supervised productive slaves, but not in New England.[25]

Preferring to retain scarce population resources at home, but wishing also to develop colonies and to counter French designs upon them, Britain seems to have stumbled on a clever solution which also eased religious and political dissent. The relocation of dissenters in colonies (including Ireland) constituted a combination of "voluntary exile" and "right of asylum," which Albert Hirschman has analyzed with respect to Latin American republics at a later time as a "conspiracy in restraint of voice."[26] Furthermore, in the early eighteenth century, when "many reasons rendered the speedy occupation of wilderness areas desirable," and since native colonists did not produce a sufficient population surplus, Britain's "efforts turned to other countries, making the encouragement of non-English subjects a distinctive feature of the new immigration policy."[27] As foreign settlers were almost necessarily refugees—given that emigration was nearly universally prohibited—their loyalty to the receiving country could be counted upon.

French policies provide an interesting contrast. Although seaboard-dwelling Huguenots were among the most colonial-minded of subjects, it was decreed when New France was restored in 1632 that settlers must be Catholic.[28] Requiring the company it chartered to provide 300 colonists a year, the state was reluctant to provide incentives for individuals to go; in consequence, there were only 2,000 settlers in New France by 1660. The state now placed the colony under direct supervision, chartered a new company, and sent 2,000 emigrants to Canada in 1665 alone. But the new company was equally unsuccessful in providing colonists. Although apparently a certain number of Huguenots had gone there as well as to the West Indies in spite of prohibitions, they were expelled from all these colonies between 1683 and 1715, ending up for the most part in mainland English ones. By then, the "English" outnumbered the French in America by twenty to one.

The British solution was very successful in the short run and contributed significantly to the expulsion of France from North America in the eighteenth century. That the United Provinces followed a policy similar to the British in southern Africa during this period suggests that their common posture may have been facilitated by the dominant position the two states occupied within the core of the world system at the time. They were mercantilists vis-à-vis each other and in relation to the rest of the world; but within the segment each controlled, a more liberal orientation emerged. As the first capitalist powers, each of them independently recognized quite early the advantages of removing obstacles to population movements within and between their possessions.[29]

As Britain's gain was viewed as everyone else's loss, while improving conditions in the New World and spreading information about opportunities there increased the transoceanic pull, concern with emigration to America definitely rose throughout Western and Central Europe in the eighteenth century. The considerations were military as well as economic. Authorities opposed emigration by a combination of legal barriers and moral exhortation:

> To emigrate was equivalent to desertion and meant forfeiture of all political and economic rights, with the penalty of imprisonment in case of return. The Bible was used to justify this position and government, fearing the loss of farmers and industrial workers, stressed the view that a person should remain in the land of his fathers. To depart was sinful, and the wage of sin was death.[30]

At the lower levels of society, serfdom and its sequels were still partly effective as a restriction on exit; with respect to the higher levels, most German principalities, Swiss cantons, and the Austrian Hapsburgs, without New World colonies of their own, imposed the sorts of sanctions already mentioned with regard to France, prohibited propaganda by the promoters of emigration, issued their own counterpropaganda, and collaborated with each other to prevent embarkation. They made it extremely difficult to dispose of property in preparation for leaving, prevented the sending of financial aid to those who departed, and cut emigrants off from their inheritances. Nevertheless, departures occurred at all levels of society. The poor had little to lose; and states began to agree in the sense that the poor, the lame, and the marginal constituted no loss to them and no gain to others. The propertied could often make arrangements of some sort. Little was done, however, to make those who had an interest in leaving want instead to stay: "It was this attempt to dam the stream without paying attention to the headwaters that in the long run made all restrictive efforts a failure."[31] Moreover there prevailed during this period, even in "absolutist" France, a great hiatus between the restrictive intent of the state and the coercive apparatus available to enforce its will.

In the course of the worldwide conflict that erupted in the late eighteenth century, ideology and national origin replaced religion as criteria of political reliability.[32] Between 1789 and 1792, for example, about 8,000 French refugees landed in Britain. In contrast to the generous self-interest that shaped the reception of their Huguenot predecessors, however, the emigrés were suspect. Popular francophobia and "fears that Jacobin emissaries had infiltrated the ranks of the refugees" produced the first Alien Bill (1793), whose preamble pointed out that "a great and unusual number of aliens have lately resorted to the kingdom." Masters were obligated to report foreigners to customs officers; foreigners had to give an account of themselves and turn in their arms; the King-in-Council could prevent them from landing and could direct those authorized to land to live in a particular district; foreigners had to register and could be deported for good cause, as defined by law-enforcement officials rather than by the courts. Similarly, revolutionary France decreed in 1795 and 1796 that all foreigners must turn in their passports and register with the municipal authorities of their place of residence. The comprehensive French passport law of 1797 constituted "the starting point for modern aliens legislation." Similar fears of political subversion motivated the imposition of parallel controls on entry in the United States (1798), Canada (1794), and Switzerland (1798 and 1799).

Although many of these laws were allowed to fall into desuetude once the alleged threat was deemed to have diminished—in Britain, however, not before 1826—the principle remained. Restrictions of this sort are revived in direct or indirect form whenever social upheavals in one or another part of the world system produce an increase of voluntary and involuntary migrations, and when those who receive temporarily give greater weight to security than to economic considerations. Far from being irrational, these restrictions are the means whereby the state can extend beyond its boundaries the police structure used at home to maintain social and political order.

## THE TRANSITION TO LIBERALISM, 1815–C. 1880

Only in a limited political sense did the Napoleonic Wars end in "A World Restored," as the Concert of Europe was established in a world system that was undergoing some profound transformations. The localized agricultural and demographic revolutions of the eighteenth century now became more generalized, having already begun to foster an industrial one. Combining economic hegemony with political paramountcy for most of the nineteenth century, Britain was able to shape an expanding segment of the world system in accordance with its interests. Within it, peace prevailed and international economic exchanges increased. Barriers to the movement of people and goods across state boundaries were progressively removed. Other early industrializers with limited political power, such as Belgium, progressively joined in. As they too industrialized, most of the other major European powers attempted to enlarge their exchange zones by constructing international economies of their own; barriers were removed within these but much less so between them. For the world system as a whole, liberalism was a central tendency emanating from the core but never fully realized even within it. Mercantilist structures persisted by adapting to new conditions. As economic imperatives brought about competition among states of the enlarged core for political control of the outer zones of the system, the balance of power ceased to function, ushering in an epoch of conflict.

The calculus of states with respect to populations was profoundly affected by the "great transformation" originally analyzed by Marx and Engels, and more recently restated by Karl Polanyi.[33] The market pattern evolved to include labor because capitalism could not function without a free labor system, and this required the removal of obstacles to the mobility of labor. The initial lack of understanding of this imperative is one of the central points in Polanyi's famous discussion of Speenhamland. Whereas Marx and Polanyi focused on the phenomenon as it occurred within states (migrations from Ireland to Britain being considered internal), there were striking, but in retrospect unsurprising, parallels in the evolution of policies concerning external population movements in the larger international market.

The factors that produced the transition from mercantilism to liberalism can best be seen in the Atlantic sector involving the British Isles and North America, which Brinley Thomas considered to have become "a single economy" in the nineteenth century, and which, incidentally, accounted for slightly over half of the estimated total European intercontinental migrations between 1820 and 1880.[34] Initially, much as on the internal scene, the generalization of a labor market at the international level produced intervention *against* market forces. When emigration from the Scottish Highlands, checked by French hostilities, resumed after the Peace of Amiens, landed proprietors pressed the government to take deterrent action. The resulting Passenger Act of 1803 introduced, according to MacDonagh, a "revolutionary principle to English law, interference of legislation with freedom of contract."[35] The act provided safer conditions for transatlantic travelers, but in doing so raised the cost of passage and thus of emigration: it was "cradled in mercantilism." Humanitarian intentions notwithstanding, its "general economic purpose ... certainly helps to explain the ease with which monstrous penalties and reckless prohibitions and injunctions were piled up."[36]

The Passenger Act reflected strategic considerations as well. If British emigration was inevitable, it should be diverted from the still-dangerous United States to the ill-defended Canadian provinces populated by recently conquered French Catholics and some American loyalists, whose long-term reliability was questionable.

Although hostility toward emigration did not disappear suddenly in Britain after the Napoleonic Wars, evidence from the 1811 census that population had grown by 15 percent in the previous decade, the steady stream of internal migration to the new industrial areas, the growing influence of the political economists, and the rise of the "dangerous poor," contributed to bring about a change of posture with respect to departure for the colonies. Adam Smith had already "provided a rationale for [colonial] emigration and settlement which was absent in the mercantilist system," namely that it would constitute a *market* for home industrial production while simultaneously meeting the problem of overpopulation in a positive instead of a negative way.[37] The rising costs of poor relief and the social disturbances occasioned by a postwar depression coupled with rapid demobilization made the colonial emigration solution an even more attractive one. "By emigration a supplicant for public handouts in Britain could become a customer for British manufacturers in the colonies. In this light the process was doubly desirable."[38]

In 1819, a select committee on the Poor Laws virtually recommended emigration to the workers. In spite of objections from the Colonial Office that emigration of paupers would merely transfer the problem from one part of the Empire to another, Parliament voted £150,000 for a project of emigration to the recently acquired Cape Colony, while the Prime Minister agreed to help Scottish weavers migrate to Upper Canada. Emigrants were also sought in Northern Ireland, in spite of Peel's concern that the departure of Protestants would reinforce the position of Catholics on the island.[39] Such schemes were facilitated, initially, by the need to send ships to repatriate 20,000 troops from North America and, subsequently, by the usefulness of emigrants as westbound paying ballast for timber ships. In keeping with these considerations, the 1803 Act was steadily pared down and the century-old ban on emigration of artisans and seamen was swept away in 1824.

Attempts to control the destination of emigrants by means of preferential fares for Canada did little good, however, as many disappeared over the border after landing: "For the Irish, St. Andrews had become a major port of entry in the United States."[40] Moreover, the interests of the shipping and timber merchants in competing against American commerce soon outweighed suspicions that the United States would use immigrants in military expeditions against Canada. By the onset of the 1827 sailing season, all existing passenger legislation that restricted and directed emigration was swept from the books. Subsequent acts reflected humanitarian restraints on the freedom of contract that were but weak palliatives to the market's awesome push and pull. All were now emigrationists, with the exception of some "Radical Tories," who appear to have anticipated a contemporary outlook by arguing that the poor were part of the nation who had the right to live in England even if it required charity and relief.[41]

Although the fear of working-class violence which contributed to passage of the Reform Act also produced more talk of assisted emigration, an

unprecedented number of departures in 1830 and 1831 led the recently constituted Emigration Commission to conclude that agencies to stimulate emigration would be superfluous. The Poor Law Amendment Act of 1834 did
include a clause enabling parishes to raise money for emigration, on the
grounds that each emigrant thus sponsored would soon be financing others;
however, the overall effect of the act left parishes with less incentive to
organize emigration from Britain. In 1838, a similar provision was established
for Ireland, where in any case eviction and soon famine provided enough
incentive to transform the stream of "free" migration into a flood. As the
advent of steam reduced the risks and financial costs of ocean-crossing, Adam
Smith's rationale became more than ever applicable to the settlement of
British possessions in North America, southern Africa, and the Pacific. British
migrants went to areas under British political and economic dominion, and
their presence there insured that this dual dominion would be maintained
and extended. Concurrently, Britain's home need for manpower was so great
that all barriers to the entry of aliens were removed as well.[42] For the time
being, however, few came, and the need was met by drawing from Ireland,
Britain's internal periphery.[43] From the 1840s on, these liberal migration
policies were coupled with free trade, including a liberal transportation
policy, all of them congruent with Britain's interests as the core of the world
capitalist system.

The established view of the United States during this period is that, with
the exception of the Alien and Sedition Act interlude and the subsequent
prohibition of the slave trade, "immigration was allowed to ebb and flow of
its own accord, guided mainly by a fluctuating economic barometer in both
Europe and America."[44] This posture, which has been characterized as an
absence of policy, in sharp contrast not only with the restrictionist orientation that prevailed later on but with contemporaneous American policies
concerning the entry of goods, has been attributed to such factors as a belief
in universal nationality, an implicit faith in the country's capacity to assimilate all comers, and a deep sense of military security.[45] In reality things were
much more complex. From the very beginning, immigration was a controversial arena in which diverse interests strove for dominance, as was the case
for tariff. Laissez-faire was a deliberate policy choice, and it was qualified by
incentives and by restrictions. That, in spite of efforts by many to the contrary, a generally open immigration policy was maintained for so long is
precisely the question on which the analysis of American policy within the
present framework leads us to focus.

Louis Jaffe has summarized the complex of interests favoring laissez-
faire as follows:

> Unlimited immigration was the logical concomitant of basic American pol-
> icy. The United States was committed very early to its philosophy of "mani-

fest destiny." The goal was the occupation and settlement of the country. . . .
The policy required men as soldiers and as workers. Immigration, therefore,
satisfied needs to which government gives highest priority: economic well-
being and defense.[46]

As a consequence of endemic conflict, the years from the American Revolution to the end of the Napoleonic Wars "comprised a period during which
immigration was hardly more than a trickle," in the course of which "a
society accustomed to constant infusions from abroad found time to adjust
itself to a condition where its people were home-born and home-bred."[47]
The most obvious indicator of what Marcus Lee Hansen called "the First
Americanization" was the almost complete victory of the English language
over its rivals.[48] Now, however, the manufacturing plants fostered by the
War of 1812 needed laborers; more generally, "unlimited manpower was
necessary if . . . projects were to be carried through on the scale of which
Americans dreamed—and immigration could supply that manpower."[49] One
might expect that those who dreamed such dreams would seek to keep the
gate wide open and even to provide incentives for immigration.

Whereas Hansen states that the United States "began its career with no
encouragement to immigrants except that offered by its opportunities . . . ,"
pointing out that Hamilton rejected the suggestion that free land grants be
used to attract Europeans in favor of the sale of land "at a price sufficient to
replenish the official coffers and to insure that the settlers would have ample
capital to tide over the first critical months," I believe this to be a misunder-
standing on his part.[50] As the state acquired land at low cost by expropriating
Indians, and as it used its income from sales to provide services for settlers,
including protection against those expropriated, the land policy should be
viewed as a form of primitive accumulation in the hands of American authorities which did serve to subsidize European settlement. Moreover, the easy
naturalization procedures instituted to reward alien supporters of the Revolution were maintained as an attraction; in America, as Hansen himself
pointed out, Europeans could obtain the rights of citizens without incurring
the obligation of military service.

On the other hand, some control was exercised from the very beginning
on the gate itself, and under circumstances which suggest that attempts were
being made to improve upon the "fluctuating economic barometer in both
Europe and America" as the regulator of immigration. Arrivals, estimated at
less than a quarter million from 1790 to 1815, reached an estimated 30,000 in
1817 alone, and perhaps an even higher level the following year.[51] According
to Hansen, the congressional investigation launched in 1818 was not
prompted by hostile sentiment toward foreigners, but was due to humanitarian concern for transatlantic passengers and the need to keep out pesti-

lence. He states that "the law of March 4, 1819, was merely a regulatory, not a restrictive measure. Recognizing overcrowding as the fundamental trouble, it forbade any transatlantic ship entering an American port to carry more than two persons for every five tons of registry. Customs officers must record the number of passengers in such vessels. Heavy penalties were inflicted on violators."[52] He also points out that the effective date of the law, September 1, 1819, marks the beginning of "federal supervision and official statistics of immigration."

There was more to this law than Hansen suggests. Whatever its intent, the law was restrictive in its effects, as was the British Act of 1803. By raising the costs of passage, the new regulations most likely selected out the least productive immigrants. Such selectivity made sense when an unlimited supply of labor seemed assured because of information in Europe concerning boom conditions in America. Incidentally, as Hansen was aware, the act affected especially those originating outside the British Isles (because the British Passenger Act mentioned earlier had already imposed similar regulations on shipping), a consequence which, if not deliberately sought, was probably not unwelcome. Finally, the establishment of statistics constituted both a symbolic extension of the domain of state concern and a foundation for the potential exercise of further regulation when circumstances changed.

When the American boom collapsed almost immediately following its passage, the law stood as a useful deterrent until market forces did their work. Meanwhile, the stream of those who had departed when the boom was still on in the spring of 1819 arrived after the bust had hit; in New York, "as the summer wore on ... the calls upon charity became insistent." The city now attempted to enforce an existing state law which "required each master of a vessel to report his passenger at the mayor's office, and authorized the municipal officials at their discretion to demand a bond not exceeding three hundred dollars for each alien likely to become a public charge."[53] Although Hansen merely concludes that New York City's restrictive efforts met with little success in the short run because shippers could easily dispose of their human cargo in other ways, it is not farfetched to surmise that regulations of this sort had a deterrent effect in the longer run. Be that as it may, these regulations indicate that during a period of economic contraction, when interests of employers, of the taxpaying middle classes, and of indigenous labor were congruent, the United States did not rely on market forces alone to regulate immigration.

When economic expansion resumed, the bonding system entailed little risk as labor would be absorbed; and, as with the British Passenger Act of 1803, it need not be enforced. This seems to have been what happened. Immigration climbed slowly in the 1820s, passing the ten thousand-mark in 1825, and averaging around 20,000 a year during the remainder of the decade.[54] The charitable institutions of Eastern seaboard cities persisted in their efforts to use a bonding system in order to shift the cost of relief to the shippers and thereby ultimately to the immigrants themselves. However, "professional bondsmen took over the task of supplying the bonds and the administration was handled so laxly that by 1828 the price had fallen so low as two dollars for bonds for a whole shipload of immigrants."[55] I would expect to find a parallel trend in the administrative history of the federal Passenger Act as well.

The attribution of the restrictive orientation of charitable institutions to economic concerns is not incompatible with Billington's interpretation of their efforts as an expression of antiforeign, and particularly anti-Catholic, prejudice. Although as of 1830, arrivals from the preceding decade and a half probably constituted no more than 2 or 3 percent of the total white population of 10.5 million, the bulk of whom were Americans of eighteenth-century standing or descent, many among them already wondered "if these thousands of foreigners could be absorbed or if they would engulf the native population."[56] The rate of immigration then climbed so rapidly in the next two decades that by 1850, the proportion foreign born reached 11.5 percent of the white population, and 15.5 percent in the Northeast alone. In a period of American economic expansion, the push and pull of the market produced a large-scale immigration which satisfied employers as it kept the supply of labor high and hence wages low. But the market created local inefficiencies, in the sense that seaboard cities became human warehouses where labor had to be maintained before it became productive. Under existing conditions of political organization, the costs of these inefficiencies (relief and social disturbances) were borne most heavily by local taxpayers. English-speaking Protestants, they used the dense network of philanthropic associations that Tocqueville so much admired as an organization for the defense of their economic interests and of their preferred way of life.

It is this class which produced and was the principal audience for "a whole school of writers . . .determined to convince Americans that immigration should be stopped or rigidly regulated," mostly on the grounds that the Irish and German Catholics, who constituted an ever-growing proportion of the total, were a "Rome-directed group of papal serfs bent on the planned destruction of the United States," or were sent by "foreign capitalists" to constitute colonies which would be so isolated as to resist Americanization, or yet that these Catholic immigrants were lawless and disorderly whiskey and beer-drinkers who would undermine the country's moral fiber.[57] If they could not be kept out altogether, they must at least be kept outside the body politic. Nativists argued that the easy naturalization procedures were not intended by the founding fathers to be permanent and were unsuitable for the new kind of foreigner, who should also be made to wait twenty-one years before being allowed to vote, as was the case for American-born men. Proposals to restrict access to citizenship and to require it for voting were major planks in the platform of the American Party organized in New York in 1843. Mostly middle-class in composition, "the nativists more and more took the opportunity to excite native workmen against immigrant competitors." They also secured support among southerners who resented the additional population weight which aliens gave to the North.

Little was done, however, until the European economic and political crises of the 1840s produced a push that outweighed the American pull. Under the impact of these crises, the governments of Germany among others "reversed their attitude of a decade before when they had looked upon every emigrant as a national loss and had hindered departure by a multitude of regulations. A strong motive was doubtless the belief that a 'bloodletting' would preclude a revival of social disorders. Among the concessions made in 1848–49 was a simplification of all the legal formalities which preceded emigration."[58] On the American side, as early as December 1846, "petitions from officials of the state and city of New York and from charitable organizations" urged Congress to institute "a more effective control" on immigration than was provided by the law of 1819.[59] The act of February 1847, "supported by all political factions," raised the standards of passenger ships and imposed more severe sanctions for violations. Attributing this action once again to humanitarian concerns, Hansen nevertheless relates that rumors in Europe "gave the impression that the new American law amounted to a prohibition of immigration."

Once again, however, middle-class urban interests clashed with others. The rapid diversion of immigrant trade to Canada "occasioned alarm among the various American interests concerned with the traffic" and prompted the Secretary of the Treasury to interpret the law very loosely. As the flood continued, New York, Massachusetts, Maryland, and Louisiana resorted to a strengthening of the bonding system by imposing a flat fee per head on shippers. Although "the people in four states had been aroused to action and had set up barriers which, though not prohibitive, indicated their belief that no longer should all classes of Europeans pass unrestricted through their gates," shippers, unable to "shift the tax to the emigrant by increasing the price of passage because conditions of competition made this inexpedient," successfully challenged the fee procedure before the Supreme Court.[60] The states then returned to the older bonding system. In 1848, Congress passed a passenger act more in keeping with shipping interests.

It is remarkable that the nativist coalition spearheaded by the Know-Nothing party, which swept the country in 1850–54 in response to the great migration, was unable to secure at the very height of its power the passage by Congress of the restrictionist legislation it advocated so vociferously and which was directed against a religious group that the majority of Americans simultaneously held in contempt and feared. This was not for lack of trying.[61] A comprehensive bill restricting immigration of the unfit and requiring a twenty-one year probation period for naturalization was buried in the Senate Judiciary committee, which recommended a year later against its passage. Opponents in both the Senate and the House insisted that the Constitution nowhere gave Congress the power to pass restrictive measures against certain classes of immigrants "no matter how desirable that might be" and urged the states to act instead under their police powers. Connecticut and Massachusetts, where Know-Nothing victories had brought in many new officeholders of modest means, then did so by imposing literacy tests on voters in 1855 and 1856 respectively, and New York and Massachusetts also prohibited the immigration of "convicts, lunatics, idiots, and paupers."

Whether these laws had a significant effect is difficult to say. The incoming tide was halved in 1855, and the level achieved in 1854 remained unequaled until 1873. Hansen acknowledges that "intolerance" contributed to the decline but insists that "other factors were more fundamental," among them the Crimean War, which caused a shortage of shipping, and a reduction of the demand for labor in the United States due to a business slump, itself attributable to drought in the West.[62] Was it coincidental that Congress, having resisted Know-Nothing pressures for restrictive legislation, passed in 1855 under these beginning slump conditions a comprehensive statute regulating tonnage and space requirements, which raised fares even above the increase produced by shipping shortages? In any case, the law worked, Hansen suggests, because commercial decline "caused shippers out of self-interest to make conditions more attractive to passengers."[63] Perhaps the Know-Nothings got their way after all, an outcome that does not appear to have occurred to Billington.[64]

The play of interests worked the other way when expansion resumed during and after the Civil War, whereas immigration did not, because economic growth in France, Germany, and elsewhere now absorbed an increasing share of the total supply of European labor while upheavals in the United States acted as a deterrent. Now, for the first time since Hamilton's rejection of land grants, the United States resorted to incentives and subsidies. The Homesteading programs made possible by the further expropriation of Indian land, brought in not only manpower to develop the land, but enough of a surplus of hopeful European peasants to insure a steady supply of industrial labor as well. In the face of severe shortages after the Civil War, Congress even passed a law authorizing employers to pay the passage of prospective immigrants by binding their services. A number of states established promotional agencies in Europe. When Manifest Destiny demanded that California be linked more efficiently with the East, a need for labor arose there as well; hence, California sentiment against Chinese notwithstanding, the United States negotiated the treaty of 1868, which guaranteed reciprocal free entry between the United States and China, an exchange of labor and trade typical of relations between core and periphery. The restrictive immigration laws of New York and Massachusetts were declared unconstitutional by the Supreme Court in 1876. Only in 1882 was a similar measure instituted at the federal level, ushering in a new policy orientation, which will be discussed in the next section.

Although a more detailed investigation is required before the links among these various strands can be established, it is evident that the American posture with respect to immigration was a much more active one than is suggested by the term laissez-faire. Why the discrepancy between widespread restrictionist sentiment and immigration policy during the half-century under consideration? The various coalitions which sought to close the door included all sections of the country, various fragments of the middle classes for the reasons shown, as well as a good part of the urban working class, in whose interest it was to limit the supply of labor. There was but one element lacking: the industrial bourgeoisie, whose project required a vast supply of labor and which profited as well from the traffic itself. Not in full control of political institutions at the state and federal levels, the weight of the manufacturers, the banks, the shippers, and the railroads was nevertheless sufficient to prevent the establishment of permanent restrictions detrimental to their interests. Their own policy was to assist the market in producing desirable outcomes. When demand and supply of labor were in equilibrium, laissez-faire sufficed, as it in effect subsidized capitalist entrepreneurs; when the supply was insufficient, incentives were provided at public cost; and when demand diminished, the restrictionists could have their way so long as they did not thereby mortgage the future.

The preceding analysis would undoubtedly benefit from a systematic comparison of the United States with Canada, where more selective policies designed to secure a better class of mostly English-speaking immigrants seem to have emerged quite early. For a Protestant regime established over a French Catholic population in a strategically vulnerable region of the Empire, the right sort of immigration was a vital necessity. The need for settlers in Upper Canada, only partly met by American loyalists, could not be met by mobilizing the French, as they would then impart to Canadian society as a whole their own cultural character. Besides, the French became restless in the 1820s and rebelled a decade later, expressing some interest in seceding from Canada to join the United States. It was also vital to keep the economy in British hands. Colonial authorities very early expressed concern to avoid becoming the guardians of an imperial poorhouse. In 1815, for example, Nova Scotia protested against the immigration of Negroes from Bermuda; and in response to the liberalization of British emigration policy in the 1820s, various provinces required masters to post a £10 bond per passenger, refundable only if the passenger survived for a year and supported himself by the end of that period. Suspended in the face of various protests, the legislation was reimposed when a cholera epidemic required the creation of health facilities for newcomers.[65]

Restrictions against the poor appear to have been coupled with incentives for those somewhat better off, as "every arrival could apply for a grant of land proportionate to the means he possessed for its cultivation. Many small farmer capitalists found Upper Canada an ideal location, English in government and society."[66] Exchanges between the United States and Canada seem to have further reinforced the relatively British and middle-class character of Canadian settlement. In 1851, a general head tax was imposed on all immigrants; the landing of disabled was prohibited in 1869, of paupers and "vicious" persons in 1872, a decade earlier than in the United States.

Those who came to Canada between 1815 and 1850 originated in the British Isles to an even greater extent than was the case in the United States; and among them an increasing proportion were Irish Catholics. This might have been a disadvantage from an imperial point of view had they merged with their coreligionists. Some did; but most chose instead to become incorporated in a society dominated by Ulstermen whose language they shared. In spite of their efforts, French Canadians were unable to attract Frenchmen to Quebec. Approximate parity between "English" (mostly Scottish and Irish) and French Canadians was reached around mid-century, after which the English gained the upper hand in spite of the French Canadians' extremely high rate of natural reproduction. On the one hand, the government subsidized immigration in a manner paralleling the recent American policy (Homestead Exemption Act, 1878; Dominion Land Acts, 1872, 1874, 1883).[67] On the other, denied the cultural facilities which might enable them to participate in the westward movement without also becoming "English," many French Canadians migrated instead to the lumber camps and industrial mills of New England, where for the time being assimilationist pressures were less intensive, and whose proximity facilitated return migrations.[68] The English did little to stem this tide, and the efforts of Quebec leaders to do so were ineffective. Through this unique process of population exchange, Canada underwent a profound transformation that consolidated the culturally specific character of its capitalist development.

In contrast with the preceding, the case of France highlights how states developed distinct migration postures in keeping with different situations in the world system. France in the nineteenth century can be viewed as a country in which two societies coexisted.[69] Although maritime capitalism had emerged in the eighteenth century, the agrarian-oriented administrative structures of the Ancien Régime outlived revolutionary upheavals. Modernized and reinforced, they prevented the "great transformation" from running its full course. The emergence of political liberalism was constrained, and the country industrialized more slowly, retaining numerous small units of agricultural production. Frenchmen, unlike Englishmen, had the choice of a viable rural way of life, so long as they kept their families small. Expelled from North America and Asia, now shut out of the mainstream Atlantic trade, France remained on the margin of the capitalist core and sought to develop an autarchic international economy by controlling a semi-periphery of its own, mostly in Eastern Europe, and a new colonial periphery in Africa. This general orientation also enhanced the likelihood of France's involvement in land wars and thereby enhanced the value of population as a military resource.

Factors of this sort, combined with demography, account better than any cultural explanation for the low rate of French emigration throughout the nineteenth century. They suggest why probably a smaller proportion of Frenchmen wanted to leave than was the case in most other European countries, and why the state maintained an ambivalent posture toward the exit of its citizens, a deterrent which further reduced the number of departures. They also appear to explain the direction of movements and France's consistently favorable posture toward immigrants, in spite of nativist pressures similar to the ones encountered in the United States.

With respect to exit, although the Rights of Man guaranteed "free sojourn and free circulation," and the Constitution of 1791 provided "freedom to move about, to remain, to leave," Article 17 of the Civil Code subsequently deprived Frenchmen of their citizenship if they established themselves abroad with no intention of returning.[70] Additional administrative restrictions on emigration were imposed during the Restoration. It is noteworthy that even Jean-Baptiste Say, the most prominent French follower of the Scottish economists, opposed emigration: "The departure of 100,000 emigrants per year is equivalent to the loss of 100,000 drowned every year with arms and baggage while crossing the border."[71] For this descendant of returned Huguenots, Adam Smith's reasoning concerning the advantages of colonial emigration was inapplicable, as France no longer controlled appropriate overseas lands.

Nevertheless, Frenchmen did leave. Legal and administrative restrictions were not enforced against the destitute by departmental authorities glad to be relieved of them; but it is possible that the restrictions deterred the departure of better-off citizens or at least influenced the choice of their destination. The low estimate of emigration, initially established on the basis of recorded arrivals in the United States, was revised upwards by Louis Chevalier in 1947 on the basis of information concerning departures and arrivals elsewhere, and now stands at considerably over 20,000 a year during the first half of the nineteenth century, with relatively little annual variation. However imprecise the data, they do reveal some significant features. French emigration consisted less of a rural "mass phenomenon" than of an aggregate of individual cases, mostly craftsmen and businessmen, suggesting that there was less emigration for the same reason that there was less internal migration, i.e., because of the lesser impact of the "great transformation" on French society as a whole during that period. Moreover, of those who left, fewer went to the emerging British-North American political and economic zone, and more to the equivalent zone France was seeking to establish in relation to contiguous countries such as Italy, Spain, and Belgium, as well as in relation to parts of Eastern Europe, of Latin America, and of North Africa.

Emigration rose suddenly, as it did elsewhere in Europe, when economic disaster hit in the 1840s, and the upheavals of 1848–51 produced a stream of political refugees and exiles as well. The Second Empire, which came into being as the rate of natural growth of the French population underwent a sharp decline, constituted an authoritarian and initially neo-mercantilist interlude, in the course of which controls on exit were reinforced. The activities of foreign recruitment agencies were restricted in order to redirect the flow of metropolitan emigration from Latin America to Algeria. Concurrently, however, the door was kept wide open to foreign labor. Its regime notwithstanding, France obviously provided an attractive market for Belgian and Italian workers, as they contributed heavily to bring up the proportion of foreigners from 1 percent of the total population in 1851 to 2 percent (740,668) in 1872. It is likely that around this time France became the first European country to achieve a positive migration balance in the nineteenth century.

In keeping with the liberal orientation of its parliamentary elite, the Third Republic eliminated formal restrictions on exit, including even the old Article 17 of the code. Nevertheless, the bureaucratic elite maintained restrictive administrative practices, and military service obligations deterred the departure not only of young men but also of their families, except for the purpose of Algerian colonization. In any case, market forces probably continued to favor a positive migration balance, as foreigners and naturalized citizens together amounted to 2.9 percent of the total population (about 1.1 million) by 1881. After recovering from the depression of the 1880s, France sought to attract foreigners by facilitating their naturalization (1889 law). As citizens, they or their children would of course be liable to military service. With respect to Algeria, it is interesting to note that France developed policies similar to those encountered in the United States and Canada: free settlement of foreigners, facilities for their naturalization, and some form of homesteading. Moreover, the land policies used to attract French and foreign settlers required the expropriation of indigenous Algerians, a policy which had the added beneficial consequence, from the French point of view, of transforming that population into a labor reserve for the mainland.[72]

It can generally be concluded that both the liberal pattern of migration policy which emerged within the enlarged and relatively peaceful Atlantic world and deviations from it illustrated by France—to which other cases, particularly some of the German states and Russia, could be added—can be accounted for by the interests of states occupying specific positions within the world system they helped to shape, interests defined by the hegemonic groups which ruled them. The migratory movements of Europeans within Europe and overseas during this period were exceptional not only in their unprecedented magnitude but also in that the preferences of most of the individuals and states involved were fairly congruent. As J. Isaac has summarized it,

> Emigration for political reasons did not cease, but it chiefly occurred where an anti-liberal, reactionary opposition came into power. The new liberal ideas, however, opened the way to a new kind of international migration, to the greatest migration history has ever witnessed. It was in harmony with the wishes and interests of the migrants and constituted at the same time a vital part of the economic system. The rapid rise in total numbers and the still more rapid rise in total wealth which were associated with the capitalist system during the century between the Napoleonic wars and the first World War could not have occurred without the migration which took place during this period.[73]

Local variations notwithstanding, it was generally the case that in the long run, under the impact of the great transformation, "one state after another was compelled to abolish serfdom and to remove other legal obstacles to free mobility."[74] Once that was done, under the conditions of political organization which then prevailed, it was well-nigh impossible to restrict that mobility to the state's own territory. As information increased and as costs of long-distance travel (in money, time, and risks) steadily decreased, migrants tended to choose optimal destinations. There, those who benefited most from such movements were sufficiently powerful to prevent the erection of permanent barriers against immigration, without relinquishing the ability to deflect the stream away from their shores when the need arose, or to select the immigrants they considered most desirable.

As one moved toward the outer reaches of the system, the liberal tendency was much less dominant; but changes occurred as well. In the zones of the world system under the direct control of Europeans, or of their descendants, slavery was gradually replaced by wage labor. It should be noted, however, that the timing of this change varied considerably and that several intermediate forms of labor were instituted, which involved active state participation in the movement of various populations. Whether political economy alone can account for these processes is doubtful.[75] Nevertheless, some of the variations seem to have been related to the position of states in relation to the system. Whereas capitalist Britain sought to eliminate the slave trade, states of the semi-periphery remained dependent on it. The rate of slave imports actually went up in South America and in Brazil from about 22,450 a year for the period 1701–1810 to 29,700 a year for the period 1811–70.[76] As pressures mounted against the Atlantic trade, the countries of South America established recruitment agencies in Europe and homesteading programs for European immigrants. Concurrently, indentured labor and various forms of corvée and government-surpervised contractual labor on European plantations emerged as alternatives to both slavery and the wage system in parts of Asia and the Pacific, as well as Africa and the Caribbean. In this as in many other respects, European states reinstated in their colonial peripheries policies drawn from the attic of their own history. Slavery persists, however, in the peripheral economic systems of the Red and Arabian seas.

## PROTECTIONISM AND NATION-BUILDING 1 8 8 0 – 1 9 6 0

Further transformations of the world system, which became most clearly manifest in the two or three decades hinged around 1890, altered not only the push and pull factors that shaped the migration calculus of a large part of the world's population, but also the outlooks of states with respect to international population movements. On the whole, between approximately 1880 and 1960, states exercised such a high degree of control over exit and entry that the migrations which in fact occurred were very different from what they might have been had free market conditions prevailed. At the very time that social scientists were devising migration theories founded on the axiom of individual choice, the activities of states were undermining the axiom itself.

The structure of the labor market changed as a function of the "second industrial revolution" and of long-term demographic processes.[77] Industrial production increasingly involved the use of nonferrous metals, petroleum, and electricity in addition to iron, coal, and steam, changes highlighted by the coming to the fore of the chemical industry and of the internal combustion engine. There was an immense expansion of the domain of markets and in the scale of the basic units of production. Fluctuations of the business cycle became broader and affected a larger proportion of the populations of more countries. Empty spaces were filled up; in most of the world, land became a commodity rather than a way of life. The capitalist imperative produced an expansionist dynamic highlighted by the completion of transcontinental railways in North America and Eurasia as well as the construction of interocean canals; combined with political concerns, it also led to the partition of Africa. For the first time in history, a world system literally encompassed the earth. Within it, the rate of growth of the population of Europe began to slow down for the first time in nearly two hundred years. Excluding Russia, Europe's share of the total world population peaked at 18 percent around 1900; and by 1950 it was down to 15.6 percent, approximately the same level as in 1800.[78] For the world as a whole, after World War I the population of the semi-periphery and of the periphery began to grow at an increasingly higher rate than that of the industrial countries of the core.

The overall effect of these changes was a mobilization of labor into the market throughout the more remote regions of the world where a growing proportion of the population was located. As had occurred among the countries that industrialized earlier, once labor mobility got under way it entailed both internal and international migrations. But the "great transformation" with respect to labor generally outpaced the industrial growth of later developers, particularly as most of them were constrained by the structure of the world economic system to orient themselves toward the production of primary goods. Propelled into a low-wage local labor market where prices for imported industrially produced goods tended to be high, labor sought to move where the terms of exchange were somewhat more favorable. Reduced costs of transportation and increased information, both of which affected the demand and supply sides of the labor market, enlarged the spatial scope of movement. Even as the total volume of population disposed to migrate increased absolutely and relatively, however, the lowered costs of movement also made it economically more feasible—from their own point of view and that of employers—for them to return. The proportion of transoceanic European migrants who did so increased significantly after 1880 (where political circumstances allowed) and was undoubtedly much higher yet within the intra-European stream, which itself constituted an increasing share of the total international movement of European peoples.[79]

Because cultural differences between populations deepen as a function of physical distance between societies, both permanent and temporary international migrations increased the cultural heterogeneity of countries of destination. Over the long term, under free market conditions, the populations of the receiving countries of the core would tend to reflect the patterns of cultural variation found in the world system as a whole. Beginning in eastern and southern Europe, whose peoples became the "new immigrants" of North America and Western Europe toward the end of the nineteenth century, the process eventually engulfed the shores and islands of the Pacific, the shores of the Mediterranean, the Caribbean Islands, the less developed countries of the American continents, and tropical Africa, producing the oft-noted directional shift of labor migrations from roughly East-West at the beginning of the period to roughly South-North by the end of it.[80]

Throughout the period, however, policies concerning exit and entry affected every component of the migratory flow so as to profoundly modify the market-produced trends. On the exit side, liberal policies among some states coexisted with coercive ones elsewhere, and several important countries of origin moved from one camp to the other. Coercive policies were applied to old and new groups, extended on the whole to cover a larger proportion of the world's population, and implemented with the unprecedented degree of thoroughness made possible by modern material and organizational technology. Much as in the mercantilist period, prohibitions against exit were associated with the creation of internal conditions that produced a desire to leave and with expulsion. The contradictions between these policies culminated in the creation of a technique of expulsion which produces no emigration at all, *Nacht und Nebel*.

On the entry side, the hallmark of the period was a general shift from relatively liberal to explicitly restrictive policies. Some were founded principally on the positive or negative selection of immigrants with respect to characteristics related to economic considerations or to political concerns. Others sought to control the duration of the migrants' stay by making residence conditional upon some sort of need on the part of the receiving country and some sort of performance on the part of the migrant. Whether or not legally defined as such, this pattern was a form of contractual migration involving not only individuals and firms but, for the most part, one state and another.

Under conditions such as these, the total number of those who actually moved in response to opportunities probably constituted a decreasing proportion of the migration-prone, as an increasing number of states where market conditions were unfavorable prevented their exit while those where conditions were favorable tended to erect barriers to entry, for reasons to be discussed in the remainder of this section. On the exit side alone, for example, the huge population of Russia remained to a considerable extent immobilized when the "great transformation" reached that region; and after a brief relatively permissive interlude, it was frozen in place (from an international point of view) except for coercive population exchanges in the wake of international conflicts. Similarly, between 1927 and 1945, for about a quarter of the period, Italy nearly ceased to feed the intra-European and transoceanic flows to which it was one of the heaviest contributors both before and after.

On the entry side, the generalization of restrictive policies probably reduced the overall numbers of international migrants because many who were inclined to leave were forced instead to make a go of it at home. Restrictive policies also fostered the emergence of different exchange patterns. For example, the actions of Britain, Canada, and the United States diverted part of the interwar and post-World War II European stream to continental countries of Western Europe and to other overseas destinations. The scarcity of labor produced by various combinations of restrictive factors triggered off new flows, such as that of Algerians to France in World War I and of Mexicans and Canadians to the United States. Incidentally, these combinations also fostered further migrations from the internal peripheries of industrial countries to their cores, as with Puerto Ricans to the mainland, southern blacks and whites to the North, Quebeckers to Ontario, Corsicans to the French mainland, and Bretons to the Paris region.

Concurrently, however, the policies of states contributed to a vast increase of permanent migrations that were much less "voluntary" than the ones occasioned by market forces alone. The Jews who left Russia and Rumania from the 1870s onward were mobilized by fear as well as by market incentives. Whereas it is difficult to specify what role each motive played in the case of these and other migrants who had some choice, many more were added over the ensuing decades who were given no choice at all. For the world as a whole, the total number of migrants in whose movement political factors played a prominent role is estimated at "some hundred or more million people" between the Balkan wars (1912–13) and 1968. Their number far outweighed the total who moved in the decades of the great migrations of the nineteenth century, and constituted a greater proportion of total international migrations during the half-century when they occurred than did voluntary ones.[81] Furthermore, as political conditions in a number of states of origin deteriorated after the relatively voluntary departure of certain waves, many who might have been temporary migrants became permanent, less voluntary ones.

The theoretical literature on migrations has little to say about the restrictive entry and coercive exit policies themselves, as sociologists and economists tend to view them as incidental "errors" that lie beyond theory's explanatory domain. Other than legal compendia, the literature on the policies per se tends to focus on them singly. Most accounts ultimately resort to some form of social psychological explanation centering on the dynamics of prejudice at the mass and/or elite levels of particular societies. Processes, usually an acceleration of social and economic change, result in an increase of "frustrations," "anomie," or something of the sort; lest they be destructive of the society in which they occur ("implosion"), these frustrations must be channeled into aggressive outlets; the outlets in turn can be external (e.g., saber-rattling, imperialism, actual war) or internal, but directed at "outsiders" (e.g., political witch hunts, persecution of ethnic minorities).[82] The reasoning applies equally well to coercion in states of origin and to restrictions in states of destination. The basic problem with this mode of explanation is that there is no way of independently charting the "level of frustration" of a society except by using "aggressive behavior"—that which is to be explained—as the indicator, nor can the level of "aggressivity," regardless of its causes, be clearly established with respect to particular groups and at different times. The result is such perfect co-variance between "cause" and "effect" as to suggest the presence of a tautology.

Granting the persistent reality of prejudice and hostility as features of social existence, as well as the possibility that their levels vary under changing circumstances, the framework used in preceding sections provides an alternative way of accounting for the policies under consideration that bypasses the theoretical and historical problems posed by psychological explanations of the behavior of entire societies. Incidentally, the framework accounts better than they do for the varying effects of prejudice in relation to specifiable conditions. Skirting the dangerous ground of overdetermination, I shall suggest that these policies arose as "solutions" to certain situations which states, conceived of as the instruments of structured groups pursuing their political and economic interests, faced as the world system underwent severe disturbances, mostly of their own making. As these processes unfolded, widespread prejudices became organized into purposeful ideologies on the basis of which support could be mustered for specific policy outcomes.

The general context is well known. As capitalism expanded in the manner shown, leading industrial countries such as the United States and Germany sought to reduce uncertainty and risks by controlling a semi-periphery and a periphery of their own, much as Britain had succeeded in doing earlier. Others, such as Russia, Japan, and France, followed suit in various ways. It was a system of competing imperialisms, in which the use of political power backed by military might, as an adjunct to the pursuit of elusive economic security, contributed to a destabilization of international politics. The efforts of hegemonic groups within countries to maintain their position in the face of growing internal challenges also contributed to imperialist expansion as well as to the projection of ideology into the international political system. Business fluctuations were exacerbated by protectionist economic policies, and they in turn reinforced the search for relative autarchy.

The destabilization of international politics in the last third of the nineteenth century is not attributable, however, to the capitalist dynamic alone. The European-centered balance of power, founded on a limited number of actors with roughly similar capabilities, gave way to a global system, in which the Pacific theater was as important as the Atlantic, as shown very early by the Spanish-American and Russo-Japanese wars, and whose leading actors required a capability for worldwide action obtainable only by a harnessing of all physical and human resources at their disposal. The course of international politics from approximately 1870 on can be viewed as a century-long contest for power among aspirants to a new role of "global power" who included some of the traditional European as well as new extra-European actors; at the same time, lesser powers were driven to find a position on a continuum ranging from satellite status to pusillanimous autarchy, within which neutrality was possible only for very few and at the convenience of the aspiring giants. The requirements of mobilization in a "Century of War" contributed to the emergence of authoritarian regimes in which the state achieved a much higher degree of control over society than the world had experienced; but even in liberal regimes, the state vastly expanded the scope of its regulatory activities and developed appropriate means for carrying them out.[83] The political-strategic stalemate achieved in the past two decades by two superpowers which appear to have reached the limits of their hegemony may be one of the elements of transition to a new phase of the world system.

Coercive exit policies emerged in regions of what was then the semi-periphery, as hegemonic groups, whose position might be undermined by the expansion of the core, sought to prevent it by rapidly reinforcing their political and economic dominance over their territory. Among the means available was the institutionalization of the regime-form earlier developed within the core: the modern bureaucratic state and the modern national community. Whereas the first wave of state-building efforts in an earlier age had produced mercantilism and the imposition of religious conformity, such efforts now and among latecomers produced economic autarchy and the imposition of national conformity over what were mostly multi-ethnic societies.

"Nation-building" entails "nation-destroying," as Walker Connor has pointed out.[84] This process, which had been under way among the countries of the core from the very beginning of the present world system, was drastically telescoped among those who launched it in the semi-periphery and later in the periphery in the late nineteenth century and in the twentieth. One of the most important consequences of this urgency was the creation of the "victim groups" identified by Hannah Arendt, the minorities and particularly the stateless, whom she viewed as "the most symptomatic group in contemporary politics."[85] Together, they constituted the bulk of the forced migrants as well as the most unfortunate among the oppressed unable to leave. What became sending countries were seeking to build nations by eliminating those deemed unassimilable while reinforcing their control over the population as a whole, to achieve both economic autarchy and strategic security; as we shall see later on, the putative states of destination responded in the same spirit, since they were engaged in similar projects. From this vantage point, it is no mere coincidence that the pogroms directed against Jews in Rumania shortly after that country achieved its independence were contemporaneous with the Chinese exclusion law legislated by California.

The involuntary migration of ethnic groups as a by-product of the tensions generated by economic modernization and nation-building has emerged in the past century as a worldwide political process. This has occurred not only because different regions of the world have successively experienced the transformations noted but also because the population movements generated by one region sometimes contributed to tensions in another. The expulsion of Jews from Rumania and Russia (either directly or by creating conditions which forced them to flee) contributed to the rise of militant anti-Semitism as a component of "nation-building" in some of the countries of destination and culminated a few decades later in the expulsion of Jews without migration from Central and Western Europe, often after a short forced re-migration to Eastern Europe. The concurrent migration of a segment of the group to its region of ethnic origin contributed to subsequent involuntary migrations in that region as well. Further involuntary ethnic migrations were generated in southeastern Europe during the Balkan wars of 1912–13 and accompanied the continent-wide international conflicts of the next four decades. It was only when a new form of empire was firmly established in Eastern Europe after World War II, and after this empire enforced a general no-exit policy, that the population movements generated in that part of the European semi-periphery three-quarters of a century earlier ground to a halt. By then, however, new involuntary migrations were being triggered off under similar structural conditions and with similar consequences in many parts of Asia and Africa.

The no-exit policy with which a forced-exit one is often coupled performs vital functions in modern autarchic regimes regardless of their ideological orientation. The primary policy is political, as it is nearly impossible to secure compliance with drastic state demands if people are able to vote with their feet. The second policy is more purely economic: to the extent that a country rejects market mechanisms, the state must exercise greater direct controls over the factors of production, including population. To these considerations must be added the general humiliation suffered by countries whose nationals become identified with menial tasks abroad or are viewed as undesirable, and, under circumstances of international tension, the value nationals take on as a strategic resource. Nowhere have I found these various concerns expressed more explicitly than in the migration policy adopted by Fascist Italy.

Ever since unification, Italian governments have encouraged emigration as a short-term solution to unemployment, to political discontent, and particularly to the problem of the South; much as Britain had done with respect to Ireland, they pushed the people out. After World War I, "passports for intending emigrants"—themselves made necessary by the generalization of passports as a device of control at entry produced by the war—"were to be delivered within twenty-four hours of applying for them. There was an emigration fund financed by the State, and specially reduced railway fares were available for Italian workers going abroad." Under Fascism, this policy was drastically reversed. Clandestine (passportless) emigration was prohibited in 1926, and the higher punishment imposed against "political" in contrast with "economic" forms of it suggests the order of priorities among the regime's concerns. The incentives for ordinary emigration were swept away in 1927 and 1928, when an official exclaimed: "Why should Italy still serve as a kind of human fish pond, to feed countries suffering from demographic impoverishment? And why should Italian mothers continue to bear sons to serve as soldiers for other nations?"[86] The target here was clearly France; but the discrimination practiced by the United States against Italians also had a feedback effect. The restrictionist exit policy, coupled with positive inducements to return and with the effects of the depression (among which must be included more severe restrictions against entry elsewhere), produced a drop in the net outflow of Italians from nearly 300,000 in 1928 to 34,000 in 1929; after a short-term increase attributable to a reopening of the "safety-valve" in 1930, emigration dwindled rapidly until it reached only 9,000 in 1936. After Italy became the semi-periphery of the German core in an autarchic segment of the world system, the two countries arranged for a controlled flow of Italian migrant workers.

The preceding account of coercive exit policies is merely the preliminary statement of a central tendency among states whose situation is similar in some respects. Only a more systematic comparative analysis could ascertain whether the many variations found within that tendency and the exceptions to it are attributable to patterned differences or to more idiosyncratic factors. On the whole, it appears that the higher the degree of human mobilization for economic and political purposes, the less can regimes afford to make exceptions to a no-exit policy by resorting to the more traditional device of exiling dissenters, by expelling the "unassimilable," or by simply allowing the emigration of such groups. In periods of high international tension, this is exacerbated by security considerations. In more normal times, however, most regimes tend to engage in some exchanges with the remainder of the world system; the advantages of a strict no-exit policy must be balanced against its costs; some groups are more valuable than others; and deviations of various sorts tend to occur.

That those countries of the capitalist core which were also politically liberal constituted the preferred destinations of the bulk of voluntary and forced migrants from other parts of the system can be taken for granted, as they offered the best environment available in the world. This was not only a function of the more advantageous terms of exchange they offered to sellers of labor with respect to individual goods. By this time, such countries conferred certain indivisible benefits upon their residents, "public" or "collective" goods in which all partake whether or not they contribute to defray their cost, such as a water supply relatively free of dangerous parasites, schools, networks of transportation and of communication, a higher degree of national security, and, much as is the case in the metropolises of today's Third World, an exciting scene that is attractive in and of itself. The total share of the economy allocated to public goods increased; government became more involved in providing them; and their costs were borne by the entire body of residents in their role of taxpayers. In one sense, residents of affluent countries, regardless of class or even recency of arrival, saw themselves in relation to subsequent waves of immigrants from the poor countries much as middle-class residents of the Eastern seaboard cities of the United States had done in the first half of the nineteenth century: they were being forced to bear an overly large share of the social costs of immigration. The emergence of restrictive immigration policies can be understood first and foremost as a necessary concomitant of the uneven distribution of geographically fixed public goods in the world, under conditions which include widespread information concerning that distribution, relatively inexpensive long-distance transportation, and demographic processes that produce a higher rate of population growth among poorer countries than among affluent ones.

Within this central tendency there were many variations that can be accounted for by the interactions of the basic factors mentioned with others. The general interests of capital and of indigenous labor, and the changing relationships between these under conditions of economic expansion or contraction, have already been discussed with respect to the previous period. For capital, with a very large supply of labor apparently assured however, it becomes possible to select those workers likely to be more productive; the costs of inefficiency are thus passed on to the country of origin without significantly raising the cost of labor in the country of destination. Appropriate policies include restrictions on the landing of the *unfit*—those unable (on physical or mental grounds) or unwilling (on moral ones) to abide by the market—such as were imposed by the United States beginning in 1882.

Expanding the supply temporarily rather than permanently (migrant rather than immigrant labor) may be advantageous because labor is least costly if renewal of the supply occurs outside the economy under consideration, and if unproductive laborers (e.g., the unemployed or the aged) can be returned to their country of origin.[87] The advocacy of restrictions by indigenous labor is constrained, on the other hand, by the possibility that a scarcity of cheap labor will provide an incentive for capital substitution and/or that capital will relocate to an area where cheap labor is abundant. It too may come to look favorably upon migrant labor, but as the lesser evil. Policies along these lines began emerging in the United States (in regard to Orientals on the West Coast during the period of railroad construction and *braceros* during and after World War II), but they were especially prominent in France, Switzerland, and Germany before and after World War I, and to a much greater extent toward the end of the period.[88]

The liberal countries of the capitalist core can be thought of as having engaged throughout the period in the exploration of various solutions to such market problems and to the conflicts they produced. Although they do not operate in quite the same way, attempts to control the entry of people parallel attempts to control the entry of goods through tariffs and import regulations. Restrictionist waves, such as the ones which engulfed the liberal world in the high-protection decades prior to and following World War I, tended to result in overly rigid policies that constituted a mortgage on the future. Flexibility with respect to the international movement of both people and goods can be achieved not only by providing "loopholes" but, more effectively, by devising more discretionary legislation with built-in provisions for adjustment to changing circumstances. Immigration policies then become merely the adjunct of manpower policies. Within the necessarily restrictive framework mentioned earlier, immigrants or migrants come to be selected on the basis of *positive* definitions of fitness, such as a set of occupational preferences.

However optimal this solution from an economic vantage point, its emergence as a pattern was prohibited by the increasing prominence among receiving countries of nation-building concerns which mirrored those of sending countries. Restrictive policies against the entry of certain groups originating in the semi-periphery and the periphery were equivalent to the policies developed by what Arendt calls the "state peoples" of the mostly multi-ethnic countries of those outer zones toward their minorities and toward those considered the unassimilable stateless. The ones sought to increase homogeneity and thereby national solidarity under conditions of international tension by expelling or forcibly assimilating ethnic minorities; the others sought to prevent the growth of heterogeneity by excluding so much as possible, within the constraints imposed by the advantages of a large labor supply, immigrants who were not ethnically cognate to the nationalities of the core. Nation-building projects on both sides contributed to the crystallization of a worldwide ideology of "scientific" racism, too notorious to require detailed discussion here, which made inchoate prejudices respectable, was useful to promote the interests of key social groups, and in turn provided a rationale for the policies themselves.

It is tempting to discern on the entry side a differentiation between types of undesirables. Entry of those who were deemed difficult to assimilate was restricted; entry of those deemed unassimilable was prohibited altogether. The unassimilable here were not so much Arendt's stateless as those whose origin was ineradicable—the non-white. In its most extreme form the prohibition was expressed in avoidance, as in a caste system, of which the modern equivalent might be ineligibility for naturalization. The United States, for example, prohibited only three categories of humanity at one time or another. The entry of Africans was in effect prohibited when the slave trade was abolished, and their special undesirability was emphasized by fostering their return to Africa when the number of free blacks increased. Native Americans were initially treated as varmint; the United States created a Pale for their survivors, and subsequent immigration—in the sense of their entry into the body of ordinary citizens—was long made well-nigh impossible. Finally came the Orientals, whose entry was also prohibited during much of the period in the white Dominions, including Canada.[89] Jews were, from this vantage point, a somewhat ambiguous group, viewed more as a separate race in Eastern Europe and more as an undesirable white ethnic group in Western Europe and North America. It is noteworthy that in Britain, during the heated debates on alien legislation at the turn of the century, the Jews were identified with the Chinese as the truest of aliens, differing only "as a matter of degree."[90] Both emerged during this period as suspects in mythical conspiracies, both were feared because of their mysterious powers founded on diasporas which lay beyond the control of ordinary rulers and could therefore result in a world conquest with the aid of gold or opium. That the Jews who erupted from the confines of the European semi-periphery were not excluded was also due in part to the presence of some of their reluctant coreligionists within the bourgeoisie of the core countries, a presence made possible by their emancipation in the course of liberal revolutions.

Although agitation against the "new immigration" from Eastern and southern Europe arose early in the United States, it was England that led the way in erecting barriers specifically against it.[91] The political process that eventuated in the passage of a restrictive act in 1905 reveals the interplay of "nation-building" concerns with class interests, complicated, in this case, by the issue of Home Rule. The entry of culturally distinct aliens who were also considered politically unreliable (mostly poor Eastern European Jews and Italians) was opposed by Tories on grounds of imperial security at a time of rising international tensions. It was a relatively low-cost policy from the point of view of capital so long as the Irish labor reserve was available. Initially in favor of restriction, the Trades Union Confederation shifted position, however, when Joseph Chamberlain advocated it with the expressed purpose of diverting working-class support from the Home-Rule Liberals. Although the Liberals who came to power in 1906 initially refused to enforce it, the act of 1905 was quite effective, mostly because it frightened away lower-class migrants. No quota system was required as *all* lower-class aliens were in a sense undesirable. The number of immigrants declined from 12,481 in 1906 to 3,626 in 1911, a period of rising immigration elsewhere; and although the severe American restrictions of the 1920s deflected much of the flow to Europe, Britain was not contaminated by it. Around 1930, the proportion of foreign-born in Britain (not including the Irish) was the lowest in Western Europe.[92] More explicitly than the mother country, the white Dominions developed restrictions against the appropriate undesirable groups; Canada, for instance, established a system of positive preferences for speakers of its two national languages which in fact worked to the advantage of English-speakers.

Viewed in this light, the case of the United States is much less idiosyncratic. It is noteworthy that although between 1881 and 1910 the United States received more immigrants than ever before, they did not constitute a larger net increment (in proportion to population) than had been the case in 1851–80. On the eve of World War I, the United States portion constituted only 60 percent of the total arriving in the four major receiving countries in the New World (including Canada, Argentina, and Brazil).[93] For nearly forty years, restrictionists concerned with nation-building sought solutions within the framework of the principle of individual selection established in 1882 and whose constitutionality had subsequently been tested and found valid.[94] Although the use of literacy tests, finally established in 1917 after repeated attempts and over Wilson's veto, outwardly conformed to that principle, its intent and its effect was group selection, as the incidence of literacy was considerably higher in countries of origin of the old immigration than of the new. When the breakthrough to the principle of group selection was made in 1921, the suitability of some nationalities against others was based not only on their alleged intelligence—a criterion which, within the heredity-minded IQ theories of the time, conveniently associated nation-building considerations with a business-minded concern for productivity—but also on their putative political disposition. Such concerns were equally explicit in 1924 and in the Walter-McCarran Act of 1952. Restrictionist policies that developed in response to the political instability of the world system during this period reflected the fear of revolutionary contagion and a desire to police the world beyond one's borders. In the twentieth century, some nationalities became identified as "anarchists," "socialists," or "communists," much as in the eighteenth French emigrés were thought to carry the Jacobin virus.

However prominent nation-building concerns responsive to international political situations became in the shaping of immigration policies, they were in turn constrained by the economic considerations discussed earlier. What to do, for example, when Senator Lodge or General Walker, President of MIT, fought the "new immigration" on grounds of national security while the National Association of Manufacturers and the Chamber of Commerce sought to keep the door open on grounds of the necessities of economic growth? The solution in the 1924 settlement was to exempt the Western Hemisphere from restrictions imposed against European immigration (in addition to Asian exclusion).[95] Although the "scientific" racists viewed other North Americans as undesirable, rating the IQ of Mexicans as "lower than Portuguese and Negroes," and of French Canadians as "about the same level as Negroes," these undesirables formed labor reserves for the U.S. regions contiguous to their home base.[96] They made the U.S. labor market more elastic as many went home when no longer needed, or if necessary, could be repatriated by administrative measures. An even more surreptitious form of flexibility was achieved with respect to Mexicans later on. In 1948, when a bitter debate took place on whether to admit 100,000 European displaced persons a year for four years, little concern was shown for the estimated 200,000 Mexican workers who entered illegally. After World War II,

> the political forces clamoring for an ever more restrictionist general immigration policy were either strangely silent with respect to the situation on our southern border or openly condoned it. The late Senator Pat McCarran defended the illegal traffic on the grounds that legal entry of Mexicans for employment in America gave the agriculture and industry involved too much red tape.[97]

What the author just quoted identified as a "social paradox" can be viewed rather as a somewhat awkward, but nevertheless effective, reconciliation of divergent interests. Flexibility was also maintained with respect to European immigration under the quota system by administrative devices which increased or decreased the amount of red tape applicants faced in the American consulates abroad.[98]

Under conditions of scarcity, the value of immigrants as manpower for economic and military purposes could fully outweigh the effects of nation-building projects and the xenophobic ideologies they produced. Like Britain and the United States, France became a country of destination for the new immigration of the 1880s.[99] Whereas in France, in contrast with the United States and Britain, Italians and Spaniards were considered easily assimilable groups, as in the English-speaking countries, Eastern Europeans (many of them Jews) were not. In 1893, Maurice Barrès rose to warn his countrymen of the consequences of the invasion; and the image of the Jew as *métèque—*

the unassimilable *metic* in the polis—figured prominently in the Dreyfus Affair a few years later. Xenophobic prejudices were at least as widespread among the general public and among the elite in France as in the United States or in Britain; and nativists were well organized politically.[100] Yet, although fifty mostly restrictionist bills were proposed between 1883 and 1914, most of them failed because of the strong resistance of employers and of the state. Beginning around 1905, Poles were brought in as contract laborers in agriculture and in the mines; when wartime conditions made this impossible, they were replaced by Algerian Moslems; and at the outbreak of war the state was even willing to extend citizenship to some African blacks in exchange for the gift of their services to the nation in arms.

The state continued to foster immigration after the war, the fears of many French citizens—shared to a considerable extent by indigenous Jews —for the "denationalization" and radicalization of their country notwithstanding.[101] The door was kept wide open at a time when it was being shut elsewhere, and naturalization requirements were even further reduced. But if it was easy to enter, it was much more difficult to stay. Granted or withdrawn by the Ministry of Labor as determined by market needs, the labor permit became in effect the equivalent for France of what the immigration visa was for the United States and it enabled the state to reinforce ordinary and political police control over foreigners.

The total number of foreign-born in France doubled in the decade after World War I. As of 1931, there were 2.7 million foreigners as well as nearly 0.4 million naturalized citizens, constituting together approximately 7.3 percent of the total population; their presence was used by many groups as a platform from which to challenge liberal democracy. Although when the depression hit, several hundred thousand were returned pell-mell to their countries of origin, as of 1936 foreigners and naturalized citizens still amounted to 6.4 percent of the French population. The system is deemed to have been extremely successful from an economic point of view as it produced entries and exits "that gave to the French labor market of that time an exceptional degree of elasticity. This contributed to the rapid recovery of the French economy after [World War I] by protecting [the] country from the grave unemployment crises its neighbors experienced."[102] Unable to impose the restrictions they advocated throughout the course of the Third Republic, the French nativists got their revenge after its demise. Vichy deprived recent immigrant Jews who had become naturalized of their citizenship, on the ground that it had been granted too easily, for political reasons, and turned them over, with all the foreign Jews they could trap, to the Nazis for disposal.[103]

The tragic irony of much of the restrictive immigration legislation erected to facilitate the national mobilization of indigenous populations was that very soon it was no longer needed to restrict the arrival of undesirables. By the late 1920s, many Europeans of the semi-periphery were no longer able to leave; within another decade, most of the others could not do so. Intentionally or not, the restrictionists had contributed their share to a conspiracy in restraint of exit which had tragic consequences. The Nazis relied heavily on such collusion for the pursuit of their policies. As the official S.S. newspaper put it in 1938, "if the world was not yet convinced that the Jews were the scum of the world, it soon would be when unidentifiable beggars, without nationality, without money, and without passports crossed their frontiers."[104] And if the beggars were seldom allowed in, could the Nazis not dispose of them at will?

## CONCLUSION

For all but a brief period, in a circumscribed segment of the world system, and with some qualifications even within that place at that time, the preferences of "those who send" and "those who receive" have shaped international migrations to a much greater extent than the preferences of "those who go." I have sought to demonstrate that the actions of states, however varied in a given period and over time, can be accounted for by means of a limited set of factors akin to the independent variables that go into the making of social theories. These factors, as well as the ones that produce population movements, take on their parametric values from the structures and processes of a historically specific world system. In that sense, migration indeed "mirrors the world as it is at the time." The present analysis is a preliminary statement to be considered as a working hypothesis for subsequent research on past and present international migrations, within which migration policies would no longer be considered as lying beyond the domain of theoretical explanation.

Without undertaking an analysis of the contemporary period, for which I have not yet done the groundwork, I would like to conclude with a brief allusion to one of its features. We have seen that even where liberalism arose, it soon gave way to coercive exit and restrictive entry policies which, together, profoundly modified the population movements—and hence the population composition of the world's countries—that would have resulted from the unbounded exercise of individual choice. Although the prevailing policies within that zone have undergone significant changes in the past two decades, it is by now evident that the trend is not toward a reinstatement of liberalism but rather toward a relatively humane form of neo-mercantilism.[105] The permanent imposition of controls on the free movement of human beings across the boundaries of societies with liberal regimes reveals some of the ultimate limitations of political liberalism in the contemporary world system. The framework set forth in this essay accounts for why such limitations must persist and thereby enables us to relate the study of international migrations to the study of more fundamental political issues.

Whereas freedom to move about, to remain, to leave, or to return is a condition of political freedom more generally, and therefore has been a concomitant of the historical growth of liberal regimes, liberalism has never been construed to require that a society be founded on the principle of freedom to enter and to become a member of the receiving polity. Although conditions of unrestricted entry appear to have been most closely approximated in the United States, Britain, and France—as well as perhaps in a few other states I have not investigated—for brief periods in the middle decades of the nineteenth century, this was in each case a matter of circumstances rather than of constitutional principle, as demonstrated by the fact that no major obstacle stood in the way of subsequent imposition of restrictions.

Why is this so? Historically, whereas a country's status in or near the core of the world system has not guaranteed that it would have a liberal regime, only countries which occupy such positions have produced them at all. As politically liberal and economically affluent societies provide the most desirable environment available to human beings imbued with modern values, they constitute the preferred locations of an increasing proportion of the world's population. It is not farfetched to assume that a very large fraction would move in accordance with these perfectly sensible preferences were they allowed to do so. Even taking into account that many more human beings than ever before are prevented from leaving their states of current residence, the potential migratory flow from the rest of the world is huge; and it is quite obvious that it includes not only the least advantaged segments of those countries but also the most fortunate among them, for whom relocation is perhaps relatively even more desirable. Under the conditions of structured spatial inequality that prevail in the world system, it is probably the case that truly free international migrations would on balance effect a radical redistribution of resources and opportunities to the benefit of the peoples originally located in the semi-periphery and the periphery.

This might in the long run benefit humanity as a whole; but it would undoubtedly impose in the short run drastic costs on the population of the affluent countries. From this point of view, all classes in the countries of the core become as one bourgeoisie in relation to all classes elsewhere, which become as one proletariat. The imposition of restrictions on entry and incorporation is a necessary condition for the reproduction of the bourgeois states. It contributes to the maintenance of international inequality but serves as well to protect the small island of political freedom mankind has achieved for the time being. Viewed in this light, the analysis of migration policies provides further support for Brian Barry's criticism of John Rawls: "The odd thing about Rawls's treatment of the question how a particular community is to be defined for the purposes of the theory of justice is that he does not discuss it."[106] Rawls is not alone in perpetrating this omission.

I agree with Barry's conclusion that any discussion of the "principles of justice" is necessarily flawed if existing states—and, I add, the existing distribution of population among them—are taken to be the units within which such principles operate.

## NOTES

1. Kingsley Davis, "The Migrations of Human Populations," *Scientific American*, 231, no. 3 (1974), p. 96.

2. For recent examples, see Everett S. Lee, "A Theory of Migration," *Demography*, 3, no. 1 (1966), pp. 47–58, as well as the articles entitled "Migrations" (Brinley Thomas and William Petersen) and "Refugees" (Louise W. Holborn) in *International Encyclopedia of the Social Sciences* (New York: MacMillan Co. and Free Press, 1968), 10, pp. 286–300, and 13, pp. 361–71.

3. Wallerstein provides an overview of his project in "The Rise and Future Demise of the World Capitalist System: Concepts for Comparative Analysis," *Comparative Studies in Society and History*, 16, no. 4 (September 1974), pp. 387–415. My theoretical understanding of the international *political* system owes a great deal to the work of Morton Kaplan. For an historical approach, see Ludwig Dehio, *The Precarious Balance* (New York: Vintage Books, 1962).

4. Baltimore: Penguin Books, 1967.

5. Hannah Arendt, *The Origins of Totalitarianism* (New York: Harcourt, Brace, Jovanovitch, 1973 ed.), p. 278.

6. J. H. Parry, *The Discovery of the Sea* (New York: Dial Press, 1974), p. 290.

7. Davis, p. 96. Unless otherwise indicated, the overview is based on his account.

8. Philip D. Curtin, *The Atlantic Slave Trade: A Census* (Madison: University of Wisconsin Press, 1969), p. 268.

9. J. S. Furnivall, *Colonial Policy and Practice* (London: Cambridge University Press, 1948), pp. 303–12.

10. Woodrow Borah, as quoted by Christopher Hill, "Caliban's Gift," *The New York Review of Books*, 23, no. 19 (November 25, 1976), p. 43.

11. Roger Mols, "Population in Europe 1500–1700," in Carlo M. Cipolla (ed.), *The Fontana Economic History of Europe*, Vol. 2, *The Sixteenth and Seventeenth Centuries* (London: Collins, 1974), pp. 59–60. Glass and Isaac (note 17) estimate the Huguenot emigration from France at 300,000; Louis Chevalier (note 70) places it at half a million.

12. Mols, p. 32.

13. Ibid., p. 35.

14. Walter Minchinton, "Patterns and Structure of Demand, 1500–1750," in Cipolla, Vol. 2, p. 153.

15. Richard Plender, *International Migration Law* (Leiden: A. W. Sythoff, 1972), p. 41.

16. On the general relationship between physical and moral control, see Michel Foucault, *Surveiller et punir: Naissance de la prison* (Paris: Gallimard, 1975).

17. Julius Isaac, *Economics of Migration* (London, 1947), pp. 14–15. Examples cited are drawn from D. V. Glass, *Population: Policies and Movements in Europe* (London: Frank Cass, 1967; originally published in 1940), pp. 91–96; John Duncan Brite, "The Attitude of European States Toward Emigration to the American Colonies and the United States, 1607–1820" (Ph.D. dissertation, Department of History, University of Chicago, 1937), pp. 194–200. On European policies more generally, see also Marcus Lee Hansen, *The Atlantic Migration 1607–1860* (New York: Harper Torchbooks, 1961; originally published in 1940), p. 19.

18. Isaac, p. 15.

19. Cecil Roth, *History of the Jews* (New York: Shocken, 1961), p. 252.

20. John Armstrong, "Mobilized and Proletarian Diasporas," *The American Political Science Review,* 70, no. 2 (June 1976), pp. 398–99.

21. Domenico Sella, "European Industries 1500–1700," in Cipolla, vol. 2, p. 400.

22. Glass, p. 96.

23. Isaac, p. 15.

24. Hill, p. 43.

25. H. J. M. Johnston, *British Emigration Policy: "Shoveling Out Paupers"* (Oxford: Clarendon Press, 1972), p. 13.

26. Albert O. Hirschman, *Exit, Voice and Loyalty* (Cambridge: Harvard University Press, 1970), pp. 60–61.

27. Hansen, p. 45.

28. Brite, p. 200.

29. Hansen, pp. 6–7. The distinctive orientation of Britain and the Netherlands accords well with the distinction between commercial and agrarian societies put forth by Edward W. Fox in *History in Geographic Perspective: The Other France* (New York: W. W. Norton, 1971).

30. Brite, p. 195; see also p. 270, and Hansen, pp. 5–8.

31. Brite, p. 198.

32. This paragraph is based on information from Plender, pp. 42ff.

33. Karl Polanyi, *The Great Transformation* (Boston: Beacon Press, 1957), pp. 77–102.

34. The estimate is from Frank Thistlethwaite, "Migrations from Europe Overseas in the Nineteenth and Twentieth Centuries," *XIe Congrès International des Sciences Historiques, Rapports,* vol. 5, *Histoire Contemporaine* (Göteborg: Almquist and Wiksell, 1960), pp. 32–60, which provides a stimulating overview of population movements during this period. The major source of statistics and other information

is Walter F. Willcox (ed.), *International Migrations,* 2 vols. (New York, 1929, 1931). Other analytic overviews are André Armengaud, "Population in Europe 1700–1914," in Carlo M. Cipolla (ed.), *The Fontana Economic History of Europe,* vol. 3, *The Industrial Revolution* (London: Collins, 1973), pp. 60–72; and Simon Kuznets, *Modern Economic Growth* (New Haven: Yale University Press, 1966), pp. 51–56.

35. Oliver MacDonagh, *A Pattern of Government Growth, 1800–1860: The Passenger Acts and Their Enforcement* (London: Macgibbon and Kee, 1961), pp. 55–66.

36. Ibid., p. 64.

37. Johnston, p. 2.

38. Ibid.

39. Ibid., pp. 14–16, 32.

40. Ibid., p. 19.

41. Ibid., p. 132.

42. Plender, p. 46.

43. For the application of the "core/periphery" concept to the United Kingdom, see Michael Hechter, *Internal Colonialism* (Berkeley: University of California Press, 1975).

44. See, for example, Robert A. Divine, *American Immigration Policy, 1924–1952* (New Haven: Yale University Press, 1957), p. 1.

45. Ibid., pp. 1–2; see also John Higham, "American Immigration Policy in Historical Perspective," *Law and Contemporary Problems,* 21, no. 2 (Spring 1956), pp. 213–15.

46. Louis L. Jaffe, "The Philosophy of Our Immigration Law," *Law and Contemporary Problems* (1956), p. 358.

47. Hansen, p. 71.

48. Ibid., p. 72.

49. Ray Allen Billington, *The Protestant Crusade: A Study of the Origins of American Nativism* (Chicago: Quadrangle Books, 1964; originally published in 1938).

50. Hansen, p. 56.

51. Ibid., p. 77.

52. Ibid., p. 102.

53. Ibid., p. 104.

54. The figures in this paragraph and the next are from U.S. Department of Commerce, *Historical Statistics of the United States* (Washington: Government Printing Office, 1960), pp. 56–66. Percentage estimates are my own.

55. Billington, p. 36.

56. Ibid., p. 34.

57. This and the following quotes are from Billington, p. 199.

58. Hansen, p. 289.

59. Ibid., p. 253.

60. Hansen, pp. 259–61.

61. Billington, pp. 411–12.

62. Hansen, p. 303.

63. Ibid., p. 300.

64. Billington states on p. 416 that the two above-mentioned state laws "were the only legislative results of a period of Know-Nothing rule." I am currently investigating the passenger acts of the period.

65. Plender, p. 46; see also MacDonagh, passim.

66. Hansen, p. 99.

67. Plender, p. 49.

68. Jacques Henripin, "From Acceptance of Nature to Control: The Demography of the French Canadians since the Seventeenth Century," in Marcel Rioux and Yves Martin, *French Canadian Society,* vol. 1 (Toronto: McClelland & Stewart, 1964), pp. 204–16.

69. See the work of Edward W. Fox cited in note 29.

70. Unless otherwise indicated, the information for the French case is from Louis Chevalier, "Emigration française au XIXeme siècle," *Etudes d'Histoire Moderne et Contemporaine,* 1 (1947), pp. 127–71, and André Armengaud, *La population française au XIXe siècle* (Paris: Presses Universitaires de France, 1971), pp. 84–106.

71. As quoted in ibid., p. 166.

72. On the origins of this process, see Malek Ath Messaoud and Alain Gillette, *L'immigration algérienne en France* (Paris: Editions Entente, 1976), pp. 9–32.

73. Isaac, p. 22.

74. Ibid., p. 20.

75. Wallerstein (1974) argues on pp. 408–9, for example, that the modern European form of slavery was a system of "high transport cost for a product of low productivity," which makes "economic sense only if the purchase price is virtually nil." As this condition was no longer met after Africa was incorporated into the world system and the manpower hitherto used for slaves was needed for cash-crop production in Africa itself, slavery was gradually replaced by wage labor. But Philip Curtin pointed out at the New Harmony conference the anachronism of Wallerstein's reasoning (cited by me in an earlier draft), as African cash-crop production under colonial supervision began long after the importation of slaves to North America was prohibited and was never very extensive.

76. Curtin, p. 268.

77. In this section, I am generally following Barraclough (see note 4); for the "second industrial revolution" and other economic change, see David Landes, *The Unbound Prometheus* (New York: Cambridge University Press, 1969), pp. 230–485.

78. E. A. Wrigley, *Population and History* (New York: McGraw-Hill, 1969), p. 205.

79. Thistlethwaite, p. 42.

80. For a detailed overview, see G. Beijer, "Modern Patterns of International Migratory Movements," in J. A. Jackson (ed.), *Migration* (Cambridge: Cambridge University Press, 1969), pp. 18ff; see also Davis, 100–102; and Dudley Kirk, *Europe's Population in the Inter-War Years* (Princeton: Princeton University Press, 1946).

81. Beijer, ibid.

82. For example, John Higham, *Strangers in the Land: Patterns of American*

*Nativism, 1860–1925* (New Brunswick: Rutgers University Press, 1955), and Bernard Gainer, *The Alien Invasion* (London: Heinemann Educational Books, 1972).

83. Harold Lasswell, "The Garrison State," *American Journal of Sociology,* 1940–41.

84. Walker Connor, "Nation-Building or Nation-Destroying?" *World Politics,* 24 (April 1972), pp. 330–31.

85. Arendt, p. 277.

86. Grandi, as cited in Glass, p. 221.

87. On the interplay of interests concerning migrant labor, see Michael Burawoy, "The Functions and Reproduction of Migrant Labor," *American Journal of Sociology,* 81, no. 5 (March 1976), p. 1082.

88. Stephen Castles and Godula Kossack, *Immigrant Workers and Class Structure in Western Europe* (London: Oxford University Press, 1973).

89. On Oriental exclusion, see Divine, p. 19; Higham (1956); and Plender, pp. 49–50. I plan to study this question more thoroughly in the future.

90. Gainer, p. 112.

91. This account is based on Gainer (note 82).

92. Kirk, p. 222.

93. Kuznets, pp. 52–53, Table 2.4.

94. For U.S. immigration legislation, I am following Higham and Divine.

95. Jaffe, on page 363, views the exemption as a "puzzle." The notion that it was a "solution" is my own.

96. For their standing and the role of IQ, see Leon J. Kamin, *The Science and Politics of I.Q.* (Potomac: Laurence Elbaum Associates, 1975; distributed by Halsted Press, John Wiley and Sons, New York), pp. 15–30.

97. Eleanor M. Haley, "A Critical Analysis of the Wetback Problem," *Law and Contemporary Problems* (1956), p. 336. Burawoy (note 87) compares the California situation with the South African one.

98. Divine, pp. 78ff.

99. Basic information in this section is from Armengaud (1971), pp. 93–106; also André Armengaud, *La population française au XXe siècle,* (Paris: Presses Universitaires de France, 1973), pp. 43–57, 62–66.

100. The theme of undesirable immigrants, particularly Jews, was prominent within various "nationalist" movements from the 1880s on. See particularly Raoul Girardet, *Le Nationalisme français, 1871–1914* (Paris: Armand Colin, 1966), and Eugen Weber, *Action Française* (Stanford: Stanford University Press, 1962).

101. Anti-immigrant sentiment played an important role in the upheaval of 1934. See particularly Maurice Chavardes, *Une campagne de presse: La droite française et le 6 février 1934* (Paris: Flammarion, 1970); and Serge Bernstein, *Le 6 février 1934* (Paris: Gallimard, 1975). On native vs. foreign Jews, see David Weinberg, *Les Juifs à Paris* (Paris: Gallimard, 1975).

102. Armengaud (1973), p. 45.

103. Robert Paxton, *Vichy France* (New York: Alfred A. Knopf, 1972).

104. Quoted by Hannah Arendt, p. 269 (see also footnote on same page).

105. In addition to Beijer (note 80), Burawoy (note 87), Castles and Cossack (note

88), see also Elliott Abrams and Franklin S. Abrams, "Immigration Policy—Who Gets In and Why?" *The Public Interest*, 38 (Winter 1975), pp. 3–29, and Charles P. Kindleberger, *Europe's Post-War Growth* (Cambridge: Harvard University Press, 1967), especially chap. 9. I am currently engaged in research on this subject.

106. Brian Barry, *The Liberal Theory of Justice* (Oxford: Clarendon Press, 1973), p. 128.

# [13]

## Towards an Understanding of Emigrational Processes

SUNE ÅKERMAN

I.

Migration research is an area of great importance in the social sciences, dealing as it does with general processes of social change as well as specific geographic movements. The student of both past and present migrations, however, is handicapped by the serious lack of empirical evidence.[1] He must deal with sources which yield only partial information, such as legislation on migration, opinions about immigrants expressed by members of the receiving society, the immigrant culture that develops in the new surroundings, the impact of the immigrants on the host society, and immigrant literature and other cultural products. On the basis of his interpretation of this slender evidence, and his application to it of insights derived from studies of other areas of human behavior, the student of migration must build models which explain this important historical phenomenon.

In order to tackle these problems according to the basic requirements of social science research, the field must be organized systematically. Essential categories of information about migration include *who* the migrants were, *when* they left, *whence* they departed and *where* they arrived, *under what circumstances* the migration took place, and *from which social and economic context* the migrants were uprooted. It is also important to ascertain the *migrants' knowledge of alternative goals* of their movements, *possible differences between the mobile and the stationary parts of a population*, and whether tangible relations existed between migrants-to-be and receiv-

287

ing areas. In addition, the phenomenon of re-migration and the structure of transport organization are of major concern to students of migration—especially those interested in the big transoceanic movements of the past century —but material about these topics is meager. And in some ways the study of internal movements is even less satisfactory. Although these migrations often reach enormous size both in agricultural and in modern industrialized societies, their timing, structure, and role is not very well documented in the available sources. A related category, the seasonal movements and labor migrations which are an important aspect of human mobility, has also been poorly recorded in official sources. Recently, researchers have begun to map patterns of commuting, an activity which has apparently been growing over both short and long distances during the postwar period.

One method of compensating for the lack of data that may exist with respect to a particular migration process is to use information that has been gathered about an analogous or contiguous migration. Migrational movements usually do not stop abruptly at national borders.[2] Thus the huge gaps in our knowledge about certain movements—for example, some of the migratory streams triggered by industrialization—may be filled by using data relating to similar movements in other countries. The rationale for such a strategy is that ecotypes of the same kind will create similar population flows.

Of course, this strategy is not free from problems. But if we have learned anything from long study of the geographical mobility of natives of the Scandinavian countries, it is the persistence over time and space of those migrations that aim at satisfying basic human needs. International migration research has revealed more and more of this constancy in population turnover. At the same time, there also seem to be great similarities between innovative migrations that reflect and that prepare structural changes in society. For this reason the psychological and social-psychological reactions of populations in motion must be carefully considered, even in a historical context. In other words, migration research ought not to be reduced to mechanical analyses of the so-called labor market. Such analyses alone cannot explain even migrations that apparently have strong economic causes.[3]

In this article I will try to illustrate some variations on this theme. We will focus upon external migratory movements, but this does not mean that the scope of our observations will be restricted to mass emigration. On the contrary, we will try to find the common denominator of most migratory movements.

II.

The various modeling techniques that have been developed in the social sciences have important implications for migration studies. In this section, therefore, I will try concisely to survey and summarize some important tendencies in model-building for emigration research.[4] Migration models tend to be derived from models developed in demography and economics, fields in which model-building is a routine practice. Such borrowed models are usually not very complicated from a quantitative point of view; they are easily adaptable to migration studies because emigration is itself a demographic and economic phenomenon.

Within this research tradition, the role of *push and pull factors* has generally been emphasized. This approach, which tries to isolate and measure the repelling and attracting powers in a migratory situation, is well suited for model formulation. Indeed, the impact of this idea has been so strong that, except among some specialists in migration research,[5] the theory of emigration may have been reduced to simple "push and pull" thinking. The long-standing dominance of this concept reflects the traditional influence of natural science on economics and on social science in general. Thus the push and pull models may be considered more or less as equilibrium constructs. These constructs reflect a mechanistic point of view which has been popular among economists, who maintain that because economic systems have a tendency to return to equilibrium, an overflow of manpower takes place when an economic system loses its balance.

Harry Jerome's writings in the 1920s served as a special inspiration for this research tradition. Jerome was able to show the impact of the American labor market on the propensity to emigrate from Europe; he strongly emphasized the importance of the pull factors. Of subsequent contributors to this field, Richard Easterlin sided with Jerome in emphasizing pull factors, while Dorothy Swaine Thomas noted the decisive importance of push factors.[6]

The writings of Brinley Thomas present a more refined version of push and pull thinking. More than his predecessors, Thomas stresses the *interplay* among factors in the sending and receiving countries. In addition to economic and demographic variables, he tries to incorporate social and spatial factors into his model. Thomas places a new emphasis on the independent role of migrational movements as agents of economic change.[7] For example, in his analysis of business-cycles Thomas draws directly upon Simon Kuznets's studies of long economic swings and the changing pattern of population-sensitive economic activities. Another important feature of Thomas's model is the concept of "the Atlantic economy," which acts as a frame for mass migrations. The center of this huge migrational system was Western Europe, with North America and other continents on the periphery.

Brinley Thomas's model was not fully formalized: it might be called semi-quantitative because some of his components and relationships are open to quantification and testing, while others are not. More formal and integrated models have been developed by other scholars of an even stronger econometric inclination, such as Wilkinson, Quigley, and Moe.[8] In general, the econometricians are not able to compete with Thomas with regard to the theoretical level of their work, but their contributions are interesting as examples of model construction and testing.

In Thorvald Moe's model (see Figure 1), the dependent variable is the *emigration rate*, which is calculated on the professionally employed group. This variable is more precisely defined as "emigrants in the most mobile age bracket of the labor force (15–30 years) in relation to 1,000 persons of the same ages in the stationary population." These calculations have been made on an annual basis.[9]

Moe uses the following function to predict Norwegian emigration: $LnMt = Lnb_0 + b_1Ln\ PYt + b_2Ln\ COt + b_3Ln\ EUSt + b_4UNt + LnV.$ The dependent variable $Mt$ = the *emigration rate* (only persons in the prime working age [15–30 years] are included). $Pyt$ = the *permanent income difference*. $COt$ = the *cohort effect* measured by the relative number of Norwegians in the age group 20–29 years, living in Norway $t$-1. $EUSt$ = *job availabilities* in the United States (Frickey's index on production for trade and transportation is used as a proxy). $UNt$ = *aggregate unemployment figures* for Norway (available from 1865). $V$ = error term.

This elaborate statistical model may, however, obscure gaps in the evidence. Although the emigration rate is of strategic importance for our evaluation of the model, Moe never presents a methodological discussion of the

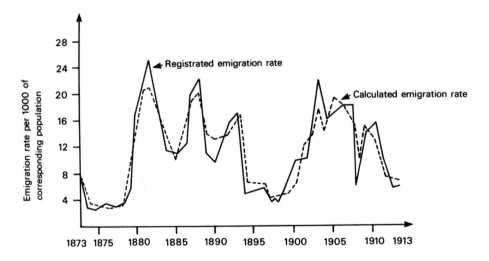

FIGURE 1. Model by Thorvald Moe compared with Norwegian emigration (ages 15–35), 1873–1913. Source: Thorvald Moe, "Demographic Development and Economic Growth in Norway, 1740–1900" (Ph.D. diss., Stanford University, 1970), p. 174.

sources from which it is derived. He does not say whether the accuracy of Norwegian emigration statistics improved between the early 1870s and 1915. Moreover, Moe does not examine the related possibility that the statistics may provide poorer coverage for the peak years of emigration than for its troughs. In interpreting his results, we must also be aware of the omitted age spans.

Another problem concerns the *permanent income gap,* which is defined as the difference between Norway and the United States in gross national product per member of the labor force. Moe does not hesitate to supply psychological interpretations of the behavior of the emigrants, postulating the emigrants' notion of the income gap as the mean value of the last five years' difference in per capita income. Here we are faced with a difficult theoretical question: how is it possible to convert a concept into a measurable variable? Other problems also arise: for example, the distribution of income might have been different in Norway from what it was in the United States. Moreover, as Moe himself emphasizes, rates of exchange usually do not serve as a good measurement of real purchasing power in different countries. Despite these reservations, we must credit Moe with introducing an interesting variable, the permanent income gap.

The so-called *cohort effect,* which is estimated on the basis of the proportion of twenty- to twenty-nine-year-old persons in the labor force, is another new feature of Moe's model. It expresses variations in the composition of the labor force, focusing on its most mobile sector. In addition to these long-term concepts, Moe also discusses some factors affecting short-term fluctuations, especially traveling costs and the cost of the inevitable period of unemployment in both the sending and receiving countries.

From Moe's example it can be seen that, for the econometricians, behavioral aspects enter the picture only occasionally. If one takes the social context as a starting-point, however, everything will of course turn out differently. This can be illustrated by the work of J. J. Mangalam, who views migration as a system-adapting mechanism with regard to the migrants' place of origin. In Mangalam's opinion, migration is the result of an inadequately functioning social organization. Thus collective migrations from an ongoing social organization create a number of changes in three systems, which he defines as *cultural, social,* and *personal.*[10] At the same time, according to Mangalam, there will also be changes within the social organization of the receiving society or area in order to accommodate the social organization that the migrants bring with them: "Thus, although migration is conceived initially as an adaptive mechanism within a single social organization, a complete understanding of migration demands that it be treated as a phenomenon that floats between and affects two social organizations, one at the place of origin and the other at the place of destination."[11] As a model, Mangalam's hypothesis is distinguished for its evident relation to Parsonian theory; its systems-analysis approach; its weak connection to economic and, even more importantly, psychological research; and the absence of recommendations for testing the model.

Another sociologist, R. C. Taylor, has concentrated on the psychological aspect of migrational processes. He has tried to classify migrants according to the nature of their motives: they are considered as either *aspiring* or *dislocated* or *resultant.*[12] An "aspiring" emigrant is one who makes a conscious effort to improve his own social and economic prospects or those of his family. This does not mean that the migrant necessarily considers himself as maladjusted in his present environment. On the other hand, the "dislocated" emigrant views his present situation as unsatisfactory. The "resultant" migrant reluctantly finds himself redundant in his present economic and social situation. Consequently, this latter type shows the least inclination to migrate and, as far as possible, tries to find an alternative. His behavior contrasts sharply with that of the aspiring and dislocated individuals, who deliberately conceive of and plan their actions.

In his empirical studies, Taylor has found logical differences between these three groups of individuals in the ways in which they evaluate their attitudes toward available information about migration and in the ways in which they make and implement their decision to migrate. More importantly, their various motives for migration appear to have a strong impact on their behavior and experiences in the receiving environments. "Aspiring" and "dislocated" individuals, for example, seem to be more ready to adjust than "resultant" individuals, who are also more inclined to re-migrate. In addition, the three groups establish different personal networks in the new environment.

It must be admitted that it is rather difficult to analyze the motivation for migration. Since Taylor ends up with a substantial residue which his three main categories are unable to accommodate, there is a need to develop a more sophisticated classification. As a contribution to the understanding of *migratory selectivity,* however, Taylor's point of view seems to be revealing and quite consistent with other empirical findings (such as the U-shaped distribution of migrants according to their qualifications).[13]

There are good reasons for investigating the psychiatric aspects of migrational movements. It has been argued hypothetically that migrants are more vulnerable to mental illness than the stationary part of a population; this is a basic theme of the classical study of Polish emigrants to North America written by W. I. Thomas and F. Znaniecki.[14] It is possible that the kind of people who choose to migrate are also more susceptible to mental disturbances than their neighbors who remain at home. This potential instability may be aggravated by the special problems of adaptation presented by migration; that is, immigrants to a foreign, and often very different, country might naturally be expected to show signs of mental distress more frequently than other people. Some attempts have been made to embody this point of view in a model which interprets migrational processes as a series of *stress-producing* elements.[15] This is a most important field of research, but currently proposed models seem to be too narrow and too biased toward the negative aspects of geographical movements. A full-fledged model needs to integrate other approaches and other findings as well.[16]

Finally, there are the probabilistic models. Perhaps the most interesting attempt in this field has been made by the geographer T. Hägerstrand.[17] A starting-point for a purely probabilistic model is the assumption that many decisions to act (or react to stimuli) can tentatively be described, in combination, as a random process: at least, this may be true if the human behavior in question results from complex causes.[18] Even though Hägerstrand worked primarily with the diffusion of innovations rather than with population movements, his so-called *Monte Carlo model* seems to be relevant to migration studies because it treats spatial processes in general. By testing such a model with random numbers, we will find that geographic concentrations of acceptances of an innovation or an innovative behavior may occur without any meaning in terms of special causes or differentials. This seems to be the case in the beginning of the spread of an innovation. So by comparing the randomly generated results and empirical observations, we are able to find out when systematic changes occur and, consequently, to interpret them.[19]

But a model that treats only the first phases of a process would be of rather restricted value to migration research. Hence Hägerstrand went on to experiment with combined random and non-random elements. This adds up to a *stochastic* construct (certain constraints are applied to an otherwise randomly determined expression). Such a model seems to fit the complex reality better. It is questionable, however, if it will ever be possible to treat a problem such as mass emigration, with its strong interactive character, as a basically randomized process.[20]

III.

Even a superficial examination of the emigration rates of the European countries which contributed to the mass emigration to the Americas reveals pronounced and repeated variations. These emigration curves look like fever charts for a pneumonia patient. Dramatic as they seem, these curves have not attracted much interest from migration scholars. This is unfortunate because key information about the function of migrational movements may well be hidden in them. As a matter of fact, current model-building efforts could profitably be concentrated on the task of trying to explain the amplitudes of emigration curves. How does it happen that migration starts at a certain level one year, then suddenly climbs to a level ten times as high the next year, then returns soon again to the starting point?

This problem has been overshadowed by discussion of the timing of the oscillations and their relation to the business cycles of the receiving and sending countries. Controversy has focused on whether pull *or* push factors best explain the changes. But there have also appeared more sophisticated attempts to treat migration patterns as the result of the interplay among several variables.

What kinds of evidence are relevant to our question about emigration rates? One important finding seems to be the *uneven geographical spread of mass emigration.* Even if cartographical analyses of European regions have not been widely performed, one might dare to say that this uneven spread is a general trait. If we consider the five Nordic countries in which geographical emigration has been thoroughly studied, we can easily distinguish mass-emigration regions from regions that have not been touched by the transoceanic exodus. Perhaps Finland shows the greatest contrast between regions; the Icelandic example is also striking. There is evidence that this pattern has been equally pronounced in the Mediterranean area and in some central parts of the continent.[21]

In addition, it has been shown that this uneven geographical spread of emigrational behavior has as a corollary a *strong continuity over time.* Although we may find important and dramatic shifts over half a century, as in the German emigration, those parts of a country or a continent which from the very beginning reacted most strongly to migration pressures frequently continue to yield great numbers of emigrants. It may be added that this constancy in the source and the direction of migrational streams is paralleled by internal movements within a country.[22]

Research has also discovered the existence of strong *relationships between certain well-defined sending and receiving areas.* This pattern includes connections between large regions such as nations in Europe and states in North America as well as links between smaller units such as parishes and townships.[23] It is particularly remarkable in urban settings, of which "Little Sicily" in Chicago is an example. We have called these connections "axes" between the end points of the emigrants' travels.

Even if the shifts in an emigration curve are sharp, it normally develops into something very much like a "growth curve."[24] (See Figure 2.) An emigration typically starts with a few scattered acceptances of an offered opportunity to move. After a while the process begins to accelerate, and grows strongly, almost exponentially, until a saturation phase is reached.[25] Thus, once more, we are reminded of the need to study migrational processes in

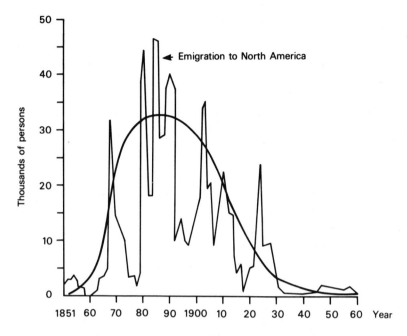

FIGURE 2. Registered Swedish emigration, 1851–1960, compared with an approximate growth curve.

depth; it is not enough to examine the changing context of the yearly fluctuations. It must be remarked, however, that depth is elusive when we are confined to aggregated statistics. Here, more work with data related to individuals is an urgent necessity.

During the mass-emigration period the agencies of the steamship companies were accused of having caused the uprooting of hundreds of thousands of inhabitants of different countries; one Swedish official, as early as 1870, criticized "the tempting persuasion and promises of the so-called emigration agents whose income depends on the greater or smaller number whom they succeed in inciting to emigrate."[26] Systematic studies have shown, however, that the activities of the agents, who were easy scapegoats for governments worried about loss of population, were not particularly important. From the perspective of current migration research, it seems that agents profited from the surges of emigration but were unable to influence them.[27]

Emigration patterns were, on the other hand, strongly dependent on the influence exerted on the primary group level by friends and relatives. In emigration studies, the term "stock effect" refers to the impact of the attitudes and experiences of former emigrants when they are transmitted back to certain areas and sub-populations. The same phenomenon can be studied through kinship analysis. It is possible to describe the structure of these personal influences in great detail.[28]

In addition, we can follow the genesis and development of a mass-emigration movement within a small administrative unit. As an example, we can consider the results of a study of Långasjö parish in southern Sweden during the years 1850–1890.[29] (See Figures 3 and 4.) Every small village within the parish is represented by a trajectory, to which emigrating individuals, families, and other groups are attached when they move away. The trajectory also serves as a time axis.[30] The location of the villages and isolated farmsteads can be seen on the map.[31]

Abundant information for this analysis exists in church records, which include catechetical examination registers, birth and death records, and in- and out-migration lists. This little information system allows us to identify members of different families and households and to examine kinship networks in general.[32] In addition, there is still a strong oral tradition about the transatlantic emigration from this area, which was tapped in the early 1960s, when many more emigrants and returning migrants were still alive. The results shed light on the receiving as well as the sending side.[33]

The links between related individuals are marked by strings.[34] Thus we can see how a family moved away, even if it took ten to fifteen years for the whole unit to leave the country. During that time, some member of the family might have made the trip across the ocean several times. Often a family or a household emigrated from one village along with relatives from neighboring villages or parishes. The ties between these emigrants are often revealed by their choice of the same or nearby destinations in North America.[35] Of course, all this does not mean that the destinations could not differ for members of the same European parish. In our investigation area there were marked differences of preference, even though the Chisago Lake district in Minnesota, parts of western Wisconsin, and (in the twentieth century) British Columbia attracted most emigrants.[36] Emigrants who traveled singly also often settled in areas—most frequently city neighborhoods—dominated by their own nationality.[37]

Returning to Figure 4, we can see how some small villages were touched early by mass emigration and continued to provide a disproportionately large number of recruits, relative to the contribution of other villages that became involved later on. This tells us something about the mechanisms that stimulate population movement. The decision to migrate overseas was made most commonly by persons who had previously taken part in internal migrations and who belonged to families or villages already involved in the exodus. Many persons who are classified as "single" emigrants in the statistical surveys actually were part of a protracted family or group migration. This

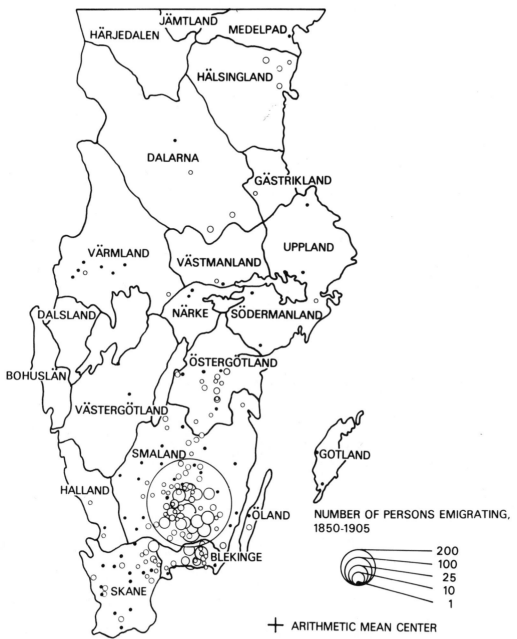

FIGURE 3. Birth field, Chisago Lake Congregation, Minnesota. Långasjö is situated in the center of the field. Source: Parish Registers of Catechetical Examination of the Augustana Church; R. C. Ostergren, "Cultural Homogeneity and Population Stability in Swedish Immigrant Communities" (unpublished paper, University of Minnesota, 1972), p. 38.

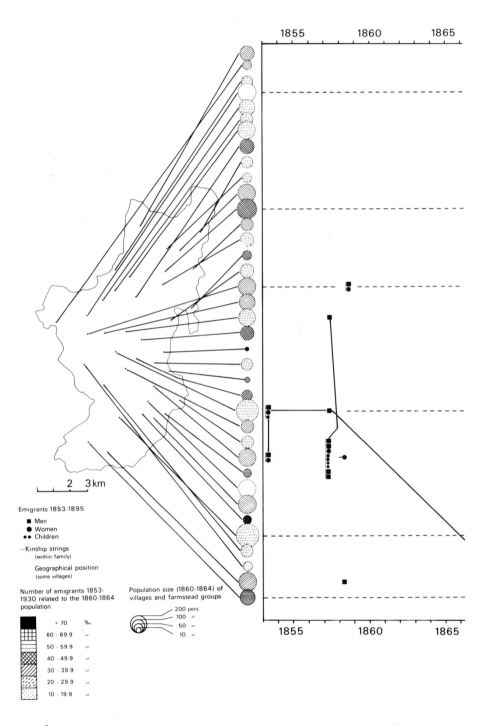

1855 1860 1865

2 3km

Emigrants 1853-1895

■ Men
● Women
■● Children

—Kinship strings
(within family)

Geographical position
(some villages)

Number of emigrants 1853-
1930 related to the 1860-1864
population

| | |
|---|---|
| > 70 | ‰ |
| 60 - 69.9 | ″ |
| 50 - 59.9 | ″ |
| 40 - 49.9 | ″ |
| 30 - 39.9 | ″ |
| 20 - 29.9 | ″ |
| 10 - 19.9 | ″ |

Population size (1860-1864) of
villages and farmstead groups

200 pers.
100 ″
50 ″
10 ″

1855 1860 1865

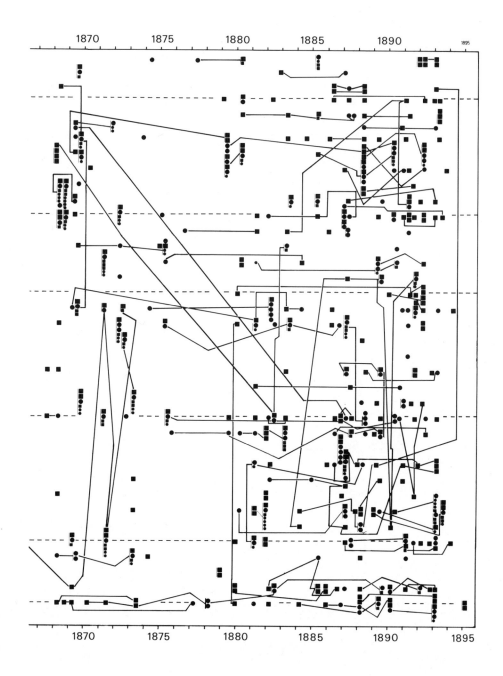

FIGURE 4. Kinship and internal migration as related to mass emigration, Långasjö, 1850–1895

shows once more that in the analysis of large-scale social phenomena the time dimension cannot be ignored.[38]

Some villages within a typical emigration parish or some parishes within a mass-emigration district may very well prove to have been almost completely resistant to the prevalent emigration pressures. This is the other side of the coin. In these cases, the alternative of emigration was not sufficiently attractive to precipitate action.[39] Clearly, a complex of factors resulted in a village population's tendency to migrate or to remain at home. Thus, a simple analysis of economic structures will not adequately explain migrational movements; similar labor market situations do not always evoke the same behavior.

The interplay between populations in the receiving and the sending countries is also revealed in the prepaid ticket system which was a prominent feature of the mass emigration. Under this system those who had already emigrated could make similar decisions for those they had left behind. A prepaid ticket was a persuasive gift from a former emigrant to his friends and relatives still in Europe; and its persuasiveness or pull was doubtless enhanced by the monetary remittances he might also send. Of course, not all prepaid tickets were purchased in order to encourage hesitant migrants. At times as much as 50–60 percent of the total tickets sold were prepaid, which doubtless reflects not only the strength of pull forces, but also a technical financial reason for buying a ticket paid for in advance in the United States or Canada. In North America there may have been some competition between the shipping lines, and the resulting lowered prices may have been especially attractive during periods of cartel agreements in Europe which considerably raised the prices of tickets bought there.[40]

All these results point to the self-generating elements that seem to be built into most migrational movements. Our next step will be to examine the extent of potential migration.

Indirect but not necessarily unreliable calculations seem to show that something like two million people, out of a population of four to five million, seriously considered leaving Sweden in the 1880s. This general mood of restlessness must have been typical of most high-emigration areas of Europe during the decades around the turn of the century; it also turns up in modern investigations based on interviews with members of migrating populations.[41]

In spite of this enormous potential willingness to emigrate, however, only a relatively small part of the population—about 25 percent—actually made the decision to move. This result points to the existence of *barriers and resistance* to population turnover, which hindered even movements between places in the same area. The study of these hindrances has led to the discovery of the so-called *rural-industrial barrier,* which has been important in the analysis of internal migration patterns.[42] Related barriers also produce resistance to external migrations. This resistance has been consistently strong over a long period, although its specific causes have varied from time to time. On the whole, these barriers seem to be more mental than physical.[43]

Without considering the individual and social psychology of the decision to migrate, it is impossible to understand the whole complicated process. It has been suggested by some scholars that migrational decisions result from what is called *value-added process.*[44] From Figure 5, we can learn how such a process is thought to work. Briefly speaking, there exists a *structural stress* of some sort. By itself, this stress does not lead to anything. It must first be recognized by the individuals, who may then react to it with manifest action. But this cannot happen until a *migration offer* appears. Still nothing will happen unless the individual concerned belongs to a *personality type* which in general is willing to pull up stakes. In addition, the *social control* must not be so strong that it hinders the decision. If all these conditions are met, the person observed will be "ripe for migration," lacking only a final impulse which *triggers off* the move. This last condition is the *situational side* of the story, which has been treated over and over by the analysis of business-cycles and other similar factors. Our approach shows how a damming up of the desire to migrate may take place within a population, and how the sills may be lowered or almost removed in certain situations, causing a tremendous effect in terms of numbers of out-migrants.[45]

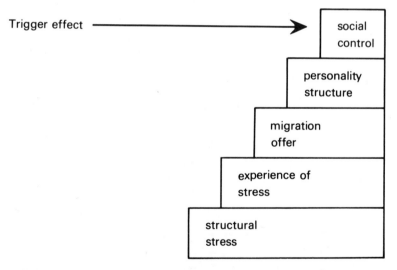

FIGURE 5. J. E. Ellemers' value-added process. Source: S. Akerman, P. G. Cassel, and E. Johansson, "Background Variables of Population Mobility: An Attempt at Automatic Interaction Analysis, A Preliminary Research Report," *The Scandinavian Economic History Review*, no. 1 (1974), p. 34.

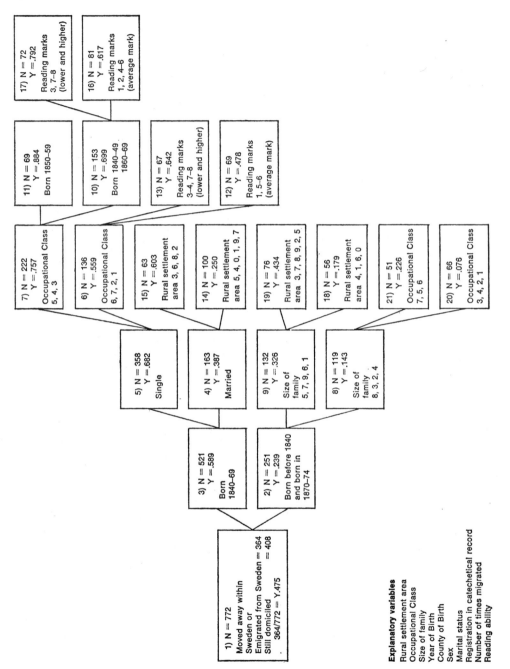

FIGURE 6. Data cleavage, Köinge, 1878–1888. N = 772. Moved away/emigrated, 1878–1888 = 1. Still domiciled, 1888 = O. Source: S. Akerman et al., "Background Variables of Population Mobility."

302]

Even if the general pattern of mass-emigration seems consistent with this social-psychological reconstruction, we need, of course, to test it more thoroughly. This has been done in a special investigation of Köinge parish, a small emigration area of southwestern Sweden.[46] In our study we used Automatic Interaction Detector analysis (AID), or data split technique, which appeared to be the most appropriate multivariate statistical technique for our theoretical level.[47] Despite many problems in interpreting the so-called tree outputs, as well as other complications related to the isolation and measurement of our concepts, it seems fair to state that the test was rather successful (see Figure 6). Repeated tests with much larger populations have given the same results.[48]

## IV.

It is now time to draw conclusions from all of this evidence. Our task was to try to understand why emigrational curves show such tremendous amplitudes and at the same time to suggest a new kind of model strategy. It must be stressed that the building and testing of our model has not been done in an orthodox way. By choosing data that were considered *crucial* and had already been tested, and by combining them into a logical structure, we have, in effect, created a prefabricated house. The various "key results" we have used in our effort have consequently acted as elements of the building.

All this adds up to the following: *An enormous potential inclination to move, a gradual ripening of the decisions to emigrate, and strong possibilities of influence on an interpersonal level within both sending and receiving populations created a situation waiting for the existing resistances to break down.* When that happened now and again the effects were astonishing. It is impossible to understand such dramatic responses to the possibility of emigration without considering the multiplier effects that were released as a consequence of the interpersonal relations.

## NOTES

1. This may seem to be a rather unfair judgment, considering the fact that a tremendous number of articles and books are devoted to migrational problems every year. What I am talking about here, however, is not research documented by aggregated statistics, net migrations, and similar evidence, but rather research based on

information about migrating individuals. I am also referring to substantial empirical research with *a longitudinal approach.*

2. Such a point of view may seem self-evident. But discussions at international conferences have shown that even subjects like historical demography, which treat very general problems, can be limited and fragmentary owing to a nationalistic approach.

3. Migration research is situated at the point of intersection of several university disciplines. Thus one might expect the specialty to be more interdisciplinarily oriented than social science in general, but this is hardly the case. As will be shown later, there exists no real communication and interaction between economic and demographic research, on the one hand, and behavioral research, on the other.

4. S. Åkerman, "Theories and Methods of Migration Research," in H. Runblom and H. Norman (eds.), *From Sweden to America: A History of the Migration* (Uppsala, 1976), pp. 17–75. The survey of migration research here is a condensed version of the 1976 text.

5. G. Olsson, *Distance and Human Interaction: A Review and Bibliography* (Philadelphia, 1965).

6. H. Jerome, *Migration and Business Cycles,* National Bureau of Economic Research, no. 9 (New York, 1926); R. Easterlin, *Population, Labor Force and Long Swings in Economic Growth* (New York, 1968); and D. S. Thomas, *Social and Economic Aspects of Swedish Population Movements 1750–1933,* Stockholm Economic Studies, 10:1 (New York, 1941).

7. B. Thomas, *Migration and Economic Growth: A Study of Great Britain and the Atlantic Economy* (Cambridge, 1954), and *Migration and Urban Development: A Reappraisal of British and American Long Cycles* (London, 1972).

8. M. Wilkinson, "Evidences of Long Swings in the Growth of Swedish Population and Related Economic Variables, 1860–1965," *Journal of Economic History,* 27 (1967), and T. Moe, "Demographic Developments and Economic Growth in Norway 1740–1940: An Econometric Study" (Ph.D. dissertation, Stanford University, 1970).

9. Moe, pp. 155ff., and Åkerman, pp. 51ff.

10. J. J. Mangalam, *Human Migration: A Guide to Migration Literature in English, 1955–62* (Lexington, Ky., 1968), pp. 1–20.

11. Mangalam, p. 15.

12. R. C. Taylor, "Migration and Motivation: A Study of Determinants and Types," in J. A. Jackson (ed.), *Migration,* Sociological Studies no. 2 (Cambridge, 1969).

13. S. Åkerman, P. G. Cassel, and E. Johansson, "Background Variables of Population Mobility: An Attempt at Automatic Interaction Analysis, A Preliminary Research Report," *The Scandinavian Economic History Review,* no. 1 (1974), pp. 32–60.

14. W. I. Thomas and F. Znaniecki, *Polish Peasant in Europe and America* (New York, 1958).

15. L. Levi and L. Andersson, *Population, Environment and Quality of Life* (Stockholm, 1975), pp. 66 ff., and Ø. Ødegaard, "Emigration and Insanity," *Acta Psychiatrica et Neurologica,* suppl. 4 (1932).

16. Levi and Andersson, pp. 67f.

17. T. Hägerstrand, *Innovation Diffusion as a Spatial Process* (Lund, 1967), and S. C. Dodd, "Diffusion Is Predictable," *American Sociological Review*, 20 (1955), pp. 392–401.

18. Compare A. Pred in Hägerstrand, p. 307.

19. Hägerstrand, pp. 140f. In other words, this is a typical *heuristic* model.

20. Hägerstrand, models II and III. Compare N. W. Henry, R. McGinnis, and H. W. Tegtmeyer, "A Finite Model of Mobility," *Journal of Mathematical Sociology* (1971).

21. Compare also the emigration to Australia from southern Europe. C. A. Price, *Southern Europeans in Australia* (Melbourne, 1963), as well as J. Puskas, *Emigration from Hungary to the United States before 1914* (Budapest, 1975).

22. See, e.g., T. Hägerstrand and D. Hannerberg, *Migration in Sweden: A Symposium* (Lund, 1957).

23. J. Rice, *Patterns of Ethnicity in a Minnesota County, 1880–1905* (Umea, 1973), and R. C. Ostergren, "Cultural Homogeneity and Population Stability in Swedish Immigrant Communities" (unpublished paper, University of Minnesota, Minneapolis, 1972).

24. S. Åkerman, *From Stockholm to San Francisco: The Development of the Historical Study of External Migrations* (Uppsala, 1975), p. 20.

25. Hägerstrand treats the implications of different levels of resistance to a behavioral alternative within a population from a theoretical viewpoint.

26. C. Erickson, *Emigration from Europe, 1815–1914* (London, 1976), p. 64.

27. B. Brattne and S. Åkerman, "The Importance of the Transport Sector for Mass Emigration," in Runblom and Norman, *From Sweden to America*, pp. 176–200.

28. Family and kinship have been studied in a migrational setting by, e.g., E. D. Smith, "Non-Farm Employment Information for Rural People," *Journal of Farm Economics*, 38 (1956), pp. 813–27. As regards contemporary migration literature, Mangalam concludes: "Not much progress has been made in developing significant frames of reference with respect to the destination of the migrants that take into account the behavioral aspects of migration" (p. 4).

29. This special study is based on a local historical study, *En smålandssocken emigrerar* [A Smaland Parish Emigrates], performed by J. Johansson, A. Redin, et al. (Växjö, 1967), as well as on the church-archive material from Långasjö parish.

30. A similar time-space representation has been suggested by T. Hägerstrand, *On the Definition of Migration* (Helsinki, 1973).

31. Population for the period 1860–64, as well as emigration frequencies for the investigation period, are also shown.

32. This is a special feature of this source material owing to the continuous registration of families and households in the *catechetical examination registers* of the Lutheran church.

33. Compare U. Beijbom, *Swedes in Chicago: A Demographic and Social Study of the 1846–1880 Immigration* (Växjö, 1971), and H. Norman, "Swedes in North America," in Runblom and Norman, *From Sweden to America*, pp. 229–241.

34. It would be possible to show most internal migration as well as the total

kinship structure, but such a picture would be more confusing than revealing. The present illustration can be seen as a *proxy* for the complete pattern of interrelationship and movements.

35. L.-G. Tedebrand, *Västernorrland och Nordamerika, 1875–1913* (Uppsala, 1972), p. 217.

36. *En smålandssocken emigrerar.*

37. Ostergren, p. 43.

38. From a theoretical point of view, this has been stressed by S. Carlsson, "Från familjeutvandring till ensamutvandring: En utvecklingslinje i den svenska emigrationens historia" [From Family Emigration to Individual Emigration] in *Emigrationer: En bok till Wilhelm Moberg* (Stockholm, 1968), pp. 101–22.

39. This fact has been stressed by F. Thistlethwaite, "Migrations from Europe Overseas in the Nineteenth and Twentieth Centuries," *XIᵉ Congrès International des Sciences Historiques, Rapports,* vol. 5 (Uppsala, 1960), pp. 32–60, but it has never been thoroughly studied.

40. B. Brattne, *Bröderna Larsson: En studie i svensk emigrant-agentverksamhet under 1880-talet* [The Larsson Brothers: The Activity of Swedish Emigrant Agents during the 1880s] (Uppsala, 1973).

41. N. H. Frijda, "Kwantitatieve analyse van een onderzoek naar de motieven van een groep emigranten," in *Emigranten/niet-emigranten* (The Hague, 1960).

42. S. Åkerman, "The Psychology of Migration," *American Studies in Scandinavia,* 8 (1972), pp. 46–52.

43. Compare P. R. Gould, "On Mental Maps" in P. W. English and R. C. Mayfield (eds.), *Man, Space, and Environment* (New York and Toronto, 1972), pp. 260–82.

44. J. E. Ellemers, "The Determinants of Emigration: An Analysis of Dutch Studies on Migration," *Sociologia Neerlandica* 2, no. 1 (1964), pp. 41ff.

45. Åkerman, Cassel, and Johansson, "Background Variables of Population Mobility."

46. Ibid.

47. J. A. Sonquist, E. L. Baker, and J. N. Morgan, *Searching for Structure* (Ann Arbor, Mich., 1974).

48. AID runs performed by K. Söderberg, Umeå University. Criticism of the AID technique as well as of our application of it has been leveled by B. Gullberg and B. Odén, "AID-analysis and Migration History," *Scandinavian Economic History Review,* 24 (1976), pp. 1–32.

# [14]

International Migration Policies: Some Demographic and Economic Contexts

GEORGE J. STOLNITZ

## MIGRATION VERSUS OTHER POPULATION POLICIES

A country's policy options concerning emigrants and immigrants differ in decided ways from those affecting its mortality and fertility. Since its international migration pattern has consequences for other countries, whether from welfare, socioeconomic, or other points of view, differential or even conflicting national objectives and impacts are to be expected. In contrast, a nation's policies designed to influence mortality or fertility tend overwhelmingly to be inner-directed—the main consequences from practical and analytical viewpoints alike are intranational. As a second contrast, whereas a national policy-maker may well feel free to encourage or inhibit net immigration, depending on circumstances, his only options for modifying mortality and associated morbidities are those aimed at reduction, at least in principle. Or again, where a country's decision to modify net migration can often take immediate effect, especially toward diminution, nothing of the sort can be contemplated in the case of fertility. This is so whether the policy goal is to reduce fertility, as through family-planning programs in low-income areas, or to raise it, as by family allowances or other incentive systems. Not only are the social norms, structures, and mechanisms for achieving quick fertility changes highly different from those involved in most migration questions, but also the comparative sizes of the target populations involved vary greatly. On the one hand, fertility changes on a major scale involve action by a mass constituency, since remarkably similar numbers of children can be produced in both palaces and huts. On the other hand, migration tends to involve comparatively small numbers of persons relative to the decision-making population, and relatively small numbers of geographical exchange points.

Moreover, and not least important from policy viewpoints, the very definition of "migrant" is often unclear. Merely the question of identifying the persons involved raises policy and associated statistical issues that have no counterparts in the counting of births or deaths. Permanent migrants may not be readily distinguishable from temporary ones, even by the migrants themselves; legal or administrative regulations affecting permanent and temporary migrants may be sharply at variance with those concerning seasonal migrants; and students and dependents of seasonal migrants may come under still other administrative headings.

To be sure, significant exceptions can be cited with respect to any or all of these distinctions. Migration-related agreements, treaties, and negotiations designed to reconcile multinational interests exist in profusion. In an era well branded by wars, genocide, and annual mass slaughter on the highways, reduction of mortality to the extent possible falls far short of being a total moral imperative. Fertility-influencing policies can be selectively focused—whether by intention or necessity—on small socioeconomic subgroups of the population, while the resistance of mass fertility patterns to programmed manipulation may yet yield to novel ways of inducing rapid change.

Further exceptions, of a converse kind, are as easily cited. For one, controls over migration suffer from inefficiencies of a considerable order. Illegal immigration in many parts of the world occurs on a substantial scale, not least in the United States itself. The net number illegally entering the United States in an average recent year may well have been 50 percent or more above the legal count, and the suspected cumulative total of the illegally entered and unapprehended population is "guesstimated" by some observers to approximate 5 to 10 million, the upper end of this range being not far short of 5 percent of the entire population. Analogous situations no doubt exist in other countries. As a further exception worth stressing, net numbers of migrants (whether they have entered for a fairly short period such as a decade or especially if counted in cumulative terms) may be substantial rather than merely minor fractions of a total population. Ireland, Switzerland, Kuwait, Israel, and a number of Caribbean areas are all strong cases in point, and there are numerous other, if less pronounced, such instances.

Despite these qualifications, to which others could be added, the above essential proposition holds. Migration policy needs to be sharply distinguished from other realms of population policy, whether one considers the range and flexibility of the most prominent policy alternatives, the immediacy with which such policies can be implemented or altered, or the extent of their anticipated effectiveness.

## SOME THEORETICAL GUIDELINES FOR ANALYSIS

Turning to some main theoretical aspects of migration policy, two in particular merit attention. Both, it might be added, apply to internal (e.g., rural-urban) as well as to international migration, after allowance for some obvious substantive adjustments. The first is that full evaluation of the desirability of a given (actual or prospective) migration flow requires a double-edged perspective: an area of origin as well as an area of destination need to be examined simultaneously for effects. Whether such effects are opposing or reinforcing is not the issue; it is enough that neither set of effects is trivial.

Important case histories of reinforcing effects can be clearly identified in the vast European out-migrations to overseas areas during the nineteenth and early twentieth centuries. Not only did these movements provide population and labor force to foster economic growth in much of the Western hemisphere, Oceania, and elsewhere; in addition, their timing probably contributed significantly to development in large originating areas as well, by siphoning off surplus population during an era of high natural increase and chronic capital scarcities.[1]

Illustrations of significant opposing effects are also not hard to find. The "brain-drain" problem, for example, goes beyond possible receiving-area benefits and also beyond opportunities for individual self-advancement as perceived by the migrants themselves. However substantial these benefits may be (and however congenial to those market-system ideologues who tend to curtail their analysis to these points of view), the sending areas have to be taken into account as well. Otherwise, possible policy options may be unduly restricted, indeed needlessly so, since allowing or disallowing migration are not the only alternatives. Compensatory arrangements, whether by governments or individuals, between origin and destination areas are another possibility. So are innovative incentive systems for equalizing or otherwise redistributing benefit-cost relations of both economic and non-economic kinds.[2]

A second key theoretical guideline, perhaps even less explored and more open to controversy than the first, is that *social* costs and benefits of migration may differ greatly from *private* costs and benefits. As the economist might put it, one must be alert to "externalities" in reaching policy judgments. On the one hand, the facts that so many millions seem ready to leave their homeland, and that so many more millions clearly prefer the city to rural places of birth or previous residence, would appear to make such preferences self-justifying beyond any question. At least, this would be so if we consider private motivations only and, to strengthen the point further, if we abstract from the inherent uncertainties of migration decisions, assume away irreversible life-cycle mistakes, and suppose that rationality on economic grounds is reinforced by non-economic considerations. This last supposition, it may be added, appears to have been borne out remarkably well in the history of main migration flows from low-income to high-income countries, or from underdeveloped to more developed parts of high-income countries, during the modern historical era. Educational, recreational, health, and intergenerational mobility inducements, among others, have often been well correlated with economic inducements to such migration.

Yet even all of this may not be enough from a policy standpoint. For on the other hand, individuals and families typically have no reason to consider whether their decisions to move or not to move entail costs to society. Roads, schools, capital requirements stemming from expanded neighborhood development, municipal services, and sometimes major amounts of housing subsidies, are all examples, abundantly encountered, of social costs that the individual can ignore but that society must consider. Obviously, such resources could be put to alternative uses if migration decisions by individuals were overruled or altered.

Whether the predominant net costs and benefits are likely to be private or social cannot be prejudged on the basis of theory alone. Quite possibly, reliance on the marketplace—in effect, on individually arrived-at migration decisions—may be the preferred alternative even after extra-individual or social considerations have been given their due. Indeed, my own predisposition has often tilted in this direction when considering rural-urban settlement problems in low-income countries. Even the vastly overcrowded primate city, with its innumerable problems and enormous social costs, may be preferable to life on the farm from key social points of view—as it obviously is for vast numbers of individuals. Nevertheless, the pendulum of a more rounded judgment might well swing the other way.

Here again, and much as in stressing the multiple-area dimensionality of migration effects, an extended theoretical framework is needed to arrive at persuasive conclusions. For migration to main cities and continued work-plus-residence in rural places are not the only alternatives. Development of hinterland cities of secondary, tertiary, or smaller size; adequate build-up of infrastructure to support such cities; and novel systems of combining farm with non-farm work for rural inhabitants—all of these are further possibilities and all require broadened accounting systems of costs and benefits for analysis and policy.

As the development economist or city planner can well attest, obstacles to persuasive policy determinations in the migration area can be manifold. But the costs of oversight can also be severe. Scholars can best serve, I believe, by disabusing us of the presumption that acceptance of what we see, *versus* the more-or-less total prevention of what we see, makes for a full listing of the only, or even the most interesting, alternatives.

## REGIONAL MIGRATION: A LOOK AHEAD IN DEMAND–SUPPLY TERMS

Although future migration policies around the world will be closely conditioned by existing regional variations in demographic and economic structure, this is not to say that demographic or economic factors alone, or even such factors in combination, are the predominant determinants of all large population movements across national borders. Nationalism, international alliances and antagonisms, religion, ethnic rivalries, desires to live under a different political system, family ties, language, and the sheer momentum of previous migrations are sure to play prominent roles in the future, as they traditionally have in the past. The usual description of voluntary migration as being predominantly economic in cause (even if true) fails to allow for the fact that most mass voluntary movements of the modern era have been associated with reinforcing non-economic influences. Certainly, the fact that a large fraction of Europe's overseas migrants returned to their home continent, and the further fact that so many non-migrants failed to move when exposed to much the same economic circumstances and prospects as were faced by migrants, should give pause to the assignment of simple causes.

However, the task of discussing non-economic or non-demographic factors affecting modern-day migration movements must be left to others, and attention in the rest of this paper is restricted to economic and demographic considerations alone. Further, in the interest of brevity, the focus below on developed and less-developed countries ("DCs" and "LDCs," respectively) as entities will deal with them as if they were internally undifferentiated groups of areas.[3] Although the use of such broad units precludes adequate study of specific migration patterns or prospects, this should not be a problem here, since the few general propositions to be made can be considered in highly aggregative terms for present purposes. "LDC," as used below, refers to very nearly all of Latin America, Africa, and Asia, with the exceptions of Japan, Israel, parts of temperate-zone South America, some non-black population sectors in Africa, and a few other small areas. "DC" refers to the rest of the world, or very nearly all of Europe, Oceania, North America (minus Mexico and the Caribbean areas), plus the above exclusions from the LDCs.

The first and simplest generalization to make may also be the most important from a global demographic viewpoint. No conceivable realistic scale of migration from LDCs to DCs can be expected to offset today's overpopulation problems in the LDC regions as a whole. To cite only one or two statistics: the great overseas migration from Europe between the Napoleonic era and today has probably not totaled much, if at all, above 75 million. Even this figure is substantially too high if one subtracts returning migrants. Moreover, the total sending population in Europe during most of this 150-year period was far below 500 million. Today, merely the growth per year among LDC populations is not far from 65 to 70 million, while their present number is already well above 2.5 billion. In India alone, merely the growth of numbers to the year 2000 will match or exceed the entire end-century population of our own country. Hence it seems nonsense to expect any but niggardly effects in quantitative terms from migration out of LDC regions as a group to DC regions. I emphasize this only because such nonsense is encountered so often.

A second generalization is that what might be called the "effective demand" globally for international migration is almost surely at a far higher level today than it has ever been in world history. To give credence to this point, one need not be a total economic determinist. Nor need one decide whether the economic disparities between today's high-income and low-income regions are substantially different from the ones that have prevailed in the past. It is enough to indicate that the disparities are very large and on average will continue to be so under all conceivable peacetime circumstances for the rest of this century and well beyond.

The above second proposition, then, follows from several considerations in combination: (a) the assumption (backed by a very considerable body of evidence) that large international economic disparities offer considerable inducement to cross national boundaries; (b) the need to take into account the sheer size of the LDC population eligible to migrate if permitted to do so; (c) the forecast that a reduction of average LDC-DC economic disparities to a point below the threshhold of inducements to migrate is far beyond the range of realistic possibility during the foreseeable future; and (d) the fact that public knowledge about the existence of LDC-DC disparities has never been greater than today, owing to the worldwide spread of continuous communications throughout the DC regions and large segments of the LDC regions, both urban and rural. While "knowledge" as a factor affecting migration is not easily assessed, research suggests that it has a very substantial bearing on migration decisions. As a final major consideration, it may be well to add: (e) the fact that costs of transportation have fallen greatly in psychic terms (for example, when health risks are taken into account), whether or not such reductions have also taken place in purely monetary terms.

Third, the supply of migration-absorbing opportunities in DC areas is extremely limited with respect to prospective LDC emigrants. Quite possibly, this is more the case today than ever before with respect to primary industries of employment, given the marked tendencies to a diminishing agricultural labor force in DC regions. The limited absorptive capacity of all DC "empty lands" relative to increasing LDC numbers can be pointed up simply. It is enough to mention again the example of India's growth of population soon matching the total size of the U.S. population.

In sum, the excess of demand for LDC-to-DC migration over the supply of viable opportunities for accommodating such demand appears hopelessly large to be overcome by policy remedies. It needs emphasis that this conclusion relates to very large regional aggregates. A great many small nations, singly and even in combination, have population sizes that can be significantly affected by migration policies.[4] The above summary conclusion should also be distinguished from judgments bearing on qualitative effects. Remittances by LDC migrants employed in DC regions may have significant effects on their home country's balance of payments, whether we are dealing with small or large sending populations. Analogously, economic development in a sending area may well be fostered as a result of the experience acquired by its native-born population while working abroad.

Hence, the thrust of the above three propositions is that it is highly selective geographic or qualitative effects such as these, rather than large-scale quantitative impacts on a region-wide scale, which should constitute the main subject matter of LDC-to-DC migration policies, if policy is to be realistic.

Fourth, the prospects for voluntary intra-LDC migration appear extremely limited, whether such migration is considered in relation to aggregate population size or even in terms of absolute numbers. Not only are there often great geographic distances within and between LDC continents, and not only are restrictionist policies widely prevalent in these areas; in addition, the potentials for large-scale intra-LDC movements again appear scant if considered from straightforward economic points of view. Some intracontinental movements in Africa probably come closest to being an exception to this anticipation, when considered relative to the population size of sending and receiving countries.

The reasons for this fourth proposition are numerous. Often, perhaps most notably in Latin America, the types of immigrants most desired by prospective LDC receiving societies do not exist in appreciable numbers in other LDC areas. Conversely, the most eager applicants for intra-LDC movements, such as those in especially impoverished rural areas, are usually not desired by prospective receiving areas, since empty agrarian spaces are few, limited in size, and destined to become rapidly occupied by home populations. Since most LDC populations are located in tropical and semi-tropical zones, only radical breakthroughs in the technical control of climate —by no means inconceivable within another century but almost surely irrelevant for many decades to come—could greatly enhance the economic attractiveness of today's tropical-type agricultural areas. For now and a long time ahead, the potential of such areas as sources of population intake must be judged to be minimal.

As to the oil-rich areas of the Middle East, these are seeking only some hundreds of thousands of persons rather than many millions. Oil, a capital-intensive industry, requires relatively few workers, and such need seems certain to diminish within a few decades, not only in the oil industry itself but also in the other sectors (in particular, service sectors) now being funded by petrodollars.

In short, if we consider the LDC regions as a whole, we find that poverty provides few inducements for the impoverished to move, even when intra-regional differentials are substantial. In this respect, migration potentials and their prospects in the world's low-income areas confront limits not unlike those affecting their mutual interchanges of commodities.

Migration prospects in the DC regions lead to a fifth general conclusion. It seems likely that the labor-shortage problems found frequently in Europe in recent decades will continue or even become exacerbated over the rest of this century, given that region's trends in fertility since World War II. Following the well-known postwar upsurge of birth rates in many European countries, declines have become nearly continent-wide, persistent, and marked. Fertility levels in many European areas today are approaching or are already at the lowest points ever encountered in their recorded history. Often, they are well below replacement. It seems doubtful that these fertility-related influences on the future size of the native labor force can be fully offset by countervailing possibilities, such as changing industrial composition, capital-labor substitution processes, or rising labor-force participation rates among women. Very probably, therefore, the most labor-short areas of Europe, which are primarily the richer ones, will continue to desire immigration of foreign labor force on a major scale.

It further seems evident, based on recent experience, that the main sources of internationally recruited labor force in Europe and North America will be relatively localized geographically. Southern Europe plus Turkey for Europe, and Mexico plus some Caribbean areas for the United States and Canada, are likely to be the chief areas of origin. If so, a sixth conclusion is that the key sending countries will tend to be positioned toward the middle or upper part of the developing-area spectrum, rather than at its low end.

This is in part because occupational, skill, and related prerequisites to successful DC employment are involved, in addition to geographic proximity. (Here as throughout, I abstract from non-economic factors, such as political arrangements within the European Economic Community or the altered immigration policies adopted by the United States during the latter 1960s.)

Seventh, so far as population movements among DCs alone are concerned, there is small reason to expect spectacular departures from the patterns of the 1960s and early 1970s. Theoretically, economic incentives to move among such populations should diminish if levels and styles of living continue to converge as they have in the recent past. Thus, the United States should no longer be expected to be the economic haven it was for Europe during the early postwar years. Similarly, the northern half of Europe should become a relatively less attractive region of destination for the southern half —especially for Italy, Spain, Greece, and Yugoslavia—in the decades ahead.

Conceivably, if the current low DC rates of natural increase were to give way to zero or even negative rates on a long-term basis, the picture with respect to LDC-to-DC migration, and even with respect to within-DC migration, might change radically. In this event, net immigration into many high-income countries could become an increasingly important fraction of total population growth, or serve as an increasingly important inhibitor of decline. But it seems best to see how the actual facts evolve before attempting to hypothesize or even speculate about contingencies that depart so sharply from historical experience.

## NOTES

1. See, for example, C. P. Kindleberger, "Mass Migrations Then and Now," *Foreign Affairs*, 43, no. 4 (July 1965), pp. 647–58, for an interpretation that stresses joint economic benefits to both receiving and sending countries during the nineteenth-century European migration experience and again within Europe since World War II. Emphasis on the importance of international economic interactions in explaining migration causes and consequences is central to the interpretive framework developed by Brinley Thomas in his well-known (and often controverted) *Migration and Economic Growth: A Study of Great Britain and the Atlantic Economy* (Cambridge, 1954), and recently again in *Migration and Urban Development: A Reappraisal of British and American Long Cycles* (London, 1972).

2. For an especially rounded and pointed review of possible adverse economic impacts of emigration in areas of origin, see Xenophon Zolotas, *International Labor*

*Migration and Economic Development,* Bank of Greece Papers and Lectures (Athens, 1966).

3. For useful detailed summaries of international migration movements in the postwar period and earlier, see United Nations, *The Determinants and Consequences of Population Trends: New Summary of Findings on Interaction of Demographic, Economic and Social Factors,* Population Studies no. 50 (1973), vol. 1, chap. 7; and also the summary and updated version in United Nations, *The Population Debate: Dimensions and Perspectives* (Papers of the World Population Conference, Bucharest), Population Studies no. 57, 1, pp. 237ff. Earlier studies providing useful overviews include D. R. Taft and R. Robbins, *International Migrations: The Immigrant in the Modern World* (London, 1955), and D. Kirk, *Europe's Population in the Interwar Years* (Princeton, N.J., 1946), chaps. 5 and 6.

4. Individual countries and populations may obviously have realistic prospects of substantial in-migration or out-migration if considered in isolation. Thus, all of the Caribbean nations and many smaller African ones could be substantially affected by such movements. However, even the combined total of such populations accounts for only a limited fraction of the LDC numbers taken as a whole, or again if taken by individual continents.

# [15]

## Freedom of Movement in International Law and United States Policy

CARL A. AUERBACH

While the nineteenth century witnessed mass migrations which the countries of origin did not attempt to halt, twentieth-century migration policy has been characterized by the use of force both to prevent and to compel the movement of people. Without the encouragement of universal codes of human rights, nation-states in the nineteenth century recognized the right of individuals to seek better lives outside their countries of origin. Despite the adoption of human rights codes in the twentieth century, governments have routinely violated individual freedom of choice by forcing or blocking emigration.

In the decade after World War II, 45 million people were expelled from their countries—a number equal to the entire overseas emigration from Europe in the century ending in 1913.[1] This total does not include the people involved in "the considerable forced movements which have taken place between countries controlled by the Soviet Union and China" because it is impossible to estimate the number so involved.[2] It is also impossible to estimate how many people today wish to emigrate but are not allowed to do so by the government of the country in which they live.

As Daniel Bell has written, it is a "fundamental tenet" of classical liberalism that "the individual—and not the family, the community, or the state—is the basic unit of society, and that the purpose of societal arrangements is to allow the individual the freedom to fulfill his own purposes."[3] According to this tenet, all nations should recognize the claims of individuals to freedom

317

of movement, including their requests (1) to leave the country of their nationality, or in which they lawfully and habitually reside, either to visit or to settle in some other country; (2) not to be forced to return to their country; (3) not to be exiled, that is, not to be forced to leave their country or prevented from returning to it; (4) to move freely from one part of their country to any other part; (5) not to be banished, that is, not to be forced to move from one part of their country to some other part; (6) to enter any country of their choice either for a visit or to settle there; and (7) to be treated, while aliens, equally with the citizens of the country in which they seek to settle.

The right to emigrate, since it involves the freedom to change one's society, is "the first and most fundamental of man's liberties."[4] It is the "right of personal self-determination"[5] because, as the United Nations Economic and Social Council has recognized, it "is essential for the protection of the full enjoyment by all of other civil, political, economic, social and cultural rights."[6] If these other rights, including the right to life, liberty and the security of the person, are not safeguarded in the country of one's nationality or habitual residence, emigration affords the only practical possibility of enjoying them.

Of course, the freedom to emigrate would be illusory if potential host states barred immigration. Yet the claim to enter any particular country in order to settle there is not recognized as a human right. Professor Maurice Cranston justifies the nonrecognition of this claim. He points out that no one disputes the proposition that freedom of movement may be limited to safeguard individual rights of privacy and property. Obviously, no one has a right to move into someone else's home. Thus restrictions on immigration may be viewed as collective exercises of these domestic rights.[7]

Justifications for denying or limiting other aspects of the freedom of movement—particularly the right to emigrate—are advanced in the name of the well-being of state and society. Three grounds are commonly advanced for rejecting the claim to emigrate or limiting it in ways more serious than imposing temporary delays upon particular individuals for reasons which are not generally questioned. It is not disputed, for example, that a state may prevent an individual from emigrating so long as the individual is serving a prison sentence; charged with a criminal offense; suspected of being a carrier of communicable disease; on active duty in the armed forces; or even attempting, by emigrating, to evade payment of outstanding civil liabilities.[8] It is accepted, too, that a state may suspend emigration generally while a war is in progress.

One ground advanced for rejecting the claim to emigrate is that it is necessary to prevent the society, particularly one in the process of development, from suffering economically because of the possible loss of highly skilled and educated persons. In addition, it is maintained, people who have been trained at public expense have an obligation to serve the community which bore the expense. Finally, considerations of national security have been used to justify refusals to permit the departure of individuals who are privy to military and other governmental secrets.

There is much to be said for the first two justifications in the case of developing countries. During the periods of mass migration in the nineteenth century, skilled manpower accompanied the flow of capital to the less developed countries. Today, most capital is invested in the more advanced countries and skilled labor from poor countries is attracted to them.[9]

Since the claim of educated and skilled people to emigrate suggests that their country of origin, whether developed or developing, has failed to create the conditions necessary to retain them voluntarily, the policy of denying that fundamental claim by keeping them within territorial bounds against their will carries a heavy burden of justification. Certainly, no justification should be accepted as valid if individuals wish to leave their country because its government is depriving them of other fundamental human rights. Nor is the economic welfare of the rest of the society sufficient justification for restricting emigration. As Professor Cranston points out, this restates "one of the worst arguments . . . ever . . . advanced in defense of slavery, namely that the misery of the enslaved persons is acceptable because it contributes to the satisfaction of the enfranchised persons."[10] The happiness of future generations, which is sometimes added as a justification, only gives this argument a "different time-dimension."[11]

The second justification for restricting emigration assumes that the cost of education represents an investment in the individual for society's purposes alone. But it may be maintained that individuals claim education to satisfy their own needs and that every civilized society should recognize this claim. Indeed, Article 26 of the Universal Declaration of Human Rights[12] proclaims that "everyone has the right to education . . . directed to the full development of the human personality." If the claim to education is acknowledged as a human right, it does not necessarily follow that there should be no obligation to repay its cost. But even if the obligation is imposed, restrictions on emigration would be justified for only so long as it took to discharge it. It would be difficult to calculate the amount to be repaid in the case of any person who has been contributing to the society by gainful employment for a number of years.

Professor Jagdish Bhagwati of MIT has proposed that professional, technical and kindred persons who emigrate from less developed countries be subjected to a special surtax on the income they earn in developed countries. The tax would be imposed either by the developed country in which the income is earned or by the United Nations; the proceeds, collected by the developed country, would be remitted either to the less developed country of origin or to a U.N. development fund for the benefit of all less developed countries.[13]

As an alternative to a special tax upon the emigrant, it has been suggested that the United Nations might be empowered to levy an assessment on the developed countries in which the emigrants earn their income and which are benefiting from the immigration. The proceeds would be earmarked for the benefit of the countries of origin.[14]

Considerations of national security may indeed require reasonable restrictions on emigration. When they do, it has been suggested, states should adopt procedures to remove persons who wish to emigrate from the positions which give them access to information vital to the national security and permit them to emigrate as soon as their acquired information is no longer vital.[15]

If we enlarge the horizons of our sympathy to encompass individual human beings all over the world and ponder our problems in the light of our common humanity, the claim to emigrate, as well as all the other claims associated with freedom of movement, would be recognized in international law and the world community would seek to make them legally enforceable rights of individuals. But of course, no country satisfies all of these claims fully; some satisfy more of them and to a significantly greater degree than others. The United Nations has given legitimacy only to some of them.

Article 1 of the Charter of the United Nations declares that it is one of the purposes of the United Nations to "achieve international co-operation . . . in promoting and encouraging respect for human rights and for fundamental freedoms for all without distinction as to race, sex, language, or religion."

Article 55 of the Charter requires the United Nations to promote "universal respect for, and observance of, human rights and fundamental freedoms for all."[16] By Article 56, all members "pledge themselves to take joint and separate action in co-operation" to achieve Article 55's purposes. To supplement Article 55, the U.N. General Assembly, on December 10, 1948, adopted the Universal Declaration of Human Rights. Article 13 of the Declaration recognizes that everyone has the right "(1) . . . to freedom of movement and residence within the borders of each state" and "(2) . . . to leave any country, including his own, and to return to his country." Article 9 recognizes everyone's right not to be subjected to arbitrary exile.

Although Professor Cranston views the human rights set forth in the Declaration as moral, not legal, rights—as rights, in other words, which individuals ought to have but which the Declaration itself does not guarantee,[17] a memorandum of the U.N. Office of Legal Affairs attaches legal significance to a U.N. Declaration. It states:

A "declaration" or a "recommendation" is adopted by resolution of a U.N. organ. As such it cannot be made binding upon Member States, in the sense that a treaty or Convention is binding upon the parties to it, purely by the device of terming it a "declaration" rather than a "recommendation." However, in view of the greater solemnity and significance of a "declaration," it may be considered to impart, on behalf of the organ adopting it, a strong expectation that members of the international community will abide by it. Consequently, in so far as the expectation is gradually justified by state practice, a declaration may by custom become recognized as laying down rules binding upon states.[18]

There are now a great number of resolutions of the U.N. General Assembly that treat the Universal Declaration of Human Rights as creating legal obligations. Professor Louis Sohn describes the Declaration as "a part of the constitutional law of the world community" which "has achieved the character of a world law superior to all other international instruments and to domestic laws."[19]

Even if the Declaration is taken to create legal obligations, these obligations are not absolute. Article 29 of the Declaration provides:

(1) Everyone has duties to the community in which alone the free and full development of his personality is possible.

(2) In the exercise of his rights and freedoms, everyone shall be subject only to such limitations as are determined by law solely for the purpose of securing due recognition and respect for the rights and freedoms of others and of meeting the just requirements of morality, public order and the general welfare in a democratic society.

(3) These rights and freedoms may in no case be exercised contrary to the purposes and principles of the United Nations.

Obviously, this general language gives individual states a great deal of discretion in determining the extent to which freedom of movement will be accorded individuals. Read broadly, it may even be taken to adopt some of the justifications for restricting freedom of movement discussed above.

To implement the rights set forth in the Declaration, covenants, conventions, and other international agreements have been entered into which have the force and effect of treaties and, according to their terms, bind the states that ratify them. For our present purposes, the International Covenant on Civil and Political Rights[20] and the International Convention on the Elimination of all Forms of Racial Discrimination[21] are the most significant. The Helsinki Final Act, agreed to on August 1, 1975,[22] will also be considered in this connection.

Article 21 of the Covenant provides:

1. Everyone lawfully within the territory of a state shall, within that territory, have the right to liberty of movement and freedom to choose his residence.

2. Everyone shall be free to leave any country, including his own.

3. The above-mentioned rights shall not be subject to any restrictions except those which are provided by law, are necessary to protect national security, public order (*ordre publique*), public health or morals or the rights and freedoms of others, and are consistent with the other rights recognized in the present Covenant.

4. No one shall be arbitrarily deprived of the right to enter his own country.

Article 13 of the Covenant provides:

An alien lawfully in the territory of a State Party to the present covenant may be expelled therefrom only in the pursuance of a decision reached in accordance with law and shall, except where compelling reasons of national security otherwise require, be allowed to submit the reasons against his expulsion and to have his case reviewed by, and be represented for the purpose before, the competent authority or a person or persons especially designated by the competent authority.

In some respects, the Covenant falls short of the Universal Declaration and, in others, it goes beyond the Declaration. For example, the Declaration recognizes the right of every one to "return to his country," but the Covenant prohibits only the "arbitrary" deprivation of the right to return—a formulation which gives the ratifying countries a discretion seemingly forbidden by the Declaration. While the Declaration also recognizes everyone's right not to be subjected to arbitrary exile, the Covenant does not mention this right, but it may be included under the right to enter one's own country. On the other hand, the Covenant gives aliens some minimum protection against arbitrary expulsion from the countries in which they lawfully reside. The Declaration is silent on this subject. Neither the Declaration nor the Covenant specifically recognizes the right not to be forced to move from one part of one's country to another; the right to immigrate to a country of one's choice; or the right to be treated equally with the citizens of the country in which one settles.

The Covenant establishes a Human Rights Committee to effectuate its provisions. In the election of its members, consideration must be given to "equitable geographical distribution" and to "the representation of the different forms of civilization and of the principal legal systems." The State Parties to the Covenant undertake to submit to the Committee, at its request and through the U.N. Secretary General, reports "on the measures they have adopted which give effect to the rights recognized [in the Covenant] and on the progress made in the enjoyment of those rights." The Committee may then comment on these reports.

Article 41 of the Covenant establishes procedures by which a State Party to the Covenant—not an individual—may file a complaint charging another State Party with violations of the Covenant.[23] Investigation of the complaint may lead to a report. The State Parties concerned must then notify the Chairman of the Human Rights Committee whether or not they accept the contents of the report. An Optional Protocol to the Covenant authorizes the Human Rights Committee to receive and consider communications from individuals claiming to be victims of violations at the hands of a State Party ratifying the Protocol. The Optional Protocol was ratified by twelve states and entered into effect, in accordance with its terms, when the Covenant did.

Article 5 of the International Convention on the Elimination of all Forms of Racial Discrimination provides:

> State Parties undertake to prohibit and to eliminate racial discrimination in all its forms and to guarantee the right of everyone without distinction as to race, colour, or national or ethnic origin, to equality before the law, notably in the enjoyment of the following rights: . . .
>
> (d) (ii) The right to leave any country, including one's own, and to return to one's country.

Because this Convention assures equality of treatment only—if a particular human right is guaranteed by a State Party to any of its inhabitants, it must be guaranteed to all—it does not seem to prohibit depriving all the inhabitants of that right.[24]

The Convention establishes a Committee on the Elimination of Racial Discrimination to examine periodic reports of the State Parties and complaints by one State Party against another. The Committee's task is to facilitate the conciliation of disputes. Article 14 grants individuals and groups of individuals the right to file complaints with the Committee against State Parties recognizing the competence of the Committee to receive such complaints. To date only four countries—Costa Rica, Netherlands, Sweden, and Uruguay—have recognized the competence of the Committee to do so.[25]

Finally, the Helsinki Final Act, agreed to by the thirty-five nations which participated in the Helsinki Conference, pledges the participating states to act "in conformity with the purposes and principles of the Charter of the United Nations and with the Universal Declaration of Human Rights." In the section of the Final Act, entitled "Cooperation in Humanitarian and other fields," the participating states profess the aim "to facilitate freer movement and contacts, individually and collectively, whether privately or officially, among persons, institutions and organizations of the participating States and to contribute to the solution of the humanitarian problems that arise in that connection."

To achieve this aim, the signatory nations declare only "their readiness . . . to take measures which they consider appropriate and to conclude agreements or arrangements among themselves, as may be needed." As an immediate matter, they express their intention (1) to "favourably consider applications for travel with the purpose of allowing persons to enter or leave their territory temporarily, and on a regular basis if desired, in order to visit members of their families"; and not to "modify the rights and obligations of the applicant [for such travel] or of members of his family"; (2) to "deal in a positive and humanitarian spirit with the applications of persons who wish to be reunited with members of their family, with special attention being given to requests of an urgent character—such as requests submitted by persons who are ill or old"; and not to "modify the rights and obligations of the applicant [for travel for the purpose of family reunification] or of members of his family"; (3) to "examine favourably and on the basis of humanitarian considerations requests for exit or entry permits from persons who have decided to marry a citizen from another participating State"; and (4) to facilitate wider travel by their citizens for personal or professional reasons.

It is difficult to see what, if anything, the Final Act at Helsinki adds substantively to the human rights documents previously considered. It does not purport to impose legal obligations upon its signatories. But states which signed the Final Act but have not ratified the International Covenant on Civil and Political Rights may thereby have assumed some additional moral, if not legal, obligations. Although the United States voted for the Universal Declaration of Human Rights, it has not signed or ratified the International Covenant on Civil and Political Rights. It signed but has not ratified the International Convention on the Elimination of All Forms of Racial Discrimination. It signed the Final Act at Helsinki.[26]

United States policy has not been motivated by the fear that the human rights specified in these documents are not secured by our domestic law.[27] Indeed, our domestic laws and practices safeguard these rights to an extent immeasurably greater than the domestic laws and practices of most of the states which have signed and ratified these documents. Freedom of movement and residence within the borders of the United States is recognized as a constitutional right and protected in a variety of contexts,[28] although the shameful evacuation of the Japanese during World War II mars the nation's record in this area.[29]

From a very early date in our history, the right of emigration and expatriation was recognized and protected. In 1779, Jefferson drafted the Virginia Code which, Jefferson wrote, "[recognized] the right expressly, and [prescribed] the mode of exercising it."[30] All men, Jefferson said, have "the natural right . . . of relinquishing the country in which birth or other accident may have thrown them, and seeking subsistence and happiness wheresoever they may be able, or may hope to find them."[31] Though the right of emigration is not mentioned in the Bill of Rights, it has been accepted as a constitutional right. So has been the right to travel generally.[32] In *Kent* v. *Dulles*, the Supreme Court declared:

> The right to travel is a part of the "liberty" of which the citizen cannot be deprived without due process of law under the Fifth Amendment. . . . Freedom of movement across frontiers in either direction, and inside frontiers as well, was a part of our heritage. . . . Freedom of travel is, indeed, an important aspect of the citizens' "liberty."[33]

The United States does not permit unrestricted travel to this country from abroad. In 1972, the Supreme Court upheld the refusal of the Attorney General to permit a Belgian journalist and Marxist theoretician to enter the country to attend academic meetings.[34]

The right not to be deprived of citizenship—without which there is no freedom of movement across frontiers in today's world—is also safeguarded as a constitutional right.[35]

Like every other country in the world, the United States does not permit unlimited immigration. The restriction of immigration, as Professor John Higham has pointed out, "inevitably conflicts with some of the deepest American values." Yet, "the conditions of the modern world have created imperative demands for defensive and regulatory action to preserve the existent goods of American life."[36] Even so, a recent study of our immigration policy concluded that the Immigration and Nationality Act of 1965 "brought into being the most humanitarian and the most sensible immigration policy in our nation's history."[37] It abolished the preexisting national origins quota system and made the reuniting of families and the admission of refugees and needed workers the keystones of our current policy. The authors go on to say:

> Despite the many criticisms that may be directed at our immigration laws, the United States remains, of all the world's countries, by far the most hospitable to immigrants. Not only do we admit more immigrants than any other country, we treat all applicants without regard to religion, race, color, or national origin. . . . Further, we allow immigrants to become full-fledged citizens after only five years. Moreover, the evidence indicates that chauvin-

istic prejudices against newcomers are rare, and opportunities for economic and social integration are widespread.[38]

Between 1920 and 1974, approximately 46,700,000 people left their countries of birth to immigrate to the United States.[39] Once admitted, aliens, like citizens, are entitled to the protections of the Fifth and Fourteenth Amendments to the United States Constitution which prohibit states, as well as the federal government, from depriving any person of life, liberty, or property, without due process of law or of the equal protection of the laws.[40] While the status of aliens has improved greatly in recent years, it still cannot be said that they are treated equally with citizens in every respect other than in the exercise of those rights, such as the right to vote, which, it is generally agreed, may be made to depend upon citizenship.[41] In particular, aliens are not protected against the possibility of deportation.[42]

Two major objections have been raised against ratifying the human rights treaties adopted by the United Nations.[43] First, it is maintained that the issue of human rights is a matter of domestic jurisdiction, that is, a matter concerning the internal affairs of the United States which is beyond the proper scope of the treaty-making power. Second, it is feared that ratification would give the federal government power to encroach upon the rights of the states in a manner that would be unconstitutional in the absence of these treaties.

These objections are not persuasive. As Professor Louis Henkin has written:

> Minimum standards of international behavior with regard to human rights were a matter of international concern and involved American foreign relations long before the U.N. Charter expressly so provided. . . . To recognize that even human rights may be matters of authentic international concern, one need only think of apartheid in South Africa, of recent events in communist countries, in Nigeria, in India and Pakistan, in Cyprus, and of other actual or potential situations where the treatment of individuals or minority groups is intimately related to war and peace among nations.[44]

With respect to the second objection, it should be recognized that the power of Congress to legislate in the field of human rights is very extensive even without a treaty to provide an additional source of federal constitutional authority. Moreover, it is always open to the United States to impose a reservation upon any treaty disclaiming the intention to use it to enlarge the scope of federal power. Finally, no one may object reasonably to the constitutional enlargement of federal power if that is necessary to guarantee the human rights of all persons in the United States.

Additionally, the arguments for ratification are impressive. In transmitting certain human rights treaties to the Senate for ratification, President Kennedy stated that they "project our own heritage on an international scale" and "our own welfare is interrelated with the rights and freedoms assured the peoples of other nations."[45] Continuing President Kennedy's effort, President Johnson added that the "rights and freedoms [which these treaties] proclaim are those which America has defined—and fights to defend around the world."[46]

Urging ratification of the U.N. Treaty on Elimination of Racial Discrimination, Professor N. L. Nathanson and Dr. Egon Schwelb advance another argument which applies to all U.N. Human Rights treaties and deserves the most thoughtful consideration. It is in the interest of the Western Powers to ratify, they write, in order to:

> secure representation of their forms of civilization and legal systems . . . on the international machinery which the Convention establishes. Without such representation, there is a danger of the Committee on the Elimination of Racial Discrimination becoming an instrument of one camp against the other.[47]

Representation would "add to the influence of the United States as protector and sponsor of all aspects of human rights throughout the world," whereas the failure to ratify "suggests an unwarranted lack of confidence by the United States in its own position with respect to equal treatment of all people within its borders."[48]

These arguments do not, however, remove the problems and contradictions involved when Western democratic states enter into treaties and other agreements concerning human rights with Communist or other totalitarian dictatorships whose continued existence depends upon the denial of these rights to their own peoples. Accepting these governments as partners in a worldwide effort to secure human rights may give them a legitimacy in this connection which they do not deserve and of which they should be deprived. At the same time, this policy may unduly raise popular hopes of enjoying fundamental human rights in these countries. When these hopes are defeated, the people of these countries may become embittered against the Western democratic countries responsible for heightening their expectations.

The Soviet Union and the Communist countries of Eastern Europe have ratified the International Covenant on Civil and Political Rights.[49] Yet the Berlin Wall and border death strips still stand in hideous witness of the fact that these countries deny their citizens the right to emigrate. Nor has the signing of the Final Act at Helsinki made an appreciable difference.[50]

Of the eleven original members of the Moscow Group organized to monitor the Helsinki Accord, three have been arrested and charged with espionage, illegal currency dealings, subversive agitation or dissemination of anti-Soviet propaganda; one is being investigated on an arson charge; one has been in Siberian exile since 1975 and three emigrated in 1976. Members of the Ukrainian and Georgian groups have also been arrested. Other repressive measures have been taken against those not yet arrested.[51]

In explaining the arrests, the official Soviet press agency Tass described the actions of one of the dissidents as "an attempt to question in the eyes of the international public the sincerity of the Soviet Union's efforts to undeviatingly implement the international obligations it assumed."[52] The Soviet Union expects the international public to assume its sincerity in this regard from the mere fact that it signed the Final Act for it has also denounced Western efforts to monitor its compliance as an interference in its internal affairs.[53]

Both Presidents Ford and Carter have concluded that even after Helsinki "most Soviet and Eastern European officials continued to view travel or emigration to the West as a privilege to be granted or refused by the state rather than as a matter of personal choice."[54] Indeed, the Soviet Union has used the Final Act to make family reunification the sole legitimate reason for emigration and thereby to limit the Universal Declaration of Human Rights and the International Covenant on Civil and Political Rights. It also defines the "family" most narrowly and even then does not always permit emigration for purposes of reunifying the family as so defined.

Contrary to the provisions of the Final Act, the USSR also "discourages emigration primarily by penalizing applicants with loss of employment and sometimes shelter, thereby creating an atmosphere which inhibits submission of applications."[55] Despite the Final Act, concluded the Moscow Monitor Group, "the USSR is surrounded by a 'Berlin wall' thousands of kilometers long."[56]

The Soviet position should not take anyone by surprise because it parallels the Soviet position regarding its domestic laws. The Soviet Union has never hesitated to violate its own laws to serve the political ends of its ruling Party.[57] Nor should Soviet policies in this regard be expected to change because the existing Soviet system could not survive if the Soviet people enjoyed fundamental human rights. As Dr. Rudolf Torovsky, a member of the legal staff in the Secretariat of the International Commission of Jurists, points out:

> refusal of freedom of exit is a generally inevitable complement of any national system built upon coercion and terror. So long as persons can avoid political pressure by leaving the country, such a system will be deprived of

complete success, and it will lead to an increasing lack of manpower resulting finally in the economic collapse of the country. . . . For the Communist
ideology, which in the view of its representatives is the basis for the best
social system and the only one with prospects for the future and whose aim
is the conquest of the whole world, it is utterly unacceptable that anyone can
voluntarily leave this social order in order to submit to an "inferior" one.[58]

While denying the human rights of their citizens, Communist countries do
not hesitate to vote for U.N. resolutions condemning other countries for
violating human rights.[59]

It may be maintained that entering into human rights treaties with the
Soviet Union and other totalitarian countries of the right or the left furnishes
a legal, as well as moral, basis upon which to ascertain and expose in the
United Nations and other forums every violation of human rights in these
countries. By refusing to enter into and ratify human rights agreements, the
United States may not only lose this basis but it may also give other states
reason to conclude that it fears to have its domestic policies judged by them
and is hypocritical in its concern for human rights throughout the world.

These are weighty considerations whose validity will depend upon the
actual use made of the human rights agreements by the Western democratic
States which are party to them.

Since the New Harmony Symposium was held and this chapter written,
Jimmy Carter was elected President of the United States and committed his
Administration to "work with potential adversaries as well as with our friends
to advance the cause of human rights."[60] To demonstrate this commitment,
President Carter informed the United Nations that he would seek ratification
of the Covenants on Civil and Political Rights and on Economic, Social, and
Cultural Rights; the Convention Against Genocide; and the Treaty for the
Elimination of all Forms of Racial Discrimination.[61] "The solemn commitments of the U.N. Charter, of the U.N.'s Universal Declaration of Human
Rights, of the Helsinki accords, and of many other international instruments," the President stated, "must be taken just as seriously as commercial
or security agreements."[62] It is also apparent that President Carter has in-
structed his U.N. representatives to oppose the United Nations' selective
morality on issues of human rights and to champion the universality essential
for the effective implementation of human rights agreements.

Despite the fact that the Helsinki Accord monitors in the Soviet Union
conclude that "the Soviet government does not intend to fulfill its international obligations in human rights,"[63] they also believe that the human rights
movement in the Soviet Union, which antedated Helsinki, can use the Final
Act as a "legal fulcrum" in its struggle.[64] Let us hope President Carter and
the courageous Soviet monitors will accomplish their aims.

NOTES

I wish to thank Professors Louis Henkin and David Weissbrodt for their helpful criticism of this paper.

1. Brinley Thomas, "Migration: Economic Aspects," 10 *International Encyclopedia of the Social Sciences* 293 (1968).
2. Ibid.
3. Daniel Bell, "On Meritocracy and Equality," 29 *The Public Interest* 40 (1972).
4. Maurice Cranston, *What Are Human Rights* 31 (Taplinger Publishing Co., Inc., New York, 1973). In the dialogue with Crito, Socrates speaks in the name of the laws as follows:

> we further proclaim and give the right of every Athenian, that if he does not like us when he has become of age and has seen the ways of the city, and made our acquaintance, he may go where he pleases and take his goods with him; and none of our laws will forbid him or interfere with him.

*Works of Plato,* tr. B. Jowett, vol. 3, p. 153 (The Dial Press).
5. Jose D. Ingles, *Study of Discrimination in Respect of the Right of Everyone to Leave any Country, Including His Own, And To Return to His Country* 9 (United Nations, 1963).
6. Draft Principles on the Freedom to Leave Any Country and Return to One's Country, adopted as Res. No. 1788 (LIV) at 1858th Plenary Meeting of U.N. Economic and Social Council, May 18, 1973, reprinted in 11 *J. Int'l. Comm. Jur.* 61 (1973).
7. Cranston, supra note 4, at 31–32.
8. Mitchell Knisbacher, "Alijah of Soviet Jews: Protection of the Right of Emigration Under International Law," 14 *Harv. J. Int'l. L.* 89, 101 (1973).
9. Thomas, supra note 1, at 297.
10. Cranston, supra note 4, at 35.
11. Ibid.
12. Adopted and proclaimed by the United Nations General Assembly resolution 217 A (III) of 10 December 1948; G.A. Res. 217, U.N. Doc. A1810 (1948).
13. See generally, Bhagwati and Partington, *Taxing the Brain Drain: A Proposal,* vol. 1 (North-Holland Publishing Co., 1976).
14. Oldman and Pomp, "The Brain Drain: A Tax Analysis of the Bhagwati Proposal," in Bhagwati and Partington, supra note 13, at 167.
15. Knisbacher, supra note 8, at 101.
16. Department of State Publication 2349, Conference Series T1 (1945).
17. See Cranston, supra note 4, at 19–23.
18. Use of the Terms "Declaration" and "Recommendation," U.N. Doc. E/CN. 4/L. 610 (1962).
19. Sohn, "The Universal Declaration of Human Rights," 8 *J. Int'l Comm. Jur.* 17, 26 (1967). The Proclamation which concluded the 1968 International Conference on Human Rights in Teheran described the Universal Declaration as reflecting "a

common understanding of the peoples of the world concerning the unalienable and inviolable rights of all members of the human family" and creating "new standards and obligations to which States should conform." U.N. Doc. O.P.I./326.

Dr. Egon Schwelb reads the Advisory Opinion of the International Court of Justice in the *Namibia (South West Africa) Case*, [1971] *I. C. J. Rep.* 16; 66 *A. J. I. L.* 145 (1972), as imposing legal obligations upon all states which signed the United Nations Charter to respect human rights and fundamental freedoms. Schwelb, "The International Court of Justice and the Human Rights Clauses of the Charter," 66 *A. J. I. L.* 337 (1972).

20. G.A. Res. 2200 A, 21 U.N. GAOR Supp. 16, at 49. U.N. Doc. A/6316 (1966). It entered into force on March 23, 1976. U.N. Office of Public Information Press Release WS/755, March 26, 1976.

21. G.A. Res. 2106, 20 U.N. GAOR Supp. 14, at 47, U.N. Doc A/6181 (1965). It entered into force on March 13, 1969. 6 U.N. monthly Chron. no. 4, at 81 (1969). The Convention was preceded by the Declaration on the Elimination of All Forms of Racial Discrimination, G.A. Res. 1964, 18 U.N. GAOR Supp. 15, at 35, U.N. Doc. A/5603, A/L. 435 (1963).

22. Conference on Security and Cooperation in Europe: Final Act, August 1, 1975, Department of State Publication 8826, General Foreign Policy Series, August 1975, at 75–135.

23. See "The U.N. Human Rights Covenants—Soon to be in Force," 15 *J. Int'l Comm. Jur.* 35, 36 (1975).

24. See Report of the Committee on the Elimination of all Forms of Racial Discrimination, 28 U.N. GAOR Supp. 18, at 12; U.N. Doc. A/9018 (1973) (Mr. Fayez A. Sayegh of Kuwait). The view expressed in this report has recently been attacked by McDougal, Lasswell and Lung-chu Chen on the ground that the "notion that a right of nondiscrimination can be established without establishing the right protected from discrimination is about as meaningful as the notion of minting a one-sided coin." Myres S. McDougal, Harold D. Lasswell and Lung-chu-Chen, "The Protection of Respect and Human Rights: Freedom of Choice and World Public Order," 25 *Amer. U. L. Rev.* 919, 1068 (1975).

With all due respect to the eminent authors, the analogy is not strong. To accept their argument would render superfluous all the other U.N. human rights instruments; ratifying this Convention would make unnecessary the ratification of any other human rights instrument. There is no violation of equal treatment if the human right in question is denied to all. That does not make the deprivation any less reprehensible, but it would not invoke the Convention on the Elimination of all Forms of Racial Discrimination.

25. The U.N. Human Rights Covenants, supra note 23, at 36.

26. Of the nineteen major multilateral treaties affecting human rights in respect of which the U.N. Secretary-General performs the depository function and the Abolition of Forced Labor Convention (adopted by the International Labour Organization in 1957, entered into force January 17, 1959, I. L. O. No. 105, 320 U. N. T. S. 291), the United States signed and ratified four and signed but has not ratified three. The four are the Slavery Convention of September 25, 1926, as amended, which entered into

force July 7, 1955 (212 U. N. T. S. 17; the United States ratified in 1929); the Protocol amending the Slavery Convention of September 25, 1926, which entered into force December 7, 1953 (182 U. N. T. S. 51; the United States ratified in 1956); the Supplementary Convention on the Abolition of Slavery, the Slave Trade, Institutions and Practices Similar to Slavery, which entered into force April 30, 1957 (226 U. N. T. S. 3; the United States ratified in 1967); and the Protocol Relating to the Status of Refugees, which incorporates the substantive provisions of the Convention Relating to the Status of Refugees and entered into force April 22, 1954. The Convention was adopted July 28, 1951, by the U.N. Conference of Plenipotentiaries on the Status of Refugees and Stateless Persons acting pursuant to General Assembly Resolution 429 (v) of December 14, 1950, 189 U. N. T. S. 137. The United States did not sign or ratify the Convention. It ratified the Protocol in 1958, 606 U. N. T. S. 267.

The three human rights treaties which the United States signed but has not ratified are the Convention on the Prevention and Punishment of the Crime of Genocide, which was adopted December 9, 1948, 78 U. N. T. S. and entered into force January 12, 1951; the International Convention on the Elimination of all Forms of Racial Discrimination and the Convention on Consent to Marriage, Minimum Age and Registration of Marriages, which was adopted November 7, 1962, 521 U. N. T. S. 231, and entered into force, December 9, 1964.

See *The Ratification of U.N. Human Rights Instruments by the United States*, prepared by the Staff of the World Peace Through Law Center (Washington, D.C. 1975); and *Human Rights: A Compilation of International Instruments of the United Nations* (United Nations Publication, Sales No. E. 68 XIV 6, 1973).

27. See generally, Zechariah Chafee, *Three Human Rights in the Constitution of 1787* (University of Kansas Press, Lawrence, Kansas, 1956); and N. L. Nathanson and Egon Schwelb, *The United States and the United Nations Treaty on Racial Discrimination: A Report for the American Society of International Law Panel on International Human Rights Law and its Implementation* (West Publishing Co., St. Paul, Minnesota, 1975).

28. See, for example, Crandall v. Nevada, 6 Wall. 35 (U.S. 1867), Edwards v. California, 314 U.S. 160 (1941), U.S. v. Guest, 383 U.S. 745 (1966), and Shapiro v. Thompson, 394 U.S. 618 (1969).

29. See Korematsu v. U.S., 323 U.S. 214 (1944).

30. Jefferson, *Writings X*, 87 (Ford ed., G. P. Putnam's Sons, New York, 1899), quoted in I-mien Tsiang, *The Question of Expatriation in America Prior to 1907*, at 26 (The Johns Hopkins Press, Baltimore, Maryland, 1942). For the provisions of the Virginia code in question, see William Waller Hening, *Statutes at Large of Virginia*, ch. LV, vol. 10, p. 129 (Richmond, Virginia, 1822–23).

31. Quoted in I-mien Tsiang, supra note 30, at 214.

32. Kent v. Dulles, 357 U.S. 116 (1958); Dayton v. Dulles, 357 U.S. 144 (1958); Aptheker v. Secretary of State, 378 U.S. 500 (1964).

33. 357 U.S. at 125–27.

34. Kleindienst v. Mandel, 408 U.S. 753 (1972). In April 1977, the United States refused visitors' visas to three labor representatives who had been invited to a long-shoremen's union gathering in Seattle to mark the retirement of Harry Bridges as

union president. President Carter rejected the Soviet Union's contention that this was a violation of the human contacts provisions of the Final Act. "We pointed out," the President reported, "that it is a longstanding U.S. policy not to recommend waivers of ineligibility [to obtain a visitor's visa] for Communist labor representatives because labor exchanges with Communist unions would equate our free and voluntary trade unions with the Communist labor organizations. There is no specific Final Act reference to travel and contacts among labor representatives, and, when signing the Final Act, all CSCE [Helsinki Conference on Security and Cooperation in Europe] participants were aware of our longstanding policy on this matter." Second Semiannual Report By the President [Carter] to the Commission on Security and Cooperation in Europe, June 1977.

35. Trop v. Dulles, 356 U.S. 86 (1958); Kennedy v. Mendoza-Martinez, 372 U.S. 144 (1963); Schneider v. Rusk, 377 U.S. 163 (1964); Afroyim v. Rusk, 387 U.S. 253 (1967). But cf., Rogers v. Bellei, 401 U.S. 815 (1971).

36. John Higham, "American Immigration Policy in Historical Perspective," 21 *Law & Contemp. Prob.* 213 (1956).

37. Elliott Abrams and Franklin S. Abrams, "Immigration Policy—Who Gets In and Why?" 38 *The Public Interest* 3 (1975).

38. Id. at 28–29.

39. "America At 200," *The New York Times Magazine,* Section 6, p. 27, July 4, 1976.

40. Yick Wo v. Hopkins, 118 U.S. 356 (1886).

41. See Hampton v. Mow Sun Wong, 96 S. Ct. 1895 (1976); Matthews v. Diaz, 96 S. Ct. 1883 (1976); Examining Board of Engineers, Architects and Surveyors v. Flores de Otero, 96 S. Ct. 2264 (1976); In re Griffiths, 413 U.S. 717 (1973); Sugarman v. Dougall, 413 U.S. 634 (1973); and Graham v. Richardson, 403 U.S. 365 (1971).

42. See, for example, Harisiades v. Shaughnessy, 342 U.S. 580 (1952); Galvan v. Press, 347 U.S. 522 (1954); cf., Rowoldt v. Perfetto, 355 U.S. 115 (1957). Our immigration laws, however, forbid the expulsion of any alien who reasonably fears persecution in the country to which the alien would be sent. These laws buttress the international Protocol Relating to the Status of Refugees which the United States has ratified.

43. See generally, The Ratification of U.N. Human Rights Instruments by the United States, supra note 26.

44. Henkin, "The Constitution, Treaties and International Human Rights," 116 *U. Pa. L. Rev.* 1012, 1025–1027 (1968).

45. Quoted in Louis B. Sohn and Thomas Buergenthal, *International Protection of Human Rights* 969 (The Bobbs Merrill Company, Inc., Indianapolis, Kansas City, New York, 1973).

46. 114 Cong. Rec. 25789 (1968).

47. Nathanson and Schwelb, supra note 27, at 15.

48. Id., at 16.

49. Multilateral Treaties in Respect of which the Secretary General Performs Depository Functions 93, U.N. Doc. St./Leg/Ser. D/7 (1973). Neither the Soviet Union nor any Eastern European country has ratified the Optional Protocol to the Covenant which authorizes the Human Rights Committee to receive and consider

communications from individuals claiming to be victims of violations of the Covenant.

50. An Act of Congress, Pub. L. 94–304, June 5, 1976, created a joint Legislative-Executive Commission on Security and Cooperation in Europe (CSCE), consisting of fifteen members, to monitor the implementation of the Helsinki Final Act. Six are U.S. Representatives appointed by the Speaker of the House of Representatives who also designates one of them as Commission chairman; six are U.S. Senators appointed by the President of the Senate; and three are representatives of the State, Defense, and Commerce Departments, respectively, appointed by the President.

The Act requires the President to submit semiannual reports to the Commission. See First Semiannual Report by the President [Ford] to the Commission on Security and Cooperation in Europe, Dec. 3, 1976; and Second Semiannual Report by the President [Carter] to the Commission on Security and Cooperation in Europe, June 3, 1977.

CSCE has also published reports of groups organized in the Soviet Union to monitor the Helsinki Accord. See Documents of the Public Groups to Promote Observance of the Helsinki Agreements in the USSR, a Partial Compilation, Edited and Prepared by the Staff of CSCE, vol. 1, Feb. 24, 1977, and vol. 2, June 3, 1977.

The conclusions in the text are based upon the two semiannual reports of the Presidents and the reports of the public groups in the USSR.

51. See Second Semiannual Report by the President to the CSCE, at 4 and Reports of Helsinki-Accord Monitors in the Soviet Union, vol. 1, at 3 and vol. 2, at 2–19. "An Amnesty International Report published in January [1977] estimates that at least 90 dissidents known to the West have been convicted in the USSR since the signing of the Final Act." Second Semiannual Report by the President to the CSCE, at 4.

52. *The New York Times*, May 16, 1976, sec. 1, p. 3, col. 1.

53. Ibid.

54. Second Semiannual Report by the President to the CSCE, at 24; First Semiannual Report by the President to the CSCE, at 39.

55. Second Semiannual Report by the President to the CSCE, at 26. See also Reports of Helsinki-Accord Monitors in the Soviet Union, vol. 2, at 42. (Document no. 20, On the Violation of the Citizens' Right to Emigrate, March–April 1977). Young people applying for a visa to emigrate have also been conscripted into the Army, through not otherwise subject to immediate induction.

56. Reports of Helsinki-Accord Monitors in the Soviet Union, vol. 1, at 62.

57. For the latest account of "the prostitution of Soviet Justice to serve State ends," see Telford Taylor, *Courts of Terror: Soviet Criminal Justice and Jewish Emigration* (New York, 1976). Professor Taylor reports that Soviet Jews seeking to emigrate are being convicted and imprisoned because of trumped-up criminal charges when the real charge is their wish to emigrate. In prison, they are being subjected to discriminatory punishments and harassments. Taylor quotes a Soviet official as saying that the Universal Declaration of Human Rights is not intended for Jews but only for Negroes. Id. at 60.

58. Rudolf Torovsky, "Freedom of Movement: Right to Exit," 4 *J. Int'l. Comm. Jur.* 63, 90–91 (1962).

59. Professor Malvina H. Guggenheim cites the following instances—by no means exhaustive—in which the Soviet Union voted for resolutions condemning other states for violating the Universal Declaration on Human Rights—Res. 2144, 21 U.N. GAOR Supp. 16, at 46, U.N. Doc. A/6316 (1966); G.A. Res. 2442, 23 U.N. GAOR Supp. 18, at 49, U.N. Doc. A/7218 (1968); G.A. Res. 2443, 23 U.N. GAOR Supp. 18, at 50, U.N. Doc. A/7218 (1968). Guggenheim, "On the Right to Emigrate and Other Freedoms: The Feldman Case," 5 *Human Rights* 75 (1975).

60. President Carter's Address at U.N. on Peace, Economy and Human Rights, March 17, 1977, reprinted in 123 Cong. Rec. S4720–S4722 (March 23, 1977).

61. Ibid.

62. Ibid.

63. Reports of Helsinki-Accord Monitors in the Soviet Union, vol. 1, at 6 (An Evaluation of the Influence of the Helsinki Agreements as They Relate to Human Rights in the USSR, 1 August 1975–1 August 1976).

64. Id., at 11.

# [16]

## Legal Regulation of the Migration Process: The "Crisis" of Illegal Immigration

In analyzing the process of migration, one can easily lose sight of the importance of international boundaries and the legal rules designed to control the movement of persons back and forth across them. These rules may seem a distraction from the study of more important matters: namely the economic, social, religious, cultural, and other considerations that apparently give rise to the desire to move. After all, large-scale migrations frequently take place within the confines of a single nation, and the forces that occasion and shape such migrations will presumably continue to control, subject to whatever incidental distortions the crossing of a border may happen to produce, when one turns to the study of international migrations. But just as it is important for those who draft the rules controlling the movement of people across borders to understand why and how people undertake such moves, it is also important for those who study migrations to examine these rules and the process that creates them.

In some situations the desire to cross the border is the very reason for the move. It is not uncommon for people to travel relatively small distances and relocate themselves in communities very much like the ones that they left behind, in order to put an international boundary between themselves and political regimes that they fear or disdain. Similarly, in some parts of the world a person who seeks improved economic opportunities can travel a short distance, cross a border, and enter a community that differs substantially in economic terms from the one he left behind. The preservation of so

336

sharp a distinction in the economic characteristics of the two communities may depend on the existence of the border. But even in those situations—presumably the most common—where the crossing of a border is incidental to the reasons for the move, the legal rules in force at the border warrant careful attention. For no matter how great the yearning for new economic opportunities, freedom from disease, or the reunification of family members, migration can take place only if the country in which the potential migrant lives is willing to let him leave (or unable to prevent his departure), and if the country he wishes to enter is willing to let him in (or unable to prevent his entry).

The United States has never made a substantial effort to establish legal barriers to the departure of its citizens, though for a short time Congress did restrict expatriation in time of war.[1] In the United States, the more controversial question regarding migration has been the erection of barriers to entry. The national debate on immigration began long before the first significant immigration restrictions were imposed in the latter part of the last century,[2] and the debate has often been very bitter. Two major issues have dominated the debate: (1) the value and feasibility of assimilating immigrants of diverse racial and national origins, and (2) the impact of immigration on the well-being of the American labor force. Pursuant to a major rethinking of immigration policy and culminating decades of debate, in 1965 Congress abandoned national origin as a touchstone of immigration policy and apparently put the first issue to rest.[3] At the same time, Congress retained the principle of numerical limitation on immigration and sharpened the requirements for prescreening of many prospective entrants by the Department of Labor in the hope of minimizing the impact of immigration on the wages and working conditions of American workers.[4]

With the termination of the national origins quota system in 1965, immigration issues receded from the forefront of political debate. But in the decade since the passage of the 1965 reforms a new issue has emerged. Congress and the national media have given so much attention to illegal immigration that a sense of crisis is now widespread. Nurturing this sense of crisis is the same psychological process of "scapegoating" that Morris and Hawkins[5] identify as a principal explanation for the widely shared belief in the existence of Organized Crime: "The common use of the orphaned pronoun 'they' teaches us that people often want and need to designate outgroups—usually for the purpose of venting hostility."[6] Illegal aliens, an invisible threat to national well-being, provide an ideal target for such hostility, and the stated reasons for decrying their presence are strongly reminiscent of the nativist arguments directed in an earlier day at certain lawful immigrants, in particular the Chinese and Japanese.[7] As with the belief in Organized Crime, it is not clear "what would be regarded as constituting significant counterevidence" to disprove the proposition that a crisis is at hand.[8] If many illegal aliens are apprehended, the gravity of the problem is thought to be self-evident. If few are apprehended, the aliens are thought to have burrowed so deeply into our society that we can no longer root them out.

Given the depth of concern with illegal immigration, it is hard to avoid astonishment at how little is known about the dimensions of the problem or its causes and effects. And little effort has been made to view the problem in the context of our immigration policy as a whole, even though the costs of losing perspective on the problem are likely to be very high. First, since the overwhelming majority of illegal immigrants are assumed to come from Mexico, Central America, and South America, the alarm over illegal immigration has increasingly given rise to suspicion of all persons of Spanish origin in the United States—native-born and naturalized citizens, lawful resident aliens, and illegal aliens alike. Singled out for stops and searches by immigration officials that other persons are spared,[9] perhaps compelled to prove the legality of their status in the United States in order to obtain employment or public benefits,[10] embarrassed and injured by the mistrusting attitude of those around them, they are all potentially the victims of the growing sense of crisis.

Second, the preoccupation with illegal immigration can affect the legislative handling of other immigration problems that Congress might more easily and quickly solve.[11] Resolution of these other problems may have to await a decision on what to do about the seemingly more urgent matter of illegal immigration.[12]

Third, an exaggerated sense of the real seriousness of the problem can distort the process of deciding how it should be handled. What is reasonable as a solution will inevitably and properly depend on how serious the situation is perceived to be. Should Congress provide the Immigration and Naturalization Service (INS) with much more law enforcement equipment and personnel? Should the borders be more effectively sealed? Should we limit or discontinue the issuance of student and tourist visas, which can easily be abused? Should employers of illegal aliens be subject to criminal penalties? Should employers be required to demand proof of lawful residence of all prospective employees? Should Congress require all citizens and lawful residents to carry a tamper-proof, machine-readable identifying card?[13] Each of these proposals would plainly involve substantial costs, but most of us would presumably be willing to bear these and even higher costs if we could be assured, first, that one or more of the proposals would really solve the problem, and second, that the problem was sufficiently serious to warrant such costly treatment. A recent Supreme Court decision illustrates the importance of that second determination. In *United States* v. *Martinez-Fuerte* the

Court rejected a constitutional challenge to the random stopping and checking of travelers by immigration officials at fixed checkpoints some distance from the border.[14] In his opinion for the Court, Mr. Justice Powell made clear that the Court perceived the problem of illegal immigration to be very serious, and he measured the reasonableness of the government's action in the light of that perception. The correctness of the decision thus turns at least to some extent on the correctness of the perception.

Finally, widespread alarm about illegal immigration can have an adverse impact on this country's relations with other countries—in particular, with Mexico. That alarm is easily translated into anger at the country from which most of the illegal entrants allegedly come. One can see signs of such an effect in the increasing demands that Mexico do more to check the movement of its citizens across the border. And the Mexican government can hardly derive much satisfaction from proposals to close the border by any means necessary, including the building of a fortified wall. Some Mexicans may already have difficulty understanding why Canadians should be so much freer than they are to enter the United States as temporary visitors. The imposition of more controls can only add to their sense of injury.

Consideration of the illegal immigration problem in its legal and historical context affords an opportunity to consider how a country goes about establishing an immigration policy. Since the great majority of illegal aliens apparently come from Mexico, the primary concern must be the immigration policy of the United States as it bears on Mexico. And the border that separates the two countries has characteristics that warrant its careful study. The line that now separates the two countries did not exist as an international legal boundary until the middle part of the last century, and the communities that have grown up on either side are similar in many respects. With relatively few natural, cultural, and linguistic barriers to impede the traffic,[15] and a strong economic incentive to move, the effective enforcement of barriers derived from law may simply not be possible. But analysis of the gap that now exists between the theory and the practice of our immigration policy may yield some insight into the ability of a nation to control the process of human migration by manipulating the rules that govern movement across its borders.

## DETERMINING THE SERIOUSNESS OF THE ILLEGAL IMMIGRATION PROBLEM

At the outset, one has to consider precisely what it is about the presence of illegal aliens that causes so much concern. Is the source of the difficulty the fact that persons are coming *illegally* to the United States, or that they are coming at all? Obviously, the illegality of their presence here is a subject of some concern. Respect for the rule of law cannot be enhanced by the spectacle of widespread defiance of our immigration laws and the ineffectuality of law-enforcement efforts. And beyond the symbolic problem, the fact that many persons are now living outside the law as an underground labor force is itself troubling. To conceal their presence, illegal entrants may feel compelled to withhold payment of taxes, keep their children out of schools, tolerate substandard wages and working conditions, decline to seek badly needed medical attention, and take other steps that may injure themselves as well as those around them. But these problems could be remedied by a simple measure: Congress could regularize the legal status of these aliens and of any others who wish to enter the United States, and bring them all within the law by declaring lawful their presence in the United States.

To put it mildly, that approach would not be viewed as a serious solution to what is perceived to be the problem. But if such a step is unacceptable —if, that is to say, these aliens would be unwelcome even if the element of illegality could be removed—then the explanation is presumably that we accept one or both of the following propositions: (1) that the illegal aliens are unwanted because they are too numerous to make possible the admission of all who would in some degree be qualitatively desirable, or (2) that they are unwanted because they have evaded any screening process and have not proved themselves qualitatively as desirable as those we would legally admit. Reasonable as these propositions appear, it is important to recognize that they rest on untested assumptions about the nature of our immigration policy and assume that we know the answers to questions that we have not even asked.

### How Many Illegal Aliens Are in the United States?

To begin with the question of numbers, one might suppose that the great concern about the presence of illegal aliens arises from a recognition that their presence in such great numbers precludes their successful absorption into our society and is inconsistent with national policies on population growth. But it is hard to see how one can realistically reach such a conclusion unless one has some understanding of how many illegal aliens are here and what our national policy on population growth might be.

In fact, no reliable information exists on the number of persons illegally in the United States, but estimates have recently run as high as 12 million.[16] In testimony before Congress, the Immigration and Naturalization Service has indicated that its own estimates of six to eight million are principally derived from the calculations of regional immigration officials who are said to have a "feel" for the situation in their own areas.[17] Their findings are concededly based on no uniform national standard and have little or no empirical value.

The one hard datum in this area is the number of deportable aliens apprehended in a year. That number has risen dramatically over the last decade from 86,597 in fiscal year 1964 to 875,915 in fiscal year 1976.[18] But extrapolations from these numbers are difficult, and the dramatic increase does not necessarily indicate that the problem is growing steadily more grave.

In the first place, growth in the number of apprehensions may be leveling off. In fiscal year 1975, as the INS reported somewhat sheepishly in that year's annual report, the number of apprehensions was down slightly from the preceding year. The number did increase in 1976, but the rate of growth has apparently slowed, perhaps indicating that the extent of the problem is stabilizing.[19]

Moreover, the increase in apprehensions over the course of recent years may have resulted more from the greater effectiveness of enforcement efforts than from any increase in the pool of illegal aliens available to be apprehended. The number of INS personnel and the size of the agency's budget have not, in fact, increased at anything like the rate at which apprehensions have increased.[20] But the Service has recently shifted more and more of its personnel to enforcement and control functions and has deployed them increasingly at border areas where the likelihood of making apprehensions is greatest.[21] It is thus possible that the number of aliens attempting illegal entry has remained fairly constant, while the rate at which they are being caught has soared.

Nor can one assume that all of the approximately 800,000 apprehended in each of the last few years are new or recent migrants. Some had presumably been living in the United States illegally for years and the fact of their very recent apprehension does not indicate that the problem has suddenly grown more serious. Of course, as a result of the concentration of enforcement efforts at border areas, most apprehensions are made within a short time after entry.[22] But the entry in question is not necessarily the alien's first: it may be simply his most recent. A substantial number of those apprehended soon after entry may have been returning to the United States after a temporary absence abroad and should not be considered new migrants. One cannot say that but for their apprehension, the total illegal alien population would have increased.[23]

Moreover, the INS data on apprehensions may exaggerate, perhaps substantially, the total number of different individuals involved. The number reported each year is the number of apprehensions made, not the number of different aliens apprehended. An alien apprehended more than once will be counted more than once. Distilling the number of individuals apprehended out of the gross number of apprehensions is a more difficult task than might at first appear, since the penalty scheme with which the aliens must contend encourages them to conceal prior apprehensions. Criminal sanctions are ordinarily imposed, if at all, only where the alien has entered illegally after previously having been deported.[24] But in view of the staggering cost of deporting all deportable aliens, the INS allows all but a very few to make a voluntary departure.[25] If caught again, an alien who has previously made a voluntary departure will not be criminally punished, but this time the INS, provided it realizes it is dealing with a multiple violator, is obviously more likely to insist on deportation.[26] An apprehended alien, accordingly, has an incentive to conceal his identity and thus reduce the likelihood of deportation.[27] In view of the difficulty and expense of detaining several hundred thousand deportable aliens long enough to determine their identities and prior records, the INS cannot make such an effort in very many cases.

Quite apart from doubts about the significance of the apprehension data, there are good reasons for skepticism about some of the recent estimates concerning illegal aliens in the United States. The INS has indicated for several years that aliens are entering the country illegally at a staggering rate, with some estimates running as high as 3–4 million new entries a year.[28] If these estimates are correct the total illegal alien population of the United States should be rising very rapidly. Yet the estimates of the total illegal alien population have not risen dramatically over the last several years, but rather have hovered around 8 million. Indeed, the INS seems more reluctant than it was several years ago to suggest that the actual number might be as much as 12 million.[29] If the total illegal alien population has in fact stabilized, then one must assume either that aliens are not entering at the extraordinary rates suggested recently or that the very high entry rates merely indicate that the population of illegal aliens is turning over very rapidly.[30] For purposes of measuring the gravity of the illegal alien problem, one needs to know the net figures on entry of illegal aliens. Yet the very high estimates offered recently on the number of entries per year do not even purport to take account of the number of illegal aliens who leave during the course of the year.

There is also good reason for skepticism about the recent estimates concerning the total illegal alien population. Where, one might reasonably ask, would it be possible to hide 8 to 12 million people who have few skills, little money, and who probably do not speak English? The conventional answer that illegal aliens, most of whom are presumably of Spanish heritage, have blended into Hispanic communities in the United States is implausible in terms of the available census data. From 1970 to 1975, a period of ostensibly stupendous growth in the illegal alien population, the number of persons of Spanish origin in the United States increased from 9,072,000 to 11,202,000.[31] The increase of slightly more than 2.1 million, or 23 percent, is large, but it certainly can be explained in terms of lawful immigration and natural population growth during the period in question.[32] If recent estimates of the illegal alien population are more or less correct and if a substantial number of the illegal aliens are reflected in the census count, one would have to assume that few, if any, persons of Spanish origin are lawfully in the United States. Of course, the census may have missed most or even all of the illegal aliens, and almost all of the 11.2 million persons of Spanish origin reported in the census may be legal residents. But even on that assumption the Hispanic population of the United States does not seem large enough to permit as many as 8 to 12 million people to disappear into it, especially when one considers that the median age of the Spanish-origin population is low. Of the 11,202,000 persons reported in 1975, only 55.7 percent, or 6,239,514, were 18 or older.[33] In short, one can account for the presence of 8 to 12 million illegal aliens only by making the extraordinary assumption that somewhere between one-half and two-thirds of the total adult Spanish-origin population of the United States, counting legal and illegal residents, is in the country illegally.

Another useful reference point in evaluating the recent estimates is provided by the Mexican census data. Commenting on a study done for the INS which reached an estimate of 8,227,800 illegal aliens, of whom 5,222,000 were said to be Mexicans, North and Houstoun point out that the 1970 Mexican census "recorded 23,229,320 men and women between the ages of 15 and 59 (the age group from which most of the 5,222,000 Mexican illegals would be drawn)," and they term "most improbable" the "implication that between one-fifth and one-quarter of all Mexican residents in that age group are illegally in the U.S."[34]

Of course, even if current estimates of the illegal alien population are much too high, the fact undoubtedly remains that a great many persons are illegally in the United States. And alarm about illegal immigration depends not so much on proof that any particular number of aliens is in the United States illegally as on the perception that the number, whatever it may be, is too high. The difficulty is that we have no yardstick for determining how many immigrants, legal or illegal, are too many.

The 1965 legislation did, to be sure, impose a ceiling on lawful immigration of 290,000 persons per year: 170,000 from the Eastern Hemisphere and 120,000 from the Western Hemisphere. Since the great majority of illegal entrants come from Mexico,[35] the impact of illegal immigration on population-growth policy should presumably be determined in light of the annual limitation of 120,000 for the Western Hemisphere. The demand for Western Hemisphere visas has consistently outstripped the number available under the statutory scheme. Indeed, the backlog is now so great that a visa applicant qualified in every respect must wait two-and-one-half years for his or her number to come up. Nearly 300,000 persons are waiting in line.[36] By entering illegally, a good many aliens escape the obligation to wait their turn, and as a result of their entry the total amount of immigration—legal and illegal—

exceeds the limits set by Congress. But the conclusion that illegal entries are inconsistent with national policies on population growth does not follow unless one can demonstrate how, if at all, the immigration ceiling relates to those policies. One has to know, in other words, why we have decided to limit the number of visas available.

The ceiling of 120,000 does not reflect any reasoned judgment about desirable levels of immigration, much less an empirical finding about the country's capacity to absorb new immigrants. The figure of 120,000 was an afterthought, an arbitrary number chosen by the Senate in 1965 as a conditional limitation on Western Hemisphere immigration pending a study on the issue by a Select Commission to be established under the Act.[37] Neither the Administration bill nor the bill that passed the House would have imposed any ceiling at all on Western Hemisphere immigration.[38] The House conferees agreed to the Senate version apparently because the ceiling was the price imposed by the Senate for acquiescence in the abandonment of the national-origins quota system.[39] The Select Commission studied the issue and reported that it was very troublesome. Although a majority of its members favored "some type of immigration limitation in the New World as in the Old," it nonetheless urged Congress to delay implementation of the ceiling for one year to permit further investigation.[40] Congress refused to act and the ceiling went into effect virtually by default.

Moreover, the figure of 120,000 is only a rough approximation of the number of persons who can enter each year as lawful immigrants from the Western Hemisphere. Not counted against the annual limitation are "immediate relatives" of United States citizens.[41] Together with a fairly small group of "special immigrants," who also may enter without regard to the ceiling, they amounted to 104,633 immigrants in 1975, with 43,994 of them from the Western Hemisphere.[42] The exemption of immediate relatives from the numerical limitation does not indicate Congressional indifference to the number of persons who enter from the Western Hemisphere. But it does suggest that Congress was willing to bend the limitation in the service of an important national policy—facilitating the reunification of families—and the number of persons entering under the exception has been far from trifling. In the case of the Western Hemisphere, the number entering outside the ceiling in 1975 amounted to more than 35 percent of the number entering under the ceiling. The figure of 120,000 was never thought, in other words, to reflect an absolute limit beyond which the nation could not safely or even profitably go.

One should also note that as a result of a very questionable administrative interpretation of the ceiling the total amount of lawful immigration from the Western Hemisphere has for several years been held below the level that

Congress apparently intended to authorize. A considerable part of the present backlog is attributable to the fact that prospective Western Hemisphere immigrants have had to compete for the limited number of visas with thousands of Cuban refugees who entered the United States in recent years. Because they did not enter as immigrants the refugees were not counted against the ceiling at the time of entry. A statute enacted in 1966 made them eligible for adjustment of status to permanent residence after living in the United States for two years.[43] The government has counted each adjustment of status against the Western Hemisphere limitation, with the effect of significantly reducing the number of visas available for more conventional immigrants from the Western Hemisphere.

In its 1968 report the Select Commission pointed out that

> the rate at which Cubans are eligible for adjustment is far in excess of normal immigration from that area and is due solely to a special humanitarian program of the U.S. Government. This should not now be a factor in delaying the admission of qualified immigrants from other countries in this hemisphere, including Canada, particularly since the 120,000 ceiling was established before the mass entry of these refugees via the airlift began.
>
> Based on the assumption of a continuing airlift, if a ceiling of 120,000 were to include Cuban adjustment cases, it could have the effect of reducing by one-third the total number of visas available for the rest of the Western Hemisphere.[44]

Because of the time lag between arrival in the United States and the filing of a petition for adjustment of status, Cuban refugees have continued to consume a large share of the 120,000 visas available each year, even though the major influx of refugees is now over. In fiscal year 1975 the INS granted 26,514 adjustments, which had the effect of reducing by more than 20 percent the number of places available for prospective Western Hemisphere immigrants. And yet at the end of the year the number of still-pending applications for adjustment of status was 74,296—more than had been pending at the end of the preceding fiscal year.[45]

Recognizing that the counting of Cuban refugees against the numerical limitation was putting too much pressure on the Western Hemisphere ceiling and made little sense in terms of the ostensible purpose of that ceiling,[46] Congress finally provided in October, 1976, that the adjustments of status should be made without regard to numerical limitation and thus without prejudice to the ability of prospective Western Hemisphere immigrants to obtain visas.[47] With the Cuban refugees finally accorded separate treatment, the total number of visas available in the Western Hemisphere—and thus the total amount of lawful immigration from the Western Hemisphere—should increase to the level that would have prevailed if the government had recognized at the outset that the case of the Cuban refugees was exceptional.[48]

In the legislation that finally resolved the Cuban refugee situation, Congress also addressed the larger problem of a numerical limitation for the Western Hemisphere and the reasons for setting it at 120,000. Most of the discussion in Congress concerned immigration from Canada and Mexico. As originally introduced by Representative Peter Rodino, the bill would have allowed Canadians and Mexicans, in view of what was said to be their countries' special relationship with the United States, to enter as immigrants without regard to numerical limitation. The House Subcommittee on Immigration, Citizenship, and International Law concluded, and Congress accepted its conclusion, that no country should enjoy special treatment. With attention focused on parity for Mexico and Canada as well as other portions of the bill, the question of an over-all ceiling for the Western Hemisphere received barely more attention than it had in 1965. Nonetheless, Congress re-enacted the limitation of 120,000 in the closing hours of the session.

The Subcommittee's report on the measure offers little in the way of explanation. The report points out that "there has been no concerted attempt or public pressure to abolish" the ceiling.[49] But how should one construe the absence of such pressure? It might be viewed as very persuasive evidence that the system is working well. But to which system does the evidence pertain—the system authorized by law, or the system that operates in the real world and consists of illegal as well as legal entries? The public is obviously concerned about the presence of illegal aliens, but one might suppose that if the problem of illegal immigration were simply one of numbers, there would be no acquiescence in the idea that the immigration system is admitting about the right number of persons. It seems unlikely that in determining whether the absorptive capacity of the country is strained, the public can distinguish between the impact of legal and illegal immigrants.

The Subcommittee's report goes on to note "the recommendation made in 1972 by the President's Commission on Population Growth and the American Future, that 'immigration levels not be increased.'"[50] But the significance of that recommendation is problematic. One of the studies undertaken for the Commission called the ceilings arbitrary in the sense that "they are unrelated to a conscious policy of population growth, labor force absorption, or any similar policy."[51] And the Commission itself conceded that population growth has "rarely been a concern of immigration policy makers."[52] Although the Commission acknowledged that the issue involves "complex moral, economic, and political considerations, as well as demographic concerns,"[53] it clearly did not make the sort of inquiry that Congress should have made as the basis for imposing the numerical limitation. It recommended that "the present level of immigration should be maintained because of the humanitarian aspects," and urged that "immigration policy be reviewed periodically to reflect demographic conditions."[54] One commentator noted that "[a]ll [the Commission recommendation] does is put off answering a very difficult question."[55] After acknowledging the Commission's recommendation and noting that "immigration would have risen above the current level without the ceiling"—in effect, after stating the question—the Subcommittee report abruptly changes the subject and declares, "[a]ttention is more appropriately focused on two [other] aspects of the immigration law."[56]

Even though Congress has failed to offer any sound basis for setting the ceiling at precisely 120,000, it might be argued that Congress did at least make a judgment about the general range of desirable immigration. Perhaps a figure slightly higher or lower than 120,000 would have been more appropriate, but that alone does not demonstrate that illegal entry at anything like the rate suggested in recent estimates is consistent with national goals. Yet it warrants repeating that the rate of increase in the illegal alien population is uncertain, and the rate may in fact put total net immigration (legal and illegal) within a reasonable distance of the ceiling. In any case, the ceiling is designed to limit the number of persons who may enter the United States for permanent residence, yet it is often said that the great majority of illegal aliens have no intention of taking up permanent residence but are working in the United States for temporary periods and at jobs most Americans would not accept. If that is true, one might conclude that present rates of illegal immigration, no matter how far beyond the ceiling they may go, are consistent with the best interests of the country. The validity of that conclusion is certainly open to dispute. But without knowing who the illegal aliens are and what they are doing in the United States, it is hard to see how one can evaluate their impact on the United States and decry their presence on the basis of numbers alone.

### Are Illegal Aliens Undesirable as Immigrants?

Just as we know little about the number of aliens now in the United States illegally, we also have relatively little reliable information about who the illegal aliens are, what they are doing in the United States, and what qualities they have that might make them desirable or undesirable as immigrants. Underlying most of the concern about illegal immigration is the assumption that illegal aliens are taking jobs from Americans. The INS clearly takes that view, and it has suggested one million as a conservative estimate of the number of jobs that could be freed for American workers if the illegal aliens could be removed.[57] To illustrate the gravity of the problem, the INS gives great publicity to the apprehension of illegal aliens who are holding desirable jobs at high rates of compensation and suggests that this "anecdotal evidence" reveals the gravity of the problem.[58] But focusing on aliens of this type can give a misleading impression of the problem as a whole. It is generally assumed that illegal aliens fall into two rough categories.[59] The first consists of relatively high-skilled persons who hold desirable jobs and are paid at about the same wage rate as citizens and resident aliens who do the same work. These illegal aliens tend to have come from the Eastern Hemisphere and to have entered the United States legally but as nonimmigrants, for example as students or tourists. They become illegal aliens by taking a job in violation of their nonimmigrant status. The second category consists of low-skilled or unskilled persons who take menial jobs at very low rates of pay. They tend to be natives of the Western Hemisphere countries and to have entered the United States from Mexico without inspection. These two types of illegal aliens present very different types of problems. The illegal aliens in the first category are the ones who hold the jobs that Americans want, but the fact that they tend to hold these jobs at the prevailing wage rate suggests at least that they are not competing unfairly with American workers. And if they did enter the United States legally as nonimmigrants, they were the subject of at least some screening by the consular and immigration officials who authorized their entry. In any case, while the number of illegal aliens of this type appears to be growing, they still apparently constitute a very small part of the total illegal alien population.[60]

The presence in the United States of a great many illegal aliens from the second category—Western Hemisphere natives, by far the majority of them Mexicans, who hold menial jobs—raises much more perplexing questions. These are the illegal aliens who are said to compete unfairly with American workers and to depress wages and working conditions. They are also the ones who are said to pay little or no taxes while they consume a substantial amount of public benefits, in particular welfare payments and free medical service. But at the same time they are the ones who are often asserted to be filling a shortage at the bottom of the labor market, taking the menial and low-paying jobs that American workers are unwilling to take. Many of these jobs are said to be in the agricultural sector, and some members of Congress have expressed reservations about legislation that would make it more difficult to employ illegal aliens on the grounds that growers in their districts have been unable, even in times of recession, to hire sufficient numbers of American workers to do low-wage, seasonal work.[61] But it has also been argued that the availability of the illegal alien labor force is crucial to the survival of certain labor-intensive enterprises in the nonagricultural sector. Michael Piore, an economist at MIT, has suggested that the new [illegal] immigration is a response to what employers perceive as a vacuum at the bottom of the labor market, a shortage, that began in the middle '60s, of workers to fill the menial, low-wage, unstable, dead-end jobs in industries like textiles, shoes and tanning, at sewing machines in the garment factories, in restaurants, hotels, laundries and hospitals. Faced with this shortage, employers began active recruitment abroad.... The labor shortage, to which this recruitment is a response, is attributed by employers to the growing reluctance of black workers to accept the kinds of low-level jobs that blacks traditionally filled.[62]

One major study has been conducted in an effort to determine who the illegal aliens are, what they are doing in the United States, and what impact they have on the American work force. Under a research and development contract with the Department of Labor, North and Houstoun interviewed 793 apprehended illegal aliens and 51 unapprehended illegal aliens to determine the characteristics of the illegal alien work force and its impact on the United States. They report that

the findings of our survey are consistent with the claim that illegals are "taking jobs that no American wants." Most respondents were working at or near the bottom of the labor market, in terms of their occupation, their wages, and their hours. Clearly, the majority of our respondents had found employment in jobs that, for the most part, offer the least in economic rewards, social status, job security and upward mobility. Few were earning incomes that would provide a family with more than a subsistence level of life, by American standards. There are few data that contraindicate the notion that ... the primary role of illegal aliens in the nation is to provide its labor markets with low-wage workers who are willing to do its dirty work.[63]

Of course, the fact that they are employed in low-level jobs does not necessarily indicate that they are needed workers, since the willingness of an American worker to take a job will presumably depend on the wages and working conditions offered. The presence of illegal aliens at the bottom of the labor market may indicate only that there are no American workers willing to take the job at the wages and working conditions that illegal aliens will accept. North and Houstoun point out that "[i]n circumstances of high unemployment and low productivity, when illegals' wages appear to be well below the norm of comparably employed U.S. workers, the claim that their presence in the U.S. labor market is symptomatic of a shortfall of low-level workers appears to us a dubious one."[64] But they go on to note, with reference to the work of Piore and others, that "labor economists are beginning to discern other, more reliable indicators that the traditional sources of low-level workers are beginning to dry up. . . . [I]t is not at all certain that [as the supply of maximally disadvantaged Americans grows smaller] high wages and short hours, even if economically feasible, will themselves prove sufficiently attractive inducements to employment in low-level jobs" to prevent a shortfall in the number of workers available to do the nation's menial and unrewarding work.[65]

This dispute over the need for illegal aliens as workers is at the heart of the controversy about illegal immigration, and one might therefore suppose that the immigration system would have faced up to this difficult issue and made some reasonable attempt to resolve it openly and on the merits. If illegal aliens were really needed workers, surely the immigration laws would have made possible their lawful entry as immigrants. The very fact of illegal entry would seem to permit the drawing of an inference that the illegal entrant is judged less desirable as an immigrant than persons who are allowed to enter lawfully. In fact, over the past decade the Western Hemisphere immigrant selection system has operated in a way that makes it more difficult than one might expect to draw that inference.

Although the 1965 Act did establish a set of priorities to control the selection of immigrants from among Eastern Hemisphere applicants (according preference to close relatives, workers with skills in short supply, and refugees),[66] the Act set forth no priorities whatsoever with regard to Western Hemisphere immigration. Had Congress continued the policy that existed until 1965 and declined to impose a numerical limitation on immigration from this hemisphere, the absence of a system of priorities would have caused little difficulty. Priorities obviously would not be needed if all qualified applicants could be admitted.[67] But the number of applications has in fact substantially exceeded the number of places available under the ceiling of 120,000. And given the absence of priorities, it has been far from clear that persons who cannot obtain visas promptly or at all—persons, in other words, who may resort to illegal entry—are presumptively the ones we would want to exclude.[68] Relatives of resident aliens and all but the closest relatives of citizens enjoy no priority, and the goal of facilitating reunification of families is accordingly jeopardized. To take an extreme but often-cited example, the spouse of a resident alien has had to wait two-and-one-half years to enter the United States legally if he or she is a native of a Western Hemisphere country. The spouse who refuses to wait and enters the United States before the visa is available is an illegal alien, but it hardly follows that he or she is unwelcome in the United States or qualitatively less desirable than aliens who have already obtained a visa. Similarly, a Western Hemisphere native whose skills are greatly in demand in the United States has enjoyed no priority over many other applicants whose services are not needed at all. The two-and-one-half year waiting period has disadvantaged not only that highly-skilled applicant but also persons in the United States who would derive benefit from the availability of those skills.

Notwithstanding the absence of a system of priorities for the Western Hemisphere, Congress did impose on prospective immigrants from this hemisphere the general requirement of obtaining a Labor Department certification that no U.S. workers are "able, willing, qualified, and available" to fill the position that the alien is seeking.[69] Aliens with certain specified family relationships to citizens of the United States and resident aliens are exempt from the requirement, and through these exemptions the great majority of persons entering lawfully from the Western Hemisphere have managed to avoid the screening process altogether.[70] A substantial number of persons now entering illegally would also apparently be exempt. But a much larger number would not,[71] and if the aliens who enter illegally are doing so because they cannot obtain the required certification, one might argue that by definition they cannot be needed workers. Still, the definition of an alien as needed or not needed is only as good as the process that formulates that definition. And the labor certification program has not proved to be an effective device for screening applicants and sorting out those who would be more desirable as immigrants from those who would be less desirable.

The House Subcommittee on Immigration, Citizenship, and International Law recently indicated that it was "disturbed by the administration of the ... requirement," and declared that it "plans to review this entire program during the next Congress."[72] Testifying before that subcommittee, a leading immigration lawyer called the program a "dismal failure" and maintained that it has produced "government lawlessness, inconsistencies, confusion, arbitrary secret action, and one of the worst phases of the Federal administrative practice."[73] In some situations the program has given the American labor force too little protection; in others it has apparently given it too much. As a device for excluding unneeded workers, the program has tended to prove ineffective, not only because so many immigrants are exempt from the requirement, but also because the immigrant who obtains certification is under no obligation to stay in the occupation for which he was certified.[74] At the same time, critics have charged that the Department has construed the certification requirement too rigidly and denied certification on the grounds that U.S. workers are available in situations where U.S. workers, whether or not theoretically available, are not in fact willing to take the work.[75] If all this were not bad enough, it also seems clear that the certification requirement has had the perverse effect of encouraging illegal immigration. For most prospective immigrants, certification cannot be made until the alien has received a specific job offer.[76] Since most aliens cannot obtain such an offer without coming to the United States, the requirement has encouraged aliens to enter the United States illegally or as nonimmigrants in order to search for work. And if they can obtain a job offer, they are likely to find that most employers will not hold the offer open for two-and-one-half years while the alien waits for the visa to become available. Thus, the alien may very well remain in the United States illegally to work at the job while waiting for the visa that will make his status lawful.[77] It seems hard to believe that his presence should be a cause for alarm the day before he receives the visa if he will be viewed as a desirable resident as soon as the visa is obtained.

It is true, of course, that an illegal entry to the United States demonstrates that the entrant is willing to disregard at least some of the country's legal rules. No matter how irrational these rules might be, the alien's willingness to disobey them gives reason for concern about his or her desirability as an immigrant to the United States. Plainly, there is unfairness in the fact that illegal entrants can enter the United States without waiting for the necessary legal authority, whereas prospective immigrants who are unwilling to flout the law must wait for months or years to gain admission, if they are able to gain admission at all. But if this is the real objection to the presence of illegal aliens in the country, one can reasonably ask whether the alarm expressed at their presence here is not substantially out of proportion to the seriousness of the problem. In the first place, if these aliens are performing services that are needed in the United States or if they are in some other way very desirable as immigrants, these facts should be weighed against the inference that can be drawn from their willingness to make an illegal entry. And as I hope to show in the next section of this article, a great many of the illegal aliens are here because our immigration system has functioned in such a way as to encourage their entry to the United States and to make possible their survival at least so long as they continued to serve a useful function. That fact should also be weighed in the balance. It could also be said that the aliens who take the initiative to enter the United States illegally will tend to be young, single, ambitious, and resourceful, and these may be the very qualities that will permit them to thrive here. While I cannot deny that the willingness of aliens to enter the United States in defiance of law is itself a source of legitimate concern, that objection is much more modest than those ordinarily made to their presence here. The objection does not seem to warrant the alarm that is so often expressed.

As part of the 1976 amendments to the Immigration and Nationality Act, Congress has at last taken steps to provide some semblance of order to immigration from the Western Hemisphere. The system of priorities or preferences that operates with regard to immigration from the Eastern Hemisphere has now been carried over to the Western Hemisphere.[78] Accordingly, visa applicants in the preferred categories—generally, persons in close family relationship to U.S. citizens and permanent resident aliens, persons with needed skills, and refugees—will get priority. For some applicants, the effect of this statutory change should be a significant reduction in the waiting time for a visa. Although the ceiling of 120,000 is still in force, a new applicant will now compete for one of the 120,000 places against persons who enjoy the same priority and not against persons without priority who may have applied long before. Of course, with the over-all ceiling unchanged, the length of the waiting period can be decreased for some persons only because it is correspondingly increased for others. Applicants without preference status will now compete for a greatly reduced number of places.

Although Congress has at last begun the hard process of choosing between the Western Hemisphere immigrants we want and those we do not, a number of very difficult questions remain unanswered. It is still too soon to know whether the carrying over of the Eastern Hemisphere system will work any significant change in the pattern of over-all immigration, legal and illegal, from the Western Hemisphere. But it does seem clear that Congress has still not faced the central question of whether illegal aliens are needed workers. The new system does give some priority to persons who can establish that their skills are needed, but the basic tool for separating needed from unneeded workers remains the labor certification requirement. Congress modified that requirement slightly, but there is little reason to assume that the certification system will suddenly operate as a more reliable indicator of the need for particular workers than it has up to now.[79] Moreover, because the preference system reserves many more visas for relatives than for those who can establish that their skills or services are needed,[80] the waiting lists for persons in the latter category are likely to be long. Relatives, by contrast, will probably find it easier to enter under the new system of priorities than before. The bias in favor of relatives might well reflect a determination by Congress that there are now no major shortages in the labor market and thus that there is no need to reserve a great many visas for persons other than relatives. But it is not clear that Congress has fully considered the ramifications of the preference system it has adopted. Despite the occasional expression of surprise and dismay at the extent to which immigration seems to beget immigration,[81] Congress often acts as if it fails to understand that the reunification of families is another name for chain migration. The extreme emphasis on family reunification, producing what has been called a "national policy of nepotism,"[82] has so far generated very little discussion, perhaps because few significant backlogs have developed in any category in the Eastern Hemisphere and in that sense the policy can be described as "working well."[83] But the real test of a system of priorities comes when the results it produces begin to diverge from the results that a process of self-selection would produce. After all, the existence of a backlog does not necessarily indicate that the policy is working badly. What it does indicate is that the policy is working at all. When the number of applicants exceeds the number of visas available and thus the entry of some persons is accomplished at the expense of others, the policy behind the system that produces these results comes sharply into focus. Substantial backlogs are certain to remain a feature of Western Hemisphere immigration so long as Congress retains the ceiling of 120,000. Now that Congress has at last established a system of priorities for this Hemisphere and made some effort to choose among the competing applicants for entry, it may be possible to focus some attention on the system that Congress has established and consider the wisdom and rationality of the choices Congress has made and the backlogs these choices have produced.

## THE HISTORICAL PATTERN OF IMMIGRATION TO THE UNITED STATES FROM MEXICO

Faced with what they perceived as a shortage of workers willing to do low-skill jobs, a number of countries in Western Europe have resorted to the large-scale importation of foreign workers. Plainly, it is still far from clear that there is now or soon will be such a shortage in the United States. But if, as argued above, the United States has not even faced the question openly and attempted to resolve it on its merits, the explanation may well be that the presence of large numbers of illegal aliens has rendered the issue moot. When one looks at the historical pattern of immigration from Mexico, it is hard to avoid the conclusion that illegal immigration, far from being an accidental phenomenon existing in defiance of the immigration policy of the country, is on the contrary a very important de facto part of that policy. Illegal aliens could well be considered the guest workers of the United States.

From World War II to the end of 1964 the United States maintained an elaborate de jure system for importing foreign laborers—the *bracero* program—that operated in several different forms and involved the entry of several hundred thousand workers from Mexico each year. The correlation in time between the end of the bracero program and the recent acceleration in the rate of apprehension of illegal aliens, most of them from Mexico, seems too close to be explained as a coincidence. The number of apprehensions from 1960–64 averaged less than 90,000 per year. During fiscal year 1965, at the mid-point of which the bracero program expired, the number jumped to 110,371. It climbed to 138,520 in 1966 and 161,608 in 1967, and it continued to climb in annual increments of 20–33 percent until fiscal year 1975.[84] To the extent that the increase in apprehensions reflects an increase in the number of aliens illegally in the United States, it would seem true, as one very instructive recent commentary on the immigration system suggested, that the bracero program is "continuing on an unofficial basis."[85]

Like the present phenomenon of illegal immigration, the bracero program generated great controversy. And the respective arguments of the program's proponents and opponents were virtually identical to the arguments that surround the current controversy over the employment of illegal aliens. Opponents maintained that employers had created the myth of a shortage of domestic workers in order to gain access to an unorganized and easily disciplined labor force that was willing to work for wages at which a domestic worker's family could not survive. Employers responded that the work was hard and that domestic workers were unwilling to take the jobs at economically feasible rates of pay.[86] The persistence of the bracero program in the form of illegal immigration, if that is a fair characterization of what has happened, says very little about the validity of either side of the argument, for either argument could explain the extra-legal continuation of the program. What it does make clear is that many employers continue to believe there is a shortage of low-level workers at appropriate rates of pay, and so long as they are willing to offer jobs to illegal aliens and the aliens are willing and able to enter the United States and take the jobs, the bracero program will remain in existence by default. A number of Representatives and Senators who have opposed legislation that would impose criminal penalties on those who knowingly hire illegal aliens will apparently remain opposed unless such a measure is accompanied by a formal revival of the bracero program.[87]

As methods of providing workers to fill what may be shortages in the labor market, the bracero program and illegal immigration have a very important characteristic in common. Neither the bracero nor the illegal alien enters the United States as an immigrant and therefore neither is on a citizenship track. No period of residence will make them eligible for naturalization and the rights that flow from citizenship. Indeed, no period of residence will even confer on them the right to remain in the United States as aliens when their services are no longer needed. Thus, if the labor shortage disappears, the worker can be sent home. If the worker is no longer able to perform the work, he can be sent home. If he is no longer willing to perform the work, perhaps because he has developed skills and aspirations for a more desirable job, he can be sent home. As convenient as it may be to fill labor shortages with workers whose legal position in the United States is so tenuous, the practice seems inconsistent with the longstanding principle of the country's immigration policy that no distinction should be drawn between "being a member of the American labor force and being a member of its society."[88] In practice, however, that principle has not always been observed, as the case of slavery dramatically illustrates.[89] With regard to immigration from Mexico, substantial evidence is available to suggest that the policy of the United States, whether by design or by default, has traditionally encouraged the entry of Mexicans as workers rather than immigrants.

The border that separates the United States and Mexico is a fairly recent invention and for much of its history it was almost completely open. Even as the population living near the border became substantial, little effort was made to impede the flow of traffic back and forth across it. McWilliams points out that for many years "the border towns not only overlapped but the mythical line ran through particular stores, buildings, and saloons."[90] The first significant restrictions on entry into the United States went into effect in the latter part of the nineteenth century, but meaningful enforcement of these restrictions at the Mexican border was more the exception than the rule. To the extent that border crossers were checked at all in the early part of this century, the effort was largely to enforce the Chinese Exclusion Acts and prevent the entry of Chinese into the United States by way of Mexico.[91] The head tax of 1882[92] and the exclusion beginning that same year of persons likely to become public charges,[93] the contract labor law of 1885[94] and the literacy test of 1917[95]—all of these statutory provisions could have significantly limited migration from Mexico. But enforcement remained lax and, at least in the years before the establishment of the Border Patrol in 1924, the border "could be crossed, in either direction, at almost any point from Brownsville to San Diego, with the greatest of ease."[96] As a result, the "statistics compiled by the Bureau of Immigration are of little value" in determining how many persons migrated from Mexico to the United States during this period since "a great number of Mexico immigrants [entered into or left] the United States without the knowledge of the immigration offices."[97]

In 1911 the Immigration Commission, chaired by Senator William P. Dillingham of Vermont, issued its massive and very important report. The significance of that report is not just that it provided the ideological foundation for the national-origins quota system that went into effect a decade later. With regard to Mexican immigration in particular, it established a pattern of analysis that has persisted ever since. On the subject of Mexican immigration the Commission pointed out that "complete records of those who cross the border have not been kept," but it reported estimates "that the number immigrating approaches 60,000 per year," which would put the rate four or five times greater than the number actually reported.[98] The xenophobic Commission reacted to these estimates with a fair degree of equanimity because it viewed the Mexican immigrants as "transient laborers, many of them alternating between their native land and the States of the Southwest, and living wherever their employment takes them."[99] The Commission found, moreover, that they were employed largely in parts of the country "which are sparsely settled and in which the climatic and other conditions are such that it has been difficult to secure laborers of any other race [in part because of the exclusion of the Chinese[100]], including the Japanese."[101] Thus,

[t]he Mexican immigrants are providing a fairly acceptable supply of labor in a limited territory in which it is difficult to secure others, and their competitive ability is limited because of their more or less temporary residence and their personal qualities, so that their incoming does not involve the same detriment to labor conditions as is involved in the immigration of other races who also work at comparatively low wages. While the Mexicans are not easily assimilated, this is not of very great importance as long as most of them return to their native land after a short time.[102]

The Commission concluded that "it is evident that in the case of the Mexican he is less desirable as a citizen than as a laborer. The permanent additions to the population, however, are much smaller than the number who immigrate for work."[103]

Within a few years Congress gave express effect to the Commission's conclusion that Mexicans make better workers than settlers. In what amounted to the first bracero program, Congress authorized the importation of workers from Mexico to meet a temporary labor shortage during World War I. Acting under the authority of legislation passed in 1917,[104] the government waived certain restrictions on entry in order to permit the importation of Mexican laborers under contract, without payment of the head tax, and without regard to literacy. Between 1917 and 1921 approximately 73,000 Mexicans entered the United States to perform temporary work in agriculture, in the mines, and for the railroads.[105] At the end of the program or when their contracts expired, they were required to return to Mexico.

With the 1920s a number of important changes occurred in the pattern of Mexican immigration. Although the national-origins quota system established by legislation in 1921 and 1924 did not apply to Mexican immigrants and they remained free of any form of numerical limitation, surveillance at the border gradually increased. It appears that one of the important reasons for the more vigilant checking of Mexican border-crossers was the desire to insure that Southern and Eastern Europeans excluded under the quota did not enter illegally through Mexico as the Chinese had earlier tried to do.[106] While Mexican immigrants were not subject to the quotas, they did have to pass the qualitative restrictions, and these restrictions were evidently enforced more vigorously in the 1920s than they had been before. As a result, the number of persons entering lawfully from Mexico declined sharply, and the number of Mexicans apprehended after entering the United States illegally began to rise.[107] Still, the border remained relatively open throughout the 1920s,[108] and Mexicans who sought work in the United States had little difficulty entering—some of them as legal immigrants, but many more as illegal aliens.

The situation changed very dramatically in the 1930s, however, as unemployment forced many Mexicans to return home and an aroused immigration service apprehended and removed from the United States a very large number who had entered without inspection in earlier years and could not establish a right to legal residence in the United States.[109] By the end of the decade the net effect was a substantial reduction in the number of Mexicans in the United States.[110] The onset of World War II turned the situation around again even before the United States had become formally involved. With business picking up rapidly, a large number of employers began to demand that Mexican workers be provided.[111] Pursuant to an agreement with Mexico signed in 1942 and legislation passed by Congress in 1943, the United States initiated a second formal program for importing Mexican workers into the United States for temporary work in agriculture and on railroad track maintenance.[112] The program originated as a response to what were thought to be severe manpower shortages during World War II, but it persisted in several different forms until 1964. When the emergency program expired in 1947, the Attorney General invoked his authority under the 1917 Act to waive the normal conditions on entry in cases where a shortage of labor was found to exist.[113] The program continued on that basis until 1951, when Congress again provided specific legislative authority, this time as an amendment to the Agricultural Act of 1949.[114] The amendment, Public Law 78, authorized the continuation of the program until December 31, 1953, but it was renewed then and several more times in succession until it was finally allowed to lapse on December 31, 1964.

Even while the bracero program was in operation, Mexicans continued to come into the United States illegally. Indeed, it seems likely that the bracero program actually stimulated illegal entry by exposing a great many Mexicans to the attractions of life in the United States, where they could work for wages that seemed very high in comparison to wage rates in Mexico.[115] By reporting these conditions to neighbors in Mexico, the returning bracero apparently encouraged others to follow in his path—as braceros if possible, but illegally if necessary. Early in the 1950s the government launched Operation Wetback, a major crackdown on illegal immigration, and apprehended hundreds of thousands of deportable aliens. In 1954 alone the service apprehended 1,075,068—more than were apprehended in any year before or since. But this massive effort to stop illegal immigration did not have the purpose or the effect of shutting off all migration from Mexico into the United States. What it did do was to change the form of the migration.[116] "As a result of the exerted efforts of the [INS] to stop the illegal entrance of aliens from Mexico, the farmers were forced to turn to [the bracero program] for required field labor."[117] In 1953 only 178,000 braceros were admitted to the United States. As the number of apprehensions under

Operation Wetback increased, so did the number of persons admitted legally as nonimmigrants under the bracero program. The program reached a peak of some 450,000 in 1957, and the number remained above 400,000 for each of the next several years.

Shortly after the bracero program expired in 1964 Congress enacted the 1965 legislation that jettisoned the system of national-origins quotas and for the first time in the nation's history imposed a numerical ceiling on immigration from the Western Hemisphere. But despite the establishment of that ceiling the amount of legal immigration from Mexico has actually risen, perhaps suggesting that persons who might earlier have entered under the bracero program are now seeking entry as immigrants.[118] And, as noted earlier, the number of persons illegally in the country has also apparently increased, indicating that many of those who cannot enter lawfully are entering outside the law.

One of the puzzling aspects of this historical pattern is the fact that so many Mexicans have entered the United States illegally or as nonimmigrants when for much of the period no numerical limitation was imposed on lawful immigration from Mexico. It is important to note that the principal explanation for most of the migration from Mexico to the United States has traditionally been economic. And it is doubtless true now, as it was at the time of the Dillingham Commission's report, that much of the migration is circular, in the sense that persons "enter this country solely for the purpose of employment, frequently for a limited period of time, and that a large number have no intention of moving here permanently."[119] North and Houstoun found that illegal aliens from Mexico are "considerably more likely than [other illegal aliens] to have come to the United States for a job, to remain closely tied to country of origin, [and] to have spouse and children at home."[120] But it is not just the illegal entrants whose migration to the United States has tended to be circular. Perhaps because of the geographic proximity of their native land and the effect this proximity has had on their attachment to it, Mexicans legally admitted to the United States for permanent residence have traditionally had a very low rate of naturalization in this country.[121] For many Mexicans who have sought jobs in the United States, an illegal entry or an entry as a nonimmigrant may have seemed adequate to accomplish their objectives.

But Mexicans are clearly not the only migrants who have come to the United States with a very strong attachment to their homeland and an expectation that they would someday go back to it. What has made Mexican immigration unique is the extent to which institutionalized patterns of circular migration have facilitated the entry of Mexicans into the United States as workers while discouraging or precluding their entry as settlers. Notwithstanding the absence of a numerical limitation, it has often been very difficult for Mexicans to obtain the visas that would permit them to enter lawfully as permanent residents. The prospective immigrant has had to pass qualitative tests and their enforcement has sometimes been vigorous. Indeed, the pressure to impose a numerical ceiling on Mexican immigration in the 1920s largely disappeared as a result of the State Department's very rigid enforcement in Mexico of the qualitative restrictions, which significantly reduced the number of immigrants.[122] For much of the period, including the years before the imposition of the numerical ceiling, substantial backlogs have existed in processing applications from Mexicans seeking to enter the United States as immigrants.[123] Thus, even an applicant who would have no difficulty passing the qualitative hurdles would still face a significant wait before the visa would become available. And finally, even if the visa could be obtained, the cost of obtaining it would likely be very high. With documentation needed not only for the principal applicant but for all dependents as well, it has been estimated that the cost could exceed a year's wages.[124] In short, even those Mexicans who would have preferred to enter the United States lawfully as immigrants have traditionally found it very difficult to do so. At the same time and in sharp contrast, they have almost always found it relatively easy to enter illegally or as nonimmigrants.[125]

The absence of significant natural obstacles to passage across the Mexican border obviously makes it difficult to control all movement back and forth across it. Although the vigorous and successful enforcement of the immigration laws in the 1930s and the early 1950s is often cited as support for the view that the United States can curtail illegal immigration if it has the will to do so, it is not entirely clear what lessons should be drawn from the experience of the 1930s and 1950s. During the Great Depression the illegal aliens, like a great many other workers, were unable to find jobs, and thus their incentive to remain in the United States largely disappeared. And in the 1950s the crackdown on illegal immigration was accompanied by a willingness to permit the entry of greater numbers of Mexicans on a lawful basis, some of them as permanent residents, but many more as nonimmigrant workers.[126] The fact remains, however, that in general the United States has not had the determination to keep the border closed. Citing "overwhelming evidence of institutionalized support" for the continued use of illegal Mexican aliens in agriculture in the Southwest, one commentator points out that the practice has been sustained by the "collusion of employers, political and legal officials, church functionaries, governmental enforcement agencies, and the governments of the two nations concerned."[127] Others point out that the Border Patrol has often performed a regulatory function, not so much excluding the illegal aliens as keeping the situation under some semblance of control.[128]

Twenty-five years ago *The New York Times* called it "remarkable how some Senators and Representatives who are all for erecting the most rigid barriers against immigration from Southern Europe suffer from a sudden blindness when it comes to protecting the southern border of the United States."[129] It is remarkable, to be sure, but certainly not inexplicable. The effectiveness of enforcement efforts in the Southwest has "ebbed and flowed according to the economic needs of the region."[130] The President's Commission on Migratory Labor reported in 1951 that "there have been times when pressure has been successfully exerted upon Washington to have the Immigration and Naturalization Service issue orders to field officers to go easy on deportations until crops have been harvested."[131] Perhaps most revealing, the Commission also found that

> [w]hen the work is done, neither the farmer nor the community wants the wetback around. The number of apprehensions and deportations tends to rise very rapidly at the close of a seasonal work period. This can be interpreted not alone to mean that the immigration officer suddenly goes about his work with renewed zeal and vigor, but rather that at this time of the year "cooperation" in law enforcement by farm employers and townspeople rapidly undergoes considerable improvement.[132]

In short, the Mexican immigration policy of the United States has rested on the view that, in the words of a Colorado farmer who testified many years ago before the Migratory Labor Commission, "any nation is very fortunate if that nation can, from sources near at hand, obtain the services on beck and call of labor, adult male labor, on condition that when the job is completed the laborer will return to his home."[133] From time to time the policy has been implemented by means of formal programs for the importation of non-immigrant foreign workers. More often it has operated through a de facto policy of sporadic enforcement of the immigration laws, allowing large numbers of Mexicans to enter the United States illegally and work in this country, but forcing them out again when their services were no longer needed.

There can be no doubt that the policy has proved distinctly advantageous to important groups in the United States. It would not have persisted if it had not. What is not at all clear, however, is first, whether the problem the policy is supposed to solve—the shortage of low-skill workers—is real or mythical, and second, assuming the problem is real, whether the policy represents a politically, diplomatically, and morally reasonable solution. A policy that permits the entry of workers for temporary employment in the United States may be a harsh but peculiarly effective solution to the problem of labor shortages, in the sense that it guarantees a continuing supply of maximally disadvantaged workers who can be depended upon to do the country's menial work without swelling the permanent labor force. As North and Houstoun put it, "[a]t bottom, a decision to use aliens—nonimmigrants or illegals—as a supply of cheap, low-skill labor is an attempt to acquire that labor and to adjure its economic and social costs."[134] Perhaps one can rationalize such a policy on the grounds that the foreign workers have voluntarily participated in very large numbers and apparently with considerable awareness of the conditions under which they would work in the United States. Many of them, after all, have come to the United States repeatedly.[135] It also appears that the government of Mexico is not opposed to the practice, at least when carried out pursuant to a formal program.[136] But whether or not one can make a reasonable defense of the practice of importing foreign workers who have no legal stake in the United States, it seems entirely clear that the issue should be brought out into the open and no longer resolved by default. Since 1964 the United States, like the countries of Western Europe, has had the benefit of a guest worker program, but it has not openly faced up to the questions raised by such a policy, nor made any effort to subject the program to even minimal legal regulation. As troublesome as a guest worker policy may be, if the alternative is an extra-legal arrangement designed to serve the same objectives—that is, a system of tolerated illegal immigration—the adoption of a formal, regulated program seems the only conscionable choice.[137]

The failure of Congress to confront the underlying questions can be explained on a number of grounds. The employers who believe a labor shortage now exists have had the benefit of the de facto labor importation program, and they have no incentive to push for a change in the status quo. Bringing the program out into the open and legalizing it would offer them few advantages, given the red tape and regulation such a legalized program would inevitably involve. As for those who deny the existence of a labor shortage and see the use of a foreign labor force as a device to avoid meeting the legitimate demands of American workers, they have always been in a difficult position on this subject. First, no one has found a painless way to terminate the de facto policy. Any of the steps that would severely limit illegal immigration would accomplish that goal by imposing significant costs on persons lawfully in the United States, for example by requiring some or all persons to carry a tamper-proof identifying card and to present it in order to obtain employment or public benefits. Second, those who sustain the largest share of the injury caused by the de facto policy are Mexican-Americans, and that community is badly divided on how the problem should be handled.[138] It is the Mexican-Americans who have the most to lose from illegal immigration since they are the ones who compete with illegal aliens for jobs, they work in precisely the areas where the availability of an illegal alien labor force may drive down wages and working conditions, and they are victimized by the cloud of suspicion that increasingly surrounds all persons of Mexican origin. But at the same time, the Mexican-Americans are as attracted to the idea of chain migration as other immigrant groups have been, and they are therefore reluctant to see steps taken that would significantly reduce migration from Mexico, legal or illegal. Since Congress has recently imposed on prospective immigrants from Mexico and the other countries of the Western Hemisphere the same annual per country limitation of 20,000 as has been imposed on countries of the Eastern Hemisphere since 1965, the number of visas available for legal immigration from Mexico will almost certainly decline.[139] Under these circumstances, and given the perception by many Mexican-Americans that much of the alarm about illegal immigration is racially motivated, it may be difficult to enlist the Mexican-American community in a drive to expel all illegal aliens and close the border to any further entries.

In the effort to explain why Congress has so far failed to come to grips with the difficult questions in this area, a factor that deserves some consideration is the traditional unwillingness of the federal judiciary to play any sort of active role in policy-making in this area. In the classic statement by Mr. Justice Frankfurter, the immigration policy of the United States "has been a political policy, belonging to the political branch of the Government wholly outside the concern and the competence of the Judiciary."[140] The Court has acted on the assumption that

> the determination of a selective and exclusionary immigration policy was for the Congress and not for the Judiciary. The conditions for entry of every alien, the particular classes of aliens that shall be denied entry altogether, the basis for determining such classification, the right to terminate hospitality to aliens, the grounds on which such determination shall be based, have been recognized as matters solely for the responsibility of the Congress and wholly outside the power of the Court to control.[141]

Pursuant to this policy of deference the Court has shown extraordinary reluctance to subject Congressional policies in this area to constitutional scrutiny. But what is perhaps more costly from the standpoint of enhancing the process of policy-making is the Court's insistence, in interpreting statutes in this area, on playing a role so deferential to Congress that it has never engaged with Congress in the kind of dialog that might improve the Congressional decision-making process. Obviously, the role of the federal Judiciary in areas of federal statutory law is generally limited. The courts do not under ordinary circumstances have the responsibility for the making of policy in the first instance. But the task of interpreting statutory rules requires courts to look behind the literal language of those rules and consider the purposes on which they rest. By means of this kind of analysis the courts have often asked questions that Congress had not considered and thereby brought difficult issues out into the open. Their decisions have often provided Congress with a framework for considering these issues and a vocabulary that can bring some precision to the task of resolving them. This is not to suggest that in the guise of interpreting federal statutes the courts have routinely arrogated to themselves the power to resolve hard questions that Congress has not considered or to substitute their own judgment for the decision of the legislative body, though surely there have been instances where precisely that has occurred. So long as the courts do not ground their decisions on constitutional principles, their interpretations and applications of federal statutory law do not preclude legislative correction. On the contrary, by making explicit the premises upon which the legislature has seemed to act, the courts invite a legislative response and in many instances improve the quality of that response by offering the legislature some indication of what precisely is involved. While continuing to play a subordinate role, the federal courts have nonetheless managed to bring some order to difficult areas and to improve the process of congressional decision-making by clarifying the issues and encouraging Congress to face up to the ramifications of its decisions. It is hard to think of any area of federal statutory law where the federal courts have done less in this regard than the area of immigration. And there seems hardly any area where the need has been greater.

In short, Congress has not yet come to grips with the hard questions posed by illegal immigration, perhaps in part because the courts have done so little to sharpen the issues and facilitate their resolution. However those issues ought to be resolved, two things seem clear. First, the issues should be brought out into the open and confronted squarely so that they will no longer be decided by default. Second, a mood of hysteria about illegal immigration can only confuse the situation and impair the ability of Congress and the public to consider the issues on their merits. With the aid of more and better information about the problem[142] and informed public discussion of the issues involved, it may at last be possible to put the problem in its proper perspective and make the hard choices that have not yet been made.

## NOTES

1. Although United States citizens have enjoyed a statutory right of voluntary expatriation since passage of the Act of July 27, 1868, c. 249, 15 Stat. 223, Congress did provide in the Act of March 2, 1907, c. 2534, §2, 34 Stat. 1228, that no citizen could

expatriate himself when the United States was at war. See 39 Op. Atty. Gen. 474 (1940). The limitation on the right was repealed in 1940.

2. The year 1875 is generally considered the watershed that separates the encouragement of immigration from its restriction. By the Act of March 3, 1875, 18 Stat. 477, Congress imposed the first qualitative restrictions on immigration by barring the entry of convicts and prostitutes. More sweeping exclusions quickly followed. See generally C. Gordon and H. Rosenfield, *Immigration Law and Procedure* §§1.1–1.4d (rev. ed. 1976).

3. Although the immigration statutes now provide that "[n]o person shall receive any preference or priority or be discriminated against in the issuance of an immigrant visa because of his nationality, place of birth, or place of residence," they also declare that "the total number of immigrant visas . . . made available to natives of any single foreign state . . . shall not exceed 20,000 in any fiscal year." 8 U.S.C. §1152(a). The per-country limitation, which originally applied only in the Eastern Hemisphere but was extended to the Western Hemisphere by the Act of October 20, 1976, 90 Stat. 2703, discussed infra, at pp. 345–47, 352–54, does have the effect of delaying the granting of visas to certain applicants because the annual quota for their country is already oversubscribed.

4. 8 U.S.C. §1182(a)(14).

5. N. Morris and G. Hawkins, *The Honest Politician's Guide to Crime Control* 232 (paperback ed. 1974).

6. Ibid., quoting from G. Allport, *The Nature of Prejudice* (1954).

7. See, e.g., J. Higham, *Strangers in the Land* (rev. ed. 1963); M. Konvitz, *The Alien and the Asiatic in American Law* 8–10 (1946); Keely, "Immigration: Considerations on Trends, Prospects, and Policy," 181, in 1 Commission on Population Growth and the American Future, *Demographic and Social Aspects of Population Growth* (1972); cf. Chew Heong v. United States, 112 U.S. 536, 565–67 (Field, J., dissenting).

8. N. Morris and G. Hawkins, supra note 5, at 205.

9. United States v. Martinez-Fuerte, 428 U.S. 543, 572 (1976) (Brennan, J., dissenting):

> Every American citizen of Mexican ancestry and every Mexican alien lawfully in this country must know after today's decision that he travels the fixed checkpoint highways at the risk of being subjected not only to a stop, but also to detention and interrogation, both prolonged and to an extent far more than for non-Mexican appearing motorists.

Cf. United States v. Brignoni-Ponce, 422 U.S. 873, 875 (1975), where the Government maintained that "trained officers can recognize the characteristic appearance of persons who live in Mexico, relying on such factors as the mode of dress and haircut." Id., at 885. The Court concluded there that the officers did not have reasonable suspicion to stop the car in question, and held that "[t]he likelihood that any given person of Mexican ancestry is an alien is high enough to make Mexican appearance a relevant factor, but standing alone it does not justify stopping all Mexican-Americans to ask if they are aliens." Id., at 886–87.

10. *Cf.* H. R. Report No. 94-506, 94th Cong., 1st Sess. 39 (1975) (dissenting views of Reps. Drinan, Badillo, Conyers, Edwards). The Bar Association of the City of New York, along with a considerable number of other organizations, has opposed legislation that would punish employers for hiring illegal aliens in part because of the danger that "[e]nactment of penalties will result in discrimination against persons with foreign appearance, foreign sounding names, and persons who do not speak English (this was the experience when the Dixon-Arnet Law which was in effect in the State of California before being declared unconstitutional as being solely within the Federal prerogative. . . .)." Hearings Before the Subcomm. on Immigration, Citizenship and Int'l. Law of the House Comm. on the Judiciary, 94th Cong., 1st Sess., Serial No. 8, at 410 (1975) (hereafter 1975 Hearings). Subsequent to that testimony the Supreme Court reversed the decision of the California Supreme Court and held the California statute constitutional. DeCanas v. Bica, 424 U.S. 351 (1976). The statute will presumably go back into effect.

11. For some examples of current statutory problems in the immigration area, see Gordon, "The Need to Modernize Our Immigration Laws," 13 *U. San. Diego L. Rev.* 1 (1975).

12. See S. Tomasi and C. Keely, *Whom Have We Welcomed?* 25, 33 (1975). Cf. 1975 Hearings, at 119. It took Congress from 1968 to 1976, with legislative proposals introduced and hearings held in the 90th through 94th Congresses, to pass a bill correcting several obvious and very serious defects in the 1965 scheme. The bill, P.L. 94-571, is discussed at pp. 345-47, 352-54 infra.

13. Each of these possible approaches has been seriously proposed. Frequently the proponent is very frank about the trade-off involved. See, e.g., American Enterprise Institute for Public Policy Research, *Proposals to Prohibit Employment of Illegal Aliens* 11 (1975), which quotes from a 1974 address by former Attorney General William B. Saxbe to the effect that with an additional $50 million and 2,200 employees, the INS could remove illegal aliens from one million jobs within a year. The INS has conducted an extensive campaign to educate the public about the seriousness of illegal immigration. See, e.g., 1975 Hearings, at 347; cf. id., at 408.

14. 428 U.S. 543 (1976).

15. J. Samora, *Los Mojados: The Wetback Story* 13–15 (1971); E. Galarza, *Merchants of Labor* 27–30 (paperback ed. 1964); C. McWilliams, *North from Mexico* 59–62 (1949).

16. See, e.g., 1975 Hearings, at 32 (testimony of Leonard F. Chapman, Jr., Comm'r, INS: 4–12 million).

17. Id., at 48 (testimony of Comm'r Chapman). With reference to the figure of 8 million, see id., at 32, and INS Press Release, December 8, 1975, referring to a study by outside contractors that arrived at that number. The Commissioner has conceded that the figure is nothing more than a very rough estimate—a figure chosen because it is mid-way between the high and low estimates. 1975 Hearings, at 32; Abrams and Abrams, "Immigration Policy—Who Gets In and Why?" 38 *Public Interest* 21 (Winter, 1975) (hereafter Abrams and Abrams). As for the validity of the findings by regional officials, an article from the *Washington Post*, Feb. 2, 1975, reproduced in 1975 Hearings, at 75, quotes an INS regional official as saying: "We just went through trying

to make an estimate. . . . I don't think any formula existed. I'm at a loss." And a public information officer quoted in that article declared: "There are formulas and there are formulas. But it sure isn't scientific."

18. The apprehension figures are included in each year's INS Annual Report. Although the figures for fiscal year 1976 have not yet been published, they were made available by Donald E. Furr, Chief of Statistics Branch, INS.

19. The annual percentage increases in apprehensions from fiscal year 1966 to fiscal year 1974 were 16%, 31%, 33%, 21%, 21%, 20%, 29%, 20%, as calculated from the figures provided in INS, Annual Report, 1975, Table 23, at 90 (1976). The number of apprehensions in fiscal year 1975 was 2.7% lower than the year earlier. The figure jumped 14% in fiscal year 1976, but that is the lowest rate of increase for a decade. And the increase over 1974 is only 11%. The fiscal year 1976 figure includes apprehensions through June 30, 1976. With regard to the current year, the apprehension rate for July 1976, according to figures provided by Mr. Furr, was 24% higher than the rate for July 1975, but the rate for August 1976 was virtually identical to the rate for August 1975.

20. D. North and M. Houstoun, *The Characteristics and Role of Illegal Aliens in the U.S. Labor Market: An Exploratory Study*, U.S. Dep't. of Labor Research and Development Contract No. 20-11-74-21, at 13–15 (1976) (hereafter North and Houstoun). According to figures provided by Leonard Pulley, Budget Officer of the INS, the total number of authorized positions for the INS has increased from 7,058 in fiscal year 1964 to 9,451 for fiscal year 1977. The Border Patrol has increased from 1,434 positions in fiscal year 1964 to 2,009 for fiscal year 1977.

21. Tomasi and Keely, supra note 12, at 37, 57; INS, Annual Report, 1975, at 13 (1976). The INS has reported that in 1975 its Remotely Monitored Sensor System (RMSS) was extended to critical segments of all Border Patrol sections at the Mexican border. Ibid.

22. In 1975, 57% of all apprehensions were made within 72 hours of entry, another 15% within 4–30 days, and 16% within 1–6 months. Ibid.

23. North and Houstoun have reported that the Mexican illegal aliens they interviewed made, on the average, "a trip home every six months or so," North and Houstoun, at 86. Each re-entry obviously does not add to the total illegal alien population.

24. 8 U.S.C. §1326.

25. Of the 766,600 deportable aliens apprehended in fiscal year 1975, only 23,438 left under formal orders of deportation. INS, Annual Report, 1975, at 19 (1976). Commissioner Chapman has suggested that INS can no longer afford even to escort all apprehended illegal aliens out of the country. He reports that the Service has "with increasing frequency" had to turn illegal aliens loose "with a letter that tells them they must go home." 1975 Hearings, at 34.

26. J. Samora, supra note 15, at 65.

27. One might assume that most illegal entrants would lack a sufficient understanding of the penalty scheme to appreciate the reasons for concealing their identities. But these reasons do not come into play until the alien has been apprehended a second time and by then he may have considerable sophistication. In any event, it

does appear that apprehended aliens are careful to reveal little information about themselves to INS officials. Id., at 64–66.

28. *Washington Star-News,* Nov. 19, 1974, reprinted in 1975 Hearings, at 71. The INS has suggested on several occasions that the 800,000 illegal aliens apprehended represent only one out of three or four of those who attempt entry. By that theory the total number of entries would fall between 2.4 and 3.2 million. See 1975 Hearings, at 32, 76. In the same general range are reported estimates of 2–2.5 million un- detected entries per year, *U.S. News & World Report,* p. 27, Feb. 3, 1975, and 40,000 –60,000 entries per week. *New York Times,* p. 20, July 25, 1976. But a more recent report indicates that the Commissioner now estimates 500,000 to 1 million entries per year, *New York Times,* p. A12, Nov. 5, 1976. And at the end of 1975 the Service stated that the illegal alien population is "conservatively estimated to be increasing by more than 250,000 a year." INS Press Release, Dec. 8, 1975.

29. Testifying before Congress, then Acting Atty. Gen. Laurence Silberman pointed out that, whereas the House Subcommittee on Immigration estimated 1–2 million illegal aliens in 1973, the Justice Department's view as of February 1975, was that between 4 and 12 million were in the country. In 1975 the Supreme Court referred to INS reports that there might be "as many as 10 or 12 million" illegal aliens. United States v. Brignoni-Ponce, 422 U.S. 873, 878 (1975). In March 1976, Commis- sioner Chapman told a Senate Subcommittee: "Our latest estimate is about 6 million. We have got some outside estimates as high as 8 million, and I have heard other guesses as high as 12 million. My own view is it is on the order of 5-1/2 or 6 million." Hearings on S. 3074, Before the Subcomm. on Immigration & Naturalization of the Senate Comm. on the Judiciary, 94th Cong., 2d Sess., 28 (1976). The most recent INS estimates talk in terms of 6–8 million illegal aliens. See, e.g., *New York Times,* p. A12, Nov. 5, 1976.

30. See note 23 supra. The INS apparently believes that the illegal alien popula- tion turns over rapidly, at least in the sense that expelled illegal aliens promptly return to the United States. See, e.g., *New York Times,* p. 20, July 25, 1976; 1975 Hearings, at 34.

31. Bureau of the Census, Current Population Reports, Population Characteris- tics, Persons of Spanish Origin in the United States: March 1975, P-20, No. 290 (1976), at 20; Bureau of the Census, 1970 Census of Population, Subject Reports, Persons of Spanish Origin PC(2)-1C (1973), at 1.

32. Of the Spanish origin population in March 1975, 12.5%, or 1,400,250 persons, were under five years old and therefore not included in the 1970 figure. Current Population Reports, supra note 31, at 20. And during the five-year interval between the 1970 and 1975 reports the lawful immigration of Spanish origin persons was substantial. Mexico alone provided 319,359 immigrants. INS, Annual Report, 1975, at 64 (1976). Total immigration for the five-year period from the independent countries of the Western Hemisphere other than Canada amounted to almost 800,000 persons, id., at 64, although plainly not all of those persons are of Spanish origin.

33. Current Population Reports, supra note 31, at 20.

34. North and Houstoun, at 153–54 n. Commissioner Chapman has several times remarked that the Mexican labor force was 16 million in 1970, Chapman, "A Look at

Illegal Immigration: Causes & Impact on the United States," 13 *U. San Diego L. Rev.* 34, 40 (1975); 1975 Hearings, at 36, without asking how plausible it is to assume that one-fourth or one-half of that labor force might have moved to the United States.

35. "The Government has estimated that 85% of the aliens illegally in the country are from Mexico." United States v. Brignoni-Ponce, 422 U.S. 873, 879 (1975). See also, Hearings on S. 3074 Before the Subcomm. on Immigration & Naturalization of the Senate Comm. on the Judiciary, 94th Cong., 2d Sess. 28, 35 (1976); 1975 Hearings, at 76. Of the deportable aliens apprehended in fiscal year 1975, 89% were Mexicans. INS, Annual Report, 1975, at 13 (1976).

36. The State Department estimated the backlog at 298,690 as of January, 1976. H.R. Rep. No. 94–1553, 94th Cong., 2d Sess. 6 (1976).

37. H.R. Rep. No. 94–1553, 94th Cong., 2d Sess. 2 (1976) ("very limited consideration"); Hearings on H.R. 981 Before Subcomm. No. 1 of the House Comm. on the Judiciary, 93d Cong., 1st Sess. 39 ("a last-minute thought"), and 313 ("conceived in haste") (1973) (hereafter 1973 Hearings); Abrams, at 5 ("ceiling pulled from the air . . . no relationship to any principle at all"); Keely, supra note 7, at 184–86. As an indication of the conditional nature of the Western Hemisphere ceiling, it is worth noting that unlike the other provisions of the 1965 Act the 120,000 limitation was not even enacted as an amendment to the basic statute in this area, the Immigration and Nationality Act of 1952. See Act of Oct. 3, 1965, §21(e), 79 Stat. 921. The ceiling was finally incorporated in the 1952 Act by P.L. 94-571, discussed below.

38. Although the Administration and House bills would have retained the traditional policy of imposing no numerical limitation on Western Hemisphere immigration, their drafters were not indifferent to the number of persons entering from the Western Hemisphere. It was assumed, however, that the qualitative restrictions, in particular the stricter labor certification requirement, would keep the number under some control.

39. H.R. Rep. No. 94-1553, 94th Cong., 2d Sess. 2 (1976); 122 Cong. Rec. No. 149, Part II, at H-11683 (testimony of Rep. Fish) (September 29, 1976).

40. Select Comm'n. on Western Hemisphere Immigration, Report 9-11 (1968).

41. 8 U.S.C. §1151(b).

42. INS, Annual Report, 1975, at 6 (1976).

43. Act of Nov. 2, 1966, 80 Stat. 1161, 8 U.S.C. §1255, note.

44. Select Comm'n., supra note 40, at 13–14.

45. INS, Annual Report, 1975, at 11 (1976).

46. The State Department "strongly support[ed]" the Select Commission's view that Cuban adjustments should not be counted toward the ceiling, and pointed out that "qualified applicants from other countries of the Western Hemisphere have suffered because of special provisions for Cuban refugees whose entry into the United States was sought and encouraged by the United States Government for political and humanitarian reasons outside the field of immigration policy." H.R. Rep. No. 94-1553, 94th Cong., 2d Sess. 25–26 (1976).

47. Act of October 20, 1976, 90 Stat. 2703.

48. The effect of the change should be substantial, as it should make available an additional 20,000 to 25,000 visas for Western Hemisphere immigrants each year for the next several years. H.R. Rep. No. 94-1553, 94th Cong., 2d Sess. 12 (1976).

49. Id., at 3.

50. Ibid., quoting from Comm'n. on Population Growth and the American Future, *Population & the American Future* 117 (1972).

51. Keely, supra note 7, at 184.

52. Comm'n., supra note 50, at 114.

53. Id., at 117.

54. Ibid.

55. Editorial from the *Washington Evening Star,* read by Rep. Joshua Eilberg at hearings held in 1973. 1973 Hearings, at 81. Any effort to determine the demographic implications of immigration would surely have to rely on net figures—immigration less emigration. But the Census Bureau has not collected data on emigration since 1957, 1975 Hearings, at 260, and policy-making without such data, as the Commission on Population Growth recognized, is very difficult. Comm'n., supra note 50, at 115. See also 1 Comm'n. on Population Growth & the American Future, *Demographic & Social Aspects of Population Growth* 175–76 (1972).

56. H.R. Rep., supra note 48, at 3.

57. See, e.g., 1975 Hearings, at 123 (chart showing type and location of jobs that could be opened up by removing illegal aliens); Hearings on S. 3074 Before the Subcomm. on Immigration & Naturalization of the Senate Comm. on the Judiciary, 94th Cong., 2d Sess. 28 (1976) (at least one million jobs and perhaps as many as 3–4 million).

58. See, e.g., 1975 Hearings, at 32, 122, 342. Cf. INS Press Release, Dec. 8, 1975, at 4 (letter to INS from ICF Inc.).

59. See North and Houstoun, at 150–51; Abrams and Abrams, at 22; Chapman, "A Look at Illegal Immigration: Causes and Impact on the United States," 13 *U. San Diego L. Rev.* 34, 37–39 (1975).

60. See note 35 supra. Of the 766,600 deportable aliens apprehended in 1975, 667,689 or 87% had entered without inspection. And 99% of the surreptitious entries, 661,997, were made across the Mexican border. Almost all of those who entered without inspection—654,836 out of a total of 667,689—were Mexicans. INS, Annual Report, 1975, at 13 (1976).

61. E.g., 1975 Hearings, at 171–72 (Rep. Richard C. White); 398 (Rep. Abraham Kazen, Jr.); cf. id., at 193; *U.S. News & World Report* 30, Feb. 3, 1975.

62. 1975 Hearings, at 424–25.

63. North and Houstoun, at 162–63.

64. Id., at 165.

65. Ibid. See also 1975 Hearings, at 409; Abrams and Abrams, at 26. One common suggestion is that unemployed U.S. workers are unwilling to do the work that illegal aliens now do because they "can receive as much compensation to sustain themselves by doing no work and drawing food stamps, welfare payments, or unemployment payments." 1975 Hearings, at 171 (testimony of Rep. White).

66. 8 U.S.C. §1153.

67. Abrams and Abrams, at 14.

68. At hearings in March 1973, Rep. Eilberg told Barbara M. Watson, Administrator of the State Department's Bureau of Security and Consular Affairs: "I trust you

will take this message back to the Secretary of State. I am particularly disturbed because it appears that the United States has developed no policy or principle regarding immigration to the United States from the Western Hemisphere. I might add that the Department has certainly had sufficient time to formulate a precise, definite policy." 1973 Hearings, at 55.

69. 8 U.S.C. §1182(a)(14).

70. Under the 1965 scheme labor certification was not required of the parents, spouses, and children of citizens and permanent resident aliens. Id. "In 1972, it is estimated that only 11.7 percent of all immigrants were required to get labor certifications." Abrams and Abrams, at 19. See also 1975 Hearings, at 118.

71. Most of the illegal aliens probably do not have relatives who are citizens or permanent residents and who could thus make possible their entry as preference immigrants. Of the apprehended Mexican aliens surveyed by North and Houstoun, 31.6% had one or more relatives in the United States, with "relatives" defined as spouse, children, parents, and siblings. North and Houstoun, at 83.

72. H.R. Rep. No. 94-1553, 94th Cong., 2d Sess. 11 (1976).

73. 1973 Hearings, at 173 (testimony of Jack Wasserman). See also H.R. Rep. No. 93-461, 93d Cong., 1st Sess. 13 (1973); Gordon, "The Need to Modernize Our Immigration Laws," 13 *U. San Diego L. Rev.* 1, 12–13 (1975); 1975 Hearings, at 119; 1973 Hearings, at 193–94.

74. See 1975 Hearings, at 128.

75. A. Fragomen, *The Illegal Alien: Criminal or Economic Refugee?* 17–18 (1973); 1973 Hearings, at 174–75; Abrams and Abrams, at 26. Of the illegal aliens surveyed by North and Houstoun, three quarters "had been working in Schedule B occupations in their most recent U.S. job." North and Houstoun, at 111. Schedule B is the list of occupations for which the Labor Department always denies certification on the grounds that U.S. workers are available.

The certification requirement in the 1965 Act required the Secretary of Labor to certify that "there are not sufficient workers in the United States who are able, willing, qualified, and available ... at the place to which the alien is destined to perform such skilled or unskilled labor." 8 U.S.C. §1182(a)(14). By a 1976 amendment Congress deleted the phrase "in the United States," P.L. 94-571, §5, Oct. 20, 1976, to "emphasize the intent that the Secretary of Labor certify on the basis of whether there are sufficient workers 'at the place' where the alien is going rather than in the United States as a whole." H.R. Rep. No. 94-1553, 94th Cong., 2d Sess. 14 (1976).

76. Prospective immigrants who are "members of the professions" or who have "exceptional ability in the sciences or the arts" and who have sought entry under the third preference, 8 U.S.C. §1153(a)(3), have been required to obtain labor certification, but the 1965 Act did not require them to obtain a specific job offer as the basis for the certification. Under the 1976 amendments, P.L. 94-571, §4(2), Oct. 20, 1976, they can no longer obtain certification without a job offer.

77. Abrams and Abrams, at 14–15.

78. P.L. 94-571, §4, Oct. 20, 1976, amending 8 U.S.C. §1153.

79. In addition to the change described in note 76 supra, Congress loosened the requirements for certification of members of the teaching profession and those with

exceptional ability in the arts and sciences, P.L. 94-571, §5, Oct. 20, 1976, amending 8 U.S.C. §1182(a)(14), because of what the Subcommittee termed a "too rigid" interpretation of the law on this point by the Labor Department. H.R. Rep. No. 94-1553, 94th Cong., 2d Sess. 11 (1976).

80. The statutory scheme defines seven preference categories and one nonpreference category. Four of the preference categories involve relatives, and Congress has reserved for these categories 74% of the available visas. The three preference categories not involving relatives (professionals, skilled workers and refugees) get 26% of the visas. Nonpreference immigrants get whatever visas are not used by applicants in one of the preference categories. See 8 U.S.C. §1153(a).

81. See Abrams and Abrams, at 12.

82. North and Houstoun, at 8.

83. Abrams and Abrams, at 16; 34 Cong. Quarterly 3008 (Oct. 16, 1976). Backlogs have developed in the third preference category—professionals—because of very heavy demand in the Philippines. But given the availability of visas in the sixth preference category (skilled workers) and the nonpreference category, many persons entitled to classification in the third preference category have found it easier to enter as skilled workers or even nonpreference immigrants. Bureau of Security & Consular Affairs, Department of State, 1974 Report of the Visa Office 9–10 (1975).

84. INS, Annual Report, 1975, at 90 (1976). See note 19 supra.

85. Abrams and Abrams, at 22. See also 1975 Hearings, at 390.

86. See J. Levy, *Cesar Chavez: Autobiography of La Causa* 129–30 (1975); 2 G. Gordon and C. Rosenfield, *Immigration Law & Procedure* §6.9 (1976); President's Comm'n. on Migratory Labor, Migratory Labor in American Agriculture 56–63 (1951).

87. 1975 Hearings, at 193, 210; *U.S. News & World Report* 30, February 3, 1975.

88. North and Houstoun, at 2.

89. Cf. Scott v. Sandford, 60 U.S. (19 How.) 393, 404 (1857), holding that Dred Scott could not be a citizen.

90. C. McWilliams, supra note 15, at 61.

91. J. Samora, supra note 15, at 34–37.

92. Act of August 3, 1882, 22 Stat. 214.

93. Ibid.

94. Act of Feb. 26, 1885, 23 Stat. 332.

95. Act of Feb. 5, 1917, 39 Stat. 874.

96. C. McWilliams, supra note 15, at 60. See also President's Comm'n., supra note 86, at 37.

97. M. Gamio, *Mexican Immigration to the United States* 3 (1969).

98. Immigration Comm'n., Abstract of Reports, S. Doc. No. 747, 61st Cong., 3d Sess. 682 (1911).

99. Ibid.

100. Chinese laborers were excluded from the United States by a series of Acts, beginning with the Act of May 6, 1882, 22 Stat. 58. The exclusion was repealed in 1943. Act of Dec. 17, 1943, 57 Stat. 600. See generally M. Konvitz, *Civil Rights in Immigration* 1–4 (1953).

101. Immigration Comm'n., supra note 98, at 684. The Commission found that Mexican laborers were brought in to "make good the deficiency of Chinese and white men available for unskilled work." Id., at 685.

102. Id., at 691.

103. Id., at 690–91.

104. Act of Feb. 5, 1917, §3, Proviso 9, 39 Stat. 878: "*Provided further,* The Commissioner General of Immigration with the Approval of the Secretary of Labor shall give rules and prescribe conditions, including exaction of such bonds as may be necessary, to control and regulate the admission of otherwise inadmissible aliens applying for temporary admission. . . ."

105. Subcomm. No. 1, House Comm. on the Judiciary, Study of Population and Immigration Problems, Special Series No. 11, at 27 (1963); President's Comm'n., supra note 86, at 37.

106. Saxbe v. Bustos, 419 U.S. 65, 85 n. 6 (1974) (White, J., dissenting); J. Samora, supra note 15, at 35.

107. Id., at 40; Cardenas, "United States Immigration Policy Toward Mexico: An Historical Perspective," 2 *Chicano L. Rev.* 66, 73–74 (1975).

108. President's Comm'n., supra note 86, at 37.

109. Study of Population and Immigration Problems, supra note 105, at 27; J. Samora, supra note 15, at 40–43; Cardenas, supra note 107, at 73.

110. President's Comm'n., supra note 86, at 37.

111. Ibid.

112. Mexicans were brought in to do railroad track work from 1943 to 1946. More than 130,000 workers were admitted under that program. Study of Population & Immigration Problems, supra note 105, at 144–45. After that time workers were admitted only to do agricultural work. On the history of the bracero program generally, see id., at 27–48; Select Comm'n. on Western Hemisphere Immigration, Report 91–93 (1968); E. Galarza, supra note 15; F. Auerbach, *Immigration Laws of the United States* 499–502 (2d ed. 1961).

113. Study of Population & Immigration Problems, supra note 105, at 33.

114. Act of July 12, 1951, 65 Stat. 119, amending Act of Oct. 31, 1949, c. 792, 63 Stat. 1051.

115. J. Samora, supra note 15, at 44–46; Cardenas, supra note 107, at 80.

116. See, e.g., E. Galarza, supra note 15, at 69–70; Cardenas, supra note 107, at 81.

117. Select Comm'n. on Western Hemisphere Immigration, Report 93 (1968). The effort to expel illegal aliens was also apparently responsible for an increase in the number of Mexican citizens seeking permanent resident status. Subcomm. No. 1, House Comm. on the Judiciary, Study of Population & Immigration Problems, Special Series No. 9, at 7, 34 (1963).

118. H.R. Rep. No. 93-461, 93d Cong., 1st Sess. 10 (1973). See also 1975 Hearings, at 50.

119. North and Houstoun, at 151. See also id., at 76–78, 82; J. Samora, supra note 15, at 90–91.

120. H.R. Rep. No. 93-461, 93d Cong., 1st Sess. 10 (1973). See also Study of Popula-

tion & Immigration Problems, supra note 117, at 14; cf. INS, Annual Report, 1975, at 117 (1976). Although Canadians also have a fairly low rate of naturalization, proximity to one's native land is clearly not the only explanation for a low naturalization rate in the case of Mexicans. See C. McWilliams, supra note 15, at 220: "Hedged in by group hostility, the [Mexican] immigrants long ago lost interest in citizenship. Lack of funds, the language difficulty, and illiteracy were important factors but not nearly as influential as segregation and discrimination. Mexicans have never been encouraged, by prevailing community attitudes, to become citizens." Indeed, until 1940 it was not altogether clear that Mexicans were eligible for citizenship as "free white persons." See M. Konvitz, supra note 7, at 96–97 and note 47.

121. Cf. Immigration Comm'n., supra note 98, at 41: The "immigration of [the Mexican] race correspond[s] somewhat to some of the southern and eastern European races coming to the eastern States. This resemblance lies chiefly in the fact that they as a rule do not come as settlers, but as a transient and migratory unskilled labor supply." See also id., at 691–92 (Japanese and Chinese).

122. Cardenas, supra note 107, at 74.

123. See Study of Population & Immigration Problems, supra note 117, at 49–50: Allen B. Moreland, Director of the Visa Office of the State Department's Bureau of Security and Consular Affairs, testified that "we have only two countries in Latin America where there is what we could call an administrative waiting list. One is Mexico and the other is the Dominican Republic. Mexico, of course, has the greatest number of people waiting in line. The waiting list in Santo Domingo is getting down to manageable proportions. But in Mexico we had 177,058 people waiting at the close of business on March 31, 1963." By contrast, Canadians, who were also permitted to enter without numerical limitation, could obtain immigrant visas with virtually no delay because of the absence of an administrative waiting list. Id., at 62.

124. 1973 Hearings, at 72.

125. Samora points out that during the last 100 years approximately 1.5 million Mexicans were admitted to the United States as legal immigrants, whereas 5,050,093 Mexicans came as nonimmigrant temporary workers from 1942 to 1968 and 5,628,712 illegal Mexican aliens were apprehended from 1924 to 1969. See also North and Houstoun, at 9. Although the figure for temporary workers and illegal aliens does not accurately reflect the total number of different individuals involved, the ratio of workers to settlers is still striking. Over the last several years the number of deportable Mexican aliens apprehended by the INS each year has been approximately 10 times the number of Mexicans entering the United States as immigrants each year.

While the immigration laws seem generally to have facilitated the entry of Mexicans as nonimmigrants, the very controversial commuter program appears at first glance to point in the opposite direction. Under the program, a great many citizens of Mexico and a much smaller number of Canadians enter the United States each day to work even though they continue to reside in their native countries. For a time the immigration service treated the commuters as nonimmigrants, but it has classified them as immigrants since 1927. For the history of the program, see Saxbe v. Bustos, 419 U.S. 65 (1974). In fact, the commuter program is consistent with the over-all pattern. The commuters have a right of permanent residence in the United States, but because they do not in fact reside in the United States they do not accumulate the years of residence needed to permit their naturalization. Moreover, perhaps because the commuters' retention of immigrant status depends on their keeping their jobs, the Mexican commuters (though apparently not the Canadians) are "subject to feelings of profound insecurity." North and Houstoun, at A-3. See also INS, Annual Report, 1975, at 8–9 (1976), which points out that while the commuters hold the same type of identifying card as conventional immigrants (I-151), the commuters' card is specially grommeted. The annual report describes the service's effort to check the commuters in order to make sure that they have not "abandoned status" by losing or giving up their U.S. jobs.

126. Apparently at the insistence of the Government of Mexico, which feared that illegal immigration would undermine its effort to control the working conditions of braceros in the United States, the government cracked down on illegal immigration in the late 1940s. See Stoddard, "Illegal Mexican Labor in the Borderlands: Institutionalized Support of an Unlawful Practice," 19 *Pac. Sociol. Rev.* 175, 184–85 (1976). The principal effect of the crackdown was the legalization of illegal aliens. Thousands were taken to the border and then instantly readmitted, this time as lawful nonimmigrant workers. See President's Comm'n., supra note 86, at 52–54; Study of Population & Immigration Problems, supra note 105, at 8; J. Samora, supra note 15, at 47–48; E. Galarza, supra note 15, at 63–69.

127. Stoddard, supra note 126, at 202–3. Cf. 8 U.S.C. §1324(a), the so-called Texas Proviso, which provides that for the purposes of the statutory section making it a crime willingly or knowingly to harbor an illegal alien, "employment (including the usual and normal practices incident to employment) shall not be deemed to constitute harboring."

128. J. Samora, supra note 15, at 48–49; North and Houstoun, at 14.

129. Editorial, Nov. 28, 1952, quoted in M. Konvitz, supra note 100, at 111.

130. North and Houstoun, at 168. See also 1975 Hearings, at 324–25, 391; J. Samora, supra note 15, at 40–55.

131. President's Comm'n., supra note 86, at 75.

132. Id., at 78.

133. Id., at 20.

134. North and Houstoun, at 169. Cf. Berger, "Those Convenient Migrants: Europe's Expendable Work Force," *The Nation* 369, Oct. 18, 1975.

135. See, e.g., J. Samora, supra note 15, at 91; Subcomm. No. 1, House Comm. on the Judiciary, Study of Population and Immigration Problems, Special Series No. 5, at 65 (1963).

136. *Washington Star-News,* Nov. 18, 1974, reprinted in 1975 Hearings, at 68; Cardenas, supra note 107, at 86.

137. The United States does have a program for the admission of temporary foreign workers, but that program permits the use of foreign workers only for work that is temporary in nature. See C. Gordon and H. Rosenfeld, *Immigration Law & Procedure* §2.14a(2) (rev. ed. 1976). Under its present form the program involves the entry of approximately 40,000 persons per year, including approximately 10,000 agri-

cultural workers. Almost all of the farm workers come from the Caribbean Islands. Commenting on a recent Congressional proposal to drop the requirement that the work be temporary in nature, the State Department noted that "an important purpose of this proposal is to facilitate the importation of seasonal farm workers, especially for employment in the Southwest," and added that it "would open the way for establishment of a system of importation of temporary foreign labor for nonagricultural employment not unlike the German 'guest worker' system." H.R. Rep. No. 94-1553, 94th Cong., 2d Sess. 21 (1976). The Department indicated that it had reservations about the proposal and urged that "the experience of European countries with this system and the social implications of its establishment in the United States be very carefully examined and considered before final action is taken on this proposal." The bill that Congress eventually enacted, P.L. 94-571, discussed earlier, did not include this controversial feature.

138. 1975 Hearings, at 325 (testimony of Manuel Fierro, Nat'l Congress of Hispanic-American Citizens); J. Samora, supra note 15, at 130; cf. 1975 Hearings, at 82–83; Select Comm'n., supra note 117, at 106–7.

139. Not counting immediate relatives, to whom the per-country ceiling will not apply, 42,218 citizens of Mexico entered as immigrants in fiscal year 1975. The application of the 20,000 ceiling will thus work a very substantial reduction in lawful immigration. See H.R. Rep. No. 93-461, 93d Cong., 1st Sess. 49 (additional views of Rep. Rodino); cf. Bonaparte, "The Rodino Bill: An Example of Prejudice Toward Mexican Immigration to the United States," 2 *Chicano L. Rev.* 40 (1975).

140. Harisiades v. Shaughnessy, 342 U.S. 580, 596 (Frankfurter, J., concurring).

141. Id., at 596–97.

142. In November, 1975, the INS announced plans for a series of surveys by outside contractors to determine how many illegal aliens are present in the United States and what their impact is on the American economy and labor force. The surveys will cost $1 million.

# [ 17 ]

Migration: An Economist's View

THEODORE W. SCHULTZ

How useful is the distinction between voluntary and involuntary migration? Although these two concepts are not defined explicitly in the papers presented here, it is fair to say that historians view most migrations over the ages as having been involuntary. According to this interpretation, people migrated because they were forced to do so by governments, or by events associated with wars and their aftermath, or by adverse natural events, e.g., crop failures and famines. Other analysts see the massive migration that occurred following the partition of India, the expulsion of non-Africans following the independence of the African nation states, and the recent migrations throughout the Middle East following the establishment of Israel, as consequences of colonialism, consistent with Marxian thought. These perceptions of migration are deemed to be involuntary; this approach treats people as pawns of government, of adverse events, and of colonialism.

From the point of view of economic behavior, it is useful to classify the actual and potential behavior of migrants as follows. The first category consists of those people who are compelled to migrate against their own self-interest, or who are not allowed to change their occupation or the location in which they live, although it would be in their self-interest to do so. Accordingly, this category includes potential migrants who are not permitted by their government to migrate either within the country in which they live or to another country. The term "involuntary" is applicable to this type of behavior. It should be noted, however, that if people are free to migrate, and

377

if they migrate because of crop failures and famine, the consequent migration is not involuntary in terms of self-interest, namely the self-interest of survival. The second category encompasses migrants who are free to leave the country in which they reside but who face various legal restrictions imposed by the country to which they prefer to migrate. It is in the self-interest of this category to migrate, provided the legal restrictions on entry do not negate fully the potential advantages of residing in and becoming citizens of the country. In the third category are people who are free to choose their occupations and their places of residence in accordance with their self-interest, whether they are immigrants or citizens.

The concept of involuntary migration is applicable to the American-Japanese who were forced to leave California during World War II, to the Germans who were expelled from parts of Eastern Europe following the war, to most of the Arabs who formerly lived in what is now Israel, to the Europeans and Indians who have been expelled by various African countries, and to the massive forced relocation of various ethnic populations within the Soviet Union. While these are all examples of recent forced migrations, history is replete with circumstances where some people were confined to a particular occupation or a given location, and other circumstances where particular people were forced to leave the country. The concept of involuntary behavior applies to all such circumstances.

What then can economic analysis add to the interpretation of migration? If people have no choice in determining where they live and what they do for a living, there obviously is no economic behavior that can be attributed to migration. It could be true that despite the large number of economic studies of migration, what they contribute is of minor importance in explaining most of the history of migration. Whether or not this is true is an issue that will not be pursued in this paper. The objectives of this paper are: (1) to indicate the effects of differences in the political economy on migration and (2) to examine migration during peaceful times when people are essentially free to migrate to improve their economic lot in satisfaction of their own preferences.


EFFECTS OF POLITICAL ECONOMY

The political and economic order has strong implications for migration. I shall comment briefly on the mercantile economy that preceded 1776, on the liberalized economy that replaced mercantilism, and then on the neo-mercantile types that have emerged since the turn of the century, mainly following World War I. There are now some indications that a neo-liberalism is emerging. In explaining these institutional developments, one following the other, it is argued that what people do privately and collectively over time is a consequence of the interactions between social, political, and economic ideas and the institutionalized order. The ideas under consideration here are those that shape social thought. When they prevail, they determine the social, political, and economic institutionalized order. These ideas are of two historical types: those that rationalize and contribute to the codification of the prevailing order, and those that arise in protest against the established order and then become embodied in social thought, eventually becoming strong enough to induce a real alteration in the prevailing institutions.[1]

The mercantile economy that prevailed for at least a century, for example in England, prior to 1776 was buttressed by the established Church and by the law. It was also rationalized by the economic "literature" of that period, which provided support for governmental restrictions on trade, on internal prices and wages, and on migration. The mercantile economy called for low wages, and one of the means of maintaining low wages was to place restrictions on out-migration.

In retrospect, the utility-of-poverty doctrine of that period is startling. The doctrine held sway in England for a century, during which the poverty of the lower classes was thought to be desirable. Between 1660 and 1776, English mercantilism produced an intricate system of foreign and domestic policies, and it sought to rationalize the utility of poverty. Edgar S. Furniss, in his prize-winning essay, devotes a long chapter to "The Doctrine of the Utility of Poverty." The beliefs of illustrious individuals of that period seem novel to us. Thomas Mun's view was that "penury and want do make a people wise and industrious." Arthur Young asserted that "everyone but an idiot knows that the lower classes must be kept poor or they will never be industrious." John Law argued that "laborers were to blame for recurring high prices because of their 'insufferable' habits of idleness contracted when food was cheap." William Petty joined in this chorus. It was thought that there should be taxes on consumption and that out-migration should be curtailed. Charity was considered the nursery of idleness. Since a larger population would keep the laborers poor, immigration should be encouraged. In support of the doctrine of the utility of poverty, George Berkeley, Bishop of Cloyne, proposed to reward parents of large families and to tax families with no children.[2]

Liberalism was in large part a protest against the adverse social and economic effects of mercantilism. The basic ideas of liberalism gradually developed into a strong, internally consistent body of social thought, and over time liberal political and social institutions replaced mercantile institutions. The year 1776 has become a convenient birth date for liberal thought. *The Wealth of Nations,* often referred to as the bible of economics, carries this date. The argument of Adam Smith rests on the proposition that in an open, competitive economy unfettered by private and public monopolies and supported by a political order in which governmental functions are greatly restricted, individuals, responding in their economic activities to their own diverse self-interests, will maximize the social product. The economics advanced by Smith became an integral part of the core of liberal social thought that profoundly altered the institutionalized functions of government over the following decades.

In Adam Smith's economy there is no room for the utility-of-poverty doctrine. The utility that matters is that revealed by what people do in serving their own self-interests. Smith's argument for an open, competitive market implies free trade and a free labor-market paying wages that are not fixed or restricted by government. It also implies that people are free to migrate from farms to towns and to leave the country if they choose to do so. Migration boomed in response to changes in institutions and to the economic opportunities associated with economic growth and the related growth in population, which in turn also induced migration. Even in backward Russia, there is August von Haxthausen's[3] account of his 1843 tour, in which he cites the liberal approach of the Russian government in according opportunities to the Mennonites and Hutterites.

The liberal political economy, in turn, gave rise to protests and dissent calling for a political and economic order in which the functions of government were even more pervasive than they had been under the mercantilism that preceded the era of economic liberalism. It was in this context that there arose a form of neo-mercantilism, ranging from centrally planned economic development to a system of command economics. The ideas that emerged from these protests called for various forms of socialism prior to those of Karl Marx. The contributions of Marx, however, came to dominate the political and economic foundations of socialism. The response to Marxian ideas has greatly altered the institutions of many nation-states, and as noted, the economic functions of the governments of these states are much enlarged.

An essential part of the argument for neo-mercantilism is that an open competitive system is blind and that the self-interests of individuals must be directed and controlled in order to achieve efficiency and equity in economic development. Controlled migration is one of the instruments of neo-mercantilism used by a government in achieving its neo-mercantilist goals.

There are now signs of a nascent neo-liberalism emerging. Because of the dependency of neo-mercantilism on a vast increase in the functions of government, which in some countries consists of extreme authoritarian nation-states, and because of the now widely observed adverse effects that the governments of these states have on personal freedom, protests akin to those of two centuries ago are once again the order of the day.

These cycles of protest and dissent and the rise and fall of liberal and mercantile social thought raise doubts about their respective underlying assumptions and theories. Economic history reveals four major developments that are not at home in either of the two long-established theories pertaining to economic processes and behavior. The first of these developments is contrary to the implications of both classical and Marxian economics. The implications are that over time Ricardian rent becomes an increasing share of personal income; in fact, the income share and the associated social and political influence of landlords have declined markedly. In the high-income countries, landlords have gradually faded away, and they are also on the decline in low-income countries. Second, contrary to Marx and not anticipated in classical theory, changes over time in the functional distribution of income have had a major effect in reducing inequality in the personal distribution of income. Third, given the imprint of Malthus, until very recently theory has been silent on the economics of the decline in fertility in high-income countries. Fourth, and most important, neither classical economic theory nor the economic theory of socialism explains the development that accounts for the extraordinary rise in the value of human time: in the United States, for example, real hourly wages increased more than fivefold from 1900 to 1972. It is obvious that the observed high price of the services of labor cannot be explained by a theory of subsistence wages or by a theory of labor exploitation. Although a very large share of national income accrues to labor (in the United States about 80 percent), Marx's labor theory of value is of no avail. Laborers have become *capitalists* as a consequence of the value of their own human capital. Human capital consists of useful abilities that people acquire by investing in themselves. This acquisition entails expenditures and the value of one's own time for the purpose of enhancing one's own future earnings and future satisfactions; thus, by means of such investments, the formation of human capital occurs.

In general, mercantile political-economic institutions seek to control migration in achieving economic development; liberal institutions tend to favor the self-interest of migrants but with increasing legal restrictions designed to protect the value of the human capital of laborers in high-income countries.

## ECONOMICS OF MIGRATION UNDER LIBERAL ECONOMIC CONDITIONS

When migrants have the opportunity to respond to their self-interest, the predominant reason that people migrate in peaceful times is to improve their human condition. The vast immigration to the United States was primarily a response to better economic opportunities as the migrants perceived these opportunities; furthermore, the extraordinary internal migration within the United States is also predominantly a form of economic behavior.

*Elements of economic logic.* Natural resources are location-specific; the location of reproducible physical capital and of people is determined by human decisions in response to the alternative opportunities. The effects of economic growth and population growth on where people live and what they do are strong, and these effects persistently call for adjustments over time. Migration is one of the major consequences of the interactions between changes in the economy and in the size and the composition of the population.

Economic theory implies that when individuals or families can improve their position by moving to a new location, they have an incentive to migrate. The expected improvement may consist of higher real earnings either without changing occupations or by entering a new occupation; it may consist of a better place to live and additional nonpecuniary satisfactions. The real incentives to migrate are as a rule some combination of the net gains in earnings and in nonpecuniary satisfactions; net gains come after account is taken of the costs of migrating. These costs vary widely, depending on human attributes and economic conditions. As a rule, they are less for individuals than for families, and less for people during their youth than during their later working years. The cost of migration has the attributes of an investment in one's own human capital. The pecuniary and nonpecuniary gains to be had at the new location imply benefits over future years. Viewed as an investment, young people have a longer future during which they can recoup their own investment in migration.

The extension of theory, by the development of the concept of human capital and of the allocation of human time, has provided a new approach to migration that is rich in terms of testable implications. A goodly number of economists have embarked on studies to test these implications. I shall comment briefly first on various types of internal migration, i.e., within countries, which encompass most migration, and then on some aspects of migration between countries.

*Upon retirement.* Individuals who for reasons of age retire from work-for-pay, find incentive to migrate in order to take advantage of better consumption opportunities using their retirement income. If the bundle of consumption services that families prefer upon retirement is to be had at a location other than the place where they have lived during their earning years, and if they can afford the preferred bundle of services and can bear the cost of moving and re-establishment and the shadow cost of leaving personal friends, there will be an incentive to migrate to the new location. The behavior of many old people in the United States who pull up stakes and head south or southwest to live their remaining years under a warmer sun strongly supports the above implication. By migration to other parts of America and to Central America, the preferred bundle of services can be had much more cheaply than in Florida, Arizona, New Mexico, or California; but understandably, however, substantial numbers of U.S. old people migrate to these states and also to other countries for the reason implied.

*Migration out of agriculture.* The modernization of agriculture in high-income countries reduces markedly the amount of farm work that is required. In the United States the total hours used for farm work declined between 1930 and 1974 from 22.9 to 5.5 billion, down by three-fourths. The decrease in the farm population was somewhat less because of the increase in off-farm work by farm people. In 1930 the U.S. farm population was 30.5 million; by 1974 it was only 9.3 million, a decline of 21.2 million. If we add to this the natural increase in the farm population between these dates, which was 11.6 million, the actual out-migration came to 32.8 million—the largest migration in modern times.

This vast migration out of agriculture did not occur because farm people suddenly acquired a distaste for farm life. They would have preferred farm life had the economic opportunities in agriculture stayed approximately equal to those in other sectors of the economy. They migrated to improve their economic lot at a substantial cost in acquiring the new skills that the non-farm occupations called for and in adapting to living under urban conditions.

*Migration in response to regional disparities in earnings.* Economic growth tends to occur unevenly among the various regions of a (large) country. Real wages become unequal. Migration redresses these wage inequalities. Predictably, laborers differ measurably in their ability to learn about better job opportunities at other locations in a country, to assess their qualifications for these better jobs, to cope with the unemployment risk associated with these jobs, and to reckon the real costs that migration would entail for them. Education has a marked effect on this particular ability: better-educated laborers are more efficient in their migration behavior than less educated laborers.[4] Thus, regional differentials in lifetime earnings of the best-educated part of the population are the lowest; for example, in adjusting to uneven economic growth, the national market for college graduates tends to approach equilibrium most rapidly.

*Effects of race and discrimination on economic opportunities.* The effects of race and discrimination on economic opportunities are complex and varied in the economic history of the United States. The story is told cogently and clearly by Thomas Sowell.[5] The migration effects of discrimination against American-born blacks are well known. Less well known are the curtailment of the opportunity of indentured servants to change their location and the frequent maltreatment of these servants while they were in bondage. The numbers of indentured servants were large: a substantial part of the work force in many of the colonies consisted of European indentured servants. Economic theory implies that indentured servants were treated even more harshly than slaves because of the different nature of the property rights in them held by those to whom they were in bondage. Sowell's findings are consistent with this implication. Religious intolerance restricted internal migration. It exacted a high price: "Shakers were flogged, Mormons were lynched, and Irish neighborhoods invaded; houses, churches, and schools were burned." German and Italian Catholics fared somewhat better than the Irish Catholics. The Scotch-Irish, Jews, and Japanese, for various reasons, managed to win entry into the better-paying occupations in less time than most of the other immigrants.

*Immigration to the United States.* The combined effects of changes in economic conditions abroad and in the United States on the ebb and flow of immigrants, as analyzed in various economic studies, tell a good deal of the story of immigration. The full play of economic incentives to enter the United States, however, has been increasingly restricted over time. What can be said is that economic considerations have dominated the peacetime periods of expansion and contraction in the vast numbers of immigrants who have entered the United States since the Civil War, as Simon Kuznets has shown.[6] Similarly, most of the changes in the movements of Puerto Ricans between the United States and Puerto Rico are thus explained. Mexican workers, who until recently temporarily entered the United States in large numbers to undertake seasonal farm work, were responding to the much higher wages to be earned in the United States compared with the prevailing wages in Mexico.

*"Brain drain" reconsidered.* In the 1960s there was a spate of conference reports and "professional" papers endeavoring to prove that the free international movement of scientists and of other highly skilled professional people should be restricted because of its adverse effects. This migration became known as the "brain drain," and it was deemed to be bad. These facile pronouncements, however, were far off the mark; they placed no value whatsoever on the gains in the welfare of the individuals who migrated and on the international contributions, to science and to other areas, of their work at the new locations. There then followed a series of economic studies[7] with strong evidence that the so-called "brain drain" was a response to economic incentives that resulted in an improvement in the welfare and in the efficiency and productivity of this highly skilled personnel. To the extent that a part of the cost of "producing" the human capital of these individuals was paid for by the country from which they came, there is an argument for compensation covering this part of that cost.

*Migration within the European Economic Community.* From an economic point of view, the efficiency of the European Economic Community

(EEC) has been much impaired by the many barriers that it has erected against imports. In one respect, however, the welfare of millions of laborers has been enhanced by the much freer movement of individuals between countries of the EEC, permitting them to respond to job opportunities. In a world suffused with nationalism and in view of the ever-increasing restrictions on what people can do privately, this greater freedom to migrate is indeed a notable exception. To argue that this migration within the EEC is wholly bad for the migrants because the receiving country does not extend citizenship to them overlooks the very substantial wages that accrue to these migrants.

## A CONCLUDING REMARK

The self-interest of migrants is thwarted in a mercantile economy. By comparison, it is much favored in a liberal economy. In a stationary, traditional economy the economic function of migration is small; it is, however, of major importance where there is economic growth and population growth. Governments can and do abridge the personal right to migrate. Public policy obviously matters. Presently, there are many indications that even in the remaining countries that have a liberal economy, the economy is being bent in ways that have adverse effects on migration. The loss of personal freedom is not reckoned by those who promote public interventions that constrain markets and competition. The motivation is of course noble: to safeguard people from unregulated competition. Although restrictions on immigration are old hat, legislatures and courts are increasingly bent on finding new ways to *regulate* internal migration to "protect" established labor, cities, states, and farmland from being used for urban settlement. Thus, sight is lost of the basic value implicit in unrestricted migration. The personal privilege to migrate is indeed precious. It is fundamental in the pursuit of circumstances that will best serve the welfare of individuals and families. It is also essential in maintaining an open efficient economy that serves human welfare.

## NOTES

1. In this section I draw on my paper, "The Economic Value of Human Time Over Time," April 1976, to be published by the Economic Research Service, U.S. Department of Agriculture, Washington, D.C.

2. See Theodore W. Schultz, "Public Approaches to Minimize Poverty," in *Poverty Amid Affluence*, Leo Fishman (ed.) (New Haven: Yale University Press, 1960).

3. August von Haxthausen, *Studies on the Interior of Russia*, edited by S. Frederick Starr and translated by Eleanore L. M. Schmidt (Chicago: University of Chicago Press, 1972).

4. See Theodore W. Schultz, "The Value of the Ability to Deal with Disequilibria," *Journal of Economic Literature*, 13 (September 1975), pp. 827–46.

5. Thomas Sowell, *Race and Discrimination* (New York: David McKay, 1975).

6. Simon Kuznets, *Modern Economic Growth* (New Haven: Yale University Press, 1966), pp. 51–54, 295–300; Simon Kuznets and Ernest Rubin, *Immigration and the Foreign Born*, National Bureau of Economic Research Occasional Paper 46 (New York, 1954).

7. See H. G. Grubel and A. D. Scott, "The International Flow of Human Capital," *American Economic Review*, Papers and Proceedings, 56 (May 1966); H. G. Johnson, "Some Economic Aspects of the Brain Drain," *Pakistan Development Review*, 7 (Autumn 1967); W. Adams (ed.), *The Brain Drain* (New York: Macmillan, 1968).

# [18]

## Migration: The Moral Framework

MARTIN E. MARTY

Morals and morality are usually considered within the context of specific social environments. Migration, because it disrupts such environments, has regularly produced both moral discourse and confusion. The confusion results from the large number of disparate experiences that can be termed "migration," and from the fact that migration itself exaggerates the issues raised by moral pluralism.

If migration represents every permanent or semipermanent movement of persons or peoples over substantial distances, it is clear that considerable diversity is implied in the designation. Different moral problems and possibilities are raised in virtually every conceivable illustration.

Migration, for example, can be purely *individual.* In that case, the migrant is forced to transport personally the whole context out of which moral decisions flow. If the movement is to a setting that is different from and even hostile to the one in which the individual's moral positions have been shaped, it is likely that the immigrant will segregate himself and spend a lifetime holding tenaciously to the values of childhood, without making a positive contribution to the new environment. Just as often, however, the individual will "pass" in the new environment, blending into its fabric. In that case, values that have been brought along will largely disappear.

If there is *group* migration, those who move have a greater opportunity both to build defensive walls against the new environment and to sustain inherited values. Or, if the migrants choose to expose themselves to the confusion of the new setting, they can make a positive, if at first unsettling, impact on others. If the imported values of the migrants are regarded as superior to those of the existing population in the new environment, then self-segregation on the part of the migrants deprives the local population of the opportunity for moral gain. Just as frequently, however, the migrant is perceived by earlier settlers as the carrier of inferior standards of moral discourse and action. In that case, migrant enclaves help protect the earlier arrivals from moral contamination, while migrant infusion represents a threat to old norms and standards.

Whether a particular migration is *voluntary* or *involuntary* raises many issues. Some students refuse to consider forced migration brought about by slavery or by military conquest to be migration at all. Others believe that refugee status is not an issue of migration. The refugee is, in effect, part of a forced migration, since the old environment allows no possibility for sustained life. Yet it is hard to rule out the "forced" aspects from discussions of migration and morals, for many reasons. In historical experience, the line between the voluntary and involuntary is normally quite vague and thin. And the involuntary migrant raises many of the same questions for the inhabitants of an environment that the voluntary migrant does.

Forced migration often results from an expression of moral flaw on the part of those who do the forcing—the conqueror, enslaver, or exploiter in the old land or region. The population in which the involuntary migrant is to arrive is faced by moral questions: should it receive him at all? Should the host be hospitable or begrudging, open or closed to influences brought by the victim, the slave, the deprived? These basic and background problems have to be addressed before one faces the first set of moral issues that we have raised.

Migration that carries *the possibility of return*—at some periods in American history up to 40 percent of the migrants did go back to their European homelands—will call forth a different style of moral conversation than will a move that is obviously *permanent.* We do not refer here to the tourist, the transient, and the overnight stranger who, obviously, do not belong in the discussion of migration. Let us consider, for example, people who head for a new locale in order to spend a few years becoming sufficiently prosperous to return home in style and with security. What attitude will such persons have toward permanent moral conditions in the place of prolonged, if still temporary, migration?

The very *distance* and *type* of change implied by migration is a matter for further confusion. Some observers will not speak of a move as being true migration if it occurs within a single social system. But what is a single social system? Would this mean that anyone who moves within the United States would *not* be considered a migrant, since on a legal basis and as far as the national memory is concerned, the United States is a single system? Yet the history of the nation is rich in debate about the meaning of internal migration precisely because it is expressive of change across the boundaries of social systems.

One could demonstrate in infinite detail the diversity occasioned by types of migrations, but the point has already been made: it is hard to link moral argument with migration simply because no single phenomenon is meant by this term. Yet the moral issue is persistently associated with all the forms of semipermanent human movement. Lest these first pages be perceived as a catalog of problems invented by a moralist, let the reader be reminded that the author is an historian who has no vocational reasons to isolate ethical and behavioral questions or to invent them—except insofar as they illumine the historical narrative.

But they do! That would have to be the verdict of anyone who listens to the record of people wherever migration has occurred within living memory or within the scope of chronicle—to say nothing of ancient saga and myth. Somehow the presence of all elements of population has to be accounted for. When the earliest settlers came to American shores, only to find someone already here, some explanations had to be offered. The explanations helped lead to fateful differences in policy. To some, the Indian was *not* a migrant from any other earthly land: God had created and hidden in the Western hemisphere a separate being. Since the biblical account was supposed to have taken care of human origins in the story of Adam, the American Indian could not therefore be human. He was thought to be a special embodiment of the demonic and subhuman—who could be evacuated or exterminated. To others, that same native was one of the lost Ten Tribes of ancient Israel, and had to be shown concern by missionaries, since such persons, having somehow migrated from the old Promised Land, obviously belonged to the plan of God that was to be unfolded in the New World. No moralist invented such an accounting; historians have reported on its consequences.

In later history, as the mythic and theological explanations began to wane in significance, the American Indian still provoked moral debate. The titles of many books on the subject are based on ethical commitments, beginning with the classic work by Helen Hunt Jackson, *A Century of Dishonor* (New York: Harper and Brothers, 1881). If there has been dishonor—as any fair-minded student of white-Indian interactions would conclude there has been—some concept of the honorable and the good must be regnant in the minds of authors like Jackson and of their appreciative or resistant readers. Removal of Indians from all productive land looked like stealing to some, like the assertion of natural rights to others. The voluntary migration of Indian tribes in the earlier American past had represented a low-efficiency, and therefore immoral, use of energy resources in the potentially rich natural environment.[1]

Equally rich in its production of moral controversy has been the forced migration of the black migrant to America from 1619 until the nineteenth century. The morality of Africans selling their brothers and sisters into bondage was always a matter of concern, if not open outrage, to abolitionists and even to the most mild demurrers against slavery. The morality of the slave-ship captains, of those who made up the selling-and-buying industry, of those who treated the slaves well or mistreated them, fill libraries of American history. If these issues should be ruled out of discussion because forced migration is not true migration, then the movement of American blacks becomes an even more intense subject after slavery and with the coming of at least putative freedom.

The movement of blacks from rural South to urban North has been much studied on moral grounds. To some, such a migration represented opportunities for self-development. To others, the migrant became nothing but a social problem. The migrant would tear apart the social fabric, it was said, because he or she might become a welfare recipient and a burden on the taxing system. Or the migrant, often innocently enough as the victim of the slave pattern, was not able to retain the firm sense of family on which existing moral frameworks had been built. In that case, other moral problems resulted.[2]

No less freighted with moral concern in the records of common people and elites alike in the United States has been the story of the peoples perceived as voluntary immigrants, first from Europe and later from Asia. In the earliest years, when colonies were distanced from each other, it was possible for new in-migrants in each of the various areas to make their place without much contact with inhabitants of other areas. One of the standard moral policies of that time was largely to ignore or to avoid the stranger to the south or to the north of one's own colony—all the while building up casual negative images of the stranger's moral worth. Many of the later problems in nation-building grew out of difficulties connected with these independent and isolated early migrations.

When the nation had been formed, however, these earlier settlers for the most part had put their name and stamp on the culture. Their understanding of the Bible, of Protestantism, of the Enlightenment, set the terms and formed the matrix for the subsequent transmission of values.[3] Those who came later—the Irish, the Continentals, especially from Southern and Eastern Europe, and the Asians—found that they either had to be sheltered from or had to adapt to this original matrix.

The people whom Oscar Handlin called "the Uprooted" became major agents in the moral development of America. What Thorstein Veblen spoke of as "the merits of borrowing" in regard to technology[4] was applicable also in the moral world. The newcomers were free to bypass many stages in the national moral evolution in order to participate in some of its fruits. Thus many began to express "the Protestant ethic" without ever having been positively related to Protestantism. The Protestant ethic came to be called "the work ethic," and it was regarded as something structural in a capitalist economy, not as the result of a specific theological commitment or historical development. The movement from "Black Power" to "Green Power" in the unfolding of the American Negro drama in the 1960s was another illustration of the way in which the accepted moral standards of a society can be borrowed and appropriated by migrants—in this case, the new northern urban blacks—at the very moment when heirs of those who first set up the moral context were deserting it.[5]

If the later-comer was often capable of adapting and even of over-adapting, the older population ordinarily viewed the new migrants with suspicion. Protestant history is rich in polemics against the Irish for what they allegedly were doing to morality in the cities. American Nativism, Know-Nothing Movements, American Protective Associations—these were all reactions to the later migrations.[6]

Another great movement of peoples that inspired moral dispute was the *Völkerwanderung* of the new middle classes from city and farm to suburb in post–World War II America. This "suburbanization of America"—the migration of individuals and families from at least slightly traditional environments to the "uprooting" suburbs, in the name of sinking down roots—was the subject of a moralistic genre of literature that developed in the 1950s. *Bachelor in Paradise, Boys Night Out, The Crack in the Picture Window, The Organization Man, The Man in the Gray Flannel Suit, No Down Payment, Please Don't Eat the Daisies, The Tunnel of Love*—these were only a few of the films and books that gave popular expression to the moral abrasions caused by this voluntary migration. Finally, in *The Suburban Myth*,[7] Scott Donaldson was able to show that much of the moral clucking and tsk-tsking was based on slight and contradictory empirical evidence. More often than not, argued Donaldson, the judgments were grounded in elitist Jeffersonian assumptions. These were the judgments of academicians and urbanites who cherished outdated myths of the agrarian scene and of the moral values that were supposed to flow from it—a scene that was being violated by the bulldozer and the builder.

We have illustrated the diversity of the moral matrices occasioned by immigration by broad-brushed depictions of several movements in a single nation during a three-century span. This effort should remind readers, if it has not so established for the first time, that moral debate about migration is not the artificial product of moralists but the natural reaction of migrants and old settlers to new circumstances. The foregoing review has demonstrated the difficulty of reducing migratory movements to patterns in which systematic moral discourse ("ethics") is clear and intelligible. Still a further complication is the fact that migration exaggerates the contradictions inherent in pluralism. Pluralism can be seen on two levels, both of which create problems for migrants. The first level is institutional pluralism, as opposed to monolithicity. In Ernest Gellner's definition, "Pluralism in the ordinary sense [is] the view that a plurality of countervailing forces, groups and institutions is the best aid towards the maintenance of both liberty and order." This kind of pluralism is at the root of the modern free democratic process, unquestioned by most members of free societies. It has produced a corollary meaning that relies more on psychological than on logical grounds, although it has been and can be defended on the basis of philosophical commitments. This "doctrinal pluralism," according to Gellner, "preaches the peaceful coexistence of any and all doctrines, not only within one society or within one person but within, so to speak, one logical universe of discourse. Everything, or very nearly, can apparently be true all at once" in such a view, complains Gellner.[8] The first of these definitions is an inevitable and sometimes welcomed issue raised by migration. The second definition makes moral patterning even more difficult for those who hold to it, as many citizens who grow weary of the attempt to speak clearly on moral issues often do.

Pluralism of the first sort is most congenial in various settled orders, spheres in which a kind of moral consensus has developed. Yet the migrant always serves to unsettle the order, bringing with him or her the potential for introducing alien or at least unfamiliar ethical standards and moral or behavioral patterns. In this image, no one sits still long enough to think things through ethically. In such circumstances, it is hard to learn what values and traditions can be transmitted to a new generation—toward whom most moral urgency is ordinarily directed. Pluralism is experienced most acutely by the migrant. Whoever moves into a traditional society, where the standards of conduct are fixed either by the code of an encompassing religious institution or by the myth and ritual system around which the society coheres, is not likely to be a victim of *anomie*. Bewilderment results, however, when the newcomer finds a jangle and jungle of competing systems. Yet the modern condition produces just such a setting, and confrontations with it have exaggerated what Peter and Brigitte Berger and Hansfried Kellner have called *The Homeless Mind.*[9] Pluralistic ignorance permits a person to make simpler, if unreflective, moral choices, since one does not know that there are alternatives to the system of which the agent is a part. Conversely, pluralistic awareness, based on critical exposure to competitive patterns, makes the development of consistent actions and responses more difficult.

We can now draw together some of these strands in setting forth the background to policy issues involving the bewildering scene of human migration. The first of these issues grows out of what has been said about pluralism as intensified by migration. In discussions of policy for dealing with human conflict there is ordinarily some sense that an arbiter or an arbitrating system exists somewhere. Thus where there is a tradition of law within a society, it is assumed that members of the society agree at least in general to some principles on which law is based. "We hold these truths to be self-evident" is a kind of creed that was given at least lip-service, before there could be a constitutional sense that "We the people" could write laws. Parties to disputes know that some sort of code exists and that its standards can be made use of in debate and eventual arbitration or settlement. But in the case of migration, where is the basis for arbitration? The answer given by history is clear: it is in the existing establishment. That is true unless the new migrants come in sufficient numbers or force that they will have political or persuasive influence strong enough to produce or impose a new moral pattern. In that event, who decides what is the good, what are bases for valuation and measurement of conduct? Even when migrants are fewer in number and the established order holds, a problem remains for the newcomer who cannot accept or comprehend the reasons for certain moral impositions. American history offers many examples of often humorous bewilderment on the part of Continental immigrants who, for example, could not understand why in the Puritan-Protestant world gambling and frolicking on Sunday were forbidden. These had never been "wrong" in the European regions left behind —regions presided over by priests or ministers as faithfully as any American communities had ever been.

In the case of migration, then, who or what is arbiter of right and wrong becomes a policy issue when the question of intervention arises. Most migrants raise problems that seem to demand some sort of intervention. Phrases like "Strategies of Intervention" often occur as chapter titles in books on migration policy.[10] Says Eugene B. Brody:

> Intervention aims at promoting the economic integration, optimal function and personal stability, in short, the adaptation of the migrant. Conversely it aims at avoiding unemployment, family fragmentation, mental illness or other forms of behavioral deviance, and the development of destructive tension between migrant and host population. Whether or not the promotion of early acculturation and eventual cultural assimilation is a legitimate goal of intervention still seems debatable.

Brody's opening lines manifest the immediacy of moral questions ("optimal," "fragmentation," "behavioral deviance," "destructive," "debatable" are all terms laden with moral significance). As he elaborates on "Public Policy Level Intrusion," "Individual Intervention," "Migration Counsellors," and the like, it is clear that someone is needed or is conceived to be needed to make decisions that affect both migrants and host populations. And the arbiter or intervener must use some standard or other. It may be based on the custom of the old culture, on appeal to absolute standards of conduct, or on some compromise with the world of the newcomer.

If enough migrants come, if they remain long enough, and if they are expressive, it is likely that they will cause at least subtle compromise in or alteration of the old standards. In any case, the collision of cultures may serve further to demonstrate the extent of the metaphysical commitments that frequently lie behind even apparently unreflective patterns of conduct, and to illumine the problems brought about by pluralism.

One of the more eloquent ponderings of this question came from the mind and pen of the late Father John Courtney Murray, S.J., in *We Hold These Truths.*[11] Whether or not one appreciates Roman Catholic ethical complexes, it is hard not to admire the power of mind and clarity of expression with which Murray addressed this matter. The Catholic was an immigrant who brought along a tradition of morality at least as old as the Protestant-Enlightened compromise he confronted upon arrival. At many points, the two systems overlapped; at others, they were in contradiction. On one set of terms, Catholics ought not be troubled by environment. Murray quoted the second-century *Letter to Diognetes:* "Every foreign land is a fatherland and every fatherland is a foreign land." But he was gifted with enough historical realism to know that half other-worldly comment did little to settle this-worldly affairs in "the civil multitude."

In a pluralist society, marked by migration, people produce and derive from separate histories: they are discrepant. As an illustration, Murray cited the conflict over the very existence, and certainly the content, of "natural law." "For the Catholic it is simply a problem in metaphysical, ethical, political, and juridical argument." For the Protestant, on the contrary, the whole doctrine of natural law is a challenge, if not an affront, to his entire style of moral thought and even to his religiosity. The doctrine is alien to him, unassimilable. He not only misunderstands it, he also distrusts it. (Here Murray did not do justice to the many Protestants and others who complicate the issue by *not* having trouble with natural law!) Murray showed the difficulties that migration created for American pluralism:

> As we discourse on public affairs, on the affairs of the commonwealth, and particularly on the problem of consensus, we inevitably have to move upward, as it were, into realms of some theoretical generality—into metaphysics, ethics, theology. This movement does not carry us into disagreement; for

disagreement is not an easy thing to reach. Rather, we move into confusion. Among us there is a plurality of universes of discourse. These universes are incommensurable.[12]

Even the statement of the problem—"we inevitably have to move upward" —would not be accepted by many people within a pluralist order. How can there be intervention based on anything but the power given by the old majority, or how can there be arbitration except on the basis of the moral views of history's winners?

For all the confusion produced in America, it is possible to say that somehow the common people have been free to fuse their particular visions with an awareness of "the common good." Some of Franklin's dream came through when he spoke up in 1749 for "the necessity of a Publick Religion." Many observers of America have noted that Americans remain loyal to their races, ethnic groups, classes, traditions, denominations, and separate value systems without losing concern for the public weal. What has resulted is a kind of ill-defined and tenuous attachment to a middle ground between simple and extreme moral absolutism and its opposite, total moral relativism. Did Americans come to this on the basis of reading formal philosophy, for example, on the model of William James's *A Pluralistic Universe?*[13] One doubts this, though James may have posed and clarified concerns for some elites. A kind of practical adjustment or adaptation seems to have occurred, as untutored people often settled for some sort of compromise in the context of recognition that moral standards had to be adhered to.

I have often been struck by the way in which citizens come fairly close to a basis for "strategies of intervention" or moral arbitration and coexistence along lines familiar in the recent but frequently criticized school of cultural anthropology collated and delineated by Clyde Kluckhohn. In any formal conference of anthropologists, his views would look dated and would be challenged from top to bottom by various newer schools of anthropology. (Pluralism is not unique to the community of theologians or of politicians!) The purpose here is not to defend Kluckhohn's specific version of the resolution of absolutist/relativist controversies in a world of migrants and pluralists. We shall show only how his depiction comes close to the practical compromise made in America, which is one product of migrations. Kluckhohn took up this issue in 1955 in an essay entitled "Ethical Relativity: Sic et Non." "From the anthropological standpoint, ethical relativity is a special case of a wider category, cultural relativity." Citing Abraham Edel and Daniel Brandt, Kluckhohn pointed to indeterminacy as the heart of the relativist position in ethical theory. A passing reminder: no agent of indeterminacy is more vivid or constant than the stranger or the migrant! He calls into question settled values simply by his arrival and his presence, assuming that he embodies aspects of social and cultural systems that are somewhat different from those which are familiar.

Kluckhohn is not content with simple indeterminacy. He tends to agree with R. E. Money-Kyrle. Wrote Kluckhohn:

> The basis of morality is . . . neither *a priori* and universal as the metaphysicians claimed, nor empirical and relative as critical philosophers and anthropologists maintain, but empirical and universal in the sense that it is a quality, like binocular vision or an articulated thumb, which is found to be common to all mankind.

Talcott Parsons and Edward Shils are further cited by Kluckhohn among those who disagree with the idea that there is "implicitly at least . . . a limitlessly pluralistic value-universe." To such analysts, migrants do not represent a total jumble; there is a limited pool of symbols and ideas out of which moral action grows. Migrants represent interdependence of humans, and thus belong to a network that already exists and is graspable. Meyer Fortes had said that "every social system presupposes such basic moral axioms. . . . These axioms are rooted in the direct experience of the inevitability of interdependence between men in society. . . . The focal field of kinship is also the focal field of moral experience."

In the light of his survey, Kluckhohn came up with a view of "the universalities in wants and the universals and near-universals in moral concepts" that "generate two fairly cheerful propositions." Are these propositions empirically discernible and defensible? Are they metaphysically grounded? I would argue that the American public and other working pluralist societies, whether on anthropological or on philosophical grounds, either have found or must find working equivalents for such "propositions" if there is to be a moral base for interventions and arbitrations, the possibility for civil discourse and resolution. The propositions, as formulated by Kluckhohn, are:

> 1. The similarities in human needs and human response-potentialities across cultures do at any rate greatly heighten the possibilities of cross-cultural communication once these core likenesses have been somewhat disentangled from their cultural wrappings.
>
> 2. While we must not glibly equate universals with absolutes, the existence of a universal certainly raises this question: If in spite of biological variation and historical and environmental diversities, we find these congruences, is there not a presumptive likelihood that these moral principles somehow correspond to inevitabilities, given the nature of the human organism and of the human situation? They may at any rate lead us to "conditional absolutes" or "moving absolutes," not in the metaphysical but in the empirical sense.[14]

We are not hitching our moral wagon to what may well be a falling star in anthropology or philosophy. This is an historian's observation: a pluralist society is a society only when, on *some* basis, people presume that there exist or that they can create some "conditional absolutes" or, more appropriate to a discussion of migration, "*moving* absolutes" as bases for intervention on policy and arbitrations of moral dispute. The alternatives would be an absolutism that gives all decisions to the powerful or to the winners, or a relativism that atomizes society and paralyzes it.

Other moral questions appropriate to all discussions of morality are connected with these basic propositions. We should cite at least two such questions.

The first issue has to do with the degree to which morality should be associated with the absence of mobility, with the possibility that an established environment should remain as the source or context for moral values. Or, is the act of migration seen as rich in creative, especially morally creative, potential? Some of these questions are posed in the following paragraph by Robert Cooley Angell:

> A whole society ... can be strained by increased heterogeneity of population. In the same way, mobility in or out of the society as a whole should be a handicap to integration. Internal migration, however, may not be a handicap. From one point of view, it would seem to be disintegrating in its effects —people need roots. On the other hand, to the degree that it acts to bring the various parts of the society to understand one another, it might be found to make for integration.[15]

From one point of view, those who worry about how morals connect with mobility seem to be saying especially to the would-be migrant family: if possible, stay home. The family that isolates itself from a larger context and sets out to move by itself finds that only with difficulty can it remain an effective transmitter of inherited moral values. Is not the strain too great, if family values are never able to be confirmed in the primary and secondary associations in the migrants' world? Eugen Rosenstock-Huessy worried about this problem in his essay, "Tribalism":

> The tribe can be defined as an institution to create marriages. Everything about it can be summed up in the one function that it is a family-making institution. The tribe is the *couche*, or the source, of families. The families themselves are transient; the tribe is eternal, the lasting form.[16]

The reader of these lines might conclude that migration by "tribe," when it occurs, is preferable to the standard pattern in free and affluent societies like America, where every fifth family moves each year, without the context of a tribe. But in the complex of modern polities and in the world of media, even tribal movement would likely be overwhelmed in new environments. So the nation tends to become the *couche,* or the source of families and values, with an increasing pressure developing to celebrate in it a "civil religion," an overarching and undergirding "religion of the republic," a semisecular public base for common moral inquiry and resolution.

Over against the accompanying threat of religious nationalism and moral statism, a number of thinkers have recently begun to point to the values in localism, in voluntary associations, in modern equivalents of the tribe. Among these are Edward Shils, *Center and Periphery: Essays in Macro-Sociology;*[17] Daniel Bell, *The Cultural Contradictions of Capitalism,*[18] with its urging that continuities in culture be perceived and nurtured; and Robert Nisbet, *Twilight of Authority.*[19] Nisbet, for example, wants a "pluralism," by which he does not mean a mere confusion, indeterminacy, or moral relativism. Instead, he seeks the polity of a *communitas communitatum,* a community of sub-communities, in which the sub-communities (as embodied by immigrant groups, tribes, and traditions) would be able to make their contributions. Such a conceived pluralism could produce "harmony."

> Tradition matters most.
> I mean reliance upon, in largest possible measure, not formal law, ordinance, or administrative regulation, but use and wont, the uncalculated but effective mechanisms of the social order, custom, folkway, and all the uncountable means of adaptation by which human beings have proved so often to be masters of their destinies in ways governments cannot even comprehend.

Nisbet looks for "revived religion, ethnicity, kinship, localism, and voluntary association" in his moral fabric—and all of these are strained by reckless migration. His concept of culture is anything but static—nor is that of Shils, who sees potential power for social change in tradition. But tradition needs nurture in locale, and too much migration makes this impossible.[20]

Bell says that "human culture is a creation of men, the construction of a world to maintain *continuity,* to maintain the "un-animal life." The past, on which people depend, is mediated by monument, artifact, and landscape. On these terms, Bell scores those who after 1910 engaged in "the withering attack on small-town life as constricting and banal."[21]

Reference to the small town, however, conjures up the opposite argument, which tells the migrant to leave. It tends to presume that traditions can be transmitted by retention of ideas and thoughts, and that values gained from an environment can easily be transported with positive effect to new environments. An ambiguous version of this argument appears in Jean B. Quandt's *From the Small Town to the Great Community: The Social Thought of Progressive Intellectuals.*[22] Quandt studies the migration of John Dewey, Jane Addams, Josiah Royce, Charles Horton Cooley, and other intellectuals. She sees that their retention of the moral norms derived from a small-town environment both gave impetus to and limited their vision of "the great community."

Similar ambivalence appears in Page Smith's *As a City Upon a Hill: The Town in American History.*[23] Smith sees the "brain drain" from small town to city to have been a tragedy for the small town and a boon to the city, because of the moral stamina that many a migrant took along. He regrets the passing of the small town, which had an ability to generate tradition and to produce "inner-directed" youth who could go to the city.

> The city needs the renewal given it by the acquisition of inner-directed youth, for the city is perhaps powerless to create its own values. It may have its fashions and fads and indeed its style, but it is too inchoate for it ever to be said of the city with much confidence that it stands for this or that; that it specifically honors integrity, skill, industry, or that it regards highly the self-effacing wisdom and human warmth that at best have counted for much in the life of the town. The most that we can say for the city is that it is tolerant, and we can seldom say that.

The covenanted community, however, is passing or has passed. Smith makes no proposals about the generation of moral values in the "inchoate" and chaotic life of the city.[24]

In contrast to this partly nostalgic and elegiac kind of writing is the genre typified by Richard Sennett in *The Uses of Disorder: Personal Identity and City Life.*[25] Sennett argues that romanticism about covenanted and cozy, ordered community is the problem—not the beginning of the solution. Unless people learn to generate values in the city, the home of the ever-shifting migrant populations, there can be no realism and little morality.

Ambiguity also characterizes the attitudes of many international migrants who had to or chose to leave Nazi Germany and its counterparts, as they are reported on by H. Stuart Hughes in *The Sea Change: The Migration of Social Thought, 1930–1965.*[26] Such a sample may not be representative, however. The group Hughes writes about was made up of self-directed (and sometimes already alienated) intellectuals, who were able to appropriate and retain what they needed from the old environment and then to move with some ease in new cultures, despite barriers of language and the like. We might describe them as having been "psychically mobile." They can hardly be seen as more than a reflective advance guard or elite among immigrants in contemporary history. Rarely are they paradigms or models for mass migrants, who have to make other kinds of adjustments.

Some scholars have been less ambivalent and more exuberant about the creative moral potentials in migration. A master's thesis by Ruth Hirsch[27] set me on the track of a number of such celebrators. One example is Frederick J. Teggart, *The Theory and Processes of History.*[28] Teggart, while hedging his bets, sees the act of migration as a stimulus for adventure and experiment, for the moral acts of bringing the new into history.

> Had there ever been but one system of ideas common to all men, advancement would have been impossible, for progress in ideas springs from comparison, and a sense of difference could not arise from contemplation of different instances of the same things. Conversely, the critical spirit is easily enough aroused by the juxtaposition of different means for attaining the same end; so that different observances for effecting the same result, different mythological explanations of the same phenomena, when brought into contact, may be expected to lead to questionings and comparisons.

There is a gloomy side of life in territories where there have been "constant warpaths and uprootings of people." But then more dramatic forms of development of criticism appear:

> The whole traditional body of customs, rites and observances tends to be overthrown, for the turmoil no longer permits of the opportunity to propitiate the slain, or to maintain the sacrifices for the dead; the lines of kindred are broken, and new groups, composed of men whom chance has thrown together, are formed under the leadership of some individual whose self-assertion, backed by strength or craft, seems to offer protection. This is the essence of all "Dark Ages," in which, through swiftly moving change, contrasts are made vividly apparent, men awake to the perception of differences in ideas, and criticism is born.
>
> The great advances of mankind have been due, not to the mere aggregation, assemblage, or acquisition of disparate ideas, but to the emergence of a certain type of mental activity which is set up by the opposition of different idea systems. . . . The stimulus is mental, and the friction springs from the contact of differing customs and explanations.

Here the migrant plays his part.[29]

More lavish in his praise of migration was Paul Tillich, who never forgot Germany or truly mastered the English language. But he found revelational and metaphysical grounding in the impulse to migrate, to "go." Thus for him, the biblical patriarch Abraham was a model; Abraham was sent out, not knowing where he was to go, and he was described as the example for later faith and action. Tillich obviously saw himself, the refugee from Nazism, as such a migrant, a person "on the boundary" or on the border—an uncomfortable, but morally creative spot.

For Tillich, migration helped people to take time utterly seriously and to overcome "the demonry of space," of tribal deity and idolatry of the known environment. Exodus, exile, and migration were normative acts for people of faith and courage. Tillich's view of the moral potential in migration, which he addressed particularly to the Christian sub-community,[30] is illustrative of the power of biblical narrative, philosophical discussion, and the evocative myths of sub-communities in our pluralistic world.

The final set of issues, if dealt with in detail, would move us beyond this discussion of migration to a consideration of policies governing refugees and involuntary migrants. This complex of problems concerns the freedom to emigrate and to immigrate, and the moral attitudes of the regions which the emigrant must leave and to which he or she might come. Soviet inhibition of Jewish migration to Israel or elsewhere, or the concern of various nations over "the brain drain" or "the talent drain," conflicts with many people's sense of their own "freedom to move." The resistance of populations to new migrations points to the contemporary relevance of such moral discussion. We have only to mention the distaste of many Americans for greeting Vietnamese refugees in 1975, Jewish refugees after 1945, or Chinese and East European immigrants before the Immigration Exclusion Acts of the mid-1920s. Such situations raise plaguing issues of international cooperation and imply the need for agencies that could intervene and arbitrate in desperate cases, something that no institution, certainly not the United Nations as it has evolved in our time, seems poised to be able to do. This topic properly belongs to the sphere of international politics. We have concentrated here on the questions of moral vantages and of the relative values in traditional moral grounding and the adventure of migration.

We have seen the migrant as an agent of moral confusion as well as a stimulus to the discussion of values. Viewed optimistically, the migrant promotes a sense of perspective, the need for common discourse, and the development of the critical principle. The question that Henri Daniel-Rops posed about the deprived migrant, the exile, that great symbol of twentieth-century disruption, still haunts: "Is not the exile, the man who has lost everything, predestined perhaps to judge the world of men who are in a secure position, to declare the hypocrisy and injustice of that world? Is he not also prepared to undergo the great spiritual experiences?"[31]

NOTES

1. On the question of the use of such energy resources, with special reference to American Indians and also to Chinese and other peoples affected by migration, see Marshall D. Sahlins and Elman R. Service (eds.), *Evolution and Culture* (Ann Arbor: University of Michigan Press, 1960).

2. For a new discussion of one phase of such movement, see Florette Henri, *Black Migration: Movement North, 1900–1920, the Road from Myth to Man* (Garden City, New York: Doubleday, 1976). Henri is concerned with straightforward narrative, but the spill-over into moral questions is persistent throughout the record.

3. How these values implied moral judgments against migrant populations is illustrated in Ruth Miller Elson, *Guardians of Tradition* (Lincoln, Nebraska: University of Nebraska Press, 1954), pp. 65ff., 101ff.

4. Sahlins and Service, p. 100.

5. This reversal of values was not lost on Theodore Roszak, *The Making of a Counter Culture* (Garden City, New York: Doubleday, 1969). Roszak argues that in American society the poor and the black are not as free as are the heirs to affluence to "drop out" and take an alternative view to that propagated by the productive capitalist system.

6. Books like Gustavus Myers, *History of Bigotry* (New York: Random House, 1943), or Ray Allen Billington, *The Protestant Crusade 1800–1860* (New York: Macmillan, 1938), contain elaborations of perceptions and actions based on older settlers' reactions to nineteenth-century immigration. Their concern about moral change was valid enough; the form their response took is usually seen as immoral.

7. New York: Columbia University Press, 1969.

8. Ernest Gellner, *Contemporary Thought and Politics* (London: Routledge and Kegan Paul, 1974), p. 13.

9. Peter and Brigitte Berger and Hansfried Kellner, *The Homeless Mind* (New York: Random House, 1973).

10. See, for example, "Preventive Planning and Strategies of Intervention: An Overview," by Eugene B. Brody in Eugene B. Brody (ed.), *Behavior in New Environments* (Beverly Hills, California: Sage Publications), pp. 437ff.

11. John Courtney Murray, S.J. in *We Hold These Truths* (New York: Sheed and Ward, 1960).

12. Murray, pp. 15–17.

13. William James, *Essays in Radical Empiricism and a Pluralistic Universe* (New York: E. P. Dutton, 1971).

14. Richard Kluckhohn (ed.), *Culture and Behavior: Collected Essays of Clyde Kluckhohn* (Glencoe, Illinois: The Free Press, 1962), pp. 264f., 269, 271, 276f., 50.

15. *Free Society and Moral Crisis* (Ann Arbor: University of Michigan Press, 1958), p. 50.

16. *I Am An Impure Thinker* (Norwich, Vermont: Argo Books, 1970), p. 121.

17. Edward Shils, *Center and Periphery: Essays in Macro-Sociology* (Chicago: University of Chicago Press, 1975). See especially the celebration of "Tradition," pp. 182ff.

18. Daniel Bell, *The Cultural Contradictions of Capitalism* (New York: Basic Books, 1976).

19. Robert Nisbet, *Twilight of Authority* (New York: Oxford University Press, 1975).

20. Nisbet, pp. 234, 236, 238, 253.

21. Bell, pp. 170, 74.

22. Jean B. Quandt, *From the Small Town to the Great Community: The Social Thought of Progressive Intellectuals* (New Brunswick, New Jersey: Rutgers University Press, 1970).

23. Page Smith, *As a City Upon a Hill: The Town in American History* (New York: Alfred A. Knopf, 1961).

24. Smith, pp. 235f., 305.

25. Richard Sennett, *The Uses of Disorder: Personal Identity and City Life* (New York: Alfred A. Knopf, 1970).

26. H. Stuart Hughes in *The Sea Change: The Migration of Social Thought, 1930–1965* (New York: Harper and Row, 1975).

27. For a rare discussion of this topic, see Ruth Hirsch, "Migration: A Problem for Theological Ethics" (Master's thesis, University of Chicago, 1957).

28. Frederick J. Teggart, *The Theory and Processes of History* (New Haven: Yale University Press, 1925).

29. Teggart, pp. 285–87.

30. Hirsch examined this view with accuracy and care in chapter 7, "Tillich's Conception of Migration as God's Election," pp. 174ff.

31. Quoted by Pieter de Jong, *Migration and the Christian Faith*, Research Group for European Migration Problems, Supplement 6, May 1964, p. 13.

# [19]

## Roots—The Sense of Place and Past: The Cultural Gains and Losses of Migration

EDWARD SHILS

I.

A plant once rooted stays where it has been. Its seeds move, a species of plant might move, but no one instance of the species, no particular plant does, except when a horticulturalist deliberately transplants it. Human beings are different. Particular human beings can and do move. They have been moving as individuals randomly and in patterns adhered to by very large numbers and as whole societies. The movements of whole societies from one place to another have come to an end. The centripetal movement from one existing society to another continues as a massive phenomenon.

Unlike plants which are rooted but have no beliefs or imagery of being rooted, human beings who are not rooted do have images of being "rooted" and of being "uprooted." Human beings become attached in sentiment to places; they have a sense of attachment to patterns of conduct and beliefs, which they attribute to past periods and which they associate with places where their "ancestors" lived. The "roots" of man, constituted by sentiments and beliefs about places and by certain classes of events which have occurred in them, are themselves states of mind and matters of belief and sentiment.

I do not know when autochthony became articulately appreciated as a desirable condition.* A. A. Zhdanov's denunciation of "rootless cosmopoli-

---

*The Oxford English Dictionary refers only to the roots of plants, trees, and beliefs, not of human beings. It contains one reference from George Eliot to a person "uprooted" from his society.

tans" was no more than a harsh echo of the Nazi denunciation of *bodenlose Intellektuellen,* of *Asphaltintellektuellen* and the Nazi praise of *Blut und Boden.* At the beginning of this century, Maurice Barrès had criticized the *déracinés;* Knut Hamsun had done the same in *Shallow Soil.* A similar attitude is implied in Maurras' disapproval of the *métèques.*

The moving about and the staying put of human beings have been taken "seriously." There is something paradoxical here. There is much sentiment about the place where one originated but it becomes articulate usually after departure from that place. As long as one remains fixed, there is little articulate expression of attachment to a place of origin. Perhaps no awareness of attachment arises until there is an actual or threatened displacement. Generalized appreciation of attachment to a place of past location occurs only after the loss of the object itself. The "need for roots" is sometimes experienced without any particular place or pattern of belief in view. It is a generalized yearning without an object.

It is interesting to observe that social philosophers, particularly liberal social philosophers, have not contended for the right to remain in the same place. Had the liberals thought of it, they undoubtedly would have acknowledged such a right, but they might not have praised its exercise. They do criticize the coercive transplantation of peoples, but this is probably more because it is coerced than because it entails removal from a place of origin. Economists of liberal beliefs have thought it to be a good thing for human beings to move to places where their labor will bring them the best returns. Freedom of movement was a plank in the platform of liberalism. Yet even in the liberal age, "vagrants," "itinerant" persons, persons of "no fixed abode," of "no known address," have been suspect—although more to the police than to liberal intellectuals. The police of the *ancien régime* in France were very distrustful of itinerant merchants or other wanderers who came into a place where everyone else was settled and known. For a long time, such attitudes persisted in France and prevailed elsewhere. In England, as late as the middle of the present century, villagers would regard as "foreigners" persons who had settled within the village twenty-five years earlier, having come from another village only a few miles away, and they distrusted them accordingly. There was an abhorrence of a "rootless" person.

Tyrants in the past ordinarily objected to the independent movement of their subjects. They often transplanted populations, sometimes as punishment; Stalin did this to certain nationalities in the Soviet Union. Tyrants transplanted populations also to strengthen their military position in certain hitherto sparsely settled areas by offering prospects of economic advantage. Aside from that, the policy of tyrants has been to make their subjects "stay put."

The situation is not too different now. The heirs of the tradition of absolutism still attempt to control, restrict, and manipulate the movement of their subjects; the heirs of the liberal and humanitarian tradition still believe in the rightness of freedom of movement, and even look with distrust on long-established residence as obstructive to innovation and bespeaking a "stick-in-the-mud" attitude. The liberals do not go so far as to insist that there is an obligation on the part of a national society to allow unlimited immigration, although there is a shadow of disapproval over such restrictions on the right of anyone not only to leave his own place of origin—it is much more than a shadow there—but also to enter any country he wishes and settle there. The liberals place the burden of proof on whoever would restrict the right of entry, although they never go so far as to state explicitly that immigration should be unlimited. The grip of nationality, which they frequently regret, has not released them entirely from its hold.

Conservatism has attributed more value to "attachment to place." In contrast with traditional, autonomist liberalism and latter-day collectivistic liberalism, both of which are strong for the right to leave and to enter and settle, conservatism regards it as desirable that those who are attached to a place should maintain their communities as they have been. Radicalism seems to have no doctrine on the matter, but its practice is to disregard the merits of a "fixed abode" and of being "rooted."

II.

With all the vicissitudes of liberalism in the present period, the right to move, to change one's place of abode, to choose one's abode, seems to be accepted by the political and intellectual classes in Western countries. Liberal and social democratic politicians have to qualify their acceptance, in principle, of unlimited immigration because of the resistance of the vested interests of trade unions and because primordial sentiments are stronger in the mass of the electorate than they are in the educated elite. From the critics of the restrictions on immigration associated with national and racial quotas in the American legislation following the First World War to the critics of residential segregation in American cities, there now seems to be unanimity about the rightfulness of departing from one's country, region, or city of birth, if one does not like it for whatever reason, and about the right, with unstated limits, to enter and take up residence wherever one wishes. There is likewise widespread insistence among those who take the "progressive" view that the newcomers to a country, region, or city should be economically "integrated," i.e., granted the same social and legal status, the same civil rights and powers, as persons who were born or resided for a longer time in the country in question. The benefits of citizenship should, it is argued, be conferred on all who reside in a given territory regardless of whether they are citizens in a legal sense. Immediate, present location in a territory is the qualification for membership in the existing society, not location for some time past. Territoriality, sheer presence in the territory of the state as such, becomes the criterion for membership in that society. There is no requirement of the "stake in society" which comes from long enduring residence in it.

In the nineteenth and early twentieth centuries, it was taken for granted that immigrants to the United States would wish to become assimilated into the central culture of the society, and it was also believed that they should do so. This view was not equally accepted in other countries; in Great Britain and France, for instance, it was thought that assimilation of ethnically alien groups would be injurious to the central culture. This is not the case today. There are very few politicians in Western countries who deem it prudent to assert that the presence of immigrants will be injurious to the national culture. While the value of a national culture is still affirmed by many persons, it is at present not in good form to assert it in public.

In the Ottoman Empire, there was no sense of a national culture, except among latter-day nationalistic Turkish intellectuals and military men; the various ethnic groups could live as they wished within their own enclaves. Unlike the present view, the Turkish view was neither relativistic nor antipathetic to the appreciation of the culture of the dominant strata of the empire.

In the United States, there were some persons who believed that assimilation would lead to cultural "bastardization" and the defacement of the dominant culture. By and large, however, whatever the reservations in America, assimilation was thought, given the fact that the immigrants had come to stay, to be the best outcome for both the newcomers and the host society. It was thought that the dominant American culture could and should be accepted by the immigrants. This view is no longer accepted by those who favor immigration. However much they insist on what is now called "integration," they are also antagonistic to the renunciations which are equally entailed in assimilation. They insist that the culture of the immigrants should be left intact. To adapt the words of a European diplomat of the 1920s, they demand *et privilèges et égalité*. They think that the immigrants should be allowed or aided to keep their old "roots" in the culture of the alien soil from which they departed, that their offspring should be educated in their "mother-tongue" and not in the language of the society to which they have come. It is contended that even though they have moved, they should be allowed and aided to retain the culture which they acquired and possessed in their place of origin. They should be allowed and encouraged to keep the memories of their primordial past and the attachments and beliefs which accompanied them. To the freedom to move, collectivistic liberalism, which is the presiding outlook of the egalitarian welfare state, adds a belief that "roots," detached and detachable from place, should be respected and protected. (Of course, it is not said quite in that way; it is expressed in the contemporary hedonistic, scientistic idiom of "ease of adjustment," "efficiency of learning," etc.) The collectivistic liberal view is far from consistent in this matter. Its approbation of the primordial attachments of immigrants—of Mexicans and Puerto Ricans entering the United States and of blacks in the American North—is not matched by its concern for family life and neighborhood, which are the loci and objects of primordial attachments, or by any solicitude for the preservation of the "roots" of the established societies and communities to which the immigrants come.

Those who move are regarded as unfortunate—in this respect collectivistic liberalism diverges from traditional autonomist liberalism, which looked to the economic advantages of migration. There is consequently a tendency to regard "moving" as undesirable and to be avoided insofar as it can be avoided. "Jobs should be brought to 'people,'" not the other way around. (At least one democratic socialist government, the present Labour government in Great Britain, acts to render movement unnecessary in the very situation for which it was declared necessary by liberal economists. Where economically provided opportunities for employment have shrunk because of the failure of local firms, the Labour government supports uneconomic firms in order to "create" employment and render movement unnecessary.)

A concern to protect the "roots"—not merely to render movement unnecessary—is apparent in recent discussions and decisions regarding the education of the offspring of immigrants. Language and history have become sublimated forms of place. "Roots," "heritage," have become separated from "place"; it is possible to protect and cultivate "roots" regardless of the loss of the place where they grew. This is how present-day collectivistic liberalism has maintained part of the liberal tradition while departing from it in other respects. The "busing" of school children in the United States, although it is greatly complicated by other considerations, seems to be indifferent to "place" or locality and to the most elementary unit of place, namely the neighborhood, in the desire of its proponents to achieve "integration" and to have justice done to blacks in the United States.

There is a complicated ambivalence here. It is believed that an individual should be free, if he so wishes, to break the primordial ties which bind him to the country and place of his birth, and that he should be entitled to enter another country to seek whatever economic and political advantages that country can offer to those who live in it. At the same time, it is thought that he should not have to renounce some of the essential ties to "the land which bore him," namely its language, its history, its customs, and its "culture." Of course, this apparent ambivalence can be washed away by the argument that it is the convenience, the material well-being, and the dignity and power of the living individual which are being considered. If one takes a wholly individualistic point of view, there is perhaps no inconsistency here —except for the high evaluation placed on "culture," "cultural identity," and "community," which are implied by the argument against assimilation into the culture of the host society and which are not matters of individual convenience. The paradox remains. Collectivistic liberalism wishes to have it both ways.

## III.

The present-day view—at least the view of those who seem to have the upper hand among those who write about it—seems to embrace simultaneously the autonomist liberal view that a human being should be able to move wherever and whenever he wishes in order to improve his lot on earth, and the conservative view that he should not be further "uprooted" by being deprived of his mother-tongue and his inherited culture and the self-image which comes from knowing the history of his ethnic community. The culture of the host country—its attachment to its own "roots" in the national territory—does not enjoy equally tender treatment,

In the nineteenth century, nationalism was in many respects liberal: the right of a nationality to be self-governing was the extension to the collectivity of the right of an individual to be self-determining and to be a member of a democratic, self-governing national polity. Yet this view bore within it an antithetical element. Whereas an individual was truly an individual if he was unencumbered by traditions, a collectivity had an enduring existence; it had a history. A national collectivity was not describable simply as a phenomenon of a single generation. It had to be rooted not just in a place; it had to be rooted in the past. A "people" was a "nation" if it had a past, a common language, common memories, and a sense of connectedness with those past events. But there was an antinomy in this combination.

The antinomy was brought to the surface by migration. On the one side, nationalists of the country of origin desired retention of the immigrants' prior culture, the retention of old roots. On the other side, nationalists in the recipient country demanded the renunciation of the immigrants' prior culture in favor of the culture of the host country; they demanded the fabrication of new "roots." The antinomy was prevented from taking an acute, easily apprehensible form as long as immigrants were admitted and neglected. If they were confined to a limited range of ill-paid occupations of low status, and as long as they were confined or confined themselves to restricted quarters of the towns in which they settled, and as long as they were excluded from the center of the host society, they could concentrate their social relationships in a circle formed by persons who came from their own villages or districts of origin and retain a good bit of the culture of their home country. But this situation presupposed relegation to humble and obscure conditions, few opportunities to emerge into the central life of the host society, and much less than the social and political equality which are now called "integration."

A high degree of linguistic and national cultural pluralism, such as was possible in the last century of the Ottoman Empire or in the empire of the Hapsburgs, could exist as long as there was a far-reaching exclusion of minorities from the center of society. Such pluralism was feasible in the United States as long as there was no ambition to "get on." Once minorities longed to enter the center of society, the "problem of assimilation" became prominent. One alternative was to renounce much of their culture—to "uproot" themselves from their inheritance of tradition and awkwardly and crudely to acquire "new roots," which were in themselves contradictions in terms. A second possibility was to return to their country of origin. A third choice was to secede from the host society and to establish a society of their own with a center of its own. Some followed the second alternative, none the third; most accepted the pressure of the center of the host society and gradually became partially assimilated.

The diasporas of the Jews, Armenians, Syrians, Lebanese, and French-Canadians could exist as long as the national culture of the host country imposed no assimilative constraint. The Ottoman Empire was ideal in this respect. Colonial countries were congenial to diaspora. The Cochin Jews, Iraqi Jews, and Ben-Israel Jews in India could survive as long as there was no effective insistence on an Indian national culture; this was the situation under alien rule. In Tsarist Russia, even popular and governmentally supported anti-Semitism did not prevent the Jews from maintaining their traditional culture because the government's policy of russianization was sporadic and half-hearted and because the Jews were barred from entry into the center of Russian society. They have fared much less well under the Communist regime. Indeed, anti-Semitism has increased with the renascence of the Jewish center in Israel.

The Syrians and the Lebanese could maintain their own culture in the West African colonies, as could the Indians in East Africa, as long as there was no pressure for "assimilation" into the culture which the rulers of the newly sovereign states were hoping to create. The Malay Muslims in South Africa could also preserve their old Islamic culture as long as the system of apartheid prevailed; once the younger generation began to be drawn to the host culture through the accessibility of mass communications, the old culture began to erode, despite official policy. The Chinese in Malaysia, Singapore, and Indonesia fit into this pattern. Under the British and Dutch colonial administrations, the Chinese diaspora could maintain itself, but after independence, the situation changed. In Singapore, the Chinese became the center of society; in Malaysia, they were sufficiently close to the center to enter into a delicately poised alliance with the newly ruling Malay elite. In Indonesia, their peripheral position and the pressure for the formation of a national culture have placed them under great strain.

The scattered fragments of a diaspora can exist as long as the host culture is weak, or indifferent, or as long as the immigrants are content to be relegated to a subordinate place. A renascence of the center of the diaspora can also strengthen the attachment to it of its periphery. This has been the case of the Jews since the establishment of the state of Israel.

The ability of an immigrant group to retain a substantial part of its autochthonous culture depends in part on its own internal life. A strictly observed domestic life helps to maintain such "roots" as can be carried over great distances; religious institutions are also transferable. This helped to preserve the Jews in Russia and to some extent those in the United States; it also helped to preserve the Italians in the United States—as long as their offspring went to parochial schools. The Jews in Tsarist Russia had a further "advantage" in the fact that they could not legally acquire ownership of land.

What alternatives are open to immigrants nowadays, when they come to societies in which the elites insist on the predominance of the central culture? They must renounce much of their traditional culture or they must leave the society to which they have immigrated. If they are residentially segregated by their own desire, or by the deliberated or unthinking policy of the host, they might for a time withstand the temptations and pressures of assimilation. If they come as short-term laborers without their families, they are in danger of losing their original culture and of not gaining the culture of the host society.

In principle, secession might have been possible in communities of immigrants—especially in societies formed by conquest or by dynastic unions —in which the immigrant community was concentrated in an area near the boundary of the country. Secession is certainly not a realistic alternative for immigrant groups which do not form more or less self-contained societies or near-societies. They must therefore capitulate or leave—insofar as they are not forced to leave by the loss even of the humble occupational opportunities which first drew them into migration.

I do not see how the fundamental antimony can be avoided. A migrant who leaves his society for one with a different culture, who leaves the place where he was born and raised, cannot avoid the diminished possession of his own original culture. As long as human beings are parts of a culture which is sustained by an elaborate social structure of familial, religious, and public authorities, and which involves a landscape, an ecological setting, an economy, and numerous particular occupations, leaving some or many of these behind is likely to attenuate his possession of his original culture and to create a void in the life of the migratory person. Even if the host society, with a rich and ascendant culture of its own, sustained by its own institutional structure, is not xenophobic but is tolerant or indifferent towards a cultural diversity which does not affront its preeminence, it is still bound to exercise both attraction and discipline on the newcomers, especially on the younger generations. Under normal circumstances, the culture of the host society attracts by the mere fact of its being a center to the immigrants and because of the advantages it offers in pecuniary rewards, deference, and proximity to authority.

At the same time, speedy assimilation is difficult for most of the newcomers. As a result, they are thrown into a trough in which their own culture is to some extent washed away, to be replaced only by a tincture of the host culture. The result pleases no one. It does not please those who are genuinely —and sometimes professionally—interested in the maintenance of the culture of origin, regardless of whether they themselves are of that culture or belong to the host society—and it does not please the proponents of the host culture. These latter look down on the unpleasant hybrid, which they regard as a threat to their own culture.

This hybrid is indeed a threat to the host culture. Threats to ascendant cultures come not only from the immigrants but also from its own bearers, from the changes in the standing of classes within its own society, and from the internal potentialities of the culture itself. Sometimes the threat is generated by the very ascendancy of the culture itself, when it is felt by its own heirs to be too "suffocating." There is, however, no doubt that even a strong culture, if its society opens itself to immigrants, is bound to be imprinted by the hybrid which is formed from the assimilation of the immigrant into the host culture. This has certainly happened in the United States; H. L. Mencken's *The American Language,* with its two *Supplements,* brings monumental evidence of this imprint.


IV.

In a society like that of the United States, where the center is very strong ecologically and has at its disposal immense legal powers and financial resources, the center would normally be culturally ascendant. At the end of the nineteenth and the beginning of the twentieth century, the center was not as strong institutionally but it was, on the whole, culturally overpowering. Its beliefs were respected by its own members, by a large indigenous middle class, and by a large immigrant working class. The immigrants had not shared much of the higher culture of their original societies. They had, however, shared its religion—except for the Jews and small persecuted sects—and they —the Jews and the sects included—brought their religions with them. They kept their religious "roots" and, at first, also their attachment to their locality of origin. Members of the next generation usually lost the parental language but retained some of the customs and religion, while acquiring some of the culture of American Protestantism. The extent of assimilation varied from one group of immigrants to the next, but except for a handful of literary men and journalists, there was generally no doubt regarding the direction in which they were to move. As long as the immigration continued, the seepage toward assimilation was compensated by new arrivals from the "old country." The patriotic fervor and repressiveness of the First World War and the years which immediately followed it pushed assimilation forward; later, renewed immigration, on a smaller scale, set it back, but during most of the ensuing decade the cessation of immigration and patriotism and prosperity pushed it forward once more.

All through these ups and downs, there was no question that the United States was a Christian, predominantly Protestant, English-speaking country with a literary culture which was primarily English and to a lesser extent American. There was also a powerful indigenous popular American culture —modes of speech, political and moral attitudes—which was somewhat scornful of but also deferential towards the higher culture. In addition, there existed a bohemian literary and political culture which was hostile towards both higher and popular cultures, particularly towards the former.

The immigrants assimilated a good deal of the popular and some of the higher culture, depending on the amount of education they received. They left their imprint on the popular culture and gave the higher, more central culture the deference accorded to an object that is respected even though not liked. The great depression in agriculture and the subsequent reduction in the cultural and political influence of the farmers weakened the force of the puritanical ethos in every sphere of American culture and it enfeebled the capacity of the dominant or central culture to impose itself.

Since the Second World War, and more especially since the early 1960s, the increased productivity of the capitalistic economies of Western Europe and North America, the propagation of the belief that education and education alone is the means of "getting on," and the extension of educational opportunity have left open the unskilled and semiskilled manual occupations which indigenous persons have not wished to accept. The result has been a flood of immigration into the United States and Western Europe: Pakistanis,

Indians, and West Indians to Great Britain; Spaniards, Algerians, and black Africans to France; Turks, Yugoslavs, Italians, and Spaniards to the Federal Republic of Germany. In the United States, Mexicans, Puerto Ricans, Haitians, Jamaicans, and other Caribbean and Latin Americans have made up the immigration from abroad. Within the country, there has been a multitudinous movement of blacks from the rural areas of the Southern states to the cities of the Northeast and Midwest. (Although the latter is an intranational immigration, it has very much in common with international immigration, insofar as it involves far wider cultural discrepancies than are ordinarily characteristic of migration from countryside to large town within a given country.)

The migrations within continental Europe purport to be temporary, and they are treated as such by the governments of the host countries, although it is no means certain that they will turn out to be so in the end. The migrations in the United States and Great Britain are probably permanent, although some migrants do return.

The immigrants to the European countries are, in the main, from the poorest classes of their own societies. Frequently peasants or agricultural laborers who lived in hierarchical societies, usually in villages and in large families under strict paternal and elderly authority which demanded deference to and observance of religious beliefs, they were only slightly educated in the higher culture of their respective societies. The attractions and pleasures of a more affluent urban existence have had unsettling effects, especially for those unmarried or separated from their families.

Immigrants to the United States, especially to the large American cities, seem to come from the more impoverished parts of poor societies. The clergy, parents, and elders have little influence over the younger generation, which is as uneducated as the continental European immigrants who have been allowed to enter only on conditions of assured employment.

One of the features of the last few decades has been the devaluation of the previously ascendant high culture and the classes which produced and bore it. This devaluation, a trickling, narrow stream a quarter of a century ago, is now a broadly rushing torrent which has swept out far beyond the banks which used to hem in the radical literary and political intellectuals. A consequence of this animosity against the inherited "WASP" culture is that there are no longer any movements to "Americanize" the immigrants such as existed in the first quarter of the present century. The curricula of the schools are not intended to create new "roots" for the children of immigrants; they are intended to enable them to "appreciate" their own ethnic past, to be "proud" of it. To do otherwise would be considered the equivalent of "neocolonialism"; it would bespeak an ethnocentric dogmatism.

The movement against the culture of the center in the teaching profession and among the persons who are in charge of what the public receives through the media of mass communication is not quite as pronounced in Europe as it is in the United States. In none of these countries is the aim simply to protect the "rootedness" of the immigrants against the power of the high culture of the host society. Radical populism in Europe has not joined with the desire to keep alive or to reanimate the "roots" of the offspring of immigrants in their traditional ethnic culture. The major intention, rather, is to discredit the hitherto prevailing high culture of the center, and to frustrate and sap the persuasive power of that culture. In consequence of this attitude, the "roots" of the immigrants have a sacredness attributed to them which is not consonant with the antitraditional progressivist outlook of those who recommend such a policy.

At present, however uneasy politicians feel about this criticism of the inherited culture of their societies, they are fearful of speaking out for it. They are afraid of being scorned as "reactionaries." Civil servants, teachers, educational administrators, and social workers have all benefited from the tremendous access of power to their central governments, from the welfare policies of their governments, and from their preoccupation with the "poor." The "poor" have become the charge and the license of these beneficiaries of the new "egalitarian" Leviathan. In Western Europe and especially in North America the "immigrants" have become invested with the sanctity of the poor. The poor—mainly the immigrants—are given immunities and privileges, among them immunity from the expectation of acquiring new "roots" in the host society. Meanwhile, the "roots" which the immigrants had in their hierarchical rural societies of origin wither. The result is further cultural impoverishment and barbarization.

Will this situation endure? Will modern Western societies undergo a process of disaggregation into a centerless pluralism? Ecologically, this is certainly not in process of occurrence: the center is more dominant, more penetrating, more saturating than it has ever been in human history. This is true in the liberal democratic societies of the West, and not just in the advanced totalitarian *soi-disant* socialist societies! More and more are careers to be made in bureaucracies, particularly in the bureaucracy of the central government. More and more are educational qualifications required for ascent in these careers. More and more attention is focused on the central authoritative institutions because the media of mass communications draw attention to them and because their actions affect lives in so many ways. It seems most unlikely that, despite the disparagement of the traditional central culture which is now so common among the educated—who revile it as "elitist"—it will lose its attractive power to the peripheral groups in society which include the poor and the immigrants. For one thing, unless their most intelligent, forceful, and ambitious offspring will be content simply to make their careers in their own peripheral ethnic groups, they will have to assimilate at least some of the traditional high culture. They will have to learn its language, they will have to master the various sciences, quasi-sciences, and pseudo-sciences which are regarded as necessary for high rewards and eminence. They will have to acquire some of the culture of the center.

Human beings, unless they change unprecedentedly, will retain a sense of "the serious," and the highly renumerated and much exhibited athletes and entertainers will not become the center of society. The individuals with better, deeper intelligences and imaginations in these immigrant groups will seek a more "serious" realization, and they will be able to find it only through the acceptance of some variant of the culture of the center. They will bridle at the attempt to enclose them within the narrow impoverished culture which the immigrant groups possess.

It seems to me that the present state of affairs is not a durable one. For the time being, it is true, the pressure of Americanization or "Germanization" or "Anglicization" is not as great as it was a half-century ago; but this relaxation of the pressure of the center is not likely to last. It is, in any case for the time being, only attenuated, not wholly obliterated. The center still attracts, and this is likely to continue. The immigrant groups will become more assimilated than their radical protectors wish them to be, or else they and their descendants will be condemned to persisting peripherality.

## V.

The anguish which some face at the loss of the emblems of their own and their ancestral past and place of origin and of the traditional culture which these nurtured has seldom been able to preserve an immigrant culture from transformation by the host culture. Nor for that matter has apprehension about the debilitating and corrupting effects of the immigrant culture on the host culture been able to preserve the latter intact. As immigrants become assimilated, they bring into the culture of the center—the dominant culture of the host society—some fragments of their own culture. They gradually acquire new "roots" very different from those which they had before and different, too, from the roots of those who have lived much longer in the host society, or who have "always" lived there. They also acquire an ambivalent attitude towards the culture of the center of their new society; they wish to acquire it and they also wish to change it.

I think that it is hopeless, and wrong as well, to argue that immigrants should keep their "roots." Unless they depart again after a rather short stay, and unless they are segregated and socially neglected and blocked, they are inevitably bound to lose much of their original culture. If they do not, they will not be able to achieve the economic and political integration which is demanded for them.

This is often a melancholy affair. The older generation mourns the infidelity of the new generation to the parochial traditional culture in which it was "rooted," in a place from which it departed; at the same time, it itself loses some of its parochial traditional culture without knowing that it is doing so. Meanwhile, the new generation renounces something which it scarcely values and acquires something, the value of which is uncertain. As they become older, some of the more sensitive members of this generation occasionally regret what they did not acquire. The new generation is left hanging "between the cut and dried" of the roots taken out of the place in which they grew and the "here and now" of a more powerful society. They do not have to renounce it all, and indeed they cannot. No culture is so unitary or so rigidly integrated that it cannot be partially renounced and partially retained. A culture, even an impoverished one, is too constitutive of the individuals who acquire it for them to lose all of it. The hybrid forms are sometimes ugly and they are often sterile. They are often shallow, and shabby. It could scarcely be otherwise. The immigrants have often come from those parts of their own society which have assimilated little of the superior culture of that society and they enter parts of their host culture which are in a parallel situation.

The immigrants are bound to have some influence on the culture of their host society, especially if the society into which they come is liberal and democratic. All the great cultures of the world have been amalgamated cultures. It is a naive romanticism to believe that the culture with which immigrants come to a foreign country has an integral purity, a mixing of which with any other culture would be a tragic loss. Is the Muslim culture of the Algerians in France, or of the Turks in Western Germany, their own original culture? Neither of them is the "pure" Arabic culture of the Arabian peninsula or the "pure" Turkic culture of Central Asia.

Those who complain about the real dangers of the "contamination" of the host culture are on no better ground, insofar as they argue from the purity of their central culture. The French, Italian, German, and English cultures, and above all the American culture, are all of heterogeneous composition and provenance. They might look unitary to their proponents and protectors; the fact that they grew more slowly and less under the scrutiny of numerous critical analysts makes the process of amalgamation less tangible. These cultures are not unitary in their origins, and it would be wrong to think that their process of growth has come to an end. They will undoubtedly continue to grow both from within and from the assimilation of new external elements.

One of the intellectual creations of modern times is populism; it is also the major source—with the idea of nationality—of the belief in the primordial unity and homogeneity of the culture of the lower classes. From a yearning for a unitary homogeneous community—in contrast to differentiated, conflictful modern society—peasant societies—and the lower classes generally—were alleged to be the bearers of a culture which was genuinely "their own." Historically viewed, however, there is little truth in this belief. The peasantry have acquired in all countries religious and cosmological beliefs which they did not themselves create, but which came to them from outside their locality. It is true that they did not abruptly lose their earlier religious beliefs, but rather assimilated the new ones and amalgamated some of the old ones into them. This is what happens to immigrants in the society to which they have come. The immigrants gradually lose the memory of place and of landscape, and this in its turn furthers the loss of culture, i.e., of languages, beliefs, and images. The loss of culture alone would not be traumatic; it becomes so on reflection. The reflection sometimes magnifies the loss.

Much grief has been caused by separation from one's original society and landscape, from the institutional practices of family life, communal organization, and occupation. The separation is sometimes painfully experienced, and the pain is compounded by the contumely—real or believed to be real—of the already settled "native" population towards the immigrants and by many of the genuine hardships of earning a livelihood. At bottom, there is little to do about this; that is what emigration is. The separation from place and society fosters the loss of culture. There is little to be done.

I think it must be accepted that immigration results in some loss of what is objectively valuable to the immigrants and to their descendants. They lose their language and a sense of historical continuity with their ancestors and their ancestral places, and they also lose the hard-won wisdom of judgment of their ancestors, built up through long and arduous experience; they lose their imagery and their consoling proverbs and adages. This is primarily a loss to the descendants of the immigrants and not necessarily to mankind, because the culture, after all, does continue to live and grow in its natural habitat, unless it is destroyed there by internal migration, urbanization, and industrialization. Much of the loss is not perceived by the losers. The cultural impoverishment of the offspring of immigrants is attributable only in part to their parents' separation from their "roots" of place and past. It might also be a consequence of the relatively impoverished character of the host culture which is offered to them by ignorant and misguided teachers in the schools and by false prophets and guides of popular literature and popular entertainment. But whether the aggravation of cultural poverty is painfully felt or is unwitting, it occurs. Cultural impoverishment is one of the consequences of migration but it is seldom an impoverishment which is a descent from great wealth.

It should be added that cultural impoverishment is not just a product of migration. It is often the result of an enthusiasm for innovation and a hostility towards tradition and towards those institutions of authority which are associated with tradition. A society can impoverish itself culturally without immigration; Western societies are already doing this by the dismantling of their educational curricula. The immigrants who would be assimilated are being offered less to be assimilated into.

Nonetheless, with all this grief and unreplaced waste, there is also a very great gain. The gain lies in the widened scope of reference—or awareness —and appreciation in the hybrid culture to which immigrants contribute. The high cultures of the great societies of the West contain much that is trivial and frivolous and of transient interest, but they all contain a great deal that is deep and serious, such as the greatest minds and the greatest experiences have discovered and elaborated. They have an immense wealth of traditions which even contemporary progressivism, scientism, and relativism have not entirely dissipated. The immigrants gain to the extent that sooner or later their more gifted descendants will acquire some of this culture. The host society gains, too. Alongside the antagonism generated in the relations between immigrant groups and the host society, there is also an increased awareness, a taking-into-consciousness of the immigrants and of the cultures from which they have come. The mental cosmos of a society is extended, over many obstacles and resistances and over much harsh judgment, by the presence and accomplishments of immigrants. A society which acquires immigrants and which in the course of time assimilates them by transmitting its own culture to them also assimilates some of their culture into itself. Not all of the growth of a central culture through immigration is "bastardization" in the pejorative sense. The results have not been uniformly happy, and much error has been mixed with truth. Still, the mind of a country which receives immigrants is extended in the passage of the years; it becomes more capacious.

VI.

Just as it is wrong to assert that any alien addition to the effective central traditions of a culture is pernicious, it is no less wrong to assert that all exogenous increments are necessarily as good as, or perhaps even better than, those practices and beliefs which they would replace. These exogenous increments sometimes impoverish the culture of the host society, they are sometimes less intelligent in their understanding of the universe, less discriminating in their aesthetic judgment, more brutal and egotistical in their moral attitude, more tribal and less civil in their sense of political obligation. There is no inevitable mechanism of moral, aesthetic, intellectual maintenance or progress inherent in any culture which prevents it from becoming dilapidated. If its heirs have been ill-educated for several generations, and if they have been encouraged to seek novelty wherever they have a chance to find it, in the idle belief that any novelty is originality and that anything novel and original is better than anything traditional, impoverishment is likely. If education neglects the great achievements of the culture or inculcates a derogatory attitude toward them, impoverishment is likely. If it comes to be thought that there is something fundamentally wrong in the inherited culture, then the way to impoverishment is opened. None of these is necessarily consequent upon immigration, but all are rendered more likely by the awareness of other cultures, their comparison and contrast. The diminished acceptance of the plausibility of the Christian articles of faith was to some extent a function of the increased awareness of the other great world religions, as disclosed by the comparative study of religion, building on the accumulated observations of travelers, merchants, explorers, and missionaries over the preceding two centuries. Immigration has a somewhat similar consequence, except that it brings into the purview of the host culture an impoverished version of another high cultural tradition or of a parochial cultural tradition.

The impoverishing cultural effect of immigration does not follow automatically from immigration—although immigration can contribute to it. Immigration can also contribute to the enrichment of a high cultural tradition: both the United States and Great Britain benefited considerably from the German immigration of 1848 and in a different way from that of the 1930s. The outcome is partly dependent on the qualities of the immigrants, on the self-esteem of the bearers of the traditional high culture of the recipient society, and on the manner and the time in which the immigrants are admitted to the center of the society and its culture.

The impoverishment of a dominant culture has other, indirect consequences which can cause disorder in a society. It is now—after a long intellectual battle—acknowledged even by social scientists that some measure of consensus is needed if a society is not to be disrupted by severe conflict. This entails some confidence in the institutions of authority, in the incumbents of positions of authority, and confidence in the rules or laws as endowed with a fundamental validity or legitimacy. It entails also the acknowledgment, even if only tacit, of the validity of the beliefs which form the context of the institutions and the rules of the exercise of authority. A society in which the incumbents of the center abdicate these beliefs will fall into disorder. Not least will this occur in a society where much is demanded of and undertaken by the center. This is a condition towards which contemporary American society has been inclining for some years.

The culture of immigrants can never become the culture of a whole society unless the immigrants are settlers in an empty or nearly unpopulated land. Where they come into a settled society, they can remain in isolated enclaves with a minimum of interaction with the society into which they have come, or they must be more or less assimilated into that society with some "give" and much "take." The interchange cannot be equal; it must be asymmetrical in the favor of the larger society. If the asymmetry favors the immigrants, the result will be disorder in the society since the mass of the settled population will not accept the culture of the immigrants as its own and will resist it. This sort of asymmetry will not come into existence without the patronage of persons in the center of society who are determined to deny the legitimacy of the main traditions of the center. The idea of a pluralism of wholly autonomous cultures of equal value is a phantasm; approximation to it will damage the society at its center or it will be accompanied by an unacceptable stratification and segregation.

The conclusion which may be drawn from all this is that the assimilation of immigrants into the society in which they settle is necessary for the well-being of the society and that this assimilation must be quite pronouncedly asymmetrical. This does not mean that the immigrants must lose all their "roots"—they have already renounced the most important part of the "root," namely "place" or "landscape." If the culture which they have brought with them or which emerges from them in the trough between the society of origin and the society of settlement (or reception) is not hideously impoverished, then there will be a loss which some of them will experience knowingly and regretfully. However, this is a price that has to be paid for life in a society different from the one in which they had their "roots." There can be no moral justification for the immigrants, or those who speak in their favor, to demand that the society to which they have come and in which they have settled should renounce its "roots" in order to accommodate them; least of all is this demand justified when the roots which they praise existed in barren soil and nurtured only a dwarfed and malformed plant. If the supporters of such a policy are successful, then their offspring and their descendants will be the losers.

VII.

The dawn of "the age of universal history"—as Raymond Aron has called it—has been accomplished by the dawn of an awareness of—and even a fellow-feeling for—human beings of other societies, other histories, other cultures. The emergence of this world society and a world culture—like *Weltliteratur*—would not be desirable if it were to become exclusive of regional cultures, national cultures, and the cultures of distinctive civilizations. This is not in prospect. But as an element in the outlook of every more parochial culture, it has a very high value. It does not necessarily entail the suppression of one's own local, or regional, or national culture, or a reduced esteem for them. The attachments, with differing objects, can remain.

The assimilation of the culture of the host society by the offspring of immigrants can never be complete because they cannot lose all of the culture of their ancestors. They might in the second generation, at least for a time, be ashamed of this, but the fact is that they do retain some of the old culture. The result is often a wider horizon of awareness of the larger world, and a wider range of sympathies. As they come closer to the center of society, they bring with them this wider horizon and this wider sympathy.

This possibility should not be exaggerated; there are many countercurrents. The "rootedness" of individuals varies; although some lose their "roots" very easily while assimilating little from their host culture, the "roots" of others, despite the loss of "place," are more tenacious. These immigrants are more resistant to the acquisition of anything new; hence what they contribute from their tradition to the common pool is very little, just as what they receive from it is also very little. Other immigrants are more capacious: they can hold to much of their transported, displaced culture while assimilating much of their host culture. They are like the creative individuals of W. I. Thomas' classification, which was indeed elaborated—although insufficiently—with the situation of immigrants in mind. The common pool of the newer culture could be the product of the best and most capacious minds, which retain some of the sustenance and attachments of their tradition, and the culture which they acquire from the society in which they themselves or their recent ancestors settled. Of course there will be very few such persons in any society. And among those few—not all of them immigrants—this culture of universal reference, and with an adherence spread over the surface of the earth, will be very patchy and fragmentary.

The result is nonetheless a movement towards a universal culture—still far from it, but closer than it would be in a world without migrations in an age of national states and national cultures and with many ethnic antagonisms passing under different names. The new, more inclusive culture may appear "rootless" to the self-conscious bearers of an established national culture or of a political ideology infused with nationalism. Of course it will not be bound to a narrow locality—but the earth's surface is also a landscape, even if very few persons have the imagination and knowledge to conceive of it as such. A few individuals might have "roots" in a place as large as the world. "Roots" are not just attachments to a place which can be seen by one person at one time. A larger culture—a culture which is shared by many whom no one person can see and which cannot ever be fully shared by everyone—can also acquire "roots." They will undoubtedly not be "roots" in a rural or village landscape. They will not be the "roots" of long-practiced handicrafts. They will reach further back in time and have a wider territorial reference. These "roots" touch on certain historical or legendary events on which attention is focused, and certain works which will be appreciated. Christianity and Islam once aspired to be such universal cultures, but neither succeeded. Marxism has aspired to be a universal culture, but it is far too empty ever to succeed, even if politicians calling themselves Marxists were to establish themselves in power everywhere in the world.

## VIII.

Appreciation of a universal culture of a high order is of course not a likelihood for the foreseeable future. And even if it were, it would not be desirable if it were exclusive of national and regional cultures and of the cultures of civilizations or continents. What was meant by *Weltliteratur* in the eighteenth century was a gallery of works originating in many countries and civilizations and going beyond the boundaries of Europe. It was a literature which any person who wanted to be a citizen of the world should have read. Its constituents were the classical works of various national literatures. The works had to be understood in terms of a common human idiom and thus they transcended the limits of parochial idiom and subject matter.

World literature can never replace national literature, it can only supplement it. Literature is too firmly "rooted" in the language in which it is written. It can never have a universal intelligibility, except to the tiny numbers of genuinely polylingual readers. For the vast majority of immigrants who are not polylingual or even genuinely bilingual, the replacement of one language by another in the course of several generations following immigration is bound to mean a loss of attachment to one of the most important constituents of culture.

The subject matter of science and the idiom in which it is analyzed and communicated do not have these limitations. There lies the prototype of a universal culture which has adherents scattered over the earth's surface and which is intelligible to and valid for all those who have undertaken the discipline of its traditions and techniques. Its establishment—in its worldwide state—is a product of migration. Scientists have emigrated from one country to another and have thus spread the scientific community. Even more important, students have migrated first to the main centers of scientific study and then back to their countries of origin to implant there the scientific ethos and discipline which they learned at the center.

A migratory scientist has his "roots" in the tradition of science, to which "place" is adventitious. Of course scientists and scholars have other kinds of roots as well, like other human beings. They may be "uprooted" in a primordial sense, but as scientists they have roots in a wider, placeless community.

The international intellectual culture was carried to North America by immigrants from Great Britain; it was later carried from Germany to the United States by short-time immigrant American students in Germany and by long-term immigrant professors moving from Germany. Sojourns of European scholars and scientists in Asia and Africa have contributed to the incipient implantation of these traditions outside of Europe and North America. Japanese, Indians, Pakistanis, Chinese, and more recently, black Africans have traveled to the centers of science and scholarship in Western Europe and North America. There they have acquired a sector of culture alien to their own indigenous traditions and thus alien to their own "roots," but nonetheless valid to them and much cherished. Some of them have returned home and to some small but growing extent have implanted this tradition of a universally valid science and scholarship. The result, unevenly spread over the earth's surface and by no means embracing all spheres of intellectual activity, is a rudimentary and substantively differentiated universal culture which transcends the parochiality of place and nationality. This rudimentary and restricted universal culture has been made possible by the migration of individuals—usually far from the poorest or the lowliest in their own countries.

The existence of this common culture has also fostered immigration. Its prior existence makes migration easier; the prospect of a more fruitful participation in it offers an incentive to migration. The social structure which sustains this culture has been, like the economic institutions of the European and American societies since 1950, more or less capable of employing renumeratively the skills of these scientific immigrants. This has of course been a spur to the immigration of the educated and the talented—just as a similar situation in the economy has been a spur to the immigration of the poor and relatively unskilled.

The result has been the "brain drain." No one, except racial and cultural "purists" in the host countries, objects to all immigration of the poor into industrial countries, where opportunities for relatively well renumerated employment are available. The migration of the highly educated in science, scholarship, and the learned professions calls forth much criticism from the countries whence the migrants come and by some persons in the countries to which they go. This criticism is based on the view that the emigration of the educated damages their countries of origin.

In the underdeveloped countries from which these scientists come, the criticism draws mainly upon economic arguments. It points to the large investment which has been made in their education and it also argues that the countries of immigration are being subsidized by the countries of emigration. It also draws upon primordial and national sentiments claiming that the emigrants have been faithless to the claims of their "roots." The liberal attitude which looks with favor on the emigration of the poor turns into a mercantilist attitude where the educated are concerned. It seems that educated persons are more cherished in their countries of origin than are uneducated ones.

It is accepted by the critics of the "brain drain" that there is a universal culture of science and scholarship and of the professions which practice them. The value of this culture is accepted—it is even vigorously affirmed—in contradiction to the attitude which views with regret, or at least apprehension, the overpowering of the traditional culture of the lower-class immigrants.

At the same time, the educated migrant is viewed in exactly the opposite manner from his lower-class countryman. His right to renounce his "roots" is questioned, while his possession of a wider, universally valid culture is appreciated. He is criticized for being "uprooted" and his emigration is regarded as evidence that this is so. This criticism is baseless. The implicit distinction between the migration of the uneducated and the migration of the educated ought to be reviewed, and what is at issue should at least be made clear. This applies as much to the host countries, which more or less welcome the educated migrant while keeping the uneducated one at arm's length, as it does to the countries of emigration, which are glad to be rid of their uneducated nationals while complaining about the emigration of their educated ones.

The migration of scientists and technologists testifies nonetheless to the existence of this very specialized stratum of a universal humanity. It stands in sharp contrast to the primordiality, localism, and nationalism which are involved in the migration of the less educated and even of those who are literarily educated.


IX.

The ethical questions which might arise about migration are terribly complicated because there are so many values involved. Of course it is desirable to maintain the traditions which have been passed on by one's ancestors. But if the immigrants have a right to this, so too do members of the host society who fear that their traditions will be "crowded out" or fundamentally changed by the persistence of the immigrants' traditional culture in the society to which they have come. If one believes in the value of national—or tribal or ethnic—culture, then what of the prerogatives of the national society which is called for by the affirmation of the value of nationality? Should the national society not enjoy the right or have the obligation to protect the culture of its own citizens? If, however, one accepts the liberal principle of nationality as entailing self-determination, individually and collectively, then what becomes of the right to move into other countries as one wishes? Do not the natives of those countries have the right of collective self-determination?

Humanity is a motley assemblage. Its various tones and hues have their distinctive values and they are entitled to respect. These diverse tones and hues are not immutable. They can fade away or they can be enriched and deepened. Migration from one society to another cannot be undertaken without cost. Immigrants who come for pecuniary advantages are not the same as settled citizens. Countries which allow immigrants to enter because they anticipate economic advantages from their labor are not entitled to harass them because they do not become perfectly assimilated or because they have a culturally degrading influence.

The gains and losses of migration to the migrants and their hosts, to the countries from which they departed, and to humanity, living and unborn, are incalculable. Economic advantages and disadvantages might be calculated, but can the cultural gains and losses of the main parties, their subsidiary parts, and the ideal of universal humanity be calculated? The whole thicket of problems touches on the most matter-of-fact economic considerations, the depths of the most opaque primordial attachments, and the heights of universal cultural values. Cost/benefit analysis is not enough.

# The Contributors

JANET ABU-LUGHOD is professor of sociology and urban affairs, Northwestern University. She is author of *Cairo: 1001 Years of the City Victorious* (1971) and co-editor with Richard Hay, Jr. of *Third World Urbanization* (1977).

RUTH S. ADAMS is executive associate of the American Academy of Arts and Sciences and editor of the *Bulletin of the Atomic Scientists*. She is editor of *Contemporary China* (1965).

SUNE ÅKERMAN is associate professor of history, Uppsala University, Sweden. He directed the Migration Research Group of Uppsala University from 1966 to 1973 and has published several articles in the field of demography and history.

CARL A. AUERBACH is dean and professor of law, University of Minnesota Law School. He is co-author of *The Legal Process* (1961) and *Federal Regulation of Transportation* (1953).

ALEXANDRE A. BENNIGSEN is visiting professor of history, University of Chicago, and professor at the École Pratique des Hautes Études, Sorbonne. He is co-author with C. Lemercier Quelquejay of *Islam in the Soviet Union* (1967). He is the author of innumerable scholarly articles on religion in the Soviet Union and on Russian-Turkish history.

PHILIP D. CURTIN is professor of history, The Johns Hopkins University, and author of *Two Jamaicas* (1955); *The Image of Africa* (1964); *The Atlantic Slave Trade: A Census* (1969); and *Economic Change in Pre-Colonial Africa* (1975).

HANS-JOACHIM HOFFMANN-NOWOTNY is professor of sociology and director of the Sociological Institute of the University of Zürich, Switzerland. He has published many scholarly articles in the field of international migration, with special attention to poverty and disadvantaged minorities.

JAMES LEE is a Ph.D. candidate in the Department of History, University of Chicago. He is completing his dissertation on the history of China's southern frontiers from ancient times through the middle of the nineteenth century.

T. G. McGEE is a senior fellow in the Department of Human Geography, Research School of Pacific Studies, Australian National University, Canberra, Australia. He has published *The Southeast Asian City* (1967); *The Urbanization Process in the Third World: Explorations in Search of a Theory* (1971); and *Hawkers in Hong Kong: A Study of Policy and Planning in the Third World City* (1974).

WILLIAM H. McNEILL is Robert A. Milliken Distinguished Service Professor of history, University of Chicago. He is the author of *The Rise of the West: A History of the Human Community* (1963), *Plagues and Peoples* (1976), and thirteen other books.

MARTIN E. MARTY is Fairfax M. Cone Distinguished Service Professor at the University of Chicago. Among his many books and articles are *The Righteous Empire* (1972); *The Pro and Con Book of American Religion* (1975); *A Nation of Behavers* (1977); and most recently, *Religion, Awakening, and Revolution.*

PETER A. MORRISON is a member of the senior research staff of The Rand Corporation, Santa Monica, California. He was on the faculty of the University of Pennsylvania and has published scholarly articles in the area of population growth and the future of America.

ORLANDO PATTERSON is professor of sociology, Harvard University. He is author of numerous scholarly articles dealing with the Caribbean and of *The Sociology of Slavery: An Analysis of the Origins, Development, and Structure of Negro Slave Society in Jamaica* (1967) and *Ethnic Chauvinism: The Reactionary Impulse* (1977).

GERALD M. ROSBERG is associate professor of law, University of Michigan Law School. He has published several articles on the constitutional rights of aliens in the United States.

THEODORE W. SCHULTZ is Charles L. Hutchinson Distinguished Service Professor of economics, University of Chicago. Among his numerous articles and books are *The Economic Value of Education* (1963); *Transforming Traditional Agriculture* (1964); *Investment in Human Capital: The Role of Education and of Research* (1971); and *Human Resources: Policy Issues and Research Opportunities* (1972).

EDWARD SHILS is Distinguished Service Professor of the Committee on Social Thought and Department of Sociology, University of Chicago. Among his numerous articles and books are *The Torment of Secrecy* (1956); *Intellectual between Tradition and Modernity: The Indian Situation* (1961); and *Center and Periphery* (1975). He was the founder and is the editor of *Minerva*.

CARL SOLBERG is professor of history, University of Washington. He is author of *Immigration and Nationalism: Argentina and China, 1890–1914* (1970), and *Oil and Nationalism in Argentina: A History* (1978).

GEORGE J. STOLNITZ is professor of economics, Indiana University, currently on leave as principal officer for Population and Development, United Nations. He has published extensively in the areas of demography and economic development.

CHARLES TILLY is professor of sociology and history, University of Michigan. Among his publications are *Migration to an American City* (1965); *The Vendee* (1964); *The Rebellious Century, 1830–1930* with Louise Tilly and Richard Tilly (1975).

JUDITH P. WHEELER is a consultant to The Rand Corporation and a former staff member of *Fortune*.

S. ENDERS WIMBUSH is a member of the research staff of The Rand Corporation and a Ph.D. candidate, Department of Political Science, University of Chicago. He has published several articles on the national problem in the Soviet Union and is co-author with Alexandre A. Bennigsen of *Muslim National Communism in the Soviet Union: A Revolutionary Strategy for the Colonial World* (1978).

ARISTIDE R. ZOLBERG is professor of political science, University of Chicago. Among his works are *Creating Political Order: The Party States of West Africa* (1966) and "Splitting the Difference: Federalization without Federalism in Belgium" in *Ethnic Conflicts in Western Societies* (1977).

# Index